Under the Human Rights Act, British courts are for the first time empowered to review primary legislation for compliance with a codified set of
fundamental rights. In this book, Aileen Kavanagh argues that the HRA
gives judges strong powers of constitutional review, similar to those exercised by the courts under an entrenched Bill of Rights. The aim of the book
is to subject the leading case law under the HRA to critical scrutiny, while
remaining sensitive to the deeper constitutional, political and theoretical
questions that underpin it. Such questions include the idea of judicial
deference, the constitutional status of the HRA, the principle of parliamentary sovereignty and the constitutional division of labour between
Parliament and the courts. The book closes with a sustained defence of
the legitimacy of constitutional review in a democracy, thus providing a
powerful rejoinder to those who are sceptical about judicial power under
the HRA.

AILEEN KAVANAGH is Reader in Law at the University of Leicester.

# CONSTITUTIONAL REVIEW UNDER THE UK HUMAN RIGHTS ACT

AILEEN KAVANAGH

CAMBRIDGE
UNIVERSITY PRESS

CAMBRIDGE UNIVERSITY PRESS
Cambridge, New York, Melbourne, Madrid, Cape Town, Singapore, São Paulo, Delhi

Cambridge University Press
The Edinburgh Building, Cambridge CB2 8RU, UK

Published in the United States of America by Cambridge University Press, New York

www.cambridge.org
Information on this title: www.cambridge.org/9780521682190

First published 2009

Printed in the United Kingdom at the University Press, Cambridge

*A catalogue record for this publication is available from the British Library*

*Library of Congress Cataloguing in Publication data*
Kavanagh, Aileen.
Constitutional review under the UK Human Rights Act / Aileen Kavanagh.
p.  cm.
Includes bibliographical references and index.
ISBN 978-0-521-76100-0
1. Great Britain. Human Rights Act 1998.   2. Human rights – Great Britain.
3. Civil rights – Great Britain.   4. Constitutional law – Great Britain.   I. Title.
KD4080.K38   2009
342.4108′5 – dc22      2009004950

ISBN 978-0-521-76100-0 hardback
ISBN 978-0-521-68219-0 paperback

For my Mother
1943–2008

# CONTENTS

# ACKNOWLEDGEMENTS

This book has not been the work of a moment and during its long gestation period, I have incurred many debts, intellectual and otherwise. I am very grateful to the University of Leicester for granting me two semesters of study leave. The first enabled me to get the project off the ground and the second facilitated its completion. I could not have written the book without these periods of research, uninterrupted by the various other demands of academic life. I am also grateful to my colleagues at Leicester (past and present), who discussed many of the issues which arose in the course of the book. These include Trevor Buck, Richard Stone, Jean McHale, John Hartshorne, Kola Abimbola, Mark Thompson and Mark Bell. I am particularly grateful to David Bonner, who read early drafts of chapters and gave me critical but always constructive feedback. His comments, and the spirit of encouragement in which they were given, have been invaluable to me throughout the process of writing this book. In the final stages, David read and commented on chapter 10 and his insightful comments made all the difference to the final product. Since some of the most important recent case law under the HRA has arisen in the area of national security, I had the benefit of David's vast expertise on this subject. Robin White was similarly supportive. He read chapter 6 and his comments helped to shape that chapter. Panu Minkkinen and Stefano Bertea helped me to run our Legal Theory Discussion Group, which provided an important intellectual backdrop for work on the book.

I have incurred many debts much further afield. At the beginning of the project, I spent a sabbatical term at the University of Toronto Law School, funded by the British Academy. I am especially grateful to David Dyzenhaus and Lorraine Weinrib for making my stay at Toronto both enjoyable and fruitful. Others who welcomed me and were willing to discuss points of mutual interest in constitutional law and theory are Alan Brudner, Mayo Moran, Stephen Moreau, Sujit Choudhry, Denise Reaume, Jennifer Nedelsky and Kent Roach. I am grateful to them all. I returned to Canada in October 2006 to participate in a colloquium in constitutional theory organised by Grant Huscroft at the University of Western, Ontario. The colloquium was as good as these events can be, and the discussion and feedback I received there were immensely helpful in refining my thoughts about the role of judicial deference in constitutional adjudication. I am very grateful to Grant for inviting me and being such a wonderful host.

Many of the arguments advanced in this book were tested initially in seminars held at the Universities of Brunel, Cambridge, Glasgow, Nottingham, Toronto and Oxford. I am grateful for the invitations to give those papers and to the various audiences, whose questions and comments forced me to think harder about the arguments I advanced. Some early attempts to grapple with constitutional review under the HRA were presented in the Civil Liberties section of the Society of Legal Scholars Annual Conference. I am grateful to Helen Fenwick and Gavin Phillipson for those opportunities, as well as for the invitation to contribute to the Symposium on Judicial Reasoning under the HRA held at the University of Durham in 2005. These events, and the discussion that ensued about adjudication under the HRA, were enormously helpful in developing my ideas for this book. I am particularly grateful to the following people for discussion and challenging questions: Trevor Allan, David Dyzenhaus, Adam Tomkins, Neil Kibble, Helen Fenwick, Gavin Phillipson, Lorenzo Zucca, George Letsas, Amanda Perreau-Saussine, Wil Waluchow, Elizabeth Palmer, Merris Amos, David Feldman, Stephen Bailey, Timothy Endicott, Philip Plowden, Kevin Kerrigan, Jeff King, Les Green, Conor Gearty, Eric Barendt, Hugh Tomlinson, Brad Miller, Jo Miles, Robert Wintemute, Nick Barber and Alison Young. Though we have never met, Mike Taggart was extremely generous with his time and willingly discussed the issues surrounding proportionality and *Wednesbury* unreasonableness with me over e-mail. His comments, together with some of his (as yet) unpublished papers on the subject, helped me to navigate this complicated area of the law.

Alison Young gave invaluable feedback on chapter 6. Her advice and encouragement were especially important in the final stages. Timothy Endicott gave me written feedback on my early thoughts on the role of parliamentary intention under the HRA, which helped me to see points I had initially overlooked or misunderstood. Jeff King and Lorenzo Zucca read chapter 7, whilst Trevor Allan and Mark Elliott generously read chapter 10. I am very grateful for their probing comments, to which I have tried to respond as best I can. In particular, Trevor Allan has always challenged me to justify my views on judicial deference and our discussion on this subject has forced me to tackle problems I might have wished to avoid. Mark Elliott read and commented on an earlier paper on proportionality and deference in preparation for a seminar at the Institute of Advanced Legal Studies in 2007 on proportionality under the HRA. I am grateful to Mads Andenas (with whom I organised that seminar) for gathering together a group of participants, whose papers and comments provided invaluable clarification and inspiration as I was finishing the second part of the book. They were Paul Craig, Jeffrey Jowell, Mark Elliott and Philip Sales. When writing the final chapters of the book, Adam Tomkins came to Leicester to give a paper on the contribution of the HRA to the protection of fundamental rights and the rule of law. As will be apparent, my attempts to grapple with, and respond to, Adam's challenging and stimulating views provided an anchor and inspiration for what eventually became chapter 13. As always, discussion with him proved immensely helpful.

As in all my endeavours, my family provided unwavering support whilst I wrote this book. In particular, I am grateful to my parents who, through their love, encouragement and humbling selflessness, have pushed me forward and always helped me to realise my aims. It is a great source of sadness to me that my mother did not live to see this book in print. For just as this book is the fruit of my labour, it is also the fruit of hers. So it is to her, in inadequate recognition of all that she has given to me, that I dedicate this book.

More than anyone, my husband, Matthew has helped in countless ways towards the completion of this book. I cannot thank him enough. He has saved me from demons in my computer a thousand times. He has been a willing sounding board for many of the ideas advanced here. His help, support and great sense of humour were indispensable in the preparation of the final manuscript. But these daily generosities are the least of Matthew's contribution. Through his love, friendship, patience and support, Matthew makes everything possible. Finally, thanks are due to our son, Sean, who helps to put it all in perspective and, together with Matthew, is the most uplifting reminder that there is much more to life than the Human Rights Act.

# 1

## Introduction

### The Human Rights Act 1998, Parliament and the courts

When the Human Rights Act 1998 (hereinafter HRA) came into force, the then Home Secretary, Jack Straw, described it as 'the first Bill of Rights this country has seen for three centuries'.[1] Admirers of the Act claimed that it would transform society for the better, providing us with a fresh set of values for a godless age.[2] Others argued that the HRA provided 'a higher order framework, a constitutional order, which constrains all public institutions and is expected to constrain even the elected legislature itself'.[3] Sir William Wade suggested that the passage of the Act 'must certainly be regarded as one of our great constitutional milestones. It makes a quantum leap into a new legal culture of fundamental rights and freedoms.'[4] Naturally, the HRA also had its detractors. Whilst accepting that the HRA was 'the UK's Bill of Rights'[5] which was 'partially entrenched',[6] some Left-leaning academic lawyers questioned 'whether the primary responsibility for the articulation of [Convention rights] ought to be taken away from the normal political processes of representative government.'[7] Keith Ewing argued that the Act represented

> an unprecedented transfer of political power from the executive and legislature to the judiciary, and a fundamental restructuring of our 'political constitution' . . . it is unquestionably the most significant formal redistribution of political power in this country since 1911, and perhaps since 1688.[8]

The particular source of consternation for lawyers like Ewing was 'the extensive shift of political authority'[9] to the judiciary. Sceptical voices from the Left were echoed in similar views on the Right, where the fear

---

[1] Speech, Institute for Public Policy Research, 13 January, 2000.
[2] Klug (2000); see also Feldman (1999b), 173, questioning whether the HRA could 'inject values which could fill the ethical vacuum at the heart of public life'.
[3] Jowell (2003a), 68.  [4] Wade (1998), 532.  [5] Tomkins (2001), 1.
[6] *Ibid.*, 2.  [7] *Ibid.*  [8] Ewing (1999), 79.  [9] Tomkins (2001), 2.

of expanding the power of unelected and unaccountable judges, at the expense of the elected representatives of the UK Parliament, was no less strongly felt.[10] Right-wing sections of the media made wild predictions that, post-HRA, the courts would be clogged with unmeritorious cases, that serious crime would go unpunished and that judges would accede to every impractical and implausible claim in the name of human rights.[11] Needless to say, such dire predictions about the future impact of the HRA have not been borne out in practice.

What is interesting about the initial academic discussion of the HRA was that, despite fervent disagreement about the merits of the Act, both admirers and detractors alike seemed to agree on its immense constitutional and institutional significance.[12] They were all agreed that the HRA transferred extensive power from the legislature and executive to the judiciary, which in turn, placed constraints on public institutions, including the legislature itself. Moreover, they all agreed on the constitutional nature of those constraints. Both admirers and critics were happy to characterise the HRA as the UK's Bill of Rights.[13] Where they disagreed was whether this transfer (and the constraints it entailed) was a good or a bad thing. Naturally, this disagreement turned, in part, on different views about the character, competence and legitimacy of the legislature, on the one hand, and the courts on the other. One of the aims of this book is to contribute to this broader constitutional debate – by examining critically the nature and extent of the alleged 'transfer' of power to the judiciary, by subjecting both the interpretive method and the substantive outcomes of the HRA case law to critical scrutiny, and finally, by taking a stance on the normative argument about the desirability and legitimacy of giving the courts strong powers of constitutional review, which have the effect of constraining the law-making powers of the democratically elected legislature.

---

[10]  Klug (2007), 704; Fenwick (2007), 142. For an overview of the political history of the 'Bill of Rights' debate, see Fenwick (2007), 141–56.

[11]  For comment on the tabloid coverage of the coming into force of the HRA, see Steyn, (2000), 552; Lester (2002a), fn. 20; see also Sedley (2008), 20ff. The *Review of the Implementation of the Human Rights Act* conducted by the Department of Constitutional Affairs in July 2006, provides some examples of the myths and misperceptions which have grown up around the HRA which have 'undoubtedly had an accumulative and corrosive effect upon public confidence both in the Human Rights Act and in the European Convention on Human Rights itself', see 'Introduction by the Lord Chancellor' (Lord Falconer) at www.justice.gov.uk/docs/full_review.pdf, 5.

[12]  Macklem (2006), 107.

[13]  Tomkins (2001), 1; Lester (1998); Klug (2001), 370; Ewing (2004), 836; Fenwick (2007), 171; Wintemute (2006a), 209; Hiebert (2006), 7.

In the UK, there is a strong intellectual tradition of opposing any enhancement of judicial power in the name of protecting human rights. This tradition draws on many different sources. The first is an intellectual hostility in mainstream British legal and political thought to abstract statements of rights, famously dismissed by Jeremy Bentham as 'nonsense upon stilts'.[14] Dicey wrote that there is 'in the English constitution an absence of those declarations or definitions of rights so dear to foreign constitutionalists',[15] but this was a strength rather than a weakness, because such rights may be constantly suspended. Dicey famously articulated another important source of opposition to Bills of Rights in the UK, namely, the belief that the existing political institutions – particularly Parliament – were perfectly capable of preserving the traditional liberties enjoyed by British citizens.[16] As a former Prime Minister once famously declared in a speech opposing a Bill of Rights for Britain: 'We have no need of a Bill of Rights because we have freedom.'[17] Belief in the value and importance of strong parliamentary government has been an important strand of British legal and political thought, which often goes hand in hand with scepticism about the desirability (and indeed, ability) of judges to enhance the protection of human rights and civil liberties.[18]

The historical belief in the ability of Parliament to protect civil liberties and the sense of complacency which sometimes accompanied it, were put under severe strain in the later part of the twentieth century. Commenting on the poor civil liberties record of governments during the 1980s, Keith Ewing and Conor Gearty suggested that the traditional political checks on government were insufficiently effective as a method of curbing the power of a determined and illiberal governing party: 'Mrs Thatcher has merely utilised to the full the scope for untrammelled power latent in the British constitution but obscured by the hesitancy and scruples of previous consensus-based political leaders.'[19] Moreover, there was an increasingly steady stream of cases brought against the UK before the European Court of Human Rights (hereinafter ECtHR) in Strasbourg. Perhaps this, more than any other fact, prompted the enactment of the HRA.[20] Writing just before the HRA was enacted, the then Home Secretary observed:

---

[14] Bentham (1843), 501.    [15] Dicey (1959), 197–8.    [16] *Ibid.*, 189–90.
[17] For discussion of this comment, see Irvine (2003a), 245.    [18] Klug (2007), 702–3.
[19] Ewing and Gearty (1990), 7; Fenwick (2007), 159; Feldman (1999a), 166. For this reason, the HRA has been described as 'Thatcher's legacy' in Fenwick (2000), 9.
[20] See Irvine (2003a), 245ff.

> What marks out the UK's record [before the European Court of Human Rights] is the serious nature of the cases brought and the absence of speedy and effective domestic remedies. This record does little for the reputation of Parliament, government or the courts. It affects the UK's international standing on human rights as well as weakening the position of individual UK citizens.[21]

Although the Labour Party had traditionally opposed a Bill of Rights enforced by the courts, eighteen years of being in Opposition combined with various shifts in the political climate,[22] led them to adopt the 'compromise solution'[23] of incorporating Convention rights into domestic law. Their election manifesto in 1997 included a commitment to incorporate the European Convention on Human Rights (hereinafter ECHR) and, after winning that election with a huge majority, the new Labour Government published a White Paper entitled *Rights Brought Home*,[24] before introducing the Human Rights Bill to the House of Lords in the same year.[25] The Human Rights Bill was thought to be a key component of the unprecedented series of major constitutional reforms set in train by the Labour Government in that initial spirit of optimism which attended their first term in office.[26] Some would have liked to see the Act, and indeed the Convention rights, constitutionally entrenched against repeal or amendment on the model of the Canadian Charter, with the rights prevailing over inconsistent primary legislation, subject to the legislature employing a notwithstanding clause to make it clear that it intended to legislate inconsistently with the right.[27] However, the traditional belief in the importance and value of strong parliamentary government, as well as a degree of reluctance to hand over such power to judges, combined to make such a solution politically unfeasible.[28] As Francesca Klug commented:

---

[21] Boeteng and Straw (1997), 74.    [22] Ewing (1999), 80ff.    [23] Feldman (1999a), 169.
[24] *Rights Brought Home: The Human Rights Bill* Cm. 3782. For discussion of the White Paper, see Wadham (1997), 141–5.
[25] 23 October 1997.
[26] Bogdanor (2004), 246. Bogdanor lists fifteen constitutional reforms carried out by the Labour Government since 1997, including *inter alia* devolution in Wales, Scotland and Northern Ireland, reform of the House of Lords and the abolition of the office of the Lord Chancellor, noting that 'any one of these reforms by itself would constitute by itself a radical change', 243. Some commentators have observed that these constitutional reforms were not the 'fruits of a grand design' but a set of 'piecemeal and politically pragmatic measures', see e.g. Lester (2002a), 80.
[27] Feldman (1999a), 168–9.
[28] See Irvine (2003a), 98: 'I doubt that consent to the Human Rights Act could have been achieved if it gave the judiciary the right to strike down Acts of Parliament in whole or part'; see also Feldman (1999a), 169; Lester (2002a), 58.

> There was concern across the political spectrum, and in judicial as well as academic circles, that incorporating broad human rights standards into UK law would lead to the demise of the British system of parliamentary supremacy (or sovereignty) over the courts... Crudely put, the debate concerned whether an elected Parliament or unelected courts should have the *final say* in determining what the law should be in a democracy.[29]

The Labour Government wanted to 'bring rights home' by making Convention rights directly enforceable in domestic courts. In this way, they could give UK citizens effective remedies for possible breaches and obviate unnecessary (and politically embarrassing) applications to Strasbourg. However, they had to find a way of achieving these aims, whilst simultaneously reassuring MPs that Parliament would remain supreme. The result was the Human Rights Act 1998.

## Aims, Structure and Themes

Under the HRA, the courts are, for the first time, empowered to review primary legislation for compliance with a codified set of fundamental rights, namely, those enshrined in the ECHR. The courts are given two main powers with respect to primary legislation: one is an interpretive power, the other is declaratory. Under section 3, they are placed under a duty to interpret legislation compatibly with Convention rights, 'so far as it is possible to do so'. If the interpretive route is impossible, they may then issue a declaration of incompatibility under section 4 HRA, which has no immediate impact on the validity of the legislation under scrutiny, but places the executive and legislature under considerable pressure to amend the legislation. In this book, the courts' powers to review primary legislation under the HRA shall be called 'constitutional review'.[30] This distinguishes it from their traditional powers of 'judicial review' with respect to public authority decision-making in administrative law. More importantly, it highlights the constitutional character of the courts' supervisory powers, and indeed, the constitutional importance of the HRA itself. By granting the courts the power to review primary legislation for compatibility with Convention rights, the HRA gives the courts a special responsibility with respect to the enforcement of Convention rights. It also places a premium on statutory interpretation as a means of achieving consistency with Convention rights, thus making explicit the

[29] Klug (2003), 126; Klug (2007), 703.
[30] For use of this term with reference to adjudication under the HRA, see Jowell (2000); Irvine (2003a), 246; Oliver (2003), 100; Palmer (2007), 33.

constitutional significance of statutory interpretation as an instrument of constitutional review. As Sir Rupert Cross observed in his classic work on statutory interpretation, written long before the HRA was on the statute books:

> The canons of interpretation represent a position taken by the judiciary on their constitutional role in relation to those who establish the political programme, those who have to carry it out, and those affected by it.[31]

The HRA strengthens the constitutional role of the courts, by allowing judges to determine the existence and content of the legal obligations flowing from Convention rights, in response to litigation. It makes rights and rights-based thinking more central to the constitutional agenda and therefore makes the courts a key participant in setting that agenda.[32] Many of the rights enshrined in the Convention have long found indirect and often implicit expression in the common law, some might say, in the 'common law constitution'.[33] To the extent that the courts now have an important role in guarding against the violation of Convention rights, judges help to ensure that legislation complies with fundamental constitutional principle.[34] The HRA calls upon the courts to act as constitutional judges and to review for compliance with principles of constitutionality.

The main aim of this book is to evaluate the nature, scope and legitimacy of the courts' powers of constitutional review under the HRA. Some commentators have argued that the HRA has elevated 'both the profile and influence of the higher courts'[35] and given the judiciary 'a newly reinvigorated position . . . in matters of public law'.[36] If this is true, then we need to subject this important constitutional development to critical scrutiny. The purpose of this book is to contribute to that enterprise. The courts' powers of constitutional review under the HRA are primarily framed by the combined workings of sections 3 and 4 HRA. In this book, I subject the case law applying those sections to critical scrutiny and, in so doing, seek to probe more deeply, the profound issues of constitutional theory underlying their application. Such issues include the constitutional relationship between Parliament and the courts and the constitutional significance of statutory interpretation, as well as broader questions about

[31] Cross (1995), 4, 10.

[32] Although they are an important participant in setting this agenda, they do not have exclusive control over it. Parliament and the Executive also contribute to this task.

[33] Allan (2006a), 46.

[34] For use of the term 'constitutional review', see also Cooke (2004), 275; Joseph (2004); Jowell (2000), 671; Oliver (2003), 100.

[35] Tomkins (2002b), 202.        [36] *Ibid.*

the nature of the British constitution and the legitimacy of constitutional review in a political system which prizes parliamentary sovereignty and the values of democratic participation. Judicial and academic debate over the scope of sections 3 and 4 HRA is a concrete manifestation of disagreement about these more fundamental issues. For this reason, I locate the doctrinal analysis of the HRA case law against the backdrop of concerns about the legitimacy of rights review in a democracy.

This book is divided into three parts. The first part charts the course of the case law applying sections 3 and 4 HRA. It evaluates the various judicial and academic attempts to articulate the alleged 'constitutional boundary' between sections 3 and 4. The central question animating this part of the book is: when is it right for the courts to flex their interpretive muscles under section 3, and when is it more appropriate for them to declare an incompatibility under section 4? This question is answered through a combination of detailed analysis of the case law, as well as broader theoretical reflections on the nature of interpretation and the constitutional significance of section 3(1) as a strong presumption of statutory interpretation. Part II sets these debates in the broader context of concerns about judicial deference and the acute power-allocation issues, to which constitutional adjudication under the HRA inevitably gives rise. The question underlying this part of the book is: how can the courts carry out their constitutional function to uphold Convention rights, whilst simultaneously exercising a constitutionally appropriate degree of judicial restraint and deference to the legislature? In other words, how can they balance the demands of judicial supervision and judicial deference? Questions about the nature, scope and justification for judicial deference have ignited intense academic and judicial controversy. Part II engages with those debates and evaluates their significance both for a theoretical evaluation of the nature of the judicial function, as well as for issues of practical application. Of crucial importance here is the case law which has arisen in the context of the Government's determination to wage a 'war on terror'. No one could have predicted that before the HRA was barely two years on the statute book, the terrorist attacks on the USA on 11 September 2001, would have generated such a critical testing ground for the UK Government's commitment to human rights protection.[37] The response of the courts when reviewing anti-terrorist legislation for

---

[37] Following the terrorist attacks in London on 7 July 2005, the Prime Minister, Tony Blair also suggested that he would consider seeking to amend the HRA if it proved to be an obstacle to the 'war on terror', see T. Blair, speaking at the monthly Downing Street press conference, 5 August 2005. (www.pm.gov.uk/output/Page8041.asp), cited in Elliott (2007b), nn. 100–1.

compliance with Convention rights in this fraught political context, is an important litmus test of the role and value of constitutional review.

Some commentators have described the acceptance into UK law of the doctrine of proportionality as one of the most profound changes brought about by the HRA.[38] Chapter 9 examines that doctrine in detail and highlights how it places a strong burden of justification on elected bodies to justify their decisions in light of human rights standards. It contributes to what many commentators have described as 'the culture of justification'.[39] The climate of constitutional justification in which the law now operates, also requires justification of the exercise of judicial power as much as any other power. The final part of this book responds to this justificatory challenge. Here, I tackle the big constitutional questions: the status of the HRA, the nature of the judicial powers under the HRA, the HRA's compatibility with the doctrine of parliamentary sovereignty and, finally, the underlying normative questions about the justification of constitutional review in a democracy. In the penultimate chapter of the book, I mount a justification for giving the courts strong powers of constitutional review. In the final chapter, I defend this against arguments rooted in democratic concerns.

This, in broad outline, is the main structure of the book. It does not seek to provide an exhaustive consideration of all the case law arising under the Act, still less an exhaustive account of how each substantive Convention right has been applied in the domestic courts. There are many other books which do precisely that.[40] The focus of this book is different. It is on the underlying questions of interpretive methodology and methods of judicial reasoning employed by the courts when carrying out their important constitutional functions under the HRA, as well as the constitutional legitimacy of those powers. As such, this book is intended as a contribution to British constitutional law, but also as a contribution to the broader literature on constitutional theory.

One terminological point should be clarified at the very outset. Whilst this book is centrally concerned with the relationship between Parliament and the courts, I avoid using the term 'the separation of powers'. This nomenclature is eschewed because it lends credence to a view which underestimates both the legitimate interaction between the three branches of government and the considerable overlap in the constitutional roles of each branch. So, in this book, I shall refer to the constitutional division

---

[38] Sedley (2002), 17.     [39] Hunt (2003), 351; Steyn (2004a), 254.
[40] Clayton and Tomlinson (2000); Fenwick (2007); Lester and Pannick (2004); Amos (2006).

of labour between the three branches of government, but will refrain from describing it as a *separation* of powers. Of course, this is in no way to deny the importance of judicial independence for the effective exercise of constitutional review. It is simply to emphasise that in order to give a meaningful account of the relationship between Parliament and the courts, we should not overlook or marginalise the various forms of inter-action, interdependence and collaboration which exist between them.

There is one important corollary of this view, which itself provides an important underlying theme of this book. This is that we should not con-sider the courts to be 'above politics'. The courts are political institutions and the power they wield is political in nature. In this book, I will argue that the ability of the courts to interact politically with the legislature and executive is part and parcel of their constitutional responsibilities under the HRA and a key component of their powers of constitutional review. The details of this claim will be worked out as the book progresses. For the moment, it suffices to note that when the courts review primary legislation for compatibility with Convention rights and decide either to interpret it compatibly with those rights or issue a declaration of incom-patibility, the courts engage in constitutional politics. As the enactment of the HRA itself shows, constitutional politics is not entirely removed from the forces and pressures that shape 'normal politics' – but the politics of constitutional rights is nonetheless marked by special features, which will be spelled out in the final two chapters of this book. What distinguishes the courts' powers of constitutional review, is not that they are apolitical, but that they respond to, and engage with, a particular type of political concern, and do so in a particular way.

## The scheme of the HRA

Before engaging with these broader themes, it may be helpful to outline the key sections of the HRA, which are relevant to the broad concerns of the book. The long title of the HRA declares that its aim is 'to give further effect to rights and freedoms guaranteed under the European Convention on Human Rights'. The Convention rights are included in a Schedule to the Act,[41] thus providing the UK with a list of codified human

---

[41] The Schedule to the HRA includes all the substantive rights in the original Convention as well several rights contained in subsequent protocols. (Article 13 on effective remedies was omitted), Articles 2–12, Article 14, Articles 1–3 of the First Protocol to the Convention and Articles 1 and 2 of the Sixth Protocol. For further discussion, see Feldman (1999a), 170–3.

rights enforceable in domestic courts.[42] There are three principal means by which the HRA gives further effect to Convention rights in domestic law. The first is by making provision for rights-compatible interpretation and amendment of primary legislation in sections 3, 4 and 10. The second is by making it unlawful for a public authority to act in a way which is incompatible with a Convention right under sections 6–9. Finally, the HRA provides a way in which Convention rights can have an impact on the legislative process. This is contained in section 19.

The primary focus of this book is on the ways in which the courts ensure that primary legislation is Convention-compatible. Therefore, its main concern will be to evaluate the combined workings of sections 3 and 4 and the broader questions of constitutional theory generated by them. Of crucial significance is section 3(1), which provides that 'so far as it is possible to do so, primary legislation and subordinate legislation must be read and given effect in a way which is compatible with the Convention rights'. This interpretive obligation has been described as an 'emphatic adjuration'[43] to the courts. It applies to all legislation 'whenever enacted',[44] so that it affects both pre- and post-HRA statutes. Crucially, the application of section 3 'does not affect the validity, continuing operation or enforcement of any incompatible primary legislation'.[45] So, although the courts have the power to interpret legislation compatibly with Convention rights, they are not given the power to invalidate it. The question then arises as to when, and under what circumstances, a court will find it impossible to interpret legislation compatibly with Convention rights. This difficult question is not answered by the terms of the HRA.

However, the Act contains an explicit acknowledgement that it will not always be possible. Section 4(2) provides that 'if the court is satisfied that the provision is incompatible with the Convention right, it may make a declaration of incompatibility'. So, in contrast to section 3, which creates a judicial *obligation* to read and give effect to legislation compatibly with Convention rights,[46] section 4 gives the court a discretion (though not a duty) to issue a declaration of incompatibility.[47] Section 4 also specifies that a declaration of incompatibility 'does not affect the validity, continuing operation or enforcement of the provision in respect of which it is

---

[42] Note that section 2(1) provides that when construing those rights, the courts are obliged to 'take into account' decisions of the ECtHR and related bodies. This obligation will be considered in chapter 6.
[43] *R. v. DPP, ex parte Kebilene* [2000] 2 A.C. 326, *per* Lord Cooke.     [44] Section 3(2)(a).
[45] Section 3(2)(b).     [46] See 'must' in section 3(1).     [47] See 'may' in section 4(2).

given'[48] and 'is not binding on the parties to the proceedings in which it is made'.[49] Thus, under the HRA, the courts are not given the power to strike down legislation, in the sense that the declaration of incompatibility does not, in itself, invalidate primary legislation or give the litigant a remedy based on such invalidation. A closer analysis of the status and implications of declarations of incompatibility is provided in chapter 10. For the moment, it suffices to note that, although declarations of incompatibility have no legal effect on the validity of legislation, the expectation is that they would put strong pressure on the executive/legislature to amend the legislation accordingly.

Provision for amendment of primary legislation following a declaration of incompatibility, is set out in section 10 entitled 'Remedial action'. Of course, Parliament may respond to a declaration of incompatibility by proceeding to amend legislation in the normal way. However, section 10(2) also provides for a 'fast-track' amendment procedure enabling a Minister to make a 'remedial order' to remove the incompatibility. It provides: 'If a Minister of the Crown considers that there are compelling reasons for proceeding under this section, he may by order make such amendments to the legislation as he considers necessary to remove the incompatibility.' Section 10 may also be used where a decision of the ECtHR suggests that a legislative provision is incompatible with the Convention.[50] Schedule 2 to the HRA provides two procedures for making a 'remedial order' which must be in the form of a statutory instrument.[51] The standard procedure is that a Minister must lay a draft of the order before Parliament for sixty days, together with an explanation of the incompatibility and a statement of the reasons for proceeding under section 10. This may provide some measure of parliamentary scrutiny of the remedial order. The alternative procedure allows the Minister to make the order before laying it before Parliament, thus taking the amendment totally outside the parliamentary process which would normally be required for primary legislation. So far, the government has shown a clear preference for using the standard procedure.[52]

The final section relevant to the preoccupations of this book is section 19 HRA. It provides that, when introducing legislation to Parliament, a Minister, before the second reading of the Bill, must 'make a statement to the effect that in his view the provisions of the Bill are compatible with the Convention (a statement of compatibility)'[53] or alternatively to 'make a statement to the effect that although he is unable to make a

---

[48] Section 4(6)(a).    [49] Section 4(6)(b).    [50] Section 10(1)(b).    [51] Section 20.
[52] See further Fenwick (2007), 205.    [53] Section 19(1)(a).

statement of compatibility the Government nevertheless wishes the House to proceed with the Bill'.[54] Whilst section 19 leaves open the possibility that a government can proceed with legislation which it believes is contrary to Convention rights, the general assumption is that it will not do so. At the very least, section 19 obliges the government to make such an intention explicit during the legislative passage of the Bill. Not only would the public statement of such an intention cause political embarrassment, it would also be seized upon by the Opposition and those who might oppose the Bill on human rights grounds. Second, a statement of intent to infringe Convention rights would be tantamount to a declaration of the government's intention to breach its obligations under international law,[55] which might provoke international condemnation leading to further political embarrassment.[56] Thus far, the ability to enact legislation without an accompanying section 19 statement of compatibility has only been used once.[57]

The impact of section 19 on the legislative process has been one of the surprises of the HRA. When it was included in the Act, it was widely believed that it would be a 'parrot provision'[58] – a mere formality which would accompany legislative proposals as a matter of course. At the time of enactment few in Whitehall or Westminster appreciated how significant its practical impact would be upon the preparation and parliamentary scrutiny of legislation.[59] What has given section 19 its political potency is the parliamentary Joint Committee on Human Rights (hereinafter JCHR), established two years after the HRA was enacted.[60] The workings of this Committee will be examined in more detail in chapters 12 and 13. For the moment, we should note that the Committee monitors the operation of section 19 and reports to each House of Parliament on the Convention-compatibility or lack of compatibility of legislative proposals. Due to lobbying from the JCHR, it is now government practice to include at least an outline of the government's views on compatibility

---

[54]  Section 19(1)(b).
[55]  As a signatory to the ECHR, the UK is under an international law obligation to observe the terms of the Convention and to secure the protection of Convention rights in domestic law.
[56]  Fenwick (2007), 206.
[57]  Communications Act 2003. See further Fenwick (2007), 208. This legislation has now been declared by the House of Lords to be compatible with the Convention, see R. (Animal Defenders International) v. Secretary of State for Culture, Media and Sport [2008] UKHL 15.
[58]  Klug (2005), 199; Sedley (2008), 21.     [59]  Lester (2002a), 76.
[60]  It had its first meeting on 31 January 2001.

in the Explanatory Notes published with every government Bill. In terms of putting pressure on the government to take seriously its obligation to ensure legislative compatibility with Convention rights, this duty to provide reasons (however brief) is much more potent than the bare requirement in section 19 to state the government's conclusion that the legislation is compatible.[61] It is widely accepted that the scrutiny work of the Joint Committee significantly influences the preparation and content of legislation, and improves parliamentary scrutiny to secure better compliance with Convention rights.

## The politics of parliamentary debates

Before embarking on the main tasks of the book, it is appropriate to enter a note of caution about the constitutional role and significance of the parliamentary debates on the Human Rights Bill prior to its enactment.[62] When we look at the terms of the HRA, it is clear that they are less than clear on important issues. For example, section 3 simply states that the courts should interpret all legislation compatibly with Convention rights 'so far as possible'. It does not specify when it is possible, and when not. Similarly, section 4 states that the courts 'may' issue a declaration of incompatibility, but gives no specific guidance on when or how the court should exercise this discretion. Moreover, the HRA provides for a fast-track amendment procedure if the Minister has 'compelling reasons' to rely on it, but does not elaborate on what those reasons might be. As Lord Nicholls remarked: 'Skilfully drawn though these provisions are, they leave a great deal of open ground. There is room for doubt and for argument. It has been left to the courts to resolve these issues when they arise.'[63]

It is perhaps natural that, in seeking to resolve these difficult issues in the first decade of the HRA's life, both judges and academic commentators alike have occasionally turned to the parliamentary record for guidance. Tellingly (though perhaps unsurprisingly), statements from *Hansard* have sometimes been used to support diametrically opposed conclusions. Take, for example, the difficult question of when the courts should adopt a Convention-compatible interpretation, and when they

---

[61] Lester (2002a), 78.
[62] For the practical and constitutional problems with reliance on parliamentary debates for the purposes of legal interpretation, see generally Kavanagh (2005a).
[63] *Parochial Church Council of the Parish of Aston Cantlow* v. *Wallbank* [2003] UKHL 37 at [36].

should issue a declaration of incompatibility instead, which is the subject-matter of Part I of this book. In *R. v. A,*[64] Lord Steyn relied on statements made by the Government Ministers who promoted the Human Rights Bill in Parliament, in order to support the conclusion that section 3 created a 'strong interpretive obligation' and section 4 should only be used as a 'last resort'.[65] For example, Lord Irvine stated in the House of Lords that 'In 99% of the cases that will arise, there will be no need for judicial declarations of incompatibility.'[66] However, some academic commentators have cited other statements from the parliamentary record to support precisely the opposite conclusion. Relying on the various statements of Government Ministers that the HRA preserves the principle of parliamentary sovereignty, these commentators claim that in order to respect that principle, the courts should rely on section 4 much more often than is the current judicial practice. In fact, they should do so in a routine way.[67]

Given that reliance on ministerial statements of this kind is prevalent in the commentary on the HRA and is often thought to provide clear evidence of Parliament's intention when enacting the HRA, we should be clear about the significance and status of such statements. Since *Pepper* v. *Hart,*[68] the courts have accepted that they can refer to *Hansard* as an aid to statutory construction where legislation is ambiguous or obscure and there is a clear ministerial statement by the Minister promoting the Bill directly on the point at issue before the court.[69] Many subsequent decisions of the House of Lords have cast doubt on the helpfulness of material from *Hansard* and have stressed that the conditions laid down in *Pepper* v. *Hart* must be strictly insisted upon.[70] In *Wilson* v. *First Country Trust,*[71] Lord Nicholls was at pains to stress that ministerial statements in Parliament should not be treated as having the same status as the enacted text of the statute.[72] Whilst statements from *Hansard* could be used as a source of background information about a statute and the mischief it was

---

[64] *R. v. A (No. 2)* [2002] 1 A.C. 45.    [65] *Ibid.* at [44].

[66] HL 585 col. 840 (5 Feb 1998). This point was reiterated by the Home Secretary (Jack Straw) in the House of Commons, see HC vol. 306 col. 778 (16 February 1998).

[67] See e.g. Tomkins (2001), 1; Gearty (2002), 248.

[68] [1993] A.C. 593.    [69] *Ibid.* at 640.

[70] See e.g. *R. v. Secretary of State for the Environment, Transport and the Regions, ex parte Spath Holme* [2001] 2 A.C. 349 at 393, 399, 409, 414. (i.e. the insistence that it can only be used where the statute is ambiguous and the statements in *Hansard* are clear).

[71] *Wilson* v. *First County Trust* [2003] 3 W.L.R. 568.

[72] *Ibid.* at [58], *per* Lord Nicholls, [139], *per* Lord Hobhouse.

designed to remedy, they should not be treated as sources of law.[73] Lord
Hobhouse articulated the constitutional underpinnings of this principle
in clear and emphatic terms:

> The constitutional means by which laws are made is by the entry of the
> statute in the statute book. The source of the new law is the document
> itself not what anyone may have said about it or some early form of it. Still
> less is it what the executive said about it or what some individual member
> of a House of Parliament may have said about it in the course of its passage
> through Parliament . . . it is a fundamental error of principle to confuse
> what a Minister or a parliamentarian may have said (or said he intended)
> with the will and intention of Parliament itself.[74]

This *dictum* reminds us of the need to be cautious about giving statements
from the parliamentary record a significance they cannot bear. It warns
us that statements made by the promoting Ministers may only reflect the
intention of the government, not Parliament as a whole. At the very least,
it counsels us to be cautious before attributing them automatically to
Parliament, simply because they are uttered by government Ministers in
emphatic terms.[75] The fact that a statement of the proposing Minister is
not controverted in parliamentary debate does not necessarily prove that it
was endorsed. As Lord Steyn remarked extrajudicially, MPs 'may agree on
only one thing, namely to vote yes. And they may have no means of voting
yes and registering at the same time disagreement with the explanation
of the Minister. Their silence is therefore equivocal.'[76] Apart from the
practical difficulties of establishing whether such ministerial statements
have received widespread endorsement, there are also constitutional (and
indeed democratic) difficulties with giving the Executive the opportunity
of clarifying the meaning of vague or ambiguous statutory provisions in
the course of parliamentary debate. In the UK, the Executive is already
hugely powerful in getting its legislative proposals enacted – it should not
therefore also have the power of determining how that legislation should
be interpreted, by filling in gaps in the legislation not clarified in the text
of the statute itself.[77]

Finally, we should always bear in mind that the purpose of parliamentary debate is political persuasion, not legal interpretation, and ministerial

---

[73] *Ibid.* at [58], *per* Lord Nicholls.     [74] *Ibid.* at [139].
[75] Steyn (2001), 65; Kavanagh (2005a), 106.      [76] Steyn (2001), 66.
[77] Steyn, (2001), 61. For a further explication of how this undermines the rationale of the
law-making process and violates the constitutional prohibition on executive law-making,
as well as encroaches on the judicial power to interpret legislation, see Kavanagh (2005a),
99–102.

statements made within this highly politicised context 'are not always conducive to a clear and unbiased explanation of the meaning of statutory language'.[78] One has to separate government rhetoric from legal principle, and appreciate the political nature and function of parliamentary debates.[79] This is not to deny that statements made by government Ministers when proposing the Human Rights Bill in Parliament may be relevant when seeking to understand the political background and mischief of the HRA. It is simply to stress that we should be wary of automatically assuming that they are 'clear evidence' of Parliament's intention as a whole and bear in mind the political context in which they are made.[80] When statements from the parliamentary debates on the Human Rights Bill have been relied on by judges or academic commentators, they are assessed at appropriate points throughout the book, but that assessment is undertaken against the backdrop of constitutional principle sketched here and the spirit of caution they recommend.

[78] *David* v. *Johnson* [1979] A.C. 264 at 349, *per* Lord Scarman.
[79] Thus, in *R. (Al-Skeini)* v. *Secretary of State for Defence* [2007] UKHL 26 (concerning the question of whether the HRA had an extra-territorial application to Iraqi civilians killed in Iraq by UK armed forces), the House of Lords rejected arguments based on the parliamentary record which suggested that the purpose of the HRA was to 'bring rights home'. As Lord Rodger observed: 'The government rhetoric was not an accurate guide to the application of the Act within the United Kingdom . . . the passages from *Hansard* to which we were referred contained nothing on which it would be safe to rely.' at [43]. Similarly, Lord Bingham noted that emphasis (both in the White Paper and parliamentary debates) on the value of the HRA to the 'British people' was natural 'for domestic political reasons', [23].
[80] Geoffrey Marshall has argued that the views of the parliamentary sponsors of the Human Rights Bill on the meaning of sections 3 and 4 fail the test of clarity or lack of ambiguity, requisite for admissibility under *Pepper* v. *Hart*: see Marshall (2003), 238–9.

# PART I

Questions of interpretation

# 2

# Sections 3 and 4 HRA: the early case law

## Introduction

In applying sections 3 and 4 HRA, the central question is: when should the courts give a section 3(1) interpretation and when is it more appropriate to issue a declaration of incompatibility? Under traditional doctrines of statutory interpretation, central emphasis is placed on the ordinary meaning of statutory words viewed in their context, as well as the intention of Parliament when enacting those words.[1] It was widely believed that section 3 enacted 'a *new* rule of statutory interpretation'[2] which departed from existing rules.[3] However, there was uncertainty about how section 3 would require the existing rules of statutory interpretation to be modified. To what extent would the traditional emphasis on ordinary contextual meaning and parliamentary intent be changed or adjusted in order to achieve compatibility with Convention rights? Just how far could judges go with this new rule of interpretation? The answer to these crucial questions would then determine when it would be more appropriate to issue a declaration of incompatibility under section 4. So, even though it was accepted that interpretation would change under section 3, the twin constraints of *express meaning* and *parliamentary intent* became *leitmotivs* in the developing jurisprudence under sections 3 and 4 HRA. It is to an examination of the early case law that we must now turn.

## Making use of section 3(1): the early case law

Within months of the HRA coming into force, the House of Lords demonstrated that it was willing to use the full amplitude of its interpretive

[1] Cross (1995), 1, 22: 'Words should generally be given the meaning which the normal speaker of the English language would understand them to bear in the context in which they are used'; see also Bankowski and MacCormick (1991), 382.
[2] Klug (2005), 195.
[3] After all, if it merely replicated existing rules of statutory interpretation, the section would have been redundant: see Marshall (1998), 168.

powers under section 3 to ensure that legislation, whenever enacted, was interpreted in a Convention-compatible way.[4] Two of its earliest decisions (*R. v. A*[5] and *Lambert*[6]) seemed to show that the judiciary was prepared to take an 'extremely vigorous stance'[7] on the question of when a Convention-compatible interpretation was possible. The first case (*R. v. A*) arose in the context of the politically sensitive and notoriously difficult question of whether (and, if so, how) to admit sexual history evidence of complainants in rape trials.[8] It is still one of the leading authorities on the scope and limits of section 3(1) HRA.[9]

The legislative provision at issue in *R. v. A* was section 41 of the Youth Justice and Criminal Evidence Act of 1999 (hereinafter YJCEA). Known as the 'rape-shield' provision, section 41 prohibited the admissibility of sexual history evidence, except with leave of the court in narrowly defined exceptions outlined in section 41(3), known as the 'gateways' to admissibility.[10] The tightly circumscribed legislative rule prohibiting such evidence was designed to replace the much-maligned section 2 of the Sexual Offences (Amendment) Act 1976 which left the question of admissibility to the largely unregulated discretion of the trial judge.[11] Section 2 had been the subject of heated criticism, on the grounds that it did not prevent the illegitimate use of sexual history evidence in rape trials, often led to the admission of irrelevant and prejudicial evidence leading to the unnecessary humiliation of complainants in rape trials and was a deterrent to women bringing rape cases at all.[12] This was the mischief Parliament sought to redress in section 41.[13]

However, given how narrowly restricted the section 41 'gateways' were, it was inevitable that the question would eventually arise in court as to whether Parliament had achieved a fair balance between the concerns of complainants and defendants' right to a fair trial in Article 6 of the Convention. This was the crux of the issue in *R. v. A*, which came up for trial within a few months of section 41 appearing on the statute

---

[4] For an overview of the case law in the first year, see Klug and Starmer (2001).
[5] *R. v. A (No. 2)* [2002] 1 A.C. 45.     [6] *R. v. Lambert* [2002] 2 A.C. 545.
[7] Fenwick (2007), 174.
[8] This was a controversial issue in many jurisdictions: see generally Kibble (2000).
[9] See e.g. *Attorney General's Reference No. 4 of 2002* [2004] 3 W.L.R. 976 at [24], *per* Lord Bingham. In *Secretary of State for the Home Department* v. *MB* [2007] UKHL 46 at [71], Baroness Hale describes *R. v. A* as a 'leading case' on section 3(1).
[10] For illuminating discussion of the 'gateways' approach, see Kibble (2000), 278.
[11] *Ibid*, 286.     [12] See e.g. Temkin (1993); Birch (2000), 247–8; McColgan (1996).
[13] For more detailed analysis of the legislative context of section 41, see Kibble (2004), 24–30.

books.[14] There, the defendant who was charged with rape, claimed that the complainant had consented to the sexual intercourse which formed the subject-matter of the charge. The question was whether evidence relating to an alleged prior consensual sexual relationship between them in the preceding weeks was admissible under section 41.

On appeal to the House of Lords, their Lordships agreed that if section 41 were construed in accordance with ordinary methods of statutory interpretation, such evidence would be inadmissible and, *prima facie*, might result in a breach of the defendant's right to a fair trial.[15] Although it contained some narrow exceptions, section 41 constituted 'a blanket exclusion of potentially relevant evidence'[16] and, as such, was simply too restrictive. It amounted to what Lord Steyn called 'legislative overkill'.[17] However, whilst ordinary methods of interpretation could not cure the 'excessive breadth'[18] of the section, this was not the end of the enquiry. Post-HRA, the courts could now tap into the potential of 'the special rule of construction embodied in section 3(1) of the HRA'.[19] Their Lordships held unanimously that it was possible to read section 41(3)(c) subject to an 'implied provision' that evidence or questioning which is required to ensure a fair trial under Article 6 ECHR could be admitted by the trial judge. They agreed on the following test of admissibility:

> [D]ue regard always being paid to the importance of seeking to protect the complainant from indignity and humiliating questions, the test of admissibility is whether the evidence is nevertheless so relevant to the issue of consent that to exclude it would endanger the fairness of the trial under Article 6 of the Convention.[20]

So, right from the start, the House of Lords showed that it was prepared to use the tools given to it by Parliament in section 3(1), in order to render statutory provisions Convention-compatible, even if this required the court to strain statutory language or to read in words which would

---

[14] In fact, the preparatory hearing of A was held only four days after the YJCEA came into force on 4 December 2000, see Kibble (2001), 27.

[15] Lord Hope disagreed with the rest of the House on this point, because he thought that it had not been shown, on the facts of A, that evidence relevant to the defendant case was in fact excluded by section 41 in a way which was incompatible with his Convention right to a fair trial, R. v. A, above n. 5 at 85–6. This will be discussed in more detail below.

[16] R. v. A, above n. 5 [39], *per* Lord Steyn. Lord Clyde pointed out that both in the UK and in other jurisdictions, attempts to legislate with 'a blanket exclusion and strictly defined exceptions' have been criticised, R. v. A [116].

[17] R. v. A, above n. 5 at [43], *per* Lord Steyn.    [18] *Ibid.* at [43].    [19] *Ibid.* at [136].

[20] Formulated by Lord Steyn, *ibid.* at [46], supported by Lord Slynn at [13]; Lord Hope at [110]; Lord Clyde at [140]; Lord Hutton at [163].

protect Convention rights. As Lord Steyn put it: 'In accordance with the will of Parliament as reflected in section 3 it will sometimes be necessary to adopt an interpretation which linguistically may appear strained. The techniques to be used will not only involve the reading down of express language in a statute but also the implication of provisions.'[21]

The transformative potential of section 3(1) can also be seen in the second major case to reach the House of Lords in the early years of the HRA. In R. v. Lambert,[22] the House of Lords had to decide whether a legal, rather than evidential, burden of proof placed on the defendant under sections 5 and 28 of the Misuse of Drugs Act 1971 was in breach of the right to a fair trial guaranteed under Article 6 ECHR. The court first established that, when read in the ordinary way, section 28 'demonstrates that what Parliament chose to do'[23] was to impose a legal burden of proof. The next stage was to assess whether this decision served a legitimate aim and satisfied the principle of proportionality. Whilst there was agreement that the statutory objective was legitimate,[24] their Lordships concluded that imposing a legal burden of proof on all defendants was a disproportionate way of satisfying that purpose. It would have been sufficient to impose an evidential burden on the accused. But all was not lost for the Misuse of Drugs Act. Their Lordships held that it was 'possible' under section 3(1) to 'read the words "to prove" as if the words used in section 28(2) were "to give sufficient evidence"'.[25] So, although the ordinary or natural meaning of the provision was that it imposed a legal burden of proof, section 3(1) enabled the court to read it so that it only imposed an evidential burden of proof.

Similarly, in Offen[26] the Court of Appeal had to determine whether section 2 of the Crime (Sentences) Act 1997 was compatible with Article 5 of the Convention. Section 2 (commonly known as the notorious 'two strikes and you're out' provision)[27] required the imposition of a mandatory life sentence where a defendant was convicted of two serious offences unless there were 'exceptional circumstances' for not doing so. 'Exceptional circumstances' was not defined in the statute and the leading pre-HRA authority on this issue[28] had interpreted it so that judges were sometimes

---

[21]  Ibid. at [44].    [22]  Above n. 6.    [23]  Ibid. at [68], per Lord Hope.
[24]  The legislative objective was to penalise the unauthorised possession of dangerous drugs, knowing that many sophisticated drugs smugglers, dealers and couriers typically secrete drugs in some container, thereby enabling them to say that they are unaware of the contents, ibid. at [36], per Lord Steyn; [71], [89], per Lord Hope.
[25]  Ibid. at [94], per Lord Steyn.    [26]  R. v. Offen [2001] 2 All E.R. 154.
[27]  It was described as 'a particularly savage legislative intervention' by Gearty (2004), 77.
[28]  R. v. Kelly [2000] Q.B. 198.

compelled to pass a sentence of life imprisonment, notwithstanding the fact that this seemed disproportionate and unjust, and potentially violated Article 5 ECHR. With section 3(1) HRA now in the judicial toolbox, such a restrictive interpretation was no longer a foregone conclusion. The Court of Appeal held that the phrase 'exceptional circumstances' should be interpreted in light of the intention of Parliament in enacting section 2 of the 1997 Act, but also the interpretive obligation under section 3 HRA. Characterising the underlying legislative purpose of the Act as the aim of protecting the public against a person who had committed serious offences,[29] the Court of Appeal concluded that only those prisoners who could be shown to be a danger to the public, would receive a life sentence. The Lord Chief Justice concluded:

> Notwithstanding the interpretation resulting from the application of section 3(1) of the 1998 Act suggested, section 2 would still give effect to the intention of Parliament. It will do so, however, in a more just, less arbitrary and more proportionate manner.[30]

Since all the evidence showed that Mr Offen presented no significant danger to the public, he was spared an automatic life sentence and instead given a determinate sentence of three years' imprisonment. Lord Woolf noted that 'section 2 therefore provides a good example of how the 1998 Act can have a beneficial effect on the administration of justice, without defeating the policy which Parliament was seeking to implement'.[31]

Although some of the reasoning in these early cases attracted controversy, three uncontroversial points about the operation of section 3(1) nonetheless emerged. The first was that under section 3(1), the judge's interpretive task can be broken down into two main stages. First, judges must establish whether legislation is *prima facie* compatible with Convention rights, i.e. 'whether on its face the provision under scrutiny is compatible or incompatible with the Convention rights'.[32] This will often require the court to assess whether the statutory provision satisfies the principle of proportionality. If the legislation (as ordinarily understood) is proportionate, and therefore compatible, then no further issue arises under the HRA. There is no need for the interpretive obligation under section 3(1). As Lord Woolf put it in *Poplar Housing*: 'Unless the legislation would otherwise be in breach of the Convention, section 3 can be ignored. So courts should always first ascertain whether, absent

---

[29] *Offen*, above n. 26 at [97], [100], *per* Lord Woolf.     [30] *Ibid.* at [99].     [31] *Ibid.* at [100].
[32] Gearty (2002), 252; Lord Steyn, in *R. v. A* at [43]; see also *Sheldrake* v. *DPP* [2004] UKHL 43 at [27], [28], *per* Lord Bingham.

section 3, there would be any breach of the Convention.'[33] However, if the legislation is thought to be disproportionate, then a *prima facie* conclusion can be drawn that the provision is incompatible with Convention rights and the interpretive duty under section 3 is engaged. Judges are then obliged to see if it is 'possible', *despite appearances*, to read and give effect to the legislation in a way which is nonetheless compatible with Convention rights. If such a reading is impossible, the courts can then issue a declaration of incompatibility. This two-stage approach has been used in all subsequent cases: the courts initially construe the legislation 'without reference to section 3',[34] before going on to construe it 'in accordance with section 3'.[35] It follows that the courts are not prevented from finding a possible Convention-compatible meaning, even if this is 'not the most obvious way to read [the legislative provision]'.[36]

The second point accepted by their Lordships in the early cases and followed in subsequent case law without exception, was that there was no need for an ambiguity in statutory language to engage section 3. As Lord Steyn stated succinctly in *R. v. A*: 'The interpretive obligation under section 3 of the 1998 Act is a strong one. It applies even though there is no ambiguity.'[37] This constituted a departure from the previous rule of statutory interpretation that judicial reliance on Convention rights was only allowed to resolve an ambiguity. The third uncontroversial point to emerge from the early case law was that the courts were no longer bound by pre-HRA authority on the interpretation of legislative provisions, given that previous case law was decided at a time when Convention rights were not part of domestic law.[38]

---

[33] *Poplar Housing & Regeneration Community Association Ltd* v. *Donoghue* [2002] Q.B. 48 at [75].

[34] See e.g. *Ghaidan v Mendoza* [2004] 3 All E.R. 411 at [24], *per* Lord Nicholls; *R. (Fuller)* v. *Chief Constable of Dorset Constabulary* [2002] 3 W.L.R. 1133 at [39], *per* Stanley Burnton J; *International Transport Roth GmbH* v. *Secretary of State for the Home Department* [2002] 3 W.L.R. 344, *per* Jonathan Parker L.J.

[35] *Roth*, above n. 34 at [149]. It is perhaps worth noting that this two-stage approach is not compelled by the terms of section 3, see Rose and Weir (2003), 40.

[36] *Lambert*, above n. 6 at [17], *per* Lord Slynn; see also *Sheldrake* v. *DPP* [2004] UKHL 43 at [28] where Lord Bingham noted that the statutory provisions under scrutiny imposed a legal burden when 'conventionally interpreted', but could nonetheless be interpreted compatibly with the Convention by imposing an evidentiary burden, at [1], [7], [27].

[37] *R. v. A*, above n. 5 at [44].

[38] See e.g. *Offen*, above n. 26; see also *Lambert*, above n. 6 at [81], *per* Lord Hope; in *Ashworth Hospital Authority* v. *MGN* [2001] 1 All E.R. 991 (CA) at [79], *per* Lord Phillips M.R.; *R. (Anderson)* v. *Secretary of State for the Home Department* [2002] 3 W.L.R. 1800 at [53], *per* Lord Steyn.

## Section 3(1) and controversy about the limits of the 'possible'

The fact that the House of Lords was prepared to read into a statute an 'implied provision' to secure the protection of one of the Convention rights, caused consternation in the academic commentary. The controversy about the application of section 3(1) in *R. v. A* was initially played out in a perceived difference of emphasis in the judgments of Lords Steyn and Hope in that case. Although Lord Hope joined the rest of the House in accepting that section 41 YJCEA could be read subject to an implied provision in order to ensure a fair trial, some of his *obiter* comments revealed his circumspection about this application of section 3(1). His reservations are encapsulated in the following statement:

> The entire structure of section 41 contradicts the idea that it is possible to read into it a new provision which would entitle the court to give leave whenever it was of the opinion that this was required to ensure a fair trial. The whole point of the section was to address the mischief which was thought to have arisen due to the width of discretion which had previously been given to the trial judge.[39]

In other words, his worry was that reading in a judicial discretion to ensure a fair trial into section 41, contravened the twin constraints of express terms and parliamentary intent, which were so central to traditional methods of statutory interpretation – or at least contravened these requirements to an unacceptable extent. Whilst Lord Hope accepted that the rule of construction laid down in section 3 was quite unlike any previous rule of statutory interpretation, he warned that 'it is *only* a rule of interpretation. It does not entitle to judges to act as legislators'.[40]

These words of caution were seized upon by academic commentators who hailed Lord Hope as the champion of the 'cautious approach'[41] and castigated Lord Steyn as the judicial 'radical'.[42] *R. v. A* was widely thought to be the 'high point of the bold approach to section 3'.[43] Critics of the decision echoed Lord Hope's worries about contravening express statutory terms and legislative intent. It was claimed that the House of Lords in *A* effectively 'rewrote'[44] section 41, and in so doing, violated

---

[39] *R. v. A*, above n. 5 at [109].      [40] *Ibid.* at [108]. Emphasis added.

[41] Rose and Weir (2003), 46; Starmer (2003), 16; Bonner *et al.* (2003), 560; Clayton (2002a), 562.

[42] See e.g. Rose and Weir (2003), 45; Bonner *et al.* (2003), 561.

[43] Rose and Weir (2003), 46; Starmer (2003), 16; Nicol (2004a), 196; Bonner *et al.* (2003), 561; Nicol (2004b), 275; Gearty (2003b), 552; see also Fenwick (2007), 174–5. For a defence of the legitimacy of the interpretive technique adopted in *R. v. A*, see Kavanagh (2005b).

[44] Nicol (2004a), 195; Nicol (2002), 443; Klug (2003), 128–9; Gearty (2002); Bonner *et al.* (2003), 560; Fenwick (2007), 175.

Parliament's intention in enacting the section. As Danny Nicol observed, 'the legislative intention [behind section 41] was transparently to restrict judicial discretion in respect of evidence of the complainants' previous sex life, yet their Lordships' interpretation reinstated the wide judicial discretion that Parliament thought it had abolished'.[45] Critics feared that the courts would hardly ever issue a declaration of incompatibility, but rather would use their interpretive powers under section 3 in 'an extremely creative fashion'[46] to render legislation Convention compatible no matter what kind of 'linguistic trick'[47] might be required to achieve such an end result.

These fears were in no way allayed and in fact were probably inflamed by Lord Steyn's candid statements on the scope of section 3(1) in his judgment in *R. v. A.* There, his Lordship pronounced that section 3 was 'more radical in its effect'[48] than ordinary methods of contextual and purposive interpretation. He concluded that section 3 'qualifies'[49] the general principle that the text is the primary source of interpretation, with other sources subordinate to it, because it 'requires the courts to find an interpretation compatible with Convention rights if it is possible to do so.'[50] The legislative history of section 3 showed that the interpretation did not have to be reasonable, merely 'possible', and straining of legislative language was therefore permissible.[51] The implication of Lord Steyn's comments was that the ordinary meaning of the statutory words would not be a barrier to the application of the interpretive obligation under section 3. A declaration of incompatibility was a measure of last resort which 'must be avoided unless it is plainly impossible to do so'.[52] In Lord Steyn's view, section 3 required the court 'to subordinate the niceties of the language of section 41'[53] to broader considerations pertaining to the defendant's right to a fair trial. For critics, the terms of the statute enacted by Parliament only a few years previously, with the explicit aim of curbing judicial discretion in this sensitive area, were more than mere 'niceties' which could be dispensed with under section 3(1).

---

[45] Nicol (2004a), 195; Nicol (2004b), 278; Klug (2003), 129.
[46] Fenwick (2007), 175; see also Nicol (2002), 442.     [47] Gearty (2002), 254.
[48] *R. v. A*, above n. 5 at [44].     [49] *Ibid.* at [44].     [50] *R. v. A*, above n. 5 at [44].
[51] In both the House of Lords and the House of Commons, Conservative amendments were laid to replace the requirement on the courts to interpret legislation compatibly with Convention rights where 'possible', with the requirement that they only do so when 'reasonable'. These amendments were rejected by the Government on the grounds that if section 3(1) contained the words 'reasonable', the courts 'would not go so far down the road of interpreting legislation as they would under the terms of clause 3 as it stands', Jack Straw, 313 HC 421–2 (3 June 1998), discussed in Klug (1999).
[52] *R. v. A*, above n. 5 at [44].     [53] *Ibid.* at [45].

However, Lord Hope's judgment was an unlikely springboard for the so-called 'cautious approach'.[54] Its most obvious limitation was the fact that Lord Hope's reservations did not lead him to dissent from the majority in *R. v. A*. He supported the rest of the House in allowing the trial judge to rely on the implied 'test' for admissibility, if to do so would ensure a fair trial. *R. v. A* was a unanimous decision of the House of Lords. Moreover, whilst his judgment was indeed infused with a cautious attitude and undoubtedly couched in cautious language, there was nothing like a set of general principles which could make up a 'general approach' with respect to section 3(1). Most likely, his reservations about the application of section 3(1) in *R. v. A* hinged on his view of the facts of the case, rather than on a general 'approach' to the judicial duties under section 3(1).[55] Subsequent case law showed that he was not averse, either in principle or in practice, to judicial 'reading in' to achieve Convention compatibility.[56] Most importantly, although his dictum that 'the whole point' of section 41 was to protect complainants was seized upon by those who favoured a cautious approach to section 3(1), when viewed in the context of Lord Hope's judgment as a whole, one could easily see that this was a hyperbolic claim.[57] In a more measured assessment, Lord Hope joined the rest of the House in acknowledging that section 41 was in fact designed to '*balance* the competing interests of the complainant to seek protection from the court and the accused's right to a fair trial'.[58] He put this point in the clearest of terms:

> A balance must be struck between the probative value of the evidence and its potential prejudice. Section 41 YJCEA has been designed to achieve that adjustment. It is clear from the background against which that section was enacted and from its own terms that this is the mischief which it was intended to address.[59]

Although the balance struck in section 41, on its ordinary meaning, may have leaned in favour of the complainant, the question raised in *A* was

---

[54] For a critical examination of Lord Hope's judgment in *R. v. A*, see Kavanagh (2005b), 262–5.

[55] *Ibid.* at [106]. See further Kavanagh (2005b).

[56] *Lambert* was decided only a few months after *R. v. A*.

[57] There are other criticisms of *R. v. A* which were, in my view, guilty of hyperbole. See e.g. the claim that the decision in *A* reinstated the unlimited judicial discretion the section was intended to remove, Klug (2003), 128; Nicol (2004a), 195. I have argued that although the discretion to admit probative evidence under section 41 was undoubtedly increased by *R. v. A*, it was not an *unlimited* discretion of the kind which existed in section 2 of the Sexual Offences Act, see Kavanagh (2005b), 267–8.

[58] *R. v. A*, above n. 5 at [72].      [59] *Ibid.* at [56].

whether this legislative provision was compatible with the defendant's right to a fair trial – whether it 'leaned too far'.[60] The important point to emerge from the decision in R. v. A was that in assessing whether this provision leaned too far, the legislation had to be interpreted in light of Convention rights. Otherwise, section 3(1) would have no work to do. There was therefore a tension in Lord Hope's judgment between his claim that section 3(1) went beyond existing methods of statutory interpretation, and the subsequent reservations about departing from express terms and legislative intention. Yet critics were uneasy with the idea that the courts could depart from those twin constraints on legitimate interpretation. At the very least, they had reservations about the degree of departure which was evidenced in R. v. A.

In what is now the leading case on section 3(1), *Ghaidan* v. *Mendoza*,[61] the House of Lords sought to dispel any suggestion that the decision in R. v. A involved 'a heterodox exercise of the power under s.3'[62] and gave a ringing endorsement to the legitimacy of the 'reading in' carried out there. It was clear that Lord Steyn's approach to the application of section 3(1) was endorsed, and the difference of emphasis between his judgment and that of Lord Hope, minimised.[63] The approach adopted in R. v. A has since been followed in recent decisions of the House of Lords.[64] However, it was undeniable that Lord Hope had tapped into some widely held

---

[60] *R. v. A*, above n. 6 at [82], [81], [72]. See further Birch (2002), 532. Given that the test proposed by the House of Lords for use by the trial judge is formulated so as to emphasise the need to take the complainant's interests into account, I would dispute Helen Fenwick's claim that their Lordships in *R. v. A* did not recognise the need to balance the defendant's right to a fair trial against the complainant's interests in being protected from humiliating questioning. Numerous *dicta* throughout the case show that all of their Lordships had this balance at the forefront of their minds, see e.g. Lord Slynn, who stressed that '*without in any way resiling from a strong insistence on the need to protect women from humiliating cross-examination* and prejudicial but valueless evidence, it seems to me clear that these restrictions in section 41 *prima facie* are capable of preventing an accused person from putting forward relevant evidence', *ibid.* at [10] (emphasis added). See also Lord Slynn at [5], Lord Steyn at [46]; Lord Hope at [51], [55], [72], [94]; Lord Clyde at [121]; Lord Hutton at [142].

[61] Above n. 34.    [62] *Ibid.* at [47].

[63] Thus, *Ghaidan* clarified that the line of academic commentary suggesting that Lord Hope's approach to section 3(1) predominated or should predominate (see e.g. Gearty (2004), 52) was rejected by the House of Lords.

[64] Followed in *R. (Hammond)* v. *Secretary of State for the Home Department* [2005] UKHL 69, where the House of Lords read section 11(1) of the Criminal Justice Act 2003 subject to 'an implied qualification' that it must be compliant with the right to a fair trial, see [29], *per* Lord Bingham, despite the fact that the section explicitly stated that prisoners would not receive an oral hearing. A similar 'reading in' is carried out in *Secretary of State for the Home Department* v. *MB* [2007] UKHL 46.

beliefs about the proper division of constitutional responsibility between the judiciary and Parliament under section 3(1). In particular, the view that section 3 does not entitle the courts to legislate, struck a chord with commentators and judges alike, and became one of the *leitmotivs* of the subsequent case law.[65] But distinguishing between the two was no easy task. It was described by Lord Woolf as 'one of the most difficult tasks which courts face under section 3'.[66] Since critics and judges rallied around the proposition that the courts should 'interpret not legislate' when applying section 3(1), it is therefore worth probing this distinction further, to see if it can help to establish when a section 3(1) interpretation is possible, and when it is not.

## Distinguishing between interpretation and legislation

If the interpretation/legislation distinction is to provide genuine guidance to judges when applying section 3(1), or equip us to assess the legitimacy of judicial decisions arising under the Act, we need to get a clearer sense of what is involved in the activity of interpretation in order to distinguish it from legislation. In this section, I will offer a theoretical account of the nature of legal interpretation and will attempt to show that the activity of interpretation involves, rather than eschews, judicial law-making. However, this law-making ability is distinguished from *legislative* law-making, because the judicial powers are much more limited in scope and effect than those possessed by Parliament. The general characterisation of interpretation outlined here will also form the basis of much of the subsequent analysis of the nature of the court's task under section 3(1) HRA.

We can begin with the uncontroversial point that the aim of a judge interpreting any legal provision is to establish its meaning. Without further reflection, this commonplace observation can give rise to widespread fallacies about the nature of interpretation. The most widespread fallacies are as follows:

(a) interpretation is entirely concerned with determining linguistic meaning, i.e. the meaning of words used in the legal provision;

---

[65] *Roth*, above n. 34 at [66], *per* Simon Brown; *R. v. A*, above n. 5 at [108], *per* Lord Hope; *Lambert*, above n. 6 at [81], *per* Lord Hope; *Poplar Housing*, above n. 33 at [59], [75], *per* Lord Woolf, [75]; *Re S, Re W* [2002] 2 A.C. 291 at [38], *per* Lord Nicholls; *R. v. Shayler* [2003] 1 A.C. 247 at [52], *per* Lord Hope; *Anderson*, above n. 38 at [30], *per* Lord Bingham, *Anderson, ibid.* at [59], *per* Lord Steyn; *Bellinger v. Bellinger* [2003] 2 A.C. 467 at [67], *per* Lord Hope.

[66] *Poplar Housing*, above n. 33 at [76].

(b) interpretation is a matter of 'discovering' meaning which is somehow contained in the wording of the provision; and

(c) interpretation is a matter of applying the law as it exists, not a matter of making new law. It is purely applicative and has no creative dimension.

These three fallacies underpin many of the common objections to so-called judicial activism under the HRA. To clarify what interpretation is and respond to some common critiques, we must refute the fallacies. Let us begin with the first. Although it is certainly the case that a judge interpreting a statutory provision must begin by attending to the meaning of the statutory language, the legal solution to an interpretive dispute will not be found in linguistic meaning alone. For example, we do not envisage that judges who disagree about the limits of the interpretive obligation under section 3(1) will find a resolution to that disagreement in the meaning of the word 'possible'. Nor do we imagine that in a case concerning the requirements of a fair trial, judges will find the legal answer by looking up the meaning of the word 'fair' in the dictionary. When legislation is drafted in broad evaluative terms (such as those contained in the HRA), interpretive disputes will not turn on the meaning of words alone, but on evaluative judgments about the ambit and limits of the judicial role as well as substantive (moral, political and legal) judgments about what fairness requires in a particular case. These judgments engage a judge's sense of justice, not just his or her sense of language. So, judicial interpretation is constrained to varying degrees by the words of the statute, but it is not determined by it. The importance of this point for understanding section 3(1) HRA was appreciated by Lord Nicholls in *Ghaidan* v. *Mendoza* when he noted that 'since section 3 relates to the "interpretation" of legislation, it is natural to focus attention *initially* on the language used in the legislative provision being considered'.[67] Whilst judges must always begin with linguistic meaning, the interpretive enquiry is not exhausted by it.

This leads us to the second fallacy. We have said that in a legal dispute about statutory meaning, the answer to the dispute will often be unclear from the meaning of the words alone. It follows that the meaning of legislative provisions is not contained within the text, waiting to be 'discovered' by the interpreting judge. Linguistic meaning will only be the

---

[67] *Ghaidan*, above n. 34 at [31], emphasis added; see also *R. (Al-Skeini)* v. *Secretary of State for Defence* [2007] UKHL 26 at [9], *per* Lord Bingham: 'The starting point [in statutory interpretation] is the language of the 1998 Act, from which the court seeks to derive the meaning of what Parliament has enacted'; see also Steyn (2004a), 247.

starting point. Beyond this, the legal provision may be 'indeterminate'. That is to say, it provides no particular solution or no single right answer to the question of how the court should decide.[68] If judges were to confine themselves to 'discovering' the meaning of statutory provisions and 'declaring' their findings, then they would simply have to declare that those terms are indeterminate. However, assuming that the parties have *locus standi*, judges are obliged to resolve the case[69] and cannot therefore arrest their enquiry at this point of 'declaration'. They are obliged to go further and interpret that provision. To interpret it, they will have to form a view on the evaluative questions it raises and offer reasons in support of their interpretive conclusion. To constitute an interpretation, judges must provide reasons supporting that outcome which show why they believe it to be correct. We may call the reasons supporting the interpretive conclusion 'justifying reasons'.[70] These evaluative considerations are not contained in the statutory text, but are added to the text by the interpreting judge in order to elucidate its meaning. When interpreting indeterminate legislative provisions, judges must supplement the bare linguistic meaning with evaluative considerations which justify their interpretive conclusion. As Ronald Dworkin puts it, the justification for a judicial decision interpreting legislative provisions cannot be found 'within the four corners' of the legislation itself – they 'must be defended as principles of political morality'.[71]

We must now confront the third fallacy, namely, that when judges interpret, their task is only to apply the law – they are not allowed to create new law. To be sure, interpretation has an applicative dimension because the judge must strive to elicit the meaning of the provision laid down by Parliament. This will involve a consideration of the linguistic meaning of the statute, Parliament's intent in enacting it,[72] as well as existing precedent which may bind the court. But clearly, application of the law as it exists does not exhaust the possibilities open to the judge interpreting legislation under the HRA. Judges are legally entitled to depart from precedents when it is inappropriate to follow them, or when it would lead to an injustice to the parties to the current dispute, or where

---

[68] For legal theoretical accounts of indeterminacy, see e.g. Hart (1994), 252, 272–3; Raz (1979), 70–2, 181–2; Endicott (1996), 669.

[69] In fact, the responsibility of judges to impose resolution in cases before them is often thought to be an aspect of the rule of law, see e.g. Endicott (1999), 14.

[70] MacCormick (1993); Kavanagh (2004b), 262.    [71] Dworkin (1985), 36.

[72] By including parliamentary intention as an aspect of the applicative dimension of interpretation, I am not overlooking the creative aspect of eliciting parliamentary intention. The issue will be examined in more detail in the next chapter.

the established line of precedent is outmoded or irrelevant to current circumstances. Moreover, many of the cases arising under the HRA will present a novel legal problem.[73] If there has not been a case in point and the judge has to decide on the basis of legal provisions which may be indeterminate on the issue, then the judge cannot decide the case without making new law. Of course, they will search for analogous cases, or look for *obiter dicta* of previous judges to support their conclusion. However, whatever material of this kind they adduce, there is no denying that judges who interpret legislation drafted in broad, evaluative terms are inevitably drawn into the task of making new law.

The fact that interpretation of legal provisions involves a combination of applying existing law and in developing new law, emphasises 'the Janus-like aspect of interpretation'.[74] Interpretation faces both backwards, aiming to elucidate the law as it is, and forwards, aiming to develop and improve it. So the judge engaging in the interpretive enterprise must interpret the words of the legal provisions (and also any relevant or analogous case law), but will also have to decide whether or how to develop the law in further directions in order to decide the case at hand. Interpretation has both an applicative and creative aspect. Nor is this creative role a novel feature of adjudication under the HRA. Even under traditional doctrines of statutory interpretation, judges have exercised a creative role by elaborating, supplementing, modifying and developing statutory meaning. This development and modification are part and parcel of the interpretive activity. So, when a court interprets an unclear statutory provision, settling its meaning will inevitably mean *giving* it a meaning. As John Gardner put it, 'it necessarily goes beyond norm-application to norm-alteration'.[75]

The question which now arises concerns the factors or considerations a judge should employ when deciding whether to apply the law as it exists or develop it in order to improve it or do justice to the parties. As Lord Irvine has noted, the challenge for the courts is to 'work out where the correct balance lies between these competing imperatives of activism and restraint'.[76] How are judges to meet this challenge? The answer is that legal interpretation involves a balance between two different sets of reasons, each pulling in different directions. Among the reasons in

---

[73] There is judicial support for the view that pre-HRA precedents on the interpretation of a statutory provision are not binding post-HRA, see e.g. *Lambert*, above n. 6 at [81], *per* Lord Hope; *Ashworth Hospital Authority* v. *MGN* [2001] 1 All E.R. 991 (CA) at [79], *per* Lord Phillips M.R.

[74] Raz (1998a), 177.    [75] Gardner (2001), 221.    [76] Irvine (1999), 354.

favour of conservation will be the values of legal continuity and stability.[77] When adjudicating, the courts should ensure coherence of purpose in the law and should integrate ongoing legislation with underlying legal doctrine. They have a role in providing stability and continuity in the legal structures and the basic principles which guide those structures, and this is especially important in relation to constitutional matters. Another reason in favour of conservation concerns the importance of legal authority. In other words, judges are interpreting and applying the law laid down by the supreme law-making body, i.e. Parliament, and they must respect that law.

However, considerations of continuity, stability and authority of law are not the only relevant ones in legal interpretation. Judges are also under a duty to arrive at a just decision for the parties in the instant case. This is why equity has an inescapable role in the interpretation of laws: the application of general rules or principles to specific cases should be mediated by equity, in order to ensure that no injustice results from their application.[78] Parliament sometimes enacts statutes in broad, evaluative terms for precisely this reason, namely, in order to allow the courts to apply it in particular cases. This provides a (stable) legal framework, but allows the courts to ensure that it is justly applied in the circumstances of different cases.

The values of equitable application of the law and legal development are evident in those cases under the HRA which have gone down the innovative rather than conservative road. Thus, although their Lordships in *R. v. A* were agreed that allowing such evidence to be admitted would require some straining of the ordinary meaning of the words, Lord Clyde commented that:

> If a case occurred where the evidence of the complainant's sexual behaviour was relevant and important for the defence to make good a case of consent, then it seems to me that the language would have to be strained *in order to avoid the injustice to the accused of excluding from a full and proper presentation of his defence.*[79]

So, while Lord Clyde was aware of the disadvantages of 'straining the language' in terms of legal certainty, he thought that the reasons in favour

---

[77] Raz (1996a), 357ff. See further Kavanagh (2004b), 268.

[78] This should not be taken as meaning that issues of 'justice' only arise when the judge decides to innovate or reform existing law. The values of having a stable framework of laws and continuity in legal doctrine are also aspects of what justice requires. The point is simply that they are not the only values.

[79] *R. v. A*, above n. 5 at [97]. Emphasis added.

of innovating the law (namely, the requirement of doing justice to the parties to the dispute) had a stronger force in the circumstances of that case. The judicial dilemma in *R. v. A* exemplifies the general tension between the values underlying legal conservatism (namely, authority, continuity and stability) on the one hand, and legal innovation on the other (just application of the law and equitable legal development). Judges have a duty to consider and balance these two sets of values (which may sometimes be in tension with each other), and give them appropriate weight in accordance with the circumstances of every case. In some cases, there will be stronger reasons in favour of preserving an existing line of authority or deferring to the current legal position as expressed in an Act of Parliament. In others, there will be stronger reasons to innovate and change the law.

This leads us to another clarification concerning common critiques of adjudication under the HRA. In an early contribution to the debate about section 3(1), Conor Gearty made the following claim:

> The way in which the senior judiciary have engaged with the Act – sometimes displaying extreme activist traits, sometimes showing enormous deference – has been rather ad hoc and unprincipled, with their Lordships and their colleagues in other quarters seemingly frequently to be uncertain about whether they are involved in interpretation or legislation.[80]

However, if one decision is 'activist' and another is 'deferential', this does not necessarily mean that judicial decision-making is '*ad hoc* and unprincipled'. It may simply mean that the reasons in favour of 'activism' are stronger in one case than another. Of course, judicial decision-making may indeed be unprincipled on other grounds or it may misjudge the reasons pulling in one direction or another. But the general point still holds true, namely, that determining the degree of activism or restraint will be a deeply contextual question, the answer to which will vary from case to case. Therefore, one cannot and should not expect consistency in judicial decision-making in the sense that those decisions would display a consistent degree of 'activism' or 'deference' in every single case. It is in the nature of interpretation that it involves a balancing between activism and restraint, and the correct resolution of this balance will vary in accordance with the facts of each individual case. Interpretation, as characterised here, involves some judicial law-making, but the *degree* of law-making required in any individual case will vary.

---

[80] Gearty (2002), 249.

We are now in a better position to evaluate the claim that, under section 3(1) HRA, the court's job is to 'interpret' not 'legislate'. The first point to note is that, at least when stated in the abstract, this slogan does not provide us with a 'litmus test'[81] for separating out legitimate from illegitimate judicial decision-making under the HRA, or indeed for choosing between section 3 or section 4. Often, it is no more than an aphoristic way of expressing the general desirability of judicial caution and wariness about going too far on the creative side of the interpretive balance.[82] The factors giving rise to such judicial caution are many and varied, and are not encapsulated in the easy slogan that judges should 'interpret' rather than 'legislate', which requires much more elucidation.

Second, the foregoing analysis shows that 'interpretation' necessarily includes rather than eschews judicial law-making. Therefore, when judges like Lord Hope say that section 3(1) is '*only* a rule of interpretation',[83] they are attempting to show that interpretation is not an unbounded activity. This is certainly true, but the acknowledged limitations on the interpretive activity do not mean that interpretation is *purely* applicative. The key to understanding the true import of the slogan that judges should 'interpret not legislate' is that it refers not to a separation of law-making powers from law-applying powers, but rather the separation of *legislative* powers of law-making from judicial powers of law-making.[84] The crucial difference between *legislation* and *judicial law-making* is contained in the fact that the judicial power to make law is a much more limited activity than the legislative ability of elected representatives.[85]

Legislators are entitled to make law simply on the basis that they think that it is desirable or beneficial – in other words, they can think about a problem purely on its merits.[86] Moreover, they can decide to reform a whole area of the law in a root-and-branch fashion, creating new frameworks or radically altering existing ones. Such radical and broad-ranging

---

[81] This expression is borrowed from a US presidential candidate who declared that his 'litmus test for judges is that . . . their passion is not to amend but to interpret the Constitution', quoted in Dworkin (1997), 1249.

[82] Allan (2006a), 37, who describes the distinction as 'empty rhetoric', and that the terms interpretation and legislation are 'ultimately labels to be attached to interpretive conclusions that one approves or disapproves'.

[83] *R. v. A*, above n. 5 at [108], *per* Lord Hope, emphasis added.

[84] See Gardner (2001), 217.

[85] For an outline of some of the limits on judicial freedom to make new law, see Irvine (1999), 354ff; for an examination of the differences between judicial and legislative law-making, see Hart (1961) 204–5; Raz (1979), 194–201; Kavanagh (2004b), 266–7.

[86] Gardner (2001), 217.

reform is generally not open to judges. This is partly due to the way in which they come to make their decisions, and partly due to limits of their expertise. In contrast to legislators, who have almost unrestricted choice in the areas of the law they can change or improve, it is not open to judges to reform any law they wish: they are limited in the decisions they can make by the vagaries of litigation. Even when a case comes before them, the issues are presented in the form of a bivalent dispute on a particular aspect of the law. They are confined to resolving that particular issue. If they stray beyond those confines, their pronouncements may be *obiter* and therefore not binding on future courts. Rarely does a case encompass an entire area of law, or allow for possible radical reform of that area.[87] The fact that judges must operate within existing legal structures and can only make law on a case-by-case basis in response to the accidents of litigation, makes it difficult for them to provide a blueprint of reform for an entire area of the law.

We have also noted the 'Janus-like' nature of interpretation. When judges make law by way of interpretation, they cannot do so in a purely forward-looking way. They are also obliged to take account of the pre-existing legal frameworks and standards set out by Parliament and previous judges. The interpretive task must take place within those boundaries. Judges are constrained by the wording and principles as laid down by Parliament and should make their decisions within the framework set out by them. While judges can look forward towards possible reform, they are nonetheless also obliged to look backwards at the terms of the legislation under scrutiny, as well as the existence and import of existing precedents. Much of judicial law-making occurs by way of filling in gaps in the existing legislative framework, resolving legal disputes through the application of general legislative provisions to particular circumstances. So judges possess the power to engage in partial and piecemeal reform, if at all, i.e. reform in one aspect of the application of the law.[88] They do this by extending existing doctrines, adjusting them to changing circumstances or introducing small alterations to avoid an injustice in their

---

[87] This is not meant to deny that there can occasionally be landmark decisions which cause widespread legal reform, or cause wider societal change. However, such decisions tend to take place against the general backdrop of incremental judicial law-making. For more detailed consideration of the role of such landmark decisions in the account of incremental judicial law-making advanced here, see Kavanagh (2003a), 74–7.

[88] The limited judicial ability to reform the law can pose a dilemma for judges since partial reform may not be successful or it may have other unforeseen bad consequences, see Raz (1979), 200–1.

application which may not have been envisaged by the legislator. They recognise, as the Court of Appeal put it, that law is best developed incrementally on a case-by-case basis and 'not with one large leap'.[89] That these concerns about the limits of judicial law-making were crucially important in understanding the limits of section 3(1) became apparent in a new series of cases handed down after *R. v. A* and *Lambert*. In these cases, the higher courts fleshed out the general pronouncements about 'interpreting not legislating', in favour of highlighting the necessarily incremental and piecemeal tool of interpretation. The first was contained in the important case of *Re S*.[90]

## The 'fundamental features' limit on section 3(1)

In *Re S*, the Court of Appeal read into the Children Act 1989 a range of new powers and procedures by which courts could supervise and monitor the implementation of care orders by local authorities, so as to protect children against violations of their rights under Article 8 ECHR. The Court of Appeal's decision was reversed unanimously by the House of Lords. It held that the introduction of these innovations into the statutory scheme was an inappropriate use of section 3(1). A fundamental and pervasive feature of the Children Act was that the courts were not empowered to intervene in the way local authorities discharged their parental responsibilities in care orders. Although the Lords accepted that, following *R. v. A*, words could be read into a statute, they opposed the particular 'reading in' undertaken by the Court of Appeal. This was because 'a cardinal principle of the Children Act 1989 is that when the court makes a care order it becomes the duty of the local authority designated by the order to receive the child into its care while the order remains in force'.[91] The decision of the Court of Appeal had the effect of undermining this 'cardinal principle'[92] or 'fundamental feature' by transferring the local authority's duty to the supervision of the courts. Giving the leading judgment in the case, Lord Nicholls concluded:

> A meaning which departs substantially from a fundamental feature of an Act of Parliament is likely to have crossed the boundary between interpretation and amendment. This is especially so where the departure has practical repercussions which the court is not equipped to evaluate. In such a case the overall contextual setting may leave no scope for rendering

[89]  *R. v. Clark* [2003] EWCA Crim 991 at [13].      [90]  *Re S, Re W* [2002] 2 A.C. 291.
[91]  *Ibid.* at [23], *per* Lord Nicholls.      [92]  *Ibid.* at [23], [27], [28], [42].

> the statutory provision Convention compliant by legitimate use of the process of interpretation. The boundary line may be crossed even though a limitation on Convention rights is not stated in express terms.[93]

His Lordship also stressed that:

> when a court, called upon to construe legislation, ascribes a meaning and effect to the legislation pursuant to its obligation under section 3, it is important that the court should identify clearly the particular statutory provision or provisions whose interpretation leads to that result.[94]

This was not done in this case. As Hale L.J. pointed out in the Court of Appeal, the appellants 'found it quite difficult to identify particular provisions of the 1989 Act which might be declared incompatible: the problem is more with what the Act does not say than with what it does'.[95] In introducing a new scheme to fill in what the Act did not say, the Court of Appeal 'exceeded the bounds of its judicial jurisdiction under section 3'.[96]

So, here we have a judicial substantiation of the boundary between interpretation and amendment, namely, that in applying section 3(1) HRA the courts should not depart from a statute's 'fundamental features'. But this raises a difficult question, namely, what makes a feature 'fundamental'? Many academic commentators on the HRA believed that Lord Nicholls' judgment in *Re S* constituted a retreat from *R. v. A* on the following grounds:

> Lord Nicholls' new principle, forbidding interpretations which conflict with fundamental features of an Act of Parliament sits uncomfortably with the result secured in *A*. Can there be much doubt that the radical restriction of evidence or questioning relating to a complainant's sexual history formed a fundamental feature of the Youth Justice and Criminal Evidence Act 1999?[97]

*Re S* is only consistent with *R. v. A* on the assumption that the change made in the latter did not depart substantially from a fundamental feature of the YJCEA.[98] Can that assumption be made? In order to show that it can, it is necessary to clarify what makes a legislative feature 'fundamental'. In order to qualify as a 'fundamental feature' of a statute as set out by Lord Nicholls in *Re S*, it is not sufficient simply to identify a statutory provision as important, or one which was clearly part of the legislative purpose or 'mischief' in enacting the statute. There is no doubt that the tightly

---

[93] *Ibid.* at [40].    [94] *Ibid.* at [41].    [95] *Ibid.* at [50].    [96] *Ibid.* at [44].
[97] Nicol (2004b), 276.    [98] Fenwick (2007), 177.

constrained restriction of sexual history evidence in section 41 YJCEA
was important in the sense that it was a significant part of the legislative
attempt to address an important and serious problem, and was clearly
an important part of the statute. But that does not make it a 'cardinal
principle'[99] or 'fundamental feature' in the sense meant by Lord Nicholls
in *Re S*. Even though Lord Nicholls thought there was a 'pressing need
for the Government to attend to the serious practical and legal problems
identified by the Court of Appeal'[100] in *Re S*, he felt that this reform could
not be brought about by the limited and piecemeal nature of the judicial
law-making power under section 3. A feature is 'fundamental' therefore,
*if it is so embedded in the fabric of the statute, that it cannot be removed
or changed by way of the necessarily piecemeal tool of judicial rectification.*
This is not a bright-line rule which will enable us to categorise statutory
provisions as 'fundamental' or not in the abstract. Rather, whether it is
appropriate to engage in piecemeal reform of a statutory provision will
depend on what Lord Nicholls calls 'the overall contextual setting'[101] of
the individual case. *Re S* clarifies that section 3(1) should not be used as
a way of radically reforming a whole statute or writing a quasi-legislative
code granting new powers and setting out new procedures to replace the
existing statutory scheme. This type of reform requires *legislative* law-
making and is therefore best undertaken by Parliament, rather than the
courts.

This understanding of the 'fundamental features' limit on section 3 is
borne out by further case law. It is supported by Lord Woolf's comments
in *Poplar Housing* that 'if it is necessary in order to obtain compliance to
*radically alter* the effect of the legislation this will be an indication that
more than interpretation is involved'.[102] The key word here is 'radical'. If
what is required is a radical change or reform to a whole set of legislative
provisions, then it is better to leave such reform to Parliament, rather than
try to rectify the problem by way of the more limited powers of judicial
rectification.[103] While judges may be entitled to 'read in' certain phrases
to render a statutory provision Convention-compatible, they cannot do
so if this will upset the fundamental workings of the Act as a whole,
or render the statute unworkable or unintelligible. This is exemplified

---

[99] *Re S*, above n. 90 at [23], *per* Lord Nicholls.          [100] *Ibid.* at [106].          [101] *Ibid.* at [40].
[102] *Poplar Housing*, above n. 33 at [73], emphasis added.
[103] See also *R. v. Shayler*, above n. 65 at [52]. If incompatibility would make the statute
*unintelligible or unworkable*, it will be necessary to leave it to Parliament to amend the
statute.

in *Roth*, where Lord Justice Simon Brown decided that a section 3(1) interpretation was not possible in that case because:

> The troubling features of the scheme are all interlinked: to achieve fairness would require a radically different approach. We cannot 'turn the scheme inside out'. As the authorities clearly indicate, the Court's task is to distinguish between legislation and interpretation, and confine itself to the latter. We cannot create a wholly different scheme so as to provide an acceptable alternative means of immigration control. That must be for Parliament itself.[104]

It was not possible to adopt an interpretation under section 3 which would remedy all the interlinked features which were incompatible with the Convention, so they could not rescue the incompatibility by the insertion of a word or phrase in one particular provision. To 'recreate' the scheme anew would effectively involve 're-writ[ing]'[105] the whole statute. This is a technique of legislation rather than that of interpretation and therefore should be left to the legislative domain.

This point is also illustrated by the decision in *Bellinger* v. *Bellinger*,[106] where the House of Lords declined to interpret 'male' and 'female' in section 11 (c) of the Matrimonial Causes Act 1973 to include a transsexual female under section 3 HRA. Giving the leading judgment in the case, Lord Nicholls explained:

> The recognition of gender reassignment for the purposes of marriage is part of a wider problem which should be considered as a whole and not dealt with in a piecemeal fashion. There should be a clear, coherent policy. The decision regarding recognition of gender reassignment for the purpose of marriage cannot sensibly be made in isolation from a decision on a like problem in other areas where a distinction is drawn between people on the basis of gender.[107]

Therefore, although the interpretation proposed by Mrs Bellinger under section 3(1) may have been linguistically and legally possible, it was constitutionally inappropriate because the resulting change in the law would have far-reaching practical ramifications, raising issues whose solution calls for extensive enquiry and the widest public consultation and discussion which was more appropriate for Parliament than the courts. It

---

[104] *Roth*, above n. 34 at [18].
[105] *Ibid.* at [156], *per* Jonathan Parker L.J.; see also Irvine (1999), 367.
[106] Above n. 65.    [107] *Ibid.* at [45].

is worth noting that *Bellinger* was not based on a rejection of the idea of 'reading in' *per se* or of engaging in judicial law reform through section 3(1). As Lord Irvine pointed out, '*Re S* does not preclude section 3 from producing unexpected, yet acceptable results; results that clarify and improve the law, and achieve compliance with the Convention. With section 3, Parliament has invited the courts to use the Convention creatively in order to find the right answer.'[108] Rather, it is based on a rejection of a particular type of law reform, namely, that which is so radical in effect, and so interlinked to reform in other areas of the law, that to attempt it by way of the necessarily piecemeal tool of the judicial rectification would be inappropriate.

So, although the interpretation in *R. v. A* undeniably went against what Parliament originally intended when enacting section 41, the discretion given to the trial judge by the section 3(1) interpretation did not require the setting up of whole new procedures or mechanisms to implement the decision. It could take place within the framework provided by section 41 YJCEA and the existing judicial decision-making power to consider exceptions from the general prohibition.[109] Moreover, whilst the judicial innovation proposed by the Court of Appeal's interpretation in *Re S* would have had far-reaching practical ramifications for local authorities and their care of children, including the authority's allocation of scarce financial and other resources,[110] in *R. v. A*, the question of the admissibility of certain evidence in the interests of a fair trial (the subject-matter of *R. v. A*) is one which lies within the traditional decision-making expertise of the courts. In sum, the type of legal reform which seemed necessary to the Court of Appeal in *Re S* to achieve Convention-compatibility was more radical in scope and effect than that which was necessary to achieve the same aim in *R. v. A*. These and other factors combine to show why the interpretation proposed in *Re S* would have violated a 'fundamental feature' of the legislation, whereas the interpretation in *R. v. A* did not.[111]

---

[108] Irvine (2003b), 320.

[109] In contrast, in *Re S*, the proposed interpretation involving the starring system would have entailed the court exercising 'a newly-created supervisory function', *ibid.* at [47], *per* Lord Nicholls.

[110] *Re S* at [43]. Lord Nicholls noted that 'it is impossible for a court to attempt to evaluate these ramifications', at [44].

[111] For more detailed consideration of how *Re S* and *R. v. A* are reconcilable, see Kavanagh (2004c), 537–40.

### Unanswered questions about the role of parliamentary intent

Whilst the House of Lords was beginning to articulate more fully some of the limits of interpretation under section 3(1), lingering doubts still remained about the constraining role of legislative intent. Many commentators still questioned the legitimacy of the decision in *R.* v. *A* on the basis that it contravened Parliament's intention when enacting the rape shield provision. These doubts were heightened by some of the *dicta* contained in the House of Lords decision in *Anderson*.[112] Mr Anderson had been convicted of two murders for which he received mandatory life sentences. Section 29 of the Crime (Sentences) Act 1997 provided:

> If recommended to do so by the parole board, the Secretary of State may, after consultation with the Lord Chief Justice together with the trial judge if available, release on licence a life prisoner.

In accordance with this section, the Secretary of State set a longer period of continued imprisonment for Mr Anderson than that recommended by the judiciary. Mr Anderson then argued that section 29 of the 1997 Act violated his right to a fair trial under Article 6 ECHR because it allowed the Home Secretary (a member of the Executive) to decide how long convicted murderers should spend in prison for purposes of punishment. Such matters should be dealt with by a court of law. The House of Lords accepted his argument. Following a recent case of the ECtHR,[113] they held that since the Home Secretary is not independent of the Executive and is not a tribunal, his decision-making power was not that of 'an independent tribunal' within the meaning of Article 6. Having decided unanimously that section 29 violated Article 6, the question then arose as to the appropriate remedy: could the court rectify the apparent incompatibility by way of section 3 or was it more appropriate to issue a declaration of incompatibility?

The House of Lords decided unanimously in favour of a declaration of incompatibility. Counsel for Mr Anderson argued that section 29 could be read in light of section 3, so that it could be understood as subject to a requirement that the maximum period to be served should not exceed the judicial recommendation. This option was emphatically rejected by the House of Lords who said that it was 'impossible' to adopt an interpretation

---

[112] Above n. 38.
[113] *Stafford* v. *UK* [2002] 35 E.H.R.R. 1121; *Benjamin and Wilson* v. *UK* [2002] 36 E.H.R.R. 1.

of section 29 which would remove the incompatibility. Lord Bingham noted that what 'emerges clearly'[114] from section 29 is that the power to release a convicted murderer is conferred on the Home Secretary. The decision is his alone. It was clear that this was what Parliament intended when they enacted section 29. The decision to give the power to the Home Secretary was 'plainly deliberate'.[115] He concluded:

> To read section 29 as precluding participation by the Home Secretary, if it were possible to do so, would not be judicial interpretation but judicial vandalism: it would give the section an effect quite different from that which Parliament intended and would go well beyond any interpretive process sanctioned by section 3.[116]

Lord Steyn rejected the possibility of a section 3 interpretation on similar grounds:

> It would not be interpretation but interpolation inconsistent with the plain legislative intent to entrust the decision to the Home Secretary, who was intended to be free to follow or reject judicial advice.[117]

These *dicta* seemed to suggest that the main reason their Lordships opposed the use of section 3 in *Anderson* was that it would be contrary to clear legislative intent. But this holding seemed to cast doubt on the legitimacy of the reasoning in *R. v. A* and *Lambert*.[118] Whatever else one could say about those two decisions, it was beyond doubt that they gave the statutory provisions at issue in each case 'an effect quite different from that which Parliament intended'. Moreover, both *A* and *Lambert* made clear that in adopting an interpretation under section 3(1), they were going against the intention of Parliament in enacting the respective statutory provisions. For example, in *Lambert*, Lord Hope had 'no doubt'[119] that it was possible to read section 28 of the Misuse of Drugs Act so as to impose merely an evidential burden on the accused, despite the fact that 'what Parliament chose to do'[120] was to impose a persuasive burden on defendants. In fact, going against the original intention contained in the legislation under scrutiny seemed to be part of the logic of the two-stage approach to interpretation under section 3(1), where the courts would form a view about the *prima facie* compatibility of

---

[114] *Anderson*, above n. 38 at [30].
[115] *Ibid.* at [30].    [116] *Ibid.* at [30].    [117] *Ibid.* at [59].
[118] Many academic commentators argued that the reasoning applied in *Anderson* could have been applied in *R. v. A* to deliver a different outcome, see e.g. Klug (2005), 196–7.
[119] *Lambert*, above n. 6 at [84].    [120] *Ibid.* at [68].

the legislation under scrutiny, before going on to render this compatible with the Convention (i.e. despite the apparent incompatibility). Neither *R. v. A* nor *Lambert* were discussed in *Anderson*, and it seemed that none of their Lordships in *Anderson* thought they were overruling a previously held understanding of section 3(1). However, it was also clear that the disparity between the *dicta* in these cases on the difficult issue of the role of parliamentary intention in adjudication under the HRA would need some serious consideration by the House of Lords. This issue came up for consideration in the leading case of *Ghaidan* v. *Mendoza*, which will be examined in the next chapter.

## 'Express terms' and 'necessary implications'

Before going on to examine *Ghaidan*, there is one other aspect of the *Anderson* case which merits attention here. After stating that the court could not avail of section 3 to rectify section 29, Lord Steyn went on to make a general statement about the limits of section 3(1). He said that section 3(1) 'is not available where the suggested interpretation is contrary to express statutory words or by implication necessarily contradicted by the statute'.[121] This seemed to be in tension with his statement in *R. v. A* that '[a declaration of incompatibility] must be avoided unless it is plainly impossible to do so. If a *clear* limitation on Convention rights is stated *in terms*, such an impossibility will arise.'[122]

   In the academic commentary on the developing jurisprudence on section 3/section 4, the difference between Lord Steyn's *dicta* in *R. v. A* and *Anderson* led many to conclude that Lord Steyn had 'recanted'[123] his former position or had 'rowed back from his earlier implication that there is a presumption that Convention rights should override the provisions of other statute unless there are express words to the contrary'.[124] It was argued (and perhaps hoped) that Lord Steyn had seen the error of his ways in *R. v. A* and was 'fall[ing] back into line'[125] with the more cautious approach of Lord Hope.[126] However, it is now clear that Lord Steyn's *dictum* in *R. v. A* was not meant to be an exhaustive statement of all the limits operating on section 3(1). Rather, his comments were specific to

---

[121] *Anderson*, above n. 38 at [59].    [122] *Ibid.* at [59].
[123] Gearty (2003b), 552; Nicol (2004b), 276; see also Tomkins (2008), 13.
[124] Klug (2005), 195; Turpin and Tomkins (2007), 63; Gearty (2004), 52–3.
[125] Gearty (2004), 53.
[126] In *R. v. A*, Lord Hope had stated that not only express terms, but also necessary implications would prevent a secondary interpretation, see above n. 5 at [108].

the context of *A*, where the House of Lords unanimously believed that it was possible (and desirable) to adopt a section 3(1) interpretation and that there was no impediment to this possibility contained either in the express terms of the YJCEA or its necessary implications.[127] Although he did not explicitly outline the range of situations in which a section 3 interpretation would be impossible in *A*, this did not necessarily show that he was unaware of such limits. This understanding of Lord Steyn's statements in *A* was supported by Lord Nicholls in *Re S*. Having articulated the 'fundamental features' limitation on the application of section 3(1), his Lordship noted that the boundary line between (legitimate) interpretation and (illegitimate) amendment:

> may be crossed even though a limitation on Convention rights is not stated in express terms. Lord Steyn's observations in *R. v. A* are not to be read as meaning that a clear limitation on Convention rights in terms is the *only* circumstance in which an interpretation incompatible with Convention rights may arise.[128]

This understanding has now been put beyond doubt by Lord Steyn in *Ghaidan* v. *Mendoza* when he acknowledged that the circumstances of *Anderson*, though not involving a linguistic impediment to the proposed interpretation, was nonetheless an inappropriate case for the use of section 3(1), because it would require radical rather than piecemeal reform of the legislation in question: 'interpretation [in *Anderson*] could not provide a substitute scheme'.[129] It seems that in *Ghaidan*, both Lords Steyn and Bingham took *Anderson* to be a case where the 'fundamental features' limitation on section 3(1) applied – a point which is borne out by the fact that they both cited Lord Nicholls' judgment in *Re S* in support of their conclusions in *Anderson* on the section 3 point.[130] The judicial consensus on the centrality of the 'fundamental features' limitation, meant that the discussion about express terms versus necessary implications was no longer central to the jurisprudence on section 3(1).[131]

However, although academic attention was drawn to the question of whether necessary implications were an additional limit on the operation of section 3(1), the difficult questions thrown up by the 'express terms' limitation (on which everyone seemed to agree), were largely ignored.

---

[127] See further Kavanagh (2004c). For discussion of the meaning of 'necessary implications', see Kavanagh (2004b), 277; Bennion (2002), 427–8; Cross (1995), 93.

[128] *Re S*, above n. 65 at [40]. Emphasis added.     [129] *Ghaidan*, above n. 34 at [49].

[130] *Anderson*, above n. 38 at [59], *per* Lord Steyn; [30], *per* Lord Steyn.

[131] Though we will see that it plays an important role in articulating the circumstances under which the presumptions of statutory interpretation are rebuttable, see further chapter 4.

There was a tension between two points of apparent judicial consensus in the early case law, concerning the constraining power of 'express terms'. On the one hand, all judges agreed from *R. v. A* right through to *Anderson* that limitations on Convention rights expressed 'in terms' would prevent the application of section 3(1). On the other, there was widespread consensus that the 'far-reaching' new rule in section 3 would apply even if the language of a statute was unambiguous. The fact that it would apply even with respect to unambiguous legislative provisions led to the need to 'strain' legislative language, or to read in or read down. But did this not go against the requirement that a section 3(1) interpretation would be impossible if it was contradicted by express terms? How could judges ensure that they did not 'distort' the meaning of legislation, whilst simultaneously departing from its plain and unambiguous meaning?[132] The apparent tension between the claim that section 3(1) could operate even if language is unambiguous and the statement that 'express terms' would pose a limit to it, needed to be resolved. These difficult questions were addressed in *Ghaidan* v. *Mendoza*, which we will consider in the next chapter.

## Conclusion

This chapter charted the course of the early case law on section 3(1)HRA. This period contained some cases where the courts relied on section 3(1) (*R. v. A, Lambert* and *Offen*), and others where the courts issued a declaration of incompatibility (*Re S, Anderson, Bellinger* and *Roth*). The section 3 cases showed that the courts were not shy about using their interpretive obligations to change the effect of statutory provisions in order to protect Convention rights, and that they were prepared not only to adopt narrow or broad readings of statutory provisions, but also to read in implied qualifications. A common feature of the section 4 cases was that section 4 was appropriate where a proposed interpretation would violate a 'fundamental feature' of the legislation under scrutiny. This limit reflects the necessarily piecemeal tool of interpretation and the way in which judges are constrained in the degree of law reform they can bring about, using this tool.

When the decisions in *Anderson, Re S* and *Bellinger* were handed down, there was a tendency amongst academic commentators to suggest that the House of Lords had 'settled'[133] the complex issue of the limits of

---

[132] For this formulation of the problem, Schaeffer (2005), 74.     [133] Nicol (2004b), 273.

interpretive possibility under section 3(1) in favour of 'restricting its use of s.3 and correspondingly availing itself more readily of s.4 declarations'.[134] It was claimed that these three cases were a reaction to, and departure from, the interpretive approach adopted by the 'more robust approach'[135] of the House of Lords in *R. v. A.*[136] The courts had allegedly retreated from the 'high water mark of the application of the interpretative obligation'[137] and were settling on a more cautious view of the interpretive possibilities sanctioned by section 3(1).

This reading of the case law was rejected by the House of Lords in *Ghaidan* where they unanimously rejected the idea that they were departing from *R. v. A.* However, the claim that the House of Lords had changed direction on this issue indicates a more fundamental problem with this line of thought, which goes to the theoretical points made earlier about the nature of interpretation. There, we saw that it is in the nature of interpretation that a judge must seek to balance competing values and the outcome of that balance will vary in accordance with the context of the case. Therefore, we should not expect the courts to 'settle' on an approach which favours section 3 or section 4 in the sense that they would consistently favour one section or the other as a general matter. As will be explained in later chapters, the question of whether an interpretation under section 3(1) is constitutionally appropriate, will depend on the array of contextual factors which pertain to that case. These will include the terms of the statutory provision, their interrelationship, as well as their relationship to the wider area of law of which they are a part. It will also depend on whether the disadvantages of a particular strained interpretation outweigh its advantages in terms of justice with the individual litigants. In short, it will depend, as Lord Nicholls rightly clarified in *Re S*, on the 'overall contextual setting'[138] of the statute in question.

There is a second general point which follows from this. This is that there is sometimes a tendency amongst academics to analyse the case law under section 3(1) by dislocating the general judicial statements about the scope of section 3 from the context in which they are made. They are then compared as abstract verbal formulae.[139] This tendency is compounded by the perhaps natural desire of lawyers to devise a single 'test' or set of 'tests' which will determine exactly when the limits of 'possibility' contained

---

[134] *Ibid.*, 280.    [135] Turpin and Tomkins (2007), 64.

[136] *R. v. A (No. 2)* [2002] 1 A.C. 45. This view also seems to be shared by Gearty (2003b), 552; Rose and Weir (2003), 46; Starmer (2003), 16; Bonner *et al.* (2003), 558.

[137] Arden (2004), 175.    [138] *Re S*, above n. 38 at [40] (Lord Nicholls).

[139] This claim is made with reference to another area of the law by Bagshaw (2006), 4.

in section 3(1) are reached in every case. The effort to identify a single 'test' with respect to the difficult judicial choice between sections 3 and 4 is futile, because interpretation involves a balancing exercise between two competing sets of values and the extent to which those values can be pursued is deeply context-dependent. One cannot say in advance what the outcome of this balancing process will be. As Lord Woolf commented in *Poplar Housing*, the best guide to understanding the operation of section 3(1) will lie in 'the practical experience of seeking to apply [it]'.[140] By dislocating the more abstract formulations of what section 3(1) requires from the practical context in which they are made, there is a risk of distorting and misunderstanding the true import of those statements. The constitutional propriety of choosing section 3 over section 4 is a deeply contextual and evaluative issue, not one which is determined by an abstract view about the merits of judicial rectification.

---

[140] *Poplar Housing*, above n. 33 at [76].

# 3

# Section 3(1) after *Ghaidan* v. *Mendoza*

## Introduction

Although there was a degree of judicial consensus about the new rule of interpretation, doubt still lingered about whether the express terms or parliamentary intent would constitute some limit on the application of section 3(1), and if so, to what extent. Controversy surrounded the legitimacy of the interpretive strategy adopted in *R.* v. *A*[1] and confusion was generated by the emphatic *dicta* in *Anderson* which seemed, on the surface, to suggest that the courts could not adopt a section 3(1) interpretation, if this would contravene legislative intent. The outstanding questions about express terms and parliamentary intent were addressed by the House of Lords in *Ghaidan* v. *Mendoza*[2] and it is to a consideration of this important case that we must now turn.

## *Ghaidan* v. *Mendoza*

Mr Mendoza claimed that that he was entitled to succeed to a secure tenancy under the Rent Act 1977 following the death of his same-sex partner who was the original tenant. Paragraph 2(2) of the first Schedule to the 1977 Act provided that 'a person who was living with the original tenant as his or her wife or husband' would be treated as the tenant's 'spouse' and was therefore entitled to a secure tenancy. The central question in *Ghaidan* was whether it was 'possible' to read and give effect to this provision in a Convention-compatible way so that 'spouse' could be read as including same-sex partners. Adopting the two-stage approach now well established in the case law, the first step for the court was to establish whether paragraph 2(2), as ordinarily understood, violated Convention rights. Only if this question was answered in the affirmative could they then go on to see if a section 3(1) interpretation was 'possible' to save it

---

[1] *R.* v. *A (No. 2)* [2002] 1 A.C. 45.    [2] *Ghaidan* v. *Mendoza* [2004] 3 W.L.R. 113.

from the apparent incompatibility. Their Lordships agreed unanimously that on an ordinary reading of paragraph 2(2), cohabiting same-sex couples were treated differently from cohabiting heterosexual couples in a way which was discriminatory towards same-sex couples, thus violating Mr Mendoza's Convention rights.[3] As Lord Nicholls put it: 'construed without reference to section 3 of the 1998 Act, [paragraph 2] violates [Mr Mendoza's] Convention right under Article 14 taken together with Article 8'.[4]

The next question was whether this apparent or *prima facie* discrimination could be eliminated by adopting a section 3(1) interpretation. In addressing this question, their Lordships had to consider two arguments which seemed to pose an obstacle to this route:

(1) that 'husband and wife' are gender-specific terms restricted to relationships between men and women; and
(2) that when Parliament enacted paragraph 2(2) it never intended it to cover same-sex couples.

As a matter of legislative history, paragraph 2(2) was the product of an amendment to the Rent Act to include cohabiting (but unmarried) heterosexual couples as those who would qualify for a statutory tenancy, but the Rent Act was 'not adapted to recognise the comparable position of cohabiting same-sex couples'.[5] In fact, the express terms and legislative intent were the basis on which the House of Lords had rejected the application of paragraph 2(2) to same-sex couples, only a few years earlier in *Fitzpatrick* v. *Sterling Housing Association*[6] on a set of facts virtually identical to those in *Ghaidan*. But this was pre-HRA, using ordinary methods of interpretation. In *Ghaidan*, the House of Lords now had at its disposal the new rule of interpretation contained in section 3(1) HRA. The question was whether the ruling in *Fitzpatrick* could survive the coming into force of the 1998 Act.

---

[3] *Ibid.* at [24], *per* Lord Nicholls; [128], *per* Lord Rodger; [55], *per* Lord Millett; [143], *per* Baroness Hale, Lord Steyn supporting the reasoning of the majority. The Convention rights at issue in *Ghaidan* were Article 14 taken together with Article 8.

[4] *Ibid.* at [24]. Note that Article 14 of the Convention does not confer a free-standing right of non-discrimination, but rather precludes discrimination in the 'enjoyment of the rights and freedoms set forth in this Convention'. Therefore, in order for Article 14 to be applicable, the facts at issue must fall within the ambit of one or more of the Convention rights. It was common ground between all parties that the facts in *Ghaidan* fell within the ambit of the right to respect for a person's home and privacy guaranteed by Article 8.

[5] *Ibid.* at [20], *per* Lord Nicholls.

[6] *Fitzpatrick* v. *Sterling Housing Association Ltd* [2001] 1 A.C. 27.

By a four to one majority (Lord Millett dissenting), their Lordships rejected the propositions that either the language of paragraph 2(2) or the intention with which it was enacted precluded a Convention-compatible interpretation under section 3(1). All judges in *Ghaidan* agreed that the interpretive obligation in section 3(1) was 'of an unusual and far-reaching character',[7] but the existence of section 4 also made it clear that there were limits to its application – such an interpretation would not be possible in every case.[8] The difficult task before the court was therefore to establish *when* the limits of possibility would be reached. Their Lordships were modest about their ability to articulate those limits in a comprehensive way. Lord Nicholls noted that 'a comprehensive answer to [the question of the standard by which "possibility" is to be judged] is proving elusive. The courts, including your Lordships' House, are still cautiously feeling their way forward has experience in the application of section 3 gradually accumulates.'[9] Lord Rodger echoed this note of humility. Whilst the existence of section 4 made it clear that 'there are limits to the obligation in section 3(1), they are not spelt out. In a number of cases your Lordships' House has taken tentative steps towards identifying those limits. The matter calls for further consideration in this case.'[10] In attempting to 'spell out' those limits more fully than in previous case law, their Lordships adopted the following approach.

Giving the leading judgment in *Ghaidan*, Lord Nicholls reiterated a point of judicial consensus from the early case law, namely, that the application of section 3(1) does not depend upon the presence of ambiguity in the legislation being interpreted:[11] 'even if . . . the meaning of the legislation admits of no doubt, section 3 may nonetheless require the legislation to be given a different meaning'.[12] The far-reaching implications of this foundational but seemingly innocuous observation, were not lost on Lord Nicholls.

> In the ordinary course, the interpretation of legislation involves seeking the intention reasonably to be attributed to Parliament in using the language in question. Section 3 may require the court to depart from this legislative intention, that is, depart from the intention of the Parliament which enacted the legislation.[13]

---

[7] *Ghaidan*, above n. 2 at [30].     [8] *Ibid.* at [27], *per* Lord Nicholls.
[9] *Ibid.* at [27].     [10] *Ibid.* at [104].
[11] Lord Nicholls, [29]–[30]; Lord Steyn, [44]; Lord Rodger, [119]; Lord Millett, [67].
[12] *Ibid.* at [29].     [13] *Ibid.* at [30].

Once it is accepted that section 3 may require legislation to bear a meaning which departs from the unambiguous meaning that legislation would otherwise bear:

> it becomes impossible to suppose Parliament intended that the operation of section 3 should depend critically upon the particular form of words adopted by the Parliamentary draftsman in the statutory provision under consideration. That would make the application of section 3 something of a semantic lottery.[14]

In other words, the language of the impugned statute would not be determinative of the question of whether a section 3(1) interpretation was possible or not. Drawing a distinction between the language of the statute and the 'concept expressed in that language'[15] Lord Nicholls pointed to the injustice of a situation whereby:

> if the draftsman chose to express the concept being enacted in one form of words, s. 3 would be available to achieve Convention-compliance. If he chose a different form of words, s. 3 would be impotent.[16]

From this, the 'inescapable'[17] conclusion was that:

> the *mere fact* the language of a consideration is inconsistent with the Convention-compliant meaning does not *of itself* make the Convention-complying interpretation under section 3 impossible.[18]

This injustice could be avoided because, under section 3(1), the courts were empowered to 'read in words which *change* the meaning of the enacted legislation, so as to make it Convention-compliant'[19] and to '*modify* the meaning, and hence the effect, of primary and secondary legislation'.[20] This seemed to put beyond doubt that giving a legislative provision an effect 'different from that which Parliament intended',[21] as suggested by the *dictum* of Lord Bingham in *Anderson*,[22] was not a general limit on the operation of section 3(1). Such change and modification was part of the interpretive contained in section 3 and was not precluded by it. However, Lord Nicholls was keen to stress that this process of

---

[14]  *Ibid.*    [15]  *Ibid.*    [16]  *Ibid.* at [31]–[32].    [17]  *Ibid.* at [31].

[18]  *Ibid.*, emphasis added.    [19]  *Ibid.* at [32].

[20]  *Ibid.*; see also *R. (Al-Skeini)* v. *Secretary of State for Defence* [2007] UKHL 26 at [15], *per* Lord Bingham: 'Section 3 provides an important tool to be used where it is necessary and possible to *modify* domestic legislation to avoid incompatibility with the Convention rights protected by the Act.' Emphasis added.

[21]  *R. (Anderson)* v. *Secretary of State for the Home Department* [2002] 3 W.L.R. 1800 at [30].

[22]  *Ibid.*

'modification' was not without limits.[23] First, the courts should not adopt a meaning which is inconsistent with a 'fundamental feature' of the legislation under scrutiny. It must be compatible with 'the underlying thrust'[24] or 'go with the grain of the legislation'.[25] Second, section 3(1) should not require the courts to make decisions for which they are not equipped because they would require 'legislative deliberation'.[26] He cited *Anderson* as an example of the first,[27] *Bellinger* as an example of the second,[28] and *Re S* as an example of both.[29]

Such limitations were not reached in this case. As Lord Rodger pointed out, to interpret paragraph 2 so as to include the survivor of a homosexual couple:

> would, of course, involve extending the reach of paragraph 2(2), but it would not contradict any cardinal principle of the 1977 Act. On the contrary, it would simply be a modest development of the extension of the concept of 'spouse' which Parliament itself made when it enacted paragraph 2(2) in 1988 . . . Nor is there any reason to fear that the proposed interpretation would entail far-reaching practical repercussions which the House is not in a position to evaluate.[30]

Their Lordships concluded that, in light of the discriminatory potential of paragraph 2(2), it was appropriate to read the words 'living together as his or her wife or husband' in paragraph 2(2) of Schedule 1 to the Rent Act 1977 to mean 'living together *as if they were* his or her wife or husband'. Thus, same-sex couples could be included within the scope of the provision, so that, like cohabiting heterosexual couples, they could succeed to a statutory tenancy on the death of their partner.

It was widely believed that the application of section 3(1) to paragraph 2(2) of Schedule 1 to the Rent Act was uncontroversial. Lord Nicholls opined that this was a case where 'no difficulty'[31] arose. Baroness Hale noted that counsel for the Secretary of State had not resisted the application of section 3(1) in *Ghaidan*, because it was 'not even a marginal case. It is well within the bounds of what is possible under s. 3(1) of the Human Rights Act 1998.'[32] *Ghaidan* received nothing like the critical attention which was heaped on *R. v. A*. Perhaps this was due to a perception that the application of section 3(1) in *Ghaidan* was uncontroversial

---

[23] These are outlined in by Lord Nicholls in *Ghaidan*, above n. 2 at [33].
[24] *Ibid.* at [33], *per* Lord Nicholls.      [25] *Ibid.*; [121], *per* Lord Rodger.
[26] *Ibid.* at [33], *per* Lord Nicholls.      [27] *Ibid.* at [34].      [28] *Ibid.*      [29] *Ibid.*
[30] *Ibid.* at [128].      [31] *Ibid.* at [35], *per* Lord Nicholls.
[32] *Ibid.* at [144], *per* Baroness Hale.

on the facts.[33] For, if anything, their Lordships' more general pronouncements on the scope of section 3(1) in *Ghaidan*, were more radical than
Lord Steyn's *dicta* in *R. v. A*. At the very least, they gave a ringing endorsement to the interpretive strategy adopted in *A*, putting beyond doubt that,
as far as the House of Lords was concerned, judicial modification of statutory terms and departure from legislative intent was part and parcel of
the interpretive obligation in section 3(1). I will consider first their Lordships' pronouncements on departure from express terms, before going on
to consider their implications for the role of parliamentary intent under
section 3(1).

## Modifying express terms

### *Express terms and the semantic lottery*[34]

The aim of this section is to show that whilst rectification of express
statutory terms is permissible under section 3(1), some of the *dicta* of the
House of Lords in *Ghaidan* overstate this point and give the misleading
impression that the express terms of the statute under scrutiny are of
no importance to the adjudicative task under section 3(1).[35] This overstatement is due, in part, to the courts' reliance on the metaphor of the
'semantic lottery', which requires some elucidation.

Lord Nicholls' fears about the unjust consequences of the 'semantic
lottery' were echoed in the other majority judgments. Lord Steyn warned
in general terms against 'an excessive concentration on linguistic features
of the particular statute'[36] and described *R. v. A* as a case which 'rejected
linguistic arguments in favour of a broader approach'.[37] Lord Rodger
elaborated in more detail on the concerns of the House about adhering
too rigidly to the language of the impugned statute which are worth
quoting in full:

> In enacting section 3(1) it cannot have been the intention of Parliament
> to place those asserting their rights at the mercy of the linguistic choices
> of the individual who happens to draft the provision in question. What
> matters is not so much the particular phraseology chosen by the draftsman
> as the substance of the measure which Parliament has enacted in those
> words. Equally, it cannot have been the intention of Parliament to place
> a premium on the skill of those called on to think up a neat way round

---

[33] See Kavanagh (2005b), 275.
[34] The following section is a revised version of the arguments advanced in Kavanagh (2007).
[35] See also Van Zyl Smit (2007), 299.    [36] *Ghaidan*, above n. 2 at [41].    [37] *Ibid*. at [47].

the draftsman's language. Parliament was not out to devise an entertaining parlour game for lawyers, but, so far as possible, to make legislation operate compatibly with Convention rights. This means concentrating on matters of substance, rather than on matters of mere language.[38]

The main problem with this analysis is that it involves a strange characterisation of the nature of statutory provisions and their relationship to the legislative process. In the majority judgments in *Ghaidan*, there was a tendency to characterise statutory provisions as if they were the product of the insignificant or arbitrary linguistic choice of the anonymous parliamentary draftsmen, hence the use of the word 'lottery'.[39] This underestimates the constitutional significance of the express terms of a statute, which have been supported by a majority of MPs in both Houses of Parliament.[40] So, as a conceptual matter, statutory terms should not be characterised merely as the insignificant linguistic choices of whoever happened to draft legislative provisions, as if the draftsman operated independently from Parliament. Rather, the particular statutory wording of all legislation is voted on by Parliament and, as such, is the constitutionally authorised vehicle through which Parliament expresses its intention.[41] The constitutional significance of statutory wording is in fact acknowledged by Lord Nicholls in *Spath Holme*,[42] where he was at pains to stress that the task of the court in statutory interpretation is to 'identify the meaning borne by the word in question in the particular context', rather than 'the subjective intention of the draftsman or of individual members or even of majority of individual members of either house'.[43]

Why did Lords Nicholls and Rodger overlook this important point which they had recognised in other (recent) case law? The House of Lords in *Ghaidan* was keen to stress that a section 3(1) interpretation was possible in that case, *despite the fact* that the statutory provision under scrutiny seemed to be drafted in gender-specific language. The potency of section 3(1) would be severely undermined, if it were to reach its limitation every time it ran contrary to statutory language which, on its ordinary construction, seemed to be incompatible with Convention rights. However, in seeking (quite rightly) to refute the argument that

---

[38] *Ibid.* at [123].     [39] Van Zyl Smit (2007), 299.
[40] For an account of the constitutional rationale of the legislative process, see further Kavanagh (2005a), 114ff.
[41] Kavanagh (2005a), 99.
[42] *R. v. Secretary of State for the Environment, Transport and the Regions, ex parte. Spath Holme* [2001] 2 A.C. 349.
[43] *Ibid.* at 397.

a section 3(1) interpretation would be impossible in a case where the ordinary meaning of legislative terms seemed to violate the Convention, their Lordships went too far in the opposite direction, by seeming to deny that there were *any* textual limits to the operation of section 3(1). This is why they overstated their position. For the purpose of disposing of *Ghaidan*, it would have been sufficient to say that textual or linguistic limits are not the only ones relevant to the section 3(1) enquiry, and that sometimes it will be necessary to modify the ordinary statutory meaning in order to achieve Convention-compatibility. They could have easily accepted that rectification of express statutory terms is part of the power given to judges under section 3(1), without committing themselves to the more extreme stance that statutory terms are of no relevance at all in determining the limits of a section 3(1) interpretation in a particular case. This more extreme position is not borne out by the case law. Nor is it supported by other important *dicta* in *Ghaidan* itself.

Take, for example, the *Anderson* case.[44] In *Ghaidan*, *Anderson* was cited by Lords Nicholls, Rodger and Steyn as a case which did not hinge on any linguistic difficulties in achieving a section 3(1) interpretation in that case, but rather because it would violate an important feature of the Crime (Sentences) Act 1997.[45] However, in coming to this conclusion, the House of Lords in *Anderson* placed much emphasis on the express terms of section 29. For example, Lord Hutton noted in *Anderson* that 'it is clear *from the wording* of section 29 of the Crime (Sentences) Act 1997 that Parliament intended that the decisions... are to be taken by the Home Secretary and not by the judiciary or by the parole board'.[46] Therefore 'having regard to the *clear provisions of section 29*' it was not possible pursuant to section 3(1) to interpret section 29 so as to take away from the Home Secretary the power to decide on the length of the tariff period and to give it to the judiciary. One of the factors leading the court to the conclusion that a section 3 interpretation was not possible in that case, was the fact that the power to release a convicted murderer was expressly conferred on the Home Secretary.[47] In reasoning in this way, Lord Hutton was not concentrating on form *rather than* substance, or adhering in a legalistic way to 'linguistic niceties'. Rather, his Lordship was making a judgment about the degree of legal reform necessary to make section 29 Convention-compatible, taking into account as one

---

[44] Above n. 21.    [45] *Ghaidan*, above n. 2 at [34], *per* Lord Nicholls.
[46] *Anderson*, above n. 21 at [80], emphasis added.
[47] *Ibid.* at [30], *per* Lord Bingham, emphasis added.

factor relevant to that judgment, the express terms of the statute under scrutiny.[48]

As it happens, the important role played by the express terms of the legislation in *Anderson* was acknowledged implicitly by their Lordships in *Ghaidan*. According to Lord Nicholls, what prevented the application of section 3(1) in *Anderson* was the fact that the proposed interpretation was 'inconsistent with an important feature *expressed clearly in the legislation*'.[49] Lord Rodger noted that it 'would have amounted to reading the section in such a way as to deprive the Home Secretary of the *express power* to release him'.[50] In these telling *dicta*, their Lordships show that the way in which legislation is drafted *is* a factor in considering whether rectification is possible under section 3(1). So, whilst it is certainly right to say that section 3(1) does not depend on linguistic possibilities *alone*, we should not be driven to the opposite extreme of denying that the express terms of the statute under scrutiny therefore have no role to play in determining whether a section 3(1) interpretation is appropriate in the context of a particular case.

*Ghaidan* itself is a further illustration of this point. Although a section 3(1) interpretation of the Rent Act was deemed possible in *Ghaidan*, both Lord Rodger and Baroness Hale made the valid point that 'the position might well have been different if Parliament had not enacted para 2(2) and had continued to confine the right to succeed to the husband or wife of the original tenant'.[51] In other words, had Parliament not already amended the Rent Act to broaden its application to unmarried couples, the degree of law reform required to extend its application to same-sex couples would have been more radical. A section 3(1) interpretation, rectifying its discriminatory impact on same-sex couples, would have been harder to justify in such a situation. As the legislation stood, the Convention-compatible result could be achieved by a 'modest'

---

[48] Lord Rodger seems to acknowledge this implicitly when he commented in *Ghaidan* that the court in *Anderson* could not deprive the Home Secretary of 'the *express* power to release' and could not 'negative the *explicit* power of the Secretary of State', *Ghaidan* at [111].

[49] *Ghaidan*, above n. 2 at [34], emphasis added.

[50] *Ibid.* at [111], emphasis added.

[51] *Ibid.* at [128], *per* Lord Rodger; [138] Baroness Hale: 'Had para 2 of Schedule 1 to the Rent Act 1977 stopped at protecting the surviving spouse, it might have been *easier* to say that a homosexual couple were not in an analogous situation. But it did not.' Emphasis added. Lord Nicholls also thought it significant that Parliament had explicitly removed marriage as a pre-condition for getting the tenancy, *ibid.* at [16]. In other words, a section 3 interpretation would have been harder to achieve and justify in such a situation.

extension of the statutory provision, more of a piece with the incremental and piecemeal nature of judicial law-reform.[52]

Moreover, it is important to remember that the express terms of the statute are crucial to the 'fundamental features' limitation on section 3(1), endorsed by their Lordships in *Ghaidan*. One of the primary ways in which we elicit the 'fundamental features' of any piece of legislation, is by reading its express terms. Lord Rodger acknowledged this when he said that judges should ensure that a section 3(1) interpretation is not inconsistent with the statute's 'essential principles *as disclosed by its provisions*'.[53] One of the insights of Lord Millett's dissenting judgment was that the essential features of the legislative scheme 'must be gathered in part at least from the words that Parliament has chosen to use'.[54] As his Lordship observes, 'whilst the courts may look behind the words of the statute, they cannot be disregarded or given no weight, because they are the medium by which Parliament expresses its intention'.[55] This is not a matter of choosing substance over form, but rather of acknowledging that statutory 'substance' is partly determined by statutory 'form', if by the latter we mean the terms in which Parliament has chosen to express its intentions.

Nor does this conclusion reduce the judicial duty under section 3 to the operation of a 'semantic lottery' or 'an entertaining parlour game for lawyers'.[56] It is simply to acknowledge that the entitlements and rights we have depend, in part, on the statutory provisions enacted by Parliament, and there are limits to what judges can achieve even through the most ingenious interpretation. By enacting section 3(1), Parliament chose to implement the HRA, in part, through techniques of judicial interpretation, thus leaving in place this dependence. Although the HRA gives judges more leeway than before to engage in a rectification of statutory provisions, it does not eradicate all the limits which inevitably beset the peculiarly judicial method of law reform. This will mean that the way in which legislation is drafted impacts on how easy or difficult it is to achieve a section 3(1) interpretation. Finding a suitable way of reading a statutory provision which protects Convention rights, whilst simultaneously causing the least change possible to the existing legislation, is one of the difficult tasks presented to judges under the HRA. To be sure, this is no

---

[52] This was expressed colourfully by Buxton L.J. in *Ghaidan* v. *Mendoza* (CA) [2002] 4 All E.R. 1162, since Parliament had already 'swallowed the camel of including unmarried partners within the protection given to married couples, it is not for the court to strain at the gnat of including such partners who are the same sex as each other', at [35].

[53] *Ghaidan*, above n. 2 at [121].    [54] *Ibid.* at [77].    [55] *Ibid.* at [70].    [56] *Ibid.* at [123].

parlour game for the entertainment of lawyers. Serious rights issues are involved. However, it *does* place a premium on the skill of judges occasionally to find ways around the language of the statute if that language seems on its face to violate Convention rights and a declaration of incompatibility is inappropriate.[57] The motivating force of the point about the semantic lottery was to signal that the courts are empowered to depart from statutory language, if to do so would protect Convention rights and not cause significant discordance in the legislation under scrutiny or the legislative framework as a whole. This is a valid point, but does not entail the more radical conclusion that statutory language is of no relevance to the judicial decision about the desirability of rectification.

Unfortunately, some of the *dicta* in *Ghaidan* have given credence to the view that *Ghaidan* presents 'a dismissive view as to the centrality of the statutory text in evaluating whether a Convention-compatible interpretation is possible'[58] and that their Lordships rejected 'both a focus on text and a focus on [legislative] purpose'[59] as possible constraints on the application of section 3(1). These natural misunderstandings are due to the unfortunately overstated judicial *dicta* in *Ghaidan*. The valid point which their Lordships sought to make in *Ghaidan* was that statutory language *alone* was not determinative or conclusive on the question of whether they should adopt a section 3(1) interpretation, not that it was of no significance whatsoever. If anything, *Ghaidan* endorses the importance and centrality of going with the grain of the impugned statute, including its express terms and legislative intent.

## *Section 3 – going with the legislative grain*

The House of Lords in *Ghaidan* acknowledged two important limits on the application of section 3. They were not entitled to (a) violate a fundamental feature of the legislation or (b) make decisions for which they were not equipped. Commenting on *Ghaidan* in a subsequent case, Lord Bingham observed that although *Ghaidan* provides us with some 'illuminating discussion'[60] on the scope and limits of section 3(1), the majority opinions in the case 'do not lend themselves easily to a brief summary'.[61] This is partly because their Lordships used 'differing expressions'[62] when explaining why a Convention-compliant interpretation may not be

---

[57] It also means that judges are, to a certain extent, 'at the mercy of the linguistic choices' contained in statutory provisions, see *ibid.* at [123], *per* Lord Rodger.
[58] Geiringer (2005), 112.     [59] *Ibid.*, 113.
[60] *Sheldrake* v. *DPP* [2004] UKHL 43 at [28].     [61] *Ibid.* at [28].     [62] *Ibid.*

possible. The aim of this section is to clarify the ideas to which these 'differing expressions' refer. This is of crucial importance in enabling us to articulate the limits on section 3(1), as enunciated in the leading case of its application.

Let us first examine the array of 'differing expressions' used by their Lordships in *Ghaidan* to express the limits on section 3(1). Lord Rodger warned that the courts must not go against the 'entire substance'[63] of the provision – a section 3(1) interpretation must not undermine 'the core and essence, the pith and substance of the measure',[64] or violate one of its 'cardinal principles'.[65] Both Lords Nicholls and Rodger accepted the requirement that a section 3(1) interpretation must 'go with the grain'[66] of the legislation and must be compatible with its 'underlying thrust'.[67] Finally, Lord Nicholls suggested that although the statutory language was not determinative, the important matter in determining the limits of section 3(1) was 'the concept expressed in the language'.[68] We will deal with Lord Nicholls' suggestion about the 'concept' expressed in the language, when we come to address the issue of parliamentary intent. There, it will be seen that the 'concept' relies on a type of purposive approach to statutory interpretation. In this section, we will concentrate on 'the pith and substance', 'cardinal principles', 'underlying thrust' and 'going with the grain'. It will be argued that these are all different ways of expressing the 'fundamental features' limitation on the operation of section 3(1).

Let us deal with the 'substance' first. Lord Rodger suggested that it is not the language but 'the entire substance of the provision'[69] which prevents the application of interpretation under section 3(1). It can be seen that this is another way of expressing the well-known 'fundamental features' limitation as originally put forward by Lord Nicholls in *Re S*. Recall that on my analysis of *Re S* and other case law, what makes a feature 'fundamental' is that *it pervades the legislative scheme to such an extent, that to remove it would require radical reform more appropriate to Parliament than the courts.* The idea of pervading the legislative scheme, combined with a prohibition on radical judicial law-making, is conveyed suggestively by Lord Rodger's claims that a section 3 interpretation should not violate 'the *entire* substance of the provision'[70] or that, 'however powerful the obligation in section 3(1), it does not allow the courts to change the

---

[63] *Ghaidan*, above n. 2 at [111].    [64] *Ibid.* at [111].    [65] *Ibid.* at [114].
[66] *Ibid.* at [33], *per* Lord Nicholls.    [67] *Ibid.*    [68] *Ibid.* at [31].
[69] *Ibid.* at [110].    [70] *Ibid.*, emphasis added.

substance of a provision *completely*.[71] In other words, some change of the statutory provision is allowed, but complete or radical change is not.

He goes on to explain that 'in considering what constitutes the substance of a provision or provisions under consideration, it is necessary to have regard to their place in the overall scheme of the legislation as enacted by Parliament'.[72] He cites *Roth* as an example of an interpretation which would have undermined the substance of a statutory provision. *Roth* was a 'fundamental features' case, because of the way in which the legislative provisions at issue in that case were interlinked. Lord Rodger also explicitly endorsed *Re S* and the idea that a section 3(1) interpretation would be impossible if it was 'inconsistent in an important respect with the scheme of the Act'.[73] To adopt such an interpretation would be 'to depart substantially from a fundamental feature of the Act'.[74] The prohibition on going against the legislative *scheme* is reiterated by Lord Rodger at various points in his judgment[75] and bolsters the view that he was concerned to preserve the 'fundamental features' limitation on the operation of section 3(1) in the sense of those features or principles which are so important to the legislative scheme that one could say that they are 'enshrined in the legislation *as a whole*'.[76] It is also supported by his disposition of *Ghaidan* on the facts: 'I cannot discern any principle underlying the Rent Act *as a whole*, or the first Schedule in particular, which requires that only the survivor of a long-term heterosexual relationship should be treated as a statutory tenant.'[77]

Both Lord Nicholls and Lord Rodger were at one in suggesting that when words are read into a statute, 'the meaning imported by application of section 3 must be compatible with the underlying thrust of the legislation being construed. Words implied must . . . go with the grain of the legislation.'[78] Both Lord Nicholls and Lord Rodger invoke the idea of going with the grain of the legislation in the context of elaborating on the fundamental features limitation as originally articulated by Lord Nicholls in *Re S*.[79] They wished to reinforce the point that whilst limited judicial rectification of statutory terms was possible under section 3(1), it was important that judges ensure that such rectification was not

---

[71] *Ibid.*, emphasis added.      [72] *Ibid.*      [73] *Ibid.* at [113].      [74] *Ibid.*
[75] *Ibid.* at [113], [118], [121], [122].      [76] *Ibid.* at [117], emphasis added.
[77] *Ibid.* at [128], emphasis added.
[78] *Ibid.* at [33], *per* Lord Nicholls, citing Lord Rodger's phrase of 'going with the grain' in support.
[79] *Ibid.* at [33], *per* Lord Nicholls; see also [115], *per* Lord Rodger (supporting the fundamental features limitation) and [115] supporting the idea of 'going with the grain'.

inconsistent with the overall legislative scheme. The suggestion that courts must go with the grain of the legislation under scrutiny gives metaphorical expression to this underlying judicial duty to try to achieve continuity in the law, even when developing it. It does not introduce to the section 3 jurisprudence a remarkable or novel new limitation on the operation of section 3.

However, Lord Rodger elaborates on the familiar 'fundamental features' limitation, in a way which gives it further substance. When discussing the interpretive technique of 'reading in', Lord Rodger notes that the courts can 'supply *by implication*'[80] words that are appropriate to ensure that legislation is Convention-compatible. He explains that if the court implies words which are consistent with the scheme of the legislation:

> it is reading the legislation in a way that draws out the full implications of [the legislative] terms and of the Convention rights. And, by its very nature, an implication will go with the grain of the legislation. By contrast, using the Convention rights to read in words that are inconsistent with the scheme of the legislation or with its essential principles as disclosed by its provisions does not involve any form of interpretation, by implication or otherwise.[81]

It seems that the idea of relying on what is *implied* by the statutory terms is key to Lord Rodger's understanding of when an interpretation is legitimate under section 3(1). One crucial point emerges from this *dictum*, the significance of which will be elaborated more fully in the next chapter. This is that Lord Rodger does not say that the courts must draw out the implications of the statutory terms *alone*. Rather, his claim is that the courts must draw out the implications of the 'legislative terms *and* of the Convention rights'. Convention rights must be used to inform and guide the interpretation of the statute under scrutiny. This bears out the insightful comment of Lord Woolf in *Poplar* that 'it is as though legislation which predates the HRA and conflicts with the Convention has to be treated as being subsequently amended to incorporate the language of section 3'.[82] By interpreting in accordance with section 3, the courts are not just trying to establish what statutory provisions under scrutiny mean in their context, but *also* what they are capable of meaning, when the importance of Convention rights are brought to bear on their interpretation.

---

[80]  *Ibid.* at [121], emphasis added.      [81]  *Ibid.*

[82]  *Poplar Housing & Regeneration Community Association Ltd* v. *Donoghue* [2002] Q.B. 48 at [75].

## Reading in precise words: interpretation versus amendment

The House of Lords in *Ghaidan* was keen to emphasise that section 3 would retain its potency, even in the face of legislation drafted in language which seemed to violate Convention rights. Under section 3, the courts could modify and qualify express statutory terms in order to achieve Convention-compliance. But when adopting the strategy of 'reading in', Lord Nicholls stressed that 'the precise form of words read in for this purpose is of no significance. It is their substantive effect which matters.'[83] Therefore, the court held that the phrase 'living together as his or her husband and wife' should be read to include same-sex partners, though their Lordships did not specify what particular words might be required to achieve that result. When judges engage in 'reading in' they do not have to produce a precise redrafting of the provision. As long it is clear, as a matter of substance, what the Convention-compatible reading involves, this is sufficient under section 3(1).[84]

In making this point, the House of Lords in *Ghaidan* rejected Lord Hope's earlier suggestion in *Lambert*[85] that the courts should 'seek to achieve the same attention to detail in their use of language to express the effect of applying section 3(1), as the Parliamentary Draftsman would have done if he had been amending the statute'.[86] Lord Hope emphasised that judges applying section 3(1) should be as careful as parliamentary draftsmen: 'It ought to be possible for any words that need to be substituted to be fitted in to the statute as if they had been inserted there by amendment.'[87] However, despite this recommendation that judges should 'read in' using the same standards of precision operated by parliamentary draftsmen, he nonetheless warned that:

> the interpretation of a statute by reading words in to give effect to the presumed intention must always be distinguished carefully from amendment. Amendment is a legislative act. It is an exercise which must be reserved to Parliament.[88]

> It ought to be possible for any words that need to be substituted to be fitted into the statute as if they had been inserted there by amendment.

These judicial *dicta* seem to be in tension with each other. Lord Hope's comments on the technique of 'reading in' make it seem remarkably

---

[83] *Ghaidan*, above at n. 2 [35], *per* Lord Nicholls.
[84] Lord Rodger said he was 'respectfully' disagreeing with Lord Hope's suggestion on this point at [124].
[85] *R. v. Lambert* [2002] 2 A.C. 545.     [86] *Ibid.* at [80], *per* Lord Hope.     [87] *Ibid.*
[88] *Ibid.* at [81].

like the process of legislative amendment. After all, he clarified that words should be read in 'as if they had been inserted there by amendment',[89] with the precision required by the parliamentary draftsman. On the other hand, we are told that judges should not amend legislation, which is an exclusively legislative act. This tension calls for some reconciliation.[90]

The overt tension is avoided by the House of Lords in *Ghaidan*, since they rejected Lord Hope's suggestion that when 'reading in' under section 3(1), the courts should emulate the standards of precision required by the parliamentary draftsman. The task of 'reading in' should not be compared to the legislative task of amendment in this sense. However, a similar tension nonetheless persists, because the House of Lords in *Ghaidan* openly endorsed the technique of 'reading in' which goes further than interpreting legislation restrictively or expansively.[91] It goes further because it allows the courts to 'read in words which change the meaning of the enacted legislation'.[92] Yet, changing and modifying the meaning of statutory provisions is precisely what is achieved when Parliament amends legislation. Nonetheless, Lord Rodger endorsed Lord Hope's general point in *Lambert* that judges should observe the boundary between (legitimate) interpretation and (illegitimate) amendment. Convention-compatibility can only be achieved by way of interpretation: 'the rest is left to Parliament and amounts to amendment of the legislation'.[93] So, even in *Ghaidan*, a similar tension exists between the statement that section 3(1) allows the courts to 'change' and 'modify' statutory meaning, but prohibits them from 'amending' legislation. How are these statements to be reconciled?

The answer is to be found in the theoretical account of the nature of interpretation presented in chapter 2. This account showed, first of all, that there is no bright line between interpretation and amendment. Just as judges make law when they interpret it, they also necessarily change law, improving some of its aspects, correcting its flaws or shortcomings, updating it so that it can be applied in just manner to contemporary problems and issues. Judicial law-making involves judicial change of the law and this applies as much to law made through the interpretation

---

[89]  *Ibid.* at [80].

[90]  For an attempt to reconcile them, see Kavanagh (2004b), 283–4. The argument advanced there was that, in his more general pronouncement about the illegitimacy of judges engaging in statutory amendment, Lord Hope underestimated or perhaps simply underemphasised the limited law-making role of judges in applying section 3(1).

[91]  *Ghaidan*, above n. 2 at [32].     [92]  *Ibid.* at [32].     [93]  *Ibid.* at [112].

of statutes, as it does to the common law.[94] When interpreting, norm-application inevitably becomes norm-alteration.[95] The transformative potential of interpretation is heightened under section 3(1), because the courts have deemed it possible to read down legislative provisions so that they have a narrower application than they seem to have on their face, and to delete statutory words, as well as to read in new words, phrases and indeed entire subsections, in order to achieve Convention-compatibility. These activities are the same as those types of legislative amendment which change a statute by deleting words or inserting new ones. To this extent, section 3 authorises a form of judicial amendment of statutory material and it seems as if the techniques of amendment employed by the judiciary under section 3(1), are the same as those employed by the legislature when engaging in similar types of amendment.[96] However, whilst the techniques are similar, the significant difference between judicial 'reading in' and legislative amendment lies in the conditions for introducing far-reaching reforms.[97] Whilst judges can engage in some statutory amendment, they are much more limited in their ability to do so and the legislature, which can reform the law root and branch, and can do so for purely forward-looking reasons. One of the important points emphasised by their Lordships in *Ghaidan* is that the judicial powers of rectification under section 3(1) are constrained by the requirement that they must 'go with the grain' of the legislative framework. This is the key to reconciling the apparent tension between the endorsement of judicial 'change' of statutory provisions and the emphatic prohibition on 'amendment'. As with the distinction between interpretation and legislation, the statement that judges must interpret rather than amend statutes is often

---

[94] Further exploration of the possibilities of changing statutory meaning through interpretation, see Kavanagh (2003a), 67–9.

[95] Gardner (2001), 221.

[96] In *R. v. Shayler* [2003] 1 A.C. 247, Lord Hope suggested at [52] that 'the techniques of judicial interpretation on the one hand and of legislation on the other are different, and this fact must be respected'. However, he clarified that what he meant was that if an interpretation 'would make the statute unintelligible or unworkable, it will be necessary to leave it to Parliament to amend the statute', *ibid.* at [52]. This point reinforces the analysis in this and the previous chapter, because it goes to show that legislative law-making powers (including powers of amendment) are more radical and broad-ranging, than those possessed by the judiciary. However, when the legislature decides to amend legislation in relatively minor ways (by inserting words, deleting them, broadening or narrowing their range of application), then the techniques used will be very similar to those employed by the judiciary, when adopting a Convention-compatible interpretation under section 3(1).

[97] Raz (1979), 200.

used as a conclusory label for the view that, when carrying out their tasks of judicial rectification, the courts must observe the proper constitutional limits of their law-making ability.

This reconciliation is evident in Lord Rodger's *dicta* in *Ghaidan*. Although his Lordship stated that judges should not amend legislation, he nonetheless clarified that it is not easy to decide in the abstract where the boundary lies between 'robust interpretation and amendment'.[98] The difficulty of identifying this boundary is due to the fact that statutory interpretation involves, rather than eschews, some judicial modification, qualification and change of statutory provisions. The idea that one can draw a line between interpretation and amendment simply on the basis that interpretation is purely applicative or conservative, whereas amendment involves change and innovation, succumbs to one of the common fallacies about the nature of interpretation described in chapter 2. Lord Rodger does not fall prey to this fallacy. He acknowledges that interpretation under section 3(1) can involve the courts in modifying statutory meaning. But, crucially, he accepted that the question of when the limits of section 3(1) are reached 'cannot be clear-cut and will involve matters of degree which cannot be determined in the abstract but only by considering the particular legislation in issue'.[99] Only when the matter is assessed in the context of a particular case, will it be possible to come to a conclusion about whether a particular interpretation is '*sufficiently* far-reaching'[100] such that it amounts to an illegitimate exercise of section 3(1): 'in that event, the boundary line will have been crossed and only Parliament can effect the necessary change'.[101]

Three important points can be deduced from this *dictum* by Lord Rodger, all of which reinforce the analysis of interpretation advanced in the previous chapter. First, the legitimacy of a section 3(1) interpretation must be assessed in light of the overall contextual setting of a particular instance of its application. Second, the question of legitimacy does not turn on *whether* the judiciary have changed the meaning of a statutory provision, but rather on the *degree* of change caused by their section 3 interpretation. Only when it is so far-reaching that it undermines the fundamental features of the legislation or draws the courts into questions they are ill-equipped to answer, can it be said that the type of reform necessary to achieve Convention-compatibility is more appropriate for

---

[98] *Ghaidan*, above n. 2 at [112].     [99] *Ibid.* at [115].
[100] *Ibid.*, emphasis added.     [101] *Ibid.*

Parliament. Third, by emphasising the limited law-making role of judges under section 3(1), Lord Rodger's comments reflect the more general point that interpretation includes rather than eschews judicial law-making. Moreover, by deeming it possible to read down, or to read words into a statute to make it Convention-compatible, the judiciary have authorised some change in the statutory terms themselves. Lord Rodger's claim that the courts cannot amend legislation under the HRA should not blind us to this fact. His aversion to the idea of judges amending legislation, reflects the point that the powers of judicial law-making are more limited than the much broader powers of amendment (if not outright repeal) possessed by Parliament. Even if it is accepted that section 3 necessarily authorises a form of judicial amendment of statutory terms, this is a limited power. Observation of those limits is the key to its legitimate exercise.

### Departing from legislative intent under the HRA

Although the issue of legislative intention was not perceived to be controversial with reference to the particular circumstances of the Rent Act, it was clear that hovering behind their Lordships' discussion of this issue in *Ghaidan*, was an acute awareness of the trenchant academic criticism of *R. v. A* on precisely this ground, i.e. that the House of Lords' interpretation in *A* flouted Parliament's clear intention when it enacted the Youth Justice and Criminal Evidence Act.[102] Commenting on what his Lordship perceived as a common misunderstanding of the scope of section 3(1) both in the case law and in the academic discussion, Lord Steyn observed in *Ghaidan*:

> There is the constant refrain that judicial reading down, or reading in, under section 3 would flout the will of Parliament as expressed in the statute under examination. This question cannot sensibly be considered without giving full weight to the countervailing will of Parliament as expressed in the 1998 Act.[103]

This idea of the 'countervailing' parliamentary intent contained in section 3(1) is a useful springboard from which to elucidate the role of parliamentary intention in adjudication under the HRA more generally.

---

[102] Nicol (2004a), 195; Nicol (2004b), 278; Klug (2003), 129.
[103] *Ghaidan*, above n. 2 at [40].

## Section 3(1): a tale of two intentions

In *Ghaidan*, the majority judgments emphasised that when the courts interpret legislation using section 3(1), there are two intentions at play. There is the original intention of Parliament in enacting the legislation under HRA scrutiny ('the original intention'), and there is the intention of Parliament as expressed in section 3(1) (the 'section 3(1) intention'). The problem is that these two intentions may conflict or seem to conflict.[104] How should the courts resolve such a conflict? As Lord Nicholls explained, the answer depends on how we are to understand the 'section 3(1) intention'. Unfortunately, section 3(1) is not clear on this issue[105] – it does not tell us how far a judge can go in departing from parliamentary intent, or indeed, if such departure is possible. However, we can nonetheless deduce the following points.

Section 3(1) places the courts under a duty to read and give effect to legislation so that it is compatible with Convention rights, wherever possible. The aim of section 3(1) is to ensure Convention-compatibility of primary legislation where possible. As Lord Hope put it in *R. v. A*: 'Compatibility with Convention rights is the sole guiding principle [of section 3(1)]. This is the paramount object which the rule seeks to achieve.'[106] If this were all we could say about section 3(1), then we would conclude that in a conflict between the 'original intention' and the 'section 3(1) intention', the latter would take priority automatically and in every case. It would amount to an instruction to judges to ensure that Convention rights are protected in domestic legislation, regardless of any conflict which may arise with the terms of that legislation or the original parliamentary intent in enacting it. However, although the aim of section 3(1) is to ensure Convention-compatibility, the means chosen by Parliament to achieve that aim, is judicial interpretation. As we saw in chapter 2, judicial interpretation is a necessarily piecemeal tool, which is ill-suited to achieving radical reform of a whole statute or indeed an entire legislative framework or scheme. It has a 'Janus-like' character, which requires that judges must respect the words and original legislative intent to some degree, whilst

---

[104] In fact, a *prima facie* conflict between the two intentions seems to be envisaged by the terms of section 3, since the interpretive obligation is only engaged when there is a *prima facie* violation of Convention rights. It is only when the 'original intention' expressed in the legislative provision under scrutiny seems to be incompatible with the Convention, that the courts are prompted by section 3 to seek to render it Convention-compliant, if at all possible, see Gearty (2002), 255; Rose and Weir (2003).

[105] *Ghaidan*, above n. 2 at [27]: 'section 3 itself is not free from ambiguity'.

[106] Above n. 1 at [108], *per* Lord Hope.

nonetheless being open to developing, modifying and improving the law. This means that when interpreting legislation compatibly with Convention rights under section 3, judges are not entitled to disregard the 'original intention' entirely. Rather, their task is to protect Convention rights to the extent that that is possible, given the terms and legislative intent in the original legislation.

So, the instruction to judges contained in section 3 is not 'protect Convention rights, regardless of original intent or legislative terms', but rather, 'when deciding what Parliament intended in passing the original statute, decide, so far as possible, in a way which protects Convention rights'.[107] This is captured by Lord Simon in *R. v. Holding*[108] when, following *Ghaidan*, he characterised the courts' duty under section 3(1) as follows: 'In looking for the intention of Parliament [in the legislation under scrutiny], due weight must be given to the intention evidenced by section 3 of the 1998 Act itself.'[109] It is also borne out by Lord Woolf's statement in *Poplar Housing*, that the task of the courts is still one of interpretation, albeit 'interpretation in accordance with the direction contained in section 3'. It is still interpretation because they must 'read and give effect' to the original legislation, but the direction contained in section 3 means that they must also seek to protect Convention rights wherever possible. The 'read and give effect' part of the instruction shows that the task of the courts under section 3(1) is limited to a degree by the terms and parliamentary intent of the legislation under scrutiny, so that the courts cannot achieve Convention-compatibility with utter disregard for them.

This is the key to understanding the way in which the traditional role of parliamentary intent in statutory interpretation has been 'adjusted' by section 3(1) HRA. Prior to the enactment of the HRA, the primary task of the court was to identify the intention of Parliament when enacting the legislation, and to give it a meaning in light of its context. Now, their task is to identify that intention, but to include as one important consideration in that identification, the importance of protecting Convention rights. This means that statutory interpretation under section 3(1) is still focused on the meaning and intention of the legislation under scrutiny, but the interpretive focus is now expanded or supplemented to include Convention rights in that deliberation. When interpreting under

---

[107] In formulating the section 3(1) duty in this way, I benefited from Timothy Endicott's written comments on a draft of Kavanagh (2006).

[108] *R. v. Holding* [2005] EWCA Crim 3185.　　[109] *Ibid.* at [47].

section 3(1), judges cannot consider the meaning of legislation in isolation from the goal of Convention-compatibility. As Lord Steyn pointed out in *Ghaidan* v. *Mendoza* 'section 3 requires a broad approach concentrating, amongst other things, in a purposive way *on the importance of the fundamental right involved*.[110] The object of interpretation under section 3 is not just the particular legislative provision under scrutiny *but also* the Convention rights themselves. In seeking to achieve the aim of Convention-compatibility, judges must ensure that the protection of Convention rights is bedded into the legislation, in a way which causes the least discordance possible with the original legislation and the legislative purpose behind it. As Lord Nicholls observed in *Ghaidan*, any departure from 'original intent' which may be required by the section 3(1) interpretation will be a matter of degree.[111] Only if such departure is to such a degree that it upsets the whole working of the statute, or causes other negative consequences will such departure be illegitimate.

### Preserving parliamentary intent whilst protecting Convention rights

The foregoing analysis reveals that whilst some departure from original legislative intent may be required under section 3(1), it is by no means true to say that the 'old lynchpin of the search for parliamentary intention' is entirely abolished post-HRA.[112] When one looks at the post-HRA case law, one can see that legislative intention is still significant to statutory interpretation under section 3(1) in the following ways. First, the reason why the courts might depart from original parliamentary intent is due to the importance of the legislative intention contained in section 3(1). As Lord Nicholls observed, the obligation to read and give effect to legislation in a way which is compatible with Convention rights 'is the intention of Parliament, expressed in section 3, and the court must give effect to this intention'.[113] At least to this extent, respect for the lynchpin of parliamentary intention is preserved and departure from intent is justified

---

[110] *Ibid.* at [41], emphasis added.

[111] This is implicit in his comments that whilst section 3 may require the courts to depart from the original intention, 'the question of difficulty is *how far*, and in what circumstances, section 3 requires a court to depart from the intention of the enacting Parliament', *ibid.* at [30].

[112] Thus, Laws L.J.'s extrajudicial comment in 1999 that 'section 3 of the 1998 Act, where it applies, will abolish the old lynchpin of the search for Parliamentary intention', seems to be overstated, see Laws (1999), xiv; reiterated in Laws (2004), 248.

[113] *Ghaidan*, above n. 2 at [26].

by reference to 'the countervailing will of Parliament'[114] as expressed in section 3. The added democratic legitimacy given to the courts by the terms of section 3(1) is often invoked by judges to justify creative interpretations under section 3(1) which depart from original legislative intent. In *R. v. A,*[115] for example, Lord Steyn noted that: 'in accordance with the will of Parliament *as reflected in section 3* it will sometimes be necessary to adopt an interpretation which linguistically may appear strained'.[116]

Moreover, the well-accepted 'two-stage' approach to section 3(1) entails that the courts will initially interpret a provision using 'ordinary methods of interpretation' before going on to give their interpretation in accordance with section 3(1). At the first stage of the interpretive enquiry, the traditional role of parliamentary intention is preserved. Thus, the traditional judicial attempts to discern legislative purpose by surveying and evaluating the usual array of internal and external contextual information, is an important part of the HRA case law. This careful evaluation of what Parliament intended is not swept aside by the section 3(1) stage of interpretation. On the contrary, a judicial practice has developed in the HRA jurisprudence whereby judges who adopt a Convention-compatible interpretation under section 3, simultaneously strive to give effect to, or reconcile this with both the express terms of the legislation and the legislative purpose or policy 'underlying' the statute under scrutiny.

In order to understand fully the ways in which the courts have sought to achieve this reconciliation, it is necessary to highlight a distinction between two different types of intention. As many judges have pointed out over the years, the phrase 'intention of the legislature' is a 'common but very slippery phrase which, popularly understood, may signify anything from intention embodied in positive enactment to speculative opinion as to what the legislature probably would have meant, although there has been an omission to enact it'.[117] Much of the confusion about the role of parliamentary intention in statutory interpretation, both before and after

---

[114] *Ibid.* at [40], *per* Lord Steyn.    [115] *R. v. A (No. 2)* [2002] 1 A.C. 45.

[116] *Ibid.* at [44], emphasis added. See also *R. v. DPP, ex parte Kebilene* [2000] 2 A.C. 326 at 345, *per* Lord Bingham; *Anderson*, above n. 21 at [18], *per* Lord Bingham; see also Lester (1998), 671. This line of reasoning has also been used in relation to section 4 HRA in *Anderson* where Lord Hutton pointed out that: 'if the courts declare that Parliament acted incompatibly with the Convention there is no question of the courts being in conflict with Parliament or of seeking or purporting to override the will of Parliament. The court is doing what Parliament has instructed them to do in section 4 of the 1998 Act.'

[117] *Saloman* v. *Saloman* [1897] A.C. 591 at 613, discussed in Greenberg (2006), 17ff.

the HRA, is caused by a failure to clarify the different ways in which 'the intention of Parliament' is used in judicial decisions, and the different notions of 'intention' on which they are based.

Of particular significance here is the distinction between 'the intention embodied in positive enactment' (here referred to as the 'enacted intention') and the legislative purpose, which is not enacted expressly in the statute.[118] When the courts refer to the 'intention of Parliament', they often mean the intention which is manifest and expressed in the words of the statute itself.[119] Therefore, as a general matter, it is assumed that legislative intention is evident from the text it enacted. As Lord Reid pointed out in the case of *Black-Clawson* in 1975:

> We often say that we are looking for the intention of Parliament, but that is not quite accurate. We are seeking the meaning of the words which Parliament used. We are seeking not what Parliament meant but the true meaning of what they said.[120]

The primacy of the enacted intention in statutory interpretation has also been endorsed more recently by Lord Hoffmann in *R. (Wilkinson)* v. *Inland Revenue Commissioners*[121] where he noted that what one normally means by the intention of Parliament is 'the interpretation which the reasonable reader would give to the statute read against its background'.[122] This clarifies that the question of legislative intention is not about the historical views of individual legislators, but rather concerns the meaning of statutory words used in context.[123]

However, when the meaning is unclear or where the meaning is clear but leads to absurd, unreasonable or undesirable results, the courts tend to rely on a different type of legislative intent which is often called 'the legislative purpose underlying the statutory provision'.[124] This gives rise to

[118] For further elaboration of the distinction between enacted intention and unenacted intention, see Kavanagh (2006), 181–3; Kavanagh (2005a), 100ff.

[119] This was famously described by Lord Radcliffe as the 'paramount rule' of statutory interpretation: *Attorney General for Canada* v. *Hallett & Carey Ltd* [1952] A.C. 427, 449. It has been described as 'one of the most ancient principles of the law and England and Wales', see Greenberg (2006), 15. It has been endorsed recently by the House of Lords in *Wilson* v. *First County Trust* [2003] 3 W.L.R. 568 at [56], *per* Lord Nicholls.

[120] *Black-Clawson International Ltd* v. *Papierwerke Waldhof-Aschaffenburg AG* [1975] A.C. 591 at 613.

[121] *R. (Wilkinson)* v. *Inland Revenue Commissioners* [2006] All E.R. 529.

[122] *Ibid.* at [18]. See also *Spath Holme*, above n. 42 at [395], *per* Lord Nicholls.

[123] See Cross (1995), 26; Dworkin (1985), 9, 18–23; Dworkin (1986), 317–27, 337–41.

[124] The Law Commission in 1969 described the purposive approach to interpretation as the 'construction that would promote the general legislative purpose underlying the provision in question', quoted in Cross (1995), 17.

a mode of statutory interpretation called the 'purposive approach'.[125] The idea is that, where possible, judges should adopt an interpretation which complies with or promotes the legislative purpose. Since this purpose is not manifest in the legislative provision under scrutiny, it must be elicited from a consideration of the statute as a whole and the context in which it was enacted, drawing on a wide range of contextual evidence in sources external to the statute itself, including the general scheme of statutory and common-law rules and principles, White Papers, Law Reform Commission Reports, and sometimes *Hansard*, where the aim of the contextual enquiry is to understand the context and circumstances in which the legislation was promulgated. However, the purposive approach to interpretation is not confined to cases where statutory meaning is unclear. In Sir Rupert Cross' classic work on statutory interpretation, he notes that 'if the ordinary meaning of the statute leads to a result which is contrary to the purpose of the statute, a judge should look for some other possible meaning of the words which would avoid that result'.[126] So if the legislative intent expressed in the text of the statute suggests one meaning, but this leads to undesirable or unjust results, the doctrine of purposive interpretation enjoins the courts to depart from the ordinary meaning (i.e. the clearly expressed 'enacted intention') in order to give effect to the background legislative purpose. This aspect of (pre-HRA) purposive interpretation is sometimes overlooked, i.e. that it includes the power to *depart from* the ordinary meaning of the statute in favour of a 'possible' meaning which conforms with the legislative purpose 'lying behind' the statute. It is for this reason that the literal and purposive approaches to interpretation are frequently juxtaposed, i.e. because the latter condones a departure from the literal or ordinary meaning.[127]

With this distinction in mind, we can return to the case law under the HRA, to see how judges have tried to reconcile their duty to read and give effect to legislation, but to do so in a way which protects Convention rights. In general, whilst the courts have been prepared to modify express terms, and therefore change or adjust the enacted legislative intent to

---

[125] On purposive interpretation generally, see Bennion (2002), 809–30.

[126] Cross (1995), 33.

[127] This point is also made by Hunt (1997), 106. This view that there is a long-established principle of statutory interpretation that 'the courts will often imply qualifications into the literal meaning of wide and general words in order to prevent them having some unreasonable consequence which Parliament could not have intended', was argued by counsel for the appellants in *R. (Jackson)* v. *Attorney General* [2006] 1 A.C. 262, quoted at [28] and accepted as a 'general principle' by the House of Lords, see [29], [30], *per* Lord Bingham.

some degree, they have simultaneously been concerned to preserve the integrity of those terms and the underlying legislative purpose to the greatest degree possible. This feat of reconciliation was claimed to be achieved in *R. v. Offen.*[128] There, Lord Woolf noted that:

> Notwithstanding the interpretation resulting from the application of section 3(1) of the 1998 Act suggested, section 2 [of the impugned legislation] will still give effect to the intention of Parliament. It will do so, however, in a more just, less arbitrary and more proportionate manner. It is a good example of how the 1998 Act can have a beneficial effect on the administration of justice without conceding the policy which Parliament was seeking to implement.[129]

By adopting an interpretation under section 3 in that case, the courts removed the injustice caused by the 'two strikes and you're out' provision, whilst simultaneously giving effect to what the court characterised as the general purpose or rationale underlying the legislation, namely, to impose a life sentence only on those criminals who were a danger to the public. Similarly, in *R. v. A*, Lord Steyn argued that if the proposed Convention-compatible interpretation were adopted 'section 41 will have achieved a major part of its objective but its excessive reach will be attenuated in accordance with the will of Parliament as reflected in section 3 of the 1998 Act'.[130] In other words, the proposed interpretation in that case did not sweep aside all of the restrictions on the admissibility of sexual-history evidence contained in section 41 (thus giving effect to the enacted intent and legislative purpose behind the provision to some extent), but nonetheless removed the potential violation of Article 6 ECHR.[131]

The judicial strategy of striving to reconcile the Convention-compatible interpretation with the legislative purpose underlying the original statute, is also in evidence in Lord Nicholls' judgment in *Ghaidan.*[132] His Lordship argued that 'the social policy underlying the 1988 extension of security of tenure under para 2 to the survival of couples living together as husband and wife is equally applicable to the survivor of homosexual couples living together in a close and stable relationship'.[133] Lord Nicholls stated the purpose of paragraph 2(2) of Schedule 1 to the Rent Act 1977 at a relatively

---

[128] [2001] 1 W.L.R. 254.    [129] *Ibid.* at [99].    [130] *R. v. A*, above n. 1 at 68, *per* Lord Steyn.

[131] See also e.g. *Lambert* above n. 85, where the section 3(1) interpretation still placed *some* burden of proof on the accused (i.e. an evidential one), just not the full legal burden as intended by Parliament.

[132] None of their other Lordships in *Ghaidan* went down this route of attempting to reconcile the social policy underlying the Act with the protection of Convention rights.

[133] *Ghaidan*, above n. 2 at [35].

high level of abstraction, which then informed the way in which he 'read' the explicit terms of the Act. Although the terms 'husband and wife' are gender-specific, the 'concept' underlying the legislative provision (i.e. the purpose of protecting people who are in stable, loving relationships who have set up home together) could include, or be applied equally to, same-sex couples.[134] He concluded that the section 3(1) interpretation adopted by the House of Lords in *Ghaidan* would 'eliminate the discriminatory aspect of paragraph 2 and would do so consistently with the social policy underlying paragraph 2'.[135]

Four points should be noted about this strategy of achieving Convention-compatibility whilst nonetheless furthering the (unenacted) legislative purpose when stated at a fairly high level of abstraction. The first is that, however much the Convention-compatible interpretation is reconciled with the 'legislative purpose', it is still the case that the courts are qualifying the effect of statutory provisions. They are modifying Parliament's 'enacted intention', albeit doing so in a way which strives to achieve some continuity with the legislative purpose behind the Act. We should not be blinded to this fact, simply because the courts stress that they are concerned to further the legislative purpose. Second, the extent to which they can achieve the desired reconciliation depends on how they characterise the legislative purpose. This characterisation is an evaluative rather than a mechanical task on which reasonable judges will disagree.[136] The legislative purpose of the draconian 'two strikes and you're out' provision in *Offen*[137] was held to be that of protecting the public from dangerous offenders. This enabled the court to come up with a restrictive interpretation of those provisions, so that it only applied to offenders who constituted a danger to the public. Whether this was in fact the Government's or Parliament's intention in enacting the legislation as a matter of historical fact, is hard to say. All one can say is that Parliament enacted legislation which gave rise to an *automatic* life sentence when someone had committed two out of a range of offences, which gave the judiciary no discretion to evaluate the severity or danger involved in committing those offences.

---

[134] For discussion of Lord Nicholls' idea of the 'concept' of the legislation (as an example of what he terms 'abstract purposive interpretation'), see Van Zyl Smit (2007), 299ff.

[135] *Ghaidan*, above n. 2 at [35].

[136] For an example of how difficult it can sometimes be to establish what the legislative purpose is, see *Countryside Alliance*, where the court accepted that the Hunting Act 2004 must have had a 'composite purpose', see Bingham at [40]; Lord Hope at [80].

[137] *R. v. Offen* [2001] 2 All E.R. 154.

The general point is that unlike the enacted intention which is manifest and clear in the words of the statute itself, any piece of legislation is likely to be accompanied by a multiplicity of (unenacted) legislative purposes both about how the individual legislative provisions will be applied, as well as the more general aims they are thought (or hoped) to fulfil. Judges must choose between various possible legislative purposes. There is a necessarily evaluative and creative element involved in the choice between one legislative purpose and another. This choice also extends to the level of abstraction at which a judge defines the legislative purpose. For example, in Lord Nicholls' judgment in *Ghaidan*, he acknowledged that, as a matter of historical fact, when amending the Rent Act in 1988, Parliament wished to phase out statutory tenancies altogether, but nonetheless allowed them to be given to unmarried cohabiting heterosexual couples in response to social pressure at that time.[138] There was no evidence of an 'intention' to include homosexual couples within the application of paragraph 2(2), and according to the maxim *expressio unius est exclusio alterius* (the mention of one thing is the exclusion of another)[139] it would normally[140] have been deduced that they were deliberately excluded. Lord Nicholls nonetheless attributed to paragraph 2(2) a more abstract 'social policy', by inquiring into the possible 'rationale'[141] for the provision, with Convention rights helping to inform that rationale. This example shows that the attribution to a statute of an abstract legislative purpose which secures the protection of Convention rights, may be in direct conflict with the actual historical intentions. Lord Nicholls imputed to Parliament an intention which gave sufficient importance to the Convention rights of cohabiting homosexual couples, even though it seems clear that concerns about the discriminatory effect of this legislation on same-sex couples, was not considered at all by Parliament in 1988.

Third, in the vast majority of cases, it will be possible to characterise the legislative purpose in such a way that it is compatible with Convention rights, no matter how much that interpretation departs from, adjusts or changes the enacted intention contained in that legislation. This is partly due to the role of the familiar presumptions of statutory interpretation,

---

[138] *Ghaidan*, above n. 2 at [20], where his Lordship noted that in 1988, the legislation was adapted 'to take account of the widespread contemporary trend from men and women to cohabit outside marriage but not adapted to recognise the comparable position of cohabiting same-sex couples.'

[139] See Cross (1995), 140ff.

[140] I say 'normally' because the maxim is just an aid to interpretation, not a blanket rule, see Cross (1995), 140.

[141] *Ghaidan*, above n. 2 at [13].

a topic which will be given more detailed attention in chapter 4. For the moment, it suffices to say that since the courts *presume* that Parliament did not intend to act in an unjust or unfair manner, or in a way which violates human rights, they tend to attribute to Parliament laudable legislative purposes. This is not because they are unaware that Parliament sometimes acts and intends to act unjustly, but because they are under an obligation to interpret their laws in light of a presumption that they do not so intend. They presume it to be the case, even if it is not the case in reality. So, the courts would not interpret the 'two strikes and you're out' provision in light of the legislative purpose of, say, securing electoral advantage or 'getting tough on crime and the sources of crime'. Rather, relying on the presumptions of statutory interpretation, the courts strive to find a legislative purpose which will lend itself to a just, fair, non-arbitrary and non-discriminatory interpretation. This presumption is enhanced by the interpretive obligation under section 3(1), which imposes a duty on the courts by Parliament to strive to adopt a Convention-compatible interpretation. The operation of section 3(1) gives support to the claim that its effect 'is equivalent to implying a supervening intention into an Act',[142] where the aim of the implication is to protect Convention rights.

Finally, the judicial practice of attempting to reconcile a creative interpretation under section 3 with the underlying purpose of the impugned statute, shows that even when judges consider it desirable overall to adopt a daring and innovative interpretation under section 3(1), they are still concerned to preserve the values of continuity and certainty to whatever degree is possible. This reflects the 'Janus-like' quality of interpretation described in chapter 2. Indeed, it is one of the general obligations of the judicial role to ensure continuity between existing law and that which is developed on an incremental case-by-case basis in the common law.[143] For this reason, the courts will often choose to resolve a case in a way which involves least legal change[144] and will tend to employ what Murray Hunt referred to as the 'classic common lawyer's technique' of stressing 'the essential continuity between what has gone before and what is being proposed'.[145] In adjudication under the HRA, one instantiation of this classic technique is the attempt to reconcile innovative interpretations with the underlying legislative purpose. However, there are other

---

[142] Schaeffer (2005), 74.     [143] See Raz (1979), 200ff.

[144] This is borne out by Lord Woolf's *obiter* comment in *Poplar Housing*, above n. 82 at [75] that the courts should 'limit the extent of the modified meaning to that which is necessary to achieve compatibility'.

[145] Hunt (1997), at 167, 120.

methods of maintaining legal continuity evident in the HRA case law, which should be noted here.

One such strategy is to suggest that the innovative (Convention-compatible) interpretation is one which Parliament *would have* endorsed had it given consideration to the issue, or being aware of the consequences for individual rights.[146] Examples of judicial reliance on this type of counterfactual attribution of intention are not difficult to find in the case law. Thus, in *R. v. A*, Lord Steyn suggested that as well as being consistent with the intention of Parliament as reflected in section 3(1):

> it is realistic to proceed on the basis that the legislature would not, if alerted to the problem, have wished to deny the right to an accused to put forward a full and complete defence by advancing truly probative material.[147]

However, such statements are rarely accompanied by a historical or psychological investigation into the veracity of these counterfactual claims. Rather, they are an indirect way of relying on the well-known presumption that an interpretation which would produce an absurd or unjust result was not intended by Parliament.[148] They show that even when judges engage in innovative decision-making, they are still concerned to preserve the values of continuity, authority and stability to the greatest degree possible.[149]

Another method of securing continuity is to point to other statutory provisions, either within the Act under scrutiny or in other more recent legislation, which are claimed to be an up-to-date indication of Parliament's support for the interpretation adopted by the court.[150] Thus, in *R. v. A*, Lord Hutton pointed out that section 41(3)(c) YJCEA already contained a limited exception to the general inadmissibility of evidence of the complainant's sexual history, thus showing that Parliament was not averse,

---

[146] For helpful discussion of the issues surrounding counterfactual attributions of intention, see Dworkin, (1986), 325–6; see also Marmor (2005), 169.

[147] *R. v. A*, above n. 1 at [67]. Lord Millett seemed to support the interpretive strategy adopted in *R. v. A* partly on this basis, see *Ghaidan* at [74]. For other examples, see also *R. v. Offen* [2001] 2 All E.R. 154 at [99], *per* Lord Woolf; *R. v. Secretary of State for the Home Department, ex parte Simms* [2000] 2 A.C. 115 at 129, *per* Lord Steyn.

[148] Cross (1995), 17.

[149] Another reason for such statements is that judges use them to underplay or even disclaim their creative, law-making powers, see Hart (1961), 135–6.

[150] See also *R. v. Holding* [2005] EWCA Crim 3185, where Simon J. observes at [48] that the section 3(1) interpretation adopted in that case followed the approach adopted in the Electoral Administration Bill going through Parliament at the time which was designed to correct the problem in the legislation under scrutiny. This judicial strategy of justifying innovative interpretations by reference to more recent developments in other statutes is discussed by Lord Rodger (2005), 59, though he also notes its dangers.

in principle, to admitting appropriate evidence in some situations.[151] Similarly, in *Lambert*, both Lord Steyn and Lord Hope noted that imposing an evidentiary rather than legal burden of proof under the Misuse of Drugs Act 1971, was consonant with the evidentiary burden of proof provided by section 118 of the Terrorism Act 2000.[152] This strategy shows that, when interpreting legislation under section 3(1), the courts do not take the legislative purpose of statutes as they find it. They add to that purpose a consideration of whether the statute gives sufficient importance to Convention rights. By highlighting the consonance between the resulting interpretation and more recent statutory provisions, the court is striving to achieve some continuity in legal development. These cases show that when the courts interpret creatively under section 3(1), they will try to take their cues from the legislation under scrutiny, or more recent legislation. Where a degree of reconciliation between the values underlying conservation and innovation is possible, or where it is possible to favour one whilst causing no substantial incursion on the other, it is legitimate for judges to point to this and use it as justificatory support for their decision.

### Parliamentary intention: to depart or not to depart?

The *dicta* in *Ghaidan* to the effect that section 3(1) may require the courts to depart from the legislative intention contained in the statute under scrutiny were, in many ways, unsurprising. They reflected a widespread academic and judicial assumption that the role of parliamentary intention would change under section 3(1).[153] However, this common perception that the courts would need to adjust the traditional role of parliamentary intention, ran alongside another view, which seemed to be in tension with it. This was expressed by the House of Lords in *Anderson* that a section 3(1) interpretation was impossible because it would violate 'the plain legislative intent to entrust the decision to the Home Secretary'.[154] The idea that departure from legislative intent was illegitimate under section 3(1) was also echoed in the academic criticism of *R. v. A* on the

---

[151] They would admit evidence in situations where the behaviour is relevant to consent and is so similar as it cannot reasonably be explained as a coincidence, see *R. v. A*, above n. 1 at [101], *per* Lord Hutton.

[152] *Lambert*, above n. 85 at [40], *per* Lord Steyn. At [92] Lord Hope opined that this showed Parliament recognised that 'as a general rule' statutory provisions which require the accused to prove something as a defence to the offence with which he has been charged, should be read and given effect to as if they imposed only an evidential burden on him.

[153] Bennion (2000), 91; Edwards (2000), 356; Feldman (1999a), 185–6; Gearty (2004), 52.

[154] *Anderson*, above n. 21 at [59], *per* Lord Steyn.

grounds that it 'turned the will of Parliament on its head'.[155] Even cases
decided after *Ghaidan* seemed to perpetuate the idea that giving effect
to parliamentary intention is a prevalent concern for judges in seeking
to discharge their duties legitimately under section 3(1). Thus, in *Secretary of State for the Home Department* v. *MB*,[156] Lord Bingham expressed
reluctance about adopting a section 3(1) interpretation of the Prevention
of Terrorism Act 2005, because 'any weakening of the mandatory language used by Parliament would very clearly fly in the face of Parliament's
intention'.[157] Although his Lordship ultimately agreed to apply section
3(1) in that case, it was nonetheless clear that his reservations about this
course of action were grounded in concerns about departing from the
express terms and parliamentary intent. So, despite the unequivocal affir-
mation in *Ghaidan* that departure from legislative intent was legitimate,
there is still a widespread view that departure from legislative intent is an
indication that an interpretation under section 3(1) has gone too far. The
tension between these two positions needs to be resolved, if we are to fully
appreciate the role of parliamentary intention in adjudication under the
HRA.

The key to resolving this tension is to bear in mind the point made
by Lord Nicholls in *Ghaidan* that departure from legislative intention is
a matter of degree. The legitimacy or illegitimacy of an interpretation
does not hinge on *whether* the courts depart from legislative intent, but
rather on the *extent* to which it so departs. If taken out of context, one can
easily find emphatic-sounding judicial *dicta* suggesting that a section 3(1)
interpretation is impossible if it would go against parliamentary intent.
The *dicta* in *Anderson* are a prime example. However, as Lord Bingham observed in *Sheldrake*, judicial pronouncements on section 3 are
'inevitably of some complexity. They must be read with reference to the
particular case with which the House was dealing.'[158] When we look more
closely at the context of the *dicta* in *Anderson* about violating parliamentary intent, it can be seen that what prevented a section 3(1) interpretation
in that case, was not departure from legislative intent *per se*, but rather that
such an interpretation would require radical reform of the statute under
scrutiny and would violate one of its fundamental features.[159] For these
reasons, the *dicta* in *Anderson* should not be taken at face value. Nor should

---

[155] Klug (2003), 128.    [156] [2007] UKHL 46.    [157] *Ibid.* at [44].
[158] *Sheldrake*, above n. 60 at [26].
[159] For a more detailed consideration of the various contextual factors preventing a section
3(1) interpretation in that case, see Kavanagh (2006), 200ff.

the *obiter* judicial reservations in *MB* be taken as proof that departure from clear wording or legislative intent is inherently illegitimate.

If the courts were prohibited from giving legislative provisions an effect not intended by the Parliament enacting it, it would completely undermine the operation of section 3(1) HRA. Section 3(1) is only engaged when the 'natural and ordinary meaning' of a statutory provision seems to conflict with the Convention. Judges are then instructed to find a possible Convention-compatible meaning, *despite* this apparent conflict. If this 'transformative potential'[160] were denied, it is difficult to see how section 3(1) would have any substantive task to perform, or if indeed it would add anything new to ordinary methods of statutory construction. If the courts were not empowered to go against the 'original intention' to some degree, then section 3(1) would be rendered otiose. It follows that departure from the express words or legislative purpose are not, in themselves, indications that a section 3(1) interpretation is prohibited. As Lord Nicholls put it: '*the mere fact* the language under consideration is inconsistent with the Convention-compliant meaning *does not of itself* make a Convention-compliant interpretation under section 3 impossible'.[161] The possibility of departing from express terms and legislative intent is part and parcel of section 3(1).

Moreover, given the fact that respecting the will of Parliament is thought to be one of the most fundamental principles of statutory interpretation (and, indeed, thought to follow from the principle of parliamentary sovereignty),[162] we should not be surprised if judges routinely say that their judgments give effect to the will of Parliament. A perusal of the case law under the HRA reveals that judges *always* tend to characterise their decisions in terms of deference to the will of Parliament, no matter how innovative that decision is. This tendency trades on the ambiguity in the idea of parliamentary intention outlined above, so that even if the courts override, change, amend or supplement Parliament's *enacted intention*, judges will tend to point out that this result is compatible with the *(unenacted) legislative purpose*. If this is not possible or desirable, they may say that their interpretation gives effect to the parliamentary intention contained in section 3(1), even if the effect of section 3(1) is, in substance, to instruct the courts to qualify or adjust the parliamentary intention expressed in the impugned legislation. Alternatively, they can rely on the 'presumptions' of parliamentary intention. In one form or

---

[160] Kavanagh (2004b), 274.     [161] *Ghaidan*, above n. 2 at [32], emphasis added.
[162] See Goldsworthy (2004), 187ff.

another, adherence to parliamentary intention is woven into the fabric of adjudication under the HRA at every point. Therefore, it is unsurprising that judges will refer to it, because it still plays an important role in post-HRA statutory interpretation.

Beyond this important role, there is also the fact that giving effect to the intention of Parliament is a way of garnering legitimacy for judicial decisions. Judicial declarations of deference to parliamentary intent are sometimes little more than a rhetorical device to express judicial subordination to Parliament.[163] As Lord Steyn said (extrajudicially): 'It is sometimes meaningful and appropriate for a judge to refer to the intention of Parliament *in recognition of its supreme lawmaking power.*'[164] By framing a judicial decision in terms of giving effect to the intention of Parliament, judges can downplay their creative role in statutory interpretation and emphasise its applicative dimension.[165] It can give very creative decisions a 'cloak of respectability',[166] by suggesting that the courts are upholding, not usurping, the legislative function. It is a way of expressing the courts' comity with Parliament. Often, the importance of deferring to clear legislative intent is used by the judiciary as a conclusory label to signal that a particular interpretation would be illegitimate or would usurp the role of Parliament. My analysis has shown that we need to be careful about which type of parliamentary intent judges are relying on, whilst bearing in mind that such reliance does not preclude a considerable amount of judicial creativity. It also shows that, in assessing the meaning and import of particular judicial *dicta*, we should be alert to the political and rhetorical dimension of judicial reasoning.

### Lord Millett's dissent

Having now explicated the sense in which the courts thought it appropriate to depart from express terms and legislative intent, it is appropriate to make some comments about Lord Millett's dissenting judgment, because they too give us some insight into the scope and limits of section 3(1).

---

[163] This point is also made by Cross (1995), 29.
[164] Steyn (2001), 64, emphasis added.    [165] See Cross (1995), 29.
[166] This phrase is borrowed from Lord Woolf (1995), 67, referring to the judicial use of the 'presumed intention' model to justify the precedence of EU law over UK legislation. As Paul Craig points out, this approach 'preserves the formal veneer of Diceyan orthodoxy while undermining its substance' and has the advantage of making Parliament rather than the courts seem responsible for the subordination of UK law to EU law: Craig (1991), 251.

This chapter endorsed Lord Millett's insight that 'the limits on the application of section 3 must be in part at least linguistic'.[167] The majority overstated the valid point that *some* departure from a statute's 'ordinary meaning' would be a legitimate application of section 3. Their overstatement led them to suggest that statutory language is of no significance at all to the judicial decision about the appropriateness of adopting a section 3 interpretation. Lord Millett's dissent is a valuable reminder of the importance of statutory language and the way in which it is the primary means of establishing what Parliament intended. However, I want to argue here that Lord Millett is also guilty of overstatement, albeit in the opposite direction. In refusing to apply section 3(1) to the Rent Act in *Ghaidan*, Lord Millett's judgment places so much weight on the 'ordinary meaning' and 'legislative purpose' of paragraph 2 of Schedule 1 to the Rent Act 1977 that it does not differ from ordinary methods of statutory interpretation. In other words, Lord Millett's understanding of section 3(1) in *Ghaidan* renders the section otiose.

Lord Millett's general pronouncements on the ambit of section 3(1) are just as noteworthy for their conformity with the majority's view on the nature of section 3(1), as they are for his ultimate dissent when applying section 3(1) to the facts of *Ghaidan*.[168] First, Lord Millett endorsed the well-known, two-stage approach to interpretation under section 3(1)[169] and agreed with the rest of the House that section 3 may require the courts to depart from the unambiguous meaning of the statutory provision and give it 'a different meaning'.[170] Following from this shared premise, Lord Millett accepted that section 3(1) introduced a novel form of interpretation which 'obliges the court to give *an abnormal construction* to the statutory language' which 'cannot be achieved by resort to standard principles and presumptions'.[171] Furthermore, Lord Millett agreed on the range of techniques which could be adopted by the courts to arrive at

---

[167]  *Ghaidan*, above n. 2 at [72].

[168]  This is explicitly acknowledged by Lord Millett at [69]; see also Van Zyl Smit (2007), 301; Young (2005), 26. Lord Millett's *dicta* are often cited alongside Lord Nicholls' *dicta* as evidence of the general principles which emerge from *Ghaidan* on the question of the proper ambit of section 3(1), see e.g. *R. v. Holding*, above n. 150 at [47], *per* Simon J. In fact, Lord Millett's suggestion that the courts can stretch statutory language almost 'to breaking point' is sometimes seen as one of the most radical general statements in *Ghaidan* on the ambit of section 3(1), see e.g. Allan J. (2006), 11.

[169]  *Ibid.* at [60].      [170]  *Ibid.* at [67].

[171]  *Ibid.* at [60], emphasis added, see also [61] where he noted that giving an 'abnormal construction to statutory language' is a task which the courts 'have not hitherto been accustomed to perform, and where they must accordingly establish their own ground rules for the first time'.

this 'abnormal construction': the courts can read in and read down and 'supply missing words so long as they are consistent with the fundamental features of the legislative scheme'.[172] He even went as far as to suggest that the courts can 'do considerable violence to the language and stretch it almost (but not quite) to breaking point'.[173] Finally, he joined the rest of the House in confirming that the interpretation adopted in *R. v. A* (often perceived as the most 'radical' case relying on section 3(1)) was a legitimate exercise of the court's powers under section 3(1). According to Lord Millett, the interpretation adopted there merely 'glossed but did not contradict anything in the relevant statute'.[174]

After reading these general pronouncements, especially the endorsement of *R. v. A*, one might have expected Lord Millett to support the majority in giving paragraph 2(2) a meaning which departed to some extent from its ordinary meaning. But Lord Millett dissented on the issue of whether section 3(1) could be applied in the circumstances of *Ghaidan* and we need to examine why. After setting out the general principles which he shared with the majority, Lord Millett went on to articulate further limits on the operation of section 3(1) which depart from the majority view and are also in tension with his own general pronouncements. Lord Millett claimed that the limits on section 3 'may also be derived from a consideration of the legislative history of the offending statute'.[175] In applying section 3, 'the court must take the language of the statute as it finds it and give it a meaning which, however unnatural or unreasonable, it is intellectually defensible'.[176] Whatever judges can achieve under section 3, this must be possible 'by a process of interpretation alone'.[177] Section 3(1) does not entitle the court 'to contradict the language of the offending statute' or to modify its effect – to do so would be to exercise a 'quasi-legislative' rather than an 'exclusively interpretative' role.[178]

It seems that Lord Millett succumbs here to one of the common fallacies about the nature of interpretation, namely, that it is purely applicative and conservative and involves no creative element. In chapter 2, we observed that it is in the nature of interpretation to *include* some modification of statutory meaning, such that it entails (rather than eschews) judicial law-making which shares some similarities with legislative law-making.[179] If this is correct, it casts doubt on Lord Millett's distinction between a

---

[172] *Ibid.* at [67].    [173] *Ibid.*
[174] *Ibid.* at [74]. For a defence of the legitimacy of *R. v. A*, see Kavanagh (2005b).
[175] *Ibid.* at [72].    [176] *Ibid.* at [67].    [177] *Ibid.* at [66].    [178] *Ibid.* at [68].
[179] Kavanagh (2004b), 266–7.

quasi-legislative and interpretative power. Even pre-HRA, statutory interpretation has had a quasi-legislative dimension, if what is meant by that is the fact that the rules of statutory interpretation give the courts devices with which they can attenuate, modify, change and improve statutory provisions. There is nothing radical in the suggestion that the courts ought not to be hide-bound by a slavish adherence to literal or 'ordinary meaning'. The 'purposive approach' to statutory interpretation has long since legitimated the power of the courts to depart from ordinary meaning, if to do so would enhance the legislative purpose. So, saying that section 3(1) restricts the courts to the devices of 'interpretation alone' does not get us very far in articulating the limits of section 3(1). Even the traditional doctrines of statutory interpretation allow and sometimes require the courts to adopt creative interpretations of statutory language, such that the ordinary meaning is modified or changed.

In fact, it is difficult to see exactly how Lord Millett can maintain his distinction between interpretation (which does not allow for modification of statutory terms) and legislation (which does) whilst simultaneously arguing that section 3(1) entitles the court to depart from the unambiguous meaning of the statutory provision and 'do considerable violence' to statutory language. One might well wonder how Lord Millett can claim that the courts can adopt an abnormal construction which is different from its unambiguous ordinary meaning, but nonetheless 'take the language of the statute as it finds it'. Lord Millett does not address the tension which exists between his general characterisation of section 3 as allowing 'unnatural', 'unreasonable' and 'abnormal' constructions of statutory language, and his more specific comments about how it should be applied in a way which is constrained by ordinary meaning. Moreover, the requirement that interpretations be 'intellectually defensible' is too vague to give us any meaningful indication about when the limits of section 3 might be reached. It is hard to imagine any judgment which would not meet this minimal criterion.[180]

This brings us to a consideration of Lord Millett's view about the role of parliamentary intent in adjudication under the HRA. Lord Millett supported Lord Steyn's comment in *R. v. A* that had Parliament been alerted to the problem, it would not have wished to deny an accused person the right to put forward full and complete deference by advancing truly probative material.[181] As noted earlier, this counterfactual attribution of

---

[180] As James Allan points out, mere intellectual defensibility is not a high hurdle to surmount, see Allan (2006), 11.

[181] *Ghaidan*, above n. 2 at [73], *per* Lord Millett.

intent to Parliament draws on the presumption of statutory interpretation that Parliament never intends to do something unjust or something which violates fundamental rights, and that this hypothetical intent need not match the 'actual' intent. But leaving this point aside, Lord Millett suggested that the type of relationship Parliament had 'in contemplation'[182] when enacting paragraph 2 of the Rent Act was an open relationship of the opposite sex. The language used was gender specific, and it seemed clear that 'Parliament contemplated an open relationship, whether legal or *de facto*, the essential feature of which is that, unlike other relationships, it subsists and can subsist only between persons of the opposite sex'.[183] In other words, Lord Millett's argument was that since the legislative purpose behind paragraph 2 was confined to heterosexual couples, this should preclude the application of section 3(1). It follows that, on Lord Millett's analysis, section 3(1) cannot be used to remedy under-inclusive legislation, where there is some evidence from the parliamentary debates that a wider range of beneficiaries was not meant to be included within the application of the statutory provision.[184]

This type of reliance on the unenacted legislative purpose as a barrier to the operation of section 3(1) is in direct contrast to the understanding of legislative intent prevalent in the majority judgments, as well as all the other judgments on section 3(1). As Lord Hoffmann pointed out in the case of *Wilkinson*,[185] the section 3(1) interpretation adopted in *Ghaidan* may have come as a surprise to the MPs who enacted paragraph 2 in 1988, but

> that is not normally what one means by the intention of Parliament. One means the interpretation which the reasonable reader would give to the statute read against its background, including, now, and assumption that it was not intended to be incompatible with Convention rights.[186]

---

[182] *Ibid.* at [78].    [183] *Ibid.* at [81].

[184] Of course, this conclusion would seem to impugn the strategy of 'reading in' carried out by the House of Lords in *R. v. A*, because there was some *Hansard* evidence that the specific purpose of the Government in enacting section 41 was to remove judicial discretion to adjudicate the issue, and replace it instead with a tightly circumscribed legislative rule. In adopting a section 3(1) interpretation in *R. v. A*, the House of Lords remedied the over-inclusive nature of that legislative rule. One would have expected Lord Millett to criticise *R. v. A* on the basis that in setting out a tightly circumscribed list of exceptions to the general prohibition on admitting sexual history evidence, Parliament deliberately omitted any other exception, which could not be supplied by the court under section 3(1). On the contrary, Lord Millett argued that in *R. v. A* 'the court supplied a missing qualification which significantly limited the operation of the statute but which did not contradict any of its fundamental features' at [73].

[185] *Wilkinson*, above n. 121.    [186] *Ibid.* at [18].

Lord Millett's particular use of legislative history here goes against the well-established principle of statutory interpretation that the search for legislative intent is an objective, not a subjective enterprise.

Moreover, the majority used the relevant Convention right (Article 8) to inform the legislative purpose they attributed to paragraph 2(2), and Lord Millett did not.[187] Lord Millett took both the language of paragraph 2(2) and the legislative purpose behind it as he found them, whereas the majority took more seriously their obligation to read and give effect to legislation *in a Convention-compatible way*. For Lord Nicholls, a crucial step in identifying the legislative purpose in the way they did was the fact that no Convention-compatible justification for paragraph 2(2) (as ordinarily understood) could be found. He was therefore driven to identify a more abstract rationale for the section which could apply to heterosexual and same-sex couples alike. This set the stage for a Convention-compatible interpretation under section 3(1).

Apart from being at variance with his own general pronouncements about the ambit of section 3(1), it is difficult to see how Lord Millett's application of section 3(1) differs in any way from traditional methods of statutory interpretation, where ordinary meaning and legislative purpose are given pride of place.[188] The key to understanding Lord Millet's view that a section 3(1) interpretation would be impossible in *Ghaidan* is contained in his characterisation of the essential features of 'living together as husband and wife'. For Lord Millett, 'living together as his or her husband and wife' had two essential features: one was that the relationship be open, the other was that it be between persons of the opposite sex.[189] But Lord Millett argued that a same-sex relationship could not be 'open', and therefore could not be included in the 'essential features' of the relationship envisaged by Parliament. Lord Millett's views on the 'openness' requirement seem out of touch with contemporary reality, since it is not uncommon for same-sex couples to set up home together and live openly in a stable, loving relationship which is, as Baroness Hale put it, 'marriage-like'. In today's world, she opined that there is 'no difficulty in applying the term "marriage-like" to same-sex relationships'.[190] Lord

---

[187] Lord Millett's judgment seemed to show that he was searching for the 'subjective' intentions behind the Act, rather than the objective meaning of the words used by Parliament.

[188] As Van Zyl Smit points out, 'nothing in Lord Millett's approach to the Rent Act, as opposed to his general *dicta*, indicate that section 3 of the HRA has made a difference to statutory interpretation', see Van Zyl Smit (2007), 301.

[189] *Ghaidan* at [78].      [190] *Ibid.* at [144].

Millett was led astray in *Ghaidan* (indeed led astray from his own general pronouncements on the ambit of section 3(1)) by an outdated understanding of the relationships same-sex couples have. This prevented him from seeing that they could have open, stable relationships *in the same way* as heterosexual couples, thus requiring a modest extension of paragraph 2 in order to remove the discrimination against them.[191]

### Section 3 after *Ghaidan* v. *Mendoza*: some general principles

*Ghaidan* is the leading case on the interpretation of statutes under section 3(1). Despite the fact that their Lordships used different modes of expression to articulate the limits on section 3(1), there was considerable agreement on what those limits were in substance. From the various judgments in *Ghaidan*, we can distil some central points of consensus, which follow from and amplify the earlier case law on section 3(1):

(1) Section 3(1) is subject to two important limits: the familiar 'fundamental features' limitation and the requirement that judges should not make decisions which 'would require legislative deliberation'.[192] The first of these limits has been explored in depth. The second will be explored more fully when we come to examine the doctrine of judicial deference in chapter 7.

(2) Whilst observing those important limits, section 3(1) allows for (and may sometimes require) judicial rectification of statutory terms, which includes the ability to modify and change statutory meaning.[193] Not only can the court read vague or general statutory provisions more restrictively or expansively, they can also use the techniques of 'reading in' or 'reading down' as exemplified most dramatically in *R.* v. *A.*

(3) When employing these techniques of rectification, judges must nonetheless ensure that the 'reading in' 'goes with the grain' of the statute and does not disturb the legislative scheme when viewed as a whole.[194] *Ghaidan* emphasises the importance of adopting a close contextual analysis of the legislation under scrutiny, when

---

[191] The point that Lord Millett's argument 'does not accurately reflect the facts about same-sex relationships in modern society' is also made by Van Zyl Smit (2007), 302.

[192] *Ibid.* at [33], *per* Lord Nicholls.

[193] *Ibid.* at [32], *per* Lord Nicholls; [124], *per* Lord Rodger.

[194] *Ibid.* at [33], *per* Lord Nicholls; [121], *per* Lord Rodger.

determining the propriety of a section 3(1) interpretation in any particular case.[195]

(4) *Ghaidan* is a ringing endorsement of the interpretive strategy of 'reading in' adopted by the House of Lords in *R. v. A.*[196] This shows that section 3(1) can be used to remedy under-inclusive as well as over-inclusive legislation.

(5) 'Reading in' does not depend on the number of words used to achieve the Convention-compatible result. As long as the words read into the statutory provision go with the legislative grain, and do not upset the legislative scheme as a whole, a 'reading in' is not illegitimate, simply because it requires a large number of words to achieve the Convention-compatible result.[197] This was a clear signal that the decision in *R. v. A* was no more illegitimate than, say, the decision in *Lambert* or *Offen*, simply because the former required judicial enunciation of a whole new judicial test for the admissibility of sexual history evidence.

(6) When 'reading in', the courts do not have to emulate the standards of precision required by the parliamentary draftsman. It suffices if they make clear what the Convention-compatible outcome will be.[198]

(7) Section 3(1) may sometimes require the court to depart from Parliament's original intention when enacting legislation which arises for judicial scrutiny under the HRA.[199] This includes the '*enacted intention*' (i.e. the intention which has been expressed in the language of the statutory provision), but also the *(unenacted) legislative purpose* lying behind that provision. *Ghaidan* endorses the view that when interpreting a statutory provision in light of section 3(1), Parliament's intention in enacting section 3(1) was that some departure

---

[195] Contrary to this analysis, Elizabeth Palmer suggests that their Lordships in *Ghaidan* were unconcerned with a close contextual analysis of the Rent Act, see Palmer (2007), 127. It may be that Palmer has been led to this conclusion by the unfortunately overstated nature of the some of their Lordships' *dicta*, which give the false impression that express terms are of no significance in determining the propriety of a section 3(1) interpretation. However, the unity of the majority behind the proposition that an interpretation must 'go with the grain' of the legislation, support its 'underlying thrust', and comply with its 'pith and substance', all emphasise the importance of legislative context in determining the appropriateness of an interpretation under section 3(1).

[196] *Ghaidan*, above n. 2 at [29], *per* Lord Nicholls; [47], *per* Lord Steyn; [67], *per* Lord Millett; [106], *per* Lord Rodger.

[197] *Ibid.* at [122], *per* Lord Rodger.

[198] *Ibid.* at [124], *per* Lord Rodger.

[199] *Ibid.* at [30], *per* Lord Nicholls.

from their intentions in previous (and indeed subsequent) legislation may be necessary to achieve Convention-compatibility. The
focus on the 'original intention' of the statute under scrutiny is not
entirely removed – rather, it should be reconciled with the 'section
3(1) intention' if possible. Various judicial strategies of reconciliation
were examined.

(8) Finally, contrary to some of the more extreme *dicta* in *Ghaidan*,
express terms and legislative intent have a constraining effect on the
possibilities of a section 3(1) interpretation, but they do not pose
an *automatic* barrier to its application.[200] The legitimacy of such
departure of a matter of degree, which needed to be evaluated in
the context of the individual case. It depends on the *extent* of the
departure, and in particular whether it departs from the fundamental
features of the legislation under scrutiny or involves the courts in
making a decision for which they are ill-equipped.

The idea that, when interpreting under section 3(1), the courts should
not place excessive concentration on the linguistic features of the statute
under scrutiny, may have been motivated by a concern to stress that the
application of section 3(1) does not depend on linguistic possibility alone.
Even if a Convention-compatible interpretation is possible linguistically, it
may not be constitutionally appropriate or desirable all things considered.
No judicial decision is justified simply on the basis that it is 'possible'. Like
any other act of statutory interpretation, interpretation under section
3(1) must be supported by strong 'justifying reasons'.[201] Therefore, mere
linguistic possibility does not *determine* the scope and limits of section
3(1). Whether it is possible to adopt an interpretation under section 3
is part of a much broader evaluative judgment related to the limits of
judicial law-making and considerations of constitutional propriety.[202]

---

[200] As Lord Nicholls observed 'the *mere fact* that the language under consideration is inconsistent with the Convention compliant meaning does not *of itself* make it Convention
compliant interpretation under section 3 impossible', emphasis added.

[201] See chapter 2, 31; see also Kavanagh (2004b), 262.

[202] That these broader considerations about 'constitutional propriety' are involved in traditional statutory interpretation seeking to elicit Parliament's intent, is emphasised in Lord
Wilberforce's judgment in *Black-Clawson* at 629–30.

# 4

## Section 3(1) as a strong presumption of statutory interpretation

### Introduction

As the leading case on section 3(1), *Ghaidan* has been followed and applied in the subsequent case law.[1] These cases have tended to show that judges will depart from ordinary meaning and legislative intent to a degree, and are prepared to rectify statutory language, whilst nonetheless observing the 'fundamental features' limitation emphasised in *Ghaidan*.[2] One case of particular note is the House of Lords decision in *R. (Wilkinson) v. Inland Revenue Commissioners*.[3] Some academic commentators have suggested that Lord Hoffmann's leading judgment in *Wilkinson* presents a 'revised rationale'[4] for the decision in *Ghaidan* and constitutes a retrenchment from some of the more radical *dicta* contained in it. They claim that *Wilkinson* 'reassert[s] the importance of text and purpose as constraints on the interpretive possibilities available in light of section 3(1).'[5] Since the role of text and purpose have been the twin *leitmotivs* of the leading case-law on section 3(1), we must examine Lord Hoffmann's judgment in *Wilkinson*, in order to clarify the current judicial understanding of the scope of section 3(1), as well as the plausibility of the view that it presents a 'rather less bold conception of the role of section 3(1)'.[6] This chapter will argue that Lord Hoffmann in fact supports a strong conception of section 3(1). Some of his *dicta* on the ambit of section 3(1) will be used as a springboard for presenting my own understanding of the nature of section 3(1), namely, that it enacts a strong presumption of statutory interpretation.

---

[1] See e.g. *Sheldrake* v. *DPP* [2004] UKHL 43; *R.* v. *Holding* [2005] EWCA Crim 3185; *Culnane* v. *Morris* [2005] EWHC 2438; *Connolly* v. *DPP* [2007] EWHC 237 (Divisional Court).

[2] *Ghaidan* v. *Mendoza* [2004] 3 W.L.R. 113.

[3] *R. (Wilkinson)* v. *Inland Revenue Commissioners* [2006] All E.R. 529.

[4] Van Zyl Smit (2007), 294.     [5] Geiringer (2008), 81.     [6] *Ibid.*, 82.

## *Wilkinson*: a weak conception of section 3(1)?

Mr Wilkinson was a widower who argued that he should receive a tax allowance that had hitherto been granted only to widows under section 262(1) of the Income and Corporation Taxes Act 1988 (hereinafter ICTA).[7] To avoid sex discrimination under the Convention, he argued that the term 'widow' should be interpreted so as to include the words 'widower' under section 3 HRA. The House of Lords rejected this possibility unanimously. Giving the leading judgment, Lord Hoffmann rested the weight of his argument on the fact that when one reads section 262 in the context of the statute as a whole, one could see that whilst Parliament had used gender-neutral terms in other sections of the Act, it specifically confined the application of section 262 to widows and did not extend it to widowers.[8] Therefore, a reasonable reader would understand Parliament to have confined its application to widows.

The question was whether section 3 HRA would allow the court to modify this understanding. Could section 3 operate as a 'counterweight'[9] to the various indications throughout the statute, that Parliament intended this section to be gender specific, but others to be gender neutral? Lord Hoffmann said that it could not. Section 3 did not entitle the courts 'to give the language of statutes acontextual meanings. That would be playing games with words'.[10] Applying *Ghaidan*, he said that it would sometimes be possible under section 3(1):

> to construe a statutory provision as referring to, or qualified by, some general concept implied rather than expressly mentioned in the language used by Parliament. Thus, in *Ghaidan* v. *Mendoza*, the words '*as* his or her wife or husband' (my emphasis) were interpreted to refer to a relationship of social and sexual intimacy exemplified by, but not limited to, the heterosexual relationship of husband and wife.[11]

This approach could not be applied in *Wilkinson* because:

> In the present case, there is no way in which any reasonable reader could understand the word 'widow' to refer to the more general concept of the surviving spouse. The contrary indications in the language of Part VII of the 1988 Act are too strong.[12]

---

[7] This section conferred a tax allowance by the words: 'where a married man whose wife is living with him dies, his widow shall be entitled . . .'
[8] *Wilkinson*, above n. 3 at [15].    [9] *Ibid.* at [16].
[10] *Ibid.* at [17].    [11] *Ibid.* at [18].    [12] *Ibid.* at [19].

Some might swiftly conclude from this statement that since the statutory provision used the word 'widow' and, in its ordinary meaning, this word is gender-specific, it is impossible to use section 3(1) to render it gender neutral. This conclusion would be too rash. It ignores the important contextual factors determining such a finding in *Wilkinson*. Just because it is impossible 'in the present case' to read the word 'widow' to include 'widower', does not mean that is impossible in all cases.[13] When we look at the legislative scheme of the ICTA, it becomes clear that entitlement to tax benefits based on gender, permeated Part VII of the ICTA.[14] Therefore, to interpret section 262 compatibly with Convention rights would have violated a fundamental feature of the legislative scheme and turned the existing scheme inside out. Moreover, it would have had broad implications for many other aspects of the social security system, which may have had legislative and financial ramifications which the courts would find difficult to assess. Therefore, following the two major limitations articulated in *Ghaidan*, the interpretation proposed in *Wilkinson* was not possible.[15] Lord Hoffmann was not suggesting that statutory wording could never be rectified or that 'reading in' or 'reading down' are illegitimate, just that it was inappropriate 'in the present case', given that the contrary indications in the legislative scheme as a whole were 'too strong'. His application of section 3(1) to the facts of *Wilkinson* was fully in accordance with the general pronouncements of the House of Lords in *Ghaidan*.

---

[13] As the example of the contextual nature of the section 3(1) enquiry, see *Sheldrake*, above n. 1, where the House of Lords held that a reverse onus provision in the Road Traffic Act 1988 did not violate Article 6 ECHR, but that a similar provision in section 11 of the Terrorism Act 2000, did violate Article 6. Lord Bingham stressed the context-specific nature of the section 3(1) enquiry, at [28].

[14] Indeed entitlement on grounds of gender has long been a feature of social security legislation, see Wikeley *et al.* (2002), 93, 144, 260ff.

[15] The 'fundamental features' limitation also explains the House of Lords' refusal to interpret various related provisions of the Social Security Contributions and Benefits Act 1992 in a Convention-compatible way in the case of *Hooper* [2005] 1 W.L.R. 1681. There, the House of Lords refused to interpret provisions of the 1992 Act in a non-discriminatory fashion (between widows and widowers). When one examines the legislative provisions in detail, one can see that the legislative scheme was permeated with gender-specific entitlements which would have been impossible for the judiciary to eliminate it by way of the piecemeal method of judicial law reform. Moreover, the 1992 Act contained some detailed specification of security benefits on gender-specific grounds, see e.g. section 37 which refers to 'pregnancy by her late husband and artificial insemination with the semen of some person other than her husband as a condition of entitlement'. In short, gender-specificity was a detailed and fundamental feature of the legislation, which would have been impossible for the judiciary to attempt to remove by interpretation.

But what about Lord Hoffmann's characterisation of the *ratio* in *Ghaidan*? It is certainly true that Lord Hoffmann offered a 'revised rationale'[16] for the decision in *Ghaidan*. He focused on the ambiguity contained in the use of general evaluative word 'as' in paragraph 2(2) of the Rent Act 1977, as opposed to the extensive powers of 'modification' under section 3(1). Lord Hoffmann made the valid point that although the words 'husband' and 'wife' were gender specific when taken in isolation, the phrase as a whole, namely, 'living together *as* his or her husband or wife', were not. The key word here is 'as', which suggests living together in a marriage-like relationship, but not one based on actual marriage. It is a curious feature of the House of Lords judgments in *Ghaidan* that none of their Lordships (not even Lord Millett) made use of this fact in justifying their interpretation under section 3(1)[17]. Lord Hoffmann's reading of *Ghaidan* gives it more 'textual grounding',[18] but in adopting this reading, his Lordship attributed to the House of Lords in *Ghaidan* a justificatory option it did not pursue. Not one of their Lordships in *Ghaidan* placed any emphasis on the fact that the word 'as' in paragraph 2 suggested relationships 'exemplified by, but not limited to' heterosexual relationships. Rather, they assumed that this provision was gender-specific (i.e. *was* limited to heterosexual relationships) and conducted their analysis of the scope of section 3(1) in the context of that assumption. They concluded that the language of paragraph 2(2) could be *modified* to achieve Convention-compatibility, *despite* the apparent gender-specificity of its terms.

However, Lord Hoffmann's articulation of a narrower and more text-bound rationale for disposing of *Ghaidan* does not necessarily entail that he endorses 'a rather less bold conception of the role of section 3(1)'[19] as a general matter. The most important premise in *Ghaidan* which led the majority to the 'inescapable'[20] conclusion that the language of the statute was not, in itself, determinative of the interpretive obligation under section 3(1), was that it allowed the court to depart from unambiguous statutory meaning. This premise is shared by Lord Hoffmann in *Wilkinson*.[21] As Lord Nicholls pointed out in *Ghaidan*, once this foundational point

---

[16]  Van Zyl Smit (2007), 294.

[17]  This oversight is even more culpable for Lord Millett, who made much in his dissenting judgment of the importance of attending to the statutory language. In fact, the inclusion of the word 'as' might have made the interpretive outcome in *Ghaidan* possible even on ordinary methods of interpretation as was argued by Ward L.J. (dissenting) in the Court of Appeal in *Fitzpatrick* [1998] Ch. 304 at 324ff.

[18]  Van Zyl Smit (2007), 304.    [19]  Geiringer (2008), 82.

[20]  *Ghaidan*, above n. 2 at [31], *per* Lord Nicholls.    [21]  *Wilkinson*, above n. 3 at [17].

is accepted, it follows that some departure from, and modification of, statutory terms must be possible under section 3(1).[22] Moreover, Lord Hoffmann acknowledged that a section 3(1) interpretation can legitimately depart from the legislative purpose behind the statutory provision under scrutiny.[23] Even if it could be shown that individual members of Parliament in 1988 either gave no thought to, or specifically objected to, the possibility of applying paragraph 2(2) to same-sex couples, this will not, in itself, preclude the application of section 3(1).[24]

So, it is far from clear that *Wilkinson* adopts a weaker or narrower conception of section 3(1) as a general matter. Lord Hoffmann's concession that the rule in section 3(1) allows the court to depart from unambiguous meaning and adopt less restrictive interpretations denies that the ordinary meaning of express statutory provisions is an absolute ban on the application of section 3(1). The scope of the interpretive obligation as characterised by Lord Hoffmann depends on what is entailed by the view that section 3(1) enacts a 'strong presumption of statutory interpretation'. In the next section, I will argue that in viewing section 3 as a strong presumption, whose application does not hinge on ambiguity in statutory language, Lord Hoffmann supports a strong rather than a weak conception of the role of section 3(1).[25] In my view, this is the correct way to understand the operation of section 3(1).

## Section 3(1) as a strong presumption of statutory interpretation

Lord Hoffmann's analysis of section 3(1) in *Wilkinson* will be seductive to those who fear and object to the 'unusual and far-reaching' potential of section 3(1), because it seems to be congruent with, or at least not jar with, traditional methods of statutory interpretation and the orthodox account of parliamentary sovereignty.[26] Relying on the

---

[22] *Ghaidan*, above n. 2 at [31].    [23] *Wilkinson*, above n. 3 at [18].    [24] *Ibid.* at [18].

[25] Claudia Geiringer claims that Lord Nicholl's concurrence with Lord Hoffmann constituted 'an implicit repudiation of the *Ghaidan* approach' by Lord Nicholls such that 'the strong interpretive approach articulated in *Ghaidan* has had its day', see Geiringer (2008), 82. My analysis suggests that this is not necessarily the case. In general, one would have expected that if a judge of the House of Lords who gave a detailed and considered leading judgments on section 3(1), wished to repudiate that approach the following year, he would have done so explicitly, providing adequate explanation for such a radical *volte-face*. Therefore, we should be sceptical of the claim that Lord Nicholls was at odds with Lord Hoffmann's judgment.

[26] For consideration of the links between parliamentary sovereignty and statutory interpretation, see chapter 11.

well-worn distinction between interpretation and legislation, Lord Hoffmann explained:

> With the addition of the Convention as background, the question is still one of interpretation, i.e. the ascertainment of what, taking into account the presumption created by section 3, Parliament would reasonably be understood to have meant by using the actual language of the statute.[27]

This renders the strong interpretive power under section 3(1) reassuringly unthreatening. But the extent to which his account of the operation of section 3(1) is more or less restrictive than *Ghaidan* depends on the meaning of the qualifications 'with the addition of the Convention as background' and 'taking into account the presumption created by section 3'. Once the full import of the operation of these presumptions is understood, it is revealed that, within this apparently traditional account of statutory interpretation, lie some features which do not sit as easily with orthodox constitutional theory as one might think. In particular, it will be seen that the presumptions of statutory interpretation give the courts strong powers to apply principles of constitutionality not easily displaced by statutory text.[28] I will argue that the constitutional dimension of these presumptions justifies Lord Hoffmann's earlier conclusion in *Matadeen* v. *Pointu* that the HRA creates 'a modified form of constitutional review' not much different than if it had been entrenched.[29]

Lord Hoffmann did not deny that section 3(1) brought about significant changes in the ordinary methods of interpretation. The most important change made by section 3 was:

> To deem the Convention to form a significant part of the background against which all statutes, whether passed before or after the 1998 Act came into force, had to be interpreted. Just as the principle of legality meant that statutes were construed against the background of human rights subsisting at common law, so now, section 3 requires them to be construed against the background of Convention rights. There is a strong presumption, arising from the fundamental nature of Convention rights, that Parliament did not intend a statute to mean something which would be incompatible with those rights.[30]

Moreover, the application of section 3 was not confined to resolving ambiguities in a statutory text. The rule in section 3:

---

[27] *Wilkinson*, above n. 3 at [17].

[28] For support for the view that the presumptions of general application possess 'an enduring constitutional status', see Allan (2006a), 30ff.

[29] *Matadeen* v. *Pointu* [1999] 1 A.C. 98 at 110.      [30] *Wilkinson*, above n. 3 at [17].

goes far beyond the old-fashioned notion of using background to resolve ambiguities in the text which had notionally been read without raising one's eyes to look beyond it. The Convention, like the rest of the admissible background, forms part of the primary materials of the process of interpretation.[31]

Lord Hoffmann is not alone amongst his judicial brethren in believing that section 3(1) enacts a strong presumption in favour of an interpretation consistent with Convention rights. Lord Steyn has consistently presented section 3(1) in this way, both in his judgments in *R.* v. *A*[32] and *Ghaidan,*[33] as well as in his extrajudicial writings.[34] It is a view widely shared by academic commentators.[35] Thus, Richard Clayton and Hugh Tomlinson argue that the proper way of understanding section 3(1) is that it combines the traditional *enacted intention* rule with a constitutional presumption in favour of Convention rights. They suggest that, when interpreting under section 3(1), we should bear in mind:

> the conventional rule that when interpreting a statute, the courts are seeking to determine 'the intention of the legislature' (i.e. what intention is either expressly or by implication conveyed by the language used). Then, in all cases in which Convention rights are at play, the effect of section 3 is equivalent to requiring the courts to act on a presumption that the intention of the legislature was to enact a provision compatible with Convention rights.[36]

A number of points need to be noted about how these presumptions operate. First, the presumptions of statutory interpretation are a familiar and long-standing judicial tool by which judges have protected fundamental rights in the common law. Even in the absence of ambiguity in the statutory language, judges have often relied on 'presumptions of general application' which are described in Sir Rupert Cross' classic work as not only supplementing the statutory text but also operating:

> at a higher level as expressions of fundamental principles governing civil liberties and the relations between Parliament, the executive and the courts. They operate here as constitutional principles which are not easily displaced by statutory text.[37]

---

[31] *Ibid.* at [17].      [32] *R.* v. *A (No. 2)* [2002] 1 A.C. 45.      [33] *Ghaidan,* above n. 2 at [50].
[34] Lord Steyn (1998), 155; Steyn (2004a), 251; see also Lord Cooke of Thornton, HL Deb vol. 582 col. 1272 (Second Reading) (27 November 1997).
[35] Kavanagh (2006), 188ff; Edwards (2000), 355; Bennion (2000), 77; Fenwick (2000), 43; Jowell (2000), 675.
[36] Clayton and Tomlinson (2000), 167.      [37] *Ibid.*, 166.

In what sense can they be said to 'supplement' the statutory text? When understanding the nature of the presumptions, it is crucial to bear in mind that Parliament's 'presumed intentions' are independent of legislators' actual historical intentions and may in fact run contrary to them.[38] Even if Parliament enacts legislation with the intention of violating the rule of law, the courts will impute to it the intention of upholding the rule of law, regardless of what the legislators actually intended.[39] So, when presumed intentions are attributed to Parliament, it is not because they reflect genuine or 'true' legislative intent as a matter of historical fact, but rather, judges apply the presumptions of statutory interpretation because they express long-standing principles of the common law.[40] The constitutional significance of these principles, has given rise to claims that they form 'a sort of common law "Bill of Rights"'.[41] In a similar vein, Lord Browne-Wilkinson remarked extrajudicially, that the judicial presumption in favour of rights-compatible statutory interpretation, meant that the common law could provide a 'half-way Bill of Rights'.[42] It is widely accepted that the judicial use of the common law presumptions of statutory interpretation is 'one of the various means by which English courts have asserted an indigenous human rights jurisdiction'.[43] They *supplement* the text because they are constitutional principles not 'contained in' the statutory text or evidenced in the legislative history. Rather, they are principles whose importance and value are recognised by the common law independently of statute and are invoked by judges to inform the interpretation of statutory texts.[44] They are one of the primary ways in which judges have always engaged in constitutional review when interpreting statutes.

---

[38] It is perhaps worth clarifying that T. R. S. Allan refers to 'presumed intentions' as 'constructive intentions' see Allan (2003), 570. This seems to be a different label for the same idea.

[39] The only exception to this is if Parliament makes its intentions clear in the words of the statute. However, in some cases, even clearly expressed *enacted intention* has been insufficient to rebut the application of certain presumptions, see e.g. *Anisminic v. Foreign Compensation Commissioners* [1969] A.C. 147. For further discussion of this point, see 102–8 below.

[40] See Woolf (1995), 66–7; Endicott (2003a), 206–8. This should not be obscured by the fact that judges often express general interpretive presumptions in the form of hypothetical, counterfactual assertions about what the legislator would or would not have intended or envisaged, see further Kavanagh (2004b), 269ff; Dworkin (1986), 325–6; Marmor (2005), 169; Bradley and Ewing (2003), 18; Cross (1995), 166; Bankowski and MacCormick (1991), 391.

[41] Willis (1938), 17; Keir and Lawson (1979), 3. Timothy Endicott argues that these presumptions are part of 'the common law of the constitution', Endicott (2003a), 203.

[42] Browne-Wilkinson (1992), 399.    [43] See also Hunt (1997), 174.

[44] Allan (2004a), 710; Endicott (2003a), 208; Jowell (2006), 575.

The most well-known presumption of constitutional significance is the principle of 'legality'. It was enunciated most famously by Lord Hoffmann in *Simms* in the form that 'even the most general words were intended to be subject to the basic rights of the individual'.[45] Following *Simms*, Lord Rodger's judgment in *Ghaidan* began with the claim that section 3(1) 'enacts the principle of legality as a rule of construction'.[46] As Lord Hoffmann explained in *Simms*, by relying on presumptions like these, 'the UK courts apply principles of constitutionality little different from those which exist in countries where the power of the legislature is expressly limited by a constitutional document'.[47] The presumptions allow the courts to rely on constitutional principles by which they can assess and ultimately qualify, limit and modify the meaning which legislation would otherwise bear, if they were not read in light of those principles. In this way, the presumptions of statutory interpretation give judges immense powers to modify the application of legislation, in ways which are not immediately apparent from Lord Hoffmann's rather conservative-sounding *dicta* in *Wilkinson*.

We should also note that the orthodox justification for applying the statutory presumptions is the fact that, in general, legislators know, or can be taken to know, that their legislation will be interpreted and understood in light of them. They are part of the known background against which Parliament legislates and of which it should be aware.[48] Thus, the presumptions are often understood as warnings to Parliament that if it does not express itself clearly, it will know that the words chosen by it in the statutory text will be interpreted in light of the presumed intentions.[49] For legislation enacted post-HRA, we can say that section 3(1) puts Parliament on notice that if it wishes to enact legislation infringing Convention rights, it will have to express that intention in clear and unequivocal terms in the statutory text.[50] However, this justification is unavailable for legislation enacted pre-1998. Section 3(1) requires that legislation enacted pre-HRA (or indeed

---

[45] See *R. v. Secretary Of State for the Home Department, ex parte Simms* [2000] 2 A.C. 115 at 132, *per* Lord Hoffmann.

[46] *Ghaidan*, above n. 2 at [104].      [47] *Simms*, above n. 45 at 131.

[48] The presumptions of statutory interpretation then form part of the 'shared interpretive Conventions that permit meaningful communication between legislators and executors (agencies and courts)': Manning (1997), 696; Raz (1996b), 267ff.

[49] See Cross (1995), 167; for the view that the law-maker's knowledge of the conventions of interpretation is a way of giving Parliament control over the law it is enacting, see Raz (1996b), 267. In American constitutional law, this is known as a 'clear statement rule', see generally Schauer (1995).

[50] Feldman (1999a), 186.

pre-ECHR), must be interpreted in accordance with a 'presumption' that it was intended to be compatible with Convention rights. Since compatibility with Convention rights was not a legal obligation when these statutes were enacted, it is not part of the 'context', in the sense of the known interpretive conventions prevailing at the time when Parliament enacted the legislation.

So, at least for legislation enacted pre-HRA, the effect of section 3(1) is more radical than the application of the ordinary presumptions of statutory interpretation. It enjoins the courts to 'deem' Convention rights to be part of the interpretive background of statutes, even though it was not part of their actual background. More importantly, in assessing the legislative context, one is interpolating into that context a set of constitutional principles (in this case the rights protected by the ECHR) which were not applicable (at least not in quite the same way) at the time of enactment. This process of interpolation may also occur with reference to post-HRA legislation, but at least in this case it can be justified by the fact that Parliament must be understood or assumed to be aware of the importance of protecting Convention rights. So, when Lord Hoffmann refers to the obligation to understand legislation in its context 'with the addition of the Convention', it has to be remembered that judges are thereby *adding* to the actual statutory context a set of rights-guarantees which may or may not have been part of the context against which Parliament enacted the original legislation.

One might think that the addition of Convention rights as background allows the courts to give statutory language 'acontextual meanings' because the courts 'deem' Convention rights to be part of that context, even though they were not part of that context in fact. However, the analysis contained in the previous chapter shows that it is exaggeration to say that the interpretive duty under section 3(1) is entirely 'acontextual'.[51] A recurring theme of the HRA case law has been that the courts will always explore the legislative history and 'linear ancestor[s]'[52] of the statutory provision under scrutiny at the first stage of the interpretive process under section 3(1). At this stage, the traditional concern of statutory interpretation to understand the words used by Parliament in the context in which they are used, is of primary importance.[53] It is at the second stage

---

[51] I thus depart from my earlier characterisation of what is involved in a section 3(1) interpretation in Kavanagh (2006), 195.

[52] *Sheldrake*, above n. 1 at [38], *per* Lord Bingham.

[53] This is described as the 'essential rule' of statutory interpretation, Cross (1995), 1.

of the interpretive process that the 'deemed background' of Convention rights is introduced, in order to see if the ordinary or apparent or obvious meaning can nonetheless be interpreted in a Convention-compatible way. Lord Hoffmann is correct to say that this does not entail that the courts should give statutory language entirely acontextual meanings. The task of the courts is to strive to protect Convention rights, in a way which accords with (or at least does not jar with) the meaning, intention and context of the legislation under scrutiny. Thus, the courts try to reconcile their Convention-compatible interpretation with the legislative history and background of the Act to the greatest degree possible. If it turns out that a section 3(1) interpretation creates too much discordance with this legislative scheme, or cannot be reformed in a way which is consistent with its 'underlying thrust', then the courts will tend not to adopt it. This reflects the expanded interpretive focus of interpretation under section 3(1) – the courts must read and give effect to the legislation under scrutiny *and* protect Convention rights.

It follows that there is some truth to Sir William Wade's observation that, under section 3 'the judges are given a new task, to interpret uncertain or ambiguous provisions not according to what they think is the true meaning, but according to the meaning which best accords with the Convention rights'.[54] This observation captures the fact that the interpretive focus under the HRA has expanded to include Convention rights, which may give rise (though not invariably) to meanings and interpretations which would not have been possible, if Convention rights were not 'deemed' to be part of the statutory context. The ordinary meaning, even if clear and unambiguous, can be modified or qualified or expanded to give effect to this duty to protect Convention rights, as long as such modification is modest rather than radical, and as long as it does not upset the overall working of the Act or undermine its cardinal principles.[55]

---

[54] Wade (1998), 529. This contrast between 'true meaning' and 'possible meaning' has been adopted in Clayton and Tomlinson (2000), 156; Bennion (2000), 91; Edwards (2000), 356; HL Deb vol. 582 col. 1272 (Second Reading) (3 November 1997); see also Cooke (1999), 253.

[55] As Lord Rodger clarifies in *Ghaidan*, 'once the HRA 1998 came into force, whenever, by virtue of section 3(1), a provision could be read in a way which was compatible with convention rights, that was the meaning which Parliament intended that it should bear. For all purposes, that meaning, and no other, is the 'true' meaning of the provision in our law', see *Ghaidan* at [106].

## How to rebut the strong presumption

In his extrajudicial writings, Lord Steyn suggested that not only does section 3(1) direct judges to find out what meanings the statutory words are 'capable of yielding', it also asks them to see if the statutory provision can be '*made to yield* a sense consistent with Convention rights'.[56] This seems to go beyond choosing one of the possible meanings of the legislation, and suggests the imposition of meaning upon a statutory provision, changing or manipulating it in order to serve the end contained in section 3(1). This imposition of meaning is achieved by way of the techniques of 'reading in' and 'reading down'. These techniques are not new to English judges. Written long before the enactment of the HRA, Sir Rupert Cross' work on statutory interpretation states:

> The judge may read in words which he considers to be necessarily implied by words which are already in the statute; and he has a limited power to add to, alter or ignore statutory words in order to prevent a provision from being unintelligible, absurd or totally unreasonable, unworkable, or totally irreconcilable with the rest of the statute.[57]

So, before the HRA was enacted, judges have had the power (in appropriate circumstances) to adopt strained constructions of statutory language, to insert words into statutory language and to delete words in order to achieve a more intelligible, reasonable or just result.[58] However, pre-HRA, the power to add to, alter or ignore statutory words has always been viewed as an extremely limited one.[59] It was only used in exceptional

---

[56] Emphasis added. This possibility has led some academic commentators to refer to section 3(1) as the 'bend me, shape me' provision, see Bonner *et al.* (2003), 555.

[57] Cross (1995), 49, 93; see also Bennion (2002), 395ff.

[58] Note: In *Inco Europe Ltd* v. *First Choice Distribution* [2000] 2 All E.R. 109 Lord Nicholls claimed at [471] that judicial power to rectify statutory language is 'confined to plain cases of drafting mistakes'. However, his Lordship cited pp. 93–103 of *Cross on Statutory Interpretation* which includes the quote cited above suggesting a much broader set of reasons which would legitimate judicial rectification. Moreover, Cross provides case citations evidencing judicial approaches to statutory interpretation which 'seem to go further than what might be added to a text by necessary implication', 95. Lord Nicholls' statements may be best understood in light of Cross' point that 'many judges will prefer not to express what they are doing as a rectification of the statutory words', 98. However, see Lord Woolf's more candid extrajudicial comment that 'it is the duty of the courts to remedy a defect in the statute by supplementing the statutory code' if statutory provisions have the result of conferring powers which could be exercised unfairly or unreasonably, Woolf (1995), 66.

[59] Cross (1995), 98.

cases where the consequence of applying the words in their ordinary meaning would be utterly unreasonable, or where there is a demonstrable mistake on the part of the drafter, or where the provision would otherwise be unintelligible or absurd or totally irreconcilable with the rest of the statute.[60]

Although judicial rectification of statutory words occurred before 1998, the HRA changes the constitutional context within which such a rectifying construction takes place. A rectification under section 3 is given a democratic pedigree since it is endorsed by Parliament in the 1998 Act. As Laws L.J. put it in *Roth*: 'The HRA 1998 now provides a democratic underpinning to the common law's acceptance of constitutional rights, and important new procedural measures for their protection.'[61] It enhances the judicial sense of legitimacy in using these techniques and allows them to be more candid about doing so.[62] Second, given the pervasive application of section 3 HRA to all legislation whenever enacted, a rectification of statutory words may become more common and less exceptional than before. Whenever possible, the courts will strive to fulfil their obligations under the HRA in a way which does not require a strained interpretation of statutory language and, as we have seen, even if the courts decide to read in words to a statutory provision, they will nonetheless attempt to give effect to the underlying purpose of Parliament in enacting that provision. However, section 3 empowers them to adopt a strained interpretation if this is necessary to achieve a Convention-compatible result, just as they were entitled pre-HRA, albeit in exceptional cases, to adopt a strained interpretation to remove an unjust or absurd result.[63]

So if the courts are entitled to depart from unambiguous statutory wording, and 'read in', 'read down' or delete words from statutory provisions, when is it ever possible to rebut the 'strong presumption' contained in section 3(1)? As pointed out in *Ghaidan*, the very existence of section 4 suggests that section 3(1) does not enact an irrebuttable presumption. It is generally thought that constitutional presumptions such as the principle of legality were rebuttable by 'express language or necessary implication

---

[60] *Ibid.*, 102.

[61] *International Transport Roth GmbH* v. *Secretary of State for the Home Department* [2002] 3 W.L.R. 344 at [71].

[62] Francis Bennion notes whilst the courts have relied on 'rectifying constructions', employing the techniques of 'reading in' and 'reading down', there was a general judicial reluctance to admit to using those techniques, see Bennion (2002), 394–5.

[63] This point is made by Lord Steyn, *R.* v. *A*, above n. 32 at 67.

to the contrary'.[64] This fits in with the view that the presumptions express 'policies of clear statement',[65] in the sense that Parliament is put on notice that if it does not express itself clearly in a statute, its language will be interpreted in light of fundamental constitutional principles, such as the rule of law. The 'express terms or necessary implications' limitation has also been used with reference to section 3(1). Thus, in *Simms*, Lord Hoffmann explained that even post-HRA, Parliament:

> can, if it chooses, legislate contrary to fundamental principles of human rights . . . but the principle of legality means that Parliament must squarely confront what it is doing and accept the political cost. Fundamental rights cannot be overridden by general or ambiguous words because there is too great a risk that the full implications of their unqualified meaning may have passed unnoticed in the democratic process.[66]

However, it has also been a point of judicial consensus that a section 3(1) interpretation is not impossible even when statutory language is unambiguous which seems to contravene Convention rights. This presents us with a fundamental (and often unacknowledged) tension which lies at the core of section 3(1). If the courts can depart from the ordinary meaning of statutory provisions, even if they are unambiguous, does it not follow that clear, unambiguous express terms will be insufficient to rebut the strong presumption enacted in section 3(1)?

Even if we leave section 3(1) out of the picture for the moment, the question about the extent to which general presumptions of constitutional significance are rebuttable, is not itself uncontroversial. This is because it is widely believed that these presumptions are not easily displaced and 'apply although there is no question of linguistic ambiguity in the statutory wording under construction'.[67] Sir Rupert Cross concluded:

---

[64] *Simms*, above n. 45 at 131, *per* Lord Hoffmann. In *A* v. *Home Secretary (Torture Evidence case)* [2006] 2 A.C. 221, the House of Lords stressed that a parliamentary intention to condone reliance by a court on torture evidence would only be accepted if there were 'express words, or perhaps the plainest possible implication', [137], *per* Lord Rodger, or 'clear express provision to the contrary', [95], *per* Lord Hoffmann.

[65] Cross (1995), 167.     [66] *Simms*, above n. 45 at 131.

[67] Cross (1995), 166; see also Browne-Wilkinson (1992), 406–7. Commenting on the common law presumption that *mens rea* is an essential ingredient of a crime unless Parliament indicates a contrary intention either by 'express terms or necessary implication' in *Attorney General's Reference (No. 4 of 2002); Sheldrake* v. *DPP* [2004] UKHL 32 at [6], Lord Bingham noted that this is 'a strong presumption, not easily displaced. The more serious the crime, and the more severe the potential consequences of conviction, the less readily will it be displaced.'

Although the points lack clear authority, it is probably true to say that some of them can only be rebutted by express words; nothing in the nature of implication, even necessary implication, will suffice.[68]

However, when examining some of the case law applying these presumptions, it is less than clear that even express words would rebut such presumptions. All public lawyers are familiar with the case of *Anisminic Ltd* v. *Foreign Compensation Commission*,[69] where the court had to consider whether section 4(4) of the Foreign Compensation Act 1950 rebutted the presumption against ousting the jurisdiction of the courts. In clear and emphatic terms, section 4 provided that a determination of the Commission 'shall not be called into question in any court of law'. Commenting on the majority finding in *Anisminic* that, despite the emphatic nature of the statutory wording, the court was not prevented from investigating whether the Commission had acted outside its jurisdiction, Sir Rupert Cross noted that 'although the presumption against ouster of jurisdiction can be displaced by express wording, it is difficult to conceive how Parliament could have been more explicit than it was in section 4'.[70] Interestingly, when the Government attempted to introduce a similarly broad ouster clause in the Asylum and Immigration Bill 2004, it backed down in the face of judicial opposition, knowing full well that the substance of this clause would have been eviscerated by the application of statutory presumptions, no matter how clearly or unequivocally expressed.[71]

Another example of the potency of these presumptions is provided in *R. (Anufrijeva)* v. *SSHD*.[72] Although the House of Lords emphasised that the constitutional principle of the rule of law would not be displaced unless Parliament legislated 'in specific and unmistakable terms',[73] it seemed as if the regulations under scrutiny there were in fact specific and

---

[68] Cross (1995), 166. For discussion of how specific a legislative provision must be in order to override constitutional legislation, see Elliott (2003), 32.

[69] *Anisminic* v. *Foreign Compensation Commissioners* [1969] A.C. 147.

[70] Cross (1995), 171; see also Turpin and Tomkins (2007), 695.

[71] See Lord Woolf's trenchant criticism of the ouster clause contained in the Asylum and Immigration Bill, Woolf (2004), 327–9. In meetings between the judiciary and Government, members of the judiciary pointed out that 'the clause was unlikely to be effective', 328. Similarly, Rawlings suggested that judicial reaction to the proposed ouster clause 'raised the possibility of the ouster clause, if enacted, being judicially "disapplied" ', Rawlings (2005), 381.

[72] [2003] 3 W.L.R. 252. For more detailed discussion of this case, see Palmer (2007), 241–54.

[73] *Ibid.* at [31], *per* Lord Steyn.

unmistakable, though this did not rebut the constitutional presumption.[74] This led Lord Cooke to observe extrajudicially that 'a principle capable of transforming statutory regulations in this way seems so potent that the depth of common law constitutional rights is virtually measureless'.[75] In another extrajudicial comment, he wondered whether what is required to rebut the presumption in favour of fundamental rights is 'unrealistically specific language'.[76] Similarly, T. R. S Allan has argued that the constitutional presumptions reflect principles of such a fundamental nature that 'the possibility even of express rebuttal may in some cases be closer to fiction than reality'.[77] On another occasion, he went so far as to suggest that in some circumstances they are 'frankly irrebuttable'.[78] At the very least, the case law and academic commentary suggest that one should be cautious before accepting at face value the 'express terms or necessary implications' limitation as a clear-cut statement of how the courts operate these presumptions.

The drastic implications of claims about the virtual irrebuttability of these presumptions may be assuaged when one remembers Lord Hoffmann's point in *Simms* that it is open to Parliament to legislate contrary to fundamental rights, as long as it is willing to accept the political cost. But it is not clear that this makes the situation any better. In practice, the government and Parliament try to incur as little as possible of this political cost. So, if what is required to rebut the presumption in favour of Convention-compatibility is a clear statement that 'we hereby intend to violate Convention rights', it is perhaps too remote and far-fetched to give much substance to the idea of an 'express terms' limitation on the presumption of compliance with Convention rights. The remoteness of such a possibility is enhanced by the fact that the courts are not precluded from applying their section 3(1) interpretive obligation to legislation containing such a clause. Even if the litigant were unsuccessful in the domestic courts, they would have the possibility of bringing an application to the ECtHR in Strasbourg, which would almost invariably find it to be in violation of the Convention. We can conclude that rebuttal of the presumption in favour of

---

[74] For further discussion of *Anufrijeva* as an example of the court relying on a constitutional presumption of statutory interpretation, despite the fact that the language of the statute was unambiguous, see Steyn (2004a).

[75] Cooke (2004), 278.    [76] Lord Cooke, cited in Joseph (2004), 341.

[77] Allan (2004a), 689; see also Allan (2006a), 31 where he argues that it is doubtful whether judges should ever rebut this presumption.

[78] Allan (2002), 105.

Convention-compatibility by express terms, will be rare and 'unusual',[79] as Lord Hoffmann suggested in *Simms*.

However, as is clear from the case law under the HRA, there are other limitations on the operation of section 3(1), most prominently, the two limits enunciated in *Ghaidan*, namely, the 'fundamental features' limitation and the prohibition on embarking on law reform which would require 'legislative deliberation'. However, these limitations are, in some ways, more demanding hurdles for Parliament to overcome, if it wished to enact legislation violating fundamental rights, because not only would it have to use express statutory wording, it would have to ensure that the rights violation permeated the legislative scheme and/or drew the courts into areas where they lack sufficient expertise. Since neither of these requirements is easy to meet, it undermines one of the traditional justifications of the statutory presumptions and calls into question their compatibility with the orthodox account of parliamentary sovereignty. This issue will be considered in more detail in chapter 11.

The fact that a statutory provision which clearly violates a Convention right, will not, in itself, constitute an automatic barrier on the operation of section 3(1), has important consequences. It means that if the House of Lords in *Ghaidan* had been faced with a Rent Act which had stated expressly that 'married couples and heterosexual cohabitees' could qualify for statutory tenancies, this would not *necessarily* preclude a section 3(1) interpretation to include same-sex couples. After all, the courts have shown that they are willing to modify express terms, to delete statutory words and to insert new words.[80] Following *Ghaidan*, it would be possible for the courts to read in the words 'or homosexual' to the hypothetical provision, or simply delete the qualification of being 'heterosexual' cohabitees, thus rendering it Convention-compatible.[81] To be sure, such an interpretation would not be taken lightly, because the courts are aware of the disadvantages of straining statutory language. The express

---

[79] *Simms*, above n. 45 at 132, *per* Lord Hoffmann.

[80] The strategy of deleting words and adding new ones was endorsed in *R. v. Holding* [2005] EWCA Crim 3185 at [48], *per* Simon J., who was 'quite satisfied' that this was within the principles enunciated in *Ghaidan* which he set out at [47].

[81] Robert Wintemute has argued that a section 3(1) interpretation would not be possible in such a case because it would amount to a 'judicial striking-down of sexual orientation discrimination that was expressly provided for in the Act, something that the current scheme of the HRA simply does not permit', Wintemute (2003), 628. For further discussion of the status of the declaration of incompatibility, including an argument that it has similarities with a judicial strike-down power, see chapter 10 at 281–93.

terms of a statute are the constitutionally authorised vehicle for conveying Parliament's intent, and the courts will strive to preserve this value to the greatest extent possible, even in creative interpretation.

It is worth noting that in *Anderson*, the courts seemed to place a lot of emphasis on the fact that to adopt a section 3(1) interpretation in that case would involve '*negativing* the explicit power of the Secretary of State'.[82] One might say that a section 3(1) interpretation of the hypothetical Rent Act, may also involve negativing or contradicting an explicit statutory term. However, whilst *Anderson* shows that the express wording of the statute has a role to play in determining the appropriateness of the section 3(1) interpretation, it is not the sole determining factor. In particular, removing the explicit power of the Secretary of State in that case, would have left a gap in the sentencing scheme of the Act, and might have required the courts to provide another in its place. This would not be the situation under the hypothetical Rent Act. It would simply extend the application of the statute to couples who displayed very similar characteristics to those mentioned in the statute. Therefore the disadvantages of a judicial rectification of such statutory language, might not outweigh the disadvantages of issuing a declaration of incompatibility, namely a failure to give any meaningful remedy to someone who has been the victim of unjust discrimination. As *Ghaidan* emphasises, what is important in assessing the degree of rectification needed to achieve Convention-compatibility is not the number of words, or the mere fact of conflict with ordinary meaning or intent, but rather the substance of the change proposed, and the broader implications of that change.

### *Ghaidan* and *Fitzpatrick* contrasted

In this chapter, I have presented the interpretive obligation under section 3(1) as a strong presumption of statutory interpretation. Whilst the application of this presumption is limited by both the 'fundamental features' and 'legislative deliberation' limitation outlined in *Ghaidan*, it could not be said that it is automatically rebutted by express terms or necessary implications alone. Viewing section 3(1) as a presumption of statutory interpretation emphasises the fact that interpretation under section 3(1) is continuous with pre-HRA statutory interpretation, whilst

---

[82] *Ghaidan*, above n. 2 at [111], *per* Lord Rodger, emphasis added.

simultaneously highlighting its important constitutional dimension.[83] Nevertheless, section 3(1) adds new content to the familiar presumption in favour of protecting human rights, because judges must now presume that Parliament does not intend to enact legislation which violates the specific rights contained in the ECHR.[84] Moreover, section 3(1) differs from the old presumption that Parliament did not intend to legislate so as so put the UK in breach of its ECHR obligations, because the latter was only held to have application in cases where the statutory provision was ambiguous.[85] No legislative ambiguity is required for judges to interpret legislation against the 'background' of Convention rights under section 3(1).[86]

Whilst section 3(1) does not mark a radical departure from interpretive methods and devices available to the courts prior to the HRA, it nonetheless changes the constitutional context in which judicial reliance on this presumption takes place, and makes it more likely that judges will do so in a robust fashion. As a way of highlighting the difference the HRA makes to traditional methods of statutory interpretation, it is instructive to consider the difference of judicial approach in *Fitzpatrick* and *Ghaidan*, since *Ghaidan* departed from the pre-HRA decision of *Fitzpatrick* v. *Sterling Housing Association Ltd*,[87] handed down only four years previously on facts virtually identical to those in *Ghaidan*. In *Fitzpatrick*, the House of Lords unanimously rejected the contention that the words 'living together as his or her husband or wife' could be read to include homosexual partners. Their rejection was based on the fact that the terms

---

[83] Laws L.J. argues that 'the challenge of the Human Rights Act will be to develop common law rules of statutory interpretation conformably with the Convention, but as part of a continuum with everything that has gone before', Laws (1999), xiii; see also Feldman (1999a), 173. On the value of continuity in legal interpretation generally, see Raz (1979), 208–9 and Raz (1996a), 357–61.

[84] This is not to deny that there may be some overlap between Convention rights and traditional common law rights, as was pointed out by Lord Hoffmann in *Simms*, above n. 45 at 131. Moreover, in the last 40 years there has been increased judicial recourse to the ECHR in the English courts, see generally Hunt (1997).

[85] See *R.* v. *Secretary of State for the Home Department, ex parte Brind* [1991] 1 All E.R. 720; Cross (1995), 166; Hope (2000), 440.

[86] This point is affirmed in *R.* v. *A*, above n. 32 at [44], *per* Lord Steyn; *R.* v. *Lambert* [2002] 2 A.C. 545 at [42], *per* Lord Steyn, [78], *per* Lord Hope; *Poplar Housing & Regeneration Community Association Ltd* v. *Donoghue* [2002] Q.B. 48 at [59], *per* Lord Woolf; *Re S, Re W* [2002] 2 A.C. 291 at [37], *per* Lord Nicholls. It is also set out in *Rights Brought Home*, Cm. 3782 (1997), paragraph 2.7.

[87] [2001] 1 A.C. 27.

'husband' and 'wife' are gender-specific,[88] and that in using the words 'as his or her husband or wife' Parliament did not intend to include homosexual partners.[89]

The first point to note is that even pre-HRA, the courts possessed the interpretive tools to hold that paragraph 2(2) of Schedule 1 to the Rent Act 1977 could be interpreted so as to include same-sex couples. Following Ward L.J. in the Court of Appeal, the House of Lords in *Fitzpatrick* could have placed more emphasis than they did on the fact that the statutory terms simply required that the couple must live together 'as' husband and wife.[90] As Lord Hoffmann pointed out in *Wilkinson*, when this phrase is read as a whole, it is 'exemplified by, but not limited to',[91] heterosexual couples. Alternatively, if they believed that the express terms of the statute were gender-specific, they could have relied on purposive interpretation to depart from the ordinary meaning of the statutory words.[92] Finally, they could have relied on one of the constitutional presumptions of statutory interpretation, such as the principle of legality. Why did they not do this?

Apart from contingent facts about the way in which the case was argued by counsel for Mr Fitzpatrick,[93] there are some fundamental differences in the method of judicial reasoning adopted in both cases, which gives us telling insights into the difference the HRA has made to traditional statutory interpretation. The first is that, in *Fitzpatrick*, no issue of discrimination was raised[94] whereas in *Ghaidan* the House of Lords was bound to consider whether paragraph 2(2) was *prima facie* discriminatory (and therefore violated Convention rights) as part of the 'first stage' of the judicial inquiry under section 3(1). Lord Nicholls set the tone of his judgment in *Ghaidan* by noting that:

> It goes without saying that Article 14 is an important article of the Convention. Discrimination is an insidious practice. Discriminatory law undermines the rule of law because it is the antithesis of fairness.[95]

---

[88] As Lord Nicholls stated at 43: 'A husband is a man and a wife is a woman', supported by Lord Clyde at 47 and Lord Slynn at 34.

[89] *Fitzpatrick*, above n. 87 at 34, *per* Lord Slynn.    [90] [1998] Ch. 304 at 324ff.

[91] *Wilkinson*, above n. 3 at [18], *per* Lord Hoffmann.

[92] In fact, when one looks at the type of judicial reasoning they adopted in order to come to the conclusion that same-sex couples could be considered as part of the original tenant's 'family', it can be seen that they adopted a type of purposive method of interpretation which was not dissimilar to that adopted by Lord Nicholls in *Ghaidan*, see Kavanagh (2007), 141–2.

[93] See Kavanagh (2007), 138.

[94] *Fitzpatrick*, above n. 87 at 35, *per* Lord Slynn, 47, *per* Lord Clyde.

[95] *Ghaidan*, above n. 2 at [9].

Given the fundamental importance of the value of non-discrimination and the need to assess whether the distinction drawn in the legislation was discriminatory, it followed that the potentially discriminatory aspect of paragraph 2(2) was a central part of the judicial reasoning in *Ghaidan*. In contrast, there was no argument in *Fitzpatrick* based on a legal right against discrimination, so that this important issue played little or no role in the judgments in *Fitzpatrick*.[96] This shows that even before section 3(1) is directly engaged, the HRA has a bearing on judicial reasoning by bringing the rights-based dimension of the case to the fore. Thus, in *Fitzpatrick*, the question was whether same-sex partners could qualify either under paragraph 2(2) or paragraph 3(1) of Schedule 1 to the Rent Act, whereas in *Ghaidan* the question was whether, *despite* a *prima facie* incompatibility with the Convention, the courts could *nonetheless* render paragraph 2(2) Convention compatible by way of interpretation under section 3(1). This changes the framework within which the arguments in both cases were considered.

The second difference between the two cases follows from this. Once the court established a difference in treatment based on sexual orientation, this placed the onus on those defending the statutory provision to provide a cogent justification for the difference in treatment in accordance with the requirements of the doctrine of proportionality.[97] As Lord Nicholls put it in *Ghaidan*, 'to be acceptable these distinctions should have a rational and fair basis'.[98] This highlights what some commentators have referred to as 'the culture of justification'[99] which attends the enactment of the HRA. This focus on the need for justification changes the legal context in which judicial decisions are made and influences the judicial reasoning and will be examined in more detail in chapter 9. The demand for justification influenced the way in which Lord Nicholls attributed to the Rent Act a Convention-compatible purpose which he then used to generate the Convention-compatible interpretation of the Rent Act.

A third and important distinction between *Fitzpatrick* and *Ghaidan* concerns the judicial approach to the express terms of paragraph 2(2). In *Fitzpatrick*, the fact that husband and wife connoted a relationship

---

[96] See e.g. *Fitzpatrick*, above n. 87 at 48, *per* Lord Clyde, 34, *per* Lord Slynn. See further Bamforth (2003a), 217 who points out that the finding that Mr Mendoza's Convention rights were violated because the legislation was discriminatory, meant that the court did not defer substantially to Parliament in approaching the issue of how the discrimination should be remedied.

[97] I will consider the doctrine of proportionality in more detail in chapter 9.

[98] *Ghaidan*, above n. 2 at [9], [19].

[99] See e.g. Hunt (2003), 351; see also Steyn (2004a), 254.

between two persons of the opposite sex led the court to reject Mr Fitz-patrick's claim without much discussion,[100] whereas in *Ghaidan* this did not mark the end of the interpretive enquiry. Post-HRA, the judiciary have demonstrated a greater willingness to depart from both the express terms of legislation and the legislative purpose underlying those terms and, as *Ghaidan* demonstrates, are more likely to interpret creatively if this will remove an incompatibility with Convention rights. Their pre-paredness to adopt even a strained interpretation, if to do so will protect Convention rights, follows from the terms of the 'strong adjuration' con-tained in section 3(1). Fourth, just before the House of Lords decision in *Ghaidan* was handed down, the ECtHR decided in *Karner* v. *Austria*[101] that legislation which prevented same-sex couples from gaining the same tenancy rights as unmarried different-sex couples was unlawful sexual orientation discrimination in violation of Convention rights. Although the House of Lords in *Ghaidan* did not seem to place much weight on *Karner*, it is clear that had the House of Lords found against him, Mr Mendoza would have been entitled to compensation from the Stras-bourg court for violation of his rights as established by *Karner*.[102] The existence of Strasbourg case law bearing directly on an issue before a UK court can influence the resolution of the case at domestic level – a matter which will be examined more fully in chapter 6.

Last but not least, there was the issue of legitimacy. In *Fitzpatrick*, many of the judges were reluctant to interpret paragraph 2(2) to include same-sex couples because they believed that law reform in this area of 'social policy' should be carried out by Parliament rather than the courts.[103] However, the issue was framed in a different way in *Ghaidan*. Due to the existence of the HRA, the question was now presented as a rights issue (an area in which the judiciary have particular expertise), whereby the judiciary had to consider the means by which they could remedy the violation.[104] Lord Slynn made this point of contrast explicit when he noted that the question of whether the non-inclusion of same-sex couples in paragraph 2(2) is discriminatory 'may have to be considered

---

[100]    *Fitzpatrick*, above n. 87 at 34, *per* Lord Slynn, 43, *per* Lord Nicholls.
[101]    *Karner* v. *Austria* (2003) 2 F.L.R. 623.    [102]   See further Wintemute (2003), 627.
[103]    See e.g. *Fitzpatrick*, above n. 87 at 33–4, *per* Lord Slynn, 66, *per* Lord Hutton, 67, 68, *per* Lord Hobhouse. This was also an important factor leading the Court of Appeal in *Fitzpatrick* to refuse to interpret paragraph 2(2) to include same-sex couples, [1998] Ch. 304 at 319, *per* Waite L.J., 324, *per* Roch L.J.
[104]    This point about the way in which the HRA prompts the courts to reframe issues which were formerly considered to be considerations of policy, into those which concern rights is borne out by Lord Hope's comments in *Lambert*, above n. 86 at [77].

when the Human Rights Act 1998 is in force. Whether the result was socially desirable in 1999 is a matter for Parliament.'[105] This highlights the crucial importance of the argument from discrimination in generating a different outcome in *Ghaidan* than in *Fitzpatrick*. It also shows how the perceived legitimacy of the court in intervening in such matters changes depending on whether it is viewed as a matter of non-discrimination protected by the HRA or a matter of what is 'socially desirable'. If the latter, then the courts are less likely to want to intervene with a legal solution to the problem. A pervasive theme of both the Court of Appeal's and House of Lords' judgments in *Fitzpatrick* was that the legal change proposed by Mr Fitzpatrick was more appropriate for Parliament than the courts.[106] However, when conceived as a rights issue a few years later in *Ghaidan*, their Lordships have an added sense of legitimacy in tackling the non-discrimination by way of interpretation, due to the fact that Parliament had given them a mandate to do exactly that when it enacted section 3(1). This combined to reassure the courts that they were not usurping Parliament's powers, but rather were carrying out the will of Parliament as expressed in section 3(1) HRA, a belief further bolstered by the assurance from counsel for the Secretary of State (who intervened in *Ghaidan*) that the Government had no objection to the application of section 3(1) in this case.[107] By adopting a more explicit 'rights-focused' approach, the courts are drawn to different conclusions and different methods of reasoning.

What emerges from an examination of the contrasting judicial approach in *Fitzpatrick* and *Ghaidan* is that the House of Lords in *Ghaidan* was more willing to 'rectify' the terms of paragraph 2(2) than they were in *Fitzpatrick*. There are two main reasons for this. The first is that, when interpreting under section 3(1), the courts must now 'deem' the Convention rights to be part of the contextual background against which they interpret legislation. The inclusion of those rights alters the interpretive matrix in which the courts operate. It shows that the courts now operate a 'strong presumption, arising from the fundamental nature of Convention rights, that Parliament did not intend a statute to mean something

---

[105] *Fitzpatrick*, above n. 87 at 34; Lord Hobhouse also considered it to be a 'matter of social policy', above n. 87 at 67.

[106] *Fitzpatrick*, above n. 87 at 66, *per* Lord Hutton, 67, *per* Lord Hobhouse.

[107] Philip Sales Q.C. Robert Wintemute argues that by adopting the section 3(1) interpretation in *Ghaidan* thereby providing an immediate remedy to the claimant, the courts are saving the UK Government and Parliament the work of removing the incompatibility and thus working in accordance with the 'division of labour' envisaged by section 3(1) HRA, Wintemute (2003), 627.

which would be incompatible with those rights'.[108] The strength of that presumption, combined with its fundamental constitutional significance, gives the courts powers of constitutional review. The second reason for the change in statutory interpretation post-HRA goes to the point about legitimacy. Through the HRA, Parliament has given the courts a mandate and responsibility to strive to ensure that primary legislation is rendered compatible with Convention rights. Not all means are justified by that important constitutional end. However, it is nonetheless the case that the courts are now under a strong adjuration to find ways of rendering legislation compatible with the Convention, even if that requires some creativity in order to achieve it. This does not mean that the HRA has ushered in a radically new type of judicial reasoning. The difference post-HRA lies more in the judiciary's willingness to use existing (creative) techniques of statutory interpretation and in their sense of legitimacy in doing so. It is not a fundamental difference in kind, but rather a different view of the appropriateness of relying on existing techniques which were formerly only used in exceptional circumstances.[109]

## Conclusion: interpretation and legitimacy

In this chapter, I have argued that section 3(1) embodies a strong presumption of constitutional interpretation, not easily displaced by express enactment to the contrary. Moreover, in the previous chapter, we saw that the type of judicial rectification employed by the courts when relying on this presumption, is not dissimilar to techniques of legislative amendment. There is no denying that section 3(1) gives the courts immense powers to modify the effect of primary legislation and depart from legislative intent. How can this be legitimate? A full answer to this question must await the discussion in the final part of this book. In chapter 12, I attempt to explain why it is legitimate for the courts to exercise strong powers of constitutional review, which necessarily limit Parliament's power to violate those rights. In chapter 13, I defend that position against objections rooted specifically in democratic concerns. Although a full defence is provided there, it may be appropriate at this juncture to make a few points about the legitimacy of interpretive method under section 3(1) HRA, particularly the power to rectify statutory meaning and depart from parliamentary intent.

---

[108]  *Wilkinson*, above n. 3 at [17].    [109]  This view is shared by Laws L.J. (2004), 245.

When assessing the question of legitimacy of constitutional review under the HRA, we should first bear in mind that section 3(1) does not give the courts radically new methods of interpretation which they did not possess pre-HRA. Judges have always possessed (and exercised) the power to rectify statutory language, if to do so would remove an injustice or violate a fundamental constitutional principle. *Anisminic* is just one graphic illustration of this point. It is easy to multiply that example. The law reports are full of (pre-HRA) cases where the courts supplied 'the omission of the legislature'[110] to protect rights such as natural justice, or refused to follow the clear implications of statutory terms where it would deny a fundamental right or cause clear injustice.[111] Similarly, even when the courts profess to be doing nothing more than giving effect to the will of Parliament, it does not follow that no law development or law reform is being carried out by the courts. Lord Steyn once remarked that 'purposive construction is like mother's milk and apple pie: who can argue against it?'.[112] Perhaps it is the beguiling effect of judicial assurances that they are loyally giving effect to Parliament's intention, which has obscured the hugely creative potential of this method of interpretation. When one examines purposive interpretation more closely, one can see that its very rationale is to allow the courts to depart from the ordinary meaning of statutory terms, in reliance on a legislative purpose attributed to the statute by the courts. Given the evaluative nature of the attribution of legislative purpose and the role which constitutional principles play in informing that attribution, it becomes clear that the ability of the courts to depart from ordinary meaning and to 'read in' and 'read down' in order to prevent a violation of those principles, was not one judges received for the first time in 1998. Therefore, if there are legitimacy concerns about interpretation under the HRA, they apply with equal force to pre-HRA adjudication.

Much of the alarm about the expanded judicial power under the HRA has perhaps been due to a mischaracterisation of the nature of statutory interpretation which existed prior to it. The idea that the only task of

---

[110] *Cooper* v. *Wandworth Board of Works* (1863) 14 C.B. 180. This example is provided by Hickman (2008), 98. For further examples of the courts adopting a rectifying construction in order to supply the omission of the legislature, see Bennion (2002), 750–62.

[111] *Adams* v. *Naylor* [1944] K.B. 750. See further the exercise of judicial law-making carried out in *R.* v. *R* [1992] 1 A.C. 599, which expanded the law of rape to include husbands who raped their wives, despite the fact that the relevant statute clearly excluded husbands from the prohibition, see Barber (2000), 146ff; see also *R.* v. *K* [2002] 1 A.C. 462 as an example of judges 'supplementing the words of a statute, to avoid what is thought to be a morally intolerable result', see Horder (2006), 75ff.

[112] Steyn (2001), 70. On purposive interpretation generally, see Bennion (2002), 809–31.

the judge before 1998 was to ascertain 'the intention of Parliament' and slavishly apply existing law, is (at least if understood in a literal or over-simplistic way) part of such a misrepresentation. If this slogan is taken to suggest that the judicial role is purely applicative, and never creative, it is clearly wrong. As Lord Wilberforce pointed out in *Black-Clawson* in 1977:

> The saying that it is the function of the courts to ascertain the will or intention of Parliament is often enough repeated, so often indeed as to have become an incantation. If too often unreflectingly stated, it leads us to neglect the important element of judicial construction; an element not confined to a mechanical analysis of today's words, but if this task is properly done, related to such matters as intelligibility to the citizen, consti-tutional propriety, considerations of history, comity of nations, reason and non-retroactive effect and, no doubt, in some contexts, to social needs.[113]

No one professes to believe any more in the fairytale of the declaratory account of the judicial role. We can now be more candid about the law-making function of judges. Therefore, we should not fall into the trap of characterising pre-HRA interpretation in terms of a fairytale, in order to cast the HRA as the big bad wolf. The Act certainly brings about changes in the judicial law-making function, and especially the constitutional context within which that law-making takes place, but it does not create that function anew. It does in a way which is continuous with the methods employed by the courts in the past.

Those who are sceptical about constitutional review under the HRA will not be appeased by this point. They will argue that, even if the courts have used these methods in the past, they have not done so to the same extent or with the same sense of legitimacy. If powers of statutory interpretation (such as the power of rectification) are used in exceptional cases, that is very different from a situation where they are becoming part of the inter-pretive 'mainstream'. Once they are used more widely, this changes the constitutional powers of the courts and alters their relationship with the other branches of government – and it is this shift in constitutional power which requires strong justification. Such justification will be provided in the final two chapters of this book. For the moment, it suffices to makes the following brief points. Although the courts have a greater sense of legitimacy in relying on the techniques of 'reading in' and 'reading down', they are also mindful of the substantial limits on their law-making role. For this reason, they have only used section 3 to rectify statutory language

---

[113]  *Black-Clawson International Ltd* v. *Papierwerke Waldhof-Aschaffenburg AG* [1975] A.C. 591 at 629, *per* Lord Wilberforce.

in a small number of cases in the first ten years of the HRA's existence.[114] Judicial rectification is not an everyday occurrence in statutory interpretation post-HRA. Moreover, in applying the doctrine of deference (which will be explored in the second part of this book), they have shown their continued sensitivity to traditional concerns about the constitutional division of labour between the legislature, executive and judiciary. They have exercised a constitutionally appropriate degree of restraint, when that is warranted by the circumstances of the case. Adjudication under the HRA has been far from 'open-ended judicial activism'[115] – it is constrained by the inherent limitations of judicial interpretation and the general constitutional obligation to treat the decisions of the legislature and the executive with respect.

Finally, it is sometimes said that judges should not be creative or activist. They should apply the law as it is, and not develop it to meet new circumstances or protect constitutional principles. This recommendation resonates with the classical picture of the judicial function, whereby judges faithfully apply the law, but never question it or create new law. Whilst the classical picture has a considerable hold on our intuitions about the proper functions of the courts, as a general characterisation of what judges do when they adjudicate disputes and interpret statutes, it is severely misleading. It is the fairytale returned. According to the general analysis of the nature of interpretation in chapter 2, interpretation necessarily includes a law-applying and law-creating element. It is both backward- and forward-looking. Therefore, the recommendation not to develop the law or make new law is an impossible one. In giving statutory provisions a meaning, the courts are 'imposing' a meaning upon it, which it did not have prior to the case being decided. Quite apart from the impossibility of the recommendation, a prohibition on judicial law-making would also be undesirable, because it would lead to profoundly unjust results. The common law has always found ways of allowing courts to rectify statutory provisions so that such results are avoided. This recalls the fact that legal certainty and authority are not the only values underlying judicial interpretation. Judges must also seek to achieve a just and equitable application of the law.

---

[114] This point is also made in Sedley (2008), 20. The point that the impact of sections 3 and 4 on primary legislation is often exaggerated is also made in the *Review of the Implementation of the Human Rights Act* (Department of Constitutional Affairs, July 2006), at www.justice.gov.uk/docs/full_review.pdf, 4.
[115] Campbell (2001), 81.

# 5

# The interplay between sections 3 and 4 HRA

## Introduction

In the previous chapter, I argued that section 3(1) enacts a strong presumption of statutory interpretation, which is difficult to rebut even by express words. It emerged that the most prominent limitations on the interpretive obligation contained in section 3 are the 'fundamental features' limitation (explored in previous chapters) and the deference limitation (which will be explored in chapters 7–9). Moreover, the question about the appropriate limits of section 3(1) is not a matter of what is 'possible', but rather what is appropriate or desirable, all things considered. The purpose of this chapter is to tie up the various strands of argument advanced thus far and to clarify aspects of the interpretive task under section 3(1) which have so far only arisen indirectly. One such issue concerns the extent to which the existence and nature of section 4 bears on the judicial decision to choose to go down the interpretive route.

## Section 3(1) as a remedial provision

Lord Steyn's comments on this issue in *Ghaidan* v. *Mendoza* provide a useful starting point. A central theme in Lord Steyn's judgment in *Ghaidan* was the idea that in order to understand section 3(1) fully, we need to appreciate its role in the 'remedial scheme'[1] of the 1998 Act. His Lordship emphasised repeatedly that section 3(1) is the 'prime remedial measure'[2] of the 1998 Act, whereas section 4 is 'a measure of last resort'.[3] In fact, this seems to provide Lord Steyn with his primary justification for eschewing 'linguistic arguments' in favour of a 'broad

---

[1] *Ghaidan* v. *Mendoza* [2004] 3 W.L.R 113 at [38], [40], [46], [49], *per* Lord Steyn.
[2] *Ibid.* at [46], [50].     [3] *Ibid.* at [46].

approach' to statutory interpretation under section 3(1), namely, that 'if the core remedial purpose of section 3(1) is not to be undermined a broader approach is required'.[4] Although the idea of section 3(1) as a 'remedial' provision is not mentioned explicitly by any of the other judges in *Ghaidan*, it is interesting to note that counsel for Mr Mendoza argued the case in these terms, i.e. by claiming that 'the *appropriate remedy* is for the court to exercise its interpretive obligation under section 3 of the 1998 Act to interpret legislation compatibly with the Convention rights'.[5] It is now quite common in judgments of the House of Lords, for the section 3(1)/section 4 point to be dealt with under the heading 'Remedy'.[6]

Lord Steyn's insight about the remedial importance of section 3(1) provides us with a key to understanding one important aspect of the interplay between section 3 and section 4.[7] The remedial nature of section 3 follows from the very nature of judicial interpretation. Statutory interpretation is not carried out in the abstract or for the pure intellectual satisfaction of discerning the meaning of unclear statutory provisions. Rather, judicial interpretations are instrumental to legal outcomes.[8] One of the factors influencing statutory interpretation is the judicial duty to strive to do justice for the individual litigant and apply the law fairly and equitably in the context of each case. Although this is not the *only* factor influencing judicial interpretation, it is certainly an important one and in the context of choosing between section 3(1) and section 4 HRA, it plays a significant role. In particular, it will sometimes create a strong judicial incentive to adopt a section 3(1) interpretation in situations where either a section 4 declaration of incompatibility would be unable to provide a remedy for the individual litigant, or where the court feels that a section 4 declaration is unlikely to result in legal change.

---

[4] *Ibid.* at [49].

[5] *Ibid.* at 563 (emphasis added). Similarly, in *R. (Anderson)* v. *Secretary of State for the Home Department* [2002] 3 W.L.R. 1800, Lord Steyn's consideration of whether it would be appropriate to adopt an interpretation under section 3(1) or issue a declaration of incompatibility under section 4 was carried out under the heading 'The remedy', [58]ff; see also Buxton L.J. (CA) in *Ghaidan* v. *Mendoza* [2002] 4 All E.R. 1162 at [34]–[35]. See further Kavanagh (2007), 127–9.

[6] See e.g. *Secretary of State for the Home Department* v. *MB* [2007] UKHL 46 at [44], *per* Lord Bingham; see also *Anderson, ibid.* at [58], *per* Lord Steyn.

[7] For a helpful overview of the issue of remedies under the HRA, see Feldman (1998) and Leigh and Lustgarten (1999), 536.

[8] Kavanagh (2004b), 262.

Take for example the difference of judicial approach in *Ghaidan*[9] and *Bellinger*.[10] If we accept that the linguistic impediment (or indeed lack of linguistic impediment)[11] to adopting a section 3(1) interpretation was very similar in both cases, what explains the fact that a section 3 interpretation was adopted in *Ghaidan*, but the interpretive route was deemed inappropriate in *Bellinger*?[12] The answer lies in the different remedial implications of the choice between section 3 and section 4 in both cases. If Mr Mendoza had received a declaration of incompatibility in *Ghaidan*, he could not have succeeded to a statutory tenancy. Nor could the Civil Partnership Bill going through Parliament at the time have been of any assistance to him, because his partner was dead.[13] However, although a section 4 declaration provided no immediate remedy for Mrs Bellinger, the courts were assured that she could get married in the near future under the forthcoming legislation.[14] Given the disadvantages of a section 3(1) interpretation in that case, the appropriate solution was to issue a declaration of incompatibility, whilst relying on assurances given to the court by the Secretary of State that Mrs Bellinger's rights would be protected in future legislation. Indeed, such legislation was provided shortly afterwards by the Gender Recognition Act 2004. Similar remedial concerns were at work in *R. v. A*.[15] In that case, a declaration of incompatibility would have provided no remedy for the defendant who risked undergoing an unfair trial. Only by adopting a section 3(1) interpretation was the court able to vindicate the defendant's rights.[16] Again, the remedial aspect of the judicial role under the HRA weighed strongly in favour of a section 3(1) interpretation rather than a section 4 declaration of incompatibility. This is not to say that the obligation to provide a remedy in the individual case overrides all other concerns. It is

---

[9] *Ghaidan*, above n. 1.
[10] *Bellinger* v. *Bellinger* [2003] 2 A.C. 467. Kavanagh (2007), 128–9.
[11] Phillipson rightly notes that purely as a matter of linguistics, a section 3(1) interpretation would have been 'almost absurdly easy' in *Bellinger*, see Phillipson (2006), 65.
[12] Thus, Francesca Klug has suggested that 'using the logic advanced in *Ghaidan*, it is possible to make the case that section 3 should have been used to reinterpret s.11 of the Matrimonial Causes Act 1973 in *Bellinger*', Klug (2005), 197; see also Palmer (2007), 129.
[13] Robert Wintemute also makes the point that a section 4 declaration would have been meaningless to Mr Mendoza, see Wintemute (2003), 627.
[14] In *Bellinger*, Lord Hobhouse noted at [79] that the appellant and Mr Bellinger wished to enter into a valid marriage as soon as the UK legislation enables them to do so.
[15] *R. v. A (No. 2)* [2002] 1 A.C. 45.    [16] See further Kavanagh (2005b), 273.

simply one important factor bearing on the choice between section 3 and section 4.[17]

## Section 4 as a 'measure of last resort'

This leads on to the second strand of Lord Steyn's analysis, namely, that a declaration of incompatibility ought to be 'a measure of last resort'.[18] In support of this conclusion, he relied on statements made by the two promoters of the Human Rights Bill as it was going through Parliament.[19] In the House of Lords, the Lord Chancellor observed that 'in 99% of the cases that will arise, there will be no need for judicial declaration of incompatibility'[20] and in the House of Commons, the Home Secretary said 'We expect that, in almost all cases, the courts will be able to interpret the legislation compatibly with the Convention.'[21] Moreover, he attached an appendix to his judgment in *Ghaidan* listing all the cases where a breach of Convention rights was found and the courts had to consider whether to opt for section 3 or section 4. This revealed that the courts issued a declaration of incompatibility more often than they used their interpretive powers under section 3(1).[22] Lord Steyn argued that 'these statistics by themselves raise a question about the proper implementation of the 1998 Act'[23] and whether the case law has taken a wrong turning, especially since the statistics in no way matched the ministerial predictions as the Human Rights Bill was going through Parliament.

There are reasons to doubt whether either of these arguments provide adequate support for Lord Steyn's conclusion. As regards the argument based on *Hansard*, it is worth questioning whether Lord Steyn's reliance on *Hansard* is compatible with his extrajudicial views published in his Hart Lecture 2000[24] about the dangers and limited value of ministerial statements as an indication of a statute's true meaning, given that they are made by members of the Executive driven by the political goal of

---

[17] For the view that section 3(1) can be a vehicle for providing a remedy for violation of Convention rights, see also Henderson (2000); Wintemute (2003), 627; Lester (2001), 691.

[18] *Ghaidan*, above n. 1 at [39], [50]. This view was also put forward by the Secretary of State for the Home Department (Jack Straw) in parliamentary debate on the Human Rights Bill, *Hansard*, HC, cols 421–2 (3 June 1998).

[19] *Ibid.* at [46].     [20] *Hansard*, HL, col. 840 (third reading) (5 February 1998).

[21] *Hansard*, HC, col. 778 (second reading) (16 February 1998).

[22] At that time, section 3(1) was only used in ten cases, a declaration of incompatibility was issued in fifteen cases, with five declarations reversed on appeal to the House of Lords.

[23] *Ghaidan* above n. 1 at [39].     [24] Steyn (2001), 59–72.

winning support for what was in this case a controversial Bill.[25] As has been recognised in recent case law of the House of Lords,[26] we should be wary of relying too heavily on statements made by members of the Executive, whose main task is to push controversial Bills through Parliament.[27] The ministerial statements cited by Lord Steyn in *Ghaidan* may simply have been politically motivated pronouncements designed to assuage the fears of opponents to the Human Rights Bill that it would greatly expand judicial power, rather than any considered opinion on the complex interplay between sections 3 and 4. Alternatively, the Executive's expectation that section 4 would only be used rarely may simply have rested on 'an unduly rosy view of British legislation'[28] in those early optimistic days of the Labour Government, that very little of their legislation was in fact contrary to the Convention.[29] As such, it is unwise to treat them as a statement of law about the complex interaction between section 3 and section 4, but rather as a political assertion designed to ensure the passing of the HRA.[30]

So the ministerial statements about Convention-compatible interpretations being possible in almost all cases are insufficient, in themselves, to ground an argument about the appropriate judicial approach to section 3(1). What about Lord Steyn's suggestion that the statistics on

---

[25] This is also questioned by Lord Phillips (2002).

[26] See e.g. *Wilson* v. *First County Trust* [2003] W.L.R. 568. For discussion of this and other cases where the House of Lords called into question the value of statements made in *Hansard* for the purposes of assisting them in statutory interpretation, see Kavanagh (2005a).

[27] Kavanagh (2005a), 105–7.

[28] Leigh and Lustgarten (1999), 536; see also Lord Falconer of Thoroton (Secretary of State for Constitutional Affairs and Lord Chancellor), 'Human Rights and Constitutional Reform', speech made at the Law Society and Human Rights Lawyers Association, 17 February 2004, available at www.dca.gov.uk/speeches/2004/lc170204.htm, where, complacent though it now sounds, he argued that the Government did not expect there to be many human rights 'faults' in their legislation. The view that the British Government did not expect the Convention to have much effect due to their assumption that UK law was already compliant, is supported in Wicks (2000).

[29] This interpretation is supported by Francesca Klug and Keir Starmer, who read them 'not as a statement of law . . . but as a frequently stated political assertion that most UK law was already compatible with the ECHR and would remain so', see Klug and Starmer (2005), 722.

[30] Whilst not overruling *Pepper* v. *Hart*, the House of Lords in *Wilson*, above n. 26, was adamant that the limits on the admissibility of ministerial statements set out in *Pepper* should be strictly observed. Geoffrey Marshall has argued that the views of the parliamentary sponsors of the Human Rights Bill on the meaning of section 3 fail the test of clarity or unambiguity requisite for admissibility under *Pepper* v. *Hart*: see Marshall (2003), 238–9.

the judicial choice between section 3 and section 4 may reflect a wrong turning in the law? As Jan Van Zyl Smit points out 'it is hard to see how a statistical generalisation over the great variety of all arguable human rights cases would affect the outcome of any particular case'.[31] The reason why this is so, goes back to the nature of the interpretive task. Judicial interpretation under the HRA requires judges to balance two sets of competing values. The relative weight of any of these factors or 'interpretative criteria'[32] varies according to the particular circumstances and context of the case at hand. In some cases (as in *Ghaidan*) the circumstances of the case combine to weigh in favour of an innovative interpretation. In *Bellinger*, they pull in the direction of a declaration of incompatibility. One cannot determine whether section 3 or section 4 will be appropriate in advance or in the abstract. All one can do is provide an analysis of the factors which influence the choice and then see how important they are in the context of a particular case. Therefore, a statistical generalisation alone cannot inform us about the appropriateness of choosing between section 3 and section 4. Assessment of this issue can only properly issue from analysing the choice in the context of particular cases.

If this more contextual approach is adopted, the need to take sides between those who argue that section 3 should be used all or nearly all the time[33] and those who argue that section 4 should be used more often,[34] is obviated. On my analysis, this issue cannot be determined in the abstract. It all depends on the details and context of the cases which get litigated under the HRA. All one can say is that section 3 should be used when it is appropriate, considering all the factors relevant to that issue in the case before the courts, and section 4 should be used when it is not. For this reason, it is misleading to depict the debate about the appropriate judicial approach to HRA adjudication as that between those who advocate reliance on section 3 no matter how creative on the one hand,[35] and those who advocate reliance on section 4 as the generally preferred alternative.[36] This highly polarised picture obscures the fact that judges and academic commentators may have no *general* preference either way, but rather will assess the appropriateness of the judicial choice

---

[31] Van Zyl Smit (2007), 298.

[32] For the idea that statutory interpretation involves the 'weighing of conflicting interpretative criteria', see Vogenauer (2005), 661.

[33] See e.g. Phillipson (2003).       [34] See e.g. Campbell (2001), 99–100; Gearty (2002), 250.

[35] These commentators are described by Conor Gearty as 'true blue human rights lawyers', see Gearty (2003b), 551.

[36] Nicol (2004b), 273; (2002), 438.

between section 3 and section 4 in light of the facts and context of the individual case. In my view, this is the correct approach.[37]

So should declarations of incompatibility be a measure of last resort for the judiciary, given the remedial nature of section 3(1)? After all, we have only shown that Lord Steyn's arguments in favour of this conclusion are problematic, not that the conclusion itself is without merit. At the very least, one can say (following the House of Lords in *Wilson* v. *First County Trust*[38]) that a section 3(1) interpretation is 'an essential *preliminary* step to making declaration of incompatibility'.[39] This follows from the terms of section 4(1) which state that section 4(2) only applies to proceedings in which a court 'determines' whether a provision is compatible with a Convention right. So, as a matter of construing the terms of the HRA, section 3(1) must be the courts' first resort because the possibility of a Convention-compatible interpretation must be explored before a declaration of incompatibility can be issued under section 4. Section 3 is given precedence over section 4 in this sense.[40]

Moreover, if we draw on Lord Steyn's insight that section 3 has a remedial function, then a further conclusion can be drawn. This is that in cases where the rights violation is substantial and a remedy is required, there will be strong reasons in favour of a 'strained' interpretation under section 3 because a declaration of incompatibility will be no remedial use to the person asserting a rights violation.[41] Whether those reasons win out in any particular case will depend on a variety of contextual factors such as how 'strained' that interpretation might be, whether it would be inconsistent with core features of the legislation under scrutiny or the legislative terms, whether it would have wide-ranging implications for the broader legislative context, whether it would involve judges in making decisions which would be more appropriate for legislative deliberation. So not only must the section 3 line of enquiry be pursued first, there may well be added reasons for judges to choose section 3 over section 4.

There is one further point which supports the view that remedial concerns will tend to lean the courts in favour of a section 3(1) interpretation

---

[37] See further Kavanagh (2004c), 544–5.    [38] Above n. 26.
[39] *Ibid.* at [14], *per* Lord Nicholls, emphasis added.    [40] Klug (2005), 722.
[41] This is not to assume that all litigants who bring human rights claims are seeking an immediate remedy. They may simply be using litigation as a way of raising the public profile of their grievance, thereby hoping to stimulate political resolution of the issue. My point is simply that in some cases (as in *Ghaidan* or *R.* v. *A*) where the main aim of the litigation must have been to seek immediate redress through the courts, there will be strong arguments in favour of choosing section 3 over section 4.

and away from a declaration of incompatibility under section 4. This is the judicial awareness of the centrality of section 3(1) to the legislative scheme of the HRA. As Lord Rodger observed in *Ghaidan*, section 3(1) is 'the means by which Parliament intended that people should be afforded the benefit of the Convention rights – "so far as it is possible", without the need for any further intervention by Parliament'.[42] A similar point was made by Lord Bingham in *Huang*,[43] where he noted that the object of the HRA was to ensure that public authorities (including, of course, the courts) 'would act to avert or rectify any violation of the Convention right, with the result that such rights would be effectively protected at home, thus (it was hoped) obviating or reducing the need for recourse to Strasbourg'.[44]

Under section 3(1), judges are given an important constitutional role in seeking to ensure that Convention rights are protected in primary legislation. The terms of sections 3 and 4 suggest that, in furtherance of that role, they should err on the side of seeking to protect rights through interpretation and only issue a declaration of incompatibility if the interpretive route is inappropriate. The choice between section 3 and section 4 is not a choice between two equally weighted statutory provisions. Judges are under an *obligation* to strive to interpret compatibly with Convention rights, but only have a *discretion* to issue a declaration of incompatibility, should that prove to be impossible. This is not to say that we can make an *a priori* assumption that a section 3(1) interpretation will be possible in almost all cases. That depends on the combination of contextual factors in any particular case, which one cannot predict. It is simply to say that the scheme of the HRA gives added weight to the interpretive option, in preference to the (discretionary) declaration of incompatibility. The declaration of incompatibility is a last resort in this sense.[45]

The point about the constitutional duty placed on the courts to ensure that primary legislation is compatible with Convention rights, is echoed in the judgment of Baroness Hale in *Secretary of State for the Home Department* v. *MB*.[46] The question there was whether the system of imposing control orders under the Prevention of Terrorism Act 2005 was compatible with the right to a fair trial under Article 6. Following the type of

---

[42] *Ghaidan* above n. 1 at [106].

[43] *Huang* v. *Secretary of State for the Home Department* [2007] UKHL 11.

[44] *Ibid.* at [8]. Lord Nicholls noted in *Ghaidan* that section 3 'is one of the primary means by which Convention rights are brought into the law of this country', [26].

[45] This view seems is supported by Klug (2005), 722.     [46] [2007] 3 W.L.R. 681.

'reading in' adopted in *R. v. A*,[47] the House of Lords supported a section 3(1) interpretation in that case, despite the fact that the statutory provision at issue was, on its ordinary meaning, clearly and unambiguously at odds with that reading. In justifying the choice of section 3 rather than section 4 in the context of this case, Baroness Hale noted that:

> In interpreting the [Prevention of Terrorism] Act compatibly we are doing our best to make it work. This gives the greatest possible incentive to all parties to the case, and to the judge, to conduct the proceedings in such a way as to afford a sufficient and substantial measure of procedural justice . . . a declaration of incompatibility, on the other hand, would allow all of them to conduct the proceedings in a way which they knew to be incompatible.[48]

This *dictum* highlights the sense in which the courts are partners working together with Parliament in order to render primary legislation compatible with Convention rights.[49] Part of the judicial perspective under section 3(1) must be to consider which solution would give better and stronger protection for Convention rights, whilst nonetheless going with the grain of existing legislation. If this can be achieved by a section 3(1) interpretation, whilst preserving at least part of the legislative objective, then the courts have a strong incentive to go down the interpretive route. It is a way in which the courts can do their best to make legislation work, whilst simultaneously protecting Convention rights.

The issue of the choice between section 3 and section 4 has elicited a range of academic responses. Gavin Phillipson has argued that included in the duty contained in section 3(1) to read 'primary and secondary legislation whenever enacted' compatibly with the Convention, is the judicial obligation to read section 3(1) itself in a Convention-compatible fashion.[50] If this premise is accepted, it follows (argues Phillipson) that section 3(1) "should be read so as to give it maximum possible scope, so that it virtually always achieves Convention compliance when reading other statutes'.[51] On this basis, he favours a reading of section 3(1) which 'maximises rather than minimises protection for Convention rights'[52] such that the courts should strive to achieve a section 3(1) interpretation in almost all cases and minimise their use of section 4. The problem with this argument is that even if we accept Phillipson's premise, it does

---

[47] *R. v. A*, above n. 15.   [48] *MB*, above n. 46 at [73].

[49] For this 'partnership' view of the relationship between Parliament and the courts under the HRA, see also Joseph (2004).

[50] See Phillipson (2003), 183ff.   [51] *Ibid.*, 187   [52] *Ibid.*

not necessarily support his conclusion. Convention-compatibility can be achieved in different ways. One option is to secure compatibility through judicial interpretation. Another is to amend legislation through the parliamentary process to remove any incompatibility. The HRA explicitly allows for both options. If Phillipson's premise is correct, then the whole of the HRA must be read in a Convention-compatible way, including section 4. The judicial obligation under section 3(1) should not be read in isolation, but rather in conjunction with the alternative option of issuing a declaration of incompatibility under section 4. The difficult judicial choice created by the interaction between section 3 and section 4 is not between maximising or minimising Convention-compatibility. Rather, it is about finding the most appropriate way of maximising protection of human rights in the context of a particular case. In some cases, this will be achieved by pursuing the interpretive route. In others, a better way of achieving Convention-compatibility will be to issue a declaration of incompatibility. In the latter cases, the justification for the judicial choice in favour of section 4 may well be (as it was in *Bellinger*, *Anderson*, *Re S* and *Roth*) that legislative law reform was required to maximise the protection of Convention rights, a result which could not be achieved (or could not be achieved to the same degree) by way of judicial interpretation.

Nor is Phillipson's argument supported or saved by his more recent claim that Article 1 of the Convention should be used as a guide to the meaning of section 3(1).[53] Article 1 requires Contracting States to secure to all within their jurisdiction the Convention rights. Phillipson emphasises the word 'secure'. It follows, he argues, that:

> Provisions in a statute that explicitly preserve to Parliament the legal ability to violate those rights (that is, ss 3(2) and 6(2)) are at the very least in some tension with this guarantee. If possible, therefore, those provisions should be read so far as is possible to be compatible with Article 1, which would mean giving them minimal effect.[54]

He concludes:

> Article 1 provides a strong argument for a reading of section 3 which minimises the circumstances in which the judiciary are forced to make a declaration of incompatibility, thus allowing a rights-violation to continue... Article 1 compels us to give the most maximal possible reading of section 3(1), so as to keep violations of Article 1 to the absolute minimum.[55]

---

[53] Phillipson (2006), 62.    [54] *Ibid.*    [55] *Ibid.*, 63.

It is not at all clear that Article 1 compels this conclusion. The crucial word to be emphasised from Article 1 is 'Contracting States'. It does not specify which institution within that state should secure the protection of Convention rights or which institutional mechanisms would best protect them.[56] Moreover, Strasbourg case law confirms that there is no requirement in the Convention that the Contracting States must adopt any particular procedure for implementing rights, let alone a requirement that it should be a judicial one.[57] Quite wisely, Article 1 is not conclusive on the question of appropriate institutional mechanism and is therefore an unsure guide to the meaning of section 3(1) and its interaction with section 4. Phillipson acknowledges that his argument based on Article 1 will appear 'mischievous'[58] since this Article was deliberately excluded from the Schedule attached to the HRA, because it was assumed to be redundant on the grounds that the HRA itself provided adequate mechanisms for securing the protection of Convention rights.[59] But this simply brings us back to the underlying question, which is how section 3 and section 4 combine to secure the protection of those rights. This difficult question is not answered by Article 1 of the Convention.

## The argument from 'dialogue'

The idea that section 4 is a 'measure of last resort' has attracted criticism from some of the leading academic commentators on the HRA. They argue that declarations of incompatibility should be used more often because they facilitate 'dialogue' between the courts and the legislature/Executive. Encouraging such dialogue was one of the purposes of the 1998 Act, to which judges can give effect by issuing declarations of incompatibility.[60] Geoffrey Marshall put the point as follows:

---

[56] For the point that the Convention, as an international treaty, is directed to states, not to any particular organ within the state, see Warbrick (2007), 30.

[57] See *Klass* v. *Federal Republic of Germany*, Series A, No. 28 (1979) 2 E.H.R.R. 214; *Silver* v. *UK*, Series A, No. 61 (1983) 5 E.H.R.R. 437. See Feldman (1998), 692. This point is supported by Francesca Klug and Keir Starmer: 'Strasbourg has long recognised that Parliament, public authorities and the courts all play their part', see Klug and Starmer (2005), 627.

[58] Phillipson (2006), 63.

[59] HL Deb, vol. 583, col. 466ff, (18 November 1997), cited by Phillipson (2006), 63.

[60] Marshall (2003), 243–4; Klug (2003), 130ff; Klug (2001), 370; Nicol (2004b), 281; Nicol (2004a), 197; Nicol (2002), 441; Hickman (2005); see generally, Roach (2001).

A declaration by the courts provides the legislature with a considered judicial view of the rights compatibility of the legislation. It can then reflect on its actions and either take the remedial steps provided for in section 10 of the Act or exercise its retained sovereign prerogative to disagree with the judicial assessment and confirm its initial view of its legislation.[61]

Supporting the idea that the courts should issue declarations of incompatibility in order to fulfil the legislative purpose of the HRA, Francesca Klug makes the following point:[62]

> [The HRA] was not enacted so that the courts could have the final say in areas where there is no settled human rights answer . . . Parliament would be entitled to choose to protect its democratic mandate on an issue where the human rights case law is far from settled. Encouraging this kind of 'dialogue' was one of the purposes of the HRA.

The issue about giving the courts the 'final say' will be addressed more fully later on in the book.[63] Clearly, the intuitive appeal of the 'dialogue' metaphor rests, in large part, on the idea that Parliament will have the 'last word' on issues related to Convention rights, thus protecting its 'sovereignty'. The plausibility of the claims underlying this idea will be addressed in more detail in chapter 11. For the moment, it suffices to make the following brief points.

First, if what is meant to be conveyed by the metaphor of 'dialogue' is simply the interaction between the courts and the legislature, then there is nothing novel in this, and it is certainly not peculiar to the declaration of incompatibility mechanism under the HRA 1998. The metaphor of 'dialogue' is equally applicable not only to section 3(1) but also to ordinary instances of statutory interpretation, whereby Parliament enacts the legislation (sometimes intentionally leaving gaps for the judiciary to fill) and the courts interpret it by determining its meaning when applied to a particular case. Parliament then has a number of 'responses'. By far the most frequent response is to do nothing, i.e. to acquiesce in the interpretation. This may have more to do with the scarcity of parliamentary time than any considered view about the correctness of the interpretation. But, of course, it also has the option (though rarely exercised) of changing the interpretation, either outright or in part. If this changed provision comes up again for interpretation in the courts, the process of so-called 'dialogue' can continue.[64]

---

[61] Marshall (2003), 243–4.    [62] Klug (2003), 132.    [63] See chapter 11, 322–4.

[64] Similarly, we are all aware of cases where the judiciary believe that it would be inappropriate (or impossible) for them to reform the law by way of interpretation despite an obvious

This familiar interaction between the branches of government is simply an aspect of the general point made at the beginning of this book, namely, that statutory interpretation involves an inter-institutional meeting between the courts and legislature. Unsurprisingly therefore, section 3(1) instantiates the same sort of 'dialogue'. Parliament enacts legislation, and if the courts decide to interpret it using the section 3(1) mechanism, it is open to Parliament to do nothing or to change the interpretation by enacting new legislation (or open to the Executive to exercise its power under section 10 HRA for fast-track amendment). So, even if we assume for the sake of argument that encouraging 'dialogue' was one of the purposes of the HRA to which the courts should give effect,[65] this does not support the conclusion that section 4 is the only or even the primary way of fulfilling that purpose. It could also be carried out by adopting an interpretation under section 3.[66] So, the argument from 'dialogue' is inconclusive on the question of how judges should choose between sections 3 and 4.

Second, the argument from 'dialogue' (at least as presented by Geoffrey Marshall) overlooks the important remedial role of section 3(1) and the duty of the courts to do justice to the litigants before them. The terms of section 3(1) make it clear that the courts have a duty to strive to achieve Convention-compatibility if at all possible, and only if this is impossible can they then go on to issue a declaration of incompatibility. In other

injustice to the litigant before them, because this would exceed their constitutional role. Even in this situation, the courts can nonetheless highlight the injustice and (in *obiter* statements) urge the government or Parliament to reform the law and this is often sufficient to prompt Parliament to reconsider its legislation.

[65] This assumption is often based on the following statement of the Home Secretary in the course of parliamentary debate on the Human Rights Bill: 'Parliament and the judiciary must engage in a serious dialogue about the operation and development of the rights in the Bill . . . this dialogue is the only way in which we can ensure the legislation is a living development that assists our citizens', 314 HC 1141 (24 June 1998), see e.g. Klug (1999), 248. However, this general (to my mind largely rhetorical) statement is an unsure basis on which to rest the claim that Parliament intended the HRA to embody any particular 'dialogue theory'. Moreover, if it is used to ground the argument that the courts should be willing to issue declarations of incompatibility in a 'routine' way (Campbell, 2001), then one would have to square this conclusion with the Home Secretary's other statements in parliamentary debate that the interpretive route under section 3 would be chosen 'in almost all cases', with resort to the declaration of incompatibility designed for 'the rare cases where that cannot be done', 306 HC 780 (16 February 1998).

[66] This point is also made by Hickman (2005), 326. Trevor Allan presents the process of interpretation of primary legislation as an 'imaginary dialogue' or 'constitutional dialogue' between Parliament and the courts, see Allan (2004a), 690, 704.

words, their first duty is to attempt to remedy the alleged rights violation through the interpretive route – the power to issue a declaration of
incompatibility only arises if this attempt fails. It may fail because such
an interpretation might violate a fundamental feature of the statute or
because it requires such a radical reform of the statute, that it would go
beyond the type of incremental judicial development of the law so characteristic of the common law method. As we shall see in the second part
of this book, it is certainly true that when carrying out their interpretive
functions under the HRA, judges ought to be sensitive to the constitutional division of labour between the three branches of government and
be alive to which institution is best placed to carry out certain types of
legal reform. However, this does not mean that judges should make their
choice between sections 3 and 4 on the basis of which option would facilitate more 'dialogue' with the elected branches. Judges have to decide cases
involving actual litigants whose rights may have been violated and they
have an obligation to arrive at a just outcome in the context of that case. If,
for example, Mr Mendoza had received a declaration of incompatibility
(as Geoffrey Marshall recommends), he would have been left without an
effective remedy for the violation of his Convention rights. It would have
been poor consolation to him to discover that a judicial decision which
failed to vindicate his rights was justified on the basis that it 'improved
the quality of political discourse.'[67]

   This is not in any way to deny that in making their decisions, judges
must bear in mind that they should respect the decisions made by the legislature and Executive. So too must they strive to ensure that they do not
attempt to make decisions for which they are ill-suited. Sometimes, the
only responsible option is to defer to the elected branches of government.
However, to renege on their remedial duty under section 3(1) would
require very strong countervailing arguments. The move from section 3
to section 4 requires strong justification as to why the interpretive route
is not possible. The judicial obligation to defer sometimes to the elected
branches may well provide such a justification. But this is very different
from the diffuse idea of 'facilitating dialogue' between the branches of
government. Those who recommend that the courts should perform a
'dialogue-enhancing' role sometimes do so on the basis that some issues
are more appropriate for Parliament rather than the courts to resolve, and

[67] Nicol (2002), 442.

if so, Parliament should not be precluded from playing a role in resolving them.[68] This justification means that the argument from dialogue no longer turns on the diffuse desirability of 'dialogue' between the branches of government. It collapses into the argument for judicial deference on the basis of superior competence and expertise. This view is examined in detail in chapter 7, where it will be argued that, in certain circumstances, this consideration may justify a court in choosing section 4 over section 3.

Finally, Francesca Klug has suggested that section 4 has come to be seen as a measure of last resort because of an assumption that it would '*force* the Executive and Parliament to change the legislation.'[69] As will be seen in chapter 10, the fact that no declaration of incompatibility issued thus far under the HRA has been ignored or defied by the Government or Parliament, gives credence to this view of their forceful nature. However, it must also be borne in mind that the declaration of incompatibility does not necessarily deliver a remedy for the individual litigant. It is precisely the relative weakness of section 4 as a remedial measure which sometimes encourages the courts to adopt an interpretation under section 3(1).[70] For example, one of the reasons for the judicial reluctance to issue a declaration of incompatibility in *R. v. A*[71] was the fear that the Government would not change the 'rape shield' provision in response to such a declaration.[72] Had the House of Lords had the option of striking down the legislation in *R. v. A*, they may well have done so, because it would have rendered the statutory provision inoperative for the purposes of the rape trial at issue, but would have simultaneously forced Parliament to reform the section so that it could protect fair trial rights in future cases. So, ironically, the fact that the declaration of incompatibility has no immediate *legal* effect, may place pressure on the UK courts to be more robust and creative in exercising their interpretive powers, than if they had the power to strike down legislative provisions.[73]

---

[68]  See e.g. Nicol (2006), 742ff.    [69]  Klug (2003), 131 (emphasis added).

[70]  This view is also shared by Lester (2001), 691; Henderson (2000) 261.    [71]  Above n. 15.

[72]  The basis of this fear and the drawbacks of issuing a declaration of incompatibility in *R. v. A* are explored in Kavanagh (2005b), 273.

[73]  It is ironic because many of those who argued against including a striking-down power in what became the HRA were largely motivated by a concern to curb judicial power. For the view that heavy reliance on section 3 is often a reaction to the relative weakness of section 4, see also Wintemute (2006a) 215.

## Predicting the political response to declarations
## of incompatibility

In many of the cases where the higher courts have issued a declaration of incompatibility, the main reason for choosing this over a section 3(1) interpretation was that judges are reluctant to engage in radical statutory reform which would be more appropriate for Parliament to undertake. *Bellinger* is a good example of a refusal to embark on a section 3(1) interpretation on the grounds that the resulting change in the law would have far-reaching practical ramifications and implications for other (inter-related) areas of the law. However, this was not the only relevant factor weighing in favour of a declaration of incompatibility in *Bellinger*. When deciding the case, the House of Lords knew that the ECtHR had handed down a recent decision holding the UK to be in breach of Articles 8 and 12 for denying legal recognition of cases of gender reassignment.[74] This decision prompted three significant developments, described by Lord Nicholls as having 'an important bearing on the outcome of this appeal'.[75] First, the Interdepartmental Working Group on Transsexual People had been reconvened to re-examine the implications of granting full legal status to transsexual people in their acquired gender in light of the *Goodwin* judgment.[76] Second, in December 2002 (i.e. a month before the *Bellinger* decision was handed down) the Government announced its intention to bring forward primary legislation which would allow transsexual people to marry in their acquired gender. Third, the Lord Chancellor accepted that since the ECtHR decision, those parts of English law which failed to give legal recognition to the acquired gender transsexual persons was in principle incompatible with Articles 8 and 12 of the Convention. Domestic law, including section 11 of the Matrimonial Causes Act 1973, would have to change. Lord Nicholls' view that these issues would be better tackled by Parliament rather than the courts, was 'more especially' the case given that the Government 'had announced its intention to introduce comprehensive primary legislation on this difficult and sensitive topic'.[77]

A similar situation obtained in the case of *Anderson*.[78] Of central importance in *Anderson* was the fact that the ECtHR had handed down two recent decisions indicating that the power exercised by the Home

---

[74] *Goodwin* v. *United Kingdom* (2002) 35 E.H.R.R. 447, cited in *Bellinger*, above n. 10 at [21], *per* Lord Nicholls.
[75] *Bellinger, ibid.* at [26].     [76] Above n. 76.
[77] *Bellinger*, above n. 10 at [37].     [78] Above n. 5.

Secretary under section 29 of the Crime (Sentences) Act 1977 violated the Convention right contained in Article 6.[79] Moreover, there was *Hansard* evidence that, in response to *Stafford*, the Home Secretary acknowledged that some of the administrative arrangements for the review and release of mandatory life sentence prisoners needed to be changed in order to give effect to that decision.[80] Finally, the *Stafford* ruling[81] provided that even if the Secretary of State's discretion under section 29 was removed, and he was obliged to follow the judicial recommendation on tariffs, this would still be in violation of Article 6, because it would be objectionable from a 'separation of powers' point of view.[82]

These factors combined to assure the House of Lords that the Government was going to change provisions like section 29, indeed was legally obliged to do so, following the ruling in *Stafford*. Therefore, there was no need to adopt a strained construction under section 3(1) HRA in this case. The more appropriate course of action was to grant a declaration of incompatibility. Moreover, even if they attempted some judicial rectification under section 3(1) to remove the Home Secretary's discretion, the judgment in *Stafford* indicated that this would be insufficient to remove the violation of Article 6 ECHR. For these reasons, a declaration of incompatibility under section 4 was a preferable and more effective judicial option than a strained interpretation under section 3.

So, it seems that in cases where the ECtHR has already pronounced on an issue and there is evidence that the Government intends to change the law in light of this, indeed is legally obliged to do so, the courts may well prefer to issue a declaration of incompatibility, rather than engaging in difficult and perhaps strained modes of interpretation under section 3. One of the reasons why judges may be reluctant to issue a declaration of incompatibility is the fear or risk that Parliament will not reform the law to comply with Convention rights.[83] It would be naive to think that considerations about whether Parliament is already prepared to change the law would not influence the judicial decision about whether to adopt an interpretation under section 3, or a declaration of incompatibility under

---

[79] *Stafford* v. *UK* (2002) 35 E.H.R.R. 1121; *Benjamin and Wilson* v. *UK* (2002) 36 E.H.R.R. 1.

[80] *Anderson*, above n. 5 at [45], *per* Lord Steyn.   [81] *Stafford*, above n. 79.

[82] This was noted in *Anderson*, above n. 5 at [44].

[83] Nicol (2004b), 273. Indeed, he points out that this may have been the reason why the House of Lords in *A* chose not to issue a declaration of incompatibility, see Nicol *ibid.*, 276. This suggestion supports the point made above that a significant distinction between *A* and *Anderson* was that in the latter, the risk of political rejection of a declaration of incompatibility was not so great, because there was reliable evidence that Parliament was going to change the law in any case.

section 4 HRA. In both *Anderson* and *Bellinger* the courts had ample evidence on which to conclude that a Convention-compatible legislative amendment would in all likelihood ensue. Therefore, a declaration of incompatibility was chosen in the knowledge that the law would be reformed in the appropriate way by Parliament. So, where the courts are aware that there may be significant disadvantage to adopting a strained interpretation under section 3, they may be encouraged to adopt a declaration of incompatibility, especially if they are reassured that Parliament is willing to reform the law. The existence of a decision of the ECtHR mandating them to carry out this amendment will be a very strong indication that Parliament will do so, indeed is already legally obliged to do so. Conversely, if the courts have reason to doubt Parliament's willingness to embark on such reform (as was the case in *R. v. A*), they may be less likely to opt for a declaration of incompatibility because the potential violation of Convention rights will not be removed from the law.

The view that the courts should take into account the likely political response to a declaration of incompatibility, is not uncontroversial. It is sometimes suggested that, in choosing between sections 3 and 4, it is illegitimate for the courts to be influenced by how the government or Parliament will react to a declaration of incompatibility.[84] Judges should decide the legal issue of principle, irrespective of how the government or Parliament will respond. If this view rests on a more general belief that it is inappropriate for the courts to engage in consequentialist reasoning or to consider matters of 'policy', I challenge it in chapter 7.[85] There, I argue that judicial reasoning includes (and ought to include) not only an evaluation of the substantive legal issue, but also much broader considerations about the institutional propriety of deciding one way or the other. Judges should not be oblivious to the (legal, social, economic and political) consequences of their decisions. In relation to the choice between sections 3 and 4, the argument that the courts should decide the matter as if they were in an institutional vacuum, raises further problems. The terms of sections 3 and 4 leaves it to the courts to decide when an interpretation is possible, and when it is more appropriate for the Executive/legislature to remedy the rights violation. This decision necessarily involves an evaluation of which institution is best placed to carry out the legal reform, and the question whether the legislature or government is willing to carry out that reform,

---

[84] Thus, Jeffrey Jowell has suggested that the courts 'ought not in any way to be influenced by the fact that Parliament may in the end disregard their pronouncements', see Jowell (2003b), 597; Nicol (2006), 744ff.

[85] See chapter 7, 183–90.

will be an important consideration in that overall deliberation.[86] Under the HRA, the courts are given an important responsibility to help to ensure that Convention rights are protected in domestic law. Therefore, they are obliged to consider whether a declaration of incompatibility will further that aim or not.[87]

Finally, it should be borne in mind that, like all the other factors weighing into the balance about whether to choose between sections 3 and 4, the existence of a Strasbourg decision will not be determinative. It depends on the other contextual factors relevant to that determination. So, for example, by the time *Ghaidan* v. *Mendoza* had reached the House of Lords, the ECtHR had handed down its decision in *Karner* v. *Austria*[88] to the effect that discrimination against same-sex couples violated the Convention. In light of *Karner*, Parliament was considering the terms of the Civil Partnership Bill when their Lordships handed down their decision in *Ghaidan*. In fact, Lord Millett queried whether it was appropriate for the House of Lords to adopt a section 3(1) interpretation 'when the government had announced its intention to bring forward corrective legislation in the form of the Civil Partnership Act'.[89] This overlooks the important remedial dimension of the decision in *Ghaidan*. Whilst the Civil Partnership Act would prevent future discrimination against same-sex couples, it would have been too late to remedy the discrimination suffered by Mr Mendoza. Moreover, the House of Lords was well aware that had he not received the statutory tenancy, he would have taken his case to Strasbourg, and in light of the principles enunciated in *Karner* (as well as the finding of incompatibility with Article 14 in the House of Lords), he was virtually certain to obtain a favourable outcome there.

---

[86] Another important factor is that the courts will be aware that if a practice develops whereby the government/Parliament always respond positively to a declaration of incompatibility, this may create a constitutional convention to that effect. Awareness of the broader constitutional significance of such a development will also play a role in the choice between sections 3 and 4, see further chapter 10, 281ff.

[87] So, my argument is not just a 'realist' observation about the practice of the courts as it has been developing, but also a normative argument that this factor of likely political response to a declaration of incompatibility *should* influence the choice between sections 3 and 4 HRA. Jan Van Zyl Smit has argued that this turns the section 3 obligation into a discretion, see Van Zyl Smit (2005), 110. In my view, considering the likely response to a declaration of incompatibility is part of a full institutional evaluation of whether a section 3(1) interpretation is desirable, i.e. it is one of the factors they must take into account when carrying out their duty under section 3(1).

[88] For consideration of the importance of the *Karner* case for the decision in *Ghaidan*, see Wintemute (2003), 627.

[89] *Ghaidan*, above n. 1 at [56].

Therefore, the section 3(1) interpretation in that case, though departing from the ordinary meaning of the legislation, satisfied the remedial concerns about Mr Mendoza's case and prevented him having to pursue costly and time-consuming litigation in Strasbourg.

## Rights and remedies returned: *Bellinger* v. *Bellinger* reconsidered

Some academic commentators have been highly critical of the House of Lords decision in *Bellinger* to issue a declaration of incompatibility, rather than remove the rights-violation by way of a section 3 interpretation. It is worth attending to these views, in order to elucidate further the nature of the judicial choice between sections 3 and 4 in the context of a particular case. One forceful critique of the unanimous decision in *Bellinger* is provided by Tom Hickman, who dismisses the House of Lords' claims about the dangers and knock-on effects of a section 3 interpretation in that case. He believes that 'there was no substance to Lord Nicholls' fears that the court had to settle government policy on the legal entitlements of transsexuals across the board, or do nothing at all'.[90] The more prudent judicial course would have been to make a narrow holding in favour of Mrs Bellinger, whilst leaving the broader issues to Parliament. This, 'would have invited prompt parliamentary action; it would have provided a remedy to Mrs Bellinger; and it would have reserved the ultimate ability of the courts to assess the principled issue'.[91]

There are a number of problems with this view. The first concerns the characterisation of what is involved in making a declaration of incompatibility. Hickman suggests that by issuing a declaration of incompatibility in *Bellinger*, the court 'did not feel able to determine for itself the question of fundamental rights that was raised'.[92] But this is not the case. The House of Lords felt well able to determine the question of fundamental rights at issue in *Bellinger*: it decided that her Convention rights had been clearly violated by the legislation and made a declaration accordingly. The problem for the court lay not in deciding 'the principled issue,'[93] but rather in finding the appropriate way of remedying the rights violation they so clearly identified. In carrying out the evaluation about appropriate remedies and the institutional division of labour in securing that remedy, the courts have an important responsibility to ensure that their decisions do more good than harm, to consider the impact on future case law and indeed, the law more generally. They also have an important

---

[90] Hickman (2005), 331.    [91] *Ibid.*    [92] *Ibid.*    [93] *Ibid.*

constitutional responsibility to ensure that they should only make those decisions which rest on an appropriate degree of expertise, law-making competence and legitimacy.[94] These are weighty factors which should not be underestimated or quickly brushed aside. They will be explored in full when we come to examine the role of deference in adjudication under the HRA in the second part of this book.

More importantly, Hickman's critique underestimates the dangers of a narrow holding in this case.[95] Judges have to be acutely aware of the risk that a decision tailored only to the facts of a particular case will nonetheless be cited in future cases, so that it will tend to influence the development of the law in damaging and unforeseen ways. In *Bellinger*, Lord Nicholls' concern was that a decision that Mrs Bellinger could be considered 'female' for the purposes of the Matrimonial Causes Act, despite the fact that she was born as a male, would have implications for a number of wider issues which *encompassed* the facts of her case. For example, even a narrow holding would have had to rely on some criteria for establishing whether Mrs Bellinger was a 'female'. Such a decision would inevitably have set a precedent on the question of whether transsexuals could marry at various stages of medical intervention. For the House of Lords, it would have been irresponsible to change the law on the basis of an assumption that Mrs Bellinger was on the 'reassigned gender side of the line'[96] since gender reassignment takes so many forms. As Lord Nicholls explained:

> Today the case before the House concerns Mrs Bellinger. Tomorrow's case in the High Court will relate to a transsexual person who has been able to undergo a less extensive course of surgery, the following week will be the case of a transsexual person who has undergone hormonal treatment but who, for medical reasons, has not been able to undergo treatment . . . by what criteria are cases such as these to be decided?.[97]

A narrow holding could not avoid making some decision about appropriate criteria – a matter of immense medical, social and psychological complexity, which a unanimous House of Lords was convinced lay beyond the expertise of the courts. Where the line should be drawn between those whose gender has been completely reassigned and those who have

---

[94] I believe that this point underlies *dictum* made in *Ghaidan* at [33] that the courts should not make decisions which would require 'legislative deliberation', *per* Lord Nicholls. The nature of this limitation on section 3(1) will be explored fully in chapter 7.
[95] This is also noted by Van Zyl Smit (2005), 107ff.    [96] *Bellinger*, above n. 10 at [39]–[40].
[97] *Ibid.* at [40].

not, was 'far from self-evident',[98] even in the case of Mrs Bellinger. Lord Nicholls rightly pointed out that there needed to be 'an adequate degree of certainty' as to when any transsexual person could marry, even if they had undergone a lesser degree of medical intervention than Mrs Bellinger.

Moreover, even if only Mrs Bellinger's marriage was recognised due to the decision, this would not eliminate the need to consider how recognition of *her* marriage would impact on her entitlements in such diverse areas as e.g. housing and residential security of tenure, inheritance, taxation, pensions, inheritance, life insurance policies and social security entitlements.[99] A decision which attempted to confine its application only to the facts of *Bellinger* would have run the risk of bringing in its wake untold and potentially negative consequences. As Lord Nicholls noted in a moment of judicial understatement, 'the circumstances in which, and the purposes for which gender reassignment are recognised are not easy questions'.[100] Judges have a responsibility to try to ensure that their decisions do not cause undue confusion and uncertainty in the law. In a subsequent case, Lord Bingham affirmed that he had 'no doubt' that the view taken unanimously in *Bellinger* that this was an area calling for comprehensive legislative reform rather than piecemeal judicial development was 'wholly correct'.[101]

Gavin Phillipson goes even further than Hickman. He argues that the decision not to opt for a section 3(1) interpretation in *Bellinger* amounted to a 'constitutional confusion'[102] because 'the role of the courts is surely to do justice to the individual – in this case remedy a violation of her rights – and leave it to Government and Legislature to sort out the overall legislative and administrative scheme'.[103] If the courts were *able* to do so (which they plainly were given the lack of linguistic impediment to a section 3(1) interpretation), Phillipson concluded that they *ought* to have done so, because doing justice to the individual is what the courts are there for. Of course, simply because the courts are able to do something, does not entail that they ought to do it. As Sedley L.J. pointed out extrajudicially: 'there are many issues lying within the courts' jurisdiction which Ministers or statutory bodies are nevertheless better equipped than judges to decide'.[104] This sentiment is echoed by Jeffrey Jowell, in the context of discussing the courts' judicial review jurisdiction:

---

[98]  *Ibid.* at [43].
[99]  These and other issues are noted by Lord Nicholls, *ibid.* at [42].     [100]  *Ibid.* at [32].
[101]  *Chief Constable of West Yorkshire Police* v. *A (No. 2)* [2005] 1 A.C. 51 at [12].
[102]  Phillipson (2006), 66.     [103]  *Ibid.*     [104]  Sedley (2004), 10.

> Having the constitutional capacity (competence) to do something is only
> the first step to judicial review. Once it is established, a further exercise is
> then required, that of justification on grounds of principle.[105]

Jowell's analysis applies with equal force to constitutional review of primary legislation under the HRA. Even though section 3(1) refers to the limits of the 'possible', a judicial decision that a rights-compatible interpretation is not possible, must be supported by a justification on grounds of principle. Mere 'possibility' is not enough: judges must advance arguments to show that their conclusions are right, just or legitimate, not simply that they have taken an available option.[106]

There is a deeper problem here, which is worth explaining in order to clarify the scope and limits of section 3(1). Phillipson seems to assume that the court's *only* duty is to do justice to the individual. Whilst this duty is indeed an important aspect of judicial decision-making, it is not the only consideration the courts must bear in mind. Inherent in the task of judicial interpretation is the need to balance their duty to do justice to the individual against values such as certainty and predictability in the law. As it happens, Phillipson concedes that if the court had adopted a section 3(1) interpretation, it would not have been 'ideal in terms of future certainty'.[107] Furthermore, whilst the courts must strive wherever possible to do justice to the individual, they must also acknowledge their institutional limitations. They are politically and legally handicapped from protecting or remedying every rights violation that comes their way, and it would be severely irresponsible of them to be oblivious to this fact. As Lord Hoffmann once put it, judges cannot 'set the world to rights'[108] and it would only discredit them if they attempted to do so. There will inevitably be cases like *Bellinger*, where although the court is 'profoundly conscious of the humanitarian considerations'[109] underlying the litigant's claim, it will be inappropriate for them to attempt to resolve them through the necessarily piecemeal tools of judicial rectification. We will explore the way in which these institutional limitations affect judicial reasoning when we come to analyse the doctrine of judicial deference.

Of importance in *Bellinger* was the fact that the remedial concerns were not so critical as to outweigh the risk of causing future problems in the law. This is partly due to the fact that whilst her marriage did not receive

---

[105] Jowell (1999), 452.
[106] See Kavanagh (2004b), 262; see also chapter 2, 31. Phillipson seems to accept this point as a general matter, see Phillipson (2006), 64.
[107] Phillipson (2006), 66.    [108] Hoffmann (2002), 144.
[109] *Bellinger*, above n. 10 at [34], *per* Lord Nicholls.

recognition by the court, she and Mr Bellinger would be able to enter into a valid marriage as soon as the legislation was in place. Moreover, interviews with Mrs Bellinger around the time of her litigation suggest that one of the reasons she brought the case was to raise the issue of transsexual rights in public discussion and achieve legal development which would benefit others like her.[110] As is often the case with constitutional test cases, her litigation was part of a broader political campaign to get transsexualism closer to the top of the political agenda.[111] This aim was achieved by having her case heard in the House of Lords, even though the outcome was a declaration of incompatibility. Mrs Bellinger's case shows that it is a mistake to assume that the only purpose of litigation is to get an individual remedy. She was assured that 'prompt parliamentary action' would ensue, regardless of whether she got a section 3(1) interpretation in her favour. In any event, both Hickman and Phillipson concede that the approach of adopting a declaration of incompatibility 'worked relatively well'[112] in that the necessary statutory reforms were indeed prompt, and that the court's decision can be explained in part by the fact that there was a Strasbourg authority binding on the government and that 'statutory reform was well progressed'.[113] This supports the argument advanced here that such factors often have an important bearing on the outcome of these cases.

Finally, Phillipson argues that an important point overlooked by my analysis of the case law (including *Bellinger*) is the fact that section 4 declarations do not legally oblige Parliament to change the law. As he puts it, 'the proposed remedy of parliamentary amendment is not and cannot be *guaranteed*'.[114] Therefore, 'judges should not depend upon it where a

---

[110] 'Transsexual mother goes public', *The Guardian*, Tuesday 13 October 1998: 'Ms Bellinger wants her marriage legalised... She wants it not just for herself but for the 10,000 in Britain who have had a sex change', Dyer (1998); see also 'Sex Change Victory after 20 Years', *The Guardian*, Tuesday 10 December 2002, Dyer (2002).

[111] See Dyer (2002), noting that Ms Bellinger invited MPs, including the Prime Minister, the Home Secretary, the Health Secretary and the Lord Chancellor, to a meeting in Parliament.

[112] Hickman (2005), 311; Phillipson (2006), 66.

[113] Hickman (2005), 332. An underlying difficulty with Hickman's analysis is his characterisation of 'the essential holding in Bellinger' as the point that 'the whole issue of transsexual starters is a matter of "social policy" for Parliament and not for the courts', see Hickman *ibid.*, 331. This view is also shared by Young (2005), 31–2; Nicol (2004a), 197; Lord Millett in *Ghaidan* at [65]. In chapter 7, I argue that the idea that the courts should defer automatically on grounds of 'social policy' is indeed flawed, but that this is not the rationale in *Bellinger*. *Bellinger* is a 'fundamental features' case.

[114] Phillipson (2006), 67, emphasis added.

Convention-compatible interpretation can be made'.[115] But the cases on which I based my argument (namely *Bellinger* and *Anderson*) were not ones where the Government announced an intention to bring forward new legislation entirely of its own political volition. Rather, these were cases where the Government accepted that they were *legally* bound to change the legislation at issue due to an adverse ruling from Strasbourg. As Lord Nicholls rightly observed in *Bellinger*: 'in the present case the Government has not sought to question the decision of the European Court of Human Rights in *Goodwin*. Indeed, it is committed to giving effect to that decision.'[116] In a subsequent case, Baroness Hale noted that the existence of the *Goodwin* decision meant that the House of Lords in *Bellinger* was 'left . . . in no doubt that UK law was incompatible with the Convention rights'.[117] If what Phillipson seeks is a legal obligation, then this exists due to the Strasbourg decision, as set out in Article 46 ECHR.

## Conclusion

Section 3(1) enacts a strong presumption in favour of an interpretation consistent with Convention rights. An evaluation of whether that presumption is rebutted in an instant case will depend on an array of contextual factors, including the terms of those provisions, their interrelationship, their relationship to the wider area of law of which they are part, and whether the original legislative purpose in enacting the legislation can be achieved to some extent. I have also attempted to show that it may also depend on other factors, such as whether Parliament is willing to reform the law, whether that reform is imminent, and in particular whether there is a ECtHR case on the issue obliging the government to change the law in any case.

I have presented the interpretive obligation under section 3(1) as one of balancing two sets of competing values: one emphasising the values of ensuring injustice from the individual litigant and equitable development of the law, the other emphasising the values of certainty, predictability and stability. In choosing between sections 3 and 4, the courts must assess whether the disadvantages of a particular strained interpretation outweigh the advantages in terms of justice for the individual litigants. Remedial concerns for the litigant may well pull the courts in favour of a section 3(1) interpretation, if a declaration of incompatibility would be

---

[115] *Ibid.*    [116] *Bellinger*, above n. 10 at [55].
[117] *R. (Countryside Alliance)* v. *Attorney General* [2008] 1 A.C. 719 at [125].

of no use to them. The remedial function of section 3(1) is an important element in understanding the judicial choice between sections 3 and 4. Moreover, *Ghaidan* and *Bellinger* alert us to the fact that mere linguistic possibility is not the only or even dominant factor in deciding whether to adopt an interpretation under section 3(1). In making that decision, the courts will also take into account the potential consequences of such an interpretation and whether it is desirable or appropriate, all things considered. One issue which is clear from the analysis contained in this chapter is the fact that, underlying the choice between sections 3 and 4, are broader evaluative questions about the appropriate constitutional division of labour between the courts, legislature and Executive. These broader questions are addressed in chapter 7, when we come to assess the role of 'judicial deference' in adjudication under the HRA. Before embarking on this task, we will first consider the impact of section 2 HRA on Convention-compatible interpretations of primary legislation. This will elucidate further both the relationship between Strasbourg and domestic case law, and will also reveal one important aspect of the status of the HRA.

# 6

## The duty of the courts under section 2

### Introduction

In determining whether primary legislation is compatible with Convention rights, section 2 HRA requires that the courts 'must take into account'[1] any relevant Strasbourg jurisprudence on the issue. In fact, the 'mandatory duty imposed on the courts by section 2'[2] is not confined to cases of statutory interpretation – it applies in any proceedings where judges are 'determining a question which has arisen in connection with a Convention right'.[3] Therefore, it seems that the courts are also obliged to take Strasbourg jurisprudence into account when developing the common law.[4] This is reinforced by the fact that the courts are public authorities under section 6 and are therefore under a general legal obligation to ensure that Convention rights are not breached, not only in cases of statutory interpretation but also in cases concerning the common law.

The central question in relation to section 2 concerns the meaning of the phrase 'take into account'. Would it suffice simply to consider the case law, only then to disapply it? Or is the Strasbourg jurisprudence binding in the same way as domestic precedents of our higher courts? On their face, the words 'take into account' are consistent with a rather weak obligation, such that the Strasbourg case law would only have minimal persuasive force in domestic case law.[5] However, the higher courts have not interpreted section 2 in that minimal way, but rather (as I shall explain below) have accorded the Strasbourg jurisprudence a binding status similar to that accorded by the House of Lords to its own precedents.[6]

---

[1] Section 2(1) HRA.

[2] *Kay* v. *Lambeth London Borough Council* [2006] UKHL 10 at [28], *per* Lord Bingham.

[3] Section 2(1) HRA.    [4] Fenwick (2007), 198.    [5] *Ibid.* 191.

[6] Helen Fenwick argues that under section 2, the Strasbourg jurisprudence 'has been treated in a fashion that comes close to giving it binding force', see *ibid.*, 192. This view is shared by Amos (2007b), 14; Masterman (2007), 59.

Before proceeding to this explanation, it should be noted that when the Human Rights Bill was going through Parliament, there was some parliamentary debate on the wording of section 2.[7] From these debates, it seems that the Government was keen to ensure that the domestic courts would retain a discretion to depart from Strasbourg case law in certain circumstances. Reasons given for this included the fact that the Convention is a 'living instrument' and since the ECtHR interprets Convention rights in a dynamic way, it would be inappropriate for the British courts to be unduly 'fettered . . . by a jurisprudence which is by definition a shifting one'.[8] Also relevant was the fact that the Convention system itself has no strict rule of precedent[9] and that the United Kingdom is, under the Convention, only bound to 'abide by' rulings of the Strasbourg court in cases in which it has been a party to the proceedings.[10] Moreover, the decisions of the Strasbourg court sometimes rely on the doctrine of the margin of appreciation, which acknowledges that the application of Convention rights may vary according to local needs and conditions.

A further objection to the notion that the domestic courts could be strictly bound to follow the Strasbourg jurisprudence in all cases, was the belief that many of the Strasbourg rulings are not suitable to be followed in this way. Strasbourg case law is addressed to the domestic authorities of the state-party in question, and whilst its judgments may be 'essentially declaratory'[11] in nature (in the sense that they declare whether a given decision or action of domestic authorities is compatible with Convention standards), some of the reasoning to that principled conclusion may involve much technical and detailed assessment of the particular facts of the case and the particular legal context of one amongst forty-six signatory states.[12] As such, it may only be the general principle (not the issues of detailed application) which will be relevant to other countries.[13]

---

[7] For discussion of the parliamentary debates on section 2, see Masterman (2007), 71ff; Wicks (2005), 406–8.

[8] Lord Browne Wilkinson, HL Debs, vol. 584, col. 1268 (19 January 1998).

[9] See further Masterman (2007), 64.    [10] See Article 46 ECHR.

[11] Harris *et al.* (1995), 26.

[12] Thus, in *R. (Gillan)* v. *Metropolitan Police Commissioner* [2006] 2 A.C. 307, Lord Bingham warned of the dangers of applying Strasbourg judgments as factual precedents, at [23]; see also *Secretary of State for the Home Department* v. *JJ* [2007] UKHL 45 at [101], *per* Lord Brown.

[13] Smith (1999), 6; Lord Hope (1999), 192.

For these and other reasons, the Lord Chancellor, Lord Irvine, was keen to ensure that the wording of section 2 would clearly 'permit UK courts to depart from Strasbourg decisions'.[14] At the report stage, the Lord Chancellor explained: 'courts will often be faced with cases that involve factors perhaps specific to the UK which distinguish them from cases considered by the European court . . . it is important that our courts have scope to apply that discretion so as to aid in the development of human rights law'.[15] However, whilst Lord Irvine wanted to ensure that the court could depart from Strasbourg authority where necessary, he assumed that British courts would follow Convention jurisprudence in the normal case. Thus, at the Committee stage, he clarified: '[courts] may depart from existing Strasbourg decisions and *on occasion* it might well be appropriate to do so . . . However, where it is relevant we would of course expect our courts to apply Convention jurisprudence and its principles to the cases before them'.[16]

## The judicial interpretation of section 2

The House of Lords has developed a clear line of authority on the meaning and scope of their duty under section 2. Whilst preserving the discretion to depart from Strasbourg case law when appropriate, it has interpreted the section 2 obligation as creating a strong presumption in favour of following Strasbourg jurisprudence, which can only be rebutted in special circumstances. The clear line of authority begins with *Alconbury*, where Lord Slynn of Hadley noted that:

> In the absence of special circumstances it seems to me that the court should follow any clear and constant jurisprudence of the European Court of Human Rights. If it does not do so there is at least a possibility that the case will go to that court which is likely in the ordinary case to follow its own constant jurisprudence.[17]

This position was subsequently endorsed by Lord Bingham in *Anderson*:[18]

> While the duty of the House under section 2(1) of the Human Rights Act 1998 is to take into account any judgment of the European Court, whose judgments are not strictly binding, the House will not without good reason

---

[14]  583 HL 514, 515 (8 November 1997); 584 HL col. 1271.
[15]  484 HL 1270, 1271 (9 January 1998).    [16]  478 HL 514–15, emphasis added.
[17]  *R. v. Secretary of State for the Environment, Transport and the Regions, ex parte Alconbury Developments Ltd* [2001] UKHL 23 at [26].
[18]  *R. (Anderson) v. Secretary of State for the Home Department* [2002] 3 W.L.R. 1800.

depart from the principles laid down in a carefully considered judgment of the court sitting as a Grand Chamber.[19]

The position was maintained by a unanimous House of Lords in *R. (Ullah)* v. *Special Adjudicator*,[20] which has become the leading case on section 2. There, Lord Bingham took the opportunity to elaborate on the rationale of the courts' approach to section 2. He explained that it:

> reflects the fact that the Convention is an international instrument, the correct interpretation of which can be authoritatively expounded only by the Strasbourg court. From this it follows that the national court subject to a duty such as that imposed by section 2 should not without strong reason dilute or weaken the effect of the Strasbourg case law. It is indeed unlawful under section 6 of the 1998 Act for a public authority, including a court, to act in a way which is incompatible with Convention rights.[21]

He went out to point out that:

> It is of course open to member states to provide for rights more generous than those guaranteed by the Convention, but such provision should not be the product of interpretation of the Convention by national courts, since the meaning of the Convention should be uniform throughout the states party to it. The duty of national courts is to keep pace with the Strasbourg jurisprudence as it evolves over time: no more, but certainly no less.[22]

Lord Bingham's pronouncements in *Ullah* have now been followed in many subsequent decisions of the House of Lords.[23] A judicial consensus has emerged on the meaning and scope of section 2 HRA. However, there are nonetheless a number of points about the courts' stance which require some clarification. The first point is that when the judiciary stress that the Strasbourg case law is not 'strictly binding' on them, what they

[19] *Ibid.* at [18]. The approach of the House of Lords to Strasbourg case law accords with that of the Strasbourg court when dealing with the issue of departing from its own previous decisions. As it stated in *Goodwin* v. *UK* (2002) 35 E.H.R.R. 18 at [74: 'While the court is not formally bound to follow its previous judgments, it is in the interests of legal certainty, foreseeability and equality before the law that it should not depart, without good reason, from precedents laid down in previous cases', see Masterman (2007), 68–9.

[20] *R.* v. *Special Adjudicator, ex parte Ullah* [2004] UKHL 26.

[21] At [20]; see also *R. (Clift)* v. *SSHD* [2007] 1 A.C. 484 at [28], *per* Lord Bingham, [49], *per* Lord Hope, [63], *per* Baroness Hale.

[22] *Ullah*, above n. 20 at [20].

[23] See *M* v. *Secretary of State for Work and Pensions* [2006] UKHL 11 at [129], *per* Lord Mance; *R. (Marper)* v. *Chief Constable of South Yorkshire Police* [2004] 1 W.L.R. 2196 at [27], *per* Lord Steyn; *Kay*, above n. 2 at [87], *per* Lord Hope; *Huang* v. *Secretary of State for the Home Department* [2007] 2 A.C. 167 at [18], *per* Lord Bingham.

mean is that they are not obliged to follow Strasbourg case law *in every case*. In other words, the binding nature of those precedents is partial rather than absolute, and the courts retain the discretion to depart from Strasbourg jurisprudence 'in special circumstances'. In effect, the courts operate a strong presumption in favour of following Strasbourg case law in the normal case, which can only be rebutted in exceptional cases. Following the Strasbourg case law is the norm – departing from it will be the exception. As Lord Bingham noted in *Kay* v. *Lambeth London Borough Council*:

> There are *isolated occasions* when the domestic courts may challenge the application by the Strasbourg court of the principles it has expounded to the detailed facts of a particular class of case peculiarly within the knowledge of national authorities. The 1998 Act gives it scope to do so. But it is ordinarily the clear duty of domestic courts, save where and so far as constrained by primary domestic legislation, to give practical recognition to the principles laid down by the Strasbourg court as governing the Convention rights specified in section 1 of the 1998 Act.[24]

Interestingly, this is the same as the approach adopted by the House of Lords in relation to its own precedents. At least since the Practice Statement in 1966,[25] the House of Lords is no longer bound 'strictly' by its previous case law, in the sense that it can never depart from it. Not only is the House of Lords entitled to distinguish its own previous case law, it is also empowered to depart from it 'when it appears right to do so'.[26] Therefore, the House of Lords' precedents are binding on it, not in a strict or absolute sense, but rather in the sense that there is a strong presumption in favour of following those cases, which can be rebutted in special circumstances. As interpreted by the House of Lords, section 2 gives the Strasbourg case law the same status or precedential weight as its own precedents. These precedents must be evaluated on their merits, both in terms of evaluating the cogency of the reasoning on which they are based, as well as their precedential weight with reference to the case before them. Moreover, a departure from either a Strasbourg or a domestic precedent would require strong justification, in order to rebut the presumption in its favour.

---

[24] Kay, above n. 2 at [28], emphasis added.
[25] *Practice Statement (Judicial Precedent)* [1966] 1 W.L.R. 1234.
[26] *Ibid.* For a critical review of the main principles used by the House of Lords when determining whether it is appropriate to overrule one of its precedents, see Cross and Harris (1991), 138ff.

## Distinguishing Strasbourg case law

The question then arises as to what might constitute such a justification. The most common way of 'departing' from a Strasbourg authority, will be to distinguish it in light of factors specific to the UK political, legal and social context. Just as domestic case law can be distinguished on grounds of difference in factual context, so too is it imperative to preserve the power of the domestic courts to distinguish Strasbourg case law, when it is applied to the particular legal, political and social context which obtains in the UK. Perhaps such a power is even more necessary with reference to Strasbourg jurisprudence, since by interpreting the Convention, the ECtHR has the daunting task of giving meaning to an international treaty which applies to over 800 million people across 47 countries. When the courts 'distinguish' Strasbourg case law on the grounds of the particular features of the UK legal, political and cultural context, this leaves the Strasbourg jurisprudence intact as a statement of general principle, but allows for its flexible application in the particular contexts presented in the various countries in which it applies.[27]

The need for sensitive, contextual application of the Convention rights in the different signatory states is acknowledged by Strasbourg itself through its reliance on the doctrine of the margin of appreciation.[28] In fact, it may be that when a Strasbourg decision relies on this doctrine, this may provide justification for the domestic courts to distinguish it.[29] Thus, Merris Amos argues that Lord Bingham's *dicta* in *Kay* suggest that it may be possible for the domestic courts to reach an interpretation of Convention rights more generous than that arrived at by the ECtHR, where the margin of appreciation applies.[30] Lord Bingham noted:

> In its decisions on particular cases the Strasbourg court accords a margin of appreciation, often generous, to the decisions of national authorities and attaches much importance to the peculiar facts of the case. Thus it is for the national authorities, including national courts particularly, to decide

---

[27] Arguably, the case of *R. (Animal Defenders International)* v. *Secretary of State for Culture, Media and Sport* [ 2008] UKHL 15 (hereinafter *ADI*), is an example where the House of Lords distinguished the Strasbourg case of *Verein gegen Tierfabriken (VgT)* v. *Switzerland* (2001) 34 E.H.R.R. 159), rather than overruled it. See Baroness Hale who opined that the conclusion that the Communications Act 2003 was not incompatible with the Convention was not contradicted by *VgT*: 'nor do I think that the decision in the *VgT* case should lead us to any different conclusion. All Strasbourg decisions are fact specific', *ADI* at [52], supported by Lord Scott at [43].

[28] *Handyside* v. *UK* (1979–80) 1 E.H.R.R. 737 at [48].

[29] See Fenwick (2007), 196, 270–2.       [30] Amos (2007a), 4ff.

in the first instance how the principles expounded in Strasbourg should be applied in the special context of national legislation, law, practice and social and other conditions. It is by the decisions of national courts that the domestic standard must be initially set.[31]

Lord Bingham's comments emphasise that the domestic courts will tend to be in a better position to evaluate the domestic context in which the Convention applies, and thus be better able to determine whether a Convention right is violated in that context. The superior expertise of the domestic courts on this aspect of the case warrants the flexibility to distinguish. Whilst it may not always be easy to detect the particular role played by the margin of appreciation, or indeed to 'detach' it from the ultimate conclusion arrived at by the ECtHR, it is nonetheless important for the domestic courts to be alert to the role it plays in the reasoning of the Strasbourg court and assess it accordingly.

### Departing from Strasbourg authority under 'special circumstances'

So much for distinguishing: what are the 'special circumstances' which might warrant a departure from Strasbourg jurisprudence? As in the domestic system of precedent, overruling requires stronger justification than distinguishing and is therefore a more exceptional course.[32] One circumstance which might weaken the presumptive force in favour of a Strasbourg decision, would be if the relevant Strasbourg case was confused or lacked clarity, or indeed if confusion were caused by a tension or apparent contradiction between different cases of the Strasbourg court. As Lord Rodger noted in *Al-Skeini*, when the judgments of the ECtHR 'do not speak with one voice',[33] this presents 'considerable difficulties for national courts who have to try to follow the jurisprudence of the European court'.[34] This ground for departure from Strasbourg case law is implicit in Lord Slynn's specification in *Alconbury* it is only obliged to follow the 'clear and constant' jurisprudence of the Strasbourg court.[35] It suggests that if the jurisprudence is not clear or constant, the presumptive force in its favour is weakened.[36]

---

[31]  *Kay*, above n. 2 at [44]. See also *Re P* [2008] UKHL 38 at [21]ff.
[32]  For an examination of the difference between distinguishing and overruling, see Raz (1979), 183–93.
[33]  *R. (Al-Skeini)* v. *Secretary of State for Defence* [2007] UKHL 26 at [67].
[34]  *Ibid.* at [67].    [35]  *Alconbury*, above n. 17.
[36]  Conversely, where a Strasbourg ruling is 'unanimous and unequivocal' and is part of 'established Strasbourg jurisprudence', it will be more difficult to justify a departure from it, see *M* v. *Secretary of State for Work and Pensions*, above n. 23 at [24]–[6], *per* Lord Nicholls.

Also of relevance in weakening the presumptive force in favour of Strasbourg jurisprudence might be the fact that the Strasbourg court did not consider all the relevant arguments[37] or gave insufficient weight to important considerations[38] or, alternatively, had not 'received all the help which was needed to form a conclusion'.[39] These reasons are implicit in Lord Bingham's *dictum* in *Anderson* that the House of Lords would not without good reason depart from a '*carefully considered judgment*'[40] of the ECtHR.[41] If there is evidence to suggest that the judgment was not carefully considered, or that it failed to consider important factors, this will weaken the presumptive force in its favour. Lord Hoffmann has also suggested that 'if an English court considered that the ECtHR had misunderstood or been misinformed about some aspect of English law',[42] this may warrant departure from it, although the lesser method of distinguishing may suffice in this situation. Another factor weakening the force of a Strasbourg authority would be if the case was decided many years ago, and the relevant social, political, cultural or medical context had changed. In such situations, the appropriate legal resolution of the issue may also need to be changed, to reflect the new social realities attending the issue.[43]

Although all these factors have been cited by the domestic courts as factors weakening the precedential force of Strasbourg authorities, it must be stressed that the presumptive force in favour of following the Strasbourg

---

[37] *ADI*, above n. 27 at [29].     [38] *Ibid.* at [32], *per* Lord Bingham; [52], *per* Hale.

[39] *R. v. Spear* [2003] 1 A.C. 734 at [12], *per* Lord Bingham; see also *Al-Skeini*, above n. 33: when assessing whether the House of Lords should be persuaded by the Strasbourg decision in *Issa*, Lord Rodger noted that the Strasbourg judgment only contained a 'short passage' on the issue before the House of Lords, which did not address some important questions, and therefore 'does not provide workable guidance for the House', see *Al-Skeini* at [80]. This is not a case of departing from the Strasbourg case, but rather a matter of determining the precedential weight of this brief passage in *Issa*. Lord Brown concluded that they 'must be regarded as *obiter dicta*', *ibid.* at [127].

[40] *Anderson*, above n. 18 at [18].

[41] In line with this requirement, Lord Steyn noted in *Anderson* that one of the reasons why the House of Lords followed the Strasbourg decision in *Stafford* was that it was 'a comprehensive and closely reasoned decision' and 'a coherent and inescapable one', *ibid.* at [58].

[42] This is contained in an *obiter* comment by Lord Hoffmann in *R. v. Lyons* [2003] 1 A.C. 976 at [46].

[43] This was thought to be a relevant factor in *N v. Secretary of State for the Home Department* [2005] 2 A.C. 296 at [92], *per* Lord Hope who observed that 'the reality is that the medicine has developed hugely since *D* [i.e. the relevant Strasbourg authority] and that a quite different problem now presents itself from that presented in *D*'. This did not rebut the presumption in favour of following *D*, but it was a factor relevant in deciding the scope of the test to be derived from the decision.

authority is nonetheless a strong one, which can only be rebutted in exceptional circumstances. As the courts sometimes observe with reference to
their own precedents, it will not suffice if the previous case is merely
wrong – it must be clearly and/or substantially wrong.[44] As pointed out
above, by far the most common reaction of the domestic courts to these
factors will be to distinguish the Strasbourg case in light of the national
context. The domestic courts will only consider themselves to be justified
in departing from Strasbourg case law, if that case law can be shown to
suffer from manifest error or flawed reasoning or would otherwise lead
to a grave injustice.

The fact that the hurdle of justifying a departure from Strasbourg
authority is a strong one, is borne out by the approach of the House of
Lords in N v. *Secretary of State for the Home Department*.[45] Despite finding
that the relevant Strasbourg jurisprudence was 'not in an altogether satisfactory state',[46] 'lacks its customary clarity',[47] did not provide adequate
guidance[48] and displayed reasoning that was not 'entirely convincing',[49]
the House of Lords nonetheless followed it. In contrast, the justificatory
hurdle was overcome in *Brown* v. *Stott*,[50] where the Privy Council did
not follow the judgment of the ECtHR in *Saunders*.[51] The reasons given
for this departure were that the reasoning of the ECtHR was 'unsatisfactory', 'unconvincing' and enunciated a 'more absolute standard than
the other jurisprudence of the court indicates'.[52] In other words, Strasbourg jurisprudence on the issue was not 'clear and constant'. Similarly,
in *Boyd*[53] the House of Lords did not follow a judgment of the ECtHR[54]
because, as Lord Bingham explained, on a number of important aspects of
the case 'the European Court did not receive all the help which was needed
to form a conclusion'.[55] However, these cases are the exception rather than
the rule. Overall, the domestic case law emphasises that, as with domestic
precedents, the presumption in favour of following Strasbourg case law
is a strong one, which is not easily rebutted.

---

[44]  Thus, the House of Lords tends to require that a decision be either 'clearly wrong' before
it can be overruled (see e.g. *O'Brien* v. *Robinson* [1973] A.C. 912 at 930), or that there be 'a
very good reason' to overrule (see e.g. *Knuller* v. *DPP* [1972] A.C. 944 at 993), both cited
in Perry (1989), 976ff. Clearly, both reasons can coincide in the one case, see further Cross
and Harris (1991), 136ff.

[45]  N v. *Secretary of State for the Home Department* [2005] 2 W.L.R. 1124.

[46]  *Ibid.* at [11], *per* Lord Nicholls.     [47]  *Ibid.* at [14], *per* Lord Nicholls.

[48]  *Ibid.* at [35], *per* Lord Hope.     [49]  *Ibid.* at [91], *per* Lord Brown.

[50]  *Brown* v. *Stott* [2003] 1 A.C. 681.     [51]  *Saunders* v. *UK* (1997) 2 B.H.R.C. 358.

[52]  *Brown* v. *Stott*, above n. 50 at 733.

[53]  *Boyd* v. *Army Prosecuting Authority* [2003] 1 A.C. 734.

[54]  *Morris* v. *UK* (2002) 34 E.H.R.R. 1253.     [55]  *Ibid.* at [12]–[13].

## The duty not to 'outpace' Strasbourg

The final issue to consider in relation to section 2(1) concerns the oft-quoted *dictum* of Lord Bingham in *Ullah* that 'the duty of national courts is to keep pace with the Strasbourg jurisprudence as it evolves over time: *no more, but certainly no less*'.[56] Whilst it is uncontroversial that the national courts are obliged to 'keep pace' with Strasbourg, some doubt has arisen as to whether domestic courts should feel inhibited about developing a more generous interpretation of Convention rights than the Strasbourg case law might suggest. If they adopt a less generous interpretation than Strasbourg (i.e. if they declare that there is no violation of a Convention right in a situation where Strasbourg has found a violation in similar circumstances), then, as Lord Slynn pointed out, this will prompt the dissatisfied litigant to bring an application to Strasbourg which, in the normal case, will follow its own jurisprudence. Not only will this be a waste of time and money for the litigant, it will also negate one of the purposes of enacting the HRA, namely, to find an effective way of resolving disputes concerning Convention rights in the domestic courts, thus obviating unnecessary applications to Strasbourg. But the same problem does not arise with reference to a *more generous* interpretation of Convention rights since then, presumably, the domestic courts would find in favour of the litigant, who would have no need to litigate the issue any further.[57] So in the case of a more generous interpretation (i.e. where the domestic court finds a violation of a Convention right where Strasbourg would not), there is no fear of correction from Strasbourg with reference to that case.

The House of Lords has resisted the view that it is entitled to develop the interpretation of Convention rights more broadly or more generously than the Strasbourg court would allow. Lord Bingham reminded us in *Ullah* that 'it is of course open to member states to provide for rights more generous than those guaranteed by the Convention', but this 'should not be the product of interpretation of the Convention by national courts, since the meaning of the Convention should be uniform throughout the state party to it'.[58] The view that the duty of the national courts is 'to keep in step with Strasbourg, neither lagging behind *nor leaping ahead*'[59] has been endorsed in a long line of subsequent decisions in the House of

---

[56] *Ullah*, above n. 20 at [20], emphasis added.
[57] Under Article 34 ECHR, a state cannot bring an application against the ruling of one of its own courts.
[58] *Ullah*, above n. 20 at [20]; see also *Secretary of State for Work and Pensions v. M*, above n. 23 at [136], *per* Lord Mance.
[59] *Al-Skeini*, above n. 33 at [90], *per* Baroness Hale.

Lords. Thus, in *R. (Clift)* v. *Secretary of State for the Home Department*,[60] Lord Hope noted that:

> The duty of national courts is to keep pace with the Strasbourg jurispru-
> dence as it evolves over time. A measure of self-restraint is needed, lest
> we stretch our jurisprudence beyond that which is shared by all the states
> parties to the Convention.[61]

In *Al-Skeini*,[62] Lord Brown went even further in emphasising the prohibition on domestic courts 'leaping ahead' of Strasbourg jurisprudence.
His Lordship suggested that the phrase at the end of Lord Bingham's
*dictum* in *Ullah* 'no more, but certainly no less', could also be inverted,
so that the duty of the national courts would be to keep pace with the
Strasbourg jurisprudence: 'no less', clarified Lord Brown, 'but certainly
no more'.[63] This sentiment was echoed in Lord Hope's judgment in *Kay*,[64]
where he stressed that the courts must not 'breach Lord Bingham's *rule*
that national courts should not outpace the Strasbourg court. The "no
more" part of this rule is just as important as the "no less" part.'[65] Even
in those cases where their Lordships have acknowledged that the Strasbourg jurisprudence might need development or improvement, they have
nonetheless resisted the temptation to undertake the task of developing
it themselves, though not always without regret.[66] Thus, in *N* v. *SSHD*[67]
Lord Hope explained:

> It is for the Strasbourg court, not for us, to decide whether its case law
> is out of touch with modern conditions and to determine what further
> extensions, if any, are needed to the rights guaranteed by the Conven-
> tion. We must take its case law as we find it, not as we would like it to
> be.[68]

In *M* v. *Secretary of State for Work and Pensions*, Lord Nicholls thought it
was axiomatic that the domestic courts should not leap ahead of Strasbourg jurisprudence on Article 8: 'It goes without saying that it would be
highly undesirable that the courts of this country, when giving effect to
Convention rights, to be out of step with the Strasbourg interpretation

---

[60] [2007] 1 A.C. 484    [61] At [49]. Lord Brown's judgment in *N* v. *SSHD* at [76].

[62] *Al-Skeini*, above n. 33.

[63] *Ibid.* at [106]. This inversion was also endorsed by Baroness Hale at [90].

[64] *Kay*, above n. 1 at [89].    [65] *Ibid.* at [89], emphasis added.

[66] See *Al-Skeini*, above n. 33 at [71], *per* Baroness Hale, [96], *per* Lord Brown; see also
*Clift*, above n. 21 at [28], where Lord Bingham applied the Strasbourg jurisprudence 'not
without hesitation'.

[67] *N* v. *SSHD*, above n. 45.    [68] *Ibid.* at [25].

of the relevant Convention article.'[69] Although he acknowledged that the Strasbourg jurisprudence on the matter before him was in a state of transition and he could envisage that the leading Strasbourg authority would be overtaken, he was clearly of the view that 'the ECtHR is the court best placed to judge when that time has arrived. It is not for the courts of this country to pre-empt that the decision'.[70]

This cautious approach to the interpretation of Convention rights has attracted some criticism from academic commentators, who have questioned whether the courts are right to refuse to develop a more generous interpretation of Convention rights than might be given at Strasbourg.[71] Thus, Roger Masterman argues that in following *Ullah*, the domestic courts have adopted a 'rigid'[72] and 'minimalist'[73] approach, which is 'overly deferential'[74] to the Strasbourg case law. He goes on to claim that the House of Lords' 'self-denying ordinance'[75] not to develop a more generous Convention jurisprudence than is provided by Strasbourg, is 'in contrast to the progressive approach [to section 2(1)] seemingly envisaged by the Government during the parliamentary debates'[76] and 'sits uneasily the [HRA's] status as a constitutional instrument and with the intentions of the Strasbourg institutions that state authorities be the primary mechanism for realising the Convention rights'.[77]

Whilst the aspiration that the domestic courts should develop its own constitutional jurisprudence of human rights beyond the acknowledged limits of the Strasbourg case law is laudable, I believe that the stance of the House of Lords with reference to its duty under section 2(1) is nonetheless correct. As Masterman rightly observes, the crucial issue here is the status of the Convention rights under the HRA, as well as the appropriate division of labour between the domestic courts and Strasbourg which follows from that status. This point needs some elaboration, in order to refute this important academic critique. We can begin with some commonplace observations. The HRA does not, technically speaking, incorporate the ECHR into domestic law. Rather, it gives legal effect to

---

[69] *M v. Secretary of State for Work and Pensions*, above n. 23 at [29].      [70] *Ibid.* at [30].

[71] Masterman (2007), 75ff; Leigh (2007a), 436–40; Clayton (2007), 18ff.

[72] Masterman (2007), 73.      [73] *Ibid.*, 85.      [74] *Ibid.*, 78.      [75] *Ibid.*, 85.

[76] *Ibid.*, 73. Robert Wintemute argues that the approach of the House of Lords to section 2(1) runs contrary to Lord Irvine's statement that 'our courts must be free to try to give a lead to Europe as well as to be led', 583 HL 515 (18 November 1997), see Wintemute (2006a), 211.

[77] Masterman (2007), 85; Richard Clayton also argues that the court's approach to section 2(1) prevents them from developing 'an indigenous human rights jurisprudence', see Clayton (2007), 19; Wicks (2005), 427.

some of the Convention rights in domestic law by enabling litigants to rely on them in domestic courts.[78] To this extent, they are domestic rights, the interpretation of which is a matter for domestic courts.[79] However, these rights are not entirely autonomous from the Convention, from which they find their original legal source. After all, the HRA is the means by which the UK gave 'domestic legal effect to the UK's international law obligations'[80] under the Convention. Therefore, the rights contained in the Schedule to the HRA have a dual status. They are part of domestic law and are therefore 'domestic rights', but they 'are not *merely* part of the domestic law'.[81] As Lord Scott observed in *ADI* they also 'remain, as they were before the 1998 Act, articles of the Convention binding on the United Kingdom under international law'.[82] It is this latter fact which gives rise to an understandable hesitancy on the part of domestic courts to depart from a clear and constant line of Strasbourg case law, even when they might wish to interpret Convention rights more generously than the Strasbourg court. If the HRA had enacted an entirely autonomous list of constitutional rights to be protected in UK law, then the courts would not be inhibited by Strasbourg case law in developing an autonomous human rights jurisprudence. But, as Lord Lester observed, the constraint on the interpretive power of the courts under section 2 is 'the price to be paid for using the Convention as a substitute for a full constitutional Bill of Rights'.[83] Regrettable though it may be, the UK courts cannot develop their constitutional rights jurisprudence on a *tabula rasa*.[84]

[78] *Huang*, above n. 23 at [8], *per* Lord Bingham. As Helen Fenwick points out, the HRA does not provide that the Convention rights are to have the 'force of law', which is the usual form of words used when international treaties are incorporated into domestic law. Instead, under section 1(2) HRA, some Convention rights are to 'have effect for the purposes of this Act', so that the rights are in a sense incorporated into domestic law when asserted against public authorities, see Fenwick (2007), 170; see also Ewing (1999), 84.

[79] See Lord Nicholls, *Re McKerr* [2004] 2 All E.R. 409: 'By enacting the 1998 Act, Parliament created domestic law rights corresponding to rights under the Convention', at [34].

[80] *Al-Skeini*, above n. 33 at [10], *per* Lord Bingham.

[81] *ADI*, above n. 27 at [44], emphasis added.

[82] *Ibid.* at [44]. In seeking to articulate the dual status of the rights contained in the Schedule to the Human Rights Act, Lord Nicholls has suggested that the articles in the ECHR are 'reproduced' as Convention right in the HRA, see *M* v. *Secretary of State for Work and Pensions*, above n. 23 at [24].

[83] Lester (1998), 672.

[84] Palmer (2007), 116. The claim that the Convention rights contained in the Schedule to the HRA have a 'dual status' is contrary to Robert Wintemute's claim that 'if the country voluntarily incorporates the exact wording of the Convention into its national law, the Convention ceases to be a European text and becomes the national text, to which national courts are free to give a more generous interpretation', see Wintemute (2006a), 211. As clarified above, my argument is that it is *both* a domestic *and* an international text, and the latter dimension does not cease to exist post-HRA.

It follows that when interpreting legislation compatibly with Convention rights, the domestic courts must recognise the interpretive supremacy of the ECtHR. The Strasbourg court is 'the highest judicial authority'[85] on the interpretation of Convention rights. As Lord Scott clarified:

> In so far as the articles [of the Convention] are part of international law they are binding on the United Kingdom as a signatory of the Convention and the European court is, for the purposes of international law, the final arbiter of their meaning and effect.[86]

The role of the European court as 'final arbiter' means that the national courts must respect the authority of the Strasbourg court and strive to interpret Convention rights consistently with it. As a result, they cannot, *without good reason*, depart from its decisions, even if such departure is on the more generous end of the spectrum. If a national court were to depart from a clear and constant line of Strasbourg authority, not on the grounds of distinguishing it in light of its application in the domestic context, but rather because the national court wishes to give a more generous interpretation of Convention rights, then this would weaken and dilute the authority of the Strasbourg court and undermine the duty of judicial comity which exists between the domestic and Strasbourg courts.[87] The higher courts are mindful of the fact that they are not just interpreting domestic rights, but are also seeking to give a ruling on the UK's obligations under the Convention.[88] Respect for the authority of the Strasbourg court to give an authoritative interpretation of Convention rights, is nonetheless necessary for an efficacious Convention system to be possible.[89] This point is driven home by Lord Bingham in *Kay*,[90] who clarified that the ECtHR is 'the highest judicial authority on the interpretation of [Convention] rights, and the effectiveness of the Convention as an international instrument depends on the loyal acceptance by member states of the principles it lays down'.[91]

Another important matter to bear in mind concerns Lord Bingham's comment in *Ullah* that the meaning of Convention rights should be 'uniform throughout the states party to it'.[92] This requires a little explanation,

---

[85] *Kay*, above n. 1 at [28], *per* Lord Bingham.     [86] *ADI*, above n. 27 at [44].

[87] See generally Amos (2007a).

[88] As Lord Hope put it in *N* v. *SSHD*: 'The argument is about the extent of the obligations under Article 3. It is about the treaty obligations of the contracting states', above n. 45 at [21].

[89] See Warbrick (2007), 33.     [90] Above n. 1.     [91] *Ibid.* at [28].

[92] *Ullah*, above n. 20 at [20]. As Lord Brown put it, the Convention 'must bear the same meaning for all states party to it', see in *Al-Skeini*, above n. 33 at [105]; see also *M* v. *Secretary of State for Work and Pensions*, above n. 23 at [24], *per* Lord Nicholls; see also

since it is sometimes misunderstood. Clearly, it does not mean that there cannot be differences in applying Convention rights or that the difference in domestic context cannot be accommodated in the Convention system. On the contrary, this difference in application is acknowledged by the Strasbourg court's reliance on the doctrine of the margin of appreciation. It is also acknowledged by the domestic courts in the UK, since the clear line of authority stretching from *Alconbury* and *Ullah* preserves the judicial discretion to distinguish Strasbourg jurisprudence if the domestic conditions render that appropriate. However, this is very different from saying that it is within the power of domestic courts to establish that Convention rights are to have a different content and meaning from one Contracting State to another.[93] This would amount to leaving it to each individual state to determine the content of Convention rights. As such, it would undermine the interpretive superiority of the Strasbourg court and the efficacy of the Convention system as a whole.

The question is one of the appropriate division of labour, expertise and authority, between the Strasbourg and domestic courts. The Strasbourg court has ultimate authority on the question of the meaning and scope of Convention rights as a matter of principle. The domestic courts must carry out their own interpretation in a way which is consistent with the Strasbourg rulings on this issue. However, as the Strasbourg court itself acknowledges, the domestic courts may have superior expertise and authority in understanding the details of the domestic legal system in which the Convention rights must apply: 'by reason of their direct and continuous contact with the vital forces of their countries, the national authorities are in principle better placed than an international court to evaluate local needs and conditions'.[94] For this reason, the domestic courts are given leeway to distinguish the Strasbourg case law at the point of application under domestic conditions. This division of labour (whereby the articulation of the general principles underlying Convention rights is a matter, ultimately, for the Strasbourg court, whereas questions of application in the domestic context are initially and primarily for the domestic courts) may underlie Lord Steyn's comments in *R. (Marper)* v.

---

in *R. (Hammond)* v. *SSHD* [2005] UKHL 69 at [11], *per* Lord Bingham, [28], *per* Lord Hoffmann. See also *Re P*, above n. 31 at [36].

[93] As Lord Nicholls commented in *SSWP* v. *M*, above n. 23 at [30], it would be 'surprising' if, as applied to same-sex couples, 'family life in Article 8 would have a different content from one Contracting State to another'.

[94] *Buckley* v. *UK* (1996) 23 E.H.R.R. 101 at 129.

*Chief Constable of South Yorkshire.*[95] There, Lord Steyn argued that the interpretation of Article 8(1) ECHR (on the scope of the right to privacy) should remain uniform throughout member states, but that in determining the question of objective justification under Article 8(2), the cultural traditions in the UK were material.[96]

The House of Lords has offered a further (related) reason why they are inhibited from interpreting Convention rights more generously than may be suggested by an established line of Strasbourg authority. This reason goes to the limited nature of the courts' powers under the HRA. The duty of the domestic courts under the HRA is to establish whether legislation or acts of public authorities are compatible with Convention rights. In so doing, domestic courts must come to a conclusion about what the Convention rights *require*. In other words, they must establish the extent of the UK's *legal obligations* under the various articles of the Convention. This important point has been a *leitmotiv* in the judgments of Baroness Hale. For example, in *Clift*, she observed that: 'It is not for us to declare legislation which Parliament has passed incompatible with the Convention rights unless the Convention and its case law *require* us to do so.'[97] Again, in *Al-Skeini*, she noted that 'If Parliament wishes to go further, or if the courts find it appropriate to develop the common law further, of course they may. But that is because they choose to do so, not because the Convention *requires* it of them.'[98] In *ADI*, her *dicta* on the limited nature of the *judicial* task under the HRA, in comparison to the much broader legislative powers of Parliament, are worth quoting in full:

> There is, of course, nothing to stop our Parliament from legislating to pro-
> tect human rights to a greater extent than the Convention and its jurispru-
> dence currently require; nor is there anything to prevent the courts from
> developing the common law in that direction. But we are here concerned
> with whether an Act of the UK Parliament is compatible with the Con-
> vention rights: if prima facie it is not, Parliament has given us the duty,
> if possible, to interpret it compatibly with those rights; and if that is not
> possible, the power to declare it incompatible. I do not believe that, when
> Parliament gave us those novel and important powers, it was giving us the

---

[95] [2004] 1 W.L.R. 3223 at [27]. See also Lord Nicholls' judgment in *M* v. *SSWP*, above n. 23 at [26]; *Re P*, above n. 31 at [118].

[96] This division of labour may also be at work in Lord Bingham's *dictum* in *Kay* when outlining 'constructive collaboration between the Strasbourg court and the national courts of member states', on which the effective implementation of the Convention depends, above n. 1 at [44].

[97] *Clift*, above n. 21 at [63], emphasis added.

[98] *Al-Skeini*, above n. 33 at [90], emphasis added.

> power to leap ahead of Strasbourg in the interpretation of the Convention
> rights. Nor do I believe that it was expecting us to lag behind.[99]

These *dicta* from Baroness Hale serve to emphasise the limited nature of the *judicial* task in giving effect to Convention rights under the HRA. The question judges have to ask themselves is: 'what do Convention rights require?', whilst acknowledging that the final arbiter on the meaning of those requirements must be the Strasbourg court. This goes back to the fact that the purpose of the HRA was not to enlarge the rights and remedies offered at Strasbourg in the domestic courts, but only to ensure that those rights and remedies can be enforced by the domestic courts without resort to Strasbourg.[100] It follows that the domestic courts are inhibited from developing a more expansive domestic Convention jurisprudence than the Strasbourg court. As Dame Arden commented extrajudicially:

> It is sufficient if the statute passes the test of compatibility with no room
> to spare. The interpretive obligation does not require the courts to give the
> fullest expression to Convention rights or to find a meaning which would
> promote them to the fullest extent.[101]

Whilst the UK courts are perfectly entitled to distinguish Strasbourg jurisprudence on grounds of domestic context, they must avoid stepping into the shoes of the Strasbourg court, attempting to enunciate the meaning of Convention rights independently from the Strasbourg case law. The task of the domestic courts under the HRA is to clarify the nature of the UK's international law obligations under the Convention, not to go beyond those obligations.

## The Convention as a 'floor not a ceiling'

Critics argue that the courts' stance on section 2 is at variance with a point made in the parliamentary debates on the Human Rights Bill, namely, that the Convention rights contained in the Schedule to the HRA were intended as a 'floor and not a ceiling' of rights protection in the UK.[102] In my view, this critique confuses the role of the different organs

---

[99]  *ADI*, above n. 27 at [53]. Although see *Re P*, above n. 31 at [119]ff.
[100]  Lord Bingham, *R. (Greenfield)* v. *SSHD* [2005] UKHL 14 at [19]; see also Lord Irvine, 583 HL 478 (18 November 1997): 'The Human Rights Act 1998 does not create new human rights or take rights away. It provides better and easier access to rights that already exist. It gives 'further effect' to those rights.'; see also *R. (Begum)* v. *Denbigh High School* [2006] 2 W.L.R. 719 at [29], *per* Lord Bingham.
[101]  Arden (2004), 170; see also *N* v. *SSHD*, above n. 45 at [17].
[102]  Wintemute (2006b), 728.

of government in giving effect to those rights. It is true that the ECHR establishes minimum standards for the protection of human rights in the forty-seven signatory states.[103] Thus, Convention rights are a 'floor' because there is nothing prohibiting Parliament from legislating in a way which is much more generous than the Strasbourg jurisprudence provides. But as we saw in earlier chapters, the interpretive powers of the courts are much more limited than the legislative powers of Parliament. The duty of the courts under the HRA is to establish what the Convention *requires*, i.e. what the floor or baseline is, in terms of the UK's legal obligations under the Convention. Baroness Hale's point is that the courts will only declare legislation to be incompatible with the Convention, if it goes beneath that baseline. If Parliament wishes to go beyond it, it is entirely free to do so, unconstrained by the determinations of the Strasbourg court. But this is not a freedom enjoyed by the courts to the same extent.[104] The domestic courts can only develop beyond Strasbourg jurisprudence in situations where the domestic context warrants such departure.

The foregoing explanation and defence of the House of Lords' stance on section 2 in no way denies that the UK courts must have flexibility to distinguish, and occasionally depart from, Convention jurisprudence when appropriate.[105] This important and necessary judicial discretion to distinguish Strasbourg case law and modify its application in the UK context is not in any way compromised by Lord Bingham's *dictum* in *Ullah* or indeed any of the subsequent case law. Moreover, there will be issues on

---

[103] *Handyside* v. *UK* (1976) 1 E.H.R.R. 737 at [47]–[9]; Clapham (1999), 135.

[104] Robert Wintemute has used Lord Woolf's comments about Convention rights being a floor not a ceiling in *R. (S)* v. *Chief Constable of the South Yorkshire Police* [2002] 1 W.L.R. 3223, to support the argument that the courts should be entitled to develop Convention jurisprudence more generously than Strasbourg, see Wintemute (2006b), 728. However, Lord Woolf's comments were made in the context of discussing the margin of appreciation which provides a justification for distinguishing not departing from Strasbourg jurisprudence. Moreover, his Lordship specified that 'there was nothing in the Convention setting a ceiling on the level of respect *which a jurisdiction* is entitled to extend to personal rights', at [34], emphasis added. The House of Lords' stance on section 2 does not preclude 'a jurisdiction' from protecting rights more generously than Strasbourg, but simply prevents the courts from doing so. Therefore, it is not clear that Lord Woolf's comments necessarily support Wintemute's claims.

[105] Therefore, I think it is exaggerated to claim that 'the House of Lords has reduced the scope of the discretion on the face of section 2(1) almost to vanishing point', see Masterman (2007), 78, because it overlooks the considerable flexibility possessed by the courts to distinguish Strasbourg decisions, as well as to depart from them.

which no pertinent Strasbourg case exists.[106] In other cases, the Strasbourg case law will be found wanting, either because it is poorly reasoned or displays inherent conflicts or contradictions. These are all factors which the domestic courts may legitimately take into account when deciding whether it is appropriate for them to follow Strasbourg case law. As the domestic courts have stressed, they will tend to follow Strasbourg when its jurisprudence is clear and constant, but are not obliged to follow it when these conditions do not obtain. In these many ways, British courts can 'give a lead' to Strasbourg, both by highlighting and explaining some of the peculiarities of the UK system to which Convention rights must apply, but also by filling in gaps in the jurisprudence where no Strasbourg case law exists.[107]

However, there is no denying that the domestic courts are nonetheless constrained to a certain degree by the Strasbourg case law. There are cases where the UK courts might like to adopt a more generous interpretation of Convention rights, but are inhibited from doing so by a clear and constant line of authority from Strasbourg. This constraint on their interpretive powers is not at odds with the HRA's status as a constitutional instrument. Under the HRA, the courts still retain the immensely important constitutional function to determine 'in the first instance'[108] the Convention-compatibility of legislation, and either to rectify that incompatibility through interpretation, or alternatively, to declare it to be incompatible, in the expectation that Parliament will change the legislation accordingly. The previous chapters testify to the fact that the courts have not been shy

---

[106]  See e.g. *Secretary of State for the Home Department, ex parte MB* [2007] 3 W.L.R. 681 at [62], where Baroness Hale pointed out that 'Strasbourg has not yet had to deal with the case exactly on all fours with the present', but she was nonetheless able to 'take several messages from those cases which are helpful for present purposes', at [63].

[107]  It may be that the constraints on judicial reasoning presented by the Strasbourg jurisprudence were under-emphasised in some of the political rhetoric used by the Government during parliamentary debate on the Human Rights Bill, especially the triumphant talk of British judges being able to 'give a lead to Europe as well as to be led.' 583 HL 515 (18 November 1997). But then, we should be cautious about attributing to such rhetoric a greater significance than it can bear. In my view, this phrase should not be understood as an accurate legal explication of the complex judicial obligation under section 2 and the appropriate relationship between domestic courts and Strasbourg. The House of Lords' stance on section 2 is perfectly in line with Lord Irvine's less rhetorical statement that whilst it is important that the courts should have the discretion to depart from Strasbourg jurisprudence in exceptional cases, he would expect the courts to follow that jurisprudence in the normal case. For the point that Government rhetoric in the parliamentary debates on the Human Rights Bill is not necessarily a reliable guide to the application of the HRA, see *Al-Skeini*, above n. 33 at [43].

[108]  *M v. Secretary of State for Work and Pensions*, above n. 23 at [131], *per* Lord Mance.

of developing a creative and robust human rights jurisprudence, albeit within the various constraints set out in the HRA. This is endorsed by Lord Woolf in an extrajudicial article, where he commented on the judicial development of 'our own domestic code of human rights jurisprudence' under the HRA, whilst nonetheless warning that this must pay 'a proper regard to the jurisprudence being developed at Strasbourg.'[109] In chapter 10, it will be shown that the powers of the courts under the HRA are not dissimilar to those possessed by constitutional courts in jurisdictions with an entrenched Bill of Rights, despite the various limitations placed on the courts, including the duty to respect Strasbourg jurisprudence.[110]

Moreover, the interpretive and declaratory powers of the courts under the HRA are exactly the sort of functions envisaged for the domestic courts by the principle of subsidiarity, which is so central to the Convention system. The idea at work in this principle is not that the domestic courts in each domestic legal system will develop their own, unique and divergent understanding of Convention rights. Rather, it is that in seeking to honour the obligation in Article 1 to secure the Convention rights in the individual states, the domestic courts will assist in this aim by resolving individual disputes based on Convention rights at the domestic level, and if possible, obviate the need to go to Strasbourg. As Lord Brown put it in *Al-Skeini*, the purpose of the HRA was 'to ensure that, from the date it took effect, it would no longer be necessary for victims to complain about alleged violations of the Convention internationally in Strasbourg instead of domestically in the United Kingdom.'[111] It means that the domestic courts perform the constitutional function of checking legislation for compatibility with Convention rights in the first instance. In carrying out that function, a delicate balance may need to be struck by the House of Lords between adherence to the interpretations of Convention

---

[109] Woolf (2004), vi. His comments suggest that he disagrees with those commentators who claim that the prevailing approach to section 2 'prevents the British courts from developing an indigenous human rights jurisprudence', see e.g. Clayton (2007), 19.

[110] Therefore, I do not see a tension between the approach that sees the HRA as a vehicle for giving easier access to the Convention domestically and one that sees it as a 'constitutional human rights instrument', see Fenwick (2007), xiv. Whilst I agree that Strasbourg jurisprudence is one of the limits on the interpretive powers of the courts under the HRA, it is one which nonetheless allows considerable room for judicial manoeuvre in terms of developing an indigenous constitutional human rights jurisprudence. Furthermore, in terms of the constitutional status of the HRA, I argue in chapter 10 that the combined role played by the domestic and Strasbourg courts, strengthens that status, rather than undermines it.

[111] *Al-Skeini*, above n. 33 at [138].

rights given by the ECtHR and its 'constitutional mandate to interpret and develop the ECHR rights in a morally defensible and culturally appropriate manner'.[112] This mandate is not eradicated by the duty to remain in tune with the Strasbourg jurisprudence, although it is limited by it.

## Conclusion

If the ECtHR has a clear and constant line of jurisprudence, which is not vitiated by any substantial flaw in its reasoning and has taken into account all the relevant considerations and there is no reason why it cannot be applied in the UK context, then it would violate the principle of comity between a national and international court, if the UK courts were not to follow it. This does not mean that the UK courts are being 'overly deferential'[113] to Strasbourg jurisprudence, but rather that they are being appropriately respectful to the court which has been given the power to determine authoritatively what Convention rights require. If there is a strong reason to depart from its case law, then the domestic courts are entitled to do so. Thus, the discretion and flexibility to evaluate Strasbourg jurisprudence on its merits is preserved by the domestic courts in their approach to the obligation under section 2. Whilst paying 'proper regard' to the Strasbourg jurisprudence, the domestic courts must nonetheless develop a human rights jurisprudence which is sensitive to the domestic context. Nothing in the House of Lords' approach to section 2 requires our domestic courts to 'routinely and uncritically apply decisions that do not sufficiently make allowance for the special qualities of our domestic jurisdiction'.[114] On the contrary, the courts have stressed that they are not 'inflexibly bound'[115] by Strasbourg jurisprudence, and can distinguish and depart from it when appropriate. However, there are limits to such development, one being that they should not be significantly more or less generous than the ECtHR would be.

---

[112]  Palmer (2007), 335; see also Woolf (2004), vi.    [113]  Masterman (2007), 78.
[114]  Woolf (2004), vi.    [115]  *Greenfield*, above n. 100 at [19], *per* Lord Bingham.

# PART II

Questions of deference

# 7

# The nature and grounds of judicial deference

## Introduction

The leading case law under the HRA is replete with judicial *dicta* to the effect that when adjudicating human rights issues, the courts should sometimes defer to Parliament and other institutions of government. But whilst the idea of deference has attracted much judicial support, there is a considerable lack of clarity both in the case law and the academic writing as to what the duty of deference might entail. In fact, the issue of deference has been described as one of the most complex issues arising under the HRA.[1] Lord Steyn has referred to the judicial and academic discussion of deference as 'a tangled story'.[2] It is tangled for a number of reasons. First, there has been very little attempt to separate out the various strands of the doctrine of deference and the different justifications for them. Second, the metaphor of the 'discretionary area of judgment' has become a popular way of articulating the nature of the doctrine, which has led to confusion and misunderstanding. Most importantly, the issue of judicial deference to the legislature or executive brings us to the heart of very difficult questions about the constitutional division of labour between the three branches of government under the HRA. It is widely believed that the HRA seeks to achieve a balance between the powers of Parliament and the courts. By preventing the courts from striking down primary legislation and accepting that the Convention rights can be qualified when 'necessary in a democratic society', the HRA is thought to preserve parliamentary sovereignty. On the other hand, the HRA gives the courts the power to test primary legislation against general human rights standards enshrined in the ECHR, which seems to envisage the courts holding the elected branches firmly to account for any breach of those rights. Reconciling the twin demands of respecting representative democracy, whilst nonetheless

[1] Pannick (1998), 548; Jowell (2003b), 592; Edwards (2002), 882.  [2] Steyn (2005a).

giving robust protection to Convention rights, has been characterised as a difficult if not impossible task.[3] The crucial question is: 'How are the courts to exercise a constitutionally appropriate degree of restraint, without ceding questions about the legality of decisions under scrutiny to the elected branches?'[4]

In this chapter, I will argue that a reconciliation between the twin demands of respecting the authority of Parliament as the primary law-maker *and* protecting Convention rights, is partly realised through the development of a doctrine of deference. This is not to say that a proper understanding of deference prevents difficult cases arising, or that the answer to the question about the constitutionally appropriate degree of restraint will be clear in every case. However, in gaining a better under-standing of the complex nature of deference and the various factors which underlie it, we are in a better position to identify how such reconciliation can be achieved, and indeed, how it ought to be achieved. At the very least, it will equip us to see the shortcomings of some misleading metaphors, which have helped to lend plausibility to misguided views about what deference entails.[5]

This chapter will proceed as follows. In the first section, I will clarify what deference is and how it operates. To this end, I will separate out the different strands of the deference doctrine and the different justifications for them. I will then go on to consider the three main reasons for defer-ence, namely, the argument from competence, expertise and democratic legitimacy. The prudential reasons judges might have for deferring to the elected branches of government are also discussed. In the final section, I will contrast the variable and contextual approach to deference advocated here, with the 'spatial' approach suggested by the idea of the 'discretionary area of judgment'. I will argue that this latter approach should be rejected. In chapter 8, I will consider how the doctrine of deference operates in par-ticular contexts, such as national security and resource-allocation cases. Finally, since the doctrine of deference has a significant bearing on the intensity of review, chapter 9 provides an analysis of this issue, focusing particularly on proportionality. For now, the task is to lay the groundwork by giving an account of what deference is and why it is desirable, if at all.[6]

---

[3] Gearty (2004), chapter 2.     [4] Palmer (2007), 127.

[5] In particular, I have in mind here the 'spatial' metaphor of the 'discretionary area of judgment' which will be examined in the final section of this chapter at 201–9.

[6] What follows is a revised and updated version of Kavanagh (2008), which focuses more closely on the UK case law.

## A variable degree of deference

I will begin my analysis with the following definition: *judicial deference occurs when judges assign varying degrees of weight to the judgment of the elected branches, out of respect for their superior competence, expertise and/or democratic legitimacy.* This is a dense definition, whose various elements need to be unpacked one by one. The first point to note is that the main rationale of deference is respect.[7] Judges owe a degree of deference to the elected branches of government because of 'that respect which one great organ of the State owes to another'.[8] It is a requirement of *inter-institutional comity*, namely, the requirement of mutual respect between the branches of government.[9] Although comity does not require the courts to agree with everything the legislature or executive does, it requires them to pay respect to their decisions.[10] The courts owe them this respect, when it can be shown that they have superior expertise, competence or legitimacy to that possessed by the courts.[11]

The question then is: *how* do they show that respect towards the decisions of the legislature or executive? The answer is that they do so by attaching an appropriate degree of weight to them, but also by treating them with courtesy. I will consider the 'courtesy' dimension of deference when we come to consider Lord Hoffmann's *dicta* on the terminology of deference.[12] For the moment, we need to explicate the idea of 'giving weight' to the judgments of the legislature, for this is the central way in which deference operates in judicial reasoning. Let us begin by noting the following general point about how deference functions. When we agree with someone on a particular issue, we do not 'defer' to them. Rather, we simply assess the pros and cons of the issue ourselves, and come to an independent conclusion which matches the other person's conclusion.

[7] For an examination of this rationale of deference in legal and non-legal contexts, see Soper (2002), 181. I will not rely on the distinction proposed by David Dyzenhaus between 'deference as respect' and 'deference as submission', see Dyzenhaus (1997), 303. On my analysis, deference is *always* due to respect, but varies *in degree* such that it sometimes amounts to what I call complete deference (what Dyzenhaus calls 'deference as submission').

[8] *Buckley* v. *Attorney General* (1950) I.R. 67 at 80, *per* O'Byrne J. (referring to the reason for the presumption of constitutionality in Irish constitutional law). See also Woolf (2003), 218, who describes deference as 'the doctrine of respect'.

[9] See e.g. *R. (Jackson)* v. *Attorney General* [2005] 3 W.L.R. 733 at [125], *per* Lord Hope: 'the delicate balance between the various institutions is . . . maintained to a large degree by the mutual respect which each institution has for the other'; see also Lord Woolf in *R.* v. *Parliamentary Commissioner for Standards, ex parte Al Fayed* [1998] 1 W.L.R. 669 at 671; McLachlin (1999–2000), 36.

[10] Endicott (2002), 286; see also Endicott (2003b), 101.

[11] Each of these reasons will be examined in detail below.    [12] See 177–81.

We only *defer* to the judgment of another when we are uncertain about what the right conclusion should be, or alternatively where we disagree with them, but nonetheless consider it appropriate to attach weight to their judgment.

These two factors apply to judicial decision-making. Deference is appropriate when the courts are uncertain about what the correct decision is, or they disagree with the legislature/Executive, but nonetheless have reasons (grounded in concerns about relative institutional competence and legitimacy) not to interfere with those decisions.[13] In chapter 8, we will see that one of the reasons why substantial judicial deference is so prevalent in the area of national security is precisely the fact that, in this context, the courts are often uncertain about what the right decision should be. For the moment, we need to get a clearer idea of how deference operates in general terms. The appropriateness of the idiom of 'giving weight' to the primary decision under the conditions of uncertainty can be illustrated by an example. Say if a judge has to assess whether a legislative scheme which penalises hauliers in various ways for unknowingly bringing illegal immigrants into the UK, violates the hauliers' right to liberty.[14] The Government claims that these penalties are necessary to counter the serious problem posed by illegal entry, and claims further that the interferences with Convention rights are justified and proportionate in light of the seriousness of this problem. In assessing the Convention-compatibility of this legislative scheme, the courts are presented with a dilemma. On the one hand, they have expertise and competence in assessing the legal implications of the legislation and their compatibility with Convention rights. On the other, they will tend to have less expertise on the broader political and social implications of the scheme. For example, they may be ill-equipped to assess the question of whether this scheme is truly 'necessary in a democratic society'. They may be uncertain about the answer to this dimension of the problem. Added to this is the fact that the democratically elected legislature has considered the issue and concluded that it is necessary in the current climate and is proportionate. Judicial uncertainty about some dimensions of the case, combined with respect for the role of Parliament as the primary decision-maker, gives rise to a presumptive weight in favour of the conclusion reached by Parliament (i.e. presumptive weight in favour of upholding the legislation).

---

[13] These are second-order reasons, see generally Perry (1989).

[14] This example is drawn from the facts of *International Transport Roth GmbH* v. *Secretary of State for the Home Department* [2002] 3 W.L.R. 344.

A number of important preliminary points arise from this example. The first is that deference is a rational response to uncertainty. The less confident we are about what the right conclusion is, the more likely we are (and indeed the more justified we are) in deferring to the judgment of another, especially if we know that the other person possesses superior expertise, competence or legitimacy in arriving at that answer.[15] So, judicial deference and uncertainty have an inverse relationship: the more certainty, the less deference, and *vice versa*. If the court is clear that a legislative scheme is 'not merely harsh but *plainly unfair*',[16] this will weigh against the arguments for deference. On the contrary, if the arguments are 'finely balanced',[17] this will weigh in favour of deference. The presumptive weight in favour of upholding the legislation means that the court will only find it to be incompatible with the Convention if it is relatively certain that it violates those rights and/or if it violates them to a substantial degree.[18] The latter qualification shows that epistemic limitations are not the only ones which factor into the question of the appropriateness of deference. Also relevant is the fact that the courts, as secondary decision-makers, cannot interfere with the primary decision unless a certain threshold of rights violation has been reached.

This factor accounts for the widespread judicial *dicta*, that the courts will not interfere with a primary decision merely on the basis that they disagree with it, but only if it violates Convention rights to a substantial degree. As Kennedy C.J. explained in the Court of Appeal: 'if the law falls within a reasonable range of alternatives the court will not find it over broad *merely because* they can conceive of a better alternative'.[19] Similarly, in *Pearson*: 'In deference to the legislature, courts should not *easily be persuaded* to condemn what has been done, especially where it has been done in primary legislation after careful evaluation.'[20] Other examples of the courts attaching a weighting threshold to decisions of the legislature

---

[15] This is why we often defer to our doctor about medical issues, financial advisers about our finances, etc. When we are uncertain about what to do due to lack of expertise, it is often rational to defer to those who possess the requisite expertise.

[16] *Roth*, above n. 14 at [26], *per* Simon Brown L.J.

[17] See e.g. *R. (Farrakhan) v. Secretary of State for the Home Department* [2002] 3 W.L.R. 481 at [79].

[18] Stephen Perry refers to these as 'epistemic' and 're-weighting' reasons, see Perry (1989), 932ff.

[19] *R. (Pearson) v. Secretary of State for the Home Department* [2001] H.R.L.R. 39 (emphasis added). Chief Justice Beverley McLachlin has described the approach of the Canadian Supreme Court in similar terms, see McLachlin (1999–2000), 29.

[20] *Ibid.* at [33], emphasis added.

or executive, are easy to find. Thus, in Lord Bingham's judgment in *Belmarsh Prison*, he stated that 'the appellants have shown *no ground strong enough* to warrant displacing the Secretary of State's decision'[21] on the derogation issue. In another case, he noted that a statute 'approved by a democratically elected Parliament . . . should *not be at all readily rejected*'.[22] These *dicta* highlight an important aspect of the judicial role, namely, that judges are not the primary decision-makers, but rather have a secondary responsibility to ensure that the primary decision-maker has acted in accordance with the requirements of legality.[23] They cannot substitute their decision for that of the primary decision-maker simply because they think it is better. These widespread *dicta* also highlight the fact that deference functions in judicial reasoning by allocating various degrees of presumptive weight in favour of the legislative decision, so that an alleged violation of Convention rights must be *substantial* and/or *clearly demonstrated* in order to outweigh the presumptive weight in its favour.[24]

This brings us to another crucial point about the nature of deference, namely, its variability: it depends on *how much* weight a judge assigns to the decisions of the elected branches.[25] It could range from treating that decision as a persuasive reason (of various strengths), through to treating it as a conclusive reason for supporting the outcome favoured by Parliament. Treating a judgment as a persuasive reason amounts to what can be called *partial deference* because it does not preclude or pre-empt the judge's own assessment of the issue. However, treating it as a conclusive reason amounts to *absolute* or *complete deference*. Here, a judge surrenders his judgment to the legislature/Executive and declines to make his own assessment on the merits of the issue.[26]

---

[21]  *A* v. *Secretary of State for the Home Department*, [2005] 2 A.C. 68 at [29], emphasis added.

[22]  *Kay* v. *Lambeth London Borough Council* [2006] UKHL 10 at [28], *per* Lord Bingham, emphasis added; see also the judgment of Baroness Hale who noted that the courts should 'think long and hard' before intervening in legislative decisions about housing policy, *Kay* at [187].

[23]  Hunt (2003).

[24]  As Lord Bingham observed in *R. (Animal Defenders International)* v. *Secretary of State for Culture, Media and Sport* [ 2008] UKHL 15 at [33]: 'the judgment of Parliament [on the issue of the propriety of a prohibition on political advertising on television and radio] should not be *lightly overridden*', emphasis added.

[25]  The variability is partly due to the fact that uncertainty is a matter of degree (see Perry (1989), 934) and partly due to the requirement that limitation of Convention rights must reach a certain threshold, which is also variable.

[26]  Thus, one could say that the House of Lords' deference to its own precedents is partial rather than absolute, because although its precedents are taken to be authoritative, their

It should be noted that when the courts decline to make their own assessment in this way, they are deciding that an issue is non-justiciable.[27] Whilst the doctrines of deference and non-justiciability are both motivated by concerns about the limited institutional expertise and legitimacy of the courts, deference differs from non-justiciability in that it does not remove an issue or subject-matter from the court's supervision altogether. Rather than being a blanket rule preventing scrutiny, deference maintains some flexibility by requiring the courts to assess their institutional competence to deal with a particular issue, and to show restraint to the extent that their competence is limited.[28] The relative flexibility of the doctrine of deference is contained in the fact that it can be partial, ranging from giving minimal through to substantial weight to the decisions of the elected branches. This is different (and significantly so) from declining to adjudicate an issue at all.[29]

These preliminary points are borne out by many of the judicial *dicta* on judicial deference in the case law arising under the Human Rights Act 1998. Many judges speak in terms of according a 'degree of deference'[30] to the legislature or Executive where the context justifies it, and many use the metaphor of attributing (a variable degree of) weight to the decisions of Parliament or the Executive.[31] Thus, in *Brown* v. *Stott*, Lord Bingham noted that the court should '*give weight to* the decisions of representative legislature and a democratic government'.[32] In *Rehman*,

Lordships are not barred from overruling previous authority. It simply means that it would take a strong reason to outweigh the force attached to the precedent. As Perry puts it, the courts tend to apply a 'high weighting threshold to overruling', see Perry (1989), 977.

[27] Note that Steyn (2005a), 349, has described deference extrajudicially as 'the idea of a court, exceptionally, out of respect for other branches of government and in recognition of their democratic decision-making role, *declining to make its own independent judgment on a particular issue*', emphasis added. It may be that what Lord Steyn has in mind here is that when judges defer, they decline to make their own judgments on the substantive legal issue. However, if judges defer completely, then this is, in effect, to make the issue non-justiciable.

[28] See Sullivan (1998), 394.

[29] For differences between deference and non-justiciability, see also King (2007), 198; Wiseman (2001), 435ff; Schokkenbroek (1998), 30. For an analysis of the doctrine of non-justiciability in Canadian law, see generally Sossin (1999).

[30] See e.g. *Poplar Housing & Regeneration Community Association Ltd.* v. *Donoghue* [2002] Q.B. 48 at [69]; *A* v. *Secretary of State for the Home Department* [2005] 2 A.C. 68 at [175], *per* Lord Rodger; see also Woolf (2003), 260.

[31] See e.g. *Brown* v. *Stott* [2001] 2 W.L.R. 817 at [39], *per* Lord Bingham; *Roth*, above n. 14 at [26], *per* Simon Brown L.J, [8], *per* Laws L.J.; *Secretary of State for the Home Department* v. *Rehman* [2002] 1 All E.R. 123 at [31], *per* Lord Steyn; *A* v. *Secretary of State for the Home Department* [2005] 2 W.L.R. 87 at [29], *per* Lord Bingham.

[32] *Brown* v. *Stott, ibid.* at [39], emphasis added.

Lord Steyn considered that it was 'self evidently right that national courts *must give great weight to* the views of the executive on matters of national security'.[33] Moreover, the case law reveals that judicial deference under the HRA tends to be *partial* rather than *absolute*.[34] As Lord Hope put it in *Wilson* v. *First County Trust*, the need for judicial deference does not mean that 'the court is absolutely disabled from forming its own view' on constitutional issues.[35] So, legislative or Executive decisions may provide persuasive reasons (of varying strengths) in favour of deferring to the solution chosen by Parliament, but they are not conclusive reasons.[36]

This has an important consequence, namely, that it is wrong to assume that judicial deference means an unquestioning acceptance of, or blind submission to, decisions made by Parliament or the Executive. Rather, it is a matter of degree that does not necessarily preclude intensive scrutiny of those decisions, or even necessarily result in a judicial decision favourable to the elected branches.[37] Thus, in *Roth* the Court of Appeal found against the Secretary of State despite according to his decision as much deference as they possibly could in the politically sensitive area of immigration control.[38] Similarly, in the *Belmarsh Prison* case (which will be discussed in more depth in chapter 8), the House of Lords declared a provision in anti-terrorist legislation incompatible with Convention rights, despite according 'great weight' to the judgment of the Home Secretary.[39] Deference and disagreement are not mutually exclusive. The primary decision of the legislature or Executive carries weight, but is not necessarily dispositive. So, deference is not anathema to the culture of justification – it is simply that, in scrutinising the justification for the legislation or Executive decision, the courts must be sensitive to the limits of their

---

[33] *Rehman*, above n. 31 at [31], emphasis added; see also *Animal Defenders International*, above n. 24 at [33], where it was decided that in the context of regulating political advertising, the Parliament's decision should be given 'great weight'. Acknowledging that this would vary from case to case, Lord Bingham noted: 'How much weight should be accorded to the judgment of Parliament depends on the circumstances and the subject matter'.

[34] As Jeff King has pointed out, under the HRA, non-justiciability has 'faded into' concerns about deference, see King (2007), 198.

[35] *Wilson* v. *First County Trust* [2003] 3 W.L.R. 568 at [116].

[36] *R.* v. *Lichniak* [2003] 1 A.C. 903 at [14].

[37] See *Roth*, above n. 14; see also *Secretary of State for the Home Department* v. *MB* [2006] EWCA Civ 1140 at [65], *per* Lord Phillips: 'Notwithstanding such deference there will be scope for the court to give intense scrutiny'; see also *Ghaidan* v. *Mendoza* [2004] 3 W.L.R. 113 at [19], *per* Lord Nicholls; see further Endicott (2002), 286.

[38] *Roth*, above n. 14 at [54], *per* Simon Brown L.J.

[39] *Belmarsh Prison* case, above n. 21 at [29], *per* Lord Bingham.

constitutional role, as well as the limits of their secondary, adjudicative function.

The variable application of deference reveals another crucial point. This is that it is no part of a proper understanding account of deference that the courts should *presume* themselves to have inferior competence, expertise or legitimacy across the board. The argument here is not that judges should always defer in every case, because they have inferior expertise, competence or democratic legitimacy. The issue of relative competence, expertise and legitimacy is a contextual one, which must be judged in the context of the case in which it arises, taking into account all the factors relevant to the deference enquiry. These will include the severity of the rights violation, the degree of confidence the courts have in their own assessment about whether a right has been violated, as well as questions about the limits of judicial expertise with respect to a particular issue and the limits of their interpretive powers under the HRA.

The example of the legislative scheme imposing penalties for hauliers also reveals that relative expertise will not tend to be an all-or-nothing matter, even within the context of one case. In any case which comes before the House of Lords, there will tend to be elements in which the courts have considerable expertise, and elements where that expertise may be less secure. This was highlighted in Lord Bingham's judgment in *R. (Baiai)* v. *Secretary of State for the Home Department*.[40] There, the question was whether various restrictions on immigrants' right to marry in the Asylum and Immigration Act 2004 were sufficiently onerous to amount to a violation of their right to marry under Article 12. Rejecting the Secretary of State's argument that 'the legislative scheme involves an area of broad social policy where the judgement of the legislature and executive should be given considerable weight', Lord Bingham concluded that this proposition was 'too sweeping'.[41] Whilst there were some features of the scheme which depended 'on a political judgement which the court is ill-qualified to assess',[42] the answer to the question of whether the scheme violated the respondents' right to marry, did not turn on broader questions of social policy 'but on an accurate analysis of the scheme and the law'.[43] The multi-dimensional aspect of these cases reinforces the need to evaluate the degree of deference in a closely contextual manner.

---

[40] [2008] All E.R. 411.    [41] *Ibid.* at [25].

[42] Examples of these features included the desirability of taking action against so-called sham marriages and the relative merits of seeking to prevent such marriages after the event of any immigration advantage might have obtained, *ibid.* at [25].

[43] *Ibid.* at [25].

The variability of deference means that it does not apply automatically when certain subject-matters arise in the case. There are no preordained areas in which deference is warranted – not even, as we will see in the next chapter, the area of national security. As Murray Hunt observed, deference must be earned rather than assumed by the elected branches, and the courts need to be vigilant in scrutinising whether there are any particular claims of superior expertise and competence in the context of the individual case, rather than adopting a crude subject-based approach which predetermines the issue.[44]

## Deference, interpretation and judicial self-restraint

One conceptual issue not yet clarified concerns the relationship between deference and interpretation. Clearly, the doctrine of deference features in the HRA case law when the courts are called upon to exercise their interpretive function under section 3 and it also influences the judicial choice between sections 3 and 4. But what is the precise relationship between deference and interpretation? In chapter 2, I argued that legal interpretation is driven by evaluative judgments.[45] I now wish to add to that claim the following clarification. This is that there are two kinds of evaluative judgment at work in interpretation under section 3 HRA.[46] The first is the *substantive evaluation*. This refers to an evaluation of the merits of interpreting a particular constitutional (or legislative) provision in one way or another.[47] The second is the *institutional evaluation*, which engages judges' views about the extent and limits of their own role (including the limits of interpretation) and the implications this has for the correct judicial decision in the circumstances of the particular case.[48] The doctrine of deference is part of the *institutional evaluation* since it concerns the desirability of the judiciary interfering with a legislative or Executive decision, based on concerns about the limits of their institutional role in the

---

[44] For a rejection of the subject-based approach to deference along similar lines, see Hunt (2003), 351; see also Allan (2004b), 294–5.

[45] See also Kavanagh (2003a), 65–6.

[46] In fact, they apply to statutory interpretation more generally.

[47] For an account of the role of 'merit' reasons (which drive the substantive evaluation) and 'non-merit' reasons (which drive the institutional evaluation), see Raz (1998b), 173–4, 187–9.

[48] See also Bickel (1962) at 74 where he distinguishes between the court's decision on the 'substantive issue' and their decision about whether (and if so, to what extent) they should adjudicate.

constitutional framework.[49] So, the doctrine of deference is indeed part of the interpretive exercise under section 3 HRA broadly speaking, but it is not part of the substantive evaluation about what the law requires. Rather, it features in an evaluation about the institutional and constitutional appropriateness of an innovative interpretation in a particular case.[50]

Deference is a doctrine of judicial self-restraint based on concerns about the appropriate roles of the different branches of government.[51] The question whether judges should defer to the legislature or Executive is not about the legal powers which judges possess. Rather, it concerns the appropriateness of judges *not* exercising those powers, or at least being restrained in exercising them. As Lord Steyn put it extrajudicially: 'The existence of jurisdiction does not mean that it ought always to be exercised.'[52] There is, after all, no *legal* bar on judges making decisions on national security or in cases which have resource implications for government. Rather, the courts sometimes restrain themselves from interfering with decisions in these areas because of concerns about the limits of the courts' expertise, competence and/or legitimacy.

Although some of Lord Hoffmann's *dicta* in *Pro-Life Alliance*[53] suggested that he viewed questions about deference as a matter of law,[54] subsequent *dicta* in *Rehman*[55] support the account developed here, namely, that deference is not a matter of the legal limits on jurisdiction, but rather a matter of judicial restraint out of respect for, and sensitivity to, the appropriate constitutional boundaries between the branches of government.[56] Thus, when commenting on the failure of

---

[49] It should be noted that whilst these two evaluations are conceptually distinct, they are often mixed and difficult to distinguish in practice.

[50] For the view that the substantive evaluation (and the merit reasons which support it) is central or primary because this defines the task of the courts in constitutional interpretation, see Raz (1998b), 187.

[51] For an overview of the various doctrines of judicial self-restraint, see Daley (2000). See also Kirk (2001).

[52] Steyn (2005a), 349; see also Sedley (2004), 10: 'there are many issues lying within the court's jurisdiction which ministers or statutory bodies are nevertheless better equipped than judges to decide' (though Lord Sedley eschews the phrase 'deference').

[53] *R. (Pro-Life Alliance)* v. *British Broadcasting Corporation* [2004] 1 A.C. 185.

[54] *Rehman*, above n. 31. Note that some of Lord Hoffmann's *dicta* in *Pro-Life Alliance* seem to challenge this view. See e.g. the following *dictum*: 'when the courts decide that a decision is within the proper competence of the legislature or executive, it is not showing deference. It is deciding the law', at [76]. Some of his *dicta* in *Pro-Life Alliance* are criticised in Jowell (2003b), 599; King (2007), 222.

[55] *Rehman*, above n. 31.      [56] *Ibid.* at [49].

SIAC to exercise 'proper deference' to the Home Secretary,[57] Lord Hoffmann noted that:

> the need for restraint is not based upon any limits to the Commission's appellate jurisdiction. The amplitude of that jurisdiction is emphasised by the express power to reverse the exercise of discretion. The need for restraint flows from a commonsense recognition of the nature of the issue and differences in the decision-making processes and responsibilities of the Home Secretary and the Commission.[58]

### Terminological concerns: comity or courtesy or both?

There is evidence in the case law that some judges are reluctant to use the term 'deference', even when they are doing exactly what deference requires on my account. Thus, despite endorsing the view that judges should accord 'appropriate weight to the judgment of a person with responsibility for given subject matter and access to special sources of knowledge and advice',[59] the House of Lords in *Huang* nonetheless emphasised that 'the giving of weight to factors such as these is not, in our opinion, aptly described as deference'.[60] Similarly, in the *Belmarsh Prison* case, Lord Bingham preferred to use the terms 'demarcation of functions' or 'relative institutional competence', whilst nonetheless giving 'great weight to the judgment of the Home Secretary'.[61] Most famously, in *Pro-Life Alliance*, Lord Hoffmann suggested that the term 'deference' is an inappropriate way of describing the relationship between the judicial and the other branches of government because of its 'overtones of servility, or perhaps gracious concession'.[62] Whilst judges have to decide on the limits of their own decision-making power, this 'does not mean that their allocation of decision-making power to the other branches of government is a matter of courtesy or deference'.[63]

These reservations about the language or terminology of deference need to be addressed before we can proceed to examine the operation

---

[57]  *Ibid.* at [49].

[58]  *Ibid.* at [58]. This understanding is also evident in his extrajudicial comments in Hoffmann (2002), 137.

[59]  *Huang* v. *Secretary of State* [2007] 2 A.C. 167 at [16].

[60]  *Ibid.* at [16].    [61]  *Ibid.* at [29].

[62]  *Pro-Life Alliance*, above n. 53 at [75], *per* Lord Hoffmann. Though see *Rehman*, where Lord Hoffmann uses the term 'deference' precisely to give expression to the nature of the judicial function in reviewing decisions of the elected branches of government, *Rehman*, above n. 31 at [49].

[63]  *Pro-Life Alliance* at [76].

of deference in practice. It should be conceded straight away that when we describe someone as 'deferential', it can carry negative connotations of behaving in an obsequious, fawning or servile way. There is a suggestion of humiliation or abasement, of kowtowing to a superior. Clearly, these connotations are inappropriate to characterise the constitutional function of the courts in reviewing the primary decisions of the legislature or Executive. However, the term 'deference' does not necessarily carry these pejorative overtones. Nor are they central to the meaning of deference. Rather, they refer to being (or appearing) *inappropriately deferential*, either by being too deferential (giving too much weight to the judgments of another) or by being misplaced (paying deference to someone to whom it is not due). So, the overtones of servility refer to a misuse of an approach to practical reasoning, which is often perfectly appropriate and sensible, and often appropriate when judges come to review decisions made by the legislature or Executive. If judges give appropriate weight to the judgments of a person who has special expertise or knowledge on a given subject-matter, they are not being servile or obsequious. Rather, they are proceeding, in the words of the House of Lords in *Huang*, 'how any rational judicial decision-maker is likely to proceed'.[64] Once we remember that deference is not necessarily absolute, but rather is a matter of according various degrees of weight to the judgments of the elected branches when it is due, the overtones of servility which Lord Hoffmann finds objectionable are subdued, if not removed altogether. Correctly understood, deference does not amount to judicial abasement or servility to the elected branches.[65] Rather, it counsels judges to be sensitive to their institutional limits and to the reasons for judicial restraint which may arise in individual cases, leading them to give appropriate but not unquestioning weight to the decisions of primary decision-makers.

Second, it may be that by saying that the 'allocation' of decision-making power of the elected branches is not one of courtesy, Lord Hoffmann was keen to emphasise that such institutional questions are of immense constitutional importance, and should not be trivialised by suggesting that they are *merely* a matter of judicial politeness. Far from being an aspect of judicial etiquette which judges can take or leave, it embodies one of the most centrally important requirements of the judicial function, namely

---

[64] *Huang*, above n. 59 at [16] (though note that this comment was made in the context of rejecting the appropriateness of the terminology of deference.)

[65] *Belmarsh Prison*, above n. 21 at [176], *per* Lord Rodger: 'Due deference does not mean abasement before [the views of government and Parliament], even in matters relating to national security.'

to 'recognise the constitutional boundaries between judicial, Executive and legislative power'.[66]

Lord Hoffmann's comments require us to clarify the role of courtesy in the doctrine of deference. As mentioned earlier, the primary rationale for deference is respect for the superior qualities possessed by the democratically elected legislature. Judges show that respect by giving an appropriate degree of weight to the primary decision, *but also* by treating those decisions with courtesy.[67] This brings out the fact that judicial deference can perform an expressive function: not only is it a way of respecting the decisions of the primary decision-maker, it is also a way of creating the *appearance* of respect for them.[68] This accounts for the fact that judges can sometimes defer to the elected branches for 'prudential reasons', i.e. to placate a hostile legislature or to avoid making an unpopular decision which might bring the judicial role into disrepute. These reasons for deference will be explored more fully in the penultimate section of this chapter. For the moment, it suffices to note that the courtesy dimension of deference means that even when judges disagree with a decision made by the elected branches, they must nonetheless do so respectfully, that is, in a way that does not belittle or ridicule those decisions or in a way which seeks to delegitimise them.[69] Whilst the importance of this requirement for the politics of judicial decision-making should not be underestimated,[70] Lord Hoffmann's comments remind us that it should

---

[66]  *Rehman*, above n. 31 at [49]. Perhaps, this is why he overstated his position by saying that these institutional questions were a matter of 'law'. It is more accurate to say that they are a matter of constitutional propriety.

[67]  See Kavanagh (2008), 188ff.

[68]  For the moral significance of deference as a way of *signalling* respect, see Soper (2002), 25; Calhoun (2000), 255; Buss (1999), 801.

[69]  This is why judges sometimes preface their disagreement with the Executive/legislature with some expression of respect, see e.g. Lord Walker's judgment in the *Belmarsh Prison* case, above n. 21, where his Lordship prefaced his conclusion that the Secretary of State's decision was 'irrational and disproportionate' with the respectful assurance that there is no attack on the good faith of the Secretary of State, nor any suggestion that he gave misleading or disingenuous reasons for his actions, at [193]. Lord Rodger points out extrajudicially that it is also part of the judicial culture in the UK to adopt a courteous (rather than confrontational) tone with respect to speeches of a fellow Law Lord, see Rodger (2002), 233.

[70]  It should be noted that deference on grounds of respect, including the duty to be courteous, is not a one-way street. The principle of inter-institutional comity also requires that the elected branches of government respect the decisions of the courts and that they refrain from comments or actions which discredit the courts or belittle their decisions. For analysis of how this type of comity has been flouted in recent years, see Bradley (2003); Le Sueur (1996).

not be overestimated either. Judicial courtesy is an important element of deference (since it is a way in which the courts express their comity with the elected branches), but it is not the *only* or even primary element in it.[71] At stake here are important matters of the constitutionally appropriate division of labour between the three branches of government.

## Minimal and substantial deference

It is now abundantly clear that the variability of deference is one of its defining characteristics. In this section, I shall argue that judges always owe a duty of *minimal deference* to parliamentary and Executive decision-making, but *substantial deference* is only owed exceptionally. *Minimal deference* is the judicial attribution of some presumptive weight to the decision taken by the elected body, but it is not a very strong presumption. It simply requires that Parliament's or the Executive's decisions are treated with respect in the sense that they should be taken seriously as a *bona fide* attempt to solve whatever social problem they set out to tackle. Whilst ordinary citizens can view parliamentary or Executive action in a sceptical way (i.e. presuming them to be erroneous or misguided unless proven otherwise) this is an inappropriate attitude for the judiciary to adopt. Judges must always give (minimal) weight to the fact that the legislation or the Executive decision is chosen by the primary decision-maker and cannot therefore be dismissed without good reason. Deference in this minimal sense means that judges (acting in their judicial capacity) cannot make light of, or be sceptical about, attempts by Parliament to solve a social problem in legislation.[72] Moreover, even if judges ultimately disagree with a legislative provision or find it incompatible with the HRA, their duty of *minimal deference* means that they should nonetheless *display* respect for it.[73]

The duty of *minimal deference* accounts for the fact that judges ought not to invalidate an Executive decision, or declare an Act of Parliament to be incompatible with the HRA, *merely* on the basis that they disagree with it or because they might have come up with a different solution if they had had the power to make the primary decision. Rather, as was shown above and exemplified in various judicial *dicta* from the HRA case

---

[71] Lord Hoffmann seems to use the terms interchangeably. He refers to 'courtesy or deference', see *Pro-Life Alliance*, above n. 53 at [76].

[72] Though note that this minimal deference does not in any way preclude intense scrutiny of those decisions.

[73] See Gavison (1999), 241.

law, the error of the legislation must be sufficiently grave to override the presumptive weight in its favour.

So, minimal deference (i.e. minimal presumptive weight in favour of the legislative or Executive decision) applies across the board in all cases. It is inherent in the role of the judges as secondary decision-makers. Not so with *substantial deference*. *Substantial deference* has to be earned by the elected branches and is only warranted where the courts judge themselves to suffer from particular institutional shortcomings with regard to the issue at hand. These are cases where they judge Parliament or the Executive to have:

(a)  more institutional competence;
(b)  more expertise; and/or
(c)  more legitimacy to assess the particular issue.

These are the three main grounds for substantial deference, and each will be considered in turn.

## The argument from institutional competence

One institutional limitation that prompts courts to defer to Parliament or the Executive is contained in the 'fundamental features' limitation examined in Part 1 of this book. When a case concerns an issue which would require widespread or radical reform of various interlinked areas of the law, a responsible judge will sometimes pay substantial defer-ence to the superior *law-making competence* of Parliament. An exam-ple of deference on this ground is provided by *Bellinger* v. *Bellinger*,[74] where the House of Lords decided that it could not interpret the Matri-monial Causes Act 1973 compatibly with the Convention because 'this would present a major change in the law, having far-reaching ramifica-tions. It raises issues whose solution calls for extensive inquiry and the widest public consultation and discussion.'[75] The uncertainty surround-ing the circumstances in which gender reassignment could be recognised for the purposes of marriage meant that it was necessary to come up with 'objective, publicly available criteria by which gender reassignment is to be assessed',[76] criteria the court was not in a position to devise. Since Parliament had the law-making ability to deal with the varied subject-matter and was able to regulate the area in a comprehensive rather than 'piecemeal fashion',[77] it was appropriate for the court to defer.

---

[74] [2003] 2 A.C. 467.    [75] *Ibid.* at [37], *per* Lord Nicholls.
[76] *Ibid.* at [42].    [77] *Ibid.* at [45].

The *Bellinger* case highlights another limitation of judicial decision-making that may account for the degree of deference they pay to Parliament or the Executive. This is that judges typically deal with a bivalent form of dispute.[78] Since the court was focused on the facts and evidence pertaining only to Mrs Bellinger, it did not feel that it would be responsible to change the law on the basis of one individual case.[79] Judges are equipped to deal with the question: 'does this legislative provision violate the Convention rights of this particular individual?', but not the more general question of how transsexuality should be regulated in disparate areas of the law. In the *Bellinger* case, the court had no difficulty in establishing that non-recognition of gender reassignment for the purposes of marriage was incompatible with Articles 8 and 12 of the European Convention[80] and made a declaration of incompatibility to this effect. No deference was needed here. It was with reference to the broader questions of how the law should be reformed in order to achieve such recognition in a fair way that the court paid deference to the superior law-making ability of Parliament.

This is not to say that substantial deference is *always* justified even in such situations. The duty of deference is not absolute even where judges have less institutional competence than Parliament or the Executive. If the existing legal doctrine has severe negative consequences for the litigant, and the court believes that Parliament is unwilling or unable to engage in the required radical reform, they may consider it necessary to engage in partial reform in order to achieve justice in the individual case, despite the possible shortcomings of this sort of reform. So, the desirability of deference in cases where radical law-reform is needed is not always the overriding concern. It is a matter of balancing the judicial obligation to do justice in the individual case against the possible disadvantages of partial or incremental reform.[81]

## The argument from expertise

One of the most common arguments advanced in favour of substantial judicial deference is that the courts should defer to Parliament and/or the

---

[78] See Endicott (1999), 15.      [79] *Bellinger*, above n. 71 at [39]–[44].      [80] *Ibid.* at [53].

[81] The Chief Justice of the Supreme Court of Canada, Beverley McLachlin, argues along similar lines that although, as a general rule, the public interest is best served if judges engage in 'cautious, incremental, case-by-case adaptation of the law to current circumstances', if the matter is of central importance to society and the rule of law, and there is a legislative inability or unwillingness to address the pressing problem at stake, the courts are justified – albeit rarely – in changing the law dramatically, see McLachlin (2001), 319.

Executive on questions of 'public policy' or matters that are in the public interest. The argument is that the expertise of the courts is in matters of law, not policy, so they should show deference when policy questions arise. The alleged dichotomy between questions of law (which are appropriate for the courts) and questions of policy (which are not) recalls Ronald Dworkin's well-known argument that judges should base their decisions on matters of principle rather than policy, where a 'principle' is defined as a 'requirement of justice or fairness or some other dimension of morality'[82] and 'policy' is defined as 'a kind of standard that sets out a goal to be reached, generally an improvement in some economic, political or social feature of the community'.[83] So, arguments of principle identify rights, whereas arguments of policy assert that some decision or law will promote the general welfare, the public interest or the collective good. Of course, the plausibility of this suggestion depends on being able to make a meaningful distinction between principles and policies, a possibility doubted by many.[84] Some argue that principles and policies are not antithetical in the way Dworkin assumes: the public interest in fact includes protecting people's fundamental rights.[85] But even if it is granted that this distinction can be made, its normative import (the claim that judges *should not* rely on policy arguments) is open to objection.

It should be noted at the outset that it is a recommendation for judges to refrain from doing something they do all the time. Any first-year law student will know that the courts consider alleged social harms when developing the common law or interpreting statutes. They do not consider rights in isolation from those harms, but rather attempt to balance one value against another. Judicial evaluation of policies and legislative goals, (including their consequences for society) is part of what one American judge called the 'traditional judicial toolkit'.[86] But this fact alone does not undermine the normative claim, because it may be (though unlikely given its pervasiveness) that these decisions are illegitimate on this basis. Luckily, the normative claim can be rejected on its own terms. Judicial decisions take effect in the world in which we live, and to be just, they must take into account the consequences or implications they may have for the various goals the law serves. So, for example, when judges are deciding medical negligence cases, it is entirely legitimate for them to consider (as they often do) the impact their decision will have on medical practice.[87]

---

[82] Dworkin (1977), 22.    [83] *Ibid.*

[84] See Greenawalt (1983); Raz (1978), 128; Finnis (1985), 315; Miller (2008), 101ff; Kyritsis (2007); Perry (1989), 981–2; Waldron (1993a), 392; MacCormick (1978), 259–64.

[85] Raz (1995).    [86] Scalia (1989), 515.    [87] Woolf (2001).

Similarly, if judges have to decide whether a member of the police force owes a duty of care to members of the public, they must consider the consequences this may have on the conduct of police business and their ability to suppress crime, as well as consequences for legal development and the role of the courts.[88]

This is the familiar floodgates argument, familiar because it is such a common and accepted feature of judicial decision-making. If judges made these decisions without any consideration of collective goals and practical consequences, their decisions would be profoundly unjust. Lord Steyn has pointed out that not only is it 'an everyday occurrence' for courts to consider matters of policy, 'it would be a matter of public disquiet if the court did not do so'.[89] The reason for this is that the just resolution of any case requires that the facts of that case should be viewed in light of the social realities that attend them. Judges have a responsibility to ensure, to the extent that they can, that their decisions are correct and one factor determining the correctness of their decisions will be whether they correctly evaluate the policy issues that inevitably arise in the course of their decisions.[90]

Aside from the moral responsibility to consider the policy implications of the decisions they make, they in fact have no alternative to do so when making many decisions under the HRA. After all, many of the freedoms protected by the Convention are expressly subject to limits necessary in a democratic society in the interests of various public goals, such as 'national security', 'public safety', 'the economic well-being of the country', and 'the prevention of disorder or crime'. All these matters involve policy issues and it would be an abdication of the judicial function to say that they are non-justiciable because judges are given a mandate by Parliament to adjudicate them under the HRA. This reflects a more general point, namely, that to the extent that a statute explicitly promotes collective goals,

---

[88] See e.g. *Hill* v. *Chief Constable of West Yorkshire* [1989] A.C. 53, *per* Lord Templeman at 65. Explicit consideration of the consequences of a particular ruling is often apparent in 'resource allocation cases', see e.g. *N* v. *SSHD* [2005] 4 All E.R. 1017: 'The consequences if the decision goes against the appellant cannot sensibly be detached from the consequences if the decision goes in her favour', *per* Lord Hope at [21].

[89] Steyn (2005a), 357. Note that many of the problems that beset the distinction between principle and policy also arise with reference to Lon Fuller's distinction between polycentric and non-polycentric issues. Lon Fuller advanced this distinction as a way of demarcating the limits of adjudication. But, as Jeff King points out, polycentricity is a pervasive feature of adjudication (and certainly a pervasive feature of adjudication under the HRA). Therefore, unless it is heavily refined, the idea of polycentricity provides weak justificatory support for judicial restraint in public law, see King (2008); Pieterse (2004), 394ff.

[90] See Ashworth (1991), 443.

judges cannot interpret those laws faithfully without some consideration of how best to promote them.[91]

The principle/policy distinction has been resurrected by Conor Gearty to show that when a case arising under the HRA is a matter of legal principle the courts should be activist, but deference is required when policy issues are involved. He relies on the metaphor of a swimming pool 'with the shallow end marked "legal principle" and the deep end marked "public policy".[92] Judges can be assured and assertive when adjudicating at the former end, but should recognise that they are 'entirely out of their depth'[93] in the latter. This claim is open not only to the objections already levelled at Dworkin's distinction, but it is also vulnerable to the following additional problem. This is that the cases under the HRA (or indeed any other constitutional document guaranteeing rights) do not arise in separate categories marked 'legal principle' or 'public policy'. Rather they are often, if not typically, entwined. In fact, all of the interesting and difficult cases involving the desirability of deference under the HRA do not lie at either end of Gearty's metaphorical pool. Rather, they are cases that simultaneously involve both legal principle of the highest constitutional order *and* public policy. One might say that they are simultaneously in the shallow and the deep end of the pool, and since this is a conceptual impossibility, the metaphor seems unhelpful as a way of illuminating the question of the desirability of judicial deference.[94]

The real distinction here is that between *the type of policy decision appropriate to the institutional features, competence and legitimacy of the courts and the type of policy decision that is beyond that competence.* Though certainly not as succinct or as pleasingly alliterative as the 'principle/policy' distinction, it brings us to the heart of the real concerns and difficulties surrounding judicial deference. First, it emphasises that if a case contains an element of public policy, this does not mean that the issue is necessarily beyond review by the courts, or that substantial deference is *automatically* required. Rather, it means that the courts must fulfil their duty of upholding constitutional principle, whilst bearing in mind any limits on their expertise, competence or legitimacy that may warrant a

---

[91] See Bell (1983), 222.     [92] Gearty (2004), 121.     [93] *Ibid.*, 122.

[94] Admittedly, Gearty seems to allow for the possibility of some cases being located on a sort of borderline between principle and policy (i.e. the middle of the pool) where judges 'assert[] an issue to be one of legal principle while all the time they are sliding into ever-deeper water', see Gearty (2004), 122. However, it is not clear how to apply this metaphorical description to the case law other than to say that such cases simultaneously involve a strong principle *and* policy dimension.

degree of deference. Second, it emphasises that the determination of how much deference is due to the elected branches of government is deeply contextual and cannot be answered by simply demarcating subject-areas where deference is appropriate. Rather, it is the (complex) task of assessing whether the court's competence, expertise and legitimacy equips them to judge this particular issue with confidence. So, instead of seeking to solve the issue of deference by asking 'is this a case involving immigration policy or housing policy or national security etc?', judges have to embark on the much more difficult and multi-faceted inquiry into relative institutional competence, expertise and legitimacy, bearing in mind all the factors relevant in the context of the individual case. These will include not only the policy context of the case and the relative expertise and competence of the courts (and the judicial process) in dealing with that context, but also the degree of intrusion into Convention rights, the nature of the right at issue and the extent (and type) of law reform necessary to rectify the alleged rights violation. So although the subject-matter of the case is relevant to the appropriate degree of deference, it is not determinative.

It should be conceded straight away that the distinction proposed here fails to provide us with a clear-cut method of identifying in advance which cases will be suitable for judicial decision-making and which will not. The allure of the seductive principle/policy distinction was that it purported to do this. But seduction and common sense do not necessarily go hand in hand. All too often, the attractions of the seducer are at best superficial and at worst, illusory. Such is the fate of the principle/policy distinction. It cannot deliver on its promise to provide us with a meaningful account of the appropriate division of labour between Parliament and the courts, partly because it exaggerates the differences between the subject-matter and decision-making processes appropriate to the judicial bodies on the one hand, and the elected branches on the other. In so doing, it distorts the extent to which *both* principle *and* policy have a role to play in both spheres. The distinction proposed here attempts to be faithful to the reality (and complexity) of the tasks facing the courts when they have to decide whether, and to what extent, to defer to the elected branches.

The more contextual approach entailed by this distinction can be illustrated by the House of Lords case of *Ghaidan v. Mendoza*.[95] Although there were precedents for substantial deference in the area of housing

---

[95] *Ghaidan*, above n. 37.

policy,[96] the House of Lords found in favour of the claimant. Whilst the court fully acknowledged that Parliament is charged with 'the primary responsibility for deciding the best way of dealing with social problems',[97] this did not mean that the court ought not to intervene. Even if a case arises in an area where 'Parliament has to hold a fair balance between the competing interests of tenant and landlords taking into account broad issues of social and economic policy', the existence of possible discrimination meant that the courts would 'scrutinise with intensity'[98] any reasons purporting to justify the apparently discriminatory regime.

Three points are worth noting about this decision. First, although the court was cognisant of, and sensitive to, the policy context in which Parliament enacted the legislation under scrutiny, this context did not preclude intense scrutiny by the courts of the justification for the policy. Second, we should note Lord Nicholl's use of the word 'primary' in his judgment in *Ghaidan*. Although Parliament is the primary decision-maker on matters of policy so that an assessment of its merits is *primarily* for Parliament, it is not *exclusively* so. We must remember that the courts have a legitimate reviewing role which requires them to make their own assessment of the legislative provision with reference to standards of legality. After all, if Parliament were the sole judge of all the advantages and disadvantages of legislative policy, this would completely emasculate the courts' reviewing role. Nor should it be assumed that simply because the courts may not have the competence to make the primary decision, they will *therefore* lack the competence to engage in (forthright) secondary review of that decision. In other words, even though we would not allocate to the courts the job of devising a comprehensive housing policy for the whole country, it does not necessarily follow that they are ill-suited to the task of reviewing part of an existing policy for compliance with legality, including the standards of Convention rights.

Finally, the court was certain that the legislation at issue in *Ghaidan* was discriminatory, especially since Strasbourg had clearly found that discrimination on grounds of sexual orientation fell within Article 14 read with Article 8.[99] Their confidence that there was a clear violation of rights led to less deference being paid to the primary decision-maker. So,

---

[96] Counsel for the defendant in *Ghaidan* relied on *Poplar Housing*, above n. 30, when arguing for a deferential judicial approach.

[97] *Ghaidan*, above n. 37 at [19].      [98] *Ibid.* at [19].

[99] The fact that the legislation was discriminatory was accepted without much discussion by all five members of the House of Lords, including Lord Millett who dissented on the issue of whether the discrimination could be removed by a section 3(1) interpretation, *ibid.* at [55]; see also Fenwick (2007), 282.

not only were they able to identify a *substantial* violation, they were also *certain* that a violation had occurred. As noted at the beginning of this chapter, there is an inverse relationship between deference and strength of a judge's conviction that the primary decision-maker has erred.[100] The more certain they are about a finding that a right has been violated, the less deferential they will tend to be. Alternatively, if it is a borderline case, where the arguments for and against the claimant's arguments are 'finely balanced',[101] this will tend to lead the courts to defer more substantially.

The approach adopted in *Ghaidan* can be contrasted with the approach of the Court of Appeal in *Poplar Housing*.[102] The question there was whether a summons for possession of a house under section 21 of the Housing Act 1988 on the ground that the tenant was 'intentionally home-less', violated Article 8. In making a decision that the claimant's rights were not violated, the Court of Appeal 'had regard' for the fact that Parliament had intended to give preference to the needs of those dependent on social housing as a whole, over those who were intentionally homeless. Lord Woolf decided to defer substantially to Parliament, which he justified as follows:

> The economic and other implications of any policy in this area are extremely complex and far-reaching. This is an area where, in our judg-ment, the courts must treat the decisions of Parliament as to what is in the public interest with particular deference. The limited role given to the court in s. 21(4) is a legislative policy decision. The correctness of this decision is more appropriate for Parliament than the courts.[103]

So it seemed as if Lord Woolf deferred to Parliament on grounds of superior expertise in matters of housing policy. This judgment has been criticised as exemplifying the crude subject-based approach to deference I have sought to reject.[104] Whilst *Poplar* is sometimes read as authority for the proposition that the courts should defer substantially in areas of complex policy, there are two factors influencing the decision (though not fully articulated in the reasoning of the court) which go against that reading. The first is that the court was uncertain about the consequences of giving the Housing Act a section 3 interpretation in favour of the claimant.[105] Uncertainty weighs in favour of more rather than less

[100] See Perry (1989) at 938, who argues that interference with the primary decision will only occur if the conviction rises above a certain epistemic threshold.

[101] *Farrakhan*, above n. 17 at [79].      [102] *Poplar Housing*, above n. 30.

[103] *Ibid.* at [69].      [104] Hunt (2003), 368.

[105] *Poplar Housing*, above n. 30 at [69]: 'There is certainly room for conflicting views as to the social desirability" of granting assured shorthold tenancies under s. 21(4) of the 1988 Act.'

deference. Second, a crucial factor tipping the scales in favour of substantial deference in this case, was the fact that the decision not to provide secure accommodation for people who were 'intentionally homeless', was a 'guiding principle' underlying the 1988 Act,[106] made in the context of an overarching and complex legislative plan to balance the competing demands for scarce social housing and against the backdrop of other elaborate legislation which, as noted by the Court of Appeal in *Poplar*, was in need of 'satisfactory review and consolidation'.[107] So, *Poplar* can be viewed as a case of deference on grounds of inferior law-making competence, not simply on grounds of inferior expertise in a complex area of social policy.[108] Understood in this way, one can see that it is not necessarily true that *Poplar* is guilty of succumbing to the errors of the crude subject-based approach.

### The argument from democratic legitimacy

The case law is replete with judicial *dicta* to the effect that the courts owe Parliament or the Executive some deference simply because they have superior democratic legitimacy to the courts.[109] The following *dictum* by Lord Woolf in *Lambert* is a good representative:

> Legislation is passed by a democratically elected Parliament *and therefore* the courts under the Convention are entitled to and should, as a matter of constitutional principle pay, a degree of deference to the view of Parliament as to what is in the interest of the public generally in upholding the rights of the individual under the Convention.[110]

The idea that substantial respect should be paid by the courts to the decisions of democratic assemblies and governments because of their

---

[106] *Ibid.* at [40].

[107] *Ibid.* at [33]. The complex nature of the legislative framework in the area of housing policy has frequently been noted by the courts, see *Kay*, above n. 22 at [53], *per* Lord Nicholls; see also Hale L.J. at [185].

[108] Thus, I would wish to clarify the claim made by Lord Bingham in *Kay* v. *Lambeth*, above n. 22 at [35] that *Poplar* is authority for the proposition that legislation will attract substantial deference 'if it is clear that the statutory scheme represents the democratic solution to the problems inherent in housing allocation'. It is not merely that the solution has had the imprimatur of democratic approval, but rather that the legislation in this area presented a complex array of interlinked provisions and pieces of legislation which represent various decisions about priority in scarce housing. The dangers of partial reform, so characteristic of the limited law reform possible in the courts, are especially acute in such an area.

[109] *Brown* v. *Stott*, above n. 31 at 703, *per* Lord Bingham, 842E–H, *per* Lord Steyn; *Lichniak*, above n. 36 at [14], *per* Lord Bingham.

[110] *R.* v. *Lambert* [2001] 2 W.L.R. 211 (CA) at [16], emphasis added; see also *Belmarsh Prison* case, above n. 21 at [39], *per* Lord Bingham.

superior democratic legitimacy, is often presented as an 'important but uncontroversial'[111] principle in the case law under the HRA. Jeffrey Jowell has sought to challenge this widely-held judicial view. He argues that whilst it is appropriate for the courts to show deference to Parliament or its agents on grounds of superior institutional competence and expertise, deference on grounds of superior democratic legitimacy is unacceptable.[112] He advances three arguments in favour of this proposition. First, if deference based on superior democratic legitimacy is accepted, the courts would be required to defer automatically, on constitutional grounds, on any occasion in which a qualified right was claimed to be limited by the public interest.[113] Second, the HRA has fundamentally altered the constitutional landscape in the UK so that 'the primacy of representative status and political accountability has been erased'.[114] The courts should not presume that elected branches are constitutionally best suited to decide a matter 'simply because of their representative character and the fact that they are politically accountable to the electorate'.[115] Finally, it would be an abdication of the court's constitutional responsibility to yield their decisions about the balance between rights and the public interest to the legislature or any other body.[116]

A number of responses can be made to these claims. First, it does not necessarily follow that if we accept superior democratic legitimacy as a factor justifying judicial deference, that the courts would therefore 'delegate'[117] all their decisions to the elected branches or 'accept the mere say-so'[118] of the elected branches. As noted earlier, deference is not an all-or-nothing matter; it is a matter of degree and will vary in accordance with the individual circumstances of the case. So, even if democratic legitimacy is accepted as a legitimate reason for judicial deference, it need not be determinative of the judicial decision in the way Jowell suggests. As Lord Bingham explained in *R. v. Lichniak*: 'the fact that a statutory provision represents the settled will of a democratic assembly is not a conclusive reason for upholding it, but a degree of deference is due to the judgments of the democratic assembly on how a social problem is best tackled'.[119] This point is driven home even more forcefully in

---

[111] *Sheldrake* v. *DPP* [2004] UKHL 43 at [23], *per* Lord Bingham; *Brown* v. *Stott*, above n. 31 at 703, 710–11.

[112] See Jowell (2003b), 596. Note that what Jowell refers to as 'institutional competence' includes both competence and expertise in the terminology used in my analysis.

[113] Jowell (2003a), 73.      [114] *Ibid.*, 75.      [115] *Ibid.*, 80.      [116] *Ibid.*

[117] Jowell (2003b), 598, (2003a), 80.      [118] Jowell (2003b), 594.

[119] *Lichniak*, above n. 36 at [14].

*R. (Countryside Alliance)* v. *Attorney General.*[120] In assessing whether there was a 'pressing need' for legislation banning fox-hunting and whether the ban was proportionate, Lord Bingham noted that:

> after intense debate a majority of the country's democratically elected representatives decided that there was a pressing need for the ban. It is of course true that the existence of duly enacted legislation does not conclude the issue . . . the degree of respect to be shown to the considered judgments of a democratic assembly will vary according to the subject matter and the circumstances.[121]

So, democratic legitimacy is not conclusive – it is just one factor weighed into the deference analysis.

Second, whilst it is certainly the case that the HRA has brought about significant changes in constitutional law, it seems hyperbolic to claim that it has 'erased'[122] the primacy of representative government and democratic accountability. That the UK courts now possess greater powers to protect rights than before, does not undermine the fact that the primary law-making powers still rest with the elected branches of government. These branches draw their legitimacy (in part) from the fact that they have been chosen by a majority of the adult population to represent them.[123] Simply put: the fact that the legislature is popularly elected and democratically accountable is one of its institutional features that warrants respect from the judiciary. The question is: *how much* respect is owed on this ground?

The worry motivating Jowell's analysis is that whilst competence and expertise will vary from case to case, the elected branches can *always* claim to have superior democratic legitimacy. Therefore, it would seem to follow that the courts will *always* have to pay deference – a worrying conclusion indeed, since this would lead to a judicial abdication of their proper reviewing function. How can we argue for deference on grounds of superior democratic legitimacy, but nonetheless prevent such an abdication? The answer is contained in the distinction adduced earlier between *minimal* and *substantial* deference. We can say that the democratic legitimacy of the elected branches of government is indeed one of the reasons why the courts owe the decisions of the elected branches deference, but that deference is only *minimal.* Our political system, being

---

[120] *R. (Countryside Alliance)* v. *Attorney General* [2007] 3 W.L.R. 922.
[121] *Ibid.* at [45].    [122] Jowell (2003a), 75.    [123] Feldman (2006).

a democratic one, necessarily values democratic legitimacy and allocates the primary law-making power to those who possess it. Therefore, *all* decisions made by those bodies are worthy of respect at least in this minimal sense. It applies independently of the merits of the legislative or Executive decision. This distinction may be lurking behind Lord Bingham's *dictum* in the *Belmarsh Prison* case that 'while any decision made by a representative democratic body must of course command respect, the degree of respect will be conditioned by the nature of the decision'.[124]

The question then is whether superior democratic legitimacy also warrants *substantial deference*? A justification for substantial deference on grounds of superior democratic legitimacy can be found in situations where judges believe that it is inappropriate for them to change the law on a particularly sensitive and controversial issue, because such a decision would have a greater chance of being accepted in society if it were introduced by the elected branches of government.[125] An example of such a situation is arguably provided by *M* v. *Secretary of State for Work and Pensions*.[126] The issue there was whether a child-support scheme which treated homosexual and heterosexual partnerships differently,[127] constituted a violation of Article 8 taken in conjunction with the prohibition on discrimination in Article 14. In rejecting this claim, Lord Bingham argued that the statutory scheme could not be stigmatised as unjustifiably discriminatory 'given the size of the overall task [of reforming the law] and the need to recruit the support of the public'.[128] He noted that 'even now there remain bodies of opinion in this country . . . for whom recognition [that difference in treatment of same-sex couples with reference to child support is discriminatory] is still a step too far'.[129] In the same case, Lord Mance observed that in times of 'changing social conditions and attitudes', the area of differences in child support for same-sex couples was one:

---

[124] *A and Others*, above n. 21 at [39].

[125] This was Lord Hoffmann's concern in *Rehman*, above n. 31 at [62]. It was also a concern underlying the House of Lords decision in *Countryside Alliance*, above n. 120, where Lord Bingham noted that 'the controversy surrounding the 2004 Act was protracted and remains acute', at [38] and that the recent legislation must be taken 'to reflect the conscience of a majority of the nation', at [45]. It seems as if concerns about the acutely controversial nature of this issue was a factor leading to judicial deference on grounds of superior democratic legitimacy.

[126] [2006] 2 A.C. 91.     [127] Pursuant to the Child Support Act 1991.

[128] [2006] 2 A.C. 91 at [6].     [129] *Ibid*.

in relation to which Parliament and the democratically elected government
should be recognised as enjoying a limited margin of discretion, regarding
the stage of development of social attitudes, when and how fast to act, how
far consultation was required and what form any appropriate legislative
changes should take.[130]

In these *dicta*, Lords Bingham and Mance are justifying judicial deference on the combined grounds of superior democratic legitimacy and
superior democratic competence. The idea that the task of 'recruiting'
public support is best carried out by the elected branches of government
is due, in part, to the resources and expertise available to the government.
Unlike the courts, the government is able to consult with those persons
or groups who are affected by the legal change and can promote and
publicise the proposed change by setting up advertising campaigns and
educational programmes in order to ensure that it has greater chances of
being accepted in society. Moreover, the elected branches have far greater
resources and capacity to ensure that there is an acceptable reconciliation
of competing social interests, when a matter is highly controversial.[131]
Often astute political judgment is required to establish when and how
law reform in controversial areas should be implemented.[132] Sometimes,
it is justified for the courts to acknowledge that they do not possess the
requisite attributes or legitimacy to make these decisions.

Beyond the institutional advantages of the legislature and Executive
which makes them 'better placed' to assess the appropriate method and
timing of controversial law reform, there is also the very fact of their superior democratic legitimacy which, depending on the circumstances, may
make reconciliation of competing social interests and eventual societal
acceptance of the legal change more likely.[133] This reason for deference

---

[130]  *Ibid.* at [153], [149].
[131]  On this point, see also Waite L.J. in *Fitzpatrick* [1998] Ch. 304 at 319 (CA) who noted
that the issue of whether housing law should give the same rights to same-sex couples
as are enjoyed by heterosexual couples is one where, 'opinions are bound to vary, and
a political judgment may in the end become necessary. That is what makes the process
of reconciliation a task better suited to the legislative function of Parliament than to the
interpretative role of the courts.' For the view that only the legislature is in a position to
'consult on, to explain, and to justify law-creation, where persons or groups interested in
or affected by it . . . in a way that can give the law creation a measure of moral, as well as
legal, authority, even in the eyes of its opponents', see Horder (2006), 78.
[132]  *Fitzpatrick, ibid., per* Waite L.J.
[133]  In his Maccabean Lecture in Jurisprudence, Lord Bingham hints at this when he comments
that a decision of the Supreme Judicial Court of Massachusetts legalising gay marriage
was 'a very significant social change to effect by judicial decision', see Bingham (2006), 22.
Although he does not claim that the decision was wrong, he suggests that 'it is perhaps

was explicitly countenanced by Lord Hoffmann in the famous postscript to his judgment in *Rehman* written post 9/11.[134] There, his Lordship observed that the judicial arm of government needed to respect the decisions of Ministers of the Crown on issues of national security not only because:

> the executive has access to special information and expertise in these matters. It is also that such decisions, with serious potential results for the community, require a legitimacy which can be conferred only by entrusting them to persons responsible to the community through the democratic process. If the people are to accept the consequences of such decisions, they must be made by persons whom the people have elected and whom they can remove.[135]

We will consider this decision in more detail when we examine deference in the context of national security in the next chapter. However, the following points about this case should be noted here. First, the argument from democratic legitimacy was not relied on in isolation. It was supplementary to the main argument on grounds of competence and expertise. The other four judges of the House of Lords supported the need for substantial deference to the Secretary of State without relying explicitly on the issue of superior democratic legitimacy. In general, they rested their conclusion on the argument that he was 'best placed' to judge what national security requires. So, even in *Rehman*, the argument from democracy was supplementary rather than determinative. Second, even if one endorses judicial deference on grounds of democratic legitimacy as a matter of principle, this does not necessarily entail the view that Lord Hoffmann correctly judged the role of democratic legitimacy in the circumstances of that case. As we will see in the next chapter, many of his other *dicta* in that case are problematic. The argument advanced here is that it may be legitimate, in some exceptional cases, for the courts to place weight on the fact of superior democratic legitimacy. They often say that the fact that a decision has been reached by a democratically elected legislature is, in itself, a reason why they should accord it respect. To be sure, judges would be shirking their responsibility to hold the legislature and Executive to the requirements of the rule of law, if they were to pay them substantial deference in a *routine* manner, *simply because* they

---

not hard to understand why it was seen, even if wrongly, as a usurpation by judges of authority that more properly belonged with the elected representatives of the people', see Bingham (2006), 23.

[134] Postscript written post 9/11.      [135] *Rehman*, above n. 31 at [62].

do not possess democratic legitimacy. My argument is that there may be *exceptional cases* where a particular law reform would cause widespread upheaval in society. In these cases, it may be that the democratic legitimacy of the elected branches of government is an advantage in securing support and consensus behind the change. As such, it would be a factor leading to a degree of judicial deference. The argument from democratic legitimacy goes a long way towards explaining the duty of *minimal deference*, but will feature in a much more subordinate and supplementary way in the question of whether substantial deference is warranted.

A final question is whether Parliament is entitled to more judicial deference than the Executive, since the latter does not have the same degree of democratic legitimacy as the former. This was suggested by Laws L.J. in the *Roth* case, where he claimed that 'greater deference is to be paid to an Act of Parliament than to a decision of the Executive or subordinate measure',[136] presumably on the basis that Parliament has a greater claim to democratic legitimacy than the Executive. This principle has not played a significant role in the case law. Moreover, a recent decision of the Court of Appeal suggests that Laws L.J. has reconsidered his position on this issue.[137] In any case, it does not seem to be a principle of general import. The reason is that the degree of deference in any particular case will be dependent on the overall context of the case, as determined by a number of different factors, such as e.g. the expertise of the primary decision-maker, the policy context in which the decision was reached, whether the court would be more or less likely to reach the right decision, which Convention right is involved and the extent of the alleged breach, and so on. Democratic legitimacy is one (often subordinate) factor in this overall assessment. If it were the only relevant factor, then it might be true to say that greater deference is to be paid to an Act of Parliament than to a decision of the Executive. But it is not the only relevant factor, often not even the most significant factor. Therefore, it is dubious as a general principle.

---

[136] *Roth*, above n. 14 at [71].

[137] In his judgment in *Huang* v. *SSHD* (CA) [2005] 3 W.L.R. 488 at [58], where Laws L.J. noted that 'In the present case the policy is given and the balance struck by the [Immigration] Rules and not by main legislation. But the balance so struck is not in our judgment entitled to less respect or deference on that account.' His Lordship does not explicitly address the tension between this *dictum* and the principle he enunciated in *Roth*, above n. 14.

## Deference for prudential reasons

Doctrines of deference are sometimes invoked by judges for what might be called prudential reasons.[138] Many judges argue (often in extrajudicial writings) that they have prudential reasons to adopt a cautious rather than an interventionist approach to adjudication. In the early days of the enactment of the HRA, such prudential concerns were prominent in the judiciary's self-portrayal of their role under the new Act. Thus, Lord Woolf argued extrajudicially that, given the extent of the change brought about by the HRA, a 'degree of conservatism' was in order: 'the objective should be to convince the legislature and the executive that the supervision of the courts is wholly constructive.'[139] Lord Bingham opined (again extrajudicially) that judges would pay due deference to the elected branches in HRA adjudication because 'to do so would certainly help to allay the fears of those who see incorporation as an objectionable judicial usurpation of democratic authority'.[140]

More generally, Lord Steyn has commented that judges should 'proceed with caution lest they undermine confidence in their judgments'.[141] This worry about adverse public reaction to their decisions, and a resulting diminution in respect for the courts, is echoed by Keene L.J. who claimed that a 'hostile public reaction to the courts overstepping their proper constitutional role' is an argument in favour of judicial restraint.[142] The desire of the courts to preserve their reputation as an impartial enforcer of the law is clearly a factor which influences judicial decision-making, as is the desire to avoid placing a strain on the court's resources.[143] In every jurisdiction, it is easy to find examples where courts

---

[138] Bickel believed that prudence (rather than principle) underpins judicial decisions to withhold judgment on the merits of a constitutional dispute, see Bickel (1962), at 49, 68, and 79.

[139] www.judiciary.gov.uk/publications_media/speeches/pre_2004/lcj100403.htm.

[140] Bingham (1998), 269–70. Similarly, it is sometimes suggested that the ECtHR is deferential to national governments out of fear that an adverse decision from the court would lead to the withdrawal of a state-party from the Convention see Marks (1995), 93; Jones (1995), 437. For some of the prudential reasons for deference adopted by the Strasbourg court, see Arai-Takahashi (2002), 99ff, 232ff.

[141] Steyn (2005a), 348; see also Hoffmann (2002), 139. It should be noted that prudential reasons for deference tend to be rooted in respect for the superior institutionally legitimacy of the elected branches and diffuse concerns about the legitimacy of judicial intervention. As such, they share the basic rationale of deference, namely, respect for the elected branches.

[142] Keene (2007), 210.

[143] For discussion of this reason for non-intervention, see Le Sueur (1995), 235ff.

demonstrate that they are not insensitive to the political responses to their actions.[144]

Reliance on prudential or strategic arguments such as these has tended to give judicial deference a bad name: it has led to claims that it is a self-denying ordinance that provides a cloak for excessive judicial timidity in the face of serious rights violations.[145] This, critics argue, is nothing short of 'an abdication by the court of its enforcement responsibilities'.[146] Furthermore, deferential decisions seem all the more objectionable because the courts sometimes conceal their prudential reasons for deferring, emphasising instead an aspect of the *substantive evaluation* that leads them to a judgment in favour of the elected branches. In fact, it is notable that whilst judges are often open about the prudential arguments in favour of deference in their extrajudicial writings, such candour is rarely reflected in their judicial decisions.

Let us deal with this objection about concealment first. It is certainly true that judges often tend to underplay the political considerations that affect their decisions. The politics of judicial decision-making are such that judges are often under considerable political pressure to make it seem as if the outcome of the case before them follows only from an assessment of the substantive legal issues involved and have nothing to do with broader political or ethical considerations. The indirect political pressure placed on judges militates against absolute candour in judicial reasoning. But it can also be self-defeating to make one's actual reasons for deference explicit. As noted at the beginning of this chapter, deference can be a way of *showing* or *manifesting* respect, and it would be counterproductive to make explicit the fact that it is only a matter of show. In other words, it would be pointless for judges to adopt a deferential decision and advance as the only reason in support of it that they wish to placate a hostile legislature. They can probably only achieve the aim of placating them, if they hand down a decision that *seems* genuinely respectful to Parliament's decision. Concealing their reservations about, or indeed outright disapproval of, a decision of the legislature may be the only way of preserving the rationale of deference.

Aside from this issue, many will find the prospect of judicial reliance on prudential reasons deeply objectionable on more substantive grounds. They will say that judges ought to confine themselves to the substantive evaluation involved in the case, and if this leads to an outcome

---

[144] For some American and Canadian examples of this phenomenon, see Tushnet (2003), 829–30.

[145] See e.g. Marks (1995), 76.    [146] See Jones (1995), 432.

unfavourable to the elected politicians, so be it. The courts should decide on the law and not get involved in prudential calculations about possible (political) consequences for them or anyone else. Their job is to enforce existing rights – the likely reaction of others is entirely irrelevant.[147] I do not agree with this argument because I believe that it relies on an unduly narrow conception of the judicial role. In my view, judges have not one but two general tasks when making their decisions: the first is to decide on the substantive merits of the individual case; the second (related) task is to make a decision on the extent and limits of their own institutional role. It would be irresponsible for judges to decide cases whilst remaining oblivious to the possible consequences of their decisions[148] and these include prudential concerns, such as whether a particular judicial decision would produce a backlash in society, whether society is ready for the legal change, whether it might be counterproductive to introduce it at this particular time or whether the legislature or government would then move to curtail the powers of the courts as a result.

Although judges have an obligation to do justice in the individual case, that is not their only obligation. They also need to ensure that the courts are respected both by the other branches of government and the general populace and that none of their decisions bring them into disrepute. Moreover, they need to understand the political context in which they operate. They are the weakest branch of government and are dependent on the other branches of government to respect and implement their decisions. Given this dependence, the continued power of the courts to make law and do justice in individual cases depends, in part, on not alienating the legislature and Executive and securing respect for their judgments in society as a whole. This is a reason in favour of restraint in judicial decision-making.[149] It means that institutional reasons can sometimes defeat substantive legal reasons in constitutional adjudication.

However, that is not to say that judges should kowtow to the elected branches whenever they issue a threat to curtail the powers of the courts or attempt to undermine their decisions. Judges must assess the seriousness of the threat, whether it is a matter of empty political posturing or,

---

[147] I take Trevor Allan to make a sophisticated version of this basic claim in Allan (2006b), 683, 688–9.

[148] As Lord Bingham pointed out (extrajudicially), the courts make their decisions 'in the light of legal principle and such authority as there is, *and having regard to the apprehended practical consequences of one decision as opposed to another*, what the law should be", see Bingham (1996/7), 16, emphasis added.

[149] See Hoffmann (2002), 140; see also *Duport Steel* [1980] 1 W.L.R. 142, *per* Lord Scarman.

alternatively, whether it is underpinned by a serious drive to change the law, whether it is made by the Prime Minister, or the leader of the Opposition whose popularity is waning, etc. Even if it is serious, this does not necessarily mean automatic or complete deference. It may simply mean that judges have to *present* their decisions in a deferential manner, even if they ultimately oppose the elected branches in the substance of their decision.[150] Or it may mean that judges should be strategic in their decision-making – they may consider it prudent to show a degree of deference in one case, in order to win themselves more freedom to do justice in future cases. Moreover, judges may be aware that their decisions will be supported by the public at large, even if it is irksome to the government of the day. This can embolden them to resist the political pressure to hand down deferential decisions. But it would be foolhardy for judges to be oblivious to any serious proposals to change the law in a significant way, in particular if it would reduce their powers. Just as they are concerned to do justice in the individual case, they must also be concerned with their more long-term ability to fulfil this role. This is not to say that prudential reasons are always of overriding importance. There are cases where the courts decide (rightly) to 'face down'[151] public criticism, or move more quickly than the pace of society and do justice in the instant case, despite (legitimate) worries about the feasibility of implementation.[152] It may be that the injustice is so heinous that the courts feel they have no other option, especially if there is no sign of reform coming from any other branch of government.

Finally, it should not be assumed that the 'prudential' reasons for deference outlined in this section are completely detached from more 'principled' or moral reasons. In fact, when judges assess the desirability of deference, the prudential and principled reasons in favour of it are deeply intertwined. For example, the argument that judges ought not to

---

[150] What I have in mind here are *obiter* judicial comments which emphasise a judicial acceptance that Parliament is the primary law-making body and that judges have a duty to respect Parliament's will, etc.

[151] This phrase is taken from a lecture given by Mr Justice Carney, the presiding judge of the Central Criminal Court in Ireland, who claimed that judges would 'face down any venom directed at them by the tabloid press' in order to ensure that the fairness of criminal trials was not threatened by abuse of the victim impact procedure, see www.ireland.com/newspaper/frontpage/2007/1011/1192007617048.html

[152] In the US context *Brown* v. *Board of Education of Topeka* 347 U.S. 483 (1954) is the classic example. However, the difficulty in implementing *Brown*, which lasted for decades, shows that the prudential and moral reasons in favour of postponing such a legal change can have tremendous force. See Marmor (2005), 162.

interfere with a legislative or Executive decision because of fear of a future legislative attack on their independence is partly based on institutional self-interest, but partly based on the (moral) concern to preserve the reputation of the courts and the laws they uphold, thus enhancing their ability to decide cases justly. A decision not to introduce a legal change because the courts believe that society is not ready for the change, or at least not ready for the change to be introduced *by them*, again presents a mixture of different types of reasons. The courts may not want to aggravate the legislature or go against the prevailing tide. But there may also be *good moral reason* not to introduce untimely change, for which the majority of people in society are not ready. It might be better (both for prudential and moral reasons) to postpone legal change until it would be better received and easier to implement. So prudential reasons and moral reasons are often deeply intertwined and mutually supportive.[153] This is not surprising. Judicial deference is part of the *institutional evaluation* judges must always undertake when they interpret legal texts. It engages concerns about the separation of powers and the relative role of institutions in the constitutional order, which is, at bottom, a matter of principle. Since these division-of-labour questions underlie the prudential reasons for deference, it follows that judges must act on the moral considerations which apply to these questions when considering whether they ought to defer.

## A contextual rather than a spatial approach

It should be abundantly clear by now that the analysis of deference presented here supports a variable and contextual approach to determining the constitutionally appropriate degree of deference in any particular case, and firmly rejects the idea that substantial judicial deference should be given to the elected branches in a routine or blanket fashion. Furthermore, the 'crude subject-based approach'[154] is also rejected here, since it entails the view that substantial deference is automatically owed in certain subject areas. The reasons for rejecting this approach also generate

---

[153] The fact that it is sometimes hard to divide judicial reasoning into moral and prudential reasons may go to support Raz's view that when we deliberate, we just consider which reasons are most pressing in a way that defies the common division of practical thought into moral and self-interested reasons. See Raz, (1999), 303. For some discussion of the implications of this insight for understanding the type of moral reasoning found in judicial decision-making, see Waldron (2008).

[154] Hunt (1997), 344ff.

substantial reservations about the idea that judicial deference should be understood or presented in terms of a 'discretionary area of judgment'. This is the idea, first given expression in the case law by Lord Hope in *Kebilene*,[155] that:

> in some circumstances it will be appropriate for the courts to recognise that there is an area of judgment within which the judiciary will defer, on democratic grounds, to the considered opinion of the elected body.[156]

This view attracted a number of supportive *dicta* in subsequent cases,[157] but has been subject to a trenchant and compelling critique by Murray Hunt.[158] As Hunt observes, the most obvious problem with the idea of the 'discretionary area of judgment' arises when we attempt to establish where the boundaries of the so-called discretionary area lie. Lord Hope suggested that it will be:

> easier for it to be recognised where the issues involve questions of social or economic policy, much less so if the rights are of high constitutional importance or of a kind where the courts are especially well-placed to assess the need for protection.[159]

But, as we know from the case law, questions involving rights of high constitutional importance (such as the right to a fair trial, the right to non-discrimination, etc.) frequently arise, perhaps even typically arise, in cases which involve questions of social or economic policy.[160] So, one cannot demarcate an 'area' where deference is appropriate in this way, because many cases contain an overlap of subject-matter. In cases where this overlap in subject-matter has occurred, the courts have tended to decide whether the questions of policy involved in the case are such that they warrant a substantial degree of deference. So, for example, in *Roth* Jonathan Parker L.J. was alive to the fact that the case involved questions of social and economic policy (arising at it did in the context of legislation to regulations to control illegal immigration) *and* issues 'of a kind where the courts are especially well-placed to assess the need for protection (issues

---

[155] *Kebilene* [2000] 2 A.C. 326.    [156] *Ibid.* at 380G.

[157] See e.g. *Roth*, above n. 14 at [69]–[79], *per* Laws L.J.; *Pearson and Martinez*, above n. 19 at [20], *per* Kennedy L.J.; *Lambert* (CA), above n. 110 at 1022E, *per* Lord Woolf (though it was not relied on in House of Lords judgments); *R. (Samaroo)* v. *SSHD* [2001] UKHRR 1139 at [29], [35]; *R. (Mahmood)* v. *SSHD* [2001] 1 W.L.R. 840 at [38], *per* Lord Phillips; *Huang* (CA), above n. 137 at [48], *per* Laws L.J.; *Kay* v. *Lambert*, above n. 22 at [77], *per* Lord Hope.

[158] Hunt (2003), 337–70.

[159] *Kebilene*, above n. 155 at 380G.    [160] This point has also made by Hunt (2003), 347.

related to a fair trial)'.[161] His Lordship decided that the importance of the social issues raised in the case, as well as the need to balance the interests of the accused, the victim and society, meant that the discretionary area of judgment should be regarded as being 'as wide as possible in this case'.[162] But what did the work here was not the accurate identification of 'an area' within which this case fell, but rather an assessment of the weight to be attached to the subject-matter with which Parliament had to deal in the overall context of the other pertinent (and possibly countervailing) factors relevant in making this determination.[163] In other words, the sort of institutional evaluation required by the deference enquiry is not avoided by the idea of a 'discretionary area'. To the extent that talk of a discretionary area of judgment suggests that such a demarcation is possible, it is misleading. It succumbs to the error of the 'crude subject-based approach' to deference and, as such, ought to be rejected.

There is another problem with presenting deference in terms of whether an issue 'falls within' Parliament's or the Executive's discretionary area of the judgment. This is that it can lead to the conflation of two separate issues. One is whether Parliament or the Executive have the expertise or (discretionary) authority to make the primary decision in this area. The second concerns the standard of scrutiny which should be adopted by the courts and whether there are particular aspects of this decision which warrant judicial deference, and to what degree. In other words, it can lead to the (false) assumption that where the primary decision-maker has authority to exercise discretion, deference by the secondary decision-maker is *therefore* required.[164] As we saw in relation to the examination of the role of deference in *Ghaidan*, simply because the courts may not have the expertise or competence to make the primary decision, should not lead the courts to assume automatically that they will therefore lack the

---

[161] *Roth*, above n. 14 at 139. See also *Re P* [2008] UKHL 38 at [48].

[162] However, despite according to Parliament the highest degree of deference in devising ways of tackling 'an extremely serious social problem' at [191], *per* Simon Brown L.J., it was held by the Court of Appeal that the scheme was so unfair that it constituted a breach of Article 6.

[163] As Jowell (2003b), 599, points out, there is no 'magic legal or other formulae to identify the discretionary area of judgment'. See also *Wilson*, above n. 35 at [70], *per* Lord Nicholls, who indicated that the subject-matter of the legislation or executive decision is only one of a number of factors which can influence the degree of deference.

[164] This assumption seems to be made by Lord Phillips in *Farrakhan*, above n. 17 at [71], where he instances as a factor in favour of according to the Secretary of State 'a particularly wide measure of discretion', the fact that it was a personal decision of the Secretary of State which was not subject to appeal. This indicated to Lord Phillips that the decision should be subjected to a less rigorous scrutiny under the province of judicial review: [74].

expertise or legitimacy to make the secondary decision, when reviewing it for legality.

This sort of error seems to be made by Lord Hope in his judgment in *R. v. A.*[165] There, his Lordship contended that 'the essential question in this case was whether Parliament acted within its discretionary area of judgment when it was choosing the point of balance [between the defendant's right to a fair trial and the complainants right not to be unduly harassed in the witness box]'.[166] Lord Hope believed that the legislation fell within the 'discretionary area' because it was one where 'Parliament was better equipped than the judges to decide where the balance lay ...'[167] Similarly, in *Kay* v. *Lambert* his Lordship noted that 'the issues addressed by this legislation [on housing policy] involve questions of social and economic policy where the choices that are to be made can easily be seen as falling within the discretionary area of judgment best left to the considered opinion of the legislature'.[168] The analysis underlying these *dicta* seems to elide two separate issues. One is whether Parliament has discretion to make the primary decision. The other is whether the review of their decision for legality by the courts should be subject to a less intrusive standard of review. This confusion is encouraged by the problematic idea of the discretionary area of judgment. The spatial metaphor obscures the fact that the real (and complex) question for the courts is whether the particular choice made by the legislature was compliant with Convention rights, and the intensity of review to be applied to that question.[169]

One judge who tends to rely heavily on the spatial metaphor in his judicial reasoning is Laws L.J. It is worth attending to his views since his dissenting judgment in *Roth* provides one of the most comprehensive judicial attempts to delineate the scope of the judicial duty of deference under the HRA. In so doing, his Lordship enunciated four principles which he deduced from the case law:[170] first, greater deference will be paid to Acts of Parliament than decisions of the Executive or subordinate measures; second, there is more scope for deference where the right

---

[165] *R. v. A (No. 2)* [2002] 1 A.C. 45.     [166] *Ibid.* at 73.     [167] *Ibid.* at 83–4.

[168] *Kay* v. *Lambert*, above n. 22 at [77].

[169] This criticism is also levelled at the application of the margin of appreciation doctrine by the ECtHR, see Schokkenbroek (1998), 32 who emphasises that it is important to keep distinct the discretion states have in implementing the Convention on the one hand, and the issue of judicial self-restraint in reviewing the choices that state has made on the other.

[170] *Roth*, above n. 14 at [83]–[86].

at stake is qualified rather than absolute; third, greater deference will
be due when the subject-matter is within the constitutional responsibility of the democratic powers; and fourth, greater or lesser deference
will be due according to whether the subject-matter lies more readily
within the actual or potential expertise of the democratic powers or
the courts. Applying these principles to the case at hand, he held that
the method of immigration control placed on hauliers entering the UK
was 'obviously far more within the competence of government than the
courts'.[171]

We have already considered, and cast doubt on, the cogency of the first
principle enunciated by Laws L.J. In fact, in his recent judgment in *Huang*,
he seems to renounce it altogether.[172] We will come to consider, and cast
doubt on, the plausibility of the second principle when we discuss the
distinction between qualified and unqualified rights in chapter 9. What
remains are his third and fourth principles about whether the subject-
matter of a case lies within the constitutional responsibility or the expertise
of the courts, or alternatively is a subject-matter more appropriate for
Parliament. Although Laws L.J. uses the expression 'the discretionary
area of judgment', he also acknowledges the context-dependent nature
of the deference enquiry and the fact that it is a matter of degree.[173]
However, his thinking about this issue, and his enunciation of the relevant
principles, is clearly dominated by the spatial metaphor and I believe
that he succumbs to the confusions to which this metaphor gives rise.
Laws L.J. sees deference in explicitly territorial terms:[174] the strength
of review is determined by whether a case falls within the 'territory of
rights'.[175] He contrasts the Executive's special responsibility for the defence
of the realm, and the special responsibility of the courts in upholding
the rule of law.[176] As Murray Hunt pointed out, 'a more transcendent
responsibility it is hard to imagine'.[177] One only has to look at the *Belmarsh
Prison* case to realise that this distinction is not helpful in demarcating
the proper constitutional role for the courts. There, the challenge for the
courts was to hold the Executive and Parliament to the demands of the rule
of law, in the context of measures adopted in defence of the realm, which
seemed to violate the rule of law. That the courts rose to the challenge in
that case is due, in no small part, to the fact that they did not adopt the
crude subject-based approach to deference, as was pleaded by the Attorney

---

[171] *Ibid.* at [87], [109].      [172] *Huang* (CA), above n. 137 at [58], *per* Laws L.J.
[173] *Roth*, above n. 14 at [77].      [174] *Ibid.* at [72], [77], [91].      [175] *Ibid.* at [72].
[176] *Ibid.* at [83].      [177] Hunt (2003), 360.

General on behalf of the Government.[178] Laws L.J. has perpetuated his territorial analysis in his recent Court of Appeal judgment in *Huang*, this time linking it explicitly to the principle/policy distinction.[179] Neither the distinction, nor the analysis on which it was based, was followed in the House of Lords decision in that case.

The question of whether judicial deference should be presented in terms of variable degrees of presumptive weight on the one hand or as a 'discretionary area of judgment' on the other, is not just 'a matter of semantics'.[180] It is a matter of great consequence because it affects our thinking about the constitutionally appropriate degree of restraint appropriate in individual cases. In an extrajudicial analysis of deference, Lord Steyn refused to make a choice between 'due deference' or the 'discretionary area of judgment' on the ground that this was a terminological issue, which ought not to 'fetter our substantive thinking'.[181] But the problem is that terminology and language *does* fetter our substantive thinking. An analysis of the case law shows that those judges who rely on the spatial metaphor tend to adopt a highly deferential approach, whereas a more contextual approach acknowledging the variability of the doctrine may have produced a better outcome. As Murray Hunt observed, it is unsurprising that Laws L.J.'s analysis in *Roth* led him to a conclusion which was 'striking in its submissiveness to Parliament and the Executive'.[182] In subsequent comments and in his judicial decision-making, Lord Steyn has in fact preferred to express the issue simply in terms of 'deference' and has eschewed the phrase 'discretionary area of judgment'. He accepted that the latter has 'overtones of a decision beyond the reach of judicial review'.[183] In *Huang*, the House of Lords noted the issues surrounding deference, the discretionary area of judgment, its relation to non-justiciability, the rationale of deference, the

---

[178] The House of Lords' rejection of the Attorney General's argument that national security issues should be non-justiciable was described by Lord Steyn extrajudicially as the 'most eloquent and magisterial judicial rebukes to an Attorney-General since Lord Denning in *Gouriet v. Union of Post Office Workers* [1977] QB 729 admonished the Attorney General to bear in mind . . . "Be you ever so high, the law is above you"', see Steyn (2005b), 350.

[179] *Huang* (CA), above n. 137 at [55] where Laws L.J. describes individual fundamental rights as 'the particular territory of the courts' and policy as 'the particular territory of the elected powers in the state'.

[180] Lester and Pannick (2004), 95.

[181] Steyn (2005a), 346ff saying that he was 'reluctant to enter into an argument about labels. It ought not to fetter our substantive thinking.'

[182] Hunt (2003), 358. See also Klug (2003), 130, who argues that Laws L.J.'s suggestion in *Roth* that deference in some areas is 'nearly absolute' is not supported by the terms and scheme of the HRA.

[183] Steyn (2004a), 255.

margin of appreciation are complex issues, which are often presented in a confusing way.[184] Given the enormous constitutional importance of these issues (as well as their complexity), we need to separate out the various elements, and clarify their nature and their interrelationship, using the most accurate and helpful terminology we can.

I have sought to emphasise the deeply contextual nature of the judicial evaluation of whether deference is appropriate and expose the perils of the crude subject-based approach. As we have seen, both conceptually and in its practical application in the case law, the idea of the 'discretionary area of judgment' has not helped to clarify these important points. In fact, there is plenty of evidence to support Murray Hunt's belief that it has hindered the proper development of the law in this area. We should be vigilant to ensure that the courts should not abdicate their proper reviewing powers, whilst nonetheless acknowledging their responsibility to exercise a 'constitutionally appropriate degree of restraint'.[185] The language we use to express this complex and multi-faceted judicial duty is crucial in establishing a clear and accurate understanding of its nature and rationale.

This brings us to a final clarification about the precise relationship between the doctrine of the 'margin of appreciation' adopted by the Strasbourg organs when applying the ECHR and the idea of a 'discretionary area of judgment' in domestic jurisprudence. Such clarification is necessary, because the case law relying on the 'discretionary area' tends to suggest that whilst the margin of appreciation has no direct application for national courts in adjudicating under the HRA, the UK courts should nonetheless recognise 'an analogous doctrine'.[186] Following the initial presentation of these issues in Lester and Pannick's influential textbook, the discretionary area of judgment is often thought of as the 'domestic counterpart of a state's margin of appreciation',[187] despite the fact that the margin of appreciation is said to have 'no application' in domestic law.[188] This has caused some confusion about the precise relationship

---

[184] *Huang,* above n. 48 at [14].      [185] Palmer (2007), 127.

[186] Following Lester and Pannick's first edition of their book (2000), 74. In this edition, the doctrine of the discretionary area of judgment is introduced in a section entitled 'Why the Doctrine of Margin of Appreciation has no Application in the Present Context'. This title was dropped in the second edition, see further Palmer (2007), 127.

[187] *Ghaidan,* above n. 37 at [21], *per* Lord Nicholls. Murray Hunt argues that the discretionary area of judgment 'has now effectively become the direct domestic equivalent of the Strasberg doctrine of the margin of appreciation', Hunt (2003), 349; see also Woolf (2003), 260.

[188] For a theoretical analysis of the 'margin of appreciation', see Letsas (2006).

between the two doctrines. Are they entirely separate or are they separate but 'analogous'? If so, what is that analogy?

The margin of appreciation is a doctrine of judicial self-restraint adopted by the Strasbourg court. It governs the extent to which, or the intensity with which, the Strasbourg court will scrutinise a decision made by a signatory state to the Convention.[189] Despite a widely held view to the contrary,[190] the margin of appreciation is not different *conceptually* or *logically* from the doctrine of deference as applied in domestic courts.[191] The structure of deference outlined in this chapter applies equally to both. Where deference and the margin of appreciation differ is in the *reasons* for deferring: supranational courts may have additional reasons to be reluctant to interfere with the decisions of national authorities – reasons which will not tend to domestic courts.[192] However, this ought not to obscure the fact that the structure and rationale of both ideas is the same.[193] Second, the term 'margin of appreciation' is a direct and unfortunately unidiomatic translation of the term used in French administrative law '*marge d'appréciation*'.[194] It refers to the latitude or leeway which States are permitted in their observance of the Convention.[195] Clearly, the idea of the 'discretionary area of judgment' owes a lot to the spatial metaphor of the 'margin of appreciation'. With both doctrines, the domestic and Strasbourg courts ask whether the subject-matter 'falls within' the margin or discretionary area and whether the margin or area should be 'wide' or 'narrow' in the instant case. The objections raised earlier to judicial reliance on the spatial metaphor apply with equal force to the doctrine of the margin of appreciation. It is merely a shorthand for the factors

---

[189] Jones (1995), 431; Mahoney (1990), 78.

[190] See e.g. Tierney (2005), 670: '[deference] is widely held to be a very different animal from the discretionary area of judgment'; see also Pannick (1998), 545.

[191] Sometimes the terminology of allowing a 'margin of discretion' has been used in UK courts, see e.g. *Samaroo*, above n. 157 at [36]; *Mahmood*, above n. 157 at [32], *per* Laws L.J.

[192] So, for example, the Strasbourg court has placed great emphasis on the fact that the Convention leaves it to each state-party in the first instance to secure the rights and freedoms it enshrined and that the role of the supranational courts is a subsidiary one, see Schokkenbroek (1998), 31; Jones (1995), 436. This concern about subsidiarity does not apply to the domestic courts.

[193] That the same idea underpins both the domestic doctrine of deference and the margin of appreciation is pointed out by other commentators: see Hunt (2003), 345; Jones (1995), 432.

[194] Arai-Takahashi (2002), 2; see also Sedley (2002), 18 who describes the margin of appreciation as 'a piece of translationese but a deadly legal device.'

[195] Jones (1995), 431; Arai-Takahashi (2002), 2; Marks (1995), 73.

which determine the intensity of review appropriate in an individual case. Indeed, it has been recommended that the Strasbourg jurisprudence would be improved, if the court were to articulate its judgments 'directly in terms of levels of scrutiny and factors determining the appropriate level of scrutiny, not indirectly in margin-of-appreciation terms'.[196] Since these spatial metaphors do not help to clarify the appropriate boundaries of legitimate judicial decision-making, and in fact cause much unnecessary confusion, we should disregard them for the purposes of analysis.

## Conclusion

It has been argued here that judges owe a degree of deference to the legislature and Executive as a matter of constitutional principle, but also for prudential or pragmatic reasons. The primary constitutional principle involved is that of inter-institutional comity. Deference requires judges to be aware of their institutional limitations and to ensure that they make the decisions to which they are best suited, but leave others to Parliament or the Executive. Sometimes judges are criticised for being too timid and asserting themselves too little against a powerful Executive or Parliament. Supine decisions give deference a bad name. They create the impression that judicial deference is to be equated with excessive or ill-placed deference.

It follows from my analysis that judicial deference is not necessarily an evasion of the judicial responsibility to uphold rights. It is only an abdication if it is excessive or is paid to elected bodies for no good reason, but it can be a virtue (what Alexander Bickel famously referred to as one of the 'passive virtues'[197]) if it is used in the context of a case where it is warranted. To be sure, sometimes standing up against the pressure exerted either by popular opinion or the actions and words of a hostile legislature requires judicial courage, and in a case where judges have the expertise to make the decision, and the justice of the case so demands and they are confident that their decision is correct, it is a weak and timid court which capitulates to those pressures. However, there are also cases where the best and most responsible judicial decision is one which is more deferential. The difficult task for the courts is to assess when deference is truly due, and when it is not. Part of that task is not to be seduced into denying their own competence and legitimacy in cases involving 'national security' or 'matters of policy'. This will be the focus of

---

[196] Schokkenbroek (1998), 36.  [197] Bickel (1961), 40.

discussion in the next chapter. Many people now argue that the HRA has ushered in a 'culture of justification'.[198] This means that there is a greater onus on the elected branches of government to justify their decisions in light of human rights concerns. The judiciary has an important role in insisting on such justifications – an insistence which is not denied by a proper understanding of the requirements of deference.

[198]  Hunt (2003), 340; Dyzenhaus (1997), 286.

# 8

# Deference in particular contexts

## Introduction

The previous chapter presented an account of the nature of deference and how it functions in judicial reasoning. The purpose of this chapter is to examine how the doctrine of deference has been applied in two particular contexts: cases involving national security and cases with resource implications. As Lord Walker pointed out in the *Belmarsh Prison* case:

> Safeguarding national security is (with the possible exception of some questions of macroeconomic policy and allocation of resources) the area of policy in which the courts are most reluctant to question or interfere with the judgment of the executive or (*a fortiori*) the enacted will of the legislature.[1]

Given that these contexts have produced some of the most notable (and perhaps notorious) cases concerning deference, closer consideration of them will help to elucidate the nature and possible dangers of the doctrine. Finally, since the desirability of judicial deference relates to the proper distribution of power between courts and Parliament, it is clearly relevant to the judicial choice between section 3 and section 4. This will be the subject of the final section.

## Deference and national security

We have seen that the subject-matter of the legislation under scrutiny is one of the factors judges take into account when deciding whether to defer to Parliament or the Executive, but it is not, in itself, a conclusive reason in favour of deferring. However, substantial, if not complete, deference has been the hallmark of judicial reasoning in the area of national security.[2] Historically, the very words 'national security' seemed to acquire 'an

---

[1] *A and Others* [2005] 2 W.L.R. 87 at [192] (hereinafter *A* or *Belmarsh Prison*).
[2] *Ibid.* at [192], *per* Lord Walker; see also Dyzenhaus (2004), 246, 259; Waldron (2003), 191.

almost mystical significance whereby the mere incantation of the phrase of itself instantly discourages the court from satisfactorily fulfilling its normal role of deciding where the balance of public interest lies'.[3] In recent years (and particularly post-HRA), the courts have shown themselves to be less awestruck by 'the mantra of national security'[4] and more ready to scrutinise the weight of claims made by the Executive under this heading. At the very least, there is now widespread judicial support for the view that national security is not non-justiciable.[5] However, there is still no denying that this is an area where substantial deference is the order of the day, with judges according the views of the Executive and Parliament 'great weight'.[6]

National security issues present the courts with a dilemma. On the one hand, judges have a constitutional mandate to ensure that decisions made by the legislature and Executive comply with the rule of law and with Convention rights. On the other, they have to acknowledge the peculiar expertise and legitimacy of the elected branches in making decisions in this area and therefore owe them substantial deference. In light of this dilemma, there are three main reasons why decisions made in the national security area tend to attract substantial deference from the courts.[7] First, when issues of national security are involved, the Executive often claims that some of the information on which their decisions are based must be kept secret.[8] The dilemma described above is heightened by the secrecy that attends many questions of national security.[9] Clearly, if a court, in carrying out its reviewing role, does not have access to all the information on which the primary decision was based, this fact alone will (quite rightly) lead it to pay more deference to the primary decision-maker, because it will be less confident that it could arrive at a better decision than the primary decision-maker. As was explained in chapter 7, deference is a rational response to uncertainty, and uncertainty will be heightened in

---

[3] Simon Brown (1994), 589; Tribe (2001), 18; Bonner (2007), 350.

[4] Simon Brown (1994), 590; Barak (2002), 157–8.

[5] *Secretary of State for the Home Department* v. *Rehman* [2002] 1 All E.R. 123 at [31], *per* Lord Steyn.

[6] *Ibid.* at [31]; see also *A*, above n. 1 at [112], *per* Lord Hope.

[7] In formulating these reasons, I benefited greatly from a talk given by Conor Gearty to the *Annual Political Theory Conference* in Oxford, January 2004.

[8] Thus, in *A*, above n. 1 at [117], where Lord Hope pointed out that the higher courts were not invited by the Attorney General to look at the closed material relevant to the case, see also at [27] Lord Bingham, [94] Lord Hoffmann.

[9] *Ibid.* at [193], *per* Lord Walker. This point about uncertainty in national security cases is also made in Poole (2008). See also Kavanagh (2008), 208ff.

a case where secrecy surrounds some of the relevant facts. The courts have no other choice but to be deferential in such a situation and to give the legislature and/or Executive the benefit of any doubts they may have either about the Executive decision itself or the intelligence on which it is based. Without access to independent sources of information or their own intelligence service, it is very difficult for the courts to challenge Executive decisions on a sure footing when they are not in possession of the information leading to the decision.[10]

Second, judges' awareness of the life and death consequences of some decisions made in the national security area will cause them to 'err, if at all, on the side of safety'.[11] The courts are aware that they could get the decision wrong, and are ever mindful of the possibly catastrophic consequences of such an error. This worry about the consequences of error in this area was made explicit in the judgment of the Special Immigration Appeals Commission (hereinafter SIAC): it stated that where there is a 'risk of destruction and mayhem on a very substantial scale, those responsible for deciding whether the risk exists and what measures are necessary to try and ensure that it is not translated into a reality must be allowed a reasonably wide margin of discretion'.[12] Judicial awareness of their limitations is therefore especially acute in the area of national security. The chances that a court would 'second-guess' some national security decisions, under these conditions of inadequate information and fear of error, are slim. Third, many decisions made in the national security area are anticipatory. They are based on factual predictions of what people might or might not do – they often involve risk assessments about possible future events. Especially when courts are prevented from seeing the intelligence on which such predictions are based, they are not well placed to challenge them.

These three reasons for deference in the national security area (uncertainty, fear of drastic consequences and the role of risk analysis) are

---

[10] Of course, this is not a knockdown argument in favour of substantial judicial deference. Rather, it could ground an argument in favour of imaginative institutional design so that specialist courts could be set up with expertise in national security matters, equipped to deal with confidential and sensitive security information. My point is simply that *if* courts are not in possession of the information on which the primary decision was based, (which, as things stand, they often are not), substantial deference may be the appropriate judicial response, see further Dyzenhaus (2007), 146ff.

[11] *A*, above n. 1 at [29], *per* Lord Bingham.

[12] The SIAC was established by the Special Immigration Appeals Commission Act 1997. For comment on SIAC's decision *A* v. *Secretary of State*, above n. 1, see Mark Elliott (2003), 339.

illustrated by the House of Lords decision in *R. (Gillan) v. Metropolitan Police Commissioner.*[13] The issue in *Gillan* was whether police powers to stop and search for articles connected to terrorism under sections 44–46 of the Terrorism Act 2000 violated Articles 5, 8, 10 and 11 of the European Convention. Despite the fact that these police powers could be exercised without the normal need for reasonable suspicion, the House of Lords nonetheless held that they did not constitute a disproportionate interference with Convention rights, partly on the basis that the legislation contained multiple safeguards and limitations.[14]

In assessing proportionality, the court had to establish whether the stop-and-search powers were a proportionate response to the Government's aim of seeking to counter the 'great danger of terrorism'. Lord Scott left no doubt about how restricted the courts were in challenging the plausibility of these claims in the context of that case. His Lordship explained that the problem with the claimants' challenge was that:

> an assessment of the reasonableness of the [legislative] response requires an assessment of the degree of seriousness of the terrorist threat to which the authorisation was a response. The latter assessment *will in most cases require some knowledge of the intelligence material* on which the police and the Home Secretary relied when making their own assessment of that threat and of what should be done in response to it.[15]

But since the court was not privy to all the intelligence information, it was labouring under uncertainty about the basis on which the decision was based, as well as uncertainty about the nature and severity of the threat. His Lordship concluded:

> In that state of the evidence the Divisional Court could not reasonably have concluded that the authorisation was a disproportionate response to the threat of terrorist activity in London appearing from the available intelligence material. Nor could the Court of Appeal and nor, in my opinion, can your Lordships. What the position would have been had the underlying intelligence material being reviewed it is impossible to tell.[16]

This case is just one amongst many which shows that when the courts are prevented from seeing intelligence evidence, substantial deference is often the only rational response. Combined with fear about the drastic

---

[13] [2006] 2 A.C. 307.

[14] For a list of the eleven constraints placed on the exercise of the power, see *Gillan, ibid.* at [14], *per* Lord Bingham.

[15] *Ibid.* at [62], emphasis added.    [16] *Ibid.* at [64].

consequences of getting it wrong and the anticipatory nature of the primary decision, it explains why deference is so common (and, however regretfully, justified) in national security cases.

It might be thought that the three reasons outlined above contradict the point made in chapter 7 that there should be no pre-determined subject-areas in which deference automatically applies. Surely cases involving national security are beyond judges' competence, expertise, and legitimacy, and should attract substantial deference across the board? This conclusion is too rash. The three grounds of deference outlined earlier go to explain why substantial deference is *sometimes* warranted in the national security area. But this is a far cry from saying that judges should *always* defer, and *never* have a useful role to play in adjudicating national security issues. Cases involving 'national security' cover a large variety of decisions, some of which may be beyond the expertise or competence of the court to challenge, some of which may not. The nature of the decision (its gravity, urgency and sensitivity, as well as the extent to which it impacts on human rights) determines the *degree* of deference which may be appropriate.[17] This can be illustrated by the House of Lords decision in *A* v. *Secretary of State for the Home Department*. Known as the 'Belmarsh Prison' case, it was described in the House of Lords as 'one of the most important cases which the House has had to decide in recent years'.[18]

There, nine people detained in Belmarsh Prison under section 23 of the Anti-Terrorism, Crime and Security Act 2001 claimed that this section violated Articles 5 and 14 ECHR. Section 23 contained the power to detain indefinitely non-nationals in circumstances where they had been determined by the Secretary of State to be a security risk but could not be deported. When enacting this provision, the Government derogated from Article 5 of the Convention, which precluded indefinite detention. The detainees had two main arguments. The first was that there was no emergency 'threatening the life of the nation' as required by Article 15 of the Convention to justify a derogation. Second, even if there were such an emergency, the decision to detain indefinitely non-nationals without trial was not 'strictly required by the exigencies of the situation' as required by Article 15. The central issue in the case concerned the appropriate standard or intensity of review with which the court should assess these

---

[17] For discussion of the 'differential character of issues for which the shield of national security may be claimed', see Feldman (1999b), 133.

[18] *A*, above n. 1 at [219], *per* Baroness Hale, [86], *per* Lord Hoffmann. For further analysis of this case, see Dyzenhaus (2007); Elliott (2007b), 7ff.

two questions. Acting on behalf of the Secretary of State, the Attorney General argued that it was for Parliament and the Executive to assess the threat facing the nation, as well as for those bodies (and not the courts) to judge the response necessary to protect the security of the public. The elected branches of government were entitled to a wide margin of appreciation on both questions, especially as they were matters of national security and the courts must accept that such matters fell within the discretionary area of judgment belonging to the democratic organs of the state. In short, the Attorney General's argument was that both issues were essentially non-justiciable.

This argument was given short shrift in the House of Lords. For the most part, the reasoning of the court supports the account of deference defended in chapter 7. First, their Lordships made clear that although substantial deference may be appropriate in matters of national security, complete deference was not. Even on the question of whether the derogation was justified, the court warned that deference 'cannot be taken too far. Deference does not mean abasement to [the views of government or Parliament], even in matters of national security.'[19] Although the decisions and views of the legislature and Executive may be worthy of respect and should therefore be given great weight in this area, deference did not mean that the court was disabled from assessing the merits of the decisions.[20] Second, the court emphasised that since 'national security' can sometimes be used as a pretext for bringing in measures that are not objectively justified, the judiciary must be vigilant to scrutinise those measures to check whether they are strictly required in the exigencies of the situation.[21] In other words, the doctrine of judicial deference did not preclude the court from subjecting decisions about national security to rigorous scrutiny.[22] Deference was not to be equated with an uncritical review or indeed with non-justiciability.

Third, Lord Bingham clarified that whilst 'any decision made by a representative democratic body must of course command respect, the degree of respect will be conditioned by the nature of the decision'.[23] Although both the derogation and the discrimination issue were reviewed on proportionality grounds,[24] their Lordships paid more deference to the Executive and Parliament on the question of the justifiability of the derogation, than on

---

[19] *Ibid.* at [176], *per* Lord Rodgers; [41], *per* Lord Bingham.

[20] See also Fenwick (2007), 283, 287.

[21] *A*, above n. 1 at [177], *per* Lord Rodger; [226], *per* Baroness Hale; [108], *per* Lord Hope; [41], *per* Lord Bingham.

[22] *Ibid.* at [42], *per* Lord Bingham.    [23] *Ibid.* at [39].    [24] *Ibid.* at [42].

the question of whether the particular means chosen by them to meet the state of emergency. The court accepted that the question of whether there is an emergency and whether it threatens the life of the nation are 'pre-eminently a matter for the executive and for Parliament. The judgment that has to be formed on these issues is outside the expertise of the courts.'[25] The different character of the derogation issue warranted more deference.[26]

It is worth noting that the court did not see some 'closed material' related to the decision to derogate and decided to defer to the judgment of the Special Immigration Appeals Commission, which had seen this material and had concluded that there was a public emergency threatening the life of the nation. Although Lord Scott expressed 'very great doubt'[27] about whether the public emergency was one that justified the description of threatening the life of the nation, he was nonetheless prepared to allow the Secretary of State 'the benefit of the doubt on this point'.[28] Similarly, Baroness Hale commented that since the circumstances of the current case took place in the aftermath of the events of 11 September 2001, and SIAC were satisfied that the open and closed material before them justified the conclusion that there was a public emergency threatening the life of the nation, she 'would not feel qualified or even inclined to disagree' with the decision to derogate.[29] She would only intervene 'if the government were to declare a public emergency where *patently* there was no such thing'.[30] These judicial *dicta* remind us of the point made in chapter 7 that deference is a rational response to uncertainty and there can be a relatively high-weighting threshold applied to decisions which are beyond the expertise of the courts. Their Lordships could not challenge the decision of the Secretary of State on a sure footing because they were not in possession of all the information on which the decision was made. Mere 'doubt', no matter how grave, cannot ground a judicial finding against the Secretary of State on matters of such immense importance, because in order to be justified as an interference with an Executive decision, the doubt must be substantiated and, given the potential consequences, clearly so. The

---

[25] *Ibid.* at [116], *per* Lord Hope.
[26] The variable character of deference leads me to disagree with Thomas Poole's suggestion that there was 'a trace of schizophrenia' in the majority's position in the *Belmarsh Prison* case, see Poole (2008), 239. The reason for the different degree of deference with respect to the two issues in *Belmarsh* is due to the differential character of the issues at stake. See Feldman (1996b), 133.
[27] *Ibid.* at [154].   [28] *Ibid.* at [154].   [29] *Ibid.* at [226].
[30] *Ibid.* at [226], emphasis added.

upshot is that if judges are in doubt, the benefit goes to the Secretary of State.[31]

On the question of whether the means chosen by Parliament to respond to the threat were 'strictly necessary', the court adopted a more stringent standard of review. They rejected the approach adopted by the Court of Appeal as excessively deferential[32] because it had decided that 'it is impossible for this court in this case to differ from the Secretary of State'[33] on the issue of whether the Secretary of State was justified in concluding that it was only necessary to detain non-national suspected terrorists. In other words, the Court of Appeal had adopted a standard of complete deference rendering it impossible for the court to form its own judgment. As Lord Hope pointed out in the House of Lords, the words 'strictly necessary' invite 'close scrutiny' of the action that has been taken, especially given that the rights of the individual are at issue.[34] Relevant here was the fact that section 23 constituted a derogation from Article 5 ECHR 'at the extreme end of the severity spectrum',[35] since the person who is detained under the section would not be accused of any crime but merely be reasonably suspected by the Secretary of State to be a terrorist. The individual could then be detained indefinitely. Many of their Lordships averted to the fact that there was a clear and substantial violation of Article 5 in this case,[36] and that the Government had provided 'no persuasive explanation'[37] why the security threat called for a power of indefinite intention in the case of non-nationals but not in the case of nationals. So this issue warranted less deference because human rights were engaged and the courts have a constitutional (and indeed democratic) mandate under the HRA to guard against their violation, in both legislative or executive decision-making.[38] Therefore, they have a particular role of vigilance with regard to them.

---

[31] Dyzenhaus (2007), 130 suggests that the House of Lords should have applied a more probing standard of scrutiny to the question of whether the derogation was justified. However, he concedes that in order to do this, the court would have needed to see the closed material on which the decision was based. In fact, he argues that more rigorous parliamentary scrutiny of the Executive decision to derogate would enhance the judicial ability to review this question, because it would place more information about it in the public domain; see also Feldman (2006), 380.

[32] *A*, above n. 1 at [44], *per* Lord Bingham; [131], *per* Lord Hope.

[33] *A and Others* (CA) pinpoint at [40], *per* Lord Woolf.

[34] *A*, above n. 1 at [116].    [35] *Ibid.* at [155], *per* Lord Scott.

[36] *Ibid.* at [178], *per* Lord Rodger (describing the inroad into the appellant's liberty in Belmarsh as 'far reaching'); see also [222], *per* Baroness Hale.

[37] *Ibid.* at [78], *per* Lord Nicholls; [43], *per* Lord Bingham.

[38] *Ibid.* at [80], *per* Lord Nicholls.

The significance of *Belmarsh* in terms of its development of the doctrine of deference in national security cases can only be fully appreciated when it is viewed against the backdrop of a long line of previous case law in this area, whose defining feature was substantial if not excessive deference to the Executive. Until very recently, decisions in the national security area were shielded from judicial scrutiny by the doctrine of non-justiciability. The *Belmarsh Prison* case was decided at a time when the British public became aware that the intelligence on which the Government based their decision to go to war in Iraq was called into question. In this context, three of their Lordships expressed doubt about the Government's claim that there was a public emergency threatening the life of the nation[39] and Lord Hoffmann denied it altogether.[40] Moreover, in asserting and emphasising the importance of their role in scrutinising Executive decisions and ensuring compliance with Convention rights, some averted to the fact that national security measures can sometimes be used as a pretext for 'repressive measures that are really taken for other reasons'.[41] These statements (and the spirit of judicial vigilance they announce) could not be further removed from the following comment by Lord Denning in the 1977 case of *Hosenball*,[42] where he noted that England was not like other parts of the world, where national security has been used 'as an excuse for all sorts of infringements of individual liberty' – in England 'successive Ministers have discharged their duties to the complete satisfaction of the people at large'.[43] Deference to the extent of *presuming* that the Executive knows best and acts honourably, is no longer a feature of the case law in this area, despite the fact judges acknowledge, as they should, that their competence and legitimacy sometimes runs out. Judges are aware that they perform an important constitutional function in holding the Executive to account and correcting abuse of power, as well as checking and scrutinising legislation for violations of human rights. They engage in constitutional review.

One final point requires comment. We have seen that, post-HRA, the courts have consistently stated that although substantial deference may be warranted in the area of national security, complete deference is inappropriate. However, some judicial comments made by Lord Hoffmann in *Rehman*[44] can be read as supporting complete deference on matters of

---

[39] *Ibid.* at [104], *per* Lord Bingham; [151], *per* Lord Scott; [155], *per* Lord Rodger.
[40] *Ibid.* at [177], *per* Lord Rodger.     [41] *Ibid.* at [177].
[42] *R. v. Secretary of State for the Home Department, ex parte Hosenball* [1977] 1 W.L.R. 766.
[43] *Ibid.* at 783.
[44] *Secretary of State for the Home Department* v. *Rehman* [2002] 1 All E.R. 123.

national security and, as such, seem to deviate from the prevailing judicial view. In *Rehman*, the House of Lords held unanimously that it was appropriate to pay substantial deference (i.e. give 'great weight' to) the views of the Secretary of State that the deportation of a Pakistani national was 'conducive to the public good' under section 3 of the Immigration Act 1971. Their Lordships accepted that the Secretary of State was 'undoubtedly in the best position to judge what national security required',[45] but they nonetheless emphasised that his decision was still open to review: it did not fall beyond the court's competence. As Lord Steyn put it 'while the national court must accord appropriate deference to the Executive, it may have to address the question: does the interference serve a legitimate objective? Is it necessary in a democratic society?'[46]

Lord Hoffmann's judgment seemed to strike a different tone. He claimed that SIAC was:

> *not entitled to differ* from the opinion of the Secretary of State on the question of whether, for example, the promotion of terrorism in a foreign country by a United Kingdom resident would be contrary to the interests of national security ... the Commission was not intended to act judicially and not to substitute its own opinion for that of the decision-maker on "questions of pure expediency".[47]

At least when viewed in isolation, this *dictum* seems to suggest that Lord Hoffmann supports absolute or complete deference in the context of national security, such that the courts are not entitled to disagree with or challenge any decision made by the Secretary of State. None of the other judges from the House of Lords in *Rehman* supported such an extreme view. Lord Hoffmann's *dicta* on judicial deference were criticised by Lord Steyn in a public address to the Judicial Studies Board, on the ground that they seemed to advocate automatic and complete judicial deference 'on any occasion when a qualified Convention right is claimed to be defeated by a particular public interest'.[48] Such an extreme view was rejected by Lord Steyn as amounting to an abdication of the judicial function of constitutional review. Lord Hoffmann's *dicta* in *Rehman* did not go unnoticed in international judicial circles either. In a delicately phrased extrajudicial comment, the President of the Israeli Supreme Court, Aharon Barak, suggested that Lord Hoffmann's comment in *Rehman* merely sought to emphasise that 'the court determines not the means of fighting terrorism

---

[45] *Ibid.* at [26].    [46] *Ibid.* at [31].    [47] *Ibid.* at [53], emphasis added.
[48] Steyn (2005a), 359.

but rather the lawfulness of the means employed'.[49] This reading is certainly more at one with the prevailing judicial understanding of the role of deference in the adjudication of national security cases under the HRA, where the courts assess whether a degree of deference is appropriate in the context of the particular case, but do not abdicate their important scrutinising function through a doctrine of non-justiciability.

Lord Steyn pointed out that later passages in Lord Hoffmann's judgment do not support the absolutist stance which seemed to be supported in some of his earlier *dicta*.[50] In particular, Lord Hoffmann clarified that if issues of human rights were involved, this would take the question outside 'the exclusive province of the executive'[51] and render it reviewable by the courts. However, there is undoubtedly a tension between the various passages in Lord Hoffmann's judgment, some of which can easily be read as an endorsement of absolute judicial deference in all cases involving national security.[52] Moreover, this apparent tension in Lord Hoffmann's judgment in *Rehman* is exacerbated when one looks at his judgment in *A*. It is one of the intriguing aspects of the decision in *A*, that whilst many of the judges sitting on the case cited Lord Hoffmann's views in *Rehman* in support of the conclusion that they should defer substantially on the question of whether there exists a public emergency threatening the life of the nation within Article 15,[53] it was only Lord Hoffmann who did not rely on them. In fact, he seemed to contradict them outright.[54]

---

[49] Barak (2002), 158. This charitable interpretation of the import of Lord Hoffmann's *dicta* is described in Dyzenhaus (2004), 261 as a 'carefully phrased rebuke' by President Barak to Lord Hoffmann. In line with President Barak's interpretation, Lord Woolf commented extrajudicially that though Lord Hoffmann's *dicta* in *Rehman* about the need to respect the superior democratic legitimacy of the elected branches 'cannot be denied', he also sought to emphasise that Lord Hoffmann's *dicta* do not undermine the constitutional obligation of the courts to 'scrutinise carefully the action which the Executive and the legislature has taken, to see whether those actions accord with the fundamental rights of the individual under the European Convention', see Woolf (2003), 261. For a critique of Lord Hoffmann's judgment in *Rehman*, see Elliott (2003), 334ff; Allan (2004b), 301–5.

[50] See e.g. *Rehman*, above n. 5 at [54].     [51] *Ibid.* at [54].

[52] The more absolutist reading is supported by Lord Hoffmann's extrajudicial statement in Hoffmann (2002), 139: 'An area *obviously not justiciable* is foreign relations or the security of the state, both of which are wholly within the competence of the Executive', emphasis added.

[53] *A*, above n. 1 at [29], [36], *per* Bingham; [112], *per* Lord Hope; at [175] Lord Rodger pointed out that it was partly in reliance on Lord Hoffmann's judgment in *Rehman*, that SIAC adopted an excessively deferential approach when making its decision in *A*.

[54] The tension between Lord Hoffmann's judgment in *A* and *Rehman* has been widely noted: see e.g. Elliott (2007b), 10; Tomkins (2005a), 264. For a critique of Lord Hoffmann's dissent in *A*, see Bonner (2007), 294ff.

Whether this is a principled change of position on the question of deference in relation to national security is difficult to say. What *is* clear is that the House of Lords in *A* supported the view that whilst the decisions of the legislature and Executive are entitled to a degree of respect and deference, the sort of unquestioning submission suggested by Lord Hoffmann in *Rehman* has been rejected as inappropriate.[55] In terms of understanding the position of the higher courts on the question of deference, we can say that Lord Hoffmann's much-maligned *dicta* in *Rehman* are something of an aberration and do not reflect the prevailing judicial view.

## Deference and resource allocation

In the previous chapter, it was argued that it is legitimate for judges to defer to the elected branches in situations where they are unable to carry out the required legal reform. It was also argued that it may be legitimate for judges to defer to the elected branches for prudential reasons, taking into account any adverse consequences their decision may have for society as a whole, or a particular section of it, or for the development of the law. The question now is: is it legitimate for the courts to defer to elected bodies, in order to avoid putting financial burden on the public purse? Should they take the financial consequences of their decision into account?

The case law is full of *dicta* to the effect that the courts are reluctant to make decisions which would be financially burdensome for the legislature or executive. So, as a matter of fact, judges *do* take the financial consequences of their decisions into account, and typically, this leads them to defer. They do so either because they are uncertain about the possible consequences of their decision or because they believe that they have insufficient expertise and/or legitimacy to make decisions of this kind. This leads to what has been called an 'economic conservativism'[56] in resource-allocation cases. A classic statement of deference on grounds of reluctance to interfere with resource allocation can be found in the pre-HRA case of *Southwark London Borough Council* v. *Tanner*.[57] There, the House of Lords refused to extend the common law of nuisance and quiet enjoyment so as to require local authorities to install soundproofing in rented accommodation. Lord Millett put the point succinctly:

---

[55] Bonner (2007), 309.    [56] Chamberlain (2003), 16.    [57] [2001] 1 A.C. 1.

> These cases raise issues of priority in the allocation of resources. Such issues must be resolved by the democratic process, national and local. The judges are not equipped to resolve them.[58]

Their Lordships claimed that their decision showed 'a proper sensitivity to the limits of permissible judicial creativity' and was 'no more than constitutional propriety requires'.[59]

In tackling cases with resource implications, the courts are faced with the same type of dilemma as was presented in the national security case law – a dilemma which is emblematic of the problem of deference more generally. On the one hand, decisions about the allocation of public resources with reference to e.g. health care, social housing, disability benefits, etc. are best made by the legislature or Executive, because they have an overview of the entire area and access to expert opinion about the advantages and disadvantages of certain priorities within the allocation, can assess the consequences of different distributive decisions and can make the decision in light of overall budgetary concerns. On the other hand, Parliament has given judges a special responsibility under the HRA to ensure that legislative and Executive decisions do not violate Convention rights, partly because the courts are well placed to make decisions in which the individual has a central role. The problem arises because a judicial decision on an individual case may have much broader implications for public expenditure. So, for example, the courts may have to adjudicate the claim that an individual's rights have been violated because a nursing home has been closed down. Clearly, a decision in favour of the claimant in this case will have significant consequences for the overall policy set by the health authority on its priorities in terms of resource allocation.

A number of familiar factors justify deference in this area. First, sometimes the courts are uncertain about whether their decision will have damaging or disruptive implications for an economic strategy where priorities are set in light of the overall picture and specialist expertise. Justice in the individual case may cause injustice overall because it may upset an overall programme of funding which has attempted to balance fairly between many different well-deserving competing claims. Second, government and local authorities have the administrative ability to gather a much broader range of information about people's needs and about the consequences of a distributive decision. This is an ability or expertise

---

[58] *Ibid.* at 26.   [59] *Ibid.* at 8, *per* Lord Hoffmann.

which judges do not possess and is a severe limitation on their competence to decide issues with resource implications.[60] Third, judges may feel inhibited from interfering with a legislative decision if they feel that their limited law-making competence may entail the dangers of partial reform. As we saw in chapter 7, these are factors to be considered in an overall evaluation of the institutional propriety of judicial intervention. Again, none of these reasons are knock-down arguments against judicial intervention. At least post-HRA, the courts have not tended to say that issues with resource implications are non-justiciable. Rather they have applied some deference when it is appropriate, but stressed that this depends on the context of the individual case.[61]

The question is, if there is an explicit human rights element to the case, does that overcome the judicial reluctance to impose financial burdens on the state, providing a counterweight to the traditional 'economic conservatism' in the case law? Not in all cases. In *Lee v. Leeds City Council*[62] it was argued that local authority housing which suffered from condensation and mould violated the claimants' right to respect for private and family life under Article 8 of the European Convention. Although it was not in contention that the property was prejudicial to the health of the occupants,[63] Chadwick L.J. placed reliance on the fact that Parliament had not implied into the tenancy agreement an obligation on the landlord to ensure that the dwelling was fit for human habitation.[64] Following the reasoning in *Southwark*, Lord Chadwick considered that in carrying out his duty of striking a balance between the resources of the local housing authority and the needs of the individual tenants, regard must be had to the fact that the financial demands of social housing is very much a matter for 'democratically determined priorities'.[65] The substantial deference paid to Parliament in this case combined with the belief that the conditions complained of did not seem sufficiently serious to amount to a violation of Article 8,[66] led to a decision in favour of the local authority.

---

[60] Cecile Fabre has described this as the strongest argument against entrenching social rights in constitutional documents, see Fabre (2000b), 176.

[61] For an examination of the 'dollars versus rights' controversy in the context of the Canadian Charter of Rights and Freedoms (1982) case law, see Miller (2008), 111ff.

[62] Decided with *Ratcliffe v. Sandwell Metropolitan Borough Council* [2002] 1 W.L.R. 1488.

[63] *Ibid.* at [41].

[64] *Ibid.* at [34]. In fact, although it had in fact created such an obligation, it decided in section 8 of the Landlord and Tenant Act 1985 that it would only apply to housing which was below a rent set in 1957 legislation, thereby rendering it effectively a dead letter.

[65] *Ibid.* at [49].    [66] *Ibid.* at [51].

However, in *Limbuela*[67] the House of Lords held that the Secretary of State was under an obligation to provide support for asylum seekers, if it appears that they face an imminent prospect of serious suffering which would amount to a violation of their Article 3 right not to be subjected to degrading or inhuman treatment. Acknowledging that this was 'an intensely political issue',[68] their Lordships were of the view that Parliament had relied on 'sound reasons of policy for wishing to take a firm line on the need for applications for asylum to be made promptly and for wishing to limit the level of support until the right to remain has been determined'.[69] They were fully aware that part of the object of the legislation under scrutiny was precisely to reduce the burden on the public purse and to restrict public support, so far as possible, to those who both need and deserve it.[70] However, section 55 of the Nationality, Immigration and Asylum Act 2002 explicitly required the Secretary of State to provide support for asylum seekers, to the extent that this would avoid a violation of Article 3.[71] So, in coming to their conclusion, many of their Lordships stressed that they were merely giving effect to the will of Parliament as expressed in section 55. Mindful of the possible opposition to the decision on the grounds that the judges were usurping the proper function of Parliament, Baroness Hale cautioned:

> there can be no question here of the court by its decision thwarting the will of Parliament. Rather your Lordships' task on these appeals is to guide the Secretary of State in the discharge of his own difficult duty of deciding when in any particular case the statutory prohibition on support becomes instead a mandatory duty to support.[72]

In other words, although the overall policy was to reduce the burden on the public purse by asylum seekers, there was an explicit statutory requirement to secure the protection of Article 3. The policy was legitimate but could not be carried too far, i.e. to the point of a rights violation. Moreover, the court was *certain* that there was inhuman and degrading treatment in this case: it was not a borderline case.[73]

There are other post-HRA cases, where the courts have overcome their general circumspection about imposing financial burdens on state bodies. For example, in *Noorkoiv* v. *SSHD*,[74] the Court of Appeal held that the

---

[67] *R. v. Secretary of State, ex parte Limbuela* [2005] UKHL 66.
[68] *Ibid.* at [13], *per* Lord Hope.  [69] *Ibid.* at [13].  [70] *Ibid.* at [2], *per* Lord Bingham.
[71] Section 55(5).  [72] [2005] UKHL 66 at [85].
[73] *Ibid.* at [7], *per* Lord Bingham, who described the claim that it was inhuman and degrading as 'plainly correct'.
[74] *Noorkoiv* v. *Secretary of State for the Home Department* [2002] 1 W.L.R. 3284.

Secretary of State could not rely on lack of resources as a justification for delays in the parole system, such that prisoners were detained after their tariff period had expired but before the Parole Board had made a decision on whether to recommend their release. As in *Limbuela*, the court was convinced that there was a *clear* violation of Article 5 of the European Convention.[75] However, this decision cannot be used as a support for the general proposition that Secretaries of State can never rely on the fact that they have limited resources. In *Noorkoiv*, the judges were assured that the change in the parole system advocated by the decision, would only give rise to 'limited additional burdens [which] should be well capable of being met, given a reasonable time'.[76] In *Napier* v. *Scottish Ministers*,[77] the Scottish Court of Session held that Mr Napier's detention in Barlinnie Prison in Glasgow violated his Article 3 right against inhuman and degrading treatment, due to the poor sanitary arrangements in his cell. The court made an interim order that Mr Napier be transferred to alternative accommodation, until the conditions at Barlinnie were improved to comply with Article 3 and rejected an argument made on behalf of the Scottish Ministers that if Mr Napier's case succeeded, it would imply that all the prisoners at Barlinnie would have a legitimate claim, resolution of which would be impracticable to implement partly on financial grounds. Rather, Lord MacFadyen preferred to consider Mr Napier's case on its own merits, without taking the other remand prisoners into account.[78]

What is it about the context of the cases outlined above which led the court to overcome their general circumspection about placing financial burdens on the state, sometimes in the context of legislation which was designed precisely to limit such burdens? A number of factors can be identified. First, in all the cases discussed, the court was convinced that there was both a *clear* and *substantial* violation of the right in question. As the courts have often pointed out with reference to Article 3, they will only intervene if the violation is above a certain threshold of severity. In all the cases outlined above, this threshold was clearly passed, so certainty about a substantial violation weighed against deference. Second, the courts are sometimes emboldened to decide in favour of the financially burdensome option, if there is evidence that Parliament or the Executive had set their priorities so that this particular claimant would be covered, but then backtrack on this commitment due to financial constraints. This was a

---

[75] See e.g. *Napier* v. *Scottish Ministers*, Outer House, Court of Session, 26 June 2001.
[76] *Ibid.* at [15].     [77] Court of Session, Lord MacFadyen, 26 June 2001.
[78] *Ibid.* at [14].

factor in the *Napier* decision. The Court of Session noted that the Scottish Ministers had been aware of the poor prison conditions at Barlinnie for a number of years, and had in fact promised to introduce internal sanitation in the prison cells by 1999.[79] In such a case, the courts do not have the same degree of uncertainty about interfering with legislative or Executive priorities set in the context of the broader picture, because they are merely enforcing such a priority rather than setting it anew. One might add that fears based on inferior democratic legitimacy are also assuaged in this situation.[80] Third, the courts have been more ready to impose a financial burden, if they are assured, as in *Noorkoiv*, that it is not excessive.[81] If the expenditure is drastic, this will be a factor weighing in favour of deference. Fourth, whilst it is difficult to generalise about cases arising under particular articles of the Convention, it is certainly the case that in Article 3 cases concerning inhuman and degrading treatment (such as *Limbuela* or *Napier*) the courts are at their most vigilant in securing protection for the individual. Sometimes, these cases are, quite literally, matters of life and death and, in such situations, the courts tend to give more weight to the rights claim involved, and consequently less weight to the uncertainty about knock-on financial consequences.[82] Even so, the courts in such cases tend to stress that the broader policy issues must

---

[79] *Napier*, above n. 75 at [9]. Although counsel for the Scottish Ministers denied that there was a contravention of Article 3 in this case, they nonetheless accepted that the sanitary conditions prevailing in Barlinnie had 'no place in a modern prison service' and maintained that the Scottish prison service was actively seeking to resolve that matter, at [11].

[80] Although not an example of striving to give effect to the priorities set by the elected branches, it is noteworthy that in his judgment in *Limbuela*, Lord Brown considered Prime Minister Tony Blair's comments in a foreword to a government paper on the scandal of people sleeping rough which he described as intolerable 'in a modern civilised society'. As Elizabeth Palmer noted, 'this observation lent weight to Lord Brown's own humane instinct that such a situation was intolerable in the case of asylum seekers', see Palmer (2007), 259.

[81] See e.g. *R. v. East Sussex County Council, ex parte Tandy* [1998] A.C. 714 where the House of Lords accepted that a local authority had reneged on its statutory duty under section 298 to provide adequate home tuition services to sick children. It is not without relevance that the potential financial outcome of this case for the local authority was negligible since only two other children had been similarly affected by the local authority policy, see Palmer (2000), 84.

[82] See e.g. the so-called 'right to die' cases such as *Airedale Trust v. Bland* [1993] 2 W.L.R. 316 where the House of Lords said that in making their decision about whether it was lawful to remove the life support, it was inappropriate for them to engage in a 'cost benefit analysis', at 896, *per* Lord Mustill. For further comment on resource implications in this type of case, see Palmer (2000), 77ff discussing *R. v. Cambridge Health Authority, ex parte B* [1995] 2 All E.R. 129.

be resolved by Parliament, including those issues which involve setting spending priorities.[83] Finally, in those cases where they have particular expertise, and can be more assured about predicting the consequences of their decisions, this will again be a factor going against deference. So, in *Noorkoiv*, the case concerned delays in the system of parole and whether there had been a breach of the right to liberty – a matter on which the courts could adjudicate with some certainty.

Support for the legitimacy of a degree of deference in some cases involving resource allocation is in no way a recommendation that the courts simply accept a claim on face value that there are insufficient resources to protect human rights. They should scrutinise such claims as far as possible, requiring the government to justify its policies both generally and in light of it implications for the individual concerned. If they did not, local authorities and government more generally could simply refer to the interdependence of competing strains on the public purse as a complete defence in all cases where claims are made against them involving financial outlay. The courts must attempt to assess the plausibility of these claims, and where a human rights claim is involved, the courts must insist that a public authority should show substantial justification on public interest grounds for violating a right.[84]

### Deference and the judicial choice between sections 3 and 4

In chapter 4, I explored some of the factors bearing on the judicial choice between section 3 and section 4. As presented there, this was largely a matter of when the limits of judicial law-making were reached. The deferential option was often that of issuing a declaration of incompatibility, rather than rectifying the legislative provision through interpretation under section 3. However, it was also clear that, underlying the choice between section 3 and section 4, are broader questions about the proper distribution of power between courts and Parliament in ensuring that Convention rights are protected. The broader considerations engage the doctrine of deference. Therefore, it is important to establish the role deference plays in making that choice.

---

[83] See *Bland, ibid.*, at 878, *per* Lord Browne-Wilkinson.
[84] Elizabeth Palmer has criticised the senior judiciary because they have 'generally recoiled from principled resolution of [welfare] disputes, distancing themselves by *routinely* pointing to the interdependence of competing strains on the public purse', see Palmer (2000), 68, emphasis added.

On my analysis, judges show deference by giving the decisions of the elected branches varying degrees of presumptive weight. The question which then arises is whether judicial deference is more likely to result in an interpretation under section 3(1) or a declaration of incompatibility under section 4. Some academic commentators on the Act advocate greater reliance on the declaration of incompatibility mechanism, on the basis that this would be more respectful and deferential to Parliament than a section 3(1) interpretation. Rather than engage in innovative interpretations which depart from the original legislative intent when enacting the legislation, judges should simply declare their view that there is an incompatibility with the Convention, but leave 'the last word' to Parliament.[85]

Whether this is in fact the more deferential option, depends on the status and legal implications of the declaration of incompatibility. That matter is addressed in detail in chapter 10 and chapter 11. There, it is argued that the declaration of incompatibility is a much stronger judicial tool than is sometimes realised and that the contrast between it and a formal strike-down power is frequently exaggerated. Moreover, in chapter 11, I question whether Parliament actually has the 'last word' in any meaningful sense, following a declaration of incompatibility. If correct, this analysis weakens the claim that a declaration of incompatibility is obviously more deferential than an interpretation under section 3.

Of course, the most deferential option would be to avoid using either section 3 *or* section 4, by finding that the legislation under scrutiny does not violate Convention rights.[86] It would give so much weight to the decision (and justification) of the legislature/Executive that it would lead the courts to accept that there was no interference with Convention rights, or that it was proportionate. Once the courts find a *prima facie* violation, then it is impossible to say, as a general matter, whether a section 3(1) interpretation or a section 4 declaration is the more deferential option. It all depends on the context of the individual case. If the legislation was enacted by a previous administration with little or no support from the government now in power, a declaration of incompatibility will be much less of a challenge to the government than a prized piece of their own legislation enacted on the heels of a widely publicised election manifesto.

---

[85] See e.g. Klug (2003).

[86] In making this point, I am not suggesting that all decisions which find that primary legislation does not violate Convention rights are necessarily deferential. Such a finding may follow probing scrutiny which pays only minimal deference to the legislature.

The declaration of incompatibility tends to grab the headlines more than a section 3(1) interpretation. Rights-compatible interpretations under section 3 tend to go unnoticed outside the legal community, whereas a section 4 declaration attracts more media attention. Section 4 cases are often reported as cases where the government has 'lost' its case and has been declared to be in violation of Convention rights. For this reason, there may be situations where the government would rather avoid the embarrassment of a public declaration that their legislation violates Convention rights and favour the more subterranean method of judicial rectification. It would be politically more advantageous for them to have the rights violation cured at source by way of judicial interpretation, because the public message delivered by such a judgment (at least to those who have little or no understanding of how the HRA works) will be that the law was found to be fully in compliance with Convention rights.[87]

As we saw in our analysis of deference for prudential reasons, concerns about how a judicial decision will be received politically is not irrelevant to judicial decision-making, since the contextual considerations about the politics surrounding a particular case will have a bearing on what constitutes the most interventionist option for the courts to take. So whilst a section 3(1) interpretation may seem like the more activist option when the matter is assessed in purely legal terms, when we view the issue in its broader political context, this is not necessarily the case. Certainly, a case like the *Belmarsh Prison* case is not thought to be inherently deferential, simply because the outcome was a declaration of incompatibility. On the contrary, it is perceived as a bold exercise of judicial power, standing up to an almighty Executive, bent on waging the 'war on terror' with less than scrupulous attention to the goal of protecting Convention rights. Finally, it should not be assumed that all section 3 interpretations will be radical either in purely legal terms, or in terms of their social or political effect.[88] If only a minor change is required in the legislation, and this change is continuous with existing legal developments and is not opposed by the government of the day, this may well be the more deferential (and less politically confrontational) option than issuing a declaration of incompatibility.

---

[87] Note that sometimes counsel for the government argues in court that the government would prefer a section 3(1) interpretation over a section 4 declaration.

[88] For the distinction between the changing the law in a way which is *legally* radical, as opposed to radical in terms of its social and political effect, see Kavanagh (2003a), 74–7.

## Conclusion

Judicial deference has become a *leitmotiv* of the HRA case law and commentary. But given that the HRA was supposed to herald an era when human rights would be more vigorously enforced, and where the standard of review would shift from the deferential *Wednesbury* standard to the more probing principle of proportionality, it may seem ironic that the doctrine of deference has been so prevalent in the judicial *dicta*. There are a number of possible reasons for the doctrine's rise to fame precisely at a time when the courts have stronger powers to review primary legislation for compliance with human rights, than ever before. First, much of the original opposition to the HRA was based on the worry about expanding judicial power. In particular, there was the concern that it would involve judges in policy-making to a greater extent than before. Therefore, it is unsurprising that the first few years of case law are replete with assurances from the judiciary that they do not wish to usurp the powers of the democratically elected Parliament, but rather will continue to show appropriate restraint and deference to them. The judiciary are aware that much of the responsibility for ensuring that the HRA is properly 'bedded in' to the legal system, lies with them. Therefore, they wish to assure the legislature that they will do so in a constructive fashion.[89]

Second, one of the recurring themes of this book is that the interpretive powers given to the courts under the HRA are not radically different from those possessed by the courts before its enactment. As I have argued, all statutory interpretation is an 'inter-institutional' meeting between the courts and Parliament, and concerns about relative institutional competence, expertise and legitimacy surface in all cases involving statutory interpretation. These concerns are in no way eliminated by the HRA, although many argue that the precise division of labour between the three branches of government has been altered by it.[90]

It ought not to be assumed, however, that simply because the case law is replete with judicial assurances that they will defer to elected bodies; this necessarily means that the case law is in fact more deferential than heretofore. Often, it is precisely in cases where judges bring about considerable legal innovation, that they rely most heavily on such assurances. A

[89] See Lord Woolf at www.judiciary.gov.uk/publications_media/speeches/pre_2004/lcj100403. htm.

[90] Conor Gearty has suggested that the culture of judicial deference was so pervasive prior to the introduction of the Human Rights Act that it did not need to be judicially noted, whereas now its very controversy is what makes it such a topic of judicial discussion, Gearty (2004), 121.

judge's statement of general principle is not always matched by practical application. Therefore, we should be careful not to view the judicial *dicta* on deference in isolation from the actual role it plays in judicial reasoning. There are many reasons to believe that the case law is, and will become, less rather than more deferential. First, as we will see in the next chapter, there is the advent of the principle of proportionality as an independent standard of review. Second, the HRA gives the courts' powers of constitutional review a 'democratic underpinning' which has enhanced the courts' sense of legitimacy in holding the legislature and the Executive to account for breaches of fundamental rights. Finally, there is generally within society, less trust in government than in previous generations and therefore less deference to those who hold public office.[91] The development of the law is not immune from the influence of these wider social changes, which have become most apparent in the emboldening of judicial spirits in the context of national security.

---

[91] See Sedley (1994), 282ff; Feldman (1999a), 167 notes that 'there is no longer a clear, ethical consensus as to how public bodies and public figures should discharge their obligations to the public'.

# 9

# Proportionality and deference under the HRA

## The meaning of proportionality

It has sometimes been observed that the introduction into UK law of the doctrine of proportionality is one of the most profound changes to judicial reasoning brought about by the HRA.[1] The doctrine of proportionality is often explained by the aphorism that one 'should not use a sledgehammer to crack a nut'.[2] Proportionality is thus presented as a relational concept – the legal response to a problem must be proportionate to the nature and severity of that problem. Thus, achieving a proportionality or balance between the legal measure and the legal aim is often thought to be the essence of the principle of proportionality.[3] However, this characterisation of the 'essence' overlooks one important aspect of proportionality, namely, that it must *also* be measured against a principle or interest which is worthy of protection. The doctrine of proportionality is only invoked when a legal measure under scrutiny harms or restricts a valuable interest. In adjudication under the HRA, that interest is the protection of Convention rights. Therefore, proportionality is invoked by the courts in order to ensure that legal measures are not excessive in relation to the social problems they are intended to solve, *but also* that it does so in a way which is not unduly restrictive of human rights. So, whilst it may seem as if the principle of proportionality does not refer to any substantive value, but rather a relationship or balance between means and ends, in fact, the proportionality enquiry is driven by the value of human rights.[4]

[1] Sedley (2002), 17; Sedley (2004), 16.
[2] *R. v. Goldsmith* [1983] 1 W.L.R. 151 at 155, *per* Lord Diplock. For an examination of the concept of proportionality in the context of Australian constitutional law, see Kirk (1997).
[3] See e.g. *R. (Samaroo) v. SSHD* [2001] UKHRR 1139 at [26], *per* Dyson L.J. Lester and Pannick (2004), 89.
[4] Lord Steyn commented in *R. v. A (No. 2)* [2002] 1 A.C. 45 at [35]: the question is 'whether, *measured against the guarantee of a fair trial,* the [legislative response] is justified and proportionate', emphasis added; see also *R. v. Lambert* [2002] 2 A.C. 545 at [17], *per* Lord Slynn, [9], *per* Lord Steyn.

For this reason, the courts have stressed that their decision about the proportionality of a legislative measure relies on a 'value judgement'.[5] It involves an evaluation of the importance of the legislative objective, as well as the importance of the particular Convention right at issue.

Under the ECHR, proportionality is the name given to a set of judicial tests used to establish whether a limitation on Convention rights is justifiable. One could say that it provides a framework for assessing the justification for limiting rights.[6] The doctrine of proportionality is not mentioned explicitly in the Convention. Rather, it is a judge-made doctrine which followed from an interpretation of the limitation clauses contained in the Convention. Some of the Convention rights provide that states may interfere with certain rights if this is 'necessary in a democratic society' or is in the pursuit of other legitimate policy aims. In *Sunday Times* v. *UK*,[7] the Strasbourg court interpreted the phrase 'necessary in a democratic society' to mean that the court must assess whether 'the interference complained of corresponded to a pressing social need, whether it was proportionate to the legitimate aim being pursued, and whether the reasons given by the national authorities to justify it are relevant and sufficient'.[8]

From this statement in *Sunday Times*, it is clear that the doctrine of proportionality is not a single or monolithic test. Rather, it comprises a range of questions which are put to the national authorities who seek to justify a legislative or administrative measure which allegedly violates Convention rights. In domestic adjudication under the HRA, there is judicial consensus on what these questions are, even if there is some controversy about how they ought to be applied in the context of individual cases. Applying the threefold set of criteria from the Privy Council case of *De Freitas*,[9] the House of Lords in *Daly* clarified, in a landmark judgment, that 'in determining whether a limitation is arbitrary or excessive ... the court would ask itself whether:

(i) the legislative objective is sufficiently important to justify limiting a fundamental right;
(ii) the legislative measures designed to meet the objective are rationally connected to it; and
(iii) the means used to impair the right of freedom are no more than is necessary to accomplish the objective'.

---

[5] *Wilson* v. *First County Trust* [2003] 3 W.L.R. 568 at [62], [63]; see also *R.* v. *Secretary of State, ex parte Limbuela* [2005] UKHL 66 at [55], *per* Lord Bingham; *Begum* v. *Denbigh High School* [2007] 1 A.C. 100 at [30], *per* Lord Bingham.
[6] Feldman (1999b), 118.    [7] *Sunday Times* (1979) 2 EHRR 245.    [8] *Ibid.* at [59].
[9] *De Freitas* v. *Permanent Secretary of Ministry of Agriculture, Fisheries, Lands and Housing* [1998] 3 W.L.R. 675.

Let us go through these questions one by one. First, the state or public authority must show that they are pursuing a legitimate aim and that the (legislative or administrative) measure adopted is rationally connected to the aim. In other words, there must be very good reason for limiting Convention rights. In the language of the Strasbourg court, the social need must be 'pressing' and the legislative aim must be important. In adjudication under the HRA, this stage of the enquiry has not tended to be particularly controversial and is often not particularly searching. Normally, it is sufficient for the state to state their legislative aim in general terms, i.e. 'national security' or 'immigration policy' or 'public health'. More often than not, this is accepted by the court as a legitimate aim. However, although it is rare for the state authority to fail at this stage, it is not impossible. For example, in *Ghaidan* v. *Mendoza*, the justification for the differential treatment of same-sex couples in the Rent Act 1977 'fell at the first hurdle: the absence of a legitimate aim'.[10] The state did not advance cogent reasons for the difference in treatment and (absent justification), their aim could not be shown to be 'legitimate' because it was discriminatory.

The second requirement is that the measure adopted must be a suitable way of achieving the aim. If there seems to be no rational connection between the aim invoked to justify the measure and the details of the measure itself, this alerts us to two possibilities. Either the alleged aim is not in fact the real or primary aim of the restrictive measure or, alternatively, if the aim is genuine, the means used to achieve it are ineffective or irrational. Either possibility can lead to a finding that the measure is 'disproportionate'. As Jeffrey Jowell observed, under proportionality 'spurious or impractical aims will not suffice'.[11] The *Belmarsh Prison* case provides us with an example of this variant of disproportionality, because the restriction in that legislation to non-nationals was not rational, given that nationals could also pose a threat to national security.

This brings us to the final stage of the proportionality analysis (often called 'proportionality in the narrow sense'): the interference with rights must be no more than is necessary to accomplish the objective – it must not interfere with rights to an unjustifiable (excessive) extent.[12] This is proportionality 'in the narrow sense' because it brings into play the main interest or value underlying the proportionality enquiry, namely, the value of protecting human rights. This is the stage of the proportionality enquiry where the courts must explicitly balance the

---

[10] *Ghaidan* v. *Mendoza* [2004] 3 W.L.R. 113 at [18], *per* Lord Nicholls.
[11] Jowell (2000), 679.        [12] See De Búrca (1993), 106; De Búrca (1997), 562ff.

reasons in favour of upholding the decision of the legislature or Executive on the one hand, and the individual human rights concerns on the other.[13]

Let us see how proportionality has been used in adjudication under the HRA with respect to primary legislation. As we know, the interpretive obligation under section 3 is only engaged if the courts find an apparent or *prima facie* incompatibility with Convention rights. If the measure under scrutiny is rights-compatible, then section 3 has no task to perform. However, if the limitation is found to be disproportionate, the court is then under an obligation to see if it can rectify the disproportionality by way of interpretation or, alternatively, issue a declaration of incompatibility. Therefore, the court's assessment of whether a limitation is proportionate or not, is a crucial preliminary step in the resolution of a compatibility challenge under the HRA. Typically, the state needs to show two things to satisfy the court that the legislative measure is proportionate. First, it must be shown to be necessary in a democratic society. Any legislative measure must not go beyond what is necessary to accomplish its legislative objective.[14] Second, there must not be 'an excessive inroad into rights'[15]. Whatever the justification in terms of legislative aim, the adverse consequences for individual rights must not be too drastic. As Simon Brown L.J. explained in *Roth*:

> It is implicit in the concept of proportionality that . . . not merely must the impairment of the individual's rights be no more than necessary for the attainment of the public policy objective sought, but also that it must not impose an excessive burden on the individual concerned.[16]

The doctrine of proportionality therefore sets limits to the acceptable legislative response to any social problem. Simon Brown L.J. highlights

---

[13] See e.g. Lord Bingham in *Razgar* v. *SSHD* [2004] 2 A.C. 368 at [20] cited with approval in *Huang* v. *Secretary of State* [2007] 2 A.C. 167 at [19], *per* Lord Bingham: making a judgment on proportionality 'must always involve the striking of a fair balance between the rights of the individual and the interests of the community which is inherent in the whole of the Convention. The severity and consequences of the interference will call for careful assessment at this stage'.

[14] *R.* v. *A*, above n. 4 at [94], *per* Lord Hope; *Lambert*, above n. 4 at [34], *per* Lord Steyn.

[15] *R.* v. *A*, *ibid.* at [36], [36], [38], [45]; also said that a measure must not be 'disproportionately restrictive' of Convention rights, see *R.* v. *A* at [13], *per* Lord Slynn; see also *Lambert*, above n. 4 at [41], *per* Lord Steyn.

[16] *International Transport Roth GmbH* v. *Secretary of State for the Home Department* [2002] 3 W.L.R. 344 at [52]. The idea that proportionality prohibits an 'excessive burden' on the individual is drawn from *James* v. *UK* (1986) 8 E.H.R.R. 123, applied in *Roth* at [52], [53].

this link between proportionality and the constitutional limits on what Parliament can do:

> Even rights which are not absolute...can be interfered with only to an extent which is proportionate. However compelling the social goal, there are limits to how far the individual's interest can legitimately be sacrificed to achieve it.[17]

Therefore, the proportionality enquiry is explicitly rights based, because it provides a way of testing or judging legislative measures (as well as the justification of those measures) in light of the importance of Convention rights. It is a crucial element in the court's ability and willingness to engage in constitutional review.

## Proportionality and deference

We now have a clearer idea of what proportionality requires. There remains the question about the relationship between proportionality and deference. In the Strasbourg jurisprudence, it has often been observed that the proportionality enquiry goes 'hand in hand' with deference.[18] This metaphor, whilst suggestive of a link between the two notions, fails to give a precise indication of how deference and proportionality are related. On my analysis, the relationship between proportionality and deference is as follows. The three questions which make up the proportionality enquiry provide the *method* of reviewing the legislative provision under scrutiny and assessing the justification advanced in support of it. It provides the court with a set of questions to be asked of the state authority. Deference refers to the *intensity* with which that method is *applied*. Therefore, deference has a crucial role to play in determinations of whether particular laws or Executive decisions satisfy the doctrine of proportionality, because it sets the intensity or intrusiveness of review which the court will adopt in assessing the importance of the competing values at stake. The more deference applied in any case, the less the court will require (in terms of strength of argument and supportive evidence) to be persuaded that the measure was disproportionate.

Thus, the proportionality enquiry can be described as a 'variable' standard. It is variable because it can be applied more or less deferentially.

---

[17] *Ibid.* at [29].

[18] *Handyside* v. *UK* (1979–80) 1 E.H.R.R. 737 at [48]; Irvine (2003a), 32 noting that the doctrine of proportionality and the concept of the margin of appreciation are 'closely allied'.

As Gráinne de Búrca explains: 'the way the proportionality principle is applied . . . covers a spectrum ranging from a very deferential approach, to a quite rigorous and searching examination of the justification for a measure which has been challenged'.[19] The factors identified by de Búrca which influence the degree of scrutiny are none other than the main grounds of deference outlined in chapter 7: 'the expertise, position and overall competence of the Court as against the decision-making authority',[20] as well as the nature and importance of the right claimed by the applicant on the one hand, and the legislative/Executive objective alleged to be served by the measure, on the other. So, whilst proportionality provides the framework in the sense of a set of questions to be asked of the legislature or Executive, deference determines the intensity with which the answers to those questions will be scrutinised and the degree of weight to be given to the decision-maker's justification.[21] This means that, rather than viewing proportionality as the extreme end of the review scale, it is more accurate to acknowledge that proportionality may itself range from a minimal control right through to a 'not manifestly inappropriate' test.[22]

This has led some commentators to suggest that there are not one, but many proportionality tests,[23] and no doubt, much scholastic energy could be spent devising a comprehensive taxonomy of tests and an accompanying list of the circumstances in which a particular test is appropriate. On my analysis, what differs from case to case is not the nature of the test itself, but the degree of deference applied and this will vary according to the multiplicity of factors which obtain in the context of an individual case. Whilst it is important to identify what those factors are, this will be a far cry from a taxonomy which would enable us to predict in advance which level of intensity a court might choose in any particular case. The combination of factors is infinitely variable and there is a degree of judgment with relation to their weight and importance. So, in the interests of clarity, and a desire not to complicate this issue unduly by burdening it with an unnecessary proliferation of terminology, we will talk of 'the

[19] De Búrca (1993), 111. Although this statement is made with reference to the case law of the European Court of Justice, the point is generalisable to Convention adjudication, as well as to the case law under the HRA.

[20] De Búrca (1993), 111.

[21] See Supperstone and Coppel (1999), 314–5. For a valuable examination of the variability of the intensity of review when using the proportionality test in the context of media law, see Fenwick and Phillipson (2006), 103ff.

[22] See De Búrca (1993), 122ff; Pillay (2007), 634; Rivers (2006), 202–3.

[23] Fenwick and Phillipson (2006), chapter 2.

proportionality test' (rather than a multiplicity of tests), but bear in mind that it is applied differently in different contexts depending on the degree of deference which is appropriate in any particular context.

The relationship between proportionality and deference means that, when assessing the proportionality of legislation, the court must be sensitive to the limits of the judicial role in terms of expertise, competence and legitimacy. This does not mean that they are entitled to sanction a limitation of rights simply because the legislature or Executive say so. The judicial task is to scrutinise the measure and the justification advanced in support of it, adjusting the degree of deference in light of the various factors mentioned above: the importance of the right, the severity of the interference with the right, as well as the importance of the social goal advanced in support of the measure. This means that the courts have to attempt to protect Convention rights, whilst simultaneously being appropriately respectful of Parliament's choice about the best legal response to a social problem. Lord Steyn encapsulates the two aspects of the task in the following statement from *R. v. A*: 'given the centrality of the right to a fair trial in the scheme of the Convention, *and* giving due weight to the important legislative goal . . . the question is whether section 41 makes an excessive inroad into the guarantee of a fair trial'.[24] Moreover, as clarified in chapter 7, the duty of deference does not mean that a court is precluded from making its own assessment of the proportionality of the legislative measure. Again, Lord Steyn notes the two aspects of this judicial task in *R. v. A*:

> Clearly the court must give weight to the decision of Parliament that the mischief encapsulated in the twin myths must be corrected. On the other hand, when the question arises whether in the criminal statute in question Parliament adopted a legislative scheme which makes an excessive inroad into the right to a fair trial, the court is qualified to make its own judgement and must do so.[25]

This idea that the court should 'make its own judgment' about proportionality is asserted frequently by the courts, and it needs to be clarified since it can generate misunderstanding about the court's task. It means that the court is entitled to make its own assessment about the weight to be attached to the various interests at stake in the proportionality enquiry – including both the importance of the legislative objective, the means used to achieve that objective and the value of the Convention rights at issue, including the severity of its violation. Judges are not required to defer

[24] *R. v. A*, above n. 4 at [38], emphasis added.      [25] *Ibid.* at [36].

absolutely to the primary decision-maker, in the sense of blindly submitting to them. Rather, their task is to scrutinise the justification advanced in support of the measure, and to assess the cogency of that justification. However, this does not mean that the courts should assess the matter as if they were the primary decision-maker. Rather, they must bear in mind that they are the secondary, rather than the primary decision-maker, and as such, owe a degree of deference to the solution adopted by Parliament. Reviewing for proportionality (however intensively) is still a type of *review*. It does not license the judiciary to retake the primary decision, without any consideration of how the legislature or Executive or administrative agency made that decision in the first place. So, although the courts are entitled to form their own judgment about the proportionality of a measure, it is not a judgment which is entirely unconstrained. It is limited both in scope (because their task is to establish whether a legislative measure is justified in light of a specific range of legal standards, not whether it is 'right' in the broadest sense) and in intensity (because of their duty of deference).

This means that the proportionality enquiry should not be equated with a 'correctness' standard of review.[26] It does not enjoin the court to come up with the best or 'correct' or 'ideal' solution to a legislative problem. Rather, it requires them to test the justification of a legislative measure to ensure that the limitation on rights is not *excessive*. As we have seen, the courts will, in general, only interfere if the rights violation is clear and substantial. Thus, the courts often say that they are testing to see if there is 'a reasonable proportionality'[27] between the means employed and the means sought to be achieved, or whether there is '*a reasonable relationship of proportionality between the means employed and the aim sought to be realised*'[28] or whether the balance struck between the general interest of the community and the personal rights of the individual was 'fair'.[29] The court is not looking for the perfect or ideal balance, but rather attempting to assess whether the one which has been struck by the primary decision-maker is fair in light of the importance of Convention rights and the legislative objective sought to be achieved. In order to justify interfering

---

[26] For the distinction between a reasonableness- and correctness standard of review, see Perry (1989).

[27] *R. v. A*, above n. 4 at [91], *per* Lord Hope.

[28] See *Lambert*, above n. 4 at [190], *per* Lord Hutton, emphasis added; *Roth*, above n. 16 at [50], *per* Simon Brown L.J.; *R. (Wilson) v. Wychavon District Council* [2007] EWCA Civ 52 (CA) at [40], *per* Richards L.J.

[29] *Lambert*, above n. 4 at [190], *per* Lord Hutton.

with the primary decision, the courts will see whether the measure is 'not merely harsh, but truly unfair'.[30] This suggests that the threshold of unfairness can be quite high to prompt a finding of disproportionality.

So, contrary to the nomenclature of the abstract formulation of the proportionality test, it is a mistake to think that the courts try to identify the measure which is the *least* restrictive on Convention rights. Rather, if they find that a measure places an excessive burden on an individual, they will try to find a *less* restrictive measure, which is simultaneously compliant with the legislative objective. Thus, in *Lambert*,[31] the court noted that the transfer of the legal burden amounts to a far more drastic interference with the presumption of innocence than the creation of an evidential burden on the accused.[32] Their Lordships were satisfied that an evidential burden was sufficient to achieve the legislative objective, whilst remaining compatible with Convention rights. The solution provided a 'reasonable relationship of proportionality' between the means employed and the aim sought to be realised. So, rather than looking for the optimally 'proportionate' solution to a problem or the best possible solution, the courts look to see if there is an unacceptable 'disproportionality', or a limitation of rights which is unjustifiable in the circumstances of the instant case.[33] Just as we think of *Wednesbury* in negative terms (i.e. as a principle of *ir*rationality or *un*reasonableness), the proportionality test is also best seen as a standard which a decision-maker can violate, rather than an *ideal* to which he must aspire.

## Justification and scrutiny

From the foregoing analysis, it will be clear that there is an important connection between proportionality and the level of justification necessary to defend legislation against a claim that it interferes with Convention rights in a disproportionate manner. This is significant for the broader themes of this book, because many commentators have argued that it is precisely this 'culture of justification'[34] which is the hallmark of strong constitutional review. Therefore, it is worth explicating the various ways

---

[30] *Roth*, above n. 16 at [31], *per* Simon Brown L.J.     [31] Above n. 4.

[32] *Lambert*, above n. 4 at [37], *per* Lord Steyn.

[33] For the view that the principle of proportionality is more accurately described as a standard of disproportionality, see *R. v. Secretary of State for the Environment, Transport and the Regions, ex parte Alconbury Developments Ltd* [2001] UKHL 23 at [169], *per* Lord Clyde.

[34] Hunt (2003), 340.

in which the doctrine of proportionality gives rise to different levels of justification with respect to primary legislation.

First, under the proportionality enquiry, the onus is squarely on the state to demonstrate that the legislative measure is proportionate.[35] The state must advance a justification of the measure showing that there was a legitimate aim, a rational connection between the aim and the legislative measure, and that it does not constitute an excessive interference with human rights. Second, the courts have consistently held (even before the HRA came into force) that when rights are claimed to be limited or infringed, the justificatory burden on the public authority is 'substantial'. Moreover, the justificatory burden is variable depending on the degree of interference with human rights. As was decided in *Smith*: 'the more substantial the interference with human rights, the more the court will require by way of justification before it is satisfied that the decision is reasonable'.[36]

Third, for the justification to be convincing, it may be necessary to produce evidence of the facts underlying the decision and its justification. Although traditionally the courts have tended to leave evidential or factual questions for the primary decision-maker, their role in evaluating the justification for limitations on rights will sometimes lead them to evaluate the evidence in support of that justification. This may be what Lord Hope had in mind when he noted in *Shayler* that under proportionality:

> a close and penetrating examination of the factual justification for the restriction is needed if the fundamental rights enshrined in the Convention are to remain practical and effective for everyone who wishes to exercise them.[37]

Fourth, in deciding whether legislation is appropriate and not disproportionate in its adverse effect, 'it is the current effect and impact of the legislation which matter, not the position when the legislation was enacted and came into force'.[38] In other words, in measuring proportionality, the courts will focus on the legislative measure and the justification advanced in its support in court. The courts will not evaluate the quality of the

---

[35]  *R. v. Shayler* [2003] 1 A.C. 247 at [45], [59], *per* Lord Hope.
[36]  *R. v. Ministry of Defence, ex parte Smith* [1996] Q.B. 517 at 554.
[37]  *Shayler*, above n. 35 at [61]; followed in *R. (Countryside Alliance) v. Attorney General* [2007] 3 W.L.R. 922 at [78], *per* Lord Hope; see also *R. v. Daly* [2001] 2 W.L.R. 1622 at [23], *per* Lord Bingham who noted that under the HRA, 'the domestic courts must themselves form a judgment of whether a Convention right has been breached (*conducting such enquiry as is necessary to form that judgment*', emphasis added; Clayton (2001), 525.
[38]  *Wilson*, above n. 5 at [52], *per* Lord Nicholls.

reasons advanced by Ministers in support of the legislation during the course of parliamentary debate. As Lord Nicholls clarified in *Wilson*: 'lack of cogent justification in the course of parliamentary debate is not a matter which "counts against" the legislation on issues of proportionality'.[39] Fifth, in order to satisfy the court that a legal measure is proportionate, the state authority does not have to show that, in deciding on the legal measure in question, it adopted a reasoning process which reflects the three-stage proportionality enquiry.[40] To be sure, the aim of the proportionality enquiry is, in part, to assess whether the state authority gave sufficient weight to the importance to Convention rights. But this does not require the legislature to adopt the three-stage *de Freitas* approach when enacting that legislation under scrutiny. It simply requires that it (or rather, their legal representation) provides a justification of the measure on Convention rights grounds when challenged in court.

## Proportionality and *Wednesbury* unreasonableness after *Daly*

We have already noted that proportionality can be applied with varying intensity, depending on the degree of deference accorded to the primary decision-maker. This would seem to have the following important consequence, namely, that proportionality is not, in itself, a more intensive standard of review than *Wednesbury* unreasonableness. As Lord Hoffmann opined extrajudicially: 'the intensity of review is not determined by which test is used.'[41] Rather, the all-important question is 'the extent of the margin of appreciation and the grounds upon which it is allowed'.[42]

However, it is widely believed that *Wednesbury* unreasonableness is inherently more deferential,[43] and often assumed that proportionality

---

[39]  *Ibid.* at [67]; followed in *R. (Wilson)* v. *Wychavon District Council*, above n. 28 at [41], *per* Richards L.J.; see also *R. (Clift)* v. *SSHD* [2007] 1 All E.R. 1.

[40]  This has not been decided in relation to Parliament, but the House of Lords rejected 'the procedural approach' i.e. an approach which demands of the decision-maker that they follow a decision-making process akin to the proportionality enquiry, in *Begum* v. *Denbigh High School*, above n. 5 at [29], *per* Lord Bingham.

[41]  Hoffmann (1999a), 112; see also Supperstone and Coppel (1999), 314–5.

[42]  Hoffmann (1999a), 112; see also Bamforth (2003b), 297. Lord Hoffmann also suggests that the academic interest in dissecting the various stages of the proportionality test and allocating cases to the various categories of 'suitability' and 'necessity' etc., is 'no better than train spotting' (112) since it overlooks the central importance of the intensity of review.

[43]  See e.g. Elliott (2001b), 322; Fordham and De La Mare (2001), 30–2; Hunt (1997), 241.

is inherently more intrusive.[44] In fact, the principal reason for the historical judicial reluctance to countenance proportionality as a ground of review in its own right pre-HRA, was precisely the assumption that proportionality embodied a more intrusive, and therefore more constitutionally suspect, method of review.[45] Put simply, the fear was that the principle of proportionality would greatly increase the opportunities for judicial intervention in, and substitution of, governmental and administrative decision-making.[46] This fear was addressed by Lord Steyn in *Daly*[47] where he outlined some important differences between *Wednesbury* and proportionality. Given that this is a landmark decision of immense importance for the courts' constitutional review jurisdiction, it is necessary to subject Lord Steyn's 'justly celebrated and much quoted opinion'[48] in *Daly* to closer scrutiny.[49]

*Daly* concerned the legality of a policy of excluding prisoners during cell searches which required prisoner officers to examine their legal correspondence. A unanimous House of Lords held that this violated the prisoner's right to legal professional privilege under Article 8(1) of the Convention. Lord Bingham placed particular emphasis on the fact that no justification was advanced for routinely excluding all prisoners while the search was being carried out.[50] However, it is the short speech of Lord Steyn concerning the appropriate standard of review post-HRA, which is most pertinent to our enquiry into proportionality and deference. With the support of the rest of the House, Lord Steyn clarified that the three-stage proportionality test set out in *De Freitas*[51] was the applicable standard in determining whether a limitation on rights was arbitrary or excessive. He was keen to stress that this test was 'materially different' from *Wednesbury* unreasonableness and, after citing with approval

---

[44] *Daly*, above n. 37 at [27], *per* Lord Steyn: 'the intensity of review is somewhat greater under the proportionality approach'; see also *Shayler*, above n. 35 at [75].

[45] See Hunt (1997), 212.

[46] This fear was very much in evidence in the negative judicial responses to the attempt to rely on proportionality as a separate ground of challenge in *R. v. Secretary of State for the Home Department, ex parte Brind* [1991] 1 A.C. 696 at 750, *per* Lord Roskill; see further De Búrca (1997), 562; Elliott (2001b), 310.

[47] *Daly*, above n. 37.    [48] *Huang v. Secretary of State* [2007] 2 A.C. 167 at [13].

[49] There is a voluminous literature on the relationship between *Wednesbury* and proportionality, see e.g. De Búrca (1997); Jowell and Lester (1987); Jowell and Lester (1988); Le Sueur (2005); Laws (1998b); Craig (1999a); Fordham and De La Mare (2001).

[50] *Daly*, above n. 37 at [19], *per* Lord Bingham.

[51] *De Freitas v. Permanent Secretary of the Ministry of Agriculture, Fisheries, Lands and Housing* [1999] 1 A.C. 69, *per* Lord Clyde at 80.

some academic commentary on the issue,[52] he outlined the differences as follows:

> First, the doctrine of proportionality may require the reviewing court to assess the balance which the decision maker has struck, not merely whether it is within the range of rational or reasonable decisions. Secondly, the proportionality test may go further than the traditional grounds of review inasmuch as it may require attention to be directed to the relative weight accorded to interests and considerations. Thirdly, even the heightened scrutiny test developed in *Smith* is not necessarily appropriate to the protection of human rights . . . the challenge based on Article 8 of the Convention . . . foundered on the threshold required even by the anxious scrutiny test.[53]

Despite this litany of differences, Lord Steyn nonetheless made the following observation:

> There is an overlap between the traditional grounds of review and the approach of proportionality. Most cases would be decided in the same way whichever approach is adopted. But the intensity of review is somewhat greater under the proportionality approach.[54]

So whilst *most* cases may be decided in the same way, it was conceivable that the proportionality approach would 'sometimes yield different results. It is therefore important that cases involving Convention rights must be analysed in the correct way.'[55] Lord Steyn was not unaware of the main fear which surrounded the introduction of the proportionality test into UK law, namely that it would inevitably result in the courts substituting their own decision for that of Ministers and would collapse into 'the forbidden appellate approach'.[56] Therefore, he concluded his judgment with the assurance that the adoption of proportionality 'does not mean that there has been a shift to merits review. On the contrary, as Professor Jowell has pointed out[57] the respective roles of judges and administrators are fundamentally distinct and will remain so.'[58]

A number of points need to be made about this judgment. First, Lord Steyn acknowledges that in most cases the proportionality approach will make no difference to the outcome of cases.[59] In fact, it may not have

[52] Jowell (2000); Craig (1999b), 561–3; Feldman (1999b), 127ff.
[53] *Daly*, above n. 37 at [27].     [54] *Ibid.*     [55] *Ibid.* at [28].
[56] R. v. *Secretary of State for the Home Department, ex parte Brind* [1991] 1 A.C. 696 at 676, *per* Lord Lowry.
[57] Jowell (2000), 681.     [58] *Daly*, above n. 37 at [28].
[59] This view is also held by Lord Cooke of Thorndon in *Daly, ibid.* at [32]; see also Sedley (2005), 9; Elliot (2001a), 174.

made any difference in *Daly* itself. After all, Lord Bingham (who gave the leading judgment in *Daly* on the substantive issue) stressed that he had reached his conclusions 'on an orthodox application of common law principles derived from the authorities and an orthodox domestic approach to judicial review'.[60] In fact, none of their Lordships (not even Lord Steyn) actually carried out the three-stage proportionality test in disposing of the issue in *Daly*.

Second, my analysis suggests that the 'overlap' in almost all cases is not accidental. It is due to the overlap in the nature of the tests themselves. Both *Wednesbury* and proportionality are different ways of asking the same question, namely, whether an infringement of Convention rights is justifiable in the context of the particular case. As we have seen, the way in which judges relying on *Wednesbury* tended to set the threshold at a high level, accounts for the view that it was 'inherently' deferential. But this high threshold has long been deemed inappropriate in the human rights context. Rather, ever since *Smith*, the courts have applied a standard of 'anxious scrutiny',[61] with an onus on the defendant to justify the alleged infringement of rights. This has led some commentators to suggest that the courts have been applying the proportionality test in all but name, even before the HRA came into force.[62] It has now become commonplace to observe that when reasonableness is intensively applied in the context of human rights, it approximates very closely to proportionality,[63] and when proportionality is applied with a substantial degree of deference, it approximates very closely to *Wednesbury*.[64] Both tests can be applied with varying degrees of intensity and this, rather than the choice of test, is what makes the difference to the outcome of a case.

However, since Lord Steyn was keen to emphasise the 'concrete differences'[65] between proportionality and review for reasonableness, we need to examine each of his claims one by one. The first point of difference noted by Lord Steyn is that proportionality may require the reviewing court to assess the balance the decision-maker has struck, not merely whether it is within the range of rational or reasonable decisions. Embedded in this claim is the assumption that these options are rivals. *Either* one assesses the balance which the decision-maker struck *or* one assesses whether the decision is within a range of rational or reasonable

---

[60] *Daly*, above n. 37 at [23].    [61] *Smith*, above n. 36 at 540.

[62] Hunt (1997), 216; De Búrca (1997), 562; Craig (1999a), 97; Craig (1999b), 615, 630; Elliott (2001b), 36; Sedley (2004), 16.

[63] Craig (1999a), 97.    [64] Elliott (2001a), 174.

[65] *Daly*, above n. 37 at [27], following Feldman (1999b), 127–8.

decisions. But this is not necessarily the case. In order to assess the reasonableness of a decision, one is necessarily drawn into assessing the balance the decision-maker has struck. Given that the decisions which come up for review are, for the most part, a matter of striking a balance between competing interests, an assessment of their reasonableness involves an assessment of whether the balance struck by the decision is reasonable. Therefore, 'balancing' and 'assessing reasonableness' are not opposing alternatives.

It may be that the distinction Lord Steyn is attempting to capture here is that between the court 'deciding for itself' whether a decision is lawful, and deciding whether that decision is reasonable. But this is also a false dichotomy. The view that under the HRA, the courts have an obligation to 'form their own judgment' on the issue of proportionality, does not mean that the courts are entitled to ignore or underestimate the relevance of the primary decision to their judgment. An independent assessment of proportionality does not eliminate deference. It follows that even if the courts decide the proportionality issue for itself, it does not necessarily follow that proportionality amounts to a correctness standard. It is not the case that, under proportionality, the courts ask themselves what they would decide and substitute that for the primary decision. Their duty of deference to the primary decision-maker constrains their ability and willingness to interfere with the primary decision.[66] In short, proportionality is, for the most part, a reasonableness standard, rather than a standard of correctness and it is the degree of deference which defines the role of the secondary decision-maker.[67]

Lord Steyn's second claim is that proportionality may go further than the traditional grounds of review inasmuch as it may require attention to be directed to the relative weight accorded to interests and considerations. This recalls the point often made in relation to *Wednesbury*, namely, that it only sanctioned the judicial intervention in the exercise of public power at the outer limits, i.e. if it was egregiously wrong or irrational. Moreover, the role of the courts was merely to see that relevant considerations were taken

---

[66] Even though David Feldman makes a similar claim to Lord Steyn about the difference between proportionality and reasonableness in general terms, he acknowledges that 'very often in the Strasbourg case law the margin of appreciation allowed to States obscures the significance of this difference' (1999b), 128. The reason for this is that when proportionality is applied deferentially, the difference between it and *Wednesbury* is not clear.

[67] Thus, proportionality is often associated with the idea of a 'fair balance', see *R. v. A*, above n. 4 at 82, *per* Lord Hope; see also Sales and Hooper (2003), 428 who claim that that there must be '*a reasonable relationship* of proportionality between the means employed and the aim pursued', emphasis added.

into account, not that they were assessed or 'weighed' in particular way. However, when one looks at the case law applying the *Wednesbury* test, especially in its 'heightened' form, it is difficult to see how the court could assess whether the public decision was reasonable (when reasonableness included protection of human rights) without assessing how the various interests at stake were balanced. As Paul Craig explains:[68]

> The realisation that the courts have been applying the test to catch less egregious administrative action itself casts doubt on the claim that *Wednesbury* review can be conducted without engaging in some form of balancing, and raises the question of the difference between this balancing and that which occurs within proportionality.

In fact, the truth of this point is acknowledged by David Feldman (on whose analysis Lord Steyn partly relies), since he accepts that both *Wednesbury* and proportionality are 'designed to allow a court to review the balance struck by a public authority between competing interests, while placing limit the scope of such review'.[69] It is also supported by Murray Hunt who notes that, even prior to *Smith*, the language of Lord Bridge in *Bugdaycay* and *Brind* shows that the 'very concept of justification involves the reviewing court in such a balancing exercise'.[70] The key phrase is that 'nothing less than an important competing public interest will be sufficient to justify' the restriction – but the reviewing court:

> cannot meaningfully decide whether a particular public interest relied on by a decision maker is important without having a view of its own as to the relative importance of a range of public interest. Similarly, to assess whether the public interest relied on is sufficient to justify the interference necessarily involves the courts taking a view as to the relative importance of the right interfered with in the seriousness of the particular infringement of it . . . in short, a reviewing court adopting Lord Bridge's approach must carry out an exercise which involves assessing the importance of the right, the seriousness of the interference and the weight of the competing public interest before it can reach a sensible view as to the sufficiency of the justification offered.[70a]

Even when we look at the Court of Appeal decision in *Smith*, the deferential conclusion reached in that case was not because the court refrained

---

[68]  Craig (1999a), 95; Craig (2003), 629. Lord Steyn enlists Paul Craig as one of the academic public lawyers who support the list of 'differences' his Lordship outlines – although this quote seems to show that Craig does not endorse the idea that proportionality involves an assessment of balance, whereas unreasonableness does not.
[69]  Feldman (1999b), 127.    [70] Hunt (1997), 217.    [70a] *Ibid.*, 217–8.

from balancing the human rights claim of the applicants against the justification advanced by the Minister. It is simply that, in assessing that balance, they gave substantial (and arguably too much) weight to the Minister's side of the argument.[71]

This leads us to Lord Steyn's final point, which is that even the heightened scrutiny test developed in *Smith* is not necessarily appropriate to the protection of human rights because the threshold was placed too high. In order to assess this claim, we need to recall what the heightened scrutiny test enunciated in *Smith* involved. As is well known, the *Smith* case concerned the legality of a policy adopted by the Minister of Defence of dismissing homosexuals from the armed forces. Giving the leading judgment for the Court of Appeal, Sir Thomas Bingham M.R. declared that the court would only interfere with an administrative discretion on substantive grounds where the court is 'satisfied that the decision is unreasonable in the sense that it is beyond the range of responses open to a reasonable decision-maker'.[72] But he went on to clarify that:

> in judging whether the decision-maker has exceeded this margin of appreciation the human rights context is important. The more substantial the interference with human rights, the more the court will require by way of justification before it is satisfied that the decision is reasonable in the sense outlined above.[73]

This became known as the 'heightened *Wednesbury* test' because it required more by way of justification before a court could be satisfied that a decision was reasonable when human rights were involved. Moreover, the imposition of a heavier evidential burden on the administration to justify its interference with a fundamental human right introduced into this 'heightened test' a classic element of the proportionality enquiry, namely, the requirement that the decision-maker must provide evidence that the measure impinges no further on a protected right than was objectively necessary to achieve its legitimate aim.[74]

---

[71] It is implicit in Mark Elliott's comments that even under *Wednesbury*, there is some scrutiny of the balance, see Elliott (2001b), 313. However, *Wednesbury* only permits judicial intervention 'if the lack of balance is so great as to be manifestly unreasonable. In contrast, the proportionality doctrine requires much closer scrutiny of the balance.' This is in line with his argument that the difference between the two standards is one of degree rather than type.

[72] *Smith*, above n. 36 at 547.

[73] *Ibid.* at 547. He claimed that this statement was merely a distillation of the principles enunciated in *R. v. Secretary of State for the Home Department, ex parte Bugdaycay* [1987] A.C. 514 and *Brind*, above n. 56.

[74] De Búrca (1997), 562.

But despite setting out this test of 'heightened scrutiny' in the human rights context, his Lordship nonetheless applied the test in a highly deferential manner and found in favour of the Minister's policy of dismissal. He did so by according a substantial degree of deference to the Minister's policy, despite the fact that it impinged upon human rights. He stated:

> the greater the policy content of the decision, the more hesitant a court must be in holding a decision to be irrational. Moreover, where decisions are of a policy-laden or security-based nature, even greater caution than normal must be shown in applying the [*Wednesbury*] test.[75]

So the *Smith* case equivocated between two abstract statements about the appropriate approach of the court in this kind of dispute, which were in tension with each other. One suggested that the courts should scrutinise decisions more closely if they seem to interfere with human rights (i.e. show minimal deference, if any). The other suggested that the courts should be 'hesitant' to scrutinise (i.e. should show substantial deference) when adjudicating a decision which is policy laden or security based.[76] Although Lord Bingham famously endorsed the 'heightened scrutiny' test combined with a demand for justification from the Minister of Defence, he failed to subject the Minister's justification to searching scrutiny, despite enunciating an abstract test which required it. So, the applicants' challenge in *Smith* foundered on the deferential way in which the test was applied, not on the test itself. As Jeffrey Jowell observed,[77] the Court of Appeal in *Smith* merely 'paid lip service to heightened scrutiny'.[78]

As is well known, the applicants then took their case to Strasbourg where they won before the ECtHR.[79] There, the justification offered by the Minister of Defence, as well as the evidence marshalled in support of that justification, were subjected to much closer scrutiny. The Strasbourg court concluded that 'convincing and weighty reasons have not been offered by the [UK] Government to justify the policy against homosexuals in the Armed Forces and for the consequent discharge of the applicants from those Forces'.[80] They concluded that the threshold at which the Court of Appeal could find the Ministry of Defence policy irrational was:

---

[75]  *Smith*, above n. 36 at 556, *per* Lord Bingham.

[76]  See also Allan (2006b), 686. The disparity between the two standards set out in *Smith* seems to be implicit in Andrew Le Sueur's analysis, since he categorises Smith as an example of *both* 'light-touch review' *and* 'anxious scrutiny'/ 'rigorous examination', see Le Sueur (2005), 39. Le Sueur's categorisation is on the basis of the abstract statements cited above, not on an analysis of how they were applied in *Smith*.

[77]  Jowell (2000), 682.      [78]  *Ibid.*; see also Allan (2004b), 299.

[79]  *Smith* v. *United Kingdom* (2000) 29 E.H.R.R. 493.      [80]  *Ibid.* at [105].

placed so high that it effectively excluded any consideration by the domestic courts of the question of whether the interference with the applicants' rights answered a pressing social need or was proportionate to the national security and public order aims pursued, principles which lie at the heart of the court's analysis of complaints under Article 8 of the Convention.[81]

This statement is often taken to show that the *Wednesbury* standard, even in its heightened form, is 'obviously' less intrusive than the proportionality enquiry, and certainly not intrusive enough to give adequate protection to human rights.[82] Thus, Lord Cooke of Thorndon pronounced that the Strasbourg decision in *Smith* has 'given the quietus' to the argument that *Wednesbury* would be sufficient for review for compatibility with Convention rights.[83] However, the ECtHR's criticism of the domestic *Smith* judgments was aimed not at the test of heightened scrutiny officially favoured by the Court of Appeal or the High Court, but rather the deferential way in which that standard was applied in the case.[84] There is no reason why Sir Thomas Bingham M.R. could not have subjected the policy to more probing scrutiny within the auspices of the 'heightened scrutiny' test, especially as he emphasised the need for the Minister to justify any limitation of human rights. It was not the supposed strictures of the *Wednesbury* test which prevented him from doing this, but rather the degree of deference he thought appropriate in a policy-laden or 'security-based' context.

So, Lord Steyn's statement of the three material differences between *Wednesbury* and proportionality seems, on closer analysis, to be less robust than is often assumed. Moreover, doubt is cast on the extent of the claimed differences by the academic commentators on which Lord Steyn relies. This analysis supports the underlying point of the chapter, which is that the form of the test adopted is less important than the willingness or ability of the courts to interfere with the decisions of the elected branches.

There is one final point to be made in relation to Lord Steyn's judgement in *Daly*. It relates to his assurance at the end of his judgment that proportionality did not amount to merits review. Beyond this bald statement, Lord Steyn did not give any further guidance on how proportionality

---

[81] *Ibid.* at [138].

[82] See Hare (2000), 6; Elliott (2001b), 304ff; Elliott, (2001a); see also Hunt (2003), 341.

[83] *Daly,* above n. 37 at [32], *per* Lord Cooke.

[84] See Le Sueur (2005) 42 where the point is made that Simon Brown L.J.'s judgment at first instance in *Smith* is an example of a court having held that an anxious scrutiny approach was appropriate, but nevertheless actually relying on a standard more akin to ordinary irrationality review.

could succeed in occupying a middle ground between deferential *Wednesbury* on the one hand, and merits review on the other. This caused some confusion in subsequent case law, especially in cases involving immigration control, where the courts seemed to be unsure about the intensity of review which might be appropriate in that context. As Laws L.J. rightly observed in the Court of Appeal decision in *Huang*, 'Daly does not tell us directly where this middle ground might be.'[85] When *Huang* came to the House of Lords, Lord Bingham noted that Lord Steyn's assurance in *Daly* that proportionality did not amount to merits review, had 'given rise to some misunderstanding'.[86] Therefore, on behalf of the House of Lords, he took the opportunity to offer the following clarification:

> The point which, as we understand, Lord Steyn wished to make was that, although the Convention calls for a more exacting standard of review, it remains the case that the judge is not the primary decision-maker. It is not for him to decide what the recruitment policy for the Armed Forces should be.[87]

This clarification is fully in line with the analysis provided here, since it draws a distinction between making the primary decision, on the one hand, and reviewing the primary decision with varying degrees of intensity, on the other. The courts can review a recruitment policy for compliance with Convention rights in a robust and intensive fashion, without trying to step into the shoes of the primary decision-maker and devise an ideal policy. Although they must decide for themselves whether the decision is compatible with Convention rights, their role is secondary in the sense that they do not substitute their decision for that of the primary decision-maker, or attempt to make it '*de novo*'.[88] Although not explicitly articulated in this way either in *Huang* or *Daly*, what prevents proportionality becoming correctness review, is the fact that when assessing the proportionality of a decision, the courts are obliged to pay due deference

---

[85] *Huang* v. *Secretary of State for the Home Department* (CA) [2005] 3 W.L.R. 488 at [49], *per* Laws L.J.; see also *R. (Samaroo)* v. *SSHD* [2001] U.K.H.R.R. 1139; *R. (Mahmood)* v. *SSHD* [2001] 1 W.L.R. 840; see Hunt (2003), 356, n. 51.

[86] *Huang* (HL), above n. 48 at [13].

[87] *Ibid.* at [13]. This is also endorsed by Lord Bingham in *Smith* because he clarified that in adopting anxious scrutiny, 'this does not mean that the court is thrust into the position of the primary decision-maker. It is not the constitutional role of the courts to regulate the Armed Forces. But it has the role of protecting rights', see *Smith*, above n. 36 at 556.

[88] One might say that the courts are the primary decision-maker with respect to the question of the compatibility of a legislative decision with Convention rights, but are the secondary decision-maker with respect to the primary decision of how to solve the particular social problem addressed in the legislation.

to the primary decision-maker. Once we realise that deference is variable in light of the context of the individual case, we are also alerted to the fact that post-*Daly* (and reinforced in *Huang*), it is no longer appropriate for the courts to assume a highly deferential position in all cases, such that 'only a very extreme degree [of unreasonableness] could bring an administrative decision within the legitimate scope of judicial invalidation'.[89] The courts have shown that they are prepared to interfere with decisions of the elected branches when variable degrees of unreasonableness are shown.

## The advantages of proportionality

It might be concluded from the preceding discussion that since the conceptual differences between proportionality and reasonableness are less marked than is sometimes assumed, there is no advantage in embracing the proportionality test in adjudication under the HRA. That conclusion would be too rash. On my analysis, the House of Lords' unequivocal adoption of the proportionality test for HRA cases in *Daly* brings about many distinct advantages. First, it *signals* that a more intrusive review of legislative or Executive action is now appropriate under the HRA. It is a strong judicial statement that the legitimacy of intensive review is now beyond doubt. It allows the courts 'to feel entitled to be more interventionist than they would be in the case of pre-HRA judicial review proceedings'.[90] This consideration about the judicial sense of legitimacy in interfering with decisions of the elected branches, has an important role to play in understanding the importance of the House of Lords' unequivocal support for proportionality in the *Daly* case. *Daly* is a clear signal to lower courts that there is, as Lord Sedley put it, 'an obligation . . . *to look considerably harder* at the proportionality of what the state does'.[91] It announces the abandonment of the high degree of deference associated with the traditional formulation of the *Wednesbury* test. It is sometimes observed that the word '*Wednesbury*' is enough to capture a period in UK public law which was marked by judicial abstention and diffidence in the face of ever-growing governmental power without any serious

---

[89] *Daly*, above n. 37 at [32], *per* Lord Cooke.        [90] Feldman (1999b), 127.
[91] Sedley (2005), 9, emphasis added. Beatson *et al.* (2005), 267 also argue that although substantive review in human rights cases was moving towards the proportionality test pre-HRA, many judgments were equivocal. *Daly* provides some clarification about this important issue.

opposition.[92] The premise of conventional *Wednesbury* review was that the court's involvement in reviewing administrative action was severely suspect, a practice requiring considerable justification.[93] Of course, in terms of applying the standard, the judges eventually responded by developing the *Wednesbury* test beyond recognition, adapting it to changing circumstances and using it to strengthen their control over the Executive.[94] However, it never completely lost its flavour of excessive deference.[95] In this sense, it is advantageous, now that the HRA is enacted, to leave this deferential baggage behind.[96] The proportionality approach is unburdened by this history and is explicitly rights-focused. So, even though there is no significant conceptual difference between heightened scrutiny and proportionality, the widespread perception that they are different, is sufficient to bring about a change in judicial culture, one which is more open to intense scrutiny of decisions made by the elected branches. It is put beyond doubt that automatic or complete deference is no longer appropriate in the human rights context. The courts should not adopt an uncritical or supine approach: they have a constitutionally important reviewing role which should not be abdicated.

Second, and perhaps most importantly, proportionality clearly places the onus on the public authority (or in the case of a human rights challenge to legislation, the state) to justify their decision with respect to the demand to give sufficient importance to human rights.[97] Moreover, that justification must be established by means of evidence.[98] Supperstone and Coppel provide a good statement of the change:

> Under proportionality, respondents to applications for judicial review will be required to produce evidence of the facts outlined in their decisions, and of the thought processes which led them to believe that the restriction on Convention rights was necessary and proportionate. This is a departure from the present *Wednesbury*-based system, where it is frequently sufficient

---

[92]  Ian Leigh refers to the 'tradition of deference' under *Wednesbury*, see Leigh (2007b), 5, 10; Elliott (2001b), 311. For a classic statement of how Wednesbury gave expression to 'the constitutional imperative of judicial self-restraint', see generally Irvine (1996); Feldman (1999b).

[93]  Craig (1999a), 98.    [94]  *Ibid.*, 95.

[95]  Murray Hunt argues that the various developments and adaptations of the *Wednesbury* test were unsatisfactory, at least in the human rights context, because they are still shackled by 'the theoretical account of the relationship between the courts and the political branches which presupposes a minimal, deferential role for judges in the review of executive and administrative discretions', Hunt (1997), 260.

[96]  It is linked to what David Feldman has referred to as the traditional judicial 'habit of deference' to Parliament's wide legislative competence, see Feldman (1999b), 139.

[97]  Fordham and De la Mare (2001), 27, 29.    [98]  *Ibid.*, 53.

for respondents merely to identify the matters which they considered without going into details as to why they chose to give one match a greater weight than another.[99]

Although the pre-HRA position (especially the approach adopted in *Smith*) seemed to place some onus on the administration to justify its interference with fundamental human rights, this was marred by the fact that the court did not place a very heavy evidential burden on them in that case. Again, *Daly* provides clarification on this issue. The state (or the public authority) is under a duty to satisfy the court that its alleged infringement of human rights is proportionate in the ways set out in the three-stage test. This shift in onus constitutes one of the most significant changes in the culture of judicial review.

There is a third advantage of proportionality which deserves mention here. This is the claim (supported by many academic commentators and judges) that, in contrast with the 'blunt' tool of *Wednesbury* unreasonableness,[100] proportionality offers the courts a more 'structured' and systematic enquiry.[101] The advantage of providing more structure to the analysis is claimed to be that it makes the various stages of the enquiry more transparent and explicit,[102] thereby constraining the judiciary in the factors they can take into account in assessing the legality of decisions taken by the elected branches of government. It is certainly the case that the proportionality enquiry provides the judiciary with a framework of separate questions they should pose to the primary decision-maker, thus implying that proportionality demands that a range of separate standards are met. However, it is probably a misleading characterisation of the case law decided under *Wednesbury* unreasonableness to suggest that unreasonableness is a monolithic or unitary standard. It is more likely that a range of different faults underlie the cases where a decision was found to be *Wednesbury* unreasonable.[103] Moreover, if we turn to the question of whether the claim about enhanced 'structure' is accurate as a characterisation of the proportionality enquiry, we can see that this is not always apparent in the case law. When courts review for proportionality, the rigour with which judges scrutinise the answers to each of the three questions will vary in accordance with the context of the case. Moreover, it is well known that the courts do not always follow the supposed 'structure'

---

[99] Supperstone and Coppel (1999), 326.        [100] Sedley (2005), 9; see also Blake (2002), 26.
[101] Craig (1999a), 99; Sedley (2002); Sedley (2008), 20; De Búrca (1993), 146.
[102] Fordham (2004), 47; Elliott (2001b), 312; Sedley (2005), 9; De Búrca (1993), 146.
[103] See also Bagshaw (2006), 18.

of the three questions – sometimes they only address one of the three or, even if all are addressed in a formal sense, one question is given priority. Even though *Daly* is the landmark case clarifying that proportionality is the appropriate standard for cases concerning Convention rights, not one of their Lordships in that case, actually went through the three stages of the proportionality enquiry, step by step. So, it may be that the claims about the advantages of the structured three-stage proportionality enquiry are overstated in light of its application in the case law. Perhaps the main advantage of proportionality is the enhanced sense of legitimacy it gives the courts and the shift in the onus of proof.

However, this does not undermine the fact that the proportionality enquiry allows the judiciary to deal separately with different aspects of the measure under review, namely, the legislative aim, its instrumentality to that aim and whether it imposes a disproportionate or excessive burden on any individual. This has the following positive consequence. While a rights claim involving a complex social problem such as e.g. national security or immigration policy may, when taken as a whole, seem to indicate that the judiciary is out of its institutional depth, the structure of the proportionality enquiry provides a means for disassembling the problem and breaking it down into more manageable questions and issues. Just as the structure of the proportionality enquiry disassembles the separate questions to be asked of the primary decision-maker, so too does it disassemble the challenges to institutional capacity and legitimacy (i.e. the grounds of deference) which underlie those questions. In so doing, the proportionality enquiry provides an opportunity for a more precise and contextual assessment both of the substantive issues, as well as the question of the degree of deference which is appropriate with reference to them.[104]

For example, although the *Belmarsh Prison* case involved a high-profile legislative initiative passed to advance the 'war on terror', the House of Lords was nonetheless able to issue a declaration of incompatibility, simply on the basis that there was no rational link between the legislative aim and the means used to achieve that aim. Or in *Ghaidan* v. *Mendoza*, the courts found a violation of Article 8 because the relevant provision of the 1977 Rent Act was not supported by a legitimate legislative aim. It is arguable that if the courts in these cases had simply been asked to assess whether these policies were 'reasonable' or 'fair', they might have

---

[104] In formulating this point, I benefited greatly from the analysis contained in Wiseman (2001), 454.

been more prone to pay substantial deference to the elected branches. There may well be cases where the courts feel more confident in their competence, expertise or legitimacy to assess whether there is a rational or logical connection between a stated legislative aim and the means used to achieve that aim, than they would in assessing the propriety, reasonableness or correctness of the legislative measure considered as a whole. Thus, the proportionality enquiry has the advantage of encouraging the courts to consider individual aspects of the measure under scrutiny, and to adopt a more precise and contextual assessment of them. This dovetails nicely with the argument advanced in chapters 7 and 8 that the question of deference must be approached in a sensitive and contextual manner.

## Proportionality and unqualified rights

We have seen that the proportionality enquiry is used by the courts in assessing the justification advanced by the state in support of the limitation. This is thought to apply straightforwardly to Articles 8–11, since those rights are stated in general terms in subsection 1 of the Article, with subsection 2 providing the legitimate grounds for limiting the right (such as e.g. national security, public safety, public health, etc.). Thus, Articles 8–11 are said to contain the 'qualified rights'. The question now is whether the proportionality enquiry is, or ought to be used, with reference to the other rights guaranteed in the Convention. Article 3 (the right against torture and inhuman and degrading treatment) contains no explicit limitation. Nor do Articles 4, 6, 7 and 14. These are known as the 'unqualified rights'. Then, there are Articles 2 and 5 which set out a number of specific instances in which limitation of the rights is allowed. These rights differ from Articles 8–11 in the sense that they are more specific about the grounds on which the rights can be limited. We can call these 'specifically qualified rights'. So, should proportionality also be used with reference to unqualified rights, or should it be confined to those which are explicitly qualified?

In the case law and academic writing on this subject, there is a widespread (though not unanimous) assumption that proportionality will only apply to the qualified rights.[105] However, for the most part, these statements about·the limited applicability of the proportionality

---

[105] See Jowell (2000), 680; For a contrasting position, see Feldman (1999b), 123, who states that proportionality is relevant in relation to 'both Convention rights which expressly or impliedly permit interferences'.

enquiry are made in passing: they assume, rather than argue for the position. Ian Leigh, by contrast, has given the matter sustained consideration and advances an array of arguments to support the idea.[106] For Leigh, proportionality has 'no place... under Articles 3, 4 or 7 which have no limitations, nor under Articles 2 or 5, where the limitations are specific'.[107] The same is true, he argues, of Article 14, although he acknowledges the difficulty that the application of Article 14 requires another Convention right to be invoked, which itself might be qualified.[108] On Leigh's analysis, the proportionality test itself 'suggests a degree of... deference'.[109] His concern is that if we allow the courts to apply the proportionality test, it will:

> become a Trojan horse by which judicial deference can be smuggled into the domestic legal system, in the absence of the margin of appreciation, into contexts where it does not belong.[110]

He explains further that where rights are unqualified:

> or contain specific exemptions without reference to proportionality, this signifies the special importance of the right in question, which should not then be diluted by reading in limitations not found in the text.[111]

Not even 'weak judicial deference' is appropriate with reference to these rights.[112] So, his objection to proportionality outside Articles 8–11 is that it entails a 'dilution'[113] of the rights which were meant to be 'unqualified' – and this goes against the importance given to them by the text of the Convention. With reference to these more important rights, a form of 'primary review' or 'merits review' is 'constitutionally mandated'.[114]

The main arguments advanced by Leigh in support of this position are essentially textual in nature. He relies on three different textual sources. First, since there are no explicit limitations in the Articles guaranteeing the so-called 'unqualified rights': therefore, the courts should not read them in. Second, section 6 HRA states 'in the plainest of terms'[115] that a public authority acts unlawfully when it violates a person's Convention rights. According to Leigh, the unqualified language of section 6 appears to require 'merits review', apart from in those cases 'where the structure

---

[106] Leigh (2002); Leigh (2007b).    [107] Leigh (2002), 284.
[108] Leigh (2002), 284284, n. 10.
[109] Leigh (2002), 278, 287, where he refers to the Convention permitting 'deference to the executive within the proportionality test' in the context of qualified Convention rights.
[110] Leigh (2002), 278.    [111] Ibid., 277.    [112] Ibid.    [113] Ibid., 284.
[114] Ibid., 287.    [115] Ibid., 283.

of the Convention invites considerations of proportionality',[116] i.e. where 'qualified rights' are at issue. Finally, Leigh relies on a statement by the ECtHR in *Chahal* v. *UK* to the effect that 'the notion of an effective remedy under Article 13 requires *independent scrutiny* of the claim that there exists substantial grounds for fearing a real risk of treatment contrary to Article 3'.[117] From this statement, Leigh deduces that where unqualified Convention rights are concerned, domestic courts must review the merits in order to comply with Article 13. In the balance of this chapter, I will attempt to show that, *contra* Leigh, deference is ineliminable in human rights adjudication and that the judicial reasoning process with reference to so-called 'unqualified rights', is not substantially different from that employed by the courts in relation to the explicitly qualified rights.

On my analysis, proportionality does not *dictate* a particular standard or intensity of review. That is determined by the three grounds of deference and the way in which they apply in the context of an individual case. Leigh's argument prompts us to enter a further clarification about the nature of deference, namely, that the appropriate degree of deference to the primary decision-maker is an omnipresent feature of human rights adjudication. As explained earlier, *minimal deference* applies across the board in every case. Moreover, the question about *whether to defer* more substantially and to what degree arises in every case. Of course, it need not be answered in the affirmative. In the majority of cases, substantial deference will be inappropriate. But the question about whether to defer is one which courts must address in every case where they have to determine whether a piece of legislation or an Executive decision is compatible with Convention rights. It must be addressed no matter what 'standard' of review is chosen as appropriate and even if it is not explicitly required by the text of the Convention.[118] Therefore, the lack of reference to proportionality or deference either in the Convention or section 6 HRA does not determine the issue either way.[119]

Leigh might respond that whilst deference may be part and parcel of *Wednesbury*, and may also feature in anxious scrutiny and proportionality, it has no place in the 'merits' or 'primary' or 'legality' review which

---

[116] *Ibid.*, 284.

[117] (1996) 23 E.H.R.R. 413 at [151], emphasis added, cited by Leigh (2002), 271.

[118] Deference is a feature of constitutional and administrative law adjudication worldwide, despite the fact that it is not mentioned in any instrument guaranteeing human rights of which I am aware.

[119] Atrill (2003), 42.

he recommends. In fact, it is precisely the lack of deference which distinguishes merits review from the traditional standards of review and this is the type of review Leigh recommends for the so-called 'unqualified rights'. However, this overlooks the fact that it is inherent in the court's role as secondary decision-maker, that it should accord some deference to the primary decision-maker. As long as the courts are called upon to review the legality of a parliamentary or Executive decision in terms of compliance with Convention rights, they will necessarily have to take into account in their decision the competence, expertise and legitimacy of the primary decision-maker. And they will have to do so regardless of whether they are adjudicating in the context of a right which is explicitly qualified or unqualified in the text of the Convention.

This is not to say that the way in which the Convention rights are expressed has no bearing on rights adjudication. On the contrary, the express terms of the Convention are always the starting point for their interpretation. It seems plausible to argue that if some rights are stated without qualification, this is suggestive of their perceived importance. However, we should be careful not to leap from this plausible premise to the conclusion that no judicial deference is appropriate in their adjudication. An alternative (and, to my mind, more plausible) conclusion is that the importance of the right is a factor indicating that less deference to the primary decision-maker may be appropriate. However, this factor alone will not determine the degree of deference. Rather, it must be balanced against other (sometimes competing) factors in an overall assessment about the extent to which deference is due. In this way, the lack of explicit qualification of the right in the text of the Convention is given some weight, but it is just one factor within a deference analysis, rather than eliminating it altogether.[120]

This approach is borne out by the case law.[121] In *R. (Bloggs 21) v. SSHD*,[122] Keene L.J. commented that even if he could accept that it is for the court to make the primary judgment in relation to unqualified rights:

---

[120] This argument is also advanced by Atrill (2003), 43; supported by Lester and Pannick (2004), 3.21 who state that 'the *greater* latitude is appropriate in relation to those rights which expressly require a balancing of competing considerations'; see also Craig (2003), 582.

[121] *R. (IR) v. Shetty* [2003] EWHC 3022, where Munby J. held that despite being a case arising under Articles 3 and 5, the court should afford the Secretary of State a margin of discretion. Heightened scrutiny is appropriate, but review on the merits was not, at [50]–[51].

[122] *R. (Bloggs 21) v. SSHD* [2003] 1 W.L.R. 2724.

the reality is that the court would have to attach considerable weight to the assessment of risk made by those with professional involvement in the areas with which the case was concerned, which in the present case means the police and the prison service.[123]

*Bloggs* concerned the removal of a prisoner from a 'protected witness unit' into a mainstream prison and whether this would breach his right to life under Article 2. Auld L.J. noted that:

> Despite the fundamental and unqualified nature of the right to life it is still appropriate to show some deference to and/or to recognise the special competence of the prison service in making a decision going to the safety of an inmate's life. However, the degree of deference to, and/or of recognition of the special competence of, the decision-maker is less and, correspondingly, the intensity of the court's review is greater – perhaps greatest in an Article 2 case – than for those human rights where the Convention requires a balance to be struck.[124]

As regards how intense the review should be, he commented that the guidance is necessarily imprecise. However, he endorsed the comment of Lord Walker of Gestingforth in *Pro-life Alliance* that 'the court's task is not to substitute its own view for that of the decision-makers, but to review their decision with an intensity appropriate to all the circumstances of the case'.[125] In other words, he denied that 'merits review' is appropriate for unqualified rights.

This leads us to a point about the nature of rights. Leigh suggests that, in relation to unqualified rights, the court's task is to ask the following 'simple question': 'have the victim's Convention rights been contravened by the public authority?'[126] In answering that question, all considerations about relative competence, expertise, political accountability and balancing are irrelevant. In the foregoing paragraphs, I have tried to show that such considerations are always relevant when courts engage in rights adjudication. Now, I wish to add to this the point that the court's task in relation to so-called unqualified rights is by no means 'simple' and is not fundamentally different from their task in relation to the qualified rights.[127] With qualified rights, the courts tend to adopt a two-stage approach. First, they establish whether there is a *prima facie* violation of

---

[123] *Ibid.* at [35].     [124] *Ibid.* at [64].     [125] *Ibid.* at [139].     [126] Leigh (2002), 287.

[127] Indeed, many judges have denied that cases arising under the so-called absolute rights involve a simplistic question of whether an action violates an absolute standard, see e.g. Jonathan Parker L.J. re Article 6 in *Roth* at [134], (discussing Article 6), citing Lord Steyn in *R. v. A*, above n. 4 at [36], in support.

the right, before then going on to assess whether the interference is proportionate or not. At the second stage of the analysis, there is a balancing exercise between the weight and importance of the Convention right on the one hand, and the severity of incursion into it, the justification for the legislative measure on the other. With respect to so-called 'unqualified rights', there is no formal division into two different stages. However, in seeking to establish whether the right has been violated, the courts assess whether the alleged violation is so severe that it can be said to go beyond the scope of the right. So, with reference to the unqualified rights, the (difficult) assessment of whether the right has been contravened is presented in the form of a delineation of the scope of the right. Take, for example, the prohibition on 'inhuman and degrading treatment' in Article 3. The difficulty in deciding Article 3 cases lies in determining the meaning and scope of the right as expressed in this vague statement. The courts have tended to say that ill-treatment must obtain a minimum level of severity, and assessment of what that minimum requires, is relative to all the circumstances of the case.[128] So, for example, when attempting to establish whether the prohibition on assisted suicide violated Diane Pretty's right to life, the court had to give weight to the legislative aim of the Suicide Act 1961 and the social function of prohibiting assisted suicide in general, whilst balancing this against Diane Pretty's claim that gaining assistance with her suicide was included within her right to life under Article 3. This sort of balancing is exactly the sort of judicial reasoning which must be carried out when reviewing for proportionality under the explicitly qualified rights. Even with the unqualified rights, the courts tend to say that violation is a matter of degree. Thus, when establishing whether certain control orders violated the right to liberty, the House of Lords initially established that the controlled persons were 'undoubtedly... deprived of their liberty' – the difficult question was whether this deprivation was sufficiently severe to warrant the conclusion that their rights under Article 5 had been violated.[129] Lord Brown explained that the issue was a question of 'degree or intensity', noting that it was difficult to identify the point at which a daily curfew 'shades into' a regime akin to house arrest.[130]

---

[128] R. (Pretty) v. DPP [2002] H.R.L.R. 10 at [90]; see also R. v. Secretary of State, ex parte Limbuela [2005] UKHL 66 at [54], per Lord Bingham.

[129] Secretary of State for the Home Department v. JJ [2007] UKHL 45 at [39], per Lord Hoffmann, [102], per Lord Brown.

[130] Ibid. at [103].

This is not fundamentally different from the *kind* of reasoning the courts adopt when adjudicating the so-called qualified rights. The difference between the two approaches is one of form rather than substance – the type of judicial reasoning is, in each case, substantially the same.[131] Therefore, the language of 'qualified' and 'unqualified' rights is misleading. All the rights contained in the Convention are subject to qualification, but in Articles 8–11, the qualifications are set out expressly in the text of the Convention. In Articles 3, 5, 6, 7 and 14, there may be no express qualifications in the text, but the courts have the task of defining the scope of those rights, which necessarily includes a determination about their limits. This task is no simpler than their task under Articles 8–11. Perhaps, due to the lack of textual guidance, the task is in fact more difficult.

This is supported by Lord Woolf's comments in *Lambert* – a case concerning the right to a fair trial under Article 6. Although Article 6 contains no express limitation clause, it is curiously omitted from Leigh's list of unqualified rights.[132] Lord Woolf claimed that the distinction between the qualified and unqualified rights is not significant in practice 'because as the ECtHR jurisprudence makes clear, the court does not have to ignore the wider interests of the public in applying those provisions of the Convention which have no express limitation'.[133] In other words, although there are no *express* limitations, Parliament and the Executive are nonetheless subject to limitations which are implicit – limitations which the courts will recognise and enforce. In support of this view, he cited Lord Hope's comments in *Kebilene* to the effect that the task of striking a balance between the demands of the general interest of the community and the protection of the fundamental rights of the individual applied 'as a matter of general principle'.[134] In other words, it applies both to the so-called 'unqualified rights', as well as those which are subject to an express limitation clause.

As we have seen, although the courts make note of the unqualified or fundamental nature of some of the Convention rights, they tend nonetheless to suggest that this does not eliminate entirely the pragmatic and constitutional reasons for deference in particular cases.[135] But what about the distinct issue of proportionality? Do the courts adopt the three-stage test with reference *only* to Articles 8–11? There are some conflicting judicial

---

[131] Atrill argues that the distinction between qualified and unqualified rights is misleading, but does so for slightly different reasons, see Atrill (2003), 44–5.

[132] *Ibid.*, 45.

[133] *Lambert*, above n. 4 at [14], citing *Murray* v. *UK* (1994) 19 E.H.R.R. 193 in support.

[134] *Ibid.* at [15].        [135] This analysis of the case law is also supported by Craig (2001), 592.

*dicta* on this issue. However, the following points should be noted. First, Lord Steyn's judgment in *Daly* sets out a proportionality test of general applicability. He did not limit its applicability to Articles 8–11.[136] True, his Lordship prefaced his comments in *Daly* with the remark that the courts should make 'due allowance for important structural differences between various Convention rights, which I do not propose to discuss'.[137] However, I do not think that this can be taken to endorse the view that proportionality is not applicable at all outside Articles 8–11. The word 'structural' seems to suggest that the difference in the rights is in the way they are expressed, rather than indicating more fundamental differences in their nature.[138] Lord Steyn's comment is thus compatible with the analysis provided here, namely, that whilst the proportionality enquiry is generally applicable, the different way in which the various Convention rights are expressed may impact on the way in which proportionality applies. Moreover, the domestic courts have often relied on proportionality with reference to the so-called unqualified rights – most notably with reference to Article 6,[139] but also in connection with Article 3,[140] Article 5[141] and Article 14.[142]

However, it cannot be denied that sometimes the courts explicitly reject proportionality as an appropriate approach with reference to unqualified rights. Thus, in *R. (Limbuela)* v. *Secretary of State*,[143] Lord Hope opined that the obligation on states to refrain from inhuman or degrading treatment was absolute, and that considerations of proportionality were inapt in this situation.[144] However, he also accepted that ill-treatment must obtain a minimum level of severity if it is to fall within the scope of Article 3 and that this assessment will be context sensitive.[145] Moreover, the

---

[136] Leigh claims that Lord Steyn's comments about the requirements of proportionality were based on 'taking Article 8 as an example', see Leigh (2002), 277, but there is no reference to Article 8, and Lord Steyn's comments seem to be general in nature.

[137] *Daly*, above n. 37 at [27], cited in Leigh (2002), 284.

[138] In fact, Leigh seems to support this reading of Lord Steyn's remark, since he goes on to argue that the differences between them are in fact 'more than structural', see Leigh (2002), 285ff.

[139] In *R. v. A*, above n. 4 at [38], Lord Steyn stated that the right to a fair trial was absolute, but that some balancing was permitted 'in respect of what the concept of a fair trial entails . . . in this context proportionality has a role to play'; see also *R. v. Offen* [2001] 2 All E.R. 154 at [95], *per* Lord Woolf; *Lambert*, above n. 4 at [17], [34], [37], *per* Lord Steyn; *Roth*, above n. 16 at [50]–[51], *per* Lord Simon Brown; see further Blake (2002), 21.

[140] See *Pretty*, above n. 128 at [92], *per* Lord Hope.

[141] *Offen*, above n. 139 at [95], *per* Lord Woolf.

[142] *Ghaidan*, above n. 10 at [18], *per* Lord Nicholls.

[143] [2005] UKHL 66.    [144] *Ibid.* at [48]ff.    [145] *Ibid.* at [54].

determination of whether treatment in any given case has obtained the necessary degree of severity to violate Article 3 will require an 'exercise of judgment'.[146] Lord Scott argued that since Article 3 was absolute and unqualified, 'there can be no room for any policy justification'.[147] Does this undercut the claim made here that both proportionality and deference are generally applicable in the context of adjudication under the HRA?

I would answer this question in the negative and for the following reasons. Whilst there may be no room for policy justification which takes the form of justifying a *prima facie* limitation on the right, there *will* tend to be policy justification which takes the form of showing that the policy does not violate the right at all, by not falling within the scope of its prohibition. Both with explicitly qualified and unqualified rights, the aim of the state will be to show that its decisions were justifiable, either by not limiting the right to an unjustifiable degree or by not violating it to an unjustifiable degree. As regards the burden of proof in, say, Article 3 cases, it is for the claimant to show that some course of conduct will, absent a justification, amount to a violation of Article 3, but it is then for those who seek to rely upon such a justification to prove convincingly that it exists.[148] Similarly, in the many cases concerning treatment in mental health institutions, once it is demonstrated that some course of conduct will, in the absence of some medical justification, amount to a violation of Article 3 then it is for those who seek to rely upon a medical justification to prove convincingly that there is a medical necessity for what is proposed. Therefore, it seems as if the courts rely on a two-stage analysis in relation to Article 3 violations even if it is not as obvious or clearly signposted as in cases relating to Articles 8–11. They look to see whether a decision or particular conduct constitutes a 'potential violation'[149] of Article 3, before going on to assess the reasons or justification for it.

In more recent writing, Leigh has softened his argument and now makes the more modest claim that post-HRA 'the courts can be seen . . . to be sensitive to the different role that they play in cases of unqualified rights'.[150] This much weaker claim is compatible with the view advanced here, namely that with reference to rights which are cast in unqualified terms, this is one factor suggesting that the courts may pay less deference to the primary decision-maker. Much of the case law does not support

---

[146] *Ibid.* at [55].      [147] *Ibid.* at [90].
[148] See discussion in *Shetty*, above n. 121 at [61], *per* Munby J.
[149] *Wilkinson* at [83], *per* Baroness Hale.      [150] Leigh (2007b), 185.

Leigh's original more unequivocal position. He notes that the 'strongest statements' in his favour come from *R. (Wilkinson)* v. *Responsible Medical Officer Broadmoor Hospital*,[151] a case concerning the need for forcible medical treatment of a mental patient detained under the Mental Health Act 1983. There, the question was whether this compulsory treatment violated the appellant's fundamental rights under Articles 2, 3 and 8. The Court of Appeal held that it was entitled to reach its own view as to the merits of the medical decision and whether it infringed the patient's human rights.[152] In support of his view that 'merits review' is warranted for unqualified rights, Leigh cites Baroness Hale's *dictum* that 'super *Wednesbury* is not enough. The appellant is entitled to a proper hearing, on the merits, of whether the statutory grounds for imposing this treatment upon him against his will are made out.'[153]

Caution needs to be exercised when assessing the import of this statement. In *Wilkinson*, Simon Brown L.J. emphasised the extent to which cases in this area depend upon the detailed facts of the individual cases.[154] He prefaced his remarks on this subject with the *caveat* that he did not intend his judgment to represent a broad statement of principle even with reference to detentions under the 1983 Act. Presumably, he would then object to it being interpreted as a broad statement of principle about the role of the courts in adjudicating unqualified rights as a whole. Second, his Lordship was keen to stress that the courts are likely to pay 'very particular regard'[155] to the views held by those specifically charged with the patient care and well-being and that 'the courts will not be astute to overrule a treatment plan decided upon by [the relevant medical practitioners]'.[156] In other words, even though he characterised the role of the courts as one of merits review, he was aware of both the principled and pragmatic need to show deference to the expertise of the primary decision-maker. In later case law, it has been emphasised that, even if it is necessary to decide some of the facts for themselves, the court's role is supervisory and does not require so-called merits review. They are not entitled to substitute their view for that of the primary decision-maker.[157] Leigh concedes that in subsequent case law there is a 'judicial reluctance'[158] to treat review of alleged breaches of unqualified rights as merits review where no deference is appropriate.

Finally, Leigh places considerable weight on the statement of the ECtHR in *Chahal* v. *UK* that 'the notion of an effective remedy under Article 13

---

[151] [2001] All E.R. 294.    [152] *Ibid.* at [26], *per* Simon Brown L.J.    [153] *Ibid.* at [83].
[154] *Ibid.* at [23].    [155] *Ibid.* at [31].    [156] *Ibid.*
[157] See e.g. *R. (IR)* v. *Shetty* above n. 121.    [158] Leigh (2007b), 185.

requires independent scrutiny of the claim that there exists a substantial grounds for fearing a real risk of treatment contrary to Article 3'.[159] From this statement about 'independent scrutiny', Leigh deduces that domestic courts must review the merits (without any deference) in order to comply with Article 13.[160] As Simon Atrill points out, 'a requirement of "independent scrutiny" is consistent with a domestic approach that falls short of substitution: the judgments of the Strasbourg court do not require the elimination of all deference in all cases under Article 3'.[161] In fact, this very point is made explicit in *Chahal* itself, where the court noted that the Convention did not require a right to judicial review

> of such breadth as to empower the court, on all aspects of the case including questions of pure expediency, to substitute its own discretion for that of the decision-making authority. The review should, however, be wide enough to bear on those conditions which are essential for the lawful detention of a person according to Article 5.[162]

Even where the Strasbourg court has been critical of the traditional *Wednesbury* standard, such as in *Smith* v. *UK*,[163] it did not go as far as to imply that judicial substitution of the Executive decision is the only means of satisfying the requirements of Article 13 where rights other than Articles 8–11 have been violated. The main reason for holding that *Wednesbury* review was inadequate for the purposes of Article 13 in the *Chahal* case, was that the reliance on national security considerations limited the English courts' power of review.[164] However, this claim may no longer hold since in the *Belmarsh Prison* case, the House of Lords asserted their willingness, indeed their duty, to scrutinise closely and rigorously decisions made in the context of national security. This standard of review, which did not amount to substitution without any deference, would seem to satisfy the requirements of Article 13.

## Conclusion

Many commentators have argued that the judicial reliance on proportionality (and rejection of *Wednesbury* unreasonableness), is one of the most significant changes brought about by the HRA. The analysis in this chapter has shown that even pre-HRA, the courts had moved towards a heightened standard of scrutiny when human rights were involved, and

---

[159] *Chahal*, above n. 117 at [151].  [160] Atrill (2003), 271.  [161] *Ibid.*
[162] *Chahal*, above n. 117 at [127].  [163] (1999) 29 E.H.R.R. 493.
[164] *Chahal*, above n. 117 at [143].

in many cases, were already relying on proportionality in all but name. However, the deferential baggage of *Wednesbury* and the sense that judicial intervention in decisions of the legislature or Executive connoted by it, meant that the judiciary were often lured into paying more deference than was due. The unequivocal support for proportionality in *Daly* put an end to that sense of illegitimacy and pointed the courts in the direction of a more probing, rights-based approach. The HRA gave the courts the necessary impetus to leave that baggage behind, thus providing a clear endorsement to the courts to scrutinise robustly and to be confident in their reviewing role.[165] This and other advantages of *Daly* were highlighted in this chapter, despite the fact that some of Lord Steyn's *dicta* seemed to exaggerate the conceptual differences between proportionality and *Wednesbury* unreasonableness. Finally, by highlighting the link between justification and proportionality, we saw that the doctrine of proportionality can contribute to the 'culture of justification' under the HRA. It highlights the way in which proportionality is a crucial component of constitutional review.

[165]  Bamforth (2003b), 291.

# PART III

## Questions of constitutional legitimacy

# 10

## The nature and status of the HRA

### Introduction

In the first part of this book, I defended some of the creative methods of interpretation employed by judges under section 3(1) HRA, including the judicial power to 'read down' and 'read in' to primary legislation. In the second part of the book, we saw that this judicial creativity is tempered, not only by the inherent limits of judicial law-making, but also by the broader institutional concerns expressed in the doctrine of deference. Therefore, this book does not advocate creativity in every case come what may. Rather, in viewing the interpretive exercise as one of balance between judicial innovation and conservation, the normative conclusion for adjudication under the HRA was that this balance ought to be carried out with care and sensitivity to all the contextual factors relevant to the case. Sometimes, the correct balance will lead the court to develop and create new law, using the interpretive obligation under section 3(1). At others, the balance of considerations will indicate that they should either not find a violation of Convention rights at all, or if they do, that they should issue a declaration of incompatibility.

But there is no denying that the HRA gives the courts considerable power to review and scrutinise legislation for compatibility with Convention rights and occasionally the power to rectify that legislation by way of statutory interpretation. In this final part of the book, I wish to address directly the question of the legitimacy of constitutional review under the HRA. In tackling this justificatory task, we need to be clear about what it is we are justifying. Such clarification will require an assessment of the status of the HRA, as well as the constitutional significance and implications of the method of adjudication entailed by it. Many commentators on the HRA believe that it is effectively a Bill of Rights and assume that the HRA takes legislative power away from the elected Parliament and gives it to the courts. In this chapter, I will subject these claims to critical scrutiny. In chapter 11, I will go on to address the justificatory challenge posed by the orthodox account of parliamentary sovereignty. It is often said that the HRA embodies an ingenious reconciliation between enhanced protection of human rights and parliamentary sovereignty. Chapter 11 will test the plausibility of that common claim. Finally, in chapters 12 and 13, I will take up the normative challenge in earnest. Chapter 12 will put forward a case for constitutional review under the HRA and chapter 13 will attempt to defend that case from important criticisms rooted in democratic concerns.

In the UK, there is a strong intellectual tradition of opposing any enhancement of judicial power in the name of protecting human rights. This opposition has both a positive and negative dimension. The positive dimension draws on a belief in the value and importance of strong parliamentary government and the right of all citizens to participate in democratic decision-making. The negative dimension is scepticism about the desirability (and indeed, ability) of judges to enhance the protection of human rights in a way which would allow them to constrain our elected representatives. I will call critics who adopt this perspective 'democratic sceptics' – 'democratic' because their arguments are firmly rooted in democratic concerns, and 'sceptics' because this captures nicely their disposition towards judicial power and is, in any case, nomenclature they are happy to ascribe to themselves.[1] Chapter 12 will address the well-known arguments along these two dimensions.

Before advancing and defending my arguments in support of constitutional review under the HRA, I need to make explicit one of my background assumptions. This is that human rights should be protected in the UK and should not be violated. In particular, those rights adumbrated in the ECHR ought to be so protected.[2] Making this assumption is justified partly because it is shared by both supporters and critics of the HRA alike. All democratic sceptics seem to endorse 'the importance of human rights within any democratic system of government'.[3] Even Keith Ewing, who has been one of the most strident critics of the HRA, stresses that whatever the problems with constitutional entrenchment of rights or increased reliance on judicial enforcement of those rights, 'no-one is denying [the] importance [of human rights], which is clear

---

[1]  See Campbell, Ewing and Tomkins (2001); Campbell (2001), 88.
[2]  In making this assumption, I in no way foreclose the possibility or desirability of protecting *more* rights than are currently protected under the Convention (e.g. so-called 'social rights'). For this claim, see e.g. Ewing (2001), 112–6. I am simply confining my justificatory task to the HRA as it is, i.e. to those rights which are currently protected under it.
[3]  Tomkins (2001), 2.

and compelling.[4] So the justificatory question posed here is not direct
at whether we should have human rights or whether they are valuable,
but rather at the institutional issue of *how* we should go about protecting them. This begs the important preliminary question of determining
exactly how the HRA goes about protecting rights, and the way in which
it affects the overall distribution of power between the three branches of
government with reference to the regulation and enforcement of Convention rights. It is to this question that we must now turn.

## The powers of the courts under the HRA

The HRA places an obligation on all public authorities to protect Convention rights. Moreover, it provides for various mechanisms to ensure
that Convention rights are taken into account in the legislative process.[5]
However, there is no doubt that some of the central powers with respect
to enforcement of Convention rights under the HRA, are given to the
courts. Responding to this fact, many democratic sceptics signed a 'mission statement' objecting to 'the extensive shift of political authority to the
judiciary which is involved in the HRA'.[6] They questioned 'whether the
primary responsibility for the articulation of these rights ought to be taken
away from the normal political processes of representative government'.[7]
This shift of power is taken to be axiomatic. 'Of course', declares Conor
Gearty, 'the HRA has already transferred extensive legislative power to the
judges.'[8] Similarly, Tom Campbell claims that the 'open-ended amount
of judicial activism' allowed by the HRA 'has the potential to remove control over a broad range of issues from the domain of ordinary, non-legal
politics'.[9] According to Campbell, creative interpretation under section
3 enables the courts 'to take to themselves matters previously reserved
for democratic decision-making as to how such moral rights ought to be
concretised and implemented'.[10]

Although these commentators are sceptical about the upshot of the
transfer they describe, they are *not* sceptical about the underlying question of whether such a transfer is actually entailed by the HRA. In posing
the problem of the HRA as they do in their mission statement, they make
two assumptions, neither of which is self-evident. The first is that the

---

[4] Ewing (1996), 45; see also Ewing and Gearty (1997), 150 who claim that it is 'self-evidently
true' that those who believe in the virtues of democracy will also believe in the value of
civil liberties and human rights.
[5] See especially the requirements under section 19.    [6] See Tomkins (2001), 10.
[7] *Ibid.*, 2.    [8] Gearty (2001), 256.    [9] Campbell (2001), 81.    [10] *Ibid.*, 88.

powers exercised by the courts under the HRA were formerly exercised by the elected, representative branches of government and then transferred to them by the Act. The second is that the powers so transferred are 'extensive'. At least the second assumption is challenged by Sandra Fredman.[11] A supporter of the HRA, she argues that, by making judges subject to a democratically enacted list of rights, rather than entirely free to develop the common law unconstrained by such a text, it actually limits rather than expands judicial power.[12] This argument should lead us to pause before accepting, without question, the claim that the HRA increases judicial power, as many of the democratic sceptics assume.

Also of significance is the fact that although there is consensus amongst democratic sceptics that the HRA embodies a transfer of power from the legislature to the judiciary, there seems to be a difference of opinion about the *nature* of that power. In their writings, reference is sometimes made to a shift of 'political authority'[13] to the judiciary which would give the courts 'primary' (though significantly not exclusive) power to 'articulate' those rights. Conor Gearty describes it as a transfer of 'legislative power'.[14] Tom Campbell describes the power as one of 'concretis[ing] and implement[ing]'[15] Convention rights. Of course, these different expressions may not necessarily reflect any deep disagreement about the nature of the power given to the judges under the HRA. They may simply be loose ways of expressing the same underlying ideas. However, it is worth giving a more precise account of the nature of the courts' powers under the HRA. This will be the task of the first section of this chapter. It is part of an attempt to answer the following two questions: (1) what *kind* of power do the courts exercise under sections 3 and 4 of the HRA? (2) To what extent have these powers been acquired from the legislature, so as to make it sensible to regard them as having been *transferred* from Parliament to the courts?[16]

## A power of review

The HRA bestows upon the courts two main powers with respect to primary legislation. The first is the power to interpret all legislation

---

[11] Fredman (2001), 197ff. Scepticism about the alleged 'extensive shift of political authority to the judiciary' is also voiced by Sedley (2002), 17.

[12] Fredman (2001), 203ff.    [13] Tomkins (2001), 10.

[14] Gearty (2001), 256.    [15] Campbell (2001), 88.

[16] In formulating these questions and arriving at answers, I benefited greatly from Macklem (2006), 108ff.

compatibly with Convention rights. The second is the power to declare legislation incompatible with Convention rights, where a Convention-compatible interpretation is not possible. The nature of the power given to the courts under section 3 is an interpretive one: the courts are empowered to determine authoritatively the content and requirements of Convention rights in the event of an individual challenge to a particular legislative provision, to review and scrutinise that legislative provision for compliance with those rights and, in some cases, to rectify legislation in order to secure such compliance, if such rectification is possible within the limits of the judicial role. So, it is a power of *review* which is carried out through *interpretation* (of both legislation and Convention rights) and includes the power to *rectify* statutory provisions.

Were these interpretive powers of review formerly exercised by Parliament and then transferred to the courts in the 1998 Act? It would seem not. When interpreting statutes pre-1998, the courts always performed the important constitutional function of ensuring that legislation complies with fundamental constitutional principle, including those rights recognised at common law.[17] They did this, for the most part, by using the familiar presumptions of statutory interpretation, many of which have constitutional significance. These powers inhered in their traditional common law jurisdiction. One of the themes of this book has been that the HRA does not give the courts a 'new found role of constitutional arbiter',[18] but rather strengthens their existing role by enhancing their powers of interpretation. So, the HRA does not bestow on the courts radically new powers of interpretation. Nor have these powers been transferred to them from Parliament. Rather, as we saw in chapters 2–6, the HRA enhances (in significant but subtle ways) the powers of interpretation the courts have always possessed. Moreover, the increase in interpretive powers has not obliterated the role of judicial deference in statutory interpretation and the courts' observance of the constitutionally appropriate degree of restraint inherent in their adjudicative task. Therefore, it is hyperbolic to claim that the HRA authorises 'an open-ended amount of judicial activism'.[19] In making the choice between sections 3 and 4, the courts have been mindful of the limits of their institutional competence, expertise and legitimacy and have, in appropriate cases, deferred to the view of the elected branches.

Thus far, we have focused on methods of statutory interpretation, and concluded that the courts' powers of interpretation prior to the

---

[17] Allan (2006a), 46.   [18] Tomkins (2001), 9.   [19] Campbell (2001), 81.

HRA were not radically changed by the Act, but nonetheless enhanced. What of the power to interpret Convention rights? The HRA gives the domestic courts the power to determine authoritatively the content and requirements of Convention rights in the event of an individual challenge to a particular legislative provision, and this is a power which the courts did not possess (or at least not to the same extent) pre-HRA.[20] Again, whilst this may be a novel power, the degree of novelty should not be exaggerated. In the decades prior to the enactment of the HRA, the courts had found ways of upholding Convention rights through the traditional methods of statutory interpretation.[21] The question now is: was this power of 'articulation' or 'concretisation' of Convention rights one which was formerly exercised by Parliament and now transferred to the courts?

If it is at all appropriate to speak of a 'transfer' of power from one institution to another, one might say that the relevant transfer is that from the ECtHR in Strasbourg to the higher courts of the UK. Since 1950, the UK has been under an international law obligation to observe the constraints of Convention rights when enacting legislation.[22] By accepting the right of UK citizens to bring an individual petition to the Strasbourg court in 1966, the UK Parliament gave to that court the power to determine authoritatively the meaning and extent of those legal obligations in the event of an alleged violation. The function performed by the courts in determining the Convention-compatibility of legislation in response to litigation, is not something that Parliament has ever done. Pre-HRA, it was performed by the ECtHR in Strasbourg. So, again, this aspect of the courts' powers under the HRA has not been transferred to them *from Parliament*, but rather transferred to them (*by* Parliament) from the ECtHR.[23] Of course, the idea of a straight 'transfer' of power from the ECtHR to the domestic courts is not itself unproblematic. Given the fact that the Strasbourg court is still the 'ultimate authority on interpretation of the European Convention',[24] the ECtHR retains final jurisdiction

---

[20] Though Murray Hunt shows that the courts relied on Convention rights in pre-HRA jurisprudence in more limited and indirect ways, see generally Hunt (1997).

[21] *Ibid.*

[22] This international law obligation still applies and is not eliminated by the HRA.

[23] Thus, writing in the context of national security case law, David Bonner has commented that, pre-1998, the question of human rights compliance was 'very much the domain of the organs of the regional system of human rights protection' (i.e. Strasbourg), but in 'the era of the HRA', these matters 'have instead to date solely been the province of United Kingdom courts, with recourse to Strasbourg as a yet-to-be-needed longstop', Bonner (2007), 289.

[24] *R. (Al-Skeini)* v. *Secretary of State for Defence* [2007] UKHL 26 at [8], *per* Lord Bingham.

to determine the meaning and scope of Convention rights. Moreover, the fact that section 2 HRA requires the domestic courts to 'take into account' Convention jurisprudence when carrying out their interpretive tasks under the HRA, means that it is perhaps more accurate to speak of the *combined* constitutional role played by the domestic courts and Strasbourg.[25] The HRA envisages a power-sharing between the two courts in the enforcement of Convention rights, rather than a straight transfer from one to the other.[26] Either way, closer analysis suggests that it is by no means self-evident that the HRA effects a transfer of *interpretive* power (let alone an extensive transfer of such power) from Parliament to the courts.

## A constitutional not a legislative power

At this point, it is appropriate to question Conor Gearty's claim that the HRA transfers 'legislative power' from Parliament to the courts. This book has not sought to hide or deny the fact that the courts have extensive law-making powers under the HRA, including the (limited) power to rectify statutory wording in order to achieve Convention-compatibility. However, in chapter 2, I relied on a distinction between legislative law-making powers and judicial law-making powers – a distinction based on the fact that the power of the courts to make law is considerably more limited than that of legislators.[27] When deciding whether they can interpret legislation compatibly with Convention rights, the courts are limited by the terms of that legislation, the broader legislative scheme of which it forms a part, as well as relevant past precedent. Moreover, whilst the courts have the power to assess whether an existing statute is compatible with Convention rights, it does not have the power to initiate and enact another statute in its place.[28] In general, judges cannot set up entirely new legal schemes to replace those which are found wanting. Parliament, on the

---

[25]  See *Kay* v. *Lambeth London Borough Council* [2006] UKHL 10 at [44] where Lord Bingham refers to the 'constructive collaboration between the Strasbourg court and the national courts of member states', on which the effective implementation of the Convention depends. Lord Steyn has remarked extrajudicially that since 2001, the Convention is 'our constitutional Bill of Rights', see Steyn (2002b), 385.

[26]  As Lord Lester points out, given the immense backlog of cases in the Strasbourg court, the jurisdiction of the domestic courts to assess ECHR claims directly under the HRA means that the case load of the ECtHR is now less burdened by British cases, since they are resolved domestically under the HRA. This is another consequence of the power-sharing between the two courts, see Lester (2005), 256.

[27]  Above, 29ff; Raz (1979), 193ff; Gardner (2001), 214–8.    [28]  Macklem (2006), 109ff.

other hand, can legislate 'on any issue, for any reason and at any time'.[29] Hence, 'legislation' is a misleading description of what judges do when they make law. Whilst judicial law-making is certainly involved in cases applying section 3(1), sometimes involving similar techniques to those employed in limited forms of legislative amendment, it is not a power to legislate which has been transferred from Parliament to the courts.[30] Parliament has not lost its power to legislate – nor has it transferred the power to legislate to the courts.

Democratic sceptics may dismiss this point as something of a fine distinction. If the courts can rectify legislation in ways which are indistinguishable from some forms of legislative amendment, we must surely conclude that the HRA has transferred at least some legislative power from Parliament to the courts. This response overlooks a number of points. The first is that the courts have always had the power to rectify statutory wording, thus casting doubt on the claim that this power has been transferred from Parliament. Second, whilst I do not deny that judicial rectification has a similar effect to some types of legislative amendment, this does not mean that the courts therefore have acquired the power to 'legislate', with all that this term entails. The distinction may be fine, but it nonetheless has important consequences for a proper understanding of the division of labour between the three branches of government. The judges' law-making ability is so severely circumscribed in comparison to the primary law-making powers of Parliament, that it is misleading to suggest that judges can legislate. In assessing the status and consequences of the HRA, we should not exaggerate either the nature or the scope of the judicial powers under the Act.

Furthermore, post-HRA, the primary power to implement Convention rights and articulate them *in legislative form* still resides in Parliament, because it must legislate in a way which complies with those rights. This is emphasised by section 19 HRA which requires the government to consider and make a statement about the perceived Convention-compatibility of legislation when it is going through the legislative process. The protection of rights under the HRA is thus driven by ongoing interaction between the legislature, Executive and the courts.[31] Thus, when enacting legislation, we expect that legislators will comply with fundamental constitutional principle and seek to 'implement' and protect human rights

---

[29] Tomkins (2005b), 27.    [30] Macklem (2006), 110.

[31] Some justification is now included in the Explanatory Notes to Bills and the explanatory memoranda to statutory instruments.

when enacting legislation. Indeed, the detailed regulation of any right in legislative form is always a task for Parliament – one which is preserved even if the courts have the power to review that legislation for compliance with those rights.[32] It is only in the event of litigation alleging a rights violation that the courts can intervene in order to 'articulate' what those rights require in the context of a particular case. Judges can only perform their corrective and supervisory role, when invited to do so *via* litigation and, as a consequence, they deal with a more limited range of decisions than the legislature. Much of the detailed regulation of rights is carried out by Parliament and the Executive in the course of their policy-making decisions, only a tiny fraction of which will be made in response to adverse judicial decisions.[33] As such, the courts provide a corrective mechanism which makes them part of the system of rights protection – but they are not, cannot and should not be the whole of that system.[34]

Therefore, it is misleading to suggest that fundamental rights are 'off-limits to our elected representatives', or even that 'the primary responsibility for the articulation of these rights [is] taken away from the normal political processes of representative government'[35] by the HRA or that it removes control over a broad range of issues from the domain of ordinary politics. The assumption made in these claims is that prior to the HRA, Parliament had the power to 'control' or 'articulate' or 'concretise' or 'implement' human rights norms – powers which have now been transferred to the courts by the Act. The foregoing analysis suggests that this is

---

[32] In fact, this power is even preserved when the courts are empowered to strike down legislation. The power to strike down is not the same as (and not as extensive as) the power to regulate that right in legislative form. The power to strike down places a veto on the enactment of certain legislative provisions (namely, those which violate rights) but it does not give the courts the task of enacting new legislation in its place, which is left to Parliament even in countries with formally entrenched Bills of Rights.

[33] This is not to deny that the class of decisions assigned to the courts can nonetheless include some very important decisions. Nor is it to deny that it can occasionally cover a wide-ranging subject-matter and have significant political and legal implications. However, it highlights the fact that constitutional review under the HRA is a decision-making procedure designed to deal with a limited range of issues, see further Kavanagh (2003a).

[34] It is sometimes suggested that the HRA heralds an entirely new 'dialogue' approach to the regulation and protection of human rights, because it gives a role to both Parliament and courts in the protection of Convention rights, rather than putting rights protection exclusively in the hands of one or the other, see e.g. Nicol (2002), 439; Nicol (2004b), 273, where he describes the HRA as a 'unique participatory instrument'. My analysis suggests that power-sharing between the three branches of government with respect to fundamental rights is not new, albeit conducted now in somewhat different terms, within a different constitutional context. See further chapter 14 at 408–11.

[35] Tomkins (2001), 2.

a questionable assumption. It overlooks the fact that even pre-HRA, Parliament did not have complete or exclusive control over whether or how rights (both Convention rights and fundamental common law rights) should be protected. The domestic courts have long performed the role of 'articulating' those rights which were perceived to be important at common law and rectifying legislation so that they upheld those rights as articulated by the courts.[36] Moreover, due to the jurisdiction of the ECtHR, Parliament was limited in its law-making power by the power of the Strasbourg court to determine authoritatively what Convention rights required in the event of an alleged violation. This is reinforced by the fact that the HRA leaves the primary legislative responsibility with Parliament, including the duty to legislate compatibly with Convention rights, albeit subject to a review mechanism enforced by the courts in the event of a challenge by an individual citizen.

So, in response to the questions posed at the outset of this section, the answer is that the power given to the courts under sections 3 and 4 is a *constitutional* power, because it enables the courts to shape the content of the human rights guarantees. Not only is it a power to enforce those rights and comply with them in common law adjudication, it is also a power to enforce those rights *against* the elected branches of government if required. The performance of this constitutional role is one which has traditionally been exercised by the courts, but has been enhanced by the HRA in various subtle ways, most notably in giving the courts a greater sense of legitimacy in opposing and limiting the law-making powers of Parliament. So, the courts did not acquire a novel *kind* of power by the enactment of the HRA – rather, their existing constitutional role was strengthened and enhanced.[37]

If the HRA merely enhances an existing constitutional power, is it meaningful to speak of a transfer of power from Parliament to the courts? Although there has been no transfer of legislative power, one might say that there has been some transfer of *constitutional* power to the courts, since the combined powers of the courts under sections 3 and 4, set limits to the power of Parliament and enhance the powers of the court to set the constitutional agenda. The HRA makes Convention rights more central to that agenda, and in giving the courts the power to determine their scope, it enhances the constitutional role of the courts *vis-à-vis* the other branches of government.[38] Crucially, it leaves to the courts the question of

---

[36] Allan (2006a); Lord Steyn (2004a), 252; Lord Irvine (2003a), 82ff.

[37] Lord Irvine (2003a), 47, 116.    [38] Ewing (1999), 99.

when it is constitutionally appropriate for the courts to rectify legislation, and when it is not. In other words, the HRA gives to the courts the power to determine the constitutionally appropriate division of labour between the legislature, Executive and the courts, in terms of implementing and enforcing Convention rights in response to litigated cases. Constitutional review has the consequence that Parliament's power to legislate is indeed constrained and limited by the courts' power to prevent violations of Convention rights – and it is this constitutional constraint on Parliament's law-making powers which requires justification in a democracy. Such justification will be provided in chapter 12.

There is one final point which is sometimes overlooked by democratic sceptics. This is that by limiting the freedom of Parliament to legislate contrary to Convention rights, the HRA gives power not only to the courts, but also to individuals.[39] By giving individuals the right to challenge legislation on the grounds that it violates their Convention rights, the HRA empowers them in ways which will be explored more fully in the next chapter. For our purposes here, it suffices to note that the distribution of power effected by the HRA is not simply (or even primarily) from Parliament to the courts. It is also from Parliament to individuals.

## The declaration of incompatibility under section 4

Thus far, we have only considered the interpretive powers of the courts under section 3(1). We have not yet considered in any depth the power to issue a declaration of incompatibility. At first glance, one might think that in terms of justifying the powers of the courts under the HRA in a democracy, declarations of incompatibility pose no problems, because they are *legally non-binding* and *negative* in nature. They are *legally non-binding* since the HRA clearly specifies that they are to have no impact on the legal validity of legislation.[40] They are declaratory of the judicial attitude to the legislation, but they do not impugn its legal validity or bind Parliament to change it. They are also *negative*, in that they allow the courts to identify an *in*compatibility, but do not require that they specify positively how to remedy the problem. To be sure, the judicial reasoning leading to a finding of incompatibility may well imply that certain legislative options are precluded, but even if Parliament decides to change the law in light of the court's declaratory pronouncement, they will tend to have room for legislative manoeuvre in deciding how to

---

[39] Macklem (2006), 112ff; Raz (1995), 41ff.  [40] Section 3(2)(b).

comply with the requirements of the Convention, as determined by the courts.

The declaration of incompatibility mechanism is sometimes celebrated by those who are opposed to an entrenched Bill of Rights on democratic grounds.[41] It would be undemocratic, they say, to give the courts the power to 'strike down' legislation enacted by Parliament, thus giving the courts 'the last word' on legislation. The democratic value of the declaration of incompatibility is that it leaves 'the last word' with Parliament. Helen Fenwick captures this line of thinking in the following way:

> Reliance mainly on section 3 tends to marginalise the democratic process: if section 3 is used, even if it emasculates a legislative provision, as in *R.* v. *A*, Parliament will not have been asked – under the section 4 procedure – to amend the provision. The whole process remains in the hands of the judiciary.[42]

In contrast, since a declaration of incompatibility has no impact on the legal validity of legislation, Parliament is given the choice about what to do and how to do it. For this reason, section 4 is thought to be a 'sovereignty-respecting provision'[43] and one that supports democratic values. As such, it does not seem to require much justification in democratic terms.

However, closer inspection reveals that the declaration of incompatibility mechanism is not as innocuous as it seems. Understanding the nature and status of the declaration of incompatibility is crucial to establishing the status of the HRA more generally, because the judicial power to strike down legislation is often thought to be one of the distinguishing features of an entrenched Bill of Rights and one of the most pernicious aspects of entrenched Bills of Rights from a democratic point of view. Let us begin with a few observations about the constitutional practice surrounding declarations of incompatibility. Since the HRA has come into force, there have been twenty-six declarations of incompatibility, many of which have led to legislative changes.[44] In every case where the courts have identified an incompatibility with the Convention, the Executive/legislature has responded positively to it, in the sense that they have come up with a solution which remedies the incompatibility. In practice, therefore, declarations of incompatibility have not been ignored

---

[41] Nicol (2006), 747; Gearty (2003a), 380–1; Campbell (2001), 99.
[42] Fenwick (2007), 189; Gearty (2004), 50; Nicol (2002), 441ff; Tomkins (2008), 13.
[43] Elliott (2002), 349.
[44] For details of the Government's response to these declarations, see www.justice.gov.uk/docs/responding-human-rights-judgments.pdf (January 2009).

or contested by Parliament.[45] On the contrary they have prompted various remedial measures in light of the requirements of the Convention, as determined by the courts. In no case has Parliament or the Government announced that they are legally and politically free to ignore a declaration of incompatibility and plan to do so.[46]

How are we to interpret these facts about the political response to declarations of incompatibility? One common interpretation is that whilst there is no legal obligation placed on Parliament to change the legislation, it is too difficult *politically* to resist the pronouncement of the courts that its legislation violates Convention rights. The political cost likely to be incurred by such resistance is too high a price for any government to pay. Rights violations look bad and governments (even ones with a strong majority) do not want to be seen to have violated rights, then adding insult to injury by defying the finding of a higher court that they have committed this violation. Indeed, the strength of these political pressures has led Lord Hoffmann to describe the difference between a judicial strike-down power and the declaration of incompatibility as merely 'a technical distinction'.[47]

This assessment seems to be supported by Keith Ewing. When commenting on the status of the declaration of incompatibility mechanism before the HRA came into force, he noted that 'although the courts would not be empowered to strike down legislation, they would *effectively* be doing so indirectly, given that government would almost certainly want to change the law'.[48] This prediction about government behaviour has been borne out in practice. Even in the highly sensitive area of national

---

[45] Fenwick (2007), 202ff.
[46] Moreover, the Government has only once availed itself of the opportunity under section 19(1)(b) to make a statement that a Bill is incompatible with the Convention, but that the Government nonetheless wish to proceed with it. This occurred in relation to the Communications Act 2003, see Helen Fenwick (2007), 209ff. However, the House of Lords has recently declared this legislation to be compatible with Convention rights nonetheless, see R. (Animal Defenders International) v. Secretary of State for Culture, Media and Sport [2008] UKHL 15. The fact that a statement of *in*compatibility is so rare, combined with the strong powers of judicial interpretation and, so far, invariably positive response to declarations of incompatibility, Helen Fenwick concludes that "in practice the Convention under the HRA is not readily distinguishable from a Bill of Rights", Fenwick (2007), 171.
[47] Hoffmann (1999b), 160; see also Elliott (2002), 348 who describes the 'overwhelming political pressure or expectation in favour of amendment' following a declaration of incompatibility.
[48] Ewing (1999), 92, emphasis added; Lester (1998), 668; Fenwick (2007), 190. For more detailed discussion of how the declaration of incompatibility operates, see Fenwick (2007), 199–204.

security, the Government and Parliament responded positively to the declaration of incompatibility issued in the *Belmarsh Prison* case. There was no suggestion from the Government that it was appropriate to ignore it or challenge the courts' authority to pronounce authoritatively on Convention-compatibility. In response to the *Belmarsh* decision, the then Home Secretary said that he 'accept[ed] the Law Lords' declaration of incompatibility' and their 'judgment that a new legislative measures *must* apply equally to nationals as well as non-nationals'.[49] He later stated that the new Bill[50] was 'designed to meet the Law Lords' criticisms that the previous legislation was both disproportionate and discriminatory'.[51] These statements show that the Government paid respect to the courts' authority to pronounce on what the law requires, and accepted that the law would need to be changed to remove the discriminatory dimension of the legislation.

But the political repercussions of ignoring a declaration of incompatibility are only part of the story of the status of the declaration of incompatibility. To get the full story, we need to consider the important role of the ECtHR. If the House of Lords issues a declaration of incompatibility to which the government fails to respond by amending legislation, this is likely to trigger an application to Strasbourg.[52] There, the applicant will argue that his or her Convention rights have been violated (as confirmed by the highest domestic court), and that the UK Government has nonetheless failed to remedy the violation. It is highly likely that, in this situation, the Strasbourg court would find that Convention rights have been violated, whereupon the UK Government would then be under an international law obligation to change the law in light of this judgment.[53] Moreover, an adverse finding in Strasbourg would increase the potential political embarrassment caused by the initial finding of the domestic court, this time attracting more international attention. In light of this fact, the UK Government will be well aware that, 'little will be achieved – and a good deal may be lost – by not amending the incompatible legislation'[54] following a declaration of incompatibility.

---

[49] C. Clarke, HC Deb, *Hansard*, col. 306 (26 January 2005), emphasis added.
[50] Prevention of Terrorism Act 2005.
[51] C. Clarke, HC Deb, *Hansard*, col. 151 (22 February 2005).    [52] Feldman (1998), 709.
[53] Lord Lester also argues that the claimant in such a situation would have a 'high probability of success' given that they were 'armed with a favourable judgment from the domestic court', see Lester (1998), 671.
[54] Elliott (2002), 348.

This combination of political and legal consequences has led Mark Elliott to conclude that the declaration of incompatibility:

> produces an outcome substantially similar to that which would have obtained if the fast-track amendment had occurred, but the applicant – and the government – would have been put to a great deal of additional time, trouble and expense. In light of this... it is likely that declarations of incompatibility will, rather automatically, prompt the amendment of domestic law. In this manner, the sovereignty-respecting declaration becomes, in substantive (but not, of course, formal) terms, to resemble a *de facto* judicial power to procure the amendment of legislation which unlawfully qualifies fundamental rights.[55]

So, in terms of understanding the status of the declaration of incompatibility under section 4, the possibility of a potential application to Strasbourg in the event of non-compliance with a declaration, is of crucial importance. It reminds us that although the declaration of incompatibility is often portrayed as a purely political mechanism,[56] it also has significant *legal* repercussions since it is the means by which the courts can 'warn Government and Parliament that, in [the court's view], the United Kingdom is in breach of its international obligations'.[57] As with other pronouncements on the requirements of the law by the higher courts, this is entitled to respect by the legislature and Executive, in accordance with the requirements of inter-institutional comity. As David Feldman observed: 'the capacity to grant a declaration of incompatibility subtly alters the allocation of powers. For the first time, Parliament has invited the judges to tell it that it has acted wrongly by legislating incompatibly with a Convention rights.'[58] But when issuing a declaration of incompatibility, the courts are doing more than identifying a non-legal wrong. They are also determining what the law of the Convention requires. As such, these declaratory pronouncements require respect from the legislature and create a 'constitutional expectation'[59] that they will be observed. For the additional pragmatic reasons outlined above, declarations of incompatibility will be taken seriously in any case.

---

[55] *Ibid.*, 349; Lester (1998), 672.    [56] Fredman (2001), 103.

[57] *Animal Defenders International*, above n. 46 at [53], *per* Baroness Hale; see also *R. (Countryside Alliance)* v. *Attorney General* [2007] 3 W.L.R. 922 at [113] where Baroness Hale opines that 'declarations [of incompatibility] have proved powerful incentives to government and Parliament to put the matter right; for if the court is right, the United Kingdom is in breach of its international obligations in maintaining such a law on the statute book'.

[58] Feldman (1999a), 187.    [59] Jowell and Cooper (2003), 3.

Some commentators have pointed out that an adverse finding from Strasbourg is not inevitable even if the House of Lords has made a declaration of incompatibility, because the ECtHR relies on the doctrine of the margin of appreciation.[60] However, it needs to be remembered that the margin of appreciation is a doctrine of deference developed by the Strasbourg court enabling it to defer to the national institutions of the signatory states, *including* the national courts. As set out in *Handyside*, the justification for applying a margin of appreciation was the fact that the ECtHR, as a supra-national body, is detached from national practices and experiences and would therefore defer to the national bodies, which are better able to evaluate the national context. But it did not exclude the courts from the application of this doctrine.[61] Therefore, it is extremely unlikely that the doctrine of the margin of appreciation would preclude the Strasbourg court from supporting the conclusion of the domestic court. On the contrary, it would be a factor weighing in favour of its endorsement, because given the historical reluctance of the ECtHR to impose on member states obligations which may seem anathema to the national culture and traditions, a finding by the House of Lords that Convention rights have been violated would arguably strengthen the resolve of the ECtHR to support this finding.[62] Moreover, given that the UK courts have tended to operate a presumption that precedents from the ECtHR are binding on them, this means that at least in a case where there is a Strasbourg precedent, the government will realise that if the House of Lords find against them, there is no point in allowing an individual petition to Strasbourg for failure to implement the declaration of incompatibility. In such situations, a decision of the House of Lords would be an accurate indication that the ECtHR would decide the same way. When one adds to this the fact that the requirements of comity between the three branches of government are such that a legal pronouncement of the highest court in the land ought to be respected by the legislature, the declaration of incompatibility begins to look like a much stronger judicial tool than might at first appear when we read the text of section 4 in isolation. If a declaration of incompatibility were ignored, it

---

[60] See Klug (2003), 132.    [61] *Handyside* v. *UK* (1979–80) 1 E.H.R.R. 737 at [48].

[62] See Lester (2002a), 67; David Feldman argues that the Strasbourg organs are likely to defer to the domestic courts' decisions, especially as the Strasbourg court considers itself to operate only a secondary, supervisory review as a court of last resort, Feldman (1998), 710. In this sense, the subsidiarity-based margin-of-appreciation doctrine will operate in favour of deference to the courts' decision on Convention-compatibility, not the other way round; see also Tushnet (2003), 837.

would threaten this comity and challenge the judges' constitutional role as the body empowered to pronounce authoritatively on the requirements of the law, including rights provisions.[63] In short, the *political* repercussions of resisting a judicial finding of a rights violation, combined with the *legal* repercussions in the (highly likely) event of an adverse finding from Strasbourg, set against the backdrop of the traditional comity between the three branches of government and the public respect for the courts, means that a declaration of incompatibility will tend to be followed rather than ignored. The combined impact of the domestic and Strasbourg courts is such as to make the declaration of incompatibility a much stronger judicial tool for limiting the power of Parliament to infringe rights than might otherwise be the case.[64]

Does this make the declaration of incompatibility tantamount to a judicial power to 'strike down' legislation enacted by Parliament? It is hard to resist Mark Elliott's conclusion that 'in substantive (as opposed to purely formal) terms, the distinction between quashing offending legislation and declaring it incompatible is not so great as may at first appear'.[65] Moreover, one can say that in those cases where Parliament decides to comply with a declaration of incompatibility and change the legislation accordingly, its effect will be similar to a judicial strike-down power, in that it leads to legislative amendment.[66] And if the Executive/legislature *always* complies with a declaration of incompatibility, then its effect will be similar across the board. Of course, the salient difference concerns the remedial shortcomings of the declaration of incompatibility for the individual litigant, which will be considered below. For the moment, the focus is on the fact that in terms of prompting legislative amendment in order to comply with fundamental rights, the declaration of incompatibility and a 'strike-down' power are similar in effect. Moreover, in light of the legal and political pressure on the Executive/legislature to comply with the declaration, the idea that Parliament is completely free to choose how to respond to a declaration and has the 'last word' on how to implement the Convention when the courts rely on section 4 rather than section 3, seems somewhat removed from reality.[67] Although *formally* Parliament has the freedom to ignore such declarations, the constitutional, political and legal

---

[63] Fenwick (2007), 190.
[64] Similarly, Timothy Macklem argues that it is the combined role of the HRA 1998 and the ECHR which gives the UK a 'Bill of Rights', see Macklem (2006), 109.
[65] Elliott (2002), 348.
[66] The different remedial implications for the individual litigant will be considered below.
[67] See also Elliott (2002), 350.

realities are such that it will need very strong justification indeed to do so. The political and legal consequences involved in ignoring or rejecting a declaration of incompatibility, may be sufficient to convert the nominally declaratory statement into one which is effectively final in almost all cases.[68]

Interestingly, this interpretation of the nature of the declaration of incompatibility as leading quasi-automatically to legislative amendment despite its nominally 'declaratory' form, was advanced by the UK Government in a number of cases before the ECtHR. Article 35 of the ECHR requires applicants to exhaust domestic remedies prior to submitting an application to the Strasbourg court. The court has developed a practice of not requiring applicants to exhaust remedies unless they are effective. The question which then arose was whether a declaration of incompatibility was an effective remedy for the purposes of Article 35 for, in those cases where it was absolutely clear that the court could not interpret a legislative provision compatibly with Convention rights under section 3, the only alternative was a declaration of incompatibility under section 4. Would such a litigant be obliged to bring a case before the domestic courts in such a situation or could it go straight to Strasbourg?[69]

In *Burden* v. *UK*,[70] the Government's argument was that a litigant would be so obliged because a section 4 declaration constituted an effective remedy. It submitted that 'the objective of giving the national courts the power under section 4 had been to provide a formal means for notifying the government and Parliament about a situation in which legislation was found not to comply with the Convention, and to provide a mechanism speedily correcting the defect'.[71] To buttress this view, it cited two statements made in the course of parliamentary debate when passing the Human Rights Bill through Parliament, most notably, the Lord Chancellor's statement in the House of Lords that 'we expect that the government and Parliament will in all cases almost certainly be prompted to change the law following a declaration of incompatibility'.[72] In light of the further fact that in all cases in which a declaration of incompatibility has been issued, the offending legislation has been amended or repealed (either by ordinary legislative amendment or by remedial order), the Government

---

[68] See also Tushnet (2003), 834ff.    [69] See generally, Kerrigan and Plowden (2007).
[70] *Burden* v. *UK* (2006) 21 B.H.R.C. 640.    [71] *Ibid.* at [21].
[72] *Ibid.* at [22]. The other was a statement by the then Home Secretary in the House of Commons that the Government's aim in enacting section 4 was to provide a mechanism to deal with incompatibilities 'in the quick and efficient way that may be necessary'.

urged the court to accept that the declaration of incompatibility was an effective remedy.

This submission was rejected by the ECtHR.[73] The court's view was that the declaration cannot constitute an effective remedy because the declaration is not binding on the parties to the litigation, and the Minister has a power, but not a duty, to amend the relevant legislation. However, acknowledging the subsidiary nature of its role and the overriding objective inherent in the Convention that Convention rights ought to be protected primarily at domestic level, it noted:

> It is possible that at some future date evidence of a long-standing and established practice of Ministers giving effect to the courts' declarations of incompatibility might be sufficient to persuade the court of the effectiveness of the procedure. At the present time, however, there is insufficient material on which to base such a finding.[74]

It is significant that the UK Government seems to interpret the section 4 declaration of incompatibility as a mechanism for addressing and remedying violations of Convention rights at domestic level in an effective and speedy fashion, rather than as a declaratory mechanism which leaves the 'last word' with Parliament. Also of significance here, is the fact that the ECtHR has signalled its willingness, at some stage in the future, to accept the declaration of incompatibility as an effective remedy. Whilst a new constitutional convention surrounding declarations of incompatibility may well be developing, it is difficult, at this relatively early stage in the application of the HRA, to be conclusive on this issue.[75] But if we reach a stage where we can say that such a convention has been established and compliance with declarations of incompatibility has become 'deeply embedded in the British constitutional culture',[76] then we will also be able to say that the declaration of incompatibility under section 4 is very similar to a judicial 'strike-down' power. Until this stage is reached, it is still clear that it is a considerably stronger judicial tool than is often assumed and often has an effect similar to a judicial 'strike-down'. If this is true, it means that the declaration of incompatibility has enhanced the powers of the courts, because prior to the HRA, judges did not have the power to make these declaratory pronouncements which have the effect of placing such immense pressure on Parliament to change the legislation, a pressure it has not yet been able or willing to resist. In short, it gives

---

[73] *Burden*, applying *Hobbs* v. *UK* (App. 63684/00) Admissibility Decision of 18 June 2002; see also *Walker* v. *UK* (App. 37212/02), Admissibility Decision of 16 March 2004.
[74] *Ibid.* at [39].    [75] See Elliott (2002), 356 ff.    [76] *Ibid.*, 365.

the courts added power (both legal and political) to prevent Parliament enacting legislation it may wish to enact – and this requires justification in a democracy, a matter which will be considered in the final two chapters.

However, the Strasbourg case law on exhaustion of domestic remedies reminds us that although there may be many similarities between the declaration of incompatibility and a strike-down power, there are also some important differences in terms of legal implications. The first is that for those litigants who know that it will be impossible for the courts to interpret legislation compatibly with Convention rights, they can bring their case straight to Strasbourg, in order to secure an appropriate remedy. More importantly, the ECtHR placed much emphasis on the fact that the declaration of incompatibility is not binding on the parties.[77] Although it may lead to future legislative amendment, it does not automatically provide a remedy for the individual litigant. Thus, the detainees in Belmarsh prison had to await new legislation in order to be released, despite the decision that their detention violated Articles 5 and 14 of the ECHR.[78] Similarly, after the declaration of incompatibility in *Bellinger* v. *Bellinger,* the amending legislation (the Gender Recognition Act 2004) did not validate retrospectively the marriages of the successful litigants who had established that the legal invalidity of their earlier marriages had been incompatible with their rights under Articles 8 and 12. As was argued in chapter 5, the remedial emptiness of the declaration of incompatibility has the consequence that there may be cases where the courts are pushed in favour of rectifying a statute by way of interpretation, whereas if they had the power to 'strike down', that option might be more appropriate. Remedial concerns mean that the courts may have to be more cautious about issuing a declaration of incompatibility in those cases where (a) an important Convention right is endangered and (b) there is a well-grounded fear that Parliament will flout the declaration of incompatibility and (c) it is unclear how Strasbourg would deal with the situation. Such an exceptional case may have been provided by *R.* v. *A.*[79] The knowledge that Parliament is not legally required to change legislation in light of a declaration of incompatibility, combined with its remedial vacuity in relation to the case before them, may push the courts in favour of an innovative interpretation to bridge the remedial

---

[77]  *Burden,* above n. 70.
[78]  Though they were released three months later, see Tomkins (2008), 31.
[79]  *R.* v. *A (No. 2)* [2002] 1 A.C. 45.

gap.[80] It also reminds us that when we are trying to learn lessons from the consistent compliance with declarations of incompatibility, we should bear in mind the possibility that the courts may only issue declarations of incompatibility in those cases where they are confident that they will be followed.

Despite this crucial difference in legal implication, the following general points should be borne in mind when contrasting the declaration of incompatibility and a judicial 'strike-down' power. The power of the courts in, say, the USA or Canada, to 'strike down' legislative provisions is a metaphorical way of expressing the point that the courts are empowered to declare that primary legislation is incompatible with a constitutional right, and that this declaration has the legal consequence of rendering that legislative provision invalid.[81] In many instances, it also places a legal obligation on the legislature to amend the legislation in order to replace the offending provision with one which complies with constitutional rights. But even in jurisdictions where this legal obligation exists, the courts are nonetheless aware that they are the weakest branch of government.[82] The courts are dependent on the elected branches of government to respect and implement their decisions. The legal obligation arising from the 'strike-down' power does not, in itself, *guarantee* that their decisions are followed.[83] It follows that the various prudential reasons for deference which exist in the UK, apply there as well. In an analysis of the US Supreme Court and the German Federal Constitutional Court, Ralf Rogowski and Thomas Gawron conclude that in order to achieve the aim of encouraging legislators to respect and ultimately implement the decisions of the respective constitutional courts, judges in both jurisdictions tend

---

[80] David Feldman has argued that the courts may be willing to 'take more risks with' issuing a declaration of incompatibility, because the courts are aware that it will have no immediate fact on the rights and obligations of the people involved, citing the *Belmarsh Prison* case as a possible instance of this, see Feldman (2007), 112. However, if my analysis is correct, the judges are not relieved of the burden of final judgment when issuing a declaration of incompatibility and it may be that that they will be extremely cautious about issuing one in a situation where they fear it will not be followed, despite the fact that it does not, in itself, automatically change the law.

[81] The point that a 'strike-down' power is a declaration of incompatibility with particular legal consequences is made by Macklem (2006), 110, n. 6.

[82] See generally Bickel (1962).

[83] I make this point partly because commentators sometimes emphasise the fact that although the declarations of incompatibility have been followed by the government and/or legislature, it does not *guarantee* that outcome, see e.g. Phillipson (2006), 67. Even when the courts have the power to strike down, this does not guarantee that the legislature or Executive will comply with it either.

to proceed cautiously and exercise various forms of self-restraint when handing down their decisions on constitutional validity.[84] The famous and protracted controversy surrounding the implementation of the US Supreme Court's decision in *Brown* v. *Board of Education*,[85] testifies to the fact that a judicial 'strike-down' power does not guarantee automatic legislative compliance with judicial decisions. It also emphasises that a power to 'strike down' is not the same as the power to regulate the content of the right in legislative form. Furthermore, it is also worth bearing in mind that judges applying a formally entrenched Bill of Rights combined with the power to 'strike down', are not simply presented with the choice to strike down or not to strike down. Rather, they also have the option of creative interpretation, allowing them to rectify statutory provisions in order to render them constitutional.[86] Commenting on the immense (but sometimes overlooked) constitutional significance of these interpretive powers, Frederick Schauer has questioned whether removing a rights violation through interpretation is a more significant incursion on Congress, than a judicial invalidation of a statutory provision.[87]

Finally, even in those jurisdictions where the courts possess a judicial 'strike-down' power, they have also tended to develop mechanisms which allow them to declare the law incompatible with the constitution, without rendering it null and void.[88] This gives the legislature time to consider various ways of revising the law in light of the broader legal and social implications, without having the law invalidated directly as a consequence of the judicial decision.[89] All of these points go to show that we should beware of exaggerating the differences between the declaration of incompatibility under the HRA and judicial power to invalidate legislation. They also warn of the dangers of exaggerating the differences between the overall dynamics of constitutional adjudication in the UK and those jurisdictions where there is a formally entrenched Bill of Rights.[90]

---

[84]  Rogowski and Gawron (2002), 15; see Baum (2002), 230. For a review article on this book, see Kavanagh (2004a).

[85]  347 U.S. 483 (1954).

[86]  For discussion of the interpretive options under the US Constitution, see Schauer (1995).

[87]  *Ibid.*, 91.

[88]  See Rinken (2002), 55–91.

[89]  The German Federal Constitutional Court thus developed a form of 'declaration of incompatibility', Rinken (2002), 70; see also the 'mandatory call' mechanism, 70ff; Mammen (2001), 437ff.

[90]  Note that I am not suggesting that there are no such differences, simply that they are less stark than sometimes assumed.

## The status of the HRA

### Lack of formal supremacy

This brings us to the central issue of the status of the HRA as a whole. Formally, the status of the HRA is no different from any other statute enacted by the UK Parliament. It contains no provision making it harder to amend or repeal than any ordinary statute. Therefore, it is not formally entrenched. Its lack of formal entrenchment is also manifested in the fact that the HRA does not preclude Parliament from enacting legislation which contradicts a judicial interpretation under section 3 and, as we have seen in the previous section, Parliament is entitled (formally) to ignore or reject a declaration of incompatibility under section 4. The power of Parliament to enact legislation contrary to Convention rights is further evidenced by section 19(1)(b), which provides that, when proposing legislation in Parliament, the Minister in charge of the Bill can state that the legislation is contrary to Convention rights, but that the government nonetheless wishes to proceed with it. These formal features combine to suggest that the orthodox doctrine of Parliamentary sovereignty is preserved and that the form of human rights protection embodied in the HRA is very different from the sort of entrenched Bill of Rights which exists in the USA. There, the Bill of Rights clearly has a higher legal status than ordinary laws and when statutes are declared by the court to violate it, they are thereby rendered invalid. In contrast, the HRA is hailed as a much more acceptable method of rights enforcement from a democratic point of view. As Helen Fenwick puts it: 'the argument from democracy has the greatest force only if a Bill of Rights can prevail over subsequent inconsistent legislation'.[91] It has much less force when Parliament can ignore and override judicial determinations on what the guaranteed rights require.

But anyone who has attempted to gain a proper understanding of the British Constitution will know that it is perilous to focus on the legal formalities alone, to the exclusion of the political practices and norms which surround them.[92] In the remainder of this chapter, I want

---

[91] Fenwick (2007), 147.

[92] See also Ewing (1999), 92 who claimed that 'as a matter of constitutional legality, Parliament may well be sovereign, but as a matter of constitutional practice, it has transferred significant power to the judiciary [under the HRA]'. Helen Fenwick also argues that a narrow legal 'doctrinal' analysis of the status of the Convention is inadequate, if not downright misleading, and should therefore be supplemented by an assessment of the political realities surrounding it, see Fenwick (2007), 162ff.

to argue that the HRA has a constitutional status superior to ordinary legislation which, when combined with the ECHR as enforced by the ECtHR in Strasbourg, effectively amounts to a Bill of Rights. Although the formalities suggest that the HRA should be viewed as an ordinary statute like any other because it has no officially declared superior status, when we look at the subject-matter of the HRA and the way in which it functions, we can see that it is different, constitutionally speaking, from ordinary statutes and is relatively entrenched.

The first point to note about the HRA is that it deals with a constitutional subject-matter. One might say that it is therefore *substantively* constitutional.[93] Where they apply, human rights guarantees establish some of the general principles under which a country is governed and, in particular, place constraints on (and therefore partly define) the relationship between the individual and the state. Furthermore, they effect a division of labour between the three branches of government.[94] These features combine to give human rights guarantees a central role in constitutional law. That the HRA is constitutional in this substantive sense is, I believe, uncontroversial. More controversial is the claim that the HRA has a superior constitutional *status* to other 'ordinary' statutes, such that it is relatively entrenched. In order to make good this claim, we need to proceed with caution.

## *The HRA's legal pervasiveness and the doctrine of implied repeal*

One of the most striking structural features of the HRA is the strength of the interpretive obligation under section 3(1), as well as its pervasive application to all other laws. As we saw in the first part of this book, section 3(1) enjoins the courts to achieve Convention-compatibility, even when faced with legislation which seems to violate Convention rights in clear and unambiguous terms. As interpreted by the higher courts, section 3(1) allows a strong rectifying construction of legislation, which in some cases, has involved reading in 'implied provisions' to protect the relevant Convention right.[95] Its legal pervasiveness is patent in the terms of section

---

[93] In making this point, I draw on the distinction made by Robert Alexy between constitutional rights which are *formally fundamental* and those which are *substantively fundamental*, see Alexy (2002), 30–2, 349–51. For the point that the content of the rights protected by the HRA is not hugely dissimilar from those contained in the US Bill of Rights, see Gardbaum (2001), 709.

[94] Raz (1998a), 153.

[95] *R. v. A (No. 2)* [2002] 1 A.C. 45; followed in *R. (Hammond)* v. *Secretary of State for the Home Department* [2005] UKHL 69, where the House of Lords read section 11(1) of the

3(1), which specifies that the courts are obliged to interpret *all* legislation, *whenever enacted*, so that it is compatible with Convention rights. Regardless of whether legislation is enacted before or after 1998, the courts are obliged to resolve a potential conflict between legislation and the HRA in favour of the latter. This is why section 3(1) is a key mechanism affording the HRA a higher status than other laws.[96] Although the courts cannot formally strike down Acts of Parliament, conformity with Convention rights is achieved through the strong powers of interpretation given to the courts under the Act. These interpretive powers give the HRA a degree of supremacy over all other legislation, whenever enacted. They are part of what Murray Hunt described in another context as 'the construction approach to supremacy'.[97]

David Feldman endorses this view. Following from the strong interpretive powers of the courts under the HRA, he draws the following conclusion:

> The Human Rights Act 1998 is thus not an ordinary statute. In a way it is like the Interpretation Act 1978, contributing to a framework which shapes the interpretation and implementation of other legislation, prior or posterior. Unlike an Interpretation Act, however, it is imbued with substantive values which are given a privileged but not unchallengeable place among the pantheon of principles, policies and values which inform and motivate legal development.[98]

He is not alone in identifying the strong interpretive powers under section 3 as the source of the HRA's superior constitutional status and the reason why the HRA is 'no ordinary law'.[99] Awareness of the fundamental

---

Criminal Justice Act 2003 subject to 'an implied qualification' that it must be compliant with the right to a fair trial, see [29], *per* Lord Bingham, despite the fact that the section explicitly stated that prisoners would not receive an oral hearing. A similar 'reading in' is carried out in *Secretary of State for the Home Department v MB* [2007] UKHL 46.

[96] David Feldman argues that the HRA has a higher status than most other legislation 'as a matter of constitutional law', see Feldman (1999a), 178ff; Fenwick (2007), 170ff.

[97] This is similar to what Murray Hunt refers to as 'the construction approach to the supremacy of community law', see Hunt (1997), 72ff.

[98] Feldman (1999a), 180.

[99] Lester (1998), 668; Feldman (1999a), 180; Palmer (2007), 115; Bogdanor (2004), 249, 259; Fenwick (2000), 46; Rivers (2002), xxii; Klug and Wildbore (2007), 232. Although Nicholas Bamforth denies that the HRA has a special constitutional status, he argues that the HRA nonetheless plays a special 'constitutional *role*, insofar as section 3 lays down 'overriding general rules of statutory interpretation', Bamforth (2007), 51. He also accepts that, partly by virtue of the 'generality' of the protection provided by section 3, Convention rights have 'considerable constitutional importance', see Bamforth (2007), 52. He does not elaborate on this distinction between constitutional status on the one hand, and constitutional role and importance on the other.

constitutional significance of the courts' interpretive powers led Lord Hoffmann to observe that, even aside from the HRA, the principle of legality (which requires that general words contained in statutes must be read subject to the basic rights of the individual) means that the UK courts 'apply principles of constitutionality little different from those which exist in countries where the power of the legislature is expressly limited by a constitutional document'.[100] Similarly, in *Matadeen* v. *Pointu*,[101] his Lordship pointed out that the HRA created a 'modified form of constitutional review' not much different from if it had been entrenched.[102] The role of the familiar presumptions of statutory interpretation (and their constitutional function) is sometimes obscured by focusing too narrowly on the fact that UK judges do not have the power to 'strike down' legislation in formal terms.[103] The previous section has shown that the declaration of incompatibility mechanism under section 4 has an effect not dissimilar to a strike-down power. Combining this with the courts' powers to rectify statutory provisions so that they conform with Convention rights, there seems to be considerable support for the view that the HRA has a superior constitutional status to other laws.

Despite the strength and pervasive application of the section 3 obligation to all laws, prior and posterior, there are many who will resist the conclusion that they, combined with the declaration of incompatibility, afford the HRA a superior constitutional status to other laws. The source of that resistance is the cherished place in orthodox British constitutional theory occupied by the principle of parliamentary sovereignty. The orthodox account of parliamentary sovereignty states that Parliament can enact any law it wishes, and cannot be prevented from carrying out this wish by any other organ of government.[104] The idea that the HRA has a superior constitutional status seems to strike at the heart of this principle, because it suggests that it enjoys a degree of entrenchment not possessed by ordinary statutes. At least with reference to post-HRA legislation, it also seems to run contrary to the doctrine of implied repeal. Full discussion of the relationship between the HRA and the principle of parliamentary sovereignty will take place in the next chapter, but the question of the

---

[100]  R. v. *Secretary of State for the Home Department ex parte Simms* [2000] 2 A.C. 115 at 131, *per* Lord Hoffmann. The view that the role of the British courts under the HRA is 'closely analogous to the role of constitutional courts in other common law countries in deciding whether legislation passes muster against the standards of constitutional Bills of Rights' is also shared by Lester (1998), 672–3.

[101]  [1999] 1 A.C. 98.     [102]  *Ibid.* at 110. See also Allan (2006a), 30.

[103]  See further Kavanagh (2007), 115–7.     [104]  Dicey (1959), 39–40.

status of the HRA requires us to confront directly the question of whether the HRA can be impliedly repealed.

In order to establish whether the HRA preserves the doctrine of implied repeal, it is necessary first to get a clearer idea of what that doctrine entails. The doctrine of implied repeal is a principle of statutory interpretation whereby, if two statutes come into conflict with each other, the courts must give precedence to the more recent Act and the earlier enactment is then impliedly repealed.[105] The application of the doctrine is triggered by a finding that there is an inconsistency or contradiction between two statutes, and when this occurs, the courts should resolve the contradiction in favour of the later statute.[106] The doctrine of implied repeal is widely thought to be a corollary of the principle of parliamentary sovereignty,[107] because it is a way of ensuring that no Parliament can bind a future Parliament, as the orthodox Diceyan account of parliamentary sovereignty requires.[108]

When we look more closely at how the doctrine of implied repeal operates in statutory interpretation, matters are less clear-cut than the orthodox account suggests. Of particular importance is the fact that the courts operate a general presumption *against* implied repeal.[109] That is to say, the courts presume that Parliament does not intend an implied repeal and interpret legislation accordingly.[110] Applying this presumption of statutory interpretation, the aim of the court is not to ensure that later statutes overturn earlier statutes, but to ensure that this only occurs when it is not possible to read later legislation in a way that does not contradict earlier legislation.[111] The courts strive to find ways of reconciling the

---

[105] Bennion (2002), 254ff.    [106] *Ibid.*, 254.

[107] See Bamforth (1998), 573; Laws, *Thoburn*, [37]; Hunt (1997), 91; Wade (1955), 174; Taylor (2004), 58ff. Recent cases cast doubt upon the constitutional orthodoxy that no statute is immune from implied repeal, see *Factortame* v. *Secretary of State for Transport* [1990] 2 A.C. 85, *R.* v. *Secretary of State for Transport, ex parte Factortame (No. 2)* [1991] 1 A.C. 603. See also the judicial *dicta* in *Jackson* v. *Attorney General* [2006] 1 A.C. 262 (to the effect that the doctrine of implied repeal does not apply to manner and form provisions).

[108] For an excellent and detailed discussion of the doctrine of implied repeal, see Young (2008), chapter 2.

[109] Bennion (2002), 255.

[110] *Ibid.*, who notes that the courts also operate a presumption against the implied revocation of a common law rule.

[111] See *Smith International Inc* v. *Specialised Petroleum Group Services Ltd* [2006] 1 W.L.R. 252; see also Bennion (2002), 225–6; Clayton and Tomlinson (2000), 171. The second countervailing principle occurs when the doctrine of implied repeal conflicts with the principle *generalis specialibus non derogant*, i.e. specific provisions of legislation are not impliedly repealed by later, general provisions of legislation.

apparently conflicting statutory interpretations, using the various interpretive tools at their disposal to do so. The general presumption against
implied repeal highlights the fact that the scope of the doctrine of implied
repeal is much more limited than is often assumed.[112] As Alison Young
puts it, 'the doctrine is not the rule, but the exception'.[113] Its exceptional
character is borne out by the fact that the courts hardly ever determine that
a statute has been impliedly repealed by a later statute. They can normally
obviate its use by removing an apparent conflict by interpretation.[114]
So, the logical steps of the interpretive exercise are as follows. Step one
requires the identification of an apparent conflict between two statutory
provisions. Step two involves applying the presumption *against* the doctrine of implied repeal. At this stage, the courts will strive to render the
apparently conflicting statutory provisions compatible with each other
through interpretation. Only if the courts fail to achieve compatibility at
this stage, will they then be forced to go to step three, which invokes the
doctrine of implied repeal. So, implied repeal is a measure of last resort.
When it applies, the later enactment takes precedence over the earlier one,
which is then impliedly repealed.[115]

The question whether the HRA preserves or contravenes the doctrine of implied repeal must be assessed against this background. In
section 3(1), Parliament enacted a different conflict-solving principle
of statutory interpretation, with respect to potential conflict between a
statute and Convention rights. Applying the two-stage approach described
in chapter 2, the first step is to identify whether there is an apparent incompatibility with Convention rights. If so, the courts go on to the second
stage, where they must strive to interpret that legislation compatibly with
Convention rights. If this is impossible, they do not have the power to
determine that this legislation has been impliedly repealed by the HRA.
Rather, they have the power to issue a declaration of incompatibility,

---

[112] For an illustration of the extent to which courts will strive to find a compatible interpretation between two apparently contradictory statutory provisions, thus avoiding the
application of the doctrine of implied repeal, see *Henry Boot Construction Ltd* v. *Malmaison Hotel (Manchester) Ltd (Malmaison)* [2001] Q.B. 388.

[113] Young (2008), 36.

[114] The doctrine of implied repeal only comes into operation if the provisions of a later Act
are 'so inconsistent with, or repugnant to, the provisions of an earlier Act that the two
cannot stand together', *West Ham Church Wardens and Overseers* v. *Fourth City Mutual
Building Society* [1892] 1 Q.B. 654 at 658.

[115] The similarity between the logical structure of this interpretive exercise and the 'two-stage'
approach to interpretation under section 3(1), supports one of the underlying themes
of the book, which is that the HRA does not give the courts radically new interpretive
powers, but rather enjoins them to interpret in ways which are continuous with traditional
methods of statutory interpretation.

which does not, in itself, affect the validity or continuing operation of the statute.[116] The view that the doctrine of implied repeal does not apply with reference to the HRA seems to be reinforced by section 3(2)(b) which declares that that section 3(1) 'does not affect the validity, continuing operation or enforcement of any incompatible primary legislation'. It also seems to be supported by one of the *Notes on Clauses* on the Human Rights Bill to the effect that 'it is not intended that the so-called doctrine of implied repeal in relation to pre-Bill legislation should apply (hence the use of the phrase "whenever enacted")'. The resistance to the application of the doctrine of implied repeal was also emphasised by the Lord Chancellor, when introducing the Bill in Parliament, who said that the Government 'did not wish to incorporate the Convention rights, and then, in reliance on the doctrine of implied repeal, allow the courts to strike down Acts of Parliament'.[117]

A number of points are warranted here. First, the doctrine of implied repeal is a principle of statutory interpretation used as a last resort when a contradiction between two statutory provisions cannot be resolved by way of interpretation. It is a conflict-solving rule for the courts to use in exceptional circumstances. When it is used, it always gives precedence to the later Act. Sections 3 and 4 of the HRA supplants the operation of this doctrine with a different conflict-solving mechanism when statutes conflict or seem to conflict with Convention rights. The scheme of the HRA introduces two important departures from the doctrine of implied repeal. The first is that the declaration of incompatibility is, at least formally, weaker than the doctrine of implied repeal. This has given rise to the claim that the HRA actually has an inferior status to other ordinary statutes, because, unlike ordinary statutes, it is unable to effect the implied repeal of earlier statutes.[118] The second (more important) point is that the conflict-solving mechanism envisaged by the combined operation of sections 3 and 4 is not confined to statutes enacted pre-HRA. Therefore, unlike the doctrine of implied repeal, it does not necessarily give precedence to a later Act of Parliament, because it also applies to Acts which post-date the HRA.

Let us take each of these points in turn. First, we must consider the idea that the HRA has an inferior status to other statutes, since it cannot not impliedly repeal them. Not only is this conclusion counter-intuitive, it ignores the fact that whilst the HRA cannot impliedly repeal earlier

---

[116] Section 4(2)(b).

[117] *Hansard*, HL col. 522 (18 November 1998). For further discussion of this issue, see Clayton and Tomlinson (2000), 170–1; Young (2002), 37ff.

[118] Fenwick (2007), 172.

statutes, it can achieve the same result by way of interpretation. As Alison Young observes, the courts 'can use principles of interpretation to achieve the same effect in practice as if s. 3(1) of the Act impliedly repealed earlier statutes that are incompatible with Convention rights'.[119] To be sure, earlier statutes are not formally disapplied, but to the extent that the courts can find ways of interpreting that statute so that the *prima facie* incompatibility with Convention rights is removed, a similar effect is achieved. Moreover, even if the courts find it impossible to rectify the incompatibility by way of interpretation under section 3, their power under section 4 to issue a declaration of incompatibility is a much stronger judicial tool than might initially appear. Although it does not affect the validity of the legislative provision in a direct way, it does so indirectly. Ultimately, it has a similar effect to implied repeal (at least to the extent of removing the incompatibility with Convention rights).

Second, the pervasive application of the HRA to legislation 'whenever enacted' means that the underlying rationale of the doctrine of implied repeal is subverted. That rationale was to ensure that Parliament is not bound by future Parliaments, and can enact legislation at any time or to repeal previous enactments. This is why the later Act always takes precedence. Under the HRA, if legislation enacted post-1998 seems to conflict with Convention rights, that legislation does not impliedly repeal Convention rights. On the contrary, the legislative provision is interpreted so as to give effect to them. The later Act is interpreted in light of the earlier one (in this case the HRA). So, the HRA is not subject to implied repeal by future enactments. Both with respect to legislation enacted before and after the HRA, the conflict with Convention rights is 'removed' by way of interpretation if at all possible. In this sense, one may say that the doctrine of implied repeal 'does not apply' with reference to the HRA. However, this apparent escape route from the conundrum of implied repeal, should not blind us to the fact that the application of the HRA to post-HRA legislation subverts the underlying rationale of the doctrine of implied repeal. The combined effect of sections 3 and 4 is to eliminate the application of the doctrine of implied repeal, partly by achieving the same results as would be reached under the doctrine, but partly by achieving the contrary result. It does the first through the combined effect of the section 3 interpretation and the declaration of incompatibility. It achieves the contrary result because the HRA is not itself open to implied repeal by later, inconsistent legislation. This is the *opposite* conclusion to that which

---

[119]  Young (2002), 37–8; see also Fenwick (2007), 172.

one would reach if one wished to conform with the doctrine of implied repeal. Both these facts must surely give rise to difficult speculation for those who wish to maintain that the HRA ensures conformity with the doctrine of implied repeal and the orthodox doctrine of parliamentary sovereignty with which it is often associated. Although the HRA does not formally challenge the traditional doctrine of implied repeal, it departs from it in substance.[120]

There is another reason to doubt the claim that the HRA has a lower constitutional status than ordinary Acts of Parliament. It relates to the constitutional significance of the HRA as a means of protecting fundamental rights. The view that statutes of 'constitutional significance' may not be subject to the doctrine of implied repeal, was voiced by Lord Wilberforce in a petition before the House of Lords' Committee of Privileges, regarding the position of the elected Irish peers to the UK Parliament in the Union with Ireland Act 1800:

> In strict law there may be no difference in status, or as regards the liability to be repealed, as between one Act of Parliament and another, but I confess to some reluctance to holding that an Act of such constitutional significance as the Union with Ireland Act is subject to the doctrine of implied repeal or of obsolescence – all the more when these effects are claimed to result from later legislation which could have brought them about by specific amendment.[121]

From this, Francis Bennion concludes that the presumption against the doctrine of implied repeal is stronger in relation to statutes of constitutional significance.[122] In *Thoburn*,[123] Laws L.J. went further and opined that 'constitutional statutes' were immune from the doctrine of implied repeal. He defined 'constitutional statutes' as those which condition 'the legal relationship between the citizen and State in some general, overarching manner'[124] and explicitly cited the HRA as an example of a constitutional statute. Laws L.J.'s *dicta* in *Thoburn* have not been greeted with

---

[120] That section 3(1) has the effect of disapplying statutory provisions to the extent that they are contrary to Convention rights leads Andrew Butler to characterise it as a 'disapplication' clause, see Butler (2000), 143. For the contrary argument that the HRA preserves the doctrine of implied repeal, see Bamforth (1998), 575. My analysis is at variance with Bamforth's conclusion that the combined effect of sections 3 and 4 allows us to avoid 'difficult speculation' about the status of Convention rights.

[121] *Earl of Antrim's Petition (House of Lords)* [1967] 1 A.C. 691.

[122] See Bennion (2002), 255, where it is suggested that the presumption against implied repeal is stronger 'the more weighty the enactment'.

[123] *Thoburn v. Sunderland City Council* [2002] 1 W.L.R. 247.   [124] *Ibid.* at [62].

universal enthusiasm in the academic commentary.[125] The suggestion that there is a hierarchy of statutes in the UK legal system is perceived to be radical and unorthodox, because it challenges one of the fundamental assumptions of the doctrine of parliamentary sovereignty, namely, that no statute has a status superior to any other.[126] Once one accepts that certain statutes are immune from implied repeal, it leaves the door open to the prospect of (at least partial) entrenchment, which in turn, raises the spectre of Parliament being bound by a previous enactment.

Without wishing (or needing) to make any pronouncements here on whether the common law recognises a special category of constitutional statutes, the following points must be made with respect to the HRA alone. The HRA is undoubtedly of immense constitutional significance, in part because of its subject-matter.[127] Also of constitutional significance is the strength of the interpretive obligation enacted in section 3, as well as the pervasive application of that obligation to all legislation whenever enacted. It is sometimes said that section 3 enacts the principle of legality of a rule of construction.[128] Central to the principle of legality, as enunciated by Lord Hoffmann in *Simms*, is the fact that Parliament only has the power to abrogate fundamental rights if it expresses its intention in the clearest of terms.[129] Broad or general words will not suffice. The reason why the principle of legality cannot be overridden by implication is because of the constitutional importance of the principle. The same conclusion has been reached by the courts with reference to section 3(1). They have clarified that Convention rights can only be repealed in subsequent legislation by clear and express terms.[130] They cannot be repealed by implication. As Lord Lester observed: 'Because of its great constitutional

---

[125]   Marshall (2002), 493; Bamforth (2003b), 283; Elliott (2002), 368ff; Tomkins (2003), 123.

[126]   See Bamforth (2003a), 48. Dicey famously said that 'there is under the English constitution no marked or clear distinction between laws which are not fundamental or constitutional and laws which are fundamental or constitutional', (1959), 89 (though this statement may only go to show that there is no formal distinction between them, not that fundamental or constitutional statutes do not exist).

[127]   In this sense, I agree with Laws L.J. when he says that the special status of a constitutional statute like the HRA follows, at least in part, 'from the special status of constitutional rights', *Thoburn*, above n. 124 at [62].

[128]   *Ghaidan v. Mendoza* [2004] 3 W.L.R. 113 at [104], *per* Lord Rodger.

[129]   *Simms*, above n. 100 at 131, *per* Lord Hoffman.

[130]   Stephen Gardbaum argues that the very existence of the declaration of incompatibility under section 4 excludes the normal rules by which a Convention right would be impliedly repealed by a subsequent incompatible statute 'for were subsequent conflicting statutes to impliedly repeal Convention rights, there would of course be no basis for a declaration of incompatibility', see Gardbaum (2001), 736.

and international importance, the courts will not treat provisions of the [HRA] as impliedly amended or repealed by subsequent legislation.'[131] This accords with the way in which the presumptions of statutory interpretation of constitutional significance, can only be rebutted by express terms or by 'necessary implication'. It would be strange if the presumption of statutory interpretation enacted in section 3(1) were to have a lesser status. On the contrary, it gives the traditional presumption embodied in the principle of legality added strength, partly because of the legitimacy given to the courts by the HRA, and partly by the strong wording of section 3(1), which reminds the courts that it is the prime remedial measure under the Act.

### The difficulty of express repeal and relative entrenchment

This raises the question of just how clear and how express a legislative provision must be, in order to rebut the presumption in favour of Convention-compatibility. In *Thoburn*,[132] Laws L.J. suggested that 'the test could only be met by express words in the later statute, or by words *so specific* that the inference of an actual determination to affect the result contended for was irresistible'.[133] This is a very strong test. Our discussion in chapter 5 suggested that a rebuttal of the presumption in favour of Convention-compatible interpretation may be extremely difficult, if not impossible to achieve, no matter how specific or unequivocally expressed Parliament's intention might be.[134] The upshot is that, not only is the HRA immune from implied repeal, it is very difficult (given the strength of the presumption of compatibility of Convention rights adopted by the courts) to repeal it expressly either. It is also worth noting that even an express provision to the effect that Parliament wished to enact legislation contrary to Convention rights is not thereby rendered immune from constitutional review under section 3 HRA. So, even if Parliament expressly legislated contrary to Convention rights, courts would still be required by section 3 to interpret the amending legislation so far as

---

[131] Lester (1998), 670. Lord Steyn has also suggested (extrajudicially) that the HRA may be immune from implied repeal because it is a 'constitutional measure', Lord Steyn (2002a), 728. He also suggested that the designation of rights as 'constitutional' 'virtually rules out arguments that such rights can be impliedly repealed by subsequent legislation', *ibid.*, 731.

[132] Above n. 123.      [133] *Ibid.* at [63], emphasis added.

[134] David Feldman argues that 'express and unequivocal words' would be needed to repeal or amend the HRA, see Feldman (1999a), 180.

possible in a manner compatible with Convention rights. The judicial duty to attempt to minimise or negate a violation of Convention rights under section 3(1) would still apply.[135] It would also apply if, in response to a section 3(1) interpretation, Parliament chose to re-enact a legislative provision in order to reinstate its pre-section 3(1) meaning. It may well be that a statutory provision which explicitly declares that Parliament 'hereby contravenes Convention rights' would present a formidable challenge to judges bent on fulfilling their duty under section 3(1). But the section 3 case law (and indeed pre-HRA case law such as *Anisminic*[136]) suggests that it is by no means a foregone conclusion that judges would inevitably decide that it was impossible to interpret this provision compatibly with Convention rights.

However, the possibility that the HRA can be repealed or amended in the same way, and with the same ease, as any other Act of Parliament must surely generate some misgivings about the alleged superior constitutional status of the HRA. The very fact that, in recent times, politicians from across the political spectrum have occasionally suggested either amending or even repealing the HRA, lends weight to the seriousness of this objection.[137] It suggests a certain precariousness in the position of the HRA.[138] However, it can nonetheless be overcome. For the most part, political statements to the effect that the HRA should be amended or repealed have been made in the context of the threat from terrorism to national security or in the area of criminal justice. Yet even in these

---

[135] *Ibid.* There is also no reason to believe that this duty would not apply if the legislation was passed without a section 19 statement having been made. This is different from the operation of the 'notwithstanding' clause under section 33 of the Canadian Charter. If the Canadian legislature decides to legislate 'notwithstanding' Charter rights or freedoms, it is generally understood that the courts are debarred from adjudicating on the compatibility of the override with Charter rights, see Gardbaum (2001), 736; Hogg (2003), chapter 36, p. 832.

[136] *Anisminic v. Foreign Compensation Commissioners* [1969] A.C. 147.

[137] David Bonner notes how government frustration with judicial constraints placed on 'effective anti-terrorist action' has produced 'headline-seeking calls for repeal or amendment of the HRA and even withdrawal from the ECHR', see Bonner (2007), 351.

[138] For example, it was reported that the Prime Minister, Tony Blair, considered limiting the courts' human rights jurisdiction under the HRA, following an embarrassing defeat for the Government in an asylum case, see *The Daily Telegraph*, 20 February 2003. Following the terrorist attacks in London on 7 July 2005, Tony Blair also suggested that he would consider seeking to amend the HRA if it proved to be an obstacle to the 'war on terror', see T. Blair, speaking at the monthly Downing Street press conference, 5 August 2005 (www.pm.gov.uk/output/Page8041.asp), cited in Elliott (2007b), nn. 100–1.

contexts, the Government never saw fit to ignore or reject a declaration of incompatibility. If they have not been prepared to pay the political cost of ignoring a declaration of incompatibility, it seems unlikely that they would be prepared to incur the far greater political cost of repealing or restricting an Act designed to enhance the protection of people's human rights and enable them to litigate rights claims more fully and directly in the domestic courts.[139]

There is a further reason why the repeal of the HRA and a return to the pre-HRA situation is an unlikely eventuality. This is the fact that, even if the HRA did not exist, the UK would still remain a signatory state to the ECHR, carrying with it an international law obligation to secure the protection of Convention rights. If the HRA is succeeding in its aim of furthering and enhancing the protection of Convention rights, it would be very difficult, both politically and legally, to justify its repeal in light of the Convention obligations which apply to the UK. One might well be able to justify *greater* protection for Convention rights than is currently afforded by the HRA, but it is not very easy to see how a lesser protection could be seriously advanced. A repeal of the HRA and a return to the pre-HRA situation is remote in practice. The only possibility (politically speaking) would be its repeal in favour of greater human rights protection, such as might be provided by a Bill of Rights with formal superior status com-bined with a judicial strike-down clause. As Francesca Klug has pointed out:

> No government is likely to pledge to repeal [the HRA] nowadays, without suggesting a replacement. Any Bill of Rights that is going to take us further than where we are now would either have to consolidate the rights in the HRA or run alongside it.[140]

This leaves the question of whether the HRA is 'entrenched'. Entrenchment refers to the degree of difficulty with which a law can be amended.[141] It is not an all-or-nothing matter. Rather, it is a matter of degree and can take many different forms. Even within one Bill of Rights, there can be varying degrees of entrenchment with respect to different

---

[139] As Robert Wintemute points out, saying you will ignore a declaration of incompatibility is one thing, doing it is another, see Wintemute (2006a), 216. The same applies to statements about repealing the HRA.

[140] Klug (2007), 717; Fenwick (2007), 298.

[141] Joseph Raz describes a constitution as 'entrenched' if 'constitutional amendments are legally more difficult to secure than ordinary legislation', see Raz (1998b), 153.

rights.[142] Some commentators suggest that the HRA is *politically entrenched* even if it is not entrenched in any formal, legal sense because, as a matter of political reality, it is extremely difficult to repeal it.[143] The HRA is certainly entrenched in this sense. But my analysis suggests that it is also entrenched in other more fundamental ways, as a matter of constitutional law.[144] As a strong presumption of statutory interpretation of immense constitutional significance, section 3(1) enables the courts to apply principles of constitutionality when interpreting legislation. At the very least, one could say that, to the extent that there is an overlap between the rights contained in the Convention and fundamental common law rights, as many judges claim,[145] then those rights are also constitutionally entrenched in the common law.[146] But once one admits the constitutional status of these rights at common law, one cannot avoid the conclusion that the rights embodied in the HRA also have a constitutional status. They form part of the fundamental constitutional principles which it is the duty of the courts to uphold and to ensure that ordinary legislation is compatible with them. It is in this sense that Sir Rupert Cross described the principle of legality and other constitutional presumptions of statutory interpretation as operating:

> at a higher level as expressions of fundamental principles governing civil liberties and the relations between Parliament, the Executive and the courts. They operate here as constitutional principles which are not easily displaced by statutory text.[147]

This may be a weaker form of entrenchment than that provided by the American Bill of Rights, but it nonetheless satisfies the condition of being

---

[142]  See e.g. the German Basic Law where the right to dignity under Article 1 is given inviolable status, such that it can never be amended. The other rights contained in the constitution are subject to a mechanism for constitutional amendment which is more difficult than for ordinary legislation.

[143]  See e.g. Gardbaum (2001), 737. It is worth noting that those commentators who emphasise that Parliament retains 'the legal right to legislate in defiance of Convention rights', nonetheless tend to accept that 'Parliament's practical freedom to legislate as it chooses is considerably narrower', see e.g. Bamforth (2007), 51.

[144]  Interestingly, in their mission statement, the democratic sceptics accept that the HRA is 'partially entrenched', though they do not elaborate on what type of entrenchment this involves, see Tomkins (2001), 2.

[145]  See e.g. Irvine (2003a), 82ff; Woolf (2008), 213; Steyn (2004a), 252ff.

[146]  For the view that presumptions of statutory interpretation can acquire a constitutional status, see Hunt (1997), 152; Allan (2006a), 46; Cooke (2004), 276ff discussing 'the depth of common law rights'.

[147]  Cross (1995), 166.

relatively entrenched. The structure of the HRA means that Convention rights cannot be repealed by implication and it is difficult to see how they could be repealed expressly. This makes them entrenched to a considerable degree.[148]

## Is the HRA a Bill of Rights?

The final issue is whether the HRA is effectively a Bill of Rights. Interestingly, there is considerable consensus amongst both supporters and critics of the HRA alike, that the HRA is tantamount to a Bill of Rights.[149] The HRA is sometimes described as a statutory Bill of Rights[150] or an interpretive Bill of Rights,[151] but a Bill of Rights nonetheless. When the HRA 1998 came into force in October 2000, the then Home Secretary, Jack Straw, described it as 'the first Bill of Rights this country has seen for three centuries'.[152] Despite this apparent consensus, it is nonetheless worth spelling out the reasons why the HRA can be viewed as a Bill of Rights. In order to do so, we need to be clear about what a Bill of Rights is. In general terms, we can say that a Bill of Rights sets out in canonical terms the fundamental rights and liberties of citizens within a country, as well as the obligations of the state (and sometimes other individuals or groups) with regard to those rights. The HRA fulfils this basis condition, since it gives legal effect to (most of) those rights enumerated in the ECHR. Therefore, we now have a list of fundamental rights enshrined in one legal document. This merely shows that the HRA exemplifies the typical content and written form of a Bill of Rights – it does not tell us whether the HRA also possesses those features of a Bill of Rights which make it a particular institutional method of enforcing those rights, i.e. whether it gives them superior constitutional status. I will take a 'Bill of Rights' to be defined by a combination of the following four general features:[153]

---

[148] This understanding of 'entrenchment' as a matter of degree is supported by Philip Alston, who characterises rights as 'entrenched' if they 'can only be overridden with significant difficulty', see Alston (1999b), 11. For the view this standard applies to the HRA, see Klug (2007), 710.

[149] Tomkins (2001), 1; Lester (1998); Klug (2001), 370; Ewing (2004), 836; Fenwick (2007), 171; Wintemute (2006a), 209; Hiebert (2006), 7 (who describes it as a 'parliamentary Bill of Rights').

[150] Fredman (2000), 99; Darrow and Alston (1999), 482; Rishworth (2004), 233ff.

[151] Lester (1998), 668.      [152] Speech, Institute of Public Policy Research, 13 January 2000.

[153] These features are adapted from Raz (1998a), 153; see also Kavanagh (2004d).

- First, it has a *superior status* to ordinary law, such that all laws contrary to it are made to conform to it or are otherwise rendered invalid or inapplicable.
- Second, it is *justiciable*, in the sense that there are judicial procedures to test the compatibility of ordinary legislation with the constitution. In other words, judges implement the superiority of the Bill of Rights.
- Third, there is a method of *individual redress* in the event of a rights violation.
- Fourth, it is relatively *entrenched*. That is to say, amendments to it are more difficult to secure than ordinary legislation.

Let us go through these features one by one. I have argued here that the HRA has a superior status to ordinary law, in that all laws contrary to it are made to conform to it, largely through judicial interpretation, but also through the declaration of incompatibility. I also argued that, as the practice has been developing, the declaration of incompatibility has a similar effect to rendering the legislation invalid. Whilst acknowledging that a judicial strike-down has some different legal implications, it was nonetheless apparent that the differences between them are often exaggerated. In short, the inclusion of the judicial strike-down clause is not a necessary feature of a Bill of Rights, as long as the judiciary have some tools at their disposal to render legislation compatible with the Bill of Rights.[154]

The second condition of *justiciability* is also met because the HRA gives judges the power to test the compatibility of ordinary legislation with a canonical list of rights – a condition which is further buttressed by the ultimate jurisdiction of the ECtHR to receive applications from aggrieved litigants. Third, the HRA allows for litigants to bring cases based on an alleged violation of Convention rights. It provides a method of individual petition and complaint, and allows for rights violations to be redressed. Finally, I specified that a Bill of Rights must be 'relatively' entrenched. This allows for the fact that entrenchment is a matter of degree and can take many different forms. I have argued that the HRA meets this criterion as well. In sum, the HRA can fairly be described as a Bill of Rights, despite the fact that there are some differences between it and the method of enforcement provided by the American Bill of Rights. This means that the Convention rights given legal force in the HRA are aptly described

---

[154] This view is also shared by Klug (2007), 705; Alston (1999b), 10.

as 'constitutional rights'[155] and review for their compliance by the courts aptly described as 'constitutional review'.[156] Finally, it should be noted that although the HRA has the status of a Bill of Rights, the fact that the rights contained in the Schedule to the HRA are derived from the European Convention, means that it is not an autonomous Bill of Rights in the American sense – it is a Bill of Rights which has a dual domestic and international law dimension, as explained in chapter 6.[157]

## Conclusion

The purpose of this chapter was to clarify the status of the HRA in general, and sections 3 and 4 in particular. I concluded that the HRA has superior constitutional status to ordinary laws – a status which is implemented through the combined workings of sections 3 and 4. Whilst the HRA strengthens and enhances the constitutional responsibility of the courts to protect human rights, this did not constitute a radical shift of authority from Parliament to the courts. It certainly did not embody an extensive transfer of legislative power, as is sometimes claimed. Rather, it gave judges greater power to set the constitutional agenda. In doing so, it was accepted that in testing legislation for compatibility with Convention rights, and then either rectifying it by way of interpretation or declaring it incompatible, judges place significant restraints and limits on what legislation Parliament can enact. These limits now need to be justified in light of serious and important democratic concerns. This is the task of the remaining chapters. However, before we can embark on this justificatory task, we must first assess whether the HRA is compatible with the principle of parliamentary sovereignty. This is the task of the next chapter.

---

[155] Rivers (2002), xxii. Note that the appropriateness of this nomenclature of 'constitutional rights' does not signal a radical departure from pre-HRA law. Some rights fundamental in the common law were characterised as 'constitutional rights' pre-HRA, see e.g. *R.* v. *Lord Chancellor, ex parte Lightfoot* [2000] Q.B. 597 at 609B; *R.* v. *SSHD, ex parte Leech* [1994] Q.B. 198 at 210A; *Thoburn* v. *Sunderland City Council* [2003] Q.B. 151 at [62]. See further Jowell (2000), 674ff; Tomkins (2003), 184–8; Steyn (2004a), 252.

[156] See Irvine (2003a), 246; Jowell (2000). For use of the term 'constitutional review' with reference to adjudication of domestic legislation subject to the requirements of EU law, see Jaconelli (1979).

[157] Lester (1998), 672.

# 11

# Parliamentary sovereignty and the HRA

## Introduction

It has become something of a constitutional trope to say that the aim of the HRA was to enhance the protection of Convention rights, whilst simultaneously preserving the constitutional principle of parliamentary sovereignty.[1] In fact, it is commonly believed that the HRA succeeded in achieving this reconciliation. Determining the legislative purpose of a complex statute is sometimes difficult, even when the statements made by the government Ministers steering it through Parliament seem emphatic and unequivocal.[2] It is certainly true that in the parliamentary debates on the Human Rights Bill, both the Lord Chancellor in the House of Lords and the Home Secretary in the House of Commons, emphasised how keen the Government was to ensure that the Act did not trespass on the sacred constitutional ground of parliamentary sovereignty. The debates are strewn with such assurances.[3] To take just one example, the Lord Chancellor stated that the aim of the HRA was to maximise 'the protection of human rights', but *only* insofar as this could be done 'without trespassing on parliamentary sovereignty'.[4]

In the first chapter, I struck a note of caution about the significance and status of such statements.[5] We need to bear in mind that they are made in a political context, where the aim of debate is to secure support for what was in this case a controversial Bill. Although the newly elected Labour Government had a huge majority when it was putting the Human Rights Bill through Parliament, the controversy (spanning decades) about whether the UK should adopt a Bill of Rights, or even

---

[1] See e.g. Feldman (1999a), 167.
[2] For the constitutional and pragmatic reasons to be cautious when determining the meaning and significance of statements made in parliamentary debate, see Kavanagh (2005a).
[3] See generally Klug (1999). The text of Lord Irvine's opening speech on the Human Rights Bill in the House of Lords is reproduced in Irvine (2003a), 7–16.
[4] HL Debs, 582, col. 1229 (November 3, 1997).      [5] Chapter 1, 13–17.

whether it should incorporate the ECHR, had been dogged by reservations based on the principle of parliamentary sovereignty. Francesca Klug observed that 'Conservative opinion tended to dismiss bills of rights as lethal to the doctrine of "parliamentary sovereignty", which was supported as an article of faith by advocates of the status quo.'[6] But reservations of this kind were not confined to the Conservative Party. Opposition from the Left was also concerned to preserve Parliament's power to enact progressive legislation, unhindered by an unaccountable, elite judiciary.[7] So, across the political spectrum, as well as in judicial and academic circles, there was concern that incorporating broad human rights standards into UK law would lead to the demise of the British system of parliamentary supremacy over the courts.[8] This opposition needed to be overcome if incorporation of Convention rights was to have any chance of success.

Whatever else we can say about the parliamentary debates on the Human Rights Bill, it is absolutely certain that, in order to secure its passing, the Government had to convince MPs from across the political spectrum, that the Act did not unduly compromise parliamentary sovereignty. The point that political prudence demanded a reconciliation with parliamentary sovereignty is borne out by some observations by Lord Lester. In 1994, Lord Lester introduced a Private Member's Bill in the House of Lords designed to give Convention rights a status similar to directly effective European Community Law. This Bill explicitly empowered the courts to strike down Acts of Parliament if they found them to be inconsistent with those rights. After his legislative proposal was 'mutilated'[9] in the House of Lords, Lord Lester was persuaded by the 'pragmatic advice' of senior Law Lords that 'given the political climate of concern about the threat to parliamentary sovereignty... it would be prudent to devise a measure that did not give the courts the express power to strike down inconsistent legislation'.[10] This comment shows that some degree of compliance with parliamentary sovereignty, even if only in formal terms,[11] was perceived to be required if a Human Rights Bill was to have any realistic chance of getting passed.[12]

---

[6] Klug (2007), 703.    [7] Ibid.    [8] Klug (2003), 126.    [9] Lester (2002a), 58.
[10] Ibid.
[11] That the courts should not be given the 'express power' to strike down inconsistent legislation is not inconsistent with giving them practical ability to strike down legislation in a way which is not express.
[12] See Lester (2002a), 58. This view that some degree of compliance with parliamentary sovereignty was needed pragmatically to secure the passing of the Act, see Feldman (1999a), 169; Black-Branch (2002), 77.

In making this observation, I am not seeking to show that the Government's belief in the importance of parliamentary sovereignty when proposing the Human Rights Bill was less than genuine.[13] I am simply pointing out that the political context of the parliamentary debates on the Human Rights Bill should lead us to be cautious before investing statements from *Hansard* with more significance than they can necessarily bear. Such caution was exercised in *Al-Skeini*,[14] which concerned the question of whether the HRA had an extraterritorial application to Iraqi civilians killed in Iraq by UK armed forces. The House of Lords rejected arguments based on *Hansard* suggesting that the purpose of the HRA was to benefit 'the British people' and 'bring rights home.' As Lord Rodger observed: 'The government rhetoric was not an accurate guide to the application of the Act within the United Kingdom... the passages from *Hansard* to which we were referred contained nothing on which it would be safe to rely.'[15] Similarly, Lord Bingham noted that emphasis (both in the White Paper and parliamentary debates) on the value of the HRA to the 'British people' was natural 'for domestic political reasons'.[16] A similar caution should be exercised when we consider the statements from *Hansard* on the importance of the principle of parliamentary sovereignty.

Furthermore, when considering the Government's statements about preserving parliamentary sovereignty, one must also bear in mind that, as with most Acts of Parliament, the HRA was enacted with various purposes in mind. Even if we accept that preserving parliamentary sovereignty was an important aim behind the HRA, it was certainly not its sole aim.[17] For many, the very purpose of enacting legislation giving the courts enhanced power to protect and enforce human rights, is precisely to limit the power of Parliament to violate those rights.[18] It was called the 'Human Rights Act', not the 'Parliamentary Sovereignty Act' – the primary aim, as manifest in the title and terms of the Act, was to provide ways of enhancing the protection of Convention rights in UK domestic law.[19] In general, the *Hansard* references to the principle of parliamentary

---

[13] In order to establish the truth of this matter, we would need to embark on an historical and political analysis far beyond the scope of this book.

[14] *R. (Al-Skeini)* v. *Secretary of State for Defence* [2007] UKHL 26.    [15] *Ibid.* at [43].

[16] *Ibid.* at [23].    [17] Klug (2007), 709.    [18] Lord Steyn (2004a), 254.

[19] The various ways in which the HRA limits Parliament (and public authorities) from violating rights leads Conor Gearty to conclude that 'the Human Rights Act appears on its face to mark a radical breach with British constitutional tradition', Gearty (2004), 21, though he simultaneously claims that it is 'clear' that the purpose of the HRA was to 'preserve Westminster's sovereignty power', Gearty (2002), 248.

sovereignty suggest that the Government wished to achieve this aim, whilst nonetheless preserving the principle of parliamentary sovereignty. But as became clear after the HRA was enacted, and especially when it was litigated before the courts, achieving a practical reconciliation between these two aims, was no easy task. Perhaps one could only preserve that principle to a degree. Unsurprisingly, the full complexity of the legal and constitutional questions surrounding this issue, was not explored in parliamentary debate.[20] Not only are there pragmatic reasons to treat statements made in parliamentary debate with caution, there are also fundamental constitutional reasons not to treat statements made by an already powerful Executive as definitive about the nature and purpose of legislation enacted by Parliament.[21] To understand the nature and purpose of the Act, we need to turn to the terms of the Act itself.

### Reconciling the HRA with parliamentary sovereignty

It is widely believed, amongst both judiciary and academic commentators alike, that the HRA preserves parliamentary sovereignty and does so in an ingenious fashion. Thus, in *Kebilene*, Lord Steyn pronounced that 'it is crystal clear that the carefully and subtly drafted Human Rights Act preserves the principle of parliamentary sovereignty'.[22] Various academic commentators have endorsed this view. One of the 'cardinal and uncontroversial features of the HRA', we are told, is that it 'ultimately preserved parliamentary sovereignty'.[23] The axiomatic and uncontroversial nature of this claim may also be endorsed by Nicholas Bamforth when he stated that 'the drafting of the Act is unambiguous in its commitment to preserving Convention rights without challenging the foundational constitutional principle of parliamentary sovereignty'.[24] So, although the HRA does not explicitly mention the principle of parliamentary sovereignty, what is it about its drafting which so clearly preserves this foundational constitutional principle?

---

[20] Even as it was, the legal dimension of parliamentary debate on the Human Rights Bill (as presented by the Lord Chancellor and Lord Lester) seemed to be too much for some of the House of Lords peers. Lord Campbell of Alloway was heard to protest about the 'esoteric lectures on law at this time of night', and that he had 'never heard anything like this after dinner' in the eighteen years he had been in the Lords. 'Why we have to be entertained for 20-something minutes with cases from here, there and everywhere totally defeats me', see HL Deb vol. 583 cols 827–8 (24 November 1997), cited in Ewing (1999), 79.
[21] Kavanagh (2005a), 102ff.      [22] *R. v. DPP, ex parte Kebilene* [2000] 2 A.C. 326 at 327.
[23] Hickman (2005), 311.      [24] Bamforth (2004), 22.

The answer is contained in the various features of the HRA examined in the previous chapter. First, the HRA has no officially declared superior status to any other Act of Parliament – it is (at least in formal terms) an ordinary Act of Parliament. Second, it can be repealed and amended in the same way as any other Act of Parliament – it is not formally entrenched. Third, the HRA does not permit judges to 'strike down' Acts of Parliament found to be in contravention of Convention rights – they can only declare them to be incompatible, but this does not create a *legal* requirement that the statute is amended accordingly. Fourth, it does not prevent Parliament from enacting legislation contrary to Convention rights. This is made explicit in section 19, which allows for the possibility that Parliament will enact legislation, notwithstanding the fact that the Government proposing that legislation believes it to be incompatible with Convention rights. Moreover, if Parliament is displeased with an interpretation under section 3, there is nothing in the HRA stopping it from re-enacting the provision in its original form, or indeed in a form which makes the intention to violate Convention rights crystal clear. The third and fourth features combine to show that, even under the HRA, Parliament has what is now referred to as 'the last word'.[25]

Before considering each of these points, we should first clarify what 'parliamentary sovereignty' entails. The classic formulation of the doctrine of parliamentary sovereignty was originally contained in an academic treatise written at the end of the nineteenth century by Professor Albert Venn Dicey.[26] Still phenomenally influential today, the following words are emblazoned on the minds of every first-year student of British constitutional law: 'Parliament . . . has, under the English constitution, the right to make or unmake any law whatever; and, further, that no person or body is recognised . . . as having a right to override or set aside the legislation of Parliament'.[27] This statement is widely thought to have both a positive and a negative dimension.[28] The positive dimension is contained in the emphatic assertion of 'parliamentary omnicompetence'[29] with respect to making, amending and repealing legislation. This explains

---

[25] See e.g. Klug (2003), 132.    [26] Dicey (1959).

[27] *Ibid.*, 39–40. Dicey's writings have an iconic status in UK public law, not dissimilar to the status attached to the writings of 'Founding Fathers' in countries with written constitutions, such as the writings of Jefferson and Madison in the USA or those of Eamon DeValera in the Republic of Ireland.

[28] See Loveland (2006), 23ff.

[29] Cooke (2004), 274 (though he describes the 'omnicompetence' attributed to Parliament by the orthodox doctrine as a fallacy).

the importance (for orthodox British constitutional theory) of ensuring that no Act of Parliament has a superior constitutional status to ordinary Acts of Parliament, because this would cast in doubt Parliament's unlimited legal power to make or repeal legislation contrary to such a fundamental statute. On the traditional account, therefore, no statute can be entrenched. The positive limb of Dicey's definition also explains the insistence that all statutes must be open to implied as well as express repeal. As Nicholas Bamforth explains, implied repeal operates 'as the cornerstone of the traditional account: for it prevents Parliament from binding itself, in relation to future legislation, in any way whatever (legally, that is rather than politically)'.[30] The negative dimension is contained in the emphatic prohibition on any other institution (including the courts) from 'overriding' or disapplying legislation enacted by the sovereign Parliament.

Does the HRA preserve both the positive and negative limb of the doctrine of parliamentary sovereignty?[31] Many commentators answer this question in the affirmative, for the reasons outlined above. As regards the positive dimension, they say that the HRA is not formally entrenched. Formally speaking, it has no superior constitutional status. They will also point out that not only can Parliament enact legislation contrary to Convention rights, it is also legally free to amend the HRA, or indeed repeal it altogether. But just notice how much one has to qualify such statements with the warning that they are only true in a formal sense. The analysis in chapter 10 revealed that if one is prepared to look beyond the bare formalities, one can see that the HRA has a constitutional status, superior to other laws. This status means that the HRA is relatively entrenched, since there is no real prospect of it being amended or repealed without replacing it with a similar or stronger system of rights protection.

One of the possible responses of those who are wedded to the doctrine of parliamentary sovereignty is to argue that the prospect of repealing the HRA (leaving nothing in its place) is, in fact, real. In support of this argument, they will tend to point to statements by politicians (both in Government and in Opposition) that they will repeal it. In chapter 10, I suggested that such statements are best understood either

---

[30] Bamforth (2004), 33.

[31] Note that Dicey's definition of parliamentary sovereignty was paraphrased in the discussion document which preceded the Human Rights Act, namely, *Rights Brought Home: The Human Rights Bill*, paragraph 2.13: 'Parliamentary sovereignty means that Parliament is competent to make any law on any matter of its choosing and no court may question the validity of any Act that it passes.'

as a matter of empty political posturing, or alternatively, as an indirect way of putting pressure on the courts to deliver deferential decisions. For various reasons, it is difficult to accept them as a serious statement of intent to dismantle the system of rights protection put in place by the HRA. The most obvious reason for doubting their veracity or plausibility as an indicator of future political action, is that if the HRA were repealed tomorrow, the UK would still remain a signatory state to the European Convention on Human Rights. Determined supporters of the traditional account of parliamentary sovereignty are not deterred even by this. They point to the fact that it is legally possible for the UK to withdraw from the Convention. We can call this type of argument *the argument from remote possibility*.[32] After all, those who rely on it do not deny that the possibility is remote – they say that the 'mere' or 'theoretical' possibility that it might occur (however improbable in reality) preserves the principle of parliamentary sovereignty. But if the preservation of the orthodox principle of parliamentary sovereignty hinges on possibilities as remote as British withdrawal from the Convention, one may well wonder whether the doctrine itself needs some rethinking.

There is a point of broader significance here. It is sometimes argued that the orthodox principle of parliamentary sovereignty as stated by Dicey has very little explanatory force.[33] That is to say, it does not provide us with an accurate account of British constitutional practice and fails to explain or illuminate important features of that practice. For, as we all know, Parliament cannot, as a matter of fact, make or unmake any law it pleases. Defenders of the traditional doctrine of parliamentary sovereignty respond by saying that although Parliament is constrained in numerous *political* ways, it is not constrained *legally*. Parliamentary sovereignty only prohibits legal constraints on Parliament's power to make or unmake any law – it does not prohibit political ones.[34] We can call this *the argument from lack of legal limits*. Although its proponents

---

[32] Mark Elliott describes the prospect of withdrawal as 'notional', Elliott (2004), 553; see also Sedley (2008), 20. The only country ever to withdraw from the Convention was Greece after a military coup, but they rejoined when the political situation settled down. According to the Copenhagen criteria established by the European Council in Copenhagen in 1993, compliance with the Convention is one of the conditions of membership of the EU. The UK Government has tended to pride itself on its contribution to the original drafting of the European Convention, so withdrawing from the Convention would mean leaving the Council of Europe and the EU. The very enactment of the HRA bears witness to its efforts to ensure compliance with it. All these factors combine to make withdrawal remote in the extreme.

[33] Elliott (2003), 30.    [34] See generally Munro (1999), 168ff.

acknowledge various practical and political erosions of Parliament's law-making powers,[35] they stress the political nature of those limits.[36] The problem with this response is that it fails to account for the considerable *legal* limitations on the power of Parliament to enact laws, most obviously, those which arise from the UK's membership of the European Union. By being a member of the European Union, the UK necessarily accepts the superior legal status of EU law and the necessary corollary that if an Act of Parliament comes into conflict with EU law, the former will be 'disapplied'.

*The argument from lack of legal limits* is frequently advanced in order to show that the HRA preserves parliamentary sovereignty. Thus, it is often said that Parliament is *legally* free to enact legislation which is incompatible with Convention rights, or that it is not *legally* prohibited from amending or repealing the HRA. *The argument from lack of legal limits* is most frequently heard in the characterisation of the nature of the declaration of incompatibility. This, we are told, is a political mechanism, not a legal one. My conclusion in chapter 10 that the HRA has a constitutionally superior status to other laws, making it relatively entrenched, did not hinge on political fact alone. It was due, in large part, to the legal constraints placed on the power of Parliament by the HRA. The first point relates to the doctrine of implied repeal. As Nicholas Bamforth explained, this doctrine is often thought to be the cornerstone of parliamentary sovereignty, because it seems to follow logically from the premise that no Parliament can bind another Parliament.[37] Those who enacted the HRA were well aware of the fact that the doctrine of implied repeal is touched by the sacrosanct principle of parliamentary sovereignty. For this reason, the terms of the HRA were drafted so as to circumvent it. However, as pointed out in chapter 10, the mode of circumvention also entailed its partial subversion, because although the HRA does not impliedly repeal other Acts of Parliament, it is not, in itself, subject to implied repeal. Time and time again, the courts have stated that if Parliament wishes to violate Convention rights, it cannot do so by implication, but rather must do so in the clearest of terms.[38] This is a legal statement about the legal status of

---

[35] *Ibid.*, 170.
[36] It should be noted that this emphasis on political rather than legal constraints is part of a wider tradition of relying on political or conventional checks and balances in the British Constitution, in preference to legal ones, see Oliver (2003), 9.
[37] Bamforth (2004), 33.
[38] See *R.* v. *Secretary of State for the Home Department, ex parte Simms* [2000] 2 A.C. 115 at 131, *per* Lord Hoffmann.

the presumption of statutory interpretation embodied in the HRA, and it is in accord with the legal status of other similar presumptions, prior to the enactment of the HRA. The status of such presumptions follows from the constitutional importance of the values they seek to protect, in this case, the rights embodied in the ECHR. These presumptions place substantive legal limits on Parliament's ability to make or unmake any law it wishes.[39]

## Interpretation under section 3(1)

There were two other legal features of the interpretive obligation in section 3 which lead us to question whether the HRA preserves parliamentary sovereignty, in anything other than purely formal ways. These were its legal pervasiveness and its interpretive robustness. The negative limb of the doctrine of parliamentary sovereignty prohibited the courts from 'overriding' or 'setting aside' primary legislation. This explains why the declaration of incompatibility is declaratory and is not, formally speaking, a power to invalidate primary legislation. But the link between interpretation and invalidation has not gone entirely unnoticed in the academic commentary. Thus, in an early contribution to the debate about section 3(1), Conor Gearty suggested that:

> if the courts were to interpret so that it was possible [to render legislation compatible with Convention rights] in every case, then a type of entrenchment against implied repeal would have been smuggled into UK law disguised as a principle of statutory interpretation.[40]

In a similar vein, Robert Wintemute has argued that if there were no limits on section 3(1), then the difference between interpretation and invalidation would disappear and section 4 become redundant".[41] Of course, Gearty and Wintemute were hypothesising about a situation which does not exist. Right from the beginning, the courts realised that the most difficult task before them was to articulate the limits on section 3(1). So, the hypothetical scenario posited by these commentators has not come about: there *are* limits to interpretation under section 3(1). However, underlying

---

[39] After all, the courts adopt a presumption *against* implied repeal and it is a rule of statutory interpretation which is hardly ever used. Therefore, in terms of statutory interpretation, it is not a doctrine of immense importance. It is only because of its links to the doctrine of parliamentary sovereignty that it is thought to have such great importance as a matter of British constitutional theory.

[40] Gearty (2002), 254.    [41] Wintemute (2000), 612.

Gearty's and Wintemute's claim is an important (though unarticulated) insight. This is that the courts' powers of statutory interpretation are not entirely separate from questions of entrenchment and validity.[42] One of the by-products of the HRA in terms of public law scholarship, is that it has highlighted the constitutional significance of statutory interpretation and shown just how powerful a tool the presumptions of statutory interpretation can be. When a court adopts a section 3(1) interpretation, it renders legislative provisions compatible with the Convention, despite the fact that they seem to violate those rights. A section 3(1) interpretation is not stopped in its tracks when faced with a statute which, in its ordinary meaning, violates Convention rights. In this way, the rights violation is removed by way of interpretation. This has led some commentators to describes rules of interpretation such as those contained in section 3(1) as 'disapplication rules'.[43] One might add that not only is the rights violation removed, but the courts sometimes supplant it with a different, Convention-compliant, meaning. In light of this point, Lord Lester has questioned whether a strained reading of legislation under section 3(1) in fact involves a greater inroad upon parliamentary sovereignty than the power to strike down inconsistent legislation.[44] Whatever the outcome of this conjectural enquiry might be, the important point lying at its core, is the insight that principles of statutory interpretation can modify, limit, extend and change statutory meaning in significant ways. As it has been interpreted by the UK courts, section 3(1) endorses the legitimacy of such modifications and has enabled the British courts to apply 'a kind of implicit constitutional-conformable interpretation'.[45] So, although the HRA preserves the formal trappings of the doctrine of parliamentary sovereignty, section 3 limits Parliament's ability to legislate contrary to those constitutional requirements in substantial and significant ways.[46]

---

[42] For the view that questions of interpretation and validity are a matter of degree, see Allan (1997), 447; Hunt (1997), 79; Jaconelli (1979).

[43] Butler (2000), 143; Taylor (2004), 63. Jeffrey Goldsworthy also suggests that some forms of reading in and reading down are 'tantamount to partial disapplication', see Goldsworthy (2004), 201.

[44] Lester (2001), 691. For the same point made in the context of US constitutional law, see Schauer (1995), 91.

[45] Limbach (2001), 6.

[46] T. R. S. Allan also supports the idea that although the HRA upholds a 'formal principle of parliamentary sovereignty', the operation of the interpretive obligation under section 3(1) places substantial limitations on the law-making power of Parliament, limitations found ultimately in the principle of the rule of law, Allan (2006a), 47.

## The declaration of incompatibility

This brings us to the question of the declaration of incompatibility and its compatibility with the doctrine of parliamentary sovereignty. Consider the following statement by Francesca Klug:

> The most unique and widely commented upon aspect of the Human Rights Act is that whilst it is intended to operate as a higher law, to which all other laws and policies must conform where possible, the Act does not allow courts to strike down statutes in the manner of judicially entrenched bills of rights. Insofar as the Human Rights Act allows courts to review and declare incompatible Acts of Parliament, it confines the British constitutional doctrine of parliamentary sovereignty but it clearly does not overturn it.[47]

Those who are wedded to the traditional doctrine of parliamentary sovereignty will undoubtedly bridle at the suggestion that the HRA operates, or was intended to operate, as a higher law. However, they will nonetheless concede that the most important weapon in their armoury in the increasingly difficult challenge to defend the orthodox account of parliamentary sovereignty under the HRA, is the declaratory nature of the declaration of incompatibility. Whatever the tortuous involutions of the academic debate about the doctrine of implied repeal, and however much it seems as if judges are interpreting legislation beyond recognition, they will fall back on the fact that the HRA differs significantly from fully entrenched Bills of Rights because it does not give the courts the power to 'strike down' legislation. As Keith Ewing observed:

> We should not diminish the importance of the fact that the Human Rights Act does not give the courts the power to strike down legislation. Nor should we diminish the reasons why the government withheld this power from the courts, grounded as they were in a desire to ensure that no court in this land, even the Judicial Committee of the House of Lords, can place itself in the position of sovereignty over the High Court of the elected Parliament.[48]

If my analysis in chapter 10 is correct, it suggests that although we should certainly bear in mind the differences between the declaration of incompatibility and a strike-down power, we should not fall into the trap of exaggerating those differences either. In fact, the trend within public law scholarship in the UK to overestimate the significance of the fact that judges do not, formally speaking, have the power to strike down Acts of

---

[47] Klug and Wildbore (2007), 232.    [48] Ewing (1999), 98.

Parliament, has contributed to a related tendency to underestimate the considerable law-making power which judges exercise (and have always exercised) when they interpret statutes.[49] It has obscured from constitutional view the fact that statutory interpretation provides the courts with subtle (though no less significant) ways in which the courts can partially control, limit and modify Acts of Parliament. The contrast with 'striking down' has also led to a misleading characterisation of the declaration of incompatibility. In chapter 10, I pointed out that although the declaration of incompatibility is often characterised as a purely political mechanism, it has important legal implications as well. This is especially important with respect to the doctrine of parliamentary sovereignty, because it is often supported by *the argument from lack of legal limits*. As pointed out in chapter 10, the immense political pressure to comply with declarations of incompatibility is only part of the picture. The rest of that picture is made up of legal pressures. First, the UK is also under an international law obligation to uphold Convention rights, and that if they fail to comply with a declaration of incompatibility, it will ultimately result in a legal finding by the Strasbourg court that the UK is in violation of those obligations. Second, although a declaration of incompatibility is formally declaratory, it nonetheless has an important legal status as a statement of legal principle by the higher courts. By issuing a declaration of incompatibility, the courts may be acknowledging the limits of their law-making powers, but they are not denying their ability to give a clear, legal view about the Convention-compatibility of a particular legislative provision. So, although a declaration of incompatibility does not have any direct legal implications for the litigant, it has important legal significance as a determination of what the law of the Convention requires by a higher court, and as such should warrant respect from Parliament in a similar way to all other legal pronouncements.

The important legal implications of the declaration of incompatibility make it difficult to argue that it only puts political pressure on the government to amend legislation in light of it. Since supporters of the orthodox account of parliamentary sovereignty argue that Parliament can only be sovereign, if it is immune from *legal* limitations, then, contrary to appearances, such immunity is not secured by the declaration of incompatibility under section 4. One might add that if the Executive decides that there are compelling reasons to do so, primary legislation can be amended by a remedial order issued by the government. In this way too, parliamentary

---

[49] See further Kavanagh (2007), 116.

sovereignty is compromised, because the remedial order under section 10 HRA allows Executive Ministers to amend primary legislation.[50]

At this point, defenders of the orthodox doctrine of parliamentary sovereignty tend to cling to the theoretical possibility of the government nonetheless defying a declaration of incompatibility. They will cite the Home Secretary's claim in parliamentary debate that the government might defy a declaration of incompatibility if a court declared the Abortion Act 1967 incompatible with the Convention.[51] This unlikely scenario brings us back into the realm of the *argument from remote possibility.*[52] One might have thought that the context of the so-called 'war on terror' would have emboldened the Government to defy a declaration of incompatibility, but even in this context, it has dutifully complied. If this constitutional practice continues, and compliance with the declaration of incompatibility becomes embedded in the British constitutional culture, the *argument from remote possibility* will become even more remote. Interestingly, the remoteness of such possibilities does not seem to deter those who are keen to shore up the principle of parliamentary sovereignty. Keith Ewing does not deny 'that in the overwhelming majority of cases, a declaration of incompatibility will be accepted by the government and Parliament of the day, thereby ensuring that the elected branch will in practice defer to the unelected branch'.[53] I would add to this diagnosis two important qualifications. The first is that, thus far, deference to the judicially declared incompatibility has been observed in every case, not just in the overwhelming majority of cases. Second, the reasons for such deference are not wholly contained in political and pragmatic concerns, but also arise from the respect for the legal authority of our higher courts to pronounce on what the law requires, as well as respect for the UK's international law obligations.

## The last word

The foregoing analysis clearly has implications for the claim that, under the HRA, Parliament has 'the last word' on how to regulate Convention rights. In the vast array of legislation bearing on Convention rights, but

---

[50] Oliver (2003), 115; Feldman (1999a), 188.

[51] *Hansard*, HC, vol. 317, col. 1301 (October 1998). For discussion, see Wintemute (2006a), 216.

[52] Presumably on the grounds that it would violate hypothetical Article 2 right to life of the foetus, though as Robert Wintemute points out (2006a), 216, the Strasbourg court declined to find such a right in *Vo v. France* (8 July 2004), at [84]–[85].

[53] Ewing (1999), 99.

not litigated before the courts, Parliament has 'the last word', in the sense that this legislation is applied, unchallenged by any other institution.[54] However, once a legislative provision is litigated in a HRA challenge, it is not at all clear that Parliament still has the 'last word'. Even in a case where the court finds that there is no violation of Convention rights, the legislative provision is upheld not just because Parliament enacted it, but also because of the court's determination that it complies with Convention rights. One might say that the court has the 'last word' in determining the Convention-compatibility of that legislation – and this is true even when it determines that the legislation satisfies that legal requirement.

But let us dwell on those cases where the court finds that there is a *prima facie* incompatibility, but rectifies its way of interpretation. In those cases, it would be more accurate to say that Parliament has the first word, in the sense that it has the power to legislate on matters related to Convention rights and to regulate those rights as it sees fit. But the courts have the last word in the sense that by interpreting it compatibly with Convention rights, they determine the legal meaning at the point of application. Moreover, unless we rely on the *argument from remote possibility*, this really is the last word on Convention compatibility. There are many political and practical reasons why Parliament hardly ever has the time or inclination to change the outcome of statutory interpretation, but there are also legal reasons to do with the requirements of inter-institutional comity, why they do not tend to do so, especially when it is contrary to a finding that there has been a rights violation.

The final possibility is where the courts find that there is an incompatibility with Convention rights which they cannot remove by way of interpretation. If they issue a declaration of incompatibility, the analysis contained in chapter 10 casts doubt on the claim that Parliament has the 'last word', even here. One might say that, legally speaking, the 'last word' in fact rests with the ECtHR in Strasbourg.[55] As was pointed out in chapter 10, Strasbourg's reliance on the doctrine of the margin of

---

[54] Of course, this point holds true even in a jurisdiction where the Bill of Rights is formally entrenched and the courts have the formal power to strike down legislation which conflicts with it. As Robert Summers explained: 'American constitutional law provides that, in matters of valid legislation, the legislature is supreme', see Summers (1991), 450.

[55] The UK complies with the Strasbourg rulings, although given that such rulings tend to identify a legal wrong, rather than necessarily prescribe how the matter should be regulated, there are various options open to any government found to be in contravention of Convention rights, so there may be controversy about the extent to which the UK has complied with particular rulings. But this does not undercut the general point that the UK Government perceives itself to be bound legally by those rulings.

appreciation, means that a ruling by the highest court in the UK that there has been a violation of Convention rights, will if anything, enhance the likelihood that Strasbourg's 'last word' will match the declaration issued by the House of Lords.[56] The fact that, thus far, the Executive/legislature has responded to all declarations of incompatibility by either amending legislation or giving a commitment to amend, and has in no instance decided to allow the incompatibility to stand, may also suggest that Parliament has the last word only in the most formal sense. Moreover, if the government decides to amend the legislation by way of remedial order without placing the order before Parliament, this means that the Executive (not Parliament) has the last word, the government has determined how the legislation should be amended in response to a declaration of incompatibility. Aside from this, the invariable practice of complying with the declarations, arising as it does from both practical and legal requirements, in itself suggests that Parliament does not have the degree of independent choice and power of determination suggested by the metaphor of the 'last word'. At most, one can say that although the HRA theoretically leaves open the possibility that Parliament can defy a declaration of incompatibility, thereby asserting its sovereignty over the courts, as a matter of legal and political practice, the last legal word is left to either the domestic courts or ultimately the ECtHR in Strasbourg.[57] Of course, the last legal word will tend to be indeterminate: a declaration of incompatibility will state that the legislative provision is incompatible with the Convention and give reasons for that conclusion, but the government and Parliament then have a choice about the appropriate legislative solution to the problem. This merely shows that Parliament has the final say on how Convention rights are implemented in legislative form – it does not show that it has the last word on determining what the Convention requires in response to a HRA challenge.

## Parliamentary sovereignty and the changing constitutional landscape

Lord Lester described the HRA as 'a subtle measure' designed to comply with 'the ceremonial forms required by the English dogma of the sovereignty of Parliament'.[58] When one looks behind the ceremonial

---

[56] Lester (2002a), 67.

[57] See also Fenwick (2007), 205–6, questioning whether the declaration of incompatibility preserves parliamentary sovereignty 'in practice'.

[58] Lester (1998), 668.

forms, both the positive and negative dimension of the traditional doctrine of parliamentary sovereignty seem to be compromised by the HRA. More importantly, I have tried to show that the formal legal structures set up by the HRA themselves compromise the claim to parliamentary omnipotence suggested by the orthodox account of parliamentary sovereignty. I argued that both the legal pervasiveness and the interpretive robustness of section 3(1) accounted, in part, for the constitutional status of the HRA, superior to other (non-constitutional) laws.

This analysis has serious and worrying implications for the doctrine of parliamentary sovereignty, at least as traditionally understood. Perhaps the 'subtlety' and 'genius' of the HRA will be enough to forestall any fundamental rethinking of so sacred and foundational a principle. The remarkable tenacity of the doctrine of parliamentary sovereignty in UK public law, notwithstanding its dislocation from constitutional practice, is borne out by the response in the legal community to the *Factortame* decision.[59] There, the House of Lords was forced to accept that EU law clearly has a superior status to domestic law, as well as the corollary that the courts can therefore disapply primary legislation. However, many judges and academic commentators nonetheless adhered to the idea that the orthodox doctrine of parliamentary sovereignty was nonetheless preserved. They did so through a combination of what I have called *the argument from lack of legal limits* and *the argument from remote possibility*. As regards the latter, it was claimed that parliamentary sovereignty was preserved because the UK could withdraw from the EU. As Mark Elliott commented 'this style of reasoning according to which the appearance of orthodoxy is preserved at the expense of the legal theory which accurately describes political reality, typifies the pragmatic British approach to constitutionalism'.[60] More importantly in relation to EU law, it was claimed that parliamentary sovereignty was ultimately preserved because the source of the (undeniable) limit on parliamentary sovereignty, was an Act of the UK Parliament which facilitated the UK's membership of the EU.[61] Parliament is still sovereign because it chose to join the EU (accepting all the constraints which went along with that membership), but could also express its sovereignty by removing itself from the EU.

---

[59] See Hunt (1997), 163, who comments that the sovereigntist perspective has proven to be 'remarkably durable'.

[60] Elliott (2003), 33. Murray Hunt (1997) also notes the 'ever-widening chasm between what constitutional actors do in practice and the roles which traditional theory purports both to describe and to justify', 1.

[61] European Communities Act 1972.

A similar type of argument is sometimes used with respect to the HRA. In response to the suggestion that the inventive and imaginative process of statutory interpretation set in train by section 3(1) HRA might constitute 'a judicial usurpation of the legislative function', some judges and commentators have responded by pointing out that 'it is Parliament itself that has used its legislative function to command the courts to interpret past and future statutes wherever possible so as to be compatible with Convention rights'.[62] Parliament is sovereign because it decided to subject itself to the various constraints provided by the HRA, and could extract itself from these constraints, if it so wished. Parliament relies on its sovereignty to limit it. However, the fact that Parliament voluntarily accepts limits on its sovereignty, does not undermine the fact that it has nonetheless limited its ability to make or unmake any law it wishes.[63] The voluntary acceptance of those limitations does not cancel those limitations out, unless one makes the assumption that it is impossible to limit parliamentary sovereignty voluntarily. This is a false assumption. Just as individuals can sell themselves into slavery, or accept various substantial limitations on their freedom of action, Parliament can voluntarily commit to substantial constraints on its freedom, including an acceptance that laws enacted by the UK Parliament will be disapplied if they conflict with laws or norms deemed to have fundamental constitutional status.

The decision in *Factortame* prompted many commentators to re-evaluate the nature of the traditional doctrine of parliamentary sovereignty and expose its limitations, not least its lack of explanatory power in the context of a changing constitutional landscape which *de facto* placed considerable legal limits on Parliament's legislative power.[64] Although there was also a notable body of extrajudicial writing challenging the absolutism of Dicey's classic definition, the general judicial approach in the case law, was to downplay the constitutional significance of membership of the EU and to smooth over possible constitutional difficulties with parliamentary sovereignty.[65] Significantly, there are now signs that, post-HRA, the courts are prepared openly to announce their ability

---

[62] Lester (1998), 671; Feldman (1999a), 186, who argues that 'strictly speaking, [section 3] does not threaten parliamentary sovereignty, because Parliament itself has decreed that judges should behave in accordance with section 3'.

[63] Hunt (1997), 71ff.

[64] See e.g. Elliott (2004), 545ff where he refers to 'the unreality of Parliamentary sovereignty'; see also Craig (1991); Wade (1996); Allan (1997); Hunt (1997), 1ff.

[65] Hunt (1997), 50ff; Elliott (2003), 29ff who noted that one of the most surprising features of the *Factortame* decision was that 'their Lordships said scarcely a word about how such a development might be accommodated in terms of constitutional theory'.

to limit parliamentary sovereignty and subject the institutions of parliamentary government to closer and greater scrutiny. Those limits were
expressed in an unprecedented fashion in *Jackson* v. *Attorney General*.[66]
Although this case was not concerned with Convention rights and no
part of the argument rested on the HRA, it is clear that the changed
constitutional landscape to which the HRA contributes, gave some of
the impetus for the remarkable *dicta* in Jackson on the limits of parliamentary sovereignty. This book is not the place to engage in a detailed
analysis of the implications of the various challenging *dicta* in *Jackson*.
For our purposes, it will suffice simply to take note of some of those *dicta*
as an indication of the changing constitutional landscape stimulated by
the HRA.

*Jackson* concerned a challenge to the constitutional validity of the
Hunting Act 2004 and the Parliament Act 1949. A nine-judge bench
of the House of Lords held unanimously that both Acts were lawful. In
the course of coming to this conclusion, some of their Lordships made
*obiter* comments on the doctrine of parliamentary sovereignty. Lord Hope
opened his judgment with the following statement:

> Our constitution is dominated by the sovereignty of Parliament. But par-
> liamentary sovereignty is no longer, if it ever was, absolute . . . step-by-step,
> gradually but surely, the English principle of the absolute sovereignty of
> Parliament which Dicey derived from Coke and Blackstone is being qual-
> ified . . . the rule of law enforced by the courts is the ultimate controlling
> factor on which our constitution is based.[67]

Echoing Lord Hope's dramatic statement, Lord Steyn opined:

> We do not in the United Kingdom have an uncontrolled constitution . . . in
> the European context the second *Factortame* decision made that clear:
> [1991] 1 AC 603 . . . moreover, the European Convention on Human Rights
> is incorporated into our law by the Human Rights Act 1998 created a new
> legal order . . . The classic account given by Dicey of the doctrine of the
> supremacy of Parliament, pure and absolute as it was, can now be seen to be
> out of place in the modern United Kingdom. Nevertheless, the supremacy
> of Parliament is still the general principle of our constitution. The judges
> created this principle. If that is so, it is not unthinkable that circumstances
> could arise where the courts may have to qualify a principle established on
> a different hypothesis of constitutionalism. In exceptional circumstances

---

[66] R. *(Jackson)* v. *Attorney General* [2006] 1 A.C. 262. For discussion of this case, see Steyn
(2006), 250ff; Young (2006); Tomkins (2008), 19–23; Jowell (2006), 562–80; Elliott (2007a)
370–9; Elliott (2006).

[67] [2006] 1 A.C. 262 at [104].

involving an attempt to abolish judicial review or the ordinary role of the courts, the Appellate Committee of the House of Lords or the new Supreme Court may have to consider whether this is a constitutional fundamental which even a sovereign parliament acting at the behest of a complacent House of Commons cannot abolish.[68]

Lord Steyn's *dictum* explicitly highlights the way in which the HRA has contributed to the changed constitutional context in which judges now operate. Moreover, in the thinly veiled reference to the planned ouster clause in the Asylum and Immigration Bill, Lord Steyn emphasised the ability and willingness of the courts to oppose an attempt by the Government to ride roughshod over Convention rights.[69] Although there is certainly much to be discussed about the various *dicta* in *Jackson* concerning the source and limitations of the doctrine of parliamentary sovereignty, for our purposes it suffices to note that they are a clear indication that the courts are now prepared to be more explicit about their constitutional ability to review, scrutinise and ultimately limit the power of Parliament. One of the underlying themes of this book has been that through the traditional doctrines of statutory interpretation, the courts have always constrained Parliament's ability to enact legislation which violates fundamental constitutional rights. Another theme has been that although the HRA has not provided the courts with radically new methods of interpretation, one of its most significant effects has been to enhance the court's sense of legitimacy about their constitutional function. The *dicta* in *Jackson* are a dramatic expression of what Lord Steyn referred to as 'the changed hypothesis of constitutionalism', i.e. the new sense of legitimacy attached to the courts' ability to engage in constitutional review.[70]

## Parliamentary sovereignty and the section 3/4 interplay

Whilst accepting that the HRA complies with the principle of parliamentary sovereignty in formal terms, I have doubted whether that is true as

---

[68]    *Ibid.* at [102]. This passage from Lord Steyn's judgment is mirrored in his extrajudicial comments in Steyn (2004b), 107–8, which were explicitly directed towards the ouster clause.

[69]    *Ibid.* at [159], *per* Baroness Hale: 'The courts will treat with a particular suspicion (and might even reject) any attempts to subvert the rule of law by removing governmental action affecting the rights of the individual from all judicial powers.'

[70]    Elliott describes these passages from *Jackson* as 'a significant staging post in the development of our unwritten constitution', Elliott (2006), 4. For further views that the HRA changes the constitutional landscape within which judges operate, see Elliott (2002), 346–52; Feldman (1999a), 187; Jowell (2006).

a matter of substance. However, it is nonetheless clear that the declaration of incompatibility in section 4 was drafted in order to prevent the courts from having a formal power to 'strike down' legislation. This has prompted some commentators to argue that judges should discharge their interpretive obligation under section 3(1), with the principle of parliamentary sovereignty in mind. Thus, Conor Gearty has argued that since the UK constitutional system (post-HRA) is still one where 'representative assemblies continue to have the final say'[71] and a judicial override is prohibited, 'a proper interpretation of the HRA should reflect this fact'.[72] The premise of this argument, namely, the claim that the HRA gives Parliament the 'final say' on matters related to Convention rights, has been questioned in this chapter. Despite this, it is still worth examining the claim that the principle of parliamentary sovereignty should inform the judicial tasks under sections 3 and 4 HRA. After all, even in *Jackson*, their Lordships did not doubt that the principle of parliamentary sovereignty was an important principle of UK constitutional law. Moreover, the principle has sometimes been invoked in the case law as a (partial) justification for a particular understanding of the judicial approach to sections 3 and 4. Thus, in *Ghaidan* v. *Mendoza*, Lord Millett noted that the judicial choice between section 3 or section 4 involved:

> a question of great constitutional importance, for it goes to the relationship between the legislature and the judiciary, and hence ultimately to the supremacy of Parliament. Sections 3 and 4 of the 1998 Act were carefully crafted to preserve the existing constitutional doctrine, and any application of the ambit of s. 3 beyond its proper scope subverts it. This is not to say that the doctrine of parliamentary supremacy is sacrosanct, but only that any change in a fundamental constitutional principle should be the consequence of deliberate legislative action and not judicial activism, however well-meaning.[73]

In chapter 4, we noted that, in terms of developing a coherent account of the nature of the judicial obligation under section 3, Lord Millett's dissent was not without its problems and contradictions. Given those contradictions, it is difficult to discern a particular approach to section 3(1) which would follow from the principle of parliamentary sovereignty. His Lordship's statement on the significance of this principle begs more questions than it answers. Even the claim that the combined workings of sections 3 and 4 were designed to preserve existing constitutional

---

[71] Gearty (2002), 269.     [72] *Ibid.*
[73] *Ghaidan* v. *Mendoza* [2004] 3 W.L.R. 113 at [57].

doctrine should not be accepted without further examination. Sections 3 and 4 may have been designed to comply only with 'the ceremonial forms'[74] of the doctrine of parliamentary sovereignty, whilst nonetheless bringing about subtle changes in the substance of the doctrine. Alternatively, since the HRA was part of 'a comprehensive programme of constitutional *reform*',[75] it is not implausible to suggest that sections 3 and 4 were crafted in order to effect a modification of existing constitutional doctrine.[76] This view is supported by David Feldman:

> The [HRA] initiates a fundamental constitutional change by introducing new values and an altered frame of reference into UK public law. These, and the mechanisms which the Act introduces for protecting human rights, will significantly affect the operation of traditional constitutional principles. At the same time, those principles, albeit in a changing form, will control the direction and speed of change.[77]

This is a far cry from accepting that the HRA simply replicates 'existing doctrine' in its current form, without changing it.[78]

Of course, these conjectures about the purpose of the HRA when enacting sections 3 and 4, say nothing about the meaning, plausibility and extent of 'the existing doctrine', which, as *Jackson* shows, is now open to question more than ever before. The impact of constitutional review under the HRA on the sovereignty of Parliament, depends on what that concept entails. Moreover, the fact that the declaration of incompatibility under section 4 is a weaker device than a formal 'strike-down' power does not necessarily support the conclusion that judges should carry out their duties under the HRA in a way which is more deferential to Parliament. In fact, many commentators have used the weakness of such features to justify precisely the opposite conclusion. Thus, Richard Clayton has claimed that the respect for Parliament:

---

[74] Lester (1998); see also Cooke (2004), 276, who observes that the HRA '*nominally* preserves the "sovereignty" of Parliament', emphasis added.

[75] Jack Straw, 306 HC 782–3 (16 February 1998); see also Irvine (2003a), 7, 17, 87.

[76] Lord Irvine argued in parliamentary debates that the Human Rights Bill 'occupied a central position in our integrated programme of constitutional *change*', 582 HL 1227 (3 November 1997), emphasis added.

[77] Feldman (1999a), 165.

[78] *R. v. Lambert* [2002] 2 A.C. 545 at [6], *per* Lord Slynn: 'If the courts are to give full effect to the HRA, long or well entrenched ideas may have to be put aside, sacred cows culled'. Even Conor Gearty, who places much emphasis on the doctrine of parliamentary sovereignty as a principle which should inform interpretation under section 3(1) denies that the HRA 'is merely duplicatory of the status quo', Gearty (2004), 5, 21 and suggests that it marks a radical change from traditional constitutional assumptions.

implicit in the structural features of the Act renders the need to defer to Parliament or the Executive less compelling, once it is acknowledged that the Human Rights Act envisages that the other branches of government will have a second bite of the cherry.[79]

In other words, the various types of deference 'built in' to the HRA mean that judges do not have to add any of their own.

The real problem with Lord Millett's *dictum* is that it does not articulate clearly the connection (if any) between the principle of parliamentary sovereignty and the 'proper scope' of section 3(1). It assumes that the proper scope of section 3(1) will be co-extensive with the principle of parliamentary sovereignty. Is this assumption justified? Recall that of central importance to the orthodox understanding of the principle of parliamentary sovereignty, was the prohibition on *any* legal limits on the ability of Parliament to make or unmake any law. If the courts were to obey the full absolutism of this principle, they would interpret section 3(1) by rendering it a dead letter, because by its nature, it is designed to limit the ability of Parliament to enact laws which violate Convention rights. In other words, if the *only* concern of the courts was to preserve parliamentary sovereignty in the traditional Diceyan sense, their duty would be to declare in every case that the legislation must stand, and should not be rectified to remove an apparent incompatibility with convention rights. Nor should it be declared incompatible. I have attempted to show that both section 3 and section 4 place practical *and legal* limits on Parliament's ability to make certain types of law. So, to preserve the full absolutism of the principle, the courts would have to avoid relying on either section.

Clearly, this would go against the clear and emphatic terms of section 3(1) and undermine the rationale of section 4. By enacting these sections, Parliament must be taken to accept the limitations which necessarily follow from them. Therefore, those who advocate a judicial approach to sections 3 and 4 which draws on the principle of parliamentary sovereignty, tend to say that it is a matter of degree, and that the courts should recognise that there are some limits on the power of interpretation under section 3(1) and that it should not be applied in every case.[80] Thus, Conor Gearty argues that section 3(1) should not be used in every case to render all legislation compatible with convention rights.[81] Reliance on section 3(1) should observe limits which neither give 'untrammelled priority'[82]

---

[79] Clayton (2004); see also Klug (2003), 128; Phillipson (2006), 68ff.    [80] Gearty (2002).
[81] *Ibid.*, 254.    [82] *Ibid.*, 250.

to rights on the one hand, nor to the power of Parliament to legislate entirely free from judicial controls on the other. However, he suggests that an approach which is respectful of the principle of parliamentary sovereignty will lead to 'more rather than fewer'[83] declarations of incompatibility – a position he suggests should be greeted with 'equanimity, almost with enthusiasm'.[84] In chapter 4, I argued that one cannot establish the propriety of the judicial choice in favour of section 3 or section 4 in the abstract – it all depends on the context of the case. This point applies equally to Gearty's suggestion that judges should issue more declarations of incompatibility. The propriety of issuing such a declaration is context dependent.

The important question for our purposes here is whether the principle of parliamentary sovereignty has any concrete implications either for interpretation under section 3(1) or for the judicial choice between sections 3 and 4. Once respect for parliamentary sovereignty is softened into the principle that, in carrying out their obligations under the HRA, the courts must respect the competence, expertise and legitimacy of Parliament and exercise a constitutionally appropriate degree of restraint in recognition of this fact, then it boils down to an argument for deference. As we saw earlier in the book, this is a context-dependent doctrine. In fact, its contextual and flexible application is its most notable advantage in comparison to the more absolute doctrine of non-justiciability. Conceived in this way, one cannot say that a proper judicial appreciation of the doctrine of deference will necessarily lead to more rather than fewer declarations of incompatibility.

## Parliamentary sovereignty and parliamentary intent

It is often assumed that the principle of parliamentary sovereignty requires deference to parliamentary intent. Thus, Jeffrey Goldsworthy argues that judicial respect for parliamentary intent is 'indispensable to sensible interpretation that is consistent with the principle of legislative supremacy'.[85] The foundational principle of statutory interpretation must be that

---

[83] *Ibid.*

[84] *Ibid.* See also Gearty (2003a), 381, where he urges us to 'celebrate' declarations of incompatibility because they show the principle of parliamentary sovereignty at work.

[85] Goldsworthy (2004), 192. The idea that there is a link between parliamentary sovereignty and respect for parliamentary intention also underlies Feldman's discussion, see Feldman (1999a), 185–6.

statutes should be interpreted according to the intention they convey, either expressly or by implication given the context in which they were enacted.[86] Goldsworthy acknowledges that interpretation is a partly creative process, but emphasises that in order for that creativity to be justified in accordance with constitutional orthodoxy, it must be justified in terms of giving effect to Parliamentary intent. As we saw in chapter 4, the notion of parliamentary intent can mean many different things. Moreover, when the courts rely on the doctrine of purposive interpretation, this does not eliminate judicial creativity, which is part and parcel of the evaluative task of establishing what the legislative purpose is. On top of this, we have the added difficulty that, when interpreting under section 3, there are two intentions at play – the intention embodied in the legislation under scrutiny and the 'section 3 intention'. How is a judge to resolve a possible conflict between these intentions, whilst simultaneously preserving an allegiance to the supremacy of Parliament? Moreover, would the sort of 'reading in' and 'reading down' endorsed by the House of Lords in cases such as *R. v. A* and *Ghaidan* be acceptable in light of 'constitutional orthodoxy'?

Goldsworthy's answer to those questions is mixed. On the one hand, he suggests that if a court is faced with a conflict between two intentions (one contained in the HRA, the other contained in a subsequent Act of Parliament) and the court gives effect to the intention contained in the HRA, then this would violate the doctrine of parliamentary sovereignty:

> The doctrine of parliamentary sovereignty requires that if they cannot be reconciled, the more recent expression of intention must prevail...if [Parliament] were bound by one of its own earlier laws, it would no longer be sovereign: it would have turned sovereignty against itself, and partially abdicated or limited its authority.[87]

Goldsworthy seeks to avoid the full consequences of this conclusion, by relying on the familiar (rebuttable) presumptions of statutory interpretation. He argues that interpretation under section 3(1) complies with the principle of parliamentary sovereignty, as long as it is justified by reference to presumed intention. In this way, one can understand the application of section 3(1) as a sort of 'standing commitment that can be treated (in the absence of sufficient evidence to the contrary) as an implicit, background assumption of every subsequent statute'.[88] Notwithstanding the fact that

---

[86] Goldsworthy (2004), 192.      [87] *Ibid.*, 296.      [88] *Ibid.*, 200.

this type of 'standing commitment' can in some cases entail the judicial power to disapply statutory provisions[89] or to read down statutes in ways which are tantamount to partial disapplication and engage in various other methods of creative interpretation, Goldsworthy asserts that it is 'crucial for the doctrine of parliamentary sovereignty that the issue be framed in this way'.[90]

It should be observed that although Jeffrey Goldsworthy's argument seems to be about which method of interpretation would be compatible with parliamentary sovereignty, his main concern is not in fact with interpretive method, but rather with the way in which the methods currently employed by the courts should be rationalised or justified, as a matter of constitutional theory. On my analysis, section 3(1) embodies a strong presumption of statutory interpretation. Like Goldsworthy, I endorsed as legitimate the various strategies of 'reading in' and 'reading down' adopted by the House of Lords in the leading case law. Moreover, I argued that judicial reliance on these strategies post-HRA, was continuous with the type of constitutional adjudication carried out by the courts in the pre-HRA era, through the familiar presumptions of statutory interpretation. But unlike Goldsworthy, I argued that the reason why the courts adopt these presumptions was to protect the constitutional values which underlie them. They are simply a way of giving effect to constitutional principle. Thus, they can be viewed as 'the courts' efforts to provide, in effect, a common law Bill of Rights'.[91] As one Canadian scholar observed, the presumptions of statutory interpretation 'no longer have anything to do with the intent of the legislature; they are a means of controlling that intent'.[92]

In an effort to square the judicial decisions under the HRA with legislative supremacy, Goldsworthy relies on what he calls 'the orthodox justification for common law presumptions',[93] namely, that the rationale of these presumptions 'lies in the assumption that the legislature would, if it intended to achieve the particular effect, have made its intention in that regard unambiguously clear'.[94] As we saw in chapter 3, in adjudication under the HRA, the higher courts in the UK have also made reference to this type of counterfactual attribution of noble intention to Parliament. There, it was argued that these assertions of counterfactual

---

[89] He puts forward the 'standing commitment' theory as justification for the power of the UK courts to disapply domestic legislation which conflicts with directly effective EU law, Goldsworthy (2004), 199ff.

[90] Ibid., 201.    [91] Pearce and Geddes (2001), 131.

[92] Section 7 of the Charter of Rights and Freedoms, Tremblay (1984), 242.

[93] Goldsworthy (2004), 206.    [94] Ibid.

intention were not accompanied with any enquiry into their veracity or plausibility as a matter of fact. The better reading of judicial statements of this nature was to view them as indirect ways in which the courts emphasise their comity with Parliament.[95] The politics of judicial law-making in the UK are such that rather than stating openly that Parliament intended to violate Convention rights, and that the courts will nonetheless remove that violation, judges tend to say that Parliament would have endorsed the interpretation (no matter how creative), if it had realised the consequences for Convention rights. This is at one with Goldsworthy's account, which emphasises the legitimacy of courts going against the ordinary meaning, when violation of Convention rights is 'inadvertent'. But the judicial practice of referring obliquely to constitutional principle *via* these statements of hypothetical intent, should not blind us to the fact that the courts apply these principles regardless of Parliament's actual intention when enacting the legislation. This applies with particular force in relation to section 3(1), because it applies to legislation enacted before the HRA came onto the statute book. The artificiality of suggesting that the presumptions of statutory interpretation are derived from the intentions of Parliament as a matter of historical fact, are particularly acute in this situation.

Finally, in terms of squaring interpretation under the HRA with constitutional orthodoxy, Goldsworthy rests much weight on the fact that these presumptions are rebuttable. He likens the statutory presumptions to 'manner and form' requirements, in that they require particular express and unequivocal words before a court will accept that a statute overrides certain common law rights. Given that he accepts that section 3(1) enacts a similar presumption, the same argument would apply to it.[96] Rather than conceiving of this as a constraint on the law-making ability of Parliament, Goldsworthy argues that it enhances rather than detracts from Parliament's ability to control its legislative agenda, because it does not restrict the ability of future legislators to change the important statute, but simply requires that they must give clear notice of any proposal to do so.[97] The courts must 'always remain open to the possibility that when enacting a subsequent statute Parliament has repudiated [its] standing commitment [to protect and uphold Convention rights]'.[98] David Feldman also stresses the significance of the fact that Parliament can enact legislation which is contrary to Convention rights for the doctrine of parliamentary sovereignty:

---

[95] See chapter 3 above, 78; Endicott (2003a), 209.     [96] Goldsworthy (2004), 198.
[97] Goldsworthy (1999), 15.     [98] *Ibid.*, 14.

> Strictly speaking, [section 3] does not threaten parliamentary sovereignty, because Parliament itself has decreed that judges should behave in accordance with section 3. It simply imposes an additional burden on drafters of legislation intended to be incompatible with the Convention right to make their intention absolutely clear and unequivocal.[99]

The analysis in chapter 4 suggests that this burden may be so onerous that it is, in effect, irrebuttable in all but the most extreme case. So, if the preservation of constitutional orthodoxy rests crucially on the rebuttable nature of the principle of legality, then we are, yet again, driven back to the *argument from remote possibility*. As Lord Hoffmann stated in *Simms*, cases in which a presumption of such constitutional importance would be rebutted, will be 'unusual'.[100] Though formally the legislature can override these presumptions, the official assumption is that it will not intend to do so – and it is this assumption which drives the operation of the presumptions and accounts for the similarity (in terms of interpretive method) between constitutional adjudication in the UK and that which is found in countries with entrenched bills of rights.

Since Goldsworthy is prepared to accept the constitutional legitimacy of the most radical reading in or reading down statutory provisions under the auspices of section 3(1), even if it is tantamount to partial disapplication, then perhaps the conclusion is that all such interpretations are compatible with the orthodox doctrine of parliamentary sovereignty – provided of course that one *justifies* those interpretations with reference to presumed or hypothetical intent. But if this is the case, we are drawn to the suggestion made in the previous section, namely, that the principle of parliamentary sovereignty may not provide us with any meaningful guidance on what constitutes legitimate statutory interpretation. At most, it provides us with an artificial rationalisation of the existing practices of statutory interpretation, which obscures from view, the way in which the courts possess an inherent common law jurisdiction to protect and enforce constitutional rights, including the ability to ensure that legislation enacted by Parliament conforms to them.

## Conclusion

The conclusion of this chapter is that the HRA only preserves the doctrine of parliamentary sovereignty in formal terms, but limits the legislative power of Parliament in substance. Although I could not substantiate

---

[99] Feldman (1999a), 186.    [100] *Simms*, above n. 38 at 131, *per* Lord Hoffmann.

my doubts in full here, I questioned whether the tension between the HRA and the orthodox principle of parliamentary sovereignty, may be more of a problem for the orthodox doctrine, than it is for the HRA. But even if one rejects the full absolutism of the orthodox doctrine of parliamentary sovereignty, one has to acknowledge its democratic underpinnings. As Lord Irvine observed, the principle of parliamentary sovereignty reflects 'the primacy which is attached to representative, democratic government'.[101] So, if the Parliament's law-making ability is limited, then this requires justification in democratic terms. Moreover, parliamentary sovereignty is a relational concept – it provides a particular account of the appropriate relationship between Parliament and the courts.[102] The HRA has important implications for the existing relationship between the three branches of government. This too requires justification. I will attempt to meet both of those justificatory challenges in the final two chapters.

[101] Irvine (2003a), 241.
[102] For an understanding of Parliamentary sovereignty as a relational concept, see Hunt (1997), 63.

# 12

# Justifying constitutional review

## Introduction

The purpose of this chapter is to justify the power of the courts to engage in constitutional review under the HRA. It will not contain an account of what makes rights special in themselves, but rather an account of why the courts are institutionally appropriate to the task of determining the meaning and scope of Convention rights and scrutinising legislation for compliance with them. The HRA gives the courts special responsibility for the enforcement of fundamental rights. In chapter 10, I argued that this did not mean that the regulation of human rights is taken out of the reach of democratic majorities completely. Rather, it meant that although this legislative and regulative power remains largely in the hands of elected representatives, the courts are given a constitutional power to check legislation for compliance with Convention rights and individuals are given powers to sue for their enforcement. This places limits on the legislative powers of Parliament.

The question posed in this chapter is: why should courts have this special responsibility? Why is it justified to allocate this supervisory function to the courts? My answer will be that the existence of an independent review procedure for compliance with rights, such as that provided by the courts under sections 3 and 4 HRA, gives individuals a meaningful opportunity to mount a rights-based challenge to primary legislation, thereby making rights protection more robust and more secure. In other words, we are more likely to enhance protection of Convention rights if we have a legal review procedure to check for their compliance, than if we leave their protection to Parliament and the Executive alone without this added safeguard. The argument proceeds by first outlining the participatory dimension of constitutional review, both in terms of allowing individuals to voice grievances based on human rights before an impartial tribunal, as well as enabling them to contribute more broadly to public discussion in ways which may not have been possible through the normal political channels. I then go on to show that constitutional review is valuable as a safeguard against the risks inherent in democratic politics. Here, the relative insulation of courts from the popular and electoral pressures often brought to bear on elected politicians, forms the cornerstone of the argument. I then attempt to show that, given the importance of Convention rights, it is valuable to have an institution which focuses specifically on individual rights and scrutinises legislation for compliance with them. Finally, I argue that having constitutional review under the HRA gives Parliament added incentives to take Convention rights seriously, not only by changing legislation in response to declarations of incompatibility, but also by encouraging it to take Convention rights seriously during the legislative process. I conclude with some comments on the need for realism and caution in responsible institutional design.

One clarification is in order before I begin. In making an argument for constitutional review, I am not suggesting the courts should provide the *only* limit on Parliament, or even the primary or most important one. On the contrary, I assume that the various political methods of encouraging and constraining democratic institutions to protect Convention rights are to be welcomed and endorsed wholeheartedly. My argument is that the various methods of political accountability should be supplemented by constitutional review, but not supplanted by it. Many democratic sceptics present the issue as one of mutually exclusive options: i.e. *either* we support political *or* legal controls.[1] The assumption is that if we endorse legal controls (especially in the form of constitutional review), we necessarily 'turn our backs on politics'.[2] This ignores the fact that political and legal controls are not mutually exclusive. They can co-exist. So, I am not arguing for the *prioritisation* of legal over political forms of accountability or that the courts should be 'absolutely centre stage'.[3] My argument is simply that they should be on the stage, sharing it with the various mechanisms of political accountability which help to ensure that Parliament and government take rights as seriously as possible.

## Participation, public discussion and individual empowerment

In chapter 10, we observed that one of the distinctive features of Bills of Rights is that they provide individuals with a means of advancing a rights claim before an independent tribunal and seeking redress for a possible violation. This followed from the fact that although the allocation of rights

---

[1] Tomkins (2005a), 3.    [2] *Ibid.*    [3] *Ibid.*, 15.

effects a distribution of power amongst state institutions, it is also a way of distributing power between institutions and individuals.[4] By allowing individuals to sue for the enforcement of their rights, one empowers them to challenge the terms of enacted legislation in a way which is different from the type of challenge one can mount in ordinary democratic politics. As such, constitutional litigation can become a second channel of political participation, parallel to ordinary parliamentary politics.[5] Of course, we know from our discussion of deference that the politics of constitutional rights is not completely immune from the influences which shape ordinary politics.[6] However, the politics of constitutional rights is nonetheless different in significant ways, and responsive to different kinds of concerns. In this section, I will show that the criteria for success in gaining access to the court, differs in important respects from those which typically obtain in normal politics.

The first such difference is that, in constitutional politics, individuals whose rights are allegedly violated have the initiative in starting the litigation process through the courts. They do not have to wait for state institutions to take up the issue. Nor do they need to rely on the government or its advisers to acknowledge a possible rights violation.[7] They can start the process themselves and bring issues to light which have not been considered by government. This is not to deny that political processes are often initiated by interest groups in normal politics, but in such cases, individuals typically need to secure widespread support in society, organise themselves into an effective pressure group or gain support in the major political organisations or parties. In constitutional politics, people do not need such a wide base of political support. They can gain access to the courts, even if they belong to marginal groups in society, have negligible political clout and little chance of pressing their grievances in the public forum, given their lack of popular support or approval. The fact that an individual's ability to advance a constitutional complaint and ultimately succeed in court do not depend to the same degree on their ability to mobilise political and popular support, is crucial in providing a justification having this institutional mechanism in place.

---

[4] Macklem (2006), 112ff; Raz (1995), 42ff.    [5] Raz (1995), 42; see also Fredman (2000).

[6] Arguably, the development of the British courts' judicial review jurisdiction in the 1980s and 1990s was a result not only of developments in 'high constitutional politics', but also (perhaps even primarily) developments in 'normal politics' i.e. the fact that the Government at that time faced little meaningful opposition in Parliament and was bent on introducing policies which seemed to disregard fundamental constitutional principles and assumptions, see Walker (1999), 145–6.

[7] Brennan (1989), 427.

This general point is exemplified by a survey of the type of cases which have been brought before the courts under the HRA. Litigants have included suspected terrorists subject to indefinite detention, mental patients, criminals (including those accused of rape), those subject to life imprisonment, prison inmates complaining about the standard of prison facilities, asylum-seekers and immigrants. These are some of the most unpopular people in our society. By allowing them some leverage on the centres of political power 'constitutional politics can empower people who are *de facto* politically disenfranchised'.[8] It can allow weak and marginalised groups to gain access to the centres of power – groups which would have negligible chances of success through the parliamentary system. Moreover, characteristically, a rights claim before the courts stands or falls on the basis of its justifiability relative to Convention rights and the previous judgments of the courts. This means that success in the constitutional realm does not depend so centrally on coalition-forming among powerful groups, but rather on the strength of the legal argument based on Convention rights.[9]

The force of this point (that constitutional litigation can be a valuable channel of political participation) may be resisted by those who believe that the courts are above or outside politics. They may argue that whilst constitutional litigation provides a *legal* remedy for violation of a right, this is an alternative to participation in the *political* process, rather than an instance of it. This view rests on a narrow conception of politics (and perhaps also a narrow conception of political participation) which blinkers its supporters to the central role which the courts play in political life.[10–11] There are many ways in which constitutional litigation can be said to provide a channel of *political* participation. One is that it enables citizens to bring a claim before the court, which is a political institution in the general sense that it is one of the three branches of government and therefore part of the political system. The second is that by making rights legally enforceable in the courts, one turns them into sources of power which are partly political. The allocation of rights is a distribution of political power in society, such that those who might otherwise be disempowered can have their claim heard in the public realm and

---

[8] Raz (1995), 44.    [9] *Ibid.*, 43.

[10–11] For an outline of the various senses of the word 'politics' which might underlie the claim that judges are, or should be, above politics, see Waldron (1990), 120–3. For the claim that attending to the constitutive foundations of the legal and political system is a central part of politics, see Elkin (1993), 134.

possibly vindicated.[12] Moreover, success before the court can have considerable impact on the allocation of resources in society and the duties which the legislature has to discharge in relation to citizens. So it is also political in the sense that it makes a difference to the allocation of power and resources in society. As Lord Steyn observed extrajudicially: 'Judges exercise power. They take decisions which affect the lives and interests of people. They make judgments on matters that affect the way in which we are governed.'[13]

There is another, albeit indirect benefit to individual litigants (especially those who are marginalised in normal politics) which is brought about by constitutional review, exemplifying its important political dimension. This is the fact that judicial decisions affecting human rights attract public attention and the issues dealt with in the higher courts inevitably become part of public discussion.[14] News reporting of a judicial decision can bring an issue to public attention and can inform public opinion and debate about an issue. A high-profile case can also underpin debate in Parliament and inform and stimulate political interrogation of MPs about a particular policy of pressing public concern.[15] Furthermore, even if the claimant loses in court, the public outcry can be such that legislators are forced to address the issue.[16] This reminds us that those who undertake constitutional litigation may not aim exclusively at winning their case in court: they can succeed in gaining publicity for an issue, raising public consciousness of the merits of the case and building up political pressure in support of it as part of a wider campaign.[17] Despite being a fervent

---

[12] This seems to be an assumption of the White Paper, *Bringing Rights Home*, where it claimed that the HRA would 'strengthen representative and democratic government . . . by enabling citizens to challenge more easily actions of the state if they fail to match the standards of the European Convention', 8. The theoretical links between democracy and this sort of 'contestation' is emphasised by Pettit (1999).

[13] Steyn (1997), 84.

[14] Ronald Dworkin has argued that the existence of a Bill of Rights can improve the quality of public discussion concerning fundamental questions of political morality, Dworkin (1996), 345. If sound, this would present a powerful reason in favour of constitutional review. I restrict myself to the more modest claim that constitutional review can contribute to public discussion by bringing issues to the fore which might otherwise have been marginalised.

[15] See David Winnick MP, Proceedings of the Select Committee on Home Affairs (8 February 2005), as cited in Gearty (2005b), 38.

[16] Sandra Fredman also points out that the rejection of Lisa Grant's claim in the Grant case (*Grant v. South West Trains Ltd* [1998] E.C.R. I-621) 'may well have created important pressure on legislators at EU level to fill a glaring gap in legislation', Fredman (2001), 213.

[17] Feldman (1992), 46.

opponent of constitutional review, even Jeremy Waldron acknowledges that:

> an issue that might otherwise have remained a marginal minority concern can be imposed on the attention of society as a whole by being brought before a court connected to some human right that in the abstract at least enjoys widespread support.[18]

Therefore, constitutional litigation can provide a way of participating in public discussion and campaigning to achieve a political outcome, by putting pressure on government through the law.[19] This can enable both individuals and courts to engage in political interaction with the elected branches of government and directly affect the policy agenda of those branches. In this way, it provides a mode of political participation which can counteract some of the ways in which normal democratic politics can disadvantage the poor and powerless in society. Arguing one's case before an impartial tribunal gives individuals more power over the determination of their rights (and therefore more influence over the basic principles on which their society is governed) than being one among the multitude in a participatory democracy, with equality of political power to all.[20] As Sandra Fredman points out:

> *Defrenne* and *Marshall* have made an important impact on the substance of European law, as have *Smith* and *Grady* on the substance of the law of the ECHR. Such principles have also filtered back into the legislative process... even if these arguments are rejected by judges, they have been articulated in an important arena, entered the public domain and exercised some influence, however oblique.[21]

There is one other factor which bolsters the foregoing argument about the individual empowerment arising from the constitutionalisation of rights. Not only does a Bill of Rights give individuals the opportunity to voice a grievance about an alleged infringement (an opportunity which may be denied to them in normal politics), it also provides them with a full hearing on that issue. A full hearing requires that both sides be heard. This means that the state must justify its actions (in this case, justify the terms of the legislation it enacted) and give an 'individualised explanation' to the victim of the alleged infringement.[22] This empowers individuals not only to get their voice heard in public discussion, but also to demand and receive an explanation from the elected branches of

---

[18] Waldron (1993a), 419.  [19] See Harlow and Rawlings (1992).  [20] Raz (1998b), 45.
[21] Fredman (2001), 213.  [22] Eylon and Harel (2006), see 1002ff.

government, which can then be assessed by an independent third party. It contributes to the 'culture of justification'.[23] Depending on the outcome of that adjudication, the elected branches of government may be compelled or encouraged to reconsider the legislation in light of the individual claim. This gives individuals considerably more power to influence legislation than they might hope to achieve through the normal political channels.

Some legal theorists have argued that whenever rights have been infringed, individuals have 'a right to a hearing', because this protects the value of human dignity underlying rights generally.[24] Since the courts are well placed to provide an independent hearing as a neutral third party to the dispute (and the elected branches are not), this justifies constitutional review. We need not embrace the full scope of this argument in order to secure the more modest conclusion which will meet our justificatory needs here. That is, simply, that part of the justification of constitutional review is that it empowers and benefits individuals by giving them additional methods of asserting their rights claims, not only by allowing marginal voices to be heard in the corridors of political power, but also by enabling individuals to demand an 'individualised explanation' and justification of the alleged infringement from the government. This conclusion is secured even if the courts ultimately find against the individual because he or she has still had the opportunity to voice a grievance and demand justification, even if they do not secure the legislative change they desire as a direct outcome of the case.[25] Individual empowerment does not depend on outcome alone, but also on the participatory aspects of litigation – of being heard and receiving an explanation.

## Responding to the risks of democratic politics

In this section, I will concentrate on three salient features of normal democratic politics and the risks entailed by those features. It will be argued that these risks are sufficiently serious to warrant the existence of an institutional mechanism which does not display those features

---

[23] Steyn (2004a), 254.

[24] Eylon and Harel (2006), 1000; Pettit (1998), 52. Interestingly, Philip Pettit also argues that if democracy is conceived of as deliberative democracy, it is necessary that legislation should be 'susceptible to challenge by individual citizens or by groups of citizens', and cites constitutional litigation as a possible forum for such 'contestatory' democracy, see Pettit (1999), 164, 179; Pettit (2001a), 729–30; Pettit (2004), 63.

[25] As the American constitutional lawyer, Laurence Tribe, points out: 'both the right to be heard, and the right to be told why, are analytically distinct from the right to secure a different outcome', Tribe (1978), 503, cited in Eylon and Harel (2006), 1006.

(at least, not to the same degree), as a useful way of minimising or counteracting those risks. Constitutional review is just such a mechanism, though not the only one. Three features of democratic politics will be considered in this regard: electoral and popular orientation, majoritarian bias and bias towards short-term interests. They will be contrasted with the corresponding features in constitutional politics.

### Responsiveness to popular views and electoral orientation

The first feature to consider is the electoral and popular orientation of normal democratic politics. MPs are accountable to the electorate, dependent on popular support for their continuance in office and can be removed if their decisions face popular disapproval. Judges, on the other hand, are not elected by the people and therefore do not need to secure popular support in order to become judges. Nor do they depend on their popularity for continuation in office. This makes them more insulated from direct political pressure than elected politicians. To be sure, they are not completely immune from such pressures, but they are much more removed from such pressures than elected politicians because judges do not stand to suffer the same adverse consequences if they make an unpopular decision. This means that, generally speaking, elected politicians have greater incentive to try to make popular decisions than judges. Whilst there may well be some indirect pressure on judges to make a decision which accords with the prevailing view, the *direct* threat of imminent removal from office is not present.[26]

Furthermore, by not being directly accountable to the people, judges do not have to engage in what Hayek referred to as the 'service-part of governmental activities'.[27] They are not subject to constituency pressures which can be exacted upon elected Members of Parliament. Responsiveness to the grievances and demands of one's constituents is, generally speaking, a valuable aspect of democratic government – it keeps politicians informed about people's needs and wants and gives them an insight into how their policies will affect others. However, there may be situations where members of a political constituency wish to press for some policy change which reflects its needs at the expense of the fundamental rights of some other citizens. In this way, the electoral orientation of democratic politics can sometimes create disincentives for elected politicians to protect human rights, if they are associated with or applied to

---

[26] See Weale (1989), 10.     [27] For this expression, see Hayek (1973), 7.

an unpopular group.[28] It creates the danger that politicians will be afraid to implement unpopular measures, or at least afraid to implement them shortly before an election.[29] If there is public outcry over a particular issue, politicians are often pressured into making popular decisions, even when these decisions go against their better judgment about what ought to happen. In recent times, where public fear has been heightened by the 'threat from global terrorism', it seems that there is often no electoral penalty for decisions adverse to human rights of suspected terrorists. In fact, there seems to be plenty of electoral gain in enacting such policies.[30] Another area notoriously subject to popular pressure to curtail rights is that of criminal justice, where the pursuit of electoral advantage tends to generate tougher sentencing and higher rates of imprisonment, than might otherwise be the case.[31]

So, the popular accountability of elected politicians generates a risk that a popular decision will sometimes be chosen, even if it is not the right decision. The structural and motivational factors which inevitably come into play in democratic decision-making mean that elected politicians are institutionally required to be responsive in various ways to popular views, and are therefore often tempted to satisfy popular wants, even when these views go against the politicians' own best judgment.[32] This is not to suggest that representative democratic government involves a slavish adherence to popular and populist views across the board. We hope and expect our politicians to have the autonomy to make the right decisions, even when they are unpopular – and it is certainly possible for a government with a strong majority in Parliament to withstand some of the pressures of popular opinion. But this should not obscure the fact

---

[28] Phillipson (2006).

[29] As David Feldman points out, 'all candidates risk losing some of their supporters in their constituencies if they do not devote a substantial amount of time to constituency affairs', see Feldman (2002), 324.

[30] Phillipson (2006). T. R. S. Allan argues that Lord Hoffmann's statement of the principle of legality in *Simms* that Parliament could legislate contrary to fundamental principles of human rights provided that it is willing to accept the political cost, should be read in light of the reality that 'there is likely to be very little political cost to curtailing prisoners' rights', see Allan (2006a), 30.

[31] For an explanation of how this tendency works, see generally Pettit (2001b); see also Pettit (2001a), 733ff; see also Steyn (2004a), 246 who argues that much legislation is this area is 'the result of governments seeking short-term political popularity'.

[32] The discussion glosses over a number of complications about the nature of the representative function in modern democracies, which cannot be addressed within the confines of this chapter. For further consideration of those issues, see Kyritsis (2006), 741ff; Waluchow (2007), chapter 3; Manin (1997); Besson (2005).

that elected representatives are nonetheless institutionally bound to pay special attention to the convictions of their constituents in various ways.[33] The personal and political dangers involved in alienating large segments of the electorate are widely felt by politicians, even if they are sometimes overcome.[34]

So, the claim is not that judges are inherently more enlightened, more honourable or more courageous then the typical legislator. The point is simply that politicians and judges make their decisions in different institutional contexts, such that it is *easier* for judges to withstand popular pressure, to ride political storms and to make the right decision in the face of widespread public opposition.[35] Judges have less to lose from making the right decision, even if it is unpopular. They enjoy a degree of immunity from popular political pressures to which 'even the most honourable and courageous politicians are subject'.[36] Judges may be political in the various ways I have described, but they are not *partisan* in the sense of being subject to pressures from a particular political party, constituency or popular view.[37]

### Responsiveness to majoritarian concerns

The second feature of normal democratic politics to consider here is its majoritarian bias. It is inherent in democratic decision-making procedure that the majority wins and the minority loses. Even if we move our focus away from election time and concentrate on ongoing democratic and parliamentary procedures, it is still the case that majority wishes

---

[33] See Kyritsis (2006), 742, 739.

[34] *Ibid.*, 739. Interestingly, when closing the parliamentary debate on the Terrorism Bill 2000, Beverley Hughes (Labour MP) considered that the 'critical test' with respect to the legislation was what members of the public – MPs' constituents – expected Parliament to do, 375 HC official report (sixth series), col. 115 (19 November 2001).

[35] This point about the difference in context and also the difference in the type of decision made by judges on the one hand and politicians on the other, is made by Waluchow (2007), 163, 255ff.

[36] *Ibid.*, 118. The guarantee of judicial independence in the UK has been strengthened by the Constitutional Reform Act 2005 (hereinafter CRA) which confines the Lord Chancellor's duties to executive or political functions and removes the power of the Lord Chancellor to sit as a judge. It also disqualifies senior judges from membership of the (parliamentary) House of Lords and creates new machinery for the appointment of judges through the new Judicial Appointments Commission. Section 3 of the CRA provides a 'guarantee of continued judicial independence'. For more detailed discussion of the CRA, see Woodhouse (2007).

[37] For the distinction between politics and partisanship, see Malleson (1999), 4.

and interests are likely to drive decision-making in representative assemblies governed by majority rule. So, democratic government is necessarily majoritarian and, by favouring majorities, it creates a risk that the views and concerns of unpopular individuals and minorities can occasionally be overridden.[38] In the case of a persistent minority, where the minority is continually outvoted, there is an even greater danger that the interests of that minority will be overlooked.[39] Majority-voting procedures, coupled with the fairly widespread belief that a representative's role is (at least in part) to vote in accordance with the views of one's constituents, create a risk that minority interests will be marginalised or overridden. In light of the risks created by the inevitably majoritarian bias of democratic politics, it is justified to think that it should be supplemented by another form of decision-making which is less responsive to majoritarian concerns – at least with reference to a specific subject-matter, in this case, fundamental constitutional rights.

### Responsiveness to short-term interests

The final distinguishing feature of normal politics concerns the susceptibility of normal politics towards short-term interests and gains. If public emotion is running high on a certain issue, there may be a case for allowing passions to cool before making a political decision. While normal politics can be subject to short-term swings and myopic or ill-considered decisions in response to strong popular demand, constitutional politics is not as vulnerable to shifts in popular opinion in the same way. Generally speaking, constitutional courts do not have to make swift decisions in response to an immediate political crisis. They generally receive a steady workload through the channels of constitutional litigation. By allocating the decision-making power over constitutional rights to the courts, we thereby give them added protection by insulating them to some degree from hasty and improvident decision-making. The fact that they are relatively insulated from direct political pressure means that judges are less likely than elected politicians to be swayed by political self-interest or a

---

[38] These generalisations about democratic government require qualification which is unnecessary for my purposes here. But just to mention one such qualification – in the UK, for example, given relatively low turnouts and the first-past-the-post system, it is in fact impossible to say that any government in the post-Second World War period has actually been supported by a majority of votes of the adult population.

[39] For the ways in which constitutional review can be valuable in the context of 'permanent minorities', such as those which exist in Northern Ireland, see Kavanagh (2004d).

desire to satisfy constituency or other popular demands when they are at variance with the protection of some (possibly minority) right. They are part of an institution which removes them to a large degree from such temptations and dangers.

Of course, it is an important and valuable feature of democratic politics that the elected branches of government are able to respond quickly to changes in the political, social and economic environment to enact legislation, or make executive decisions, swiftly.[40] These are valuable characteristics to possess when one is exercising legislative and governmental power. But they are not necessarily qualities that best fit the exercise of a constitutional power such as that exercised by the courts when upholding and enforcing Convention rights. Thus, the characterisation of the power of the courts under the HRA as constitutional rather than legislative in chapter 10 must be borne in mind here, as it is an important component in the justification of constitutional review under the HRA.

When commenting on the moral justification of the rule of law in Britain, Joseph Raz noted that the function of the rule of law in judicial decisions is 'to facilitate the integration of particular pieces of legislation with the underlying doctrines of the legal system.'[41] The courts have to carry out their interpretive functions in a way which is 'both faithful to the legislative purpose and principled in integrating it with traditional doctrines of the liberties of the citizens.'[42] Traditionally, this role of integrating legislation with constitutional principles was carried out through the presumptions of statutory interpretation. Now, this constitutional function is enhanced and clarified by the particular presumption embodied in section 3 HRA. In carrying out the constitutional function of ensuring that ongoing legislation is attuned to constitutional principles, it is an institutional advantage to be relatively insulated from direct political pressure. The courts' relative immunity from the day-to-day pressures of normal politics makes them less likely to follow a passing trend or be influenced by short-term swings in democratic politics. Legislators, on the other hand, tend naturally to have a greater preoccupation with current problems. This, combined with their felt need to secure re-election

---

[40] This is not to deny that the various stages of the legislative process are designed to slow down the enactment of legislation and ensure that it is not unduly hasty. However, it is also the case that, when legislation is required in a perceived emergency, it is possible (at least with a strong majority) to rush through new legislation in a matter of days, see e.g. Anti-Terrorism, Crime and Security Act 2001. This example is discussed further in chapter 13 at 382.

[41] Raz (1994), 375.    [42] *Ibid.*

by a public all too susceptible to the influences of the short term, makes them more liable to short-term swings and panic measures. Those effects can be mitigated by the courts, who can check legislation for compliance with fundamental principle and the long-established traditions of liberty, especially since some of the concerns presented as rights claims before the court may be unlikely to receive support in an institutional context directly responsive to popular and majoritarian views. Therefore, it is an advantage in adjudicating those claims if the institution allocated that task is not directly accountable to popular views and not as responsive to short-term concerns. So, the courts' relative independence from direct political pressure and short-term swings in the prevailing mood provide some reasons why rights should be given a constitutional status and why the courts should be given special responsibility for their protection.

The point that constitutional review is justified because it is institutionally designed so as to insulate it from short-term pressures, is prone to misunderstanding, and therefore requires some clarification here. Such misunderstanding is engendered by the fact that some advocates of constitutional review rely on a misleading metaphor. They argue that review by the courts offers the opportunity of an 'appeal from the "people drunk" to the "people sober".'[43] Since the legislature may be swayed by the mood of the moment into enacting hasty and ill-considered legislation, the courts are justified in placing limits on the elected branches because 'unlike politics, [the court] speaks dispassionately in the cool language of reason and logic'.[44] Adam Tomkins claims that the assumption underpinning this claim is as follows: 'that it is *only* the political branches that are capable of acting arbitrarily; the courts of law, apparently, *never* can'.[45] Since this extreme claim is obviously false, the argument about the relative institutional advantages of the court, such as its relative insulation from short-term political pressures, can be quickly dismissed.

Tomkins' assumption attributes to defenders of constitutional review implausible, extreme and unrealistic beliefs, which are not made here. It is no part of my argument that all or even most decisions made by our elected representatives are driven by self-serving motives, expediency and hot-headed passion which leads them to oppress the vulnerable. Nor do I make the naive assumption that the courts are *never* guilty of succumbing to 'passion' or capitulating to the political pressures of the day.

---

[43] Hayek (1960), 179.    [44] Tomkins (2005b), 13.

[45] *Ibid.*, emphasis added. An extreme reading of the point about the ability of the courts to 'tame politician's passions' is adopted by Nicol (2006), 738.

This much should be evident from my analysis of the various reasons motivating judicial deference, especially those grounded in prudential considerations. Moreover, I rejected the principle/policy distinction as a meaningful way of demarcating the functions of the courts and Parliament, on the grounds that both these institutions employ a type of reasoning which combines principle and policy.[46] Reliance on principle is not the exclusive property of the courts, with expediency the hallmark of 'political' decisions. For these reasons, I share Tomkins' reservations about reliance on the metaphor of 'people drunk and people sober' as a general characterisation of the differences between judicial and legislative reasoning. It suggests an unduly negative and derogatory picture of democratic politics and an unduly rosy picture of judges and courts.

However, the rejection of this extreme way of demarcating the respective functions of Parliament and courts, does not mean that we must rule out the much more modest claim that normal politics is designed in such a way to make it more responsive than constitutional politics to short-term pressures. Since this responsiveness sometimes threatens to compromise constitutional principles, it may be appropriate, at least with reference to a narrow range of such principles (say, individual rights), to subject them to a corrective mechanism enforced by the courts. Whilst it is not an all-or-nothing matter, the institutional structure of the courts is such that the courts are better placed to resist popular opinion and the hostility of powerful groups in some circumstances. The courts are less prone to short-term pressures and are not designed to be responsive to them. To be sure, they are not immune from such pressures, and sometimes capitulate to them in an unjustifiable manner. Judges are not infallible. But the institutional context within which judges operate is of a different nature and dynamic to that which is inhabited by elected politicians, and this gives judges an institutional advantage in holding elected politicians to account if they sometimes violate rights or other fundamental constitutional principles in the course of carrying out their vast legislative and policy-making agenda.[47] So, whilst the metaphor of an appeal from the people drunk to the people sober may be misleading as a *general characterisation* of the differences between judicial and legislative reasoning, it nonetheless captures an important aspect of the factors which can bear

[46] See chapter 7, 183ff.
[47] Therefore, I would dispute Nicol's conclusion that we can rely on judges '*no more than on legislators*' to exercise the dispassionate application of reason, see Nicol (2006), 739, emphasis added.

on one rather than the other, given the different institutional structure in which elected politicians and judges operate.

## The judicial focus on individuals and rights

Thus far, I have offered some reasons why it is justified to remove constitutional rights from some of the pressures of normal politics and allow some decisions about their scope and ambit to be taken by the courts. There are other features of judicial decision-making which bolster these points. The first is that the courts are particularly suited to claims where the individual has special standing and which relate to a self-contained set of facts. Judges are trained and educated to assess such facts which are disputed between two parties[48] and to establish whether they give rise to a claim in law. They are ill suited to dealing with issues, the determination of which depends on the balancing of multiple alternatives or the resolution of conflict of different interests as required in general policy determinations, but good at deciding upon an individual claim about the legal protection given to an individual interest by a piece of legislation already in place. For this reason, judges are better suited to reacting to issues concerning the implications of a law and the claims of an individual under that law, rather than setting up a range of policies to deal with a complex social problem in advance.

This is simultaneously a point in favour of giving judges power to decide some matters related to constitutional rights, and a point against giving them the power to decide a wider range of legislative and political issues. Since Convention rights are, for the most part, individual rights, and since the courts are well suited to judging disputes where the individual has special standing, this focus on the individual is an advantage in providing a checking mechanism to uphold those rights. Hearing individual grievances and assessing their legal merits in the context of an existing legal framework as applied to a concrete-fact situation, is what the courts are designed to do best.[49] In normal politics, one tends to need a wider base of political support or organisation in an interest group in order to advance one's claim. It is rare that the concerns of one individual or a small group of individuals can be brought to the attention of the government through the normal political channels, such that they

---

[48] This has been described by Endicott as 'the bivalent form of judicial disputes', see Endicott (1999), 15; for this point, see also BeVier (1984), 9.

[49] Eylon and Harel (2006), 998.

would receive an individualised explanation about the implications of a legislative programme for them.

Not only are courts focused on the individual, they are also focused on human rights. When assessing legislation in response to an individual challenge, the court does not consider the merits of the legislation generally. Rather, it has the narrower task of checking to see if the legislation gives due weight to Convention rights and other requirements of legality. When governing the country and responding to all the multifarious concerns thrown up in political life, human rights are just one factor amongst many which MPs must consider when making a policy decision. Given the vast range of subject-matter contained in legislation, it may not be easy for legislators to see what issues of rights are embedded in a legislative proposal brought before them, or at least not easy for them to predict this in advance of its application in concrete cases. As David Feldman pointed out, 'most legislation does not involve the risk of overt conflict with Convention norms . . . the risk usually arises more incidentally'.[50] When the implications for Convention rights 'may not be facially prominent in the legislation'[51] and are difficult in any case to predict in advance, it is advantageous to have an institutional mechanism which focuses specifically on the issue of rights compliance and can therefore draw Parliament's attention to an issue it might otherwise neglect.[52]

Important though they are, human rights are not (and should not be) the be all and end all of the legislative or governmental agenda – they are just one amongst many other values and goals which ought to be realised in public decision-making.[53] An exclusive or even primary focus

---

[50] Feldman (2004), 102.

[51] Waldron (2006), 1370. For the point that legislators have much more on their minds than human rights, see Feldman (2004), 94.

[52] Danny Nicol, who is otherwise a critic of constitutional review, accepts that this is a strong argument in favour of constitutional review, see Nicol (2006), 743; see also Waldron (2006), 1370 arguing that this is a 'respectable' argument in favour of some degree of judicial review of legislation.

[53] Nicol (2006), 743. Lucia Zedner engages in 'a little gentle human rights scepticism' by arguing that there are limits and even hazards involved in relying on rights-based opposition to control orders because 'although they articulate an important necessary minimum, human rights fail to enunciate a fully developed conception of the society' and therefore are 'not an adequate basis of public policy-making', Zedner (2007), 187. This is true, but it only supports scepticism directed at those advocates of human rights who believe that human rights should be the sole or even primary basis of public policy-making. No such view is advocated here. As Wil Waluchow reminds us: 'one can recognise the importance of rights without thinking that they exhaust the normative landscape', see Waluchow (2007), 178.

on them may not be a good quality to possess when exercising legislative or executive functions. But given that human rights form an important part of fundamental constitutional principle, it is useful to have an institution set up with the specific and focused mandate of reviewing the legislative (and Executive) output of the elected branches of government for compliance with these principles. As Lord Nicholls pointed out in the *Belmarsh Prison* case, there may be many reasons why legislation is less than ideal, but the courts will intervene '*only* when it is apparent that, in balancing the various considerations involved, the primary decision-maker must have given insufficient weight to the human rights factor'.[54] In this way, the relatively narrow focus of judicial decision-making is an institutional advantage in upholding constitutional principle. Many violations of Convention rights occur because the legislature was (quite legitimately) focused on concerns other than human rights. An institutional structure which includes a review mechanism by an independent, impartial body, staffed by unelected office-holders with security of tenure, whose primary task is to assess democratic decision-making for compliance with human rights at the instance of the aggrieved individual, is a better way of protecting rights than leaving their protection and implementation in the hands of elected politicians alone.

It may strike some readers as strange to rely on the court's narrow focus (both on the individual claimant and the human rights dimension of the case) as an advantage of constitutional review and one of the sources of its justification. After all, many critics argue that this narrowness is one of the woeful shortcomings of judicial decision-making and one of the reasons why we should be cautious about giving judges power to adjudicate human rights claims. How can judges make the right decision about whether human rights have been violated, they ask, when their assessment is so narrowly constrained by limited experience, expertise and the narrow, legalistic confines of the facts of an individual case as presented to them in litigation? Adam Tomkins provides a good statement of this worry:

> Decision-making through the bipolar adjudicative techniques of the court room allows precious little room for compromise or negotiated settlement . . . as such, neither the range nor the variety of argument in court is anything like as plural or as open as is the case with parliamentary forms of decision-making.[55]

---

[54] *A and Others* [2005] 2 W.L.R. 87 at [192] at [80], emphasis added.
[55] Tomkins (2005b), 29.

Constitutional litigation 'squeezes out any room for the *res publica*, the public interest, along with any third party interests'.[56] Similar reservations about the limitations of using the adjudicative mechanisms of litigation in protecting rights are voiced by Conor Gearty who argues that there is 'no greater enemy of strategic thinking than adversarial litigation'.[57]

The empirical basis of some of the details of these claims is open to question. Take, for example, the claim that judicial decision-making leaves no place for consideration of the public interest. One of the central tasks of the court in adjudication under the HRA is to determine what is in the public interest, since the courts are explicitly required by the text of the Convention to determine whether an alleged infringement of Convention rights is necessary in a democratic society. Furthermore, many of those involved in day-to-day litigation before the courts will, no doubt, dispute the bald assertion that litigation leaves little room for compromise or negotiated settlement. Certainly, in my analysis of the ways in which the courts have used the doctrine of deference, such compromise is readily apparent in judicial reasoning. Many commentators claim that the HRA is itself an embodiment of one large (constitutional) compromise between parliamentary sovereignty and the protection of human rights – a compromise negotiated between interest groups arguing for a Bill of Rights on the one hand and other groups arguing for the preservation of unlimited parliamentary sovereignty on the other.[58]

But Tomkins and Gearty are undeniably correct in their central claim, namely, that the variety of argument canvassed in court when considering a bivalent dispute between two parties, is narrower than that which can be considered in the normal political sphere. The problem with Gearty's and Tomkins' claim is that it relies on an unexplored and unacknowledged conflation of legislative/Executive power on the one hand, and constitutional power on the other. The narrow focus of the courts is only a problem if the task the courts have to perform is the same as that performed by the elected branches. But it is not the same. The courts do not have, and should not have, the power to design legislative schemes to regulate the various Convention rights. If they had this broad legislative power, then Tomkins' and Gearty's claim would hold true because, in order to exercise it, they would need to be aware of the array of arguments and interests which help Parliament and the Executive to do their

---

[56] Tomkins (2001), 8; Fredman (2001), 206.    [57] Gearty (2001), 259.
[58] Feldman (1999a), 165; Phillipson (2006), 69.

job well. The job of the courts is different. Judges are required to carry out the constitutional function of assessing the application of particular legislative provision to the facts of an individual case, in light of the (narrow) range of considerations and values presented to them in the ECHR. In carrying out this task and in discharging their 'ancient function of deciding as between two competing parties on which side the law should come down',[59] their independence from normal politics and constituency pressures as well as their focus on the particular concerns of the individual in relation to that law, becomes an advantage rather than a disadvantage – they are qualities which help the courts to perform their *constitutional* functions. As such, the narrow focus of the courts is part of the argument in favour of constitutional review, rather than a point against it.[60]

## Enforcing constitutional limits on Parliament

My assumption has been that the UK is under a moral obligation to protect fundamental rights and that this obligation pervades all of Parliament's law-making activities. This assumption is shared by democratic sceptics. What I wish to argue here is that the existence of constitutional review under the HRA enhances Parliament's ability to discharge this duty in one important way, namely, that judicial decisions under the HRA give the Executive/legislature prudential reasons to be more vigilant in their protection of human rights.[61] So, if the government is aware that an unwelcome eventuality will come about if it fails to protect rights, then this provides a 'prudential reason' for it to comply with human rights standards. The threat of an adverse decision from the courts is just such an eventuality – it is an institutional sanction for violation of Convention rights. Coupled with a desire to avoid incurring such an adverse judgment, the HRA gives the Executive/legislature prudential reasons to be vigilant in protecting rights, over and above what we might call its reasons of virtue. Of course, court decisions and their anticipated effect are not the only factors encouraging Parliament to be vigilant in protecting rights.

---

[59] Gearty (2001), 259.

[60] This is not to deny the value of third-party interventions in human rights cases, see Hannett (2003), 128; Fredman (2001), 206. Nor do I wish to deny that that the courts sometimes lack sufficient information on which to base their decisions and could benefit from specialist interventions.

[61] One has a prudential reason to perform an act if performing it will in some way advance one's interests or prevent them being adversely affected. For an explanation of how the law can provide prudential reasons to its subjects, see Hart (1982), 254–5.

A watchful opposition in Parliament may actively monitor the governing majorities' compliance with a Bill of Rights, not to mention the scrutiny and possible criticism from non-governmental human rights organisations, the public and the press. The central role which these factors play in ensuring that Parliament upholds Convention rights are not denied here. It is simply that the existence of constitutional review as an extra checking mechanism or safeguard, enhances the likelihood of compliance with human rights, both before and after legislation is enacted.

Given that review under the HRA operates in relation to legislation which has already been enacted, it may seem surprising to suggest that constitutional adjudication can have an impact on the legislative programme prior to enactment. However, this would be to underestimate the role which anticipation of adverse judicial decision plays in legislative deliberations.[62] This anticipatory effect is borne out by the fact that in many countries where constitutional review exists, it is customary to have legal experts attached to the government in order to evaluate the possibility of proposed laws being referred to the courts and invalidated as unconstitutional.[63] In the UK, we now have the Joint Committee on Human Rights (hereinafter JCHR) which monitors human rights compliance as a Bill is going through Parliament. One of the significant factors in the reports of this Commission is the anticipated judicial reaction in the event of litigation under the HRA.[64]

Anticipation of possible litigation is widely acknowledged to play a role in preventing Parliament from restricting rights. Commenting on the passage of what became the Terrorism Act 2000, Conor Gearty noted that the combined effect of section 19 HRA and 'the probability of legal challenge in the future'[65] meant that some of the discussion of the Bill in Parliament was conducted in the language of human rights, and some concessions on the Bill relating to human rights were secured 'which arguably might not have been obtained without the 1998 legislation'.[66] In recent times, the role of anticipated judicial decisions in constraining Parliament was seen most dramatically in relation to the extraordinarily broad ouster clause contained in the Asylum and Immigration Bill 2004. Judges excoriated this ouster clause in public

---

[62] The force of such an anticipatory reaction is, of course, difficult to verify empirically. However, its role as an aspect of governmental 'auto-limitation' is well documented in studies of constitutional law across Europe, see Stone-Sweet (2000), 60, 73, 75–9. 196–7.
[63] Stone-Sweet (2000), 77; see also Landfried (1992), 9.
[64] Feldman (2004), 112.    [65] Gearty (2005a), 23.    [66] *Ibid.*

lectures,[67] warning extrajudicially that the clause violated the rule of
law to such an extent that judges might disapply it, if it came before the
courts.[68] Rick Rawlings characterised these 'just try me' statements vividly
as 'effectively raising the constitutional stakes in a game of high-level
poker'.[69] The serious possibility that the senior judiciary would indeed
disapply the provision cast:

> an increasing shadow in the parliamentary proceedings on the Bill, most
> obviously in the Upper House. Ministers could not say but that they
> had been warned. In the event, having struggled through the Commons,
> Ministers abandoned the ouster on reaching the House of Lords.[70]

Explaining his reasons for abandoning the clause, the Minister proposing
the Bill admitted that in reaching his decision, he had listened carefully
to the arguments put by the senior judiciary, including the views of the
former Lord Chancellor who had 'forcibly made representations about
the Bill'.[71]

This provides a good, recent example where the anticipated effect of
a judicial decision put pressure on Parliament to change its legislative
agenda, in favour of enhancing the rights protection for some of the vulnerable in our society, namely those seeking asylum, without ever needing
to reach the courtroom. It reminds us that the HRA can enhance Parliament's ability and willingness to protect human rights, both *ex ante*
and *ex post*. Under section 19, the government Minister proposing a Bill
has to make a statement about the government's view of its compatibility
with Convention rights. Whilst this statement is not legally binding, it
requires, at the very least, that the government should address the issue
of compatibility with Convention rights to some degree. Thus far, the
existence of section 19 has not necessarily ensured that there has been
in-depth consideration in Parliament of the human rights implications of
all legislation.[72] However, it nonetheless shows that part of the aim of the
HRA is to ensure that all branches of government give weight to human
rights concerns and ensure that they are respected in all governmental and
legislative activities. At the very least, it impresses upon Ministers proposing Bills in Parliament that consideration of Convention-compatibility

---

[67] Woolf (2003); see also Steyn (2004b), 107–8; Fordham (2004), 86ff.
[68] See generally Tomkins (2008), 16.    [69] Rawlings (2005), 406.    [70] *Ibid.*
[71] Hansard, HL vol. 659, col. 51 (15 March 2004).
[72] See Wadham (2001), 623ff. Though this article was at a very early stage in the HRA's life,
before the work of the JCHR was fully underway.

should be an important part of the legislative process.[73] When one adds to this requirement the fact that the JCHR can question and get evidence from the relevant Minister about the Convention-compatibility of proposed legislation, it becomes clear that the prudential incentives for MPs to take Convention rights seriously, are greatly enhanced.[74] The HRA can thus stimulate pre-enactment scrutiny of legislation within Parliament, rather than relying purely on the post-enactment scrutiny provided by the courts. The Government's wish to avoid the political costs of enacting legislation without the stamp of human rights approval provided by the section 19 statement, has one other important consequence, namely, that provisions have been included in Bills specifically to make them comply with the Convention.[75] One instance of this was the inclusion in section 55 of the Nationality, Immigration and Asylum Act 2002 (which denied all assistance and benefits to asylum seekers who did not claim asylum promptly on arrival) of a proviso that this could only occur as long as it did not result in a breach of asylum seekers' Convention rights.[76] The explicit inclusion of this proviso was the springboard from which the House of Lords could justify its decision in *Limbuela*[77] that the denial of assistance to destitute asylum seekers may violate Article 3 ECHR, whilst emphasising that in so doing, it was merely giving effect to the intention of Parliament.[78]

There is one final, albeit indirect, way in which the existence of constitutional review can contribute towards, and enhance, Parliament's ability and willingness to protect Convention rights. This is that by having in place a mechanism whereby citizens can challenge legislation and demand that it be reviewed to ensure that it is compatible with fundamental rights,

---

[73] Thus far, there has only been one instance in which the proposing Minister has felt unable to make a statement pursuant to section 19 HRA, to the effect that in her view, the provisions of the Bill were compatible with the Convention rights. This is the Communications Act 2003. For comment, see Fenwick (2007), 209ff. This legislation has now been held to be compatible with the Convention in *R. (Animal Defenders International)* v. *Secretary of State for Culture, Media and Sport* [ 2008] UKHL 15.

[74] See Lester (2002b), 434, 442. Lester also points out that in response to representations from the Joint Committee, the Government has agreed (since 1 January 2002) to include an outline of the Government's views on compatibility in the Explanatory Notes published with every Government Bill, 448; see also Feldman (2002), 339.

[75] See Sedley (2008), 21–2.

[76] Nationality, Immigration and Asylum Act 2002, section 55(5). For discussion of some early cases brought under section 55 and the 'ill-tempered outburst' of the Home Secretary in response to them, see Bradley (2003), 397ff.

[77] *R. (Limbuela)* v. *SSHD* [2005] UKHL 66.

[78] *Ibid.* at [75], *per* Baroness Hale. For further discussion, see chapter 8 at 225.

it can impress on the public mind the importance of these rights, includ-ing the importance in which they are held by the state organs.[79] It may give citizens added assurance that their rights are central concerns for the government. Not only is there vigilance against their violation, there is also a public commitment by government that legislation will undergo a judicial checking mechanism which can find fault with it on human rights grounds. It demonstrates that the main organs of government have committed themselves not only to respecting rights but also to 'adopting an attitude of rigorous respect'.[80] In this way, constitutional review under a Bill of Rights can have a beneficial side-effect of assuring the public of the importance in which human rights are held, because it enables elected branches to display a principled willingness to respect rights and to reconsider legislation if it transpires that the court finds an unjustified infringement. When the HRA was enacted, Jack Straw (the then Home Secretary) captured something of this idea when he observed that the HRA was 'an important part of Labour's programme for restoring trust in the way we are governed'.[81] He also suggested that the HRA would 'nurture a culture of understanding our rights and responsibilities'.[82] It can encour-age such a culture by confirming publicly the important status of rights and an acknowledgement that even the legislature is not above them.[83] Of course, this public assurance (and the culture of rights which may attend it) is somewhat undermined if politicians display irritation and impa-tience with adverse judicial decisions and attempt to discredit and belittle judges when they challenge their decisions on human rights grounds.[84] This merely goes to show that elected politicians also have a role to play in ensuring that Convention rights and the HRA which gives effect to them, are respected and that public confidence in the judiciary is maintained. They do that by observing the requirements of inter-institutional comity, but also by showing that they are willing to subject themselves to the constraints contained in the Convention rights, however irksome it may be in particular situations to be challenged and have to amend legislation to comply with their requirements.[85]

---

[79] Hayek (1960), 217.    [80] Pettit (1989), 153; Ingram (1994), 180.

[81] Boateng and Straw (1997), 79.    [82] *Ibid.*

[83] The claim that one of the advantages of having a Bill of Rights is that it demonstrates a public commitment to rights and thereby gives rights a more prominent place within public space and consciousness is also supported by Waluchow (2007), 120–2, 244.

[84] See Bradley (2003).

[85] Under section 3 of the Constitutional Reform Act 2005, MPs are placed under an obligation to 'uphold the independence of the judiciary', and they are prohibited from seeking 'to

## Democracy, distrust and institutional design

For many democratic sceptics, the claim that constitutional review is necessary to protect individual and minority rights 'is only plausible as long as it is reasonable to think that proper regard will not be paid to individual rights in the democratic and representative processes'.[86] They conclude that the argument for legal limits on the elected branches enforced by the courts, rests on an 'ambivalence about government'[87] and a worrying lack of faith or distrust in politicians and ordinary citizens to protect rights.[88] Jeremy Waldron urges us to accept the opposite assumption, namely, that:

> voters and legislators are capable of focusing their deliberations on the general good and on some sense of the proper balance that should be held among individual interests in society.[89]

Once we adopt this view of the democratic process and the people operating within it, the justification for constitutional review is undermined.[90]

It is no part of my argument that public representatives or people in general lack the *capacity* to deliberate about rights or strive for their protection. Nor is there any assumption that people will *only* vote in a self-interested, immoral or prejudiced way with no concern for the common good.[91] But even if we accept people's *capacity* to make the right decisions when they act politically, we are still faced with the prospect that they might not always do so. They may make the wrong decision, either because they give preference to their own self-interest over the common good, or because they fail to consider the long-term effects of their decision or the effect it might possibly have on others, or simply because they are moved by a knee-jerk emotional response to a particular issue.[92] The question then becomes: how should we deal with these facts when we come to think about institutional design? When designing political and

---

influence particular judicial decisions through any special access to the judiciary', see further Woodhouse (2007), 157.

[86] Waldron (1993a), 416.     [87] Tomkins (2005b), 17.     [88] See Kavanagh (2003b).

[89] Waldron (1993a), 417. For further discussion of the question of whether legislators are capable of addressing rights concerns responsibly, see also Waldron (2006), 1349.

[90] This view is advanced by many writers, see Waldron, (1993a), 417; Gauthier (1993), 315; Weale (1999), 170.

[91] The point that arguments of principle permeate the deliberation and decision-making of ordinary politics (i.e. that the court is not the *only* principled institution in democratic government) is a widespread criticism of Dworkin's distinction between principle and policy, see Finnis (1985), 311; see also Waldron (1993a), 418; Weale (1999), 170; Sunstein (1993), 146.

[92] For an outline of the various risks inherent in decision-making made by popular political control, see Pettit (2001a), 733ff.

legal institutions, we should put the possibility of rights violation into the equation rather than basing it purely, as Waldron seems to suggest, on the assumption that citizens and politicians can decide well.[93] We have to seriously confront questions about the likelihood that political institutions will perform their functions well and if not, whether any safeguards can be put in place to minimise error. Therefore, it is important to consider the relative advantages and disadvantages of various state institutions, based on their composition, their decision-making processes, the context in which they make their decisions, as well as the risks inherent in their design.[94] Given that we value human rights, guarding against risk should be a strong motivating factor in setting up institutions, placed alongside any optimism we may have about people's willingness to do the right thing.[95] We should err on the side of vigilance rather than complacency when it comes to designing institutions to uphold rights,[96] taking into account the possibility of a wicked government gaining power or a good government being susceptible to electoral, popular, majoritarian or sectarian pressures to thwart them. But this vigilance is not based on distrust or scepticism about our fellow human beings; it is simply due to a realistic acknowledgement of our limitations. In recognition of these limitations in ourselves and our procedures, we must structure our constitutional system so as to overcome them.[97]

The suggestion that the case for constitutional review rests on an unacceptable distrust of politics and politicians is further called into question by the following point. Many violations of Convention rights occur through no fault of the legislator. It may simply be that Parliament did not

---

[93]  Waluchow accuses Waldron of being too idealistic when it comes to characterising democratic institutions, whilst being realistic, if not downright sceptical about judicial procedures, see Waluchow (2007), 248ff. In response to the charge that he adopts a naively optimistic view of legislators, Waldron admits that opponents of judicial review sometimes 'do this deliberately' in order to counter the perceived idealism adopted by defenders of constitutional review, see Waldron (2006), 1379. In my view, the best way of approaching the institutional question is to attempt to be realistic about both institutions, rather than idealistic about one or the other.

[94]  This approach to institutional design is supported by Kyritsis (2006), 747; see also Pettit (1997), 210ff.

[95]  Ely (1980), 181. For further comment on the element of idealism in Waldron's characterisation of democratic decision-making and the problems it poses when we consider issues of institutional design, see Waluchow (2007), 248–9.

[96]  For the distinction between assuming that people are inevitably corrupt and assuming that people in power may be inherently corruptible, see Pettit (1997), 211ff. For a defence of the view that vigilance does not necessarily entail distrust, see *ibid.*, 263–5.

[97]  Waluchow (2007), 152.

have the protection of a particular right in the forefront of its concerns when enacting a particular piece of legislation. Similarly, a rights violation can occur due to the unforeseeability of the impact on an individual right. This is partly due to the inherent human limitations in anticipating all the cases which may arise, but is also due to the facts of social life – changes in society may mean that a statute which did not originally violate anyone's rights, do so when applied to a changed social context. This may only become apparent after years of being on the statute books. Moreover, the terms of the HRA apply to legislation 'whenever enacted'. This means that legislation enacted prior to the HRA, or even before the UK became a signatory to the European Convention, could now be found wanting in terms of Convention rights. Such a violation would not be the fault of the legislature, who may well have enacted the legislation in a good faith effort to comply with the legal norms applicable at the time. Nor should we assume that every time the higher courts issue a declaration of incompatibility, MPs are furious that they did not get their way or did not get away with a rights violation. In many cases, they may have failed to anticipate a rights violation and are happy for the courts to rectify the problem by way of interpretation or, alternatively, by drawing their attention to it through a declaration of incompatibility. This sort of constructive collaboration between the branches of government is precisely what was envisaged when Parliament enacted the HRA.

The fact that many rights violations occur without any hostility to rights protection does not undermine the case for constitutional review. In fact, it strengthens it, because it shows that even if we assume that legislators will always strive to protect rights in every case, and never succumb to pressures to do otherwise, the possibility of rights violations still exists. Even on the best-case scenario (where no political actor is swayed from their moral duty to protect rights) there is still room for a case for constitutional review. It is justified because it can deal with the inadvertent violation of rights, as well as violations based on failure to anticipate future cases. Having a review mechanism which can be activated by the person whose right is allegedly violated can be a useful way of bringing violations of rights to light, of empowering individuals to do so, and helping Parliament to rectify shortcomings in legislation as they occur.

Of course, the foregoing argument about the need for vigilance and realism in institutional design applies equally to courts. As democratic sceptics rightly point out, advocates of constitutional review are often realistic (if not downright pessimistic) when it comes to democratic institutions, but don their rose-coloured spectacles when it comes to the courts.[98] My support for the institution of constitutional review is not based on idealistic or naive views about the abilities of judges or the courts to deliver rights protection. Judges suffer from the same human limitations as everyone else. They are not immune from making the wrong decision or misjudging the significance of particular rights claims. But it is impossible to design a perfect institutional decision-making procedure for these sorts of political decisions.[99] There is always the possibility of human error. All we can do is take account of this possibility, by putting in place various institutional safeguards. Providing an independent third party to supervise the elected branches on questions related to constitutional rights is just such a safety mechanism which operates as a corrective to the potential risks inherent in democratic decision-making. Similarly, the fact that we give judges life tenure and do not make them popularly elected or accountable, the fact that we circumscribe the scope of their decision-making power by requiring them to concentrate on ensuring compliance with a limited range of legal guarantees, that judges are educated and trained in the law, etc. – these are all institutional features which operate as safety mechanisms to ensure that judges fulfil the function they are institutionally designed to realise. This, coupled with the requirement that all judicial decisions have to be supported by reasoned, public justification based in part on previous case law, constitutional principle and Convention rights all seek to ensure, so far as possible, that judges are constrained by the social, public and peer-group pressures involved in handing down their judgments. To be sure, these institutional safeguards do not provide *guarantees* of perfect decisions upholding the rights of the vulnerable and the downtrodden in every case. But they go some way towards the realisation of this institutional aim and, as I will attempt to show in chapter 13, this is an aim which is in fact realised to a sufficient degree since the enactment of the HRA.

## Conclusion

Advocates of constitutional review are sometimes branded as the enemies of the legislature and democracy. The purpose of this chapter was to mount a case for constitutional review which does not rest on animosity towards democratic institutions or scepticism about democratic values.

---

[98] See e.g. Waldron (2006), 1379.
[99] See Rawls (1971), 85ff: 'No political procedure is an instance of perfect procedural justice'.

Rather, the assumption was that although democracy is a valuable method of political decision-making, it is nonetheless subject to some limits in the interests of protecting rights to an optimal degree. I have tried to show that we have good reason to protect constitutional fundamentals (including constitutional rights) through the courts. Having constitutional review in place empowers individuals, by allowing them to have their constitutional complaint heard and providing them with a forum in which the criteria for success in having those complaints vindicated are significantly different than in the normal political channels. It was the court's relative insulation from political pressure and short-term concerns which provided the cornerstone of this part of the argument. This factor was crucial in understanding the ability of the courts to withstand certain types of pressure which, I argued, posed dangers for the adequate protection of constitutional rights in normal politics. On my account, the justification of constitutional review was that it can provide *additional* (though by no means exclusive or guaranteed) protection against the sacrifice of fundamental and long-term interests for short-term political gains.

The added security against the contingency of rights violation was not the whole of the case for constitutional review. It was also based on the way in which constitutional litigation can become a second channel of (political) participation, parallel to that provided by normal politics. Furthermore, the narrow judicial focus on compliance with human rights, as well as on individual interests, strengthens the case in favour of constitutional review. In the final section, I tried to show that my case for constitutional review did not rest on a crude 'politics bad, law good'[100] approach. My argument was that politics is good at certain things and law is good at others. I attempted to show that the courts are well placed to carry out the *constitutional* function given to them under the HRA, a function which includes the constitutional duty to ensure that the elected branches of government protect Convention rights when enacting legislation and making executive decisions.

---

[100] This crude view is attributed to legal constitutionalists in Tomkins (2005b), 13. Although space prevents me from elaborating on this point here, I will just note that despite supporting constitutional review, I do not subscribe to any of the six tenets ascribed to legal constitutionalism by Tomkins (2005b), 11ff.

# 13

# Constitutional review and participatory democracy

## Introduction

The previous chapter presented arguments in support of the type of review function allocated to the courts under sections 3 and 4 of the HRA. This case was, for the most part, institutional in nature, in that it relied on various distinctive features of the courts and constitutional politics to argue that constitutional review was a useful corrective to some of the tendencies of normal democratic politics. An inevitable consequence of this argument is that judges are given the power to limit the decision-making power of our elected representatives – a prospect which will give cause for concern in a democracy. John Hart Ely captures the nerve of this democratic worry when he observes that: 'a body that is not elected or otherwise politically responsible in any significant way is telling the people's elected representatives that they cannot govern as they'd like'.[1]

Worries of this kind mean that the arguments in chapter 12 will fail to convince democratic sceptics. They will bemoan the fact that judges are unelected and unaccountable and can therefore claim no democratic legitimacy for the decisions they make. Furthermore, they will maintain that, whatever the force of the arguments about the advantages of constitutional review, they do not take into account its major drawback from a democratic point of view, namely, that it involves a limit on the equal right of each citizen to participate in democratic government and an unjustifiable limit on the power of Parliament. Curtailment of the equal right to participate cannot be justified, no matter what the gain in terms of human rights protection. Finally, they will deny the practical force of those arguments in any case, because they will claim that judges do a very bad job in practice of furthering and protecting human rights. The alleged gain in terms of human rights protection is, they will argue, illusory – particularly in times of emergency. They will try to show that the judicial

---

[1] Ely (1980), 4–5. This worry is articulated in similar terms in Ewing (1996), 41.

record under the HRA does not provide any ground for optimism that judges in the UK will enhance the protection of human rights.

In this chapter, I wish to defend the case for constitutional review under the HRA against these powerful democratic objections. In so doing, I hope to provide satisfactory answers to the following three questions, posed by Keith Ewing just as the HRA was enacted:

- Why should the outcome of the democratic process (legislation) be subject to scrutiny by those (judges) who are in general not part of the process of democratic election and accountability?
- Why should the outcome of the democratic process (legislation) be determined on the basis of standards of democracy determined by those (judges) who are not accountable for the values they develop and impose on the rest of the community?
- Why should the people be denied the opportunity to determine the nature of the democracy in which they wish to live, particularly as modern Europe presents us with competing visions, both in terms of principles and procedures?[2]

Before embarking on these tasks, I will first sketch briefly what I mean by democracy and how constitutionalism is sometimes in tension with it. On my account, democracy is, simply, a system of governance which allows individuals opportunities for participation in the political process – it is government 'by the people'. Whilst accepting that the purpose of this system is the promotion of sound decisions which protect the interests of the people (i.e. government 'for the people'),[3] I nonetheless take the participatory decision-making procedure to be the essence of democracy. As such, I support what Ronald Dworkin described as a 'procedural' rather than a 'constitutional' conception of democracy.[4] The procedural conception relies on a relatively uncontroversial and thin notion of democracy, which takes as its central feature the idea that in democratic government, the rules which define and order public life should be the product of decision-making by a body that is, in some systematic way, dependent upon the views of those who are citizens of that society.[5] It follows that

---

[2] Ewing (2001), 109.    [3] Raz (1994), 117.
[4] For this distinction, see Freeman (1990), 335; see also Waluchow (2007), 106–9. For an outline of some of the advantages of adopting a procedural conception of democracy, see Sypnowich (2007), 766–7, including that it does not obscure the tension between constitutionalism and democracy and makes salient the 'democratic dilemma'.
[5] Albert Weale claims that this is a point on which all the varying conceptions of democracy agree, see Weale (1989), 43.

the democratic institutions of government are those which are elected by the people and designed to be representative of them. It also follows that the courts are not, in themselves, democratic institutions. Rather, on my account, the rationale of giving the courts a constitutional function is to place limits on the decision-making powers of the democratic institutions in light of constitutional principle. In the course of this chapter, I will try to show that whilst democracy is a valuable form of government, it is not an absolute value – some limits on its operation are justified, though they are not without a democratic cost.[6]

### The argument that judges are unelected and unaccountable

The first question raised by Ewing concerns the common refrain that constitutional review is illegitimate because judges are unelected and unaccountable and therefore lack the democratic legitimacy to challenge, revise or even scrutinise the decisions of the elected branches of government.[7] Of course, if it is unacceptable that public decision-making on our behalf is carried out by unelected and unaccountable officials, then this would impugn the vast number of such decisions made by unelected but hugely influential civil servants, who are far less accountable and visible to the public than judges. It would also cast serious doubt on the legitimacy of Acts of Parliament, since the second chamber of the UK Parliament (the House of Lords) is entirely unelected. Even the legitimacy of government decisions is rendered dubious because one does not have to be democratically elected to be a member of the Cabinet.

Leaving this aside, there are other more fundamental problems with the 'unelected and unaccountable' refrain. The main problem is that it conflates two types of power, one constitutional and the other legislative. In chapter 11, I argued that given the nature of the *constitutional* power exercised by the court, the fact that judges were unelected and unaccountable is actually an institutional advantage. It might be a disadvantage if the task of the courts under the HRA were the same as the

---

[6] This is not the only way of reconciling the tension between constitutionalism and democracy. Other strategies are e.g. to show that constitutional limits are a precondition of democracy, see e.g. Dworkin (1995), 2–11; (1996), 14ff; Waluchow (2007), 106; Fabre (2000a), 96; Harel (2003); Eisgruber (2001); Freeman (1990). Others argue that only *some* constitutional restraints are democracy reinforcing, namely those without which democratic government could not function see e.g. Ely (1980); Jones (1994), 173–5; Holmes (1988); Holmes (1995); Sunstein (1988), 328; Dahl (1989), 182; Weale (1999), 171ff; Cohen (1998), 202.
[7] Sedley (2005), 148.

task of the elected branches in formulating policy, enacting legislation and making swift executive decisions. But judges do not perform these functions. Therefore, it is misguided and counterproductive to suggest that they should possess the qualities which are appropriate for carrying out these varied tasks.[8] So, in response to Ewing's question why should legislation be 'subject to scrutiny by those judges who are in general not part of the process of democratic election and accountability?', the answer contained in chapter 12 is that they should be given that scrutinising power *precisely because of* these features. If judges were popularly elected and accountable to the general populace in the same way as MPs, it would be counterproductive because it would severely undermine their ability to perform their important constitutional functions. The fact that they can make decisions without being concerned about whether they will be re-elected or being unduly swayed by the popularity of their decision, provides the rationale for allocating to them the task of reviewing legislation for compliance with Convention rights. The independence of the judiciary from sectional interests and electoral orientation is one of the pre-conditions for the effectiveness of a Bill of Rights such as the HRA – without it, it would be difficult to imagine how the courts could succeed in enforcing it.

Moreover, the fact that the courts are not subject to direct accountability to the public in the sense that they cannot be removed from office if they fall from popular favour, should not lead us to conclude that they are completely unaccountable. Judges are subject to public influence in other more subtle and indirect ways. If accountability is at least partly defined as 'the duty of a public decision-maker to explain, legitimate and justify a decision',[9] then we can see that judges are subject to various mechanisms of accountability.[10] All judicial decisions have to be supported by written, publicly available reasons. This makes the courts susceptible to public criticism, as well as occasional criticism from Members of Parliament. Whereas judges in the UK were traditionally considered to be above criticism, this is no longer the case. They are regularly subjected to media scrutiny and are increasingly willing to engage in public debate about the judicial role and broader legal issues of public concern.[11] The judiciary is aware that the effective discharge of their functions depends, to some extent, on public confidence in the courts and in the belief that the courts

---

[8] See also Macklem (2006), 109.    [9] Oliver and Drewry (1996), 134.
[10] For detailed examination of such mechanisms, see Malleson (1999), chapter 3; Sedley (2002), 18.
[11] Malleson (1999), 2.

operate an impartial and fair system of adjudication.[12] A perusal of the case law of the higher courts reveals that judges are often sensitive to concerns about how their judgments are publicly received and reported in the press.[13] They know all too well that their judgments will be subject to detailed scrutiny within the legal profession, both by the judges' peer-group on the bench, as well as practising lawyers and academics. Judicial decisions are also scrutinised within government and Parliament as a whole, and if a decision is thought to be incorrect, it is open to Parliament to reverse it. In fact, post-HRA, there seems to be a move towards greater accountability of the judiciary.[14] This is exemplified by the Constitutional Reform Act 2005 which establishes a 'Judicial Appointments and Conduct Ombudsman', whose job it is to investigate alleged maladministration by the judiciary, following an application from 'any interested party'.[15] All of these mechanisms combine to make the courts indirectly accountable for their decisions in significant and public ways.[16]

## The argument from the equal right of participation

Ewing's third question forces us to confront the charge that constitutional review denies, or at least limits, the right to democratic participation, i.e. the equal right of citizens to determine the rules under which they should be governed. Jeremy Waldron is one of the most formidable and sophisticated opponents of constitutional review, whose opposition rests centrally on this claim. For Waldron, the right to 'participate on equal terms in social decisions' is nothing less than the 'right of rights'.[17] By taking decisions about rights away from participatory majoritarian institutions, and placing them in the hands of the courts, constitutional review involves an unjustifiable 'disempowerment of ordinary citizens on matters of the highest moral and political importance'.[18] Crucially, Waldron does not view the right to participate as one (albeit important) value to be included in a balance with others. For him, participation is *fundamental*: a participatory majoritarian resolution of political disputes should be adopted,

---

[12] See Steyn (2002b), 388–9.

[13] See e.g. *A* v. *Home Secretary (Torture Evidence)* [2006] 2 A.C. 221, Lord Rodger lamented the fact that the CA decision in that case 'has been subjected to sweeping criticisms which to a large extent ignored their reasoning and the very factors which led them to their conclusion', at [128].

[14] Malleson (1999), chapter 3.     [15] CRA 2005, section 110.

[16] See Waluchow (2007), 150.

[17] Waldron (1993b), 20; for a response to Waldron's arguments, see Kavanagh (2003b).

[18] Waldron (1993b), 45.

even if this would lead to worse outcomes than any other decision-making mechanism. Thus, the likelihood that constitutional review under a Bill of Rights might offer better protection to human rights is insufficient justification to restrict or limit the 'right of rights'. The reason is that:

> If a process is democratic and comes up with the correct result, it does no injustice to anyone. But if the process is non-democratic, it inherently and necessarily does an injustice, in its operation, to the participatory aspirations of the ordinary citizen. And it does this injustice, tyrannises in this way, whether it comes up with the correct result or not.[19]

Waldron thus assigns a special status to the right of participation that makes it inappropriate to limit it for the sake of protecting other rights or furthering other principles of political morality. Not only is the right to participate given primacy within political morality, it is also given primacy in the hierarchy of rights.[20] While most people would accept that rights can be limited, especially if they come into conflict with other rights, Waldron and other democratic sceptics give the right to participate fundamental status which renders it immune from such limitations. It means that the right to participation 'is . . . a moral right the violation of which cannot be traded off against minimising the violations of other rights'.[21]

Jeremy Waldron's famous article launching his critique based on the right to participate (originally published in the *Oxford Journal of Legal Studies*) was partly written with a view to influencing the debate in the UK about the propriety of introducing a Bill of Rights.[22] Waldron succeeded in this aim. His views have been immensely influential on the UK debate and are invariably cited by those who are opposed to a UK Bill of Rights or wish to challenge and criticise the power given to judges under the HRA.[23] If democratic scepticism were a religion, Waldron would be the High Priest.[24] Keith Ewing endorses wholeheartedly Waldron's idea that the right to participate is fundamental. In language redolent of Waldron's analysis, he argues that 'the first principle of any social democratic society is the right of the people of the community to political equality – a right

---

[19] *Ibid.*, 50.
[20] The view is also supported by Conor Gearty, who described the right to vote as 'the key liberty' because it is the 'entitlement upon which the utility of the remaining liberties depend', see Gearty (2004), 34–5.
[21] For this description of Waldron's idea of participation, see Alexander (2003), 279.
[22] Waldron (1993b), 18.
[23] Ewing (1996), 43; Walker (2001), 122ff; Nicol (2002), 439; Hiebert (2006), 8.
[24] Though there are signs that his faith is weakening, see Waldron (2006).

which may be regarded as one of the most fundamental of all human rights'.[25] Drawing on this foundational principle, he proceeds to make the following claims:

> I understand that there are problems about the efficiency of Parliament. I understand also that there may be a strong case for its reform. But I cannot understand how we can remain faithful and loyal to this first principle – the right of equality in decision-making – by transferring power from Parliament to the courts. The effect of such a move would be to transfer sovereign power and the right to participate in the supreme political decision-making body of the state to a small group of public officials over whom we have no control and to a process from which we are effectively excluded, unlike rulemaking through sovereign Parliament in the election of which everyone potentially plays an equal part and in which everyone is entitled to equal respect.[26]

He concludes that if constitutional review under a Bill of Rights is in place, 'the people have no say in making the most fundamental of all the rules by which they are all to be governed'.[27]

In making this formidable critique, Ewing endorses the central tenets of Waldron's analysis, four of which should be highlighted here. The first is that the right to participate is not one right or principle amongst many, but rather 'our most cherished principle'.[28] It is *fundamental*. The second is its *egalitarian* emphasis – the right to participate is a right to have an *equal* say in public decision-making. Third, Ewing echoes Waldron's concerns about the importance of participation as a way of *including* all citizens in public decision-making, regardless of how just or fair or desirable the outcome of that decision is. Waldron puts the point succinctly:

> There is a certain dignity in participation and an element of insult and dishonour in exclusion that transcends issues of outcome.[29]

Finally, there is the *empowerment* dimension of participation. This is the view that by allowing decisions to be taken by way of participatory majoritarianism, one empowers individuals by giving them 'a say'. Conversely, by limiting this decision-making procedure by way of constitutional review, one disempowers them.

In responding to this critique, I will pursue two main lines of argument. The first will challenge the alleged *primacy* of the right to participate. Whilst the importance and (intrinsic) value of the right to participate is accepted, I will argue that it does not have the fundamental status which

---

[25] Ewing (2006), 43, citing Waldron.    [26] *Ibid.*    [27] *Ibid.*
[28] *Ibid.*, 48; see also Nicol (2002), 439.    [29] Waldron (1993b), 38.

Waldron and Ewing attribute to it. The second line of argument will attempt to show that participation through the channels of normal politics does not deliver on the *egalitarian, inclusive* and *empowerment* features Ewing and Waldron claim for it. By having constitutional review in place, there is no doubt that we limit the (formally) equal right to participate in normal politics, but in so doing, we enhance the real chances of effective participation for some of those who tend to be excluded, marginalised and disempowered in society. So, *even if* the right to participate were our most cherished principle, as Waldron and Ewing claim, we would be more loyal to it and more likely to achieve its underlying aims, if we limit it in various ways, including through the mechanism of constitutional review.

Let us begin by addressing the question of whether the right to participate has a special status which makes it inappropriate to limit it for the sake of protecting other rights or furthering other principles of political morality. I can concede at the very outset that popular participation in, and popular control of, public decision-making is of undoubted importance. As the procedural conception of democracy confirms, popular participation is the central tenet of democratic government. Not only is it valuable instrumentally to achieving democratic goals, it is also intrinsically valuable, because it gives people the opportunity of contributing to the public life of their country and exerting popular control over their representatives.[30] Thus, one can agree with Waldron and Ewing when they say that the intrinsic importance of participation is contained (at least in part) in the dignity of being included in political decisions and the concomitant insult of being excluded.[31]

Does it follow that the intrinsic importance of participation gives it the special status claimed by Waldron and Ewing, such that it should never be limited? Not necessarily. The reason is that although we care about popular participation in public decision-making, it is not the only thing we care about. The justification for limiting the scope of democratic decision-making by constitutional review is, quite simply, that the value of participatory democratic procedures is not absolute. We also care deeply about the outcomes of those procedures i.e. whether democratic decision-making delivers good, sound, fair, just decisions which benefit the country

---

[30] See e.g. Phillips (1995), 28–29.

[31] For further discussion of the intrinsic value of participation, see Kavanagh (2003b), 458ff; see also Dworkin (1987), 4–5, 19–23; Beitz (1983), 74–5; Lively (1975), 134–5; Rawls (1971) 233–4; Hyland (1995), 189.

and its citizens.[32] So, even if we value participation, it does not necessarily follow that we must value it to the exclusion of all else or that it is never justifiable to limit it to some degree. There are other values which a political system must realise (even a democratic political system) and these include fundamental rights.

Let me also concede one other point. This is that the intrinsic importance of democratic participation means that, in a democracy, there is a presumption in favour of participatory political decision-making, which places non-participatory decision-making mechanisms (such as constitutional review) under a burden of justification. However, it does not rule them out completely. The burden of proof shifts to those who wish to argue for limits on citizen participation or exceptions to it.[33] We must have positive and weighty reasons to think that such a procedure would improve the quality of political decisions if it is to justify a limitation on the important right to participate. In my view, such weighty reasons are contained in chapter 12, namely, that the existence of constitutional review makes it more likely that human rights will be better protected, especially when they are asserted by those who have little chance of success in having their voice heard in normal politics. Both Waldron and Ewing support wholeheartedly the value of protecting human rights, but are nonetheless prepared to see those rights left unprotected (or at least less robustly protected), if this involves any compromise on the right to participate.[34] In my view, it is justifiable to limit the right to participate with reference to a small range of decisions, if by doing so, we secure an enhanced protection of human rights.

There are further reservations about the faith invested by Waldron and Ewing in the 'equal right to participate' in terms of what it can deliver.[35] In particular, one can question whether giving people a right to participate is actually a way of including them, empowering them and giving them an 'equal say' in what Ewing calls 'the democratic decisions

---

[32] Raz argues that the moral quality of political decisions is sufficiently important to establish what he calls 'the instrumentalist condition of good government'. Raz (1994), 117; see also Rawls (1971), 3, 227, 232; Nelson (1980), 100ff; Dworkin (1996), 34.

[33] Kavanagh (2003b), 459; Phillips (1995), 29; Beitz (1983), 79. Neil Walker also argues that the importance of democratic values means that democratic forms of decision-making attract 'strong presumptive legitimacy', see Walker (2001), 127.

[34] Phillipson (2006), 67ff.

[35] Though it should be noted that in his most recent writings, Waldron concedes that constitutional review may be justified if it can be shown that legislative institutions are dysfunctional or if democratic decision-making is partly based on prejudice or hostility to the rights of particular members in society, see Waldron (2006).

of the community'.[36] Waldron characterises democratic participation on issues concerning fundamental rights as 'a situation where the community *as a whole* is attempting to resolve some issues concerning *the rights of all the members of the community* and attempting to resolve it on the basis of equal participation'.[37] By participating in majoritarian politics, 'each individual acts, to some extent, as a voice for her own interests which ought to be taken seriously in politics'.[38] Writing sceptically about the HRA, Tom Campbell also argues for the importance of preserving 'the democratic right of the citizens of the UK to determine the basic principles on which their society is to be governed and to have an equal say in how these principles are to be embodied in binding rules'.[39]

Many readers of these claims will find them deeply unrealistic, either as a general characterisation of the way democratic majoritarian politics works or, more particularly, as an accurate characterisation of the nature of democratic participation in the UK. The most obvious way in which the rhetoric about the 'equal right of individuals to participate on issues which affect them' obscures rather than illuminates the way in which democracy works, is that it creates the misleading impression that democracy is direct i.e. that citizens vote directly on substantive issues.[40] But in modern democracies like the UK, it is invariably the case that political decisions are made by public representatives rather than directly by us – the people who are affected by them.[41] So the question about the protection of rights is not whether we should make these decisions ourselves *or* whether we should

---

[36] Ewing (1996), 44. In fact, one could doubt the claim that the right to participate is our most cherished principle, on the empirical basis that most people have no interest in participating in politics. Adam Tomkins gives the following blunt, but I think accurate, characterisation: 'Most of us, of course, could not be bothered [with participation in political affairs]. We really could not care less. Even the meagre act of voting is just too much effort for many these days', see Tomkins (2002a), 175. Of course, the widespread disillusionment with voting and political participation more generally, does not undermine the normative argument that we *ought* to cherish political participation, but it casts considerable doubt on the empirical claim that we do in fact cherish it.

[37] Waldron (1999), 297, emphasis added.       [38] Waldron (1993b), 37.

[39] Campbell (2001), 99.

[40] Kryitsis (2006) argues that an unacknowledged assumption underlying the image of the citizen's 'equal right to participate' is that it equates democratically elected legislatures with the people conceived as a self-governed collective. In highlighting this assumption, Kyritsis mounts a formidable challenge to Waldron's claim that constitutional review accords the views of a few judges superior voting weight to those of ordinary citizens. Kyritsis argues that the same is true of representative government.

[41] In fact, it is questionable whether direct plebiscitary democracy would be desirable, even if it were not unfeasible under modern conditions. For an argument that it would be 'wholly inimical' to deliberative democracy, see Pettit (2004), 52ff.

hand them over to judges. It is about who should make decisions about rights *on our behalf* – elected representatives or judges?[42] The indirect nature of contemporary democracy means that individual citizens do not have the opportunity to determine directly the rules and laws on which they are governed. All we have is the opportunity to choose one elected representative in our own constituency, from an extremely limited range of political parties once every four or five years.[43]

It follows that it is misleading to suggest democratic politics empowers people to have an equal say in decisions *about human rights*. Still less is it plausible to sustain more grandiose claims about citizens' ability to '*determine* the basic principles on which their society is to be governed'.[44] If we consider voting as a central instantiation of democratic participation, we have to agree with Sandra Fredman's conclusion that 'a vote at a general election is scarcely an opportunity to participate in decisions about human rights'.[45] Nor could it be considered to be 'a vote for a particular interpretation of a human right'.[46] Looking at the realities of the way in which democratic politics functions in the UK, she concludes:

> under the current system, the right of citizens to participate in decisions about rights is so attenuated as to be almost fictional, largely because of the weakness of Parliament relative to an all-powerful executive.[47]

The effective dominance of Parliament by the Executive, combined with the first-past-the-post electoral system and strong party discipline, means that, in effect, policy decisions (including the fundamental rules by which we are all governed) are made by a small group of politicians, backed up by an influential and anonymous civil service.

There is another misleading element in these characterisations of political participation, namely, Waldron's suggestion that major decisions about human rights concern the 'rights of all members of the community'. This is misleading because, typically, important decisions about human rights concern the application of a relatively uncontroversial general right to individual members of society, who may represent

---

[42] It is thus misleading when Waldron says 'We should distinguish between a court's deciding things by a majority, and lots and lots of ordinary men and women deciding things by a majority', (1993b), 49.

[43] Lord Hoffmann also points out extrajudicially that, under the current system, voters are forced by 'buy the complete packages of one or other of the three major parties', see Hoffmann (1999b), 161, though with the first-past-the-post system, this choice is normally limited to two major parties.

[44] Campbell (2001), 99, emphasis added.      [45] Fredman (2001), 199.

[46] *Ibid.*, 206.      [47] *Ibid.*, 208.

unpopular or marginal interests. Thus, whilst Convention rights may, in abstract terms, concern the rights of all members of the community, when they come up for discussion in Parliament or before the courts, the question tends to be whether an uncontroversial, abstract right such as the right to liberty can be applied to protect, say, suspected terrorists, or whether the prohibition on discrimination entails the legalisation of gay marriage or gay adoptions. These issues are more accurately characterised as decisions about the rights of one particular group – often unpopular ones. Given this characterisation, it is no longer self-evident, that the best way of dealing with them, is to subject them exclusively to a decision-making procedure marked by its popular and electoral orientation.[48]

Of importance here is the distinction between formal and effective participation. People with concerns of marginal political importance, who are unpopular and lack the ability to mobilise the support of an interest group may be effectively excluded from participating in the normal political process and therefore be unable to stand up for their rights through the normal political channels. If they are persistently outvoted by more powerful groups, they will become a permanent minority which *de facto* has little if any power to influence political decision-making.[49] Although these people may have a *formal* right to vote, associate and assemble, they are *effectively* disenfranchised because they cannot gain support or recognition for their claims and concerns.[50] Normal representative politics, operating as it does on a massive scale with competing interests fighting for protection and support, creates a systemic risk that those who fail to mobilise popular and/or political support or whose interests are not represented by a Member of Parliament, will be effectively excluded and disenfranchised. As one democratic sceptic concedes:

> simplistic appeals to political equality leave the most intractable difficulties unanswered in this context. 'Each citizen shall count for one' fails to account for those situations where certain individuals are a permanent minority and whose concerns are not adequately represented within the political process.[51]

---

[48] For a more detailed consideration of the role of 'impact on the rights-bearer' as a factor in considering a just institutional decision-making procedure for dealing with rights, see Kavanagh (2003b), 469ff.

[49] On the potentially valuable role of a Bill of Rights in countries with permanent minorities of this kind, see generally Kavanagh (2004d), discussing the role of a Bill of Rights in Northern Ireland.

[50] For the distinction between formal and effective participation, see Gewirth (1982).

[51] Malik (2001), 293, though she suggests that the solution to this problem is reform of representative institutions.

Thus, whilst it may well be the case that each individual's voice '*ought* to be taken seriously in politics',[52] as Waldron tellingly puts it, the reality is that those who wish to voice unpopular or marginal concerns, will often by silenced in normal politics.

The distinction between formal and effective participation also casts doubt on the egalitarian claims made for the right to democratic participation. In supporting the idea that the right to participate embodies the principle of political equality, Keith Ewing clarifies that 'political equality means equality of influence over decision-making'.[53] Ewing will not be unaware that differences in wealth, education and popular support all create disparities between people's political power and their ability to achieve or influence their political goals.[54] Clearly, these inequalities will enable those who are better situated, either financially or politically, to exercise a larger influence over legislation and a greater chance to ensure the protection of their interests.[55] Organisation skills, time, money, easy access to agents of government, parties or the media, are all necessary to the construction of effective political action and are attributes which are relatively inaccessible to many. So, having an equal right to participate does not mean that one's actual ability to participate effectively is equal. Nor does it mean that everyone will be able to get their voice heard or be able to influence policy to the same extent.[56]

The possibility of exclusion is precisely the situation where the existence of an independent tribunal to review and assess the Convention-compatibility of legislation is valuable, because it enables those groups at least to get their case heard in a forum which is relatively independent of the political power structures which may otherwise prevent them from getting to protection of their rights. Unless other social inequalities leading to inequality of political leverage are removed or mitigated, the idea that genuinely equal participation can be achieved simply by giving everyone the right to participate is no more than a 'pious aspiration'.[57] As

---

[52] Ewing also (tellingly) says that everyone 'potentially' plays an equal part in democratic decision-making, not that they actually play an equal part, see Ewing (2006), 43, emphasis added.

[53] *Ibid.*

[54] Kyritsis (2006) also makes a convincing case that elected representatives have a far greater influence over public decision-making than ordinary citizens.

[55] Lively (1975), 22; see also Sandalow (1981), 449.

[56] Beitz (1983), 73, calls this the difference between potential and actual political influence; see also Dworkin (1987), 12.

[57] Phillips (1995), 30. As Alan Gewirth points out in relation to American democracy: 'the democratic process is itself characterised by the same inequalities as characterise the other, substantive aspects of American society see Gewirth (1982), 322; see also Gewirth (1996), 340.

John Rawls puts it, we must be prepared to take 'compensating steps'[58] in order to preserve the fair value of this right for all. A willingness to investigate such options displays an appreciation of the gap between formal and substantial equality, as well as a desire to narrow this gap in order to enhance real political and social inclusion.[59] The options are many and varied. They could include various reforms of parliamentary procedures, making television time or newspaper space available freely to the poor or placing limits on the funding of political parties.[60] Another mechanism is that provided by constitutional review.

This means that securing effective participation in a way which pays tribute to people's fundamental equality, may itself require some inequalities in formal participation. If it can be shown that the interests underlying participation (namely, autonomy, dignity, inclusion, etc.) are better protected by having democratic government combined with constitutional review, then this combination of institutional procedures should be chosen. Here, the limits on the right to equal participation are set by the goal of achieving maximum effective participation for all.

Democratic sceptics will respond by pointing out that access to court is just as blighted with real-life social inequalities as access to the centres of power through the normal political channels. Not only can the more powerful in our society pursue litigation as a way of achieving political aims, limitations on legal aid and the time and money required to advance litigation to the highest level effectively exclude the worst off in society from accessing this channel also. The argument advanced here is not that everybody with a worthwhile claim about rights can succeed in bringing their case to court. It is merely that access to court (and the likelihood of success in court) is susceptible to different forces and influences than access and success through the normal political channels. The differences are highlighted when one observes that some of the most prominent litigants under the HRA (e.g. destitute asylum seekers, terrorist suspects imprisoned without trial, prisoners, mental patients, immigrants, etc.),[61] come from the worst-off and unpopular groups in society. It is difficult to

---

[58] Rawls (1971), 225.     [59] Phillips (1995), 35.

[60] For an outline of these and other measures that could be instituted in order to make more available to groups the 'effective ability to press their claims in public communication', see Gewirth (1982), 324–5. For discussion of party funding in the UK see Ewing (2006).

[61] Andrew Clapham also points out that the major beneficiaries of the judicial provision for Strasbourg jurisprudence based on the Convention have been prisoners, mental patients, immigrants and children, Clapham (1999), 131.

see how they would have succeeded in vindicating their rights in normal politics.[62]

When one considers litigants like these, it sheds a harsh and unforgiving light on claims that what matters most in political morality is the right to participate only in normal politics, but not through other channels. It is difficult to sustain the claim that that formally participatory decision-making procedures, outweighs the prospect of securing an outcome which actually protects their rights in substantive terms.[63] It also exposes as unrealistic, the idea that such a right is the best means of ensuring every citizen's empowerment, inclusion and equality. Such litigants would respond by saying that they want participation to be an effective way of getting their voice heard and, ultimately, having their interests respected. They do not care whether the channel they pursue to achieve those aims is democratic or not. As it happens, many of the beneficiaries of human rights adjudication enumerated above (namely, prisoners, mental patients and immigrants) do not possess the right to vote in any case, so are also excluded formally from the primary method of democratic participation.[64] But even if this option were formally open to them, any real sense of inclusion, empowerment or equal respect will depend on success in gaining a lever on the centres of power, and if this is achieved through constitutional review, then this will be (at least to them in their situation of marginalisation) the means by which these values are realised. Certainly, it would be difficult to convince them that they would enjoy a greater level of empowerment and inclusion, if left to pursue their case through the normal political channels. The various features of the democratic process outlined in chapter 12 (especially its popular/electoral orientation and its majoritarian bias) conspire to make their chances of success remote.

## The argument from the poor judicial record under the HRA

### The HRA: futility or utility?

As presented in chapter 12 and defended here, the case for constitutional review rested mainly on the peculiar institutional features of the courts, which suggest that rights claims will be considered in a different light when they come before the courts. Clearly, institutional structure alone

---

[62] Kateb (1983), 150.    [63] See also Phillipson (2006), 56ff.

[64] See the Representation of the People Act 1983; prisoners: section 3(1); mental patients: section 7(1); and children under eighteen: section 1(1). This point is also made in Clapham (1999), 131.

does not *guarantee* that the aims of this institutional design are realised. Democratic sceptics argue that even though the judiciary now have the tools under the HRA to give more robust protection of human rights, they have (for the most part) failed to use those tools in order to protect them. Therefore, it is unjustifiable to limit the valuable right to democratic participation, because the alleged gains in terms of rights protection since the HRA has been enacted are nowhere to be seen.

The most damning critique of this nature was delivered by Keith Ewing in an article entitled 'The Futility of the HRA'.[65] There, he pointed out that although we now have a Bill of Rights in the form of the HRA, we nonetheless 'live in a period of unparalleled restraint in liberty, with more restraints on the way'.[66] This was partly blamed on the draconian statutory initiatives introduced by the Labour Government post 9/11 as part of the so-called 'war on terror',[67] and partly on what he considers to be the dismal judicial response to such measures: 'what we find is that rather than use the new powers which they craved, the judges have in fact failed to engage in areas which concern the protection of the individual who comes face to face with the state'.[68] In short, he argues that the HRA 'has been scarred by the continuing deference shown by the courts to the government'.[69]

A number of points need to be made in response to Ewing's indictment of the judicial record under the HRA. First, it is a mistake to blame the judges for the enactment of legislation which encroaches on liberty or human rights more generally. The case for constitutional review under the HRA is partly based on the fact that it provides some constraint on normal politics, both by preventing and correcting legislation which violates Convention rights. The existence of constitutional review under the HRA gives Parliament added incentives to protect those rights. But the existence of these constraints, incentives and various (limited) institutional sanctions in the event of violation, in no way *guarantees* that a government bent on violating rights will be prevented from doing so. Ewing's examples show that, even though we have constitutional review under the HRA, we do not live under a 'juristocracy'[70] as democratic sceptics sometimes rhetorically declare. The limited nature of the courts'

---

[65] Ewing (2004), 829.    [66] *Ibid.*, 836.    [67] *Ibid.*, 836–9    [68] *Ibid.*, 840.    [69] *Ibid.*, 846.
[70] *Ibid.*, 831; Tomkins (2005b), 7. The limited scope of constitutional review as a decision-making procedure is often overlooked by those who contrast 'juristocracy' and democracy. The reality is that unlike, say, democracy, monarchy or aristocracy, judicial review is not a complete theory of political authority. It is a decision-making procedure designed to deal with the limited range of issues, see Kavanagh (2003b), 454; see also Dworkin (1985), 27.

powers mean that Parliament still retains immense legislative and policy-making powers, including the power to violate Convention rights in ways the courts find difficult or impossible to oppose. The argument advanced in chapter 12 was that the HRA can contribute in various ways to enhancing the protection of Convention rights, not that it delivers a utopia where no human right is ever violated by any branch of government.

Interestingly, all of the legislative examples Ewing adduces arise in the area of national security. What these examples show is that governments under pressure to respond quickly and effectively to an emergency situation, and eager to pacify a fearful public, are all too prone to hasty and populist decisions, which pay scant regard to the human rights of marginalised groups. The most notorious example of this is one which Ewing uses, namely, the Anti-Terrorism, Crime and Security Act 2001, which, despite its staggering length, breadth and draconian implications, was rushed through Parliament in a matter of days.[71] This is not a wonderful example of the allegedly participatory, democratic decision-making procedures so prized by Ewing. It is one (albeit a particularly notorious and egregious) example of the 'well-established tradition of rushing terrorist legislation through Parliament'.[72] The Executive and legislative response to the threat from global terrorism has left a lot to be desired, both in terms of democratic procedure and in terms of substantive outcome concerning individual liberty. If anything, the examples Ewing adduces cry out for the need for multiple safeguards, including a review procedure enforced by officials who are free from electoral accountability and the short-term political pressures to which elected politicians succumb.

The real question with reference to the anti-terrorist legislation is whether the Government's response to 9/11 would have been better or worse in terms of rights protection, if the HRA had not been enacted. The HRA can only be deemed 'futile', if it can be shown that the level of rights protection would have been the same or worse without it. Like any claim involving a counterfactual, the suggestion that we would have got better rights protection without the HRA is an extremely difficult proposition to assess.[73] Verifying the counterfactual would inevitably involve

---

[71] See Tomkins (2002c), 205, who points out that the Government only allowed sixteen hours of debate on this Bill in the Commons, and it received nine days in the House of Lords.

[72] Tomkins (2002c), 205; see also Tomkins (2002b), 203, who points out that in the field of national security, 'parliamentary scrutiny continues to be meagre'.

[73] For an exploration of some of the difficulties involved in verifying such counterfactual claims, see also Waluchow (2007), 168ff; Waldron (1999), 168.

some conjecture, given that the social and political situation did not remain constant once the HRA was enacted. In particular, one would need to investigate whether the response of the Government to the threat from 'global terrorism' post 9/11 would have been more or less vigilant about protecting rights, than it would have been if the HRA had not been enacted. Ewing fails to engage in such a comparative and admittedly difficult conjectural analysis.[74]

We can look to his former co-author, Conor Gearty, for some of the comparative, empirical analysis we require in order to assess Ewing's claim that the HRA is futile. Gearty's analysis reveals that the HRA contributed in various subtle ways to make the Terrorism Act 2000 less draconian than it might otherwise have been.[75] Concessions were made in the course of its passage through the two Houses of Parliament which eliminated some of its worst excesses. Some of these concessions were due to concern about potentially adverse judicial findings under the HRA.[76] Gearty argues that the same is true of the Anti-Terrorism, Crime and Security Act 2001 (another of Ewing's allegedly damning examples of the futility of the HRA). He concludes that 'some concessions were secured which arguably might not have been obtained without the 1998 legislation'[77] and that the critical response to the legislation 'drew strength and energy'[78] from the 1998 Act.[79] After examining the passage of these Bills through Parliament, and the 'apocalyptic' tenor of the then Prime Minister's public pronouncements on global terrorism, Gearty's appropriately tentative conclusion was that if the government of the day had been given 'the free legislative rein that existed in pre-Convention days', it would 'surely

[74] Though he concedes that the Anti-Terrorism, Crime and Security Act 2001 removes 'one of the most obnoxious provisions of the Prevention of Terrorism Act 1989', in response to a decision of the Strasbourg court, see Ewing (2004), 837. In other words, he concedes that the existence of Convention case law made the Terrorism Act less objectionable from a human rights point of view than it might otherwise have been.

[75] Gearty (2005a), 21; see also Nicol's detailed analysis of the parliamentary debates on the Anti-Terrorism Crime and Security Act, see Nicol (2005), 457–62. He concludes that although Convention rights did not play a central role in the House of Commons debates, they were an important feature of debate in the House of Lords, where a large number of peers used them to attack a wide range of the Bill's proposals. His analysis shows that a 'Convention consciousness' was also a prevalent concern in the parliamentary debates on the Nationality, Immigration and Asylum Bill 2002, see Nicol (2005), 467.

[76] Nicol also concludes that concerns about Convention-compatibility in the House of Lords led the Government to amend the burden of proof provisions, see Nicol (2005), 461.

[77] Gearty (2005a), 23.    [78] Ibid.

[79] Of crucial importance in securing these concessions was the Joint Committee on Human Right's questioning of the Home Secretary regarding Part Four of the Bill, see Lester (2002), 444.

have been likely . . . to have resulted in more rather than less invasions of liberty'.[80] These conclusions are supported by the former legal adviser to the JCHR, David Feldman, who suggested that even if the outcome of the debates on the Anti-Terrorism, Crime and Security Bill were 'not entirely satisfactory from a human rights standpoint',[81] it should still be recognised that:

> the consideration given to human rights was far more systematic and sophisticated than anything that took place in respect of the Prevention of Terrorism (Temporary Provisions) Act 1974 with the Official Secrets Act 1989, let alone the Public Order Act 1936, the Official Secrets Act 1911, or the Defence of the Realm regulations in the two World Wars.[82]

These conclusions, based on close, detailed analysis of the legislative passage of these controversial Bills, weaken Ewing's drastic claim that the HRA is futile. They suggest that the HRA was useful in protecting rights to a greater degree than might have been possible without it.

Leaving the legislative programme aside for the moment, let us now turn to the judicial response to it. This is surely the critical issue with respect to assessing the effectiveness of the HRA. Of course, before criticising judges for failing to 'oppose' draconian legislation, one has to bear in mind that judges do not have control over the issues they can adjudicate. If they believe that a statute or statutory provision is objectionable from a human rights point of view, they can only do something about it, if it is litigated before them. They are not always given this opportunity, because a suitable case does not present itself. Sometimes governments try to oust their jurisdiction altogether. However, such an opportunity was provided when the *Belmarsh* detainees brought a case under Part IV of the Anti-Terrorism, Crime and Security Act 2001. In line with his deep-seated scepticism about judges, Ewing predicted that the 'experience of the Convention rights in the domestic courts is likely to be one of abject disappointment and growing disillusionment'.[83] As Lord Lester pointed out in a response to Ewing entitled 'The Utility of the HRA', this 'proved to be an over-hasty verdict'.[84] The House of Lords condemned the system of Executive detention without trial contained in the 2001 Act.

---

[80]  Feldman (2004), 26.     [81]  Feldman (2002), 348.
[82]  *Ibid.*; Feldman (2004), 91ff, where he argues that legislative provisions are now drafted and justified with more sensitivity to their human rights implications than they were prior to the creation of the JCHR in January 2001.
[83]  Ewing (2004), 852.     [84]  Lester (2005), 253.

Widely thought to be an 'extraordinary'[85] and 'remarkable'[86] decision, *Belmarsh* shows how constitutional review can enable the courts to stand up against an all too powerful Executive, by defending the human rights of the vulnerable and marginalised when they come face to face with the might of the state in a highly sensitive area.[87]

## Democratic scepticism and judicial deference

Ewing's prediction about the judicial record may well have been wrong in relation to the *Belmarsh Prison* case, but fellow democratic sceptics have not been deterred. Though conceding that the *Belmarsh Prison* case was indeed 'remarkable',[88] Adam Tomkins warns that we ought not to get carried away by its alleged vindication of individual liberty. He advances four reasons to subdue any premature or unwarranted jubilation about the case. First, he points out that what makes the *Belmarsh Prison* case remarkable is that it departed from a long line of twentieth-century cases which were notoriously deferential to the elected branches in times of emergency.[89] Second, after *A* was decided, those detained under the 2001 Act remained in detention: none was released. Third, when Parliament responded to the declaration of incompatibility in *A*, they did so by replacing indefinite detention with a new system of control orders, which, to varying degrees, have withstood legal challenge under Article 5 ECHR. Finally, the decision in *A* has been succeeded, according to Tomkins, by subsequent case law which has been deferential to the Executive and legislature in the national security context.

---

[85] Tomkins (2005a), 259.

[86] Tomkins (2008), 28, 30, 33; Gearty (2005a), 28; Gearty (2005b), 37 who describes it as 'the finest assertion of civil liberties that has emerged from a British court since at least *Entick* v. *Carrington*'.

[87] Another decision Ewing criticises for being unduly deferential, is *R. (Abbasi)* v. *Secretary of State for Foreign and Commonwealth Affairs*, where the House of Lords refused to challenge the Foreign Secretary's consular representations on behalf of a UK citizen detained at Guantanamo Bay. It is worth noting that although the court did not think it their place to tell the Foreign Secretary how to conduct foreign relations, it nonetheless made powerful *obiter* comments about how objectionable it was that Mr Abbasi was detained without trial in territory over which the USA had exclusive control. As Rodney Austin pointed out, 'this is a remarkable step for a UK court to take, even if the court was not prepared to provide relief against the Foreign Secretary', see Austin (2007), 99, 117.

[88] Tomkins (2008), 28.

[89] *Ibid.*, 30: "what is so immediately arresting about the decision in *A* is precisely its novelty"; see also Gearty (2005b), 40–41.

Each point made by Tomkins is undeniably correct, yet the criticism of the courts they are intended to support is, I believe, misguided. In this section, I will address the points about judicial deference, because they go to the heart of the sceptical critique. Tomkins points out, quite rightly, that the general trend in judicial decision-making on national security issues prior to A was highly deferential.[90] Moreover, he points to some decisions handed down after A which also display deference.[91] He therefore concludes that A should not be heralded triumphantly as the end of judicial deference, because this doctrine of restraint is alive and well in other decisions. There are two problems with this point, at least when pressed into service of a critique of A in the way Tomkins hopes. The first is that it relies on a misunderstanding of the nature, rationale and legitimacy of judicial deference. The second is that, ironically, it expects too much of judges and court structures, subjecting them to standards they can rarely if ever achieve and are generally not designed to achieve.[92] Both problems are interlinked and require explanation.

As we saw in the second part of this book, judicial deference is highly contextual and depends on all the factors relevant to the case. Therefore, if the courts are less deferential in one case, it does not mean that they will not or cannot (legitimately) be more deferential in another. Judicial deference involves a determination about the constitutionally appropriate degree of judicial restraint in the context of a particular case. It is a ubiquitous feature of constitutional decision-making. To criticise A for not eliminating deference altogether, is to criticise it for not achieving the impossible. What is remarkable about A is not that it rejected the idea that some deference was appropriate in the context of national security, but that it was an emphatic rejection of the idea that cases involving national security are non-justiciable. In A, the House of Lords repeatedly emphasised its important and legitimate scrutinising role, although it acknowledged that it must nonetheless be appropriately respectful of the expertise, competence and superior democratic legitimacy of the elected branches. This marks a subtle but nonetheless significant change in the direction of the case law in this area, which does not mean that deference will never be appropriate. Moreover, the fact that A marked a departure from a long line of extraordinarily deferential decisions which existed prior to it, is surely a point in favour of constitutional review under the HRA, rather

---

[90] Tomkins (2008), 31.    [91] *Ibid.*

[92] The irony is contained in the fact that democratic sceptics argue for a limited judicial role, but simultaneously criticise judges for not playing a more expansive role.

than a point against it. It suggests that the enhanced democratic legitimacy of the courts' review jurisdiction under the HRA has emboldened them to stand up to the Executive in a time of alleged crisis, in order to check Executive (and indeed legislative) abuse of power.[93]

There are more fundamental problems with Ewing's and Tomkin's critique – problems which go to the heart of their democratic scepticism. On my analysis, a variable degree of judicial deference may be *justified* because judges owe the elected branches of government respect, on grounds of their superior expertise, competence and a democratic legitimacy. It is curious, therefore, that democratic sceptics do not celebrate deferential decisions. After all, what occurs when judges are deferential (and especially when they are absolutely supine) is that the elected branches of government are given free rein to do whatever they want, unencumbered by any constitutional or legal restraints placed on them by unelected and unaccountable judges. One might add that, in such cases, the 'equal right of all citizens to participate in the fundamental decisions on which they are governed', is left completely unimpaired. The important (and often ignored) question which needs to be asked when judges are criticised for handing down deferential decisions is 'who have the judges failed to stand up *to*?'[94] In most cases, the answer is, of course, Parliament and the Executive, and one would expect democratic sceptics to celebrate the fact that those who are elected and accountable face no meaningful judicial opposition.

This might seem like a disingenuous point, since we all know what is wrong with supine judicial decisions which fail to stand up to an almighty Executive. They are objectionable because they are an abdication of the constitutional function of the courts in ensuring that decisions of the Executive and legislature comply with fundamental constitutional principles, such as *habeas corpus*. The rationale of having independent judges to assess claims brought by individual citizens is that they can use their impartiality to ride political storms, oppose unjust decisions made by a panicked Executive and defend the liberty of the individual. And it is

---

[93] See Sedley (2007), vii, who observes that under the HRA, the courts have been given 'a parliamentary mandate to enforce the executive's compliance, and to oversee the legislature's compliance, with the ECHR'. One of the underlying themes of David Bonner's book (to which Lord Sedley wrote the Foreword) is that, armed with the HRA, the domestic judiciary has become more confident in scrutinising national security measures: 'The HRA era has witnessed a more empowered and less deferential judiciary – witnessed most markedly by the approach of the house in *A and others*...', see Bonner (2007), 351.

[94] Phillipson (2006), 58, emphasis added.

important that they do this, precisely in situations where it goes against popular and short-term concerns to which normal politics sometimes falls victim. In their more abstract arguments, both Ewing and Tomkins invite us to give primacy to democratic politics and to reject the legitimacy of judicial challenge to that primacy. It is curious then, that they do not support the democratic justification for judicial deference.

Aside from matters of principle, democratic sceptics seem to overlook some of the pragmatic limitations under which courts labour when assessing national security cases. The case law in this area shows that even if the courts wished to oppose the elected branches, they are often inhibited if not completely incapacitated from doing so, because they are prevented from seeing the intelligence evidence on which the primary decision was taken. As we saw in chapter 8, deference is a rational response to uncertainty: it would be irresponsible for judges to seek to overturn Executive decisions or reinterpret legislation if they have insufficient information on which to make such a decision, possibly with drastic consequences. This point was vividly illustrated by the case of *R. (Gillan)* v. *Metropolitan Police Commissioner*[95] – another case which Tomkins describes as 'dismal'[96] and 'disturbing'[97] from a civil liberties perspective. The analysis in chapter 7 demonstrates how constrained the court was in challenging the legislation in the case, given that it was precluded from seeing the intelligence information on which the primary decision was based.[98]

## Democratic sceptics as disappointed absolutists

When reading the writings of democratic sceptics, one is reminded of H. L. A. Hart's astute observation that sceptics are often 'disappointed absolutists'.[99] They expect everything, and when it does not materialise, they are thrown into 'abject disappointment'.[100] Take for example Tomkins' criticism of the decision in *A* that it did not lead to the automatic release of the *Belmarsh* detainees (though they were released three months later).[101] The reason they were not automatically released is that

---

[95]  *R. (Gillan)* v. *Metropolitan Police Commissioner* [2006] 2 A.C. 307.
[96]  Tomkins (2008), 28.    [97]  *Ibid.*, 27.    [98]  See chapter 8, 214.
[99]  Hart (1961), 135 (discussing 'rule-sceptics' in particular).    [100]  Ewing (2004), 852.
[101]  The House of Lords judgment was handed down on 16 December 2004, but the detainees were not released until March 2005, largely due to the fact that the 2001 Act was about to expire, see *Guardian*, 12 March 2005; see also Wintemute (2006a), 219, though contrary to the democratic sceptics, Wintemute uses the shortcoming of the declaration of incompatibility mechanism to mount a case in favour of a full judicial strike-down power under the HRA.

Parliament did not give the courts the power to do any such thing under the HRA. The remedial limits of the declaration of incompatibility meant that it had no immediate legal consequences for the parties to the legal dispute. Had the courts been given the power to strike down the legislation, perhaps the consequence that Tomkins desires would have been possible. The irony here is that it was partly due to the forceful arguments of democratic sceptics, that the courts were not given this power under the HRA, but were left with the more limited mechanism of the declaration of incompatibility.[102] Again, there is a tension here between the democratic sceptics' celebration of the limited nature of the declaration of incompatibility (and in some cases advocacy of a greater use of this mechanism precisely because of its limited nature) and their criticism of the courts when the result of applying that mechanism is that the individual is not given an immediate remedy.

Tomkins' absolutist stance is also evident in his criticisms of the other case law arising under the HRA. Whilst acknowledging that there have been 'some surprisingly welcome and progressive decisions',[103] he criticises such decisions for being 'heavily qualified'.[104] Tomkins argues that when we look at progressive decisions like *Limbuela*,[105] we should be hesitant to conclude that they 'herald a new general direction in the law'.[106] 'Even the most apparently progressive decisions', he concludes, 'are limited and heavily qualified, either in their own terms or when read in the light of other cases. None can yet be said to have made general changes in the overall direction of the law.'[107] Even worse, he suggests that there are some illiberal decisions on the post-HRA judicial record.[108]

Although it is not possible within the confines of this chapter to engage with all the examples adduced by Tomkins, I wish to make the following general points about his mode of analysis. First, only a disappointed absolutist would be shocked to find some illiberal decisions on the judicial record and reject the whole institution of constitutional review on that basis. Like all the other branches of government, the courts are staffed by human beings who are humanly fallible. Just as the record of Parliament and the Executive is not without blemish post-HRA, the record of the courts may also have its shortcomings.[109] More importantly, when

---

[102] See Klug (2005), 198.    [103] Tomkins (2008), 25.    [104] *Ibid.*
[105] *R. v. Secretary of State for the Home Department, ex parte Limbuela* [2005] UKHL 66.
[106] Tomkins (2008), 35.    [107] *Ibid.*    [108] *Ibid.*
[109] Gavin Phillipson goes further and claims that 'in almost every case cited as the judicial failure [by democratic sceptics] . . . the role of Parliament and the then government has been worse, or at least as bad', see Phillipson (2006) 58.

one looks more closely at the cases Tomkins selects, what emerges is that the apparently illiberal outcomes are often due to the particular factual matrix of a case or the way the case was argued before the court. In fact, he concedes that in two out of the four cases he cites as illiberal,[110] the facts of those cases were 'unpromising in terms of a search for effective judicial protection of liberty and fundamental rights'.[111] He claims that no such problem arises with respect to *Gillan*.[112] This assessment of *Gillan* is open to challenge on the following grounds. One of the reasons why sections 44–46 of the Anti-Terrorism, Crime and Security Act were upheld in that case was that these legislative provisions contained multiple safeguards and constraints, which meant that the authorisation and exercise of the power to stop and search was very closely regulated.[113] Furthermore, the fact that neither claimant in this case was stopped for longer than thirty minutes influenced the court in concluding that the claimants were not detained 'in the sense of confined or kept in custody'.[114] In other words, the particular factual context led to the court's conclusion that there was no significant deprivation of liberty in this case. Moreover, given the evidence provided on behalf of the Metropolitan Police and the Home Secretary, the authorisation in the particular circumstances of *Gillan* was shown to be within the power granted by section 44 of the Anti-Terrorism, Crime and Security Act.[115] Finally, and perhaps most importantly, counsel for the claimants in *Gillan* accepted in the course of argument that the giving of a section 44 authorisation to stop and search would sometimes be a proportionate response to the threat of terrorist activity, and that a balance must be struck between the degree of interference with ordinary liberties and the degree of risk to the public posed by the terrorist threat.[116] Once these points were conceded, it severely weakened the claimants' case, and made it very difficult for the courts to find that the legislation was a disproportionate interference with Convention

---

[110] *R. v. Shayler* [2003] 1 A.C. 247; *R. v. Z* [2005] 2 A.C. 645.

[111] Tomkins (2008), 26.     [112] *Gillan*, above n. 95.

[113] For a list of the eleven constraints placed on the exercise of the power, see *Gillan*, *ibid.* at [14], *per* Lord Bingham.

[114] *Ibid.* at [25], *per* Lord Bingham.

[115] *Ibid.* at [16]–[19]. Rodney Austin also suggested that the fact that the appellants were taking actions in the county court against the police officers and the Metropolitan Police Commissioner, was also significant to the outcome of the judicial review application because the House of Lords attached significance to this alternative source of redress, see Austin (2007), 115, citing *Gillan*, above n. 95 at [36] and [66].

[116] *Ibid.* at [62], *per* Lord Scott.

rights, especially in light of the limited intelligence material available to them.[117]

This case illustrates a general feature of judicial decision-making, instantiated in adjudication under the HRA. This is that whilst all of these cases raise deeply important (moral, political and legal) issues, the courts are not asked to pronounce upon those issues in the abstract. The courts have no roaming brief to ensure that every piece of legislation enacted by Parliament is ideal from a civil liberties perspective. Rather, they have the much narrower task of determining whether a particular litigant's Convention rights have been violated in the context of the particular circumstances of that case. Even when particular legislative provisions are litigated before them, judges do not have the task of deciding whether the legislation as a whole is liberal or illiberal, never mind the more difficult task of rendering it liberal, should they wish to do so. They have the more limited task of assessing the Convention-compatibility of a particular legislative provision, bearing in mind their duty to respect the decisions made by the elected branches, and in light of all the other limitations on their powers outlined in earlier chapters. This means that, when assessing the case law, we have to take into account the factual context in which it arises and bear in mind the necessarily limited nature of judicial adjudication. It is not the judges' job to set about liberalising statutes across the board – it is their job to assess the Convention-compatibility of one particular section of that Act in light of the facts of the case before them, and if those facts are unpromising, then the courts' already limited law-making and law-reforming ability is severely constrained. They should not be criticised for observing those constraints, which are the key to their legitimacy.

This general point is illustrated by one of the House of Lords' decisions on control orders which were introduced by the Prevention of Terrorism Act 2005. That Act allows either the court or the Secretary of State to impose 'obligations' on individuals whom the Secretary of State 'suspects', but cannot prove, have been involved in terrorist-related

---

[117] This point that the way in which a case is argued can determine the outcome of a case is acknowledged by Tomkins in relation to the *R. (Pro-Life Alliance)* v. *British Broadcasting Corporation* [2004] 1 A.C. 185, see Tomkins (2005b), 28, where he points out (quite rightly) that the House of Lords was not *asked* to address the question of whether the rules prohibiting broadcasters from screening pictures offensive to public feeling complied with the principle of freedom of political expression, but rather *the much narrower question* of whether the broadcasters correctly applied those rules in this particular case.

activity. In *Secretary of State for the Home Department* v. *JJ*,[118] the House of Lords held (three to two) that a control order imposing an eighteen-hour curfew was such a severe restriction on the liberty of the 'controlled persons' that it infringed their right to liberty under Article 5. In so doing, Lord Brown stated emphatically that the courts would resist the 'siren voices'[119] urging it to accept that the borderline between deprivation of liberty and restriction of liberty of movement should be shifted to accommodate 'today's need to combat terrorism'. The decision was hailed as a 'devastating blow' to the Government.[120]

Unsurprisingly, the vindication of liberty contained in *JJ* did not persuade Adam Tomkins. He claimed that 'it was not the overall system of control orders that was held to be unlawful in this case: it was merely that particular control orders affecting the claimant had been made by the Secretary of State and not by a court'.[121] Again, the disappointment that the courts only achieve a qualified (rather than an absolute) victory for liberty is evident in Tomkins' critique. However, the courts were not asked to assess the merits of the 'overall system of control orders'. As Keir Starmer pointed out, whether control orders were 'a good idea or a bad idea was not the issue before the court'.[122] Rather, the issue before them was whether the particular controls imposed on these particular claimants amounted to a 'deprivation of their liberty' or merely a 'restriction on movement' in accordance with the Strasbourg jurisprudence on Article 5 ECHR. These litigants did not ask the courts to assess whether the overall system of control orders violated Convention rights. When handing down their judgment in the House of Lords, Lord Brown expressed this point about the appropriate division of labour between Parliament and the courts in terms one might have expected democratic sceptics to applaud. His Lordship stressed that the broader question of whether control orders are necessary to safeguard public security 'is a debate for the House in its legislative capacity, not for your Lordships in

---

[118] [2007] UKHL 45.    [119] *Ibid.* at [107].

[120] Ford, 'Judges deal blow to "draconian" anti-terror laws', *The Times*, 2 August 2006.

[121] He also criticised the decision for dividing three to two and not coming to a unanimous conclusion. What matters most from a legal point of view (and certainly from the point of view of the controlled persons) is that the House of Lords handed down a decision in their favour. As democratic sceptics are fond of pointing out, the cases which come before the House of Lords concern matters on which reasonable people can disagree. We should not be surprised and disappointed if there is some disagreement in the House of Lords, particularly if the majority decision is commendable on civil liberties grounds.

[122] Starmer (2007), 125.

the Appellate Committee'.[123] In carrying out their more limited task of assessing the legality of the control order regime in light of the particular facts presented to them in *JJ*, the House of Lords found that these particular control orders violated Convention rights. To criticise the court for not sweeping aside the whole legislative framework, is to criticise them for engaging in a task to which they are not suited or equipped, a task which they do not want – and a task which democratic sceptics would, in any case, deny that they should be given because they are unelected, unaccountable and possess insufficient legitimacy or expertise to carry out.

A similar problem of expecting more from judges than they can possibly deliver, underlies Tomkins' claim that none of the progressive decisions he identifies can be said to 'herald a new general direction in the law'.[124] 'Even the most apparently progressive decisions are limited and heavily qualified, either in their own terms or when read in the light of other cases. None can yet be said to have made general changes in the overall direction of the law.'[125] The point is that we should *expect* judicial decisions to be limited and qualified, because of the limited nature of their role. In general, judges are not equipped to achieve radical reform of the law or make 'general changes in the overall direction of the law'. Their abilities, institutional structure, expertise and legitimacy all indicate that when they make law, they should do so in an incremental way, case by case – in small steps rather than big leaps. By criticising them for not making big leaps, we are holding them to the standards of a different type of institution.

The arguments contained in chapter 12 were modest in scope. They showed that it can be useful to place the Executive and legislature under certain constraints, giving them various incentives to ensure that they do not violate Convention rights. The utility of the HRA was also contained in the fact that constitutional review provides some institutional sanctions in the event of a violation occurring (a sanction which does not rest entirely on post-enactment constitutional review, but also in

---

[123] *JJ*, above n. 118 at [86]. The fact-specific nature of this type of adjudication is also evident in the other cases on control orders, see *Secretary of State for the Home Department* v. *MB* [2007] 3 W.L.R. 681, [3], *per* Lord Bingham, where he characterises one of the questions before the court as 'whether the cumulative impact of the obligations imposed on AF by the control order dated 11 September 2006 and pursuant to the 2005 Act amounted to a deprivation of liberty within the meaning of Article 5(1) ECHR'; see also *Secretary of State* v. *E* [2008] 1 All E.R. 699 at [7], *per* Lord Bingham.

[124] Tomkins (2008), 35.     [125] *Ibid.*

pre-enactment anticipation of such review). That these mechanisms of enforcement have their limits is one of the recurring themes of this book. It is democratic sceptics who tend to lament the fact that even if the HRA has prevented some degree of human rights violation, it has not led to their 'bald elimination'.[126] But the absolute elimination of rights violations is not the aim of the ECHR and certainly not the task of judges when implementing it. All that needs to be shown for the purposes of mounting a case for constitutional review under the HRA, is that the courts are making some advances in holding the legislature and Executive to account for potential violations of Convention rights, and is helping to ensure that the human rights dimension of legislation is borne in mind, both before and after legislation is enacted.

This less absolute standard is met, both when we consider the anticipatory effect of potential litigation on the pre-enactment legislative agenda, as well as cases such as those which Tomkins rightly deems progressive, such as e.g. the *Belmarsh Prison* case,[127] *Limbuela*,[128] and *Laporte*.[129] The case law in the area of national security has not stopped the assiduous 'war on terror' waged by the UK Government, but it has mitigated some of its worst excesses. Take for example the three key House of Lords' decisions on control orders: *JJ*,[130] *MB*[131] and *E*.[132] Those who think that control orders are inherently unacceptable from a civil liberties point of view will share Tomkins' disappointment that the courts did not prohibit control orders altogether. These cases establish that the difference between (illegitimate) deprivation of liberty and (legitimate) restriction on liberty

---

[126] Gearty (2005a), 21. In a similar vein, Lucia Zedner criticised the decision in *JJ* because the courts did not eliminate control orders entirely: 'the result [in *JJ*] was no more than a partial relaxation of the terms of the orders, for example reducing the curfew from 18 to 14 hours per day . . . granted the new restrictions may as the result comply with human rights standards but the fundamental question over the very institution of the control order remains to be addressed', Zedner (2007), 186. Indeed, this more fundamental question was not put to the courts, and in any case, it is not the type of question to which they are ideally suited to adjudicate.

[127] *A and others* [2005] UKHL 71   [128] Above n. 105.

[129] *R. (Laporte)* v. *Chief Constable of Gloucestershire* [2007] 2 A.C. 105. It should be noted that in the *Review of the Implementation of the Human Rights Act* conducted by the Department of Constitutional Affairs in July 2006, it was emphasised that the impact of the Act on policy formation was not only due to the need to respond to litigation, but also through the formalisation of the process of ensuring compatibility with Convention rights through section 19 and scrutiny by the JCHR, see 'Introduction by the Lord Chancellor' (Lord Falconer) at www.justice.gov.uk/docs/full_review.pdf, p. 4.

[130] Above n. 118.   [131] *Secretary of State for the Home Department* v. *MB* [2007] UKHL 46.

[132] *Secretary of State for the Home Department* v. *E* [2007] UKHL 47. For further discussion of these cases, see Starmer (2007).

is one of degree, such that an eighteen-hour curfew (*JJ*) amounts to a deprivation, but a twelve-hour curfew (*E*) does not. However, the subtle but nonetheless potent force of these decisions is contained in the way in which the courts used section 3 HRA to ensure that rules prohibiting the Secretary of State from revealing evidence contrary to the public interest, should be read subject to a judicial discretion to order more disclosure, if this is warranted by a fair trial.[133] Whilst not eliminating control orders altogether, this is a powerful judicial sting in the tail of these cases, because the obligation to disclose such information may force or encourage the Home Secretary to pursue a criminal prosecution instead of imposing a control order in the first place.[134] It has always been the Government's stated position that a criminal prosecution of those suspected of terrorist offences is preferable to preventative measures such as control orders, though it seems as if the Government is not always as diligent as one might expect in referring such cases to the Crown Prosecution Service.[135] The House of Lords' decisions on control orders mitigate the worst effects of the control order regime in some instances, by placing added pressure on the Government to comply with their stated position favouring criminal prosecution. This is not an obvious, dramatic or headline-grabbing victory for liberty, but it is nonetheless of crucial importance in showing how the HRA can help to curtail the Government's tendency to avoid the constraints of the criminal justice system when dealing with suspected terrorists.

Other cases Tomkins does not mention are *Offen*[136] (which eliminated the notorious injustice of the three-strikes-and-you're-out legislation), as well as the various cases on reverse burdens of proof.[137] The latter cases arose in the context of the Government's increased use of reverse onus provisions in response to concerns about global terrorism and organised crime, especially drug trafficking. As Helen Fenwick has commented, 'the "reading down" under section 3 HRA of reverse burdens to evidential ones, has provided something of a check to this governmental tendency and a reassertion of the fundamental right encapsulated in Article 6(2)'.[138] In *Attorney General's Reference (No. 4 of 2002); Sheldrake v. DPP*,[139] Lord Bingham noted that 'until the coming into force of the HRA 1998, the issue

---

[133] See *MB*, above n. 131.    [134] I owe this point to David Bonner.
[135] Starmer (2007), 128.    [136] *R. v. Offen* [2001] 2 All E.R. 154.
[137] *R. v. Lambert* [2002] 2 A.C. 545; *R. v. DPP, ex parte Kebilene* [2000] 2 A.C. 326; *R. v. Johnstone* [2003] UKHL 28; *Attorney General's Reference (No. 1 of 2004)* [2004] 1 W.L.R. 211; *Sheldrake v. DPP* [2004] UKHL 43.
[138] Fenwick (2007), 178.    [139] Above n. 137.

[of "reading down" such reverse burdens of proof] could scarcely have arisen'[140] because the statutory provisions at issue[141] were not obscure or ambiguous. Finally, the unequivocal endorsement of proportionality in *Daly*[142] will have a pervasive effect on adjudication for compliance with human rights, as can be seen in the immigration context by the House of Lords' decision in *Huang*.[143]

The sum total of all of these cases, combined with the increasing appreciation of the importance of Convention rights during the legislative process and within government departments, may not amount to a new legal order, or a radical difference in the fundamental principles by which we are governed. However, one of the underlying points of this section has been to show that the question of the utility of the HRA should not be judged by this absolutist standard, but rather by the more qualified demand that it is useful to some degree in ensuring that rights receive enhanced protection. It is noteworthy that many of the most useful decisions have arisen in the context of national security.

### The argument from political rather than legal limits

The potential for rights violation by Parliament and the Executive is not denied by democratic sceptics. They acknowledge that there are problems about the efficiency of Parliament and strong arguments in favour of its reform.[144] Many lament the notorious Executive dominance of Parliament in the UK, which places so much power in the hands of so few. But rather than turning to legal constraints, they argue that we should concentrate instead on political ones. As Keith Ewing notes, 'you cannot reduce the democratic deficit by doubling it'.[145] They argue that political methods of constraining the Executive and Parliament to observe Convention rights should be prioritised. One should 'democratise' human rights, rather than 'juridify' them.[146]

As noted earlier, this is a false dichotomy. We do not need to choose between parliamentary reform and constitutional review. We can have

---

[140]  Above n. 137 at [7].

[141]  Anti-Terrorism, Crime and Security Act 2001, section 11 and Road Traffic Act 1988, section 5.

[142]  *R. v. Daly* [2001] 2 W.L.R. 1622.     [143]  *Huang v. Secretary of State* [2007] 2 A.C. 167.

[144]  Tomkins (2005b), 10; Gearty (2004), 210.

[145]  Ewing (1996), 43; Ewing believes that 'there is a crisis of democratic engagement reflected not only in electoral turnout (with only 3 in 4 electors voting in 2005), but also declining party memberships', see Ewing (2006), 16.

[146]  For this contrast, see Campbell (2001), 96.

both. Constitutional review does not supplant the work of Parliament: it supplements it. The same is true of participation: we can have democratic participation through the normal political channels, together with the additional channel of constitutional litigation. In advance of the HRA coming into force, democratic sceptics warned that once judicial review under the HRA was in place 'institutions such as Parliament, the Ombudsman and others are likely to find it more difficult to make their scrutiny voice fully heard'.[147] We were told that 'by inflating the power and responsibility of the judiciary, the influence and contribution which could be offered from other less well-dressed, but perhaps better suited, institutions has been sidelined and overlooked'.[148] In even more apocalyptic terms, we were warned that:

> locating the task of enforcing rights in the courts can lead to the suffocating of alternative avenues of dispute resolution. What fate awaits ministerial responsibility, or the parliamentary Commissioner for Administration (the Ombudsman) after the HRA?.[149]

These dire predictions have not been borne out in practice. The immense law-making and policy-making power of Parliament is, for the most part, left intact. There is no evidence to suggest that the Ombudsmen have been thwarted or 'suffocated' in any way by the HRA. In fact, since the enactment of the HRA, the various Ombudsman offices have multiplied and strengthened,[150] the number of complaints received by them has increased and various reforms have been proposed and introduced to enhance their effectiveness and accessibility.[151] Moreover, the current Parliamentary Commissioner for Administration (Ann Abraham) sees the current reform and strengthening of the office of the Ombudsman, as *part of* the wider process of constitutional reform 'that began in the 1990s with the Human Rights Act, devolution and reform of the Upper Chamber'.[152] There is no suggestion that the HRA has thwarted the expansion and development of the various Ombudsman schemes. Moreover, since 1997, many procedural changes have been introduced in the House of Commons in order to improve the quality of parliamentary scrutiny of legislation, in an effort to ensure that it is conducted in a more systematic and probing

---

[147] Tomkins (2001), 9.    [148] *Ibid.*, 10.    [149] *Ibid.*, 9.    [150] Abraham (2008a), 9.
[151] See e.g. Regulatory Reform Act 2007, Regulatory Reform (Ombudsman) Order 2007; see Turpin and  Tomkins (2007), 629–30; For an overview of the number and variety of claims handled by the Public Sector Ombudsmen in 2006–2007, see Abraham (2008a), 2.
[152] Abraham (2008c), 215, 207; see also Abraham (2008b), 377 where she stresses 'the inherent alliance between Ombudsmen and human rights'.

way.[153] For example, the new Constitution Committee in the House of Lords[154] has as one of its aims the scrutiny of Bills for compliance with constitutional norms and principles.[155] These and other developments make it difficult to accept the assertions that the HRA has swallowed up all other initiatives to scrutinise legislation in Parliament. If anything, the enactment of the HRA has coincided with (and arguably stimulated) many other initiatives to develop and enhance parliamentary scrutiny of legislation in order to ensure it is rights compatible.

Of immense significance in this regard is the Joint Committee on Human Rights (hereinafter JCHR), composed of members of both Houses of Parliament and overseen by a full-time legal adviser. The main function of the Committee is to assist Parliament in providing independent scrutiny of Executive policies and legislation which impact on Convention rights, as well as alerting Parliament to potential violations of Convention rights before legislation is enacted.[156] It is widely accepted that it greatly enhances the parliamentary scrutiny of legislation in terms of Convention rights.[157] It does so by publishing reports to each House of Parliament on its views as to the Convention-compatibility of legislation and particularly draft legislation, after taking evidence from Ministers, government departments, legal experts and Non-Governmental Organisations.[158] If the Committee has concerns about a Bill's compliance with human rights, it recommends appropriate amendments. The Joint Committee's reports are often relied on by MPs in the course of parliamentary debate, in order to support opposition to a Bill or an amendment to it.[159] There is also growing evidence that the reports of the JCHR (as well as the

---

[153] This is largely a result of the work of the Select Committee on modernisation of the House of Commons, see First Report, The Legislative Process (1997–98 HC 190); Second Report, Programming of Legislation and Timing of Votes (1999–2000 H.C. 589); First Report, Programming of Legislation (2000–2001 H.C. 382).

[154] It had its first meeting in February 2001.

[155] See Feldman (2002), 343. See Select Committee on the Constitution, First Report, Reviewing the Constitution: terms of reference and method of working with evidence, 2001–2002 HL 11.

[156] See Klug and Wildbore (2007), 235.

[157] For more detailed analysis of how this Committee works, see Lester (2002b); Klug and Wildbore (2007); Palmer (2007), 112–14.

[158] See Feldman (2002), 33.

[159] Klug and Wildbore (2007), 241 argue that one of the three ways in which the JCHR advises and influences Parliament is that it may impact on parliamentary debates, contribute to amendments to legislation, and inform and influence Parliamentarians more generally. For an example of influence on parliamentary debate, see the JCHR's report on the Anti-Terrorism, Crime and Security Bill which was quoted by many critics of the Bill during the parliamentary debates, see Lester (2002b), 439–40 (and debates cited there).

responses it elicits from the relevant government Ministers), are proving helpful to the courts when assessing the Convention-compatibility of legislation.[160]

It is difficult to see how or why it would have been more difficult for Parliament to introduce this method of scrutiny, if the HRA had not been enacted. Since its inception, this Committee has employed an expert legal adviser who is well placed to predict adverse judicial decisions, both in the domestic courts and in Strasbourg. The workings of that Committee interact with, and feed on, judicial decisions about Convention-compatibility – both existing case law of the domestic and Strasbourg courts, as well as anticipated decisions in light of existing jurisprudence.[161] Drawing on her experience as a specialist adviser to the JCHR, Francesca Klug concluded that, when writing its scrutiny reports, the JCHR 'was largely engaged in an exercise of "second guessing" the likely judgments of the courts, and in particular the European Court of Human Rights'.[162] Therefore, parliamentary and judicial forms of scrutiny and constraint are not mutually exclusive. If anything, the work of the JCHR highlights 'the collaborative nature of the human rights endeavour'[163] set in train by the HRA, because it is a way in which Parliament, the Executive and the courts can play a collaborative role in enhancing protection of human rights in the UK.

The example of the JCHR begs the question of why we should not rely exclusively on political control mechanisms like this. Why not adopt those forms of political accountability which do not have the disadvantage that they are enforced by unelected and unaccountable officials? The reason is that, however well one reforms Parliament, by increasing

---

[160] Reports of the JCHR were cited extensively in the *Belmarsh Prison* case; see also *R. (Animal Defenders International) v. Secretary of State for Culture, Media and Sport* [2008] UKHL 15 at [14]–[21]; *Secretary of State for the Home Department v. MB* [2007] UKHL 46 at [16].

[161] See Klug and Wildbore (2007), 243. Lord Lester noted that the Joint Committee does so in a way similar to the approach adopted by the courts when assessing claims of human rights violations, namely, by adopting the method of analysis provided by the proportionality principle, Lester (2002b), 438.

[162] Klug and Wildbore (2007), 243. Though it should be noted that Klug objects to the idea that the Committee should adopt such a 'quasi-judicial' role. She recommends that it should think more broadly about Convention-compliance. However, the current focus of the Committee on the likelihood of a judicial finding that there is an incompatibility with Convention rights, merely reflects prudential concerns about an adverse judicial finding on Convention-compatibility. In my view, fear of being found to be in contravention of the Convention is one of the benefits of the HRA.

[163] Palmer (2007), 113.

accountability and eliminating the concentration of power in the Executive, one is still left with institutions which are (quite rightly) responsive to popular opinion and majoritarian concerns, orientated to some extent towards re-election and (thankfully) equipped to make swift decisions with immense consequences. The point made in chapter 12 was that even when democracy was functioning *as it ought to do*, the distinguishing features of normal politics will still be present, exerting various degrees of pressure on elected politicians.[164] Therefore, in addition to any internal constraints which such institutions may set up, it is beneficial to have some checks on the decisions of the elected branches by an institution which is removed (as far as possible) from such concerns and pressures. Constitutional litigation also has other positive side-effects, such as empowering individuals who might otherwise be excluded from normal politics and enhancing the real (as opposed to formal) ability to participate in public life. Even if there were wonderful political methods of attempting to ensure Convention-compliance within Parliament, they would still be a case for constitutional review.

## Conclusion

In the course of this chapter and the last, I have put forward and defended an institutional argument for constitutional review under the HRA. For the most part, the argument was based on the institutional advantages of the courts in performing a constitutional review role in ensuring that legislation is compatible with Convention rights. In this chapter, I responded to important democratic objections to this type of review and in doing so, clarified why constitutional review is partly justified by the constraints it places on normal democratic politics, not in spite of those constraints. Constitutionalism helps to ensure that democratic government is held to the fundamental principles of the constitutional order and that democratic decisions are informed by the duty to protect Convention rights. Whilst acknowledging the value of democratic government, I tried to show that democratic values are not and should not be the whole of

---

[164] The deleterious impact of the electoral and popular orientation of democratic politics on counter-terrorist policy has led Gavin Phillipson to conclude that effective political protection of civil liberties in this politically sensitive context is a myth, see Phillipson (2006), 45ff, and that democratic sceptics should face up to the fact that 'their proposed electoral accountability to the violation of civil liberties is largely a fiction', see Phillipson (2006), 51 (written in the context of an examination of the political forces underlying the anti-terrorist legislation introduced by the Labour Government post 9/11).

our political morality. There are appropriate limits on political decision-making which applied no matter how much support the government has amongst the populace.

In these concluding comments, I wish to show how the limits placed by the courts on democratic institutions nonetheless support and strengthen democratic rule and give greater protection to the values which underlie that rule. In particular, I want to highlight the ways in which constitutional rights and popular participation are mutually supportive ideas.[165] First, constitutional litigation can provide an added channel of participation, which can benefit those who might have difficulty getting their voice heard in normal politics. Constitutional review is partly justified by the fact that it helps secure effective political participation by those who are disadvantaged in a system of unlimited participatory majoritarianism. So, the reasons for being committed to participation are also reasons for being committed to constitutional litigation under the HRA.[166] Second, not only does constitutional review provide a means of participation, it also offers enhanced protection for what we may call 'democratic rights'. These rights (such as the right to vote, associate, assemble, freedom of expression) are said to be constitutive of the democratic process, rather than limits on it. They are often thought to be 'preconditions for a well-functioning democracy'[167] and the fact that majorities cannot intrude on these rights should not obscure their democratic nature. If Convention rights receive enhanced protection through the mechanisms provided by the HRA, then democratic rights will also benefit from this enhanced protection. In this way, constitutional review can underpin and reinforce democratic rule by strengthening the protection of democratic rights. Finally, whilst constitutional review does indeed restrict democratic decision-making, it does so for reasons which are congruent with the reasons why we value participation in the first place. As we saw earlier, at the most basic level, the point of having participatory rights was to ensure that people could get their voice heard in the public forum. Furthermore, it was valued because it gave people a sense of belonging in their community, a feeling of being respected as a full member in that community. The restriction of democratic decision-making procedures by constitutional review does not reflect a disregard for any section of the community or a denial of any

---

[165] For an outline of some supportive links between rights and democracy, see also Jones (1994), 173–7.

[166] *Ibid.*, 177; the idea that the right to a hearing before the court and democratic participation rest on the same underlying values is also made by Eylon and Harel (2006), 1018ff.

[167] Holmes and Sunstein (1995), 278.

person's membership. On the contrary, it is partly justified on the basis that it helps to redress the loss of membership an individual may feel if they are effectively excluded from and disenfranchised by the political process. This sort of restriction is very different in its justification, from one which has the aim of diluting the influence of one particular group in society. Constitutional review shares the egalitarian premise of participation itself.

This chapter began by noting the tension between constitutionalism and democracy and ends by noting the mutually supportive connections which nonetheless exist between them. One of the purposes of adopting a procedural conception of democracy was to keep in full view the central fact that constitutional review limits the law-making powers of Parliament. Within the acknowledged limits of the adjudicative function, the HRA allows the courts to constrain the law-making powers of Parliament. Another way of approaching the tension between constitutionalism and democracy is to dissolve it, by emphasising the mutually supportive connections between them.[168] Those who adopt this strategy tend to argue that human rights and the rule of law underpin democracy itself, and that since the courts seek to protect those values, they are performing a democratic function. This way of resolving the tension is often supported by the judiciary, both in the case law and in extra-curial writings. Defending themselves against the charge that they are 'undemocratic', they sometimes argue that by upholding the rule of law, they protect, rather than undermine, the democratic ideal.[169] In this spirit, Lord Bingham declared in the *Belmarsh Prison* case that the courts were entitled to adjudicate robustly anti-terrorist legislation for compliance with Convention rights, because there is 'no distinction between the democratic institutions and the courts'.[170] Whilst I have sought to highlight the ways in which constitutional review and democracy can work together, supporting the same ultimate values, I do not go so far as to say that there is no distinction between democratic institutions and the courts. Following the procedural conception of democracy, the defining feature of *democratic* decision-making is that it is carried out in a way which is responsive in a meaningful way to popular opinion and input. It follows that judicial decision-making cannot be characterised as inherently 'democratic',

---

[168] Ely (1980); Jones (1994), 173–5; Holmes (1988); Holmes (1995); Sunstein (1988), 328; Dahl (1989), 182; Weale (1999), 171ff; Cohen (1998), 202.

[169] See e.g. Steyn (2006), 246; Steyn (2002a), 724; Hoffmann (1999b), 161. Laws (1995), 72ff; Laws (1998a), 254ff.

[170] *Belmarsh Prison* [2005] UKHL 71 at [42].

because judges are unelected and are not responsive in any meaningful way to popular views and opinions.[171] But this is in no way to deny the legitimacy of judicial decision-making, including the legitimacy of placing limits on democratic government. In this sense, my analysis supports Lord Bingham's conclusion, namely, that the courts must never abdicate their important and legitimate scrutinising function of the elected branches of government. This may not be democratic, but nor should it be stigmatised as illegitimate. Imposing and enforcing constitutional constraints on Parliament is one of the rationales of having constitutional review.

[171] That is not to say that they have absolutely no democratic credentials, but as Waldron points out, if comparative democratic legitimacy is the basis for the objection to constitutional review, pointing to the democratic credentials of the courts is 'a staggeringly inadequate response', Waldron (2006), 1391.

# 14

## Concluding comments and future directions

### Introduction

Rendering legislation compatible with Convention rights is a weighty responsibility. By placing much of this responsibility on the shoulders of the courts, the HRA gives judges strong powers of constitutional review, including the power to modify statutory provisions to conform with fundamental rights. It enables them to rely on principles of constitutionality which supplement statutory text and augment statutory meaning. The task of this book has been to evaluate the exercise of those powers and to probe more deeply, the profound issues of constitutional theory underlying their application. In many ways, the conclusions reached in this book will seem modest. One of the underlying themes has been that section 3 affirms and strengthens an interpretive approach which already existed in common law adjudication and, in turn, reflects the existence of constitutional principles embedded in the common law based on respect for fundamental rights. In arguing that section 3 should be understood as a strong presumption of statutory interpretation, I highlighted the way in which the interpretive duty under section 3 follows from the traditional function of the court as the 'constitutional arbiter' of statutory meaning, but post-HRA, the discharge of this function is more rights based. Though I endorsed the various creative methods of interpretation employed by the courts under section 3(1) (including those employed in *R. v. A*), I argued that judicial supervision must be tempered by judicial deference. Even when the courts are called upon to engage in constitutional review, they are still the secondary decision-maker. As such, they must pay an appropriate degree of respect and deference to the primary law-making ability of Parliament. Both of these ideas (judicial supervision and judicial deference) must be put in their rightful place in an account of the distribution of power between Parliament and the courts.

The modest nature of these conclusions should not obscure their fundamental implications for the theoretical foundations of British public law. Traditionally, debate about the nature and legitimacy of the judicial role in the UK Constitution, has tended to be conducted in highly polarised terms. The debate has been dominated (and, to my mind, atrophied) by the following contrasts: parliamentary sovereignty versus judicial supremacy, the political versus the legal constitution, democracy versus juristocracy, democratic dialogue versus judicial monopoly. Academic discussion of the legitimacy of constitutional review under the HRA has not been spared this type of polarisation. Echoing (and, no doubt, instantiating) all of the strident polar opposites just mentioned, those who celebrate and rejoice in the declaration of incompatibility are placed in one corner, and those who enthuse about a robust interpretive role for the courts, are placed in the other. Other polarisations are added into the familiar mix. *Either* one agrees that the most significant and valuable effect of the HRA is the parliamentary scrutiny of legislation via the Joint Committee of Human Rights (JCHR) *or* one supports the primacy or even dominance of the 'judicial perspective' on matters of Convention rights. The debate over which institution has 'the last word' under the HRA (Parliament or the courts) is another casualty of the polarised framework. The idea that the most important question under the HRA is 'who has the last word?' sometimes blinds interlocutors to the fact that the division of labour between Parliament and the courts is not a 'winners takes all' competition between them, with both institutions vying for ultimate supremacy. Parliament and the courts may have different functions, with the courts possessing the last legal word in some senses when a matter is litigated before them, and Parliament retaining a huge amount of legislative power to regulate Convention rights in primary legislation. As we saw in the last chapter, it also retains the power to violate those rights, or at least to test the concept of a proportionate infringement to its limits. The problem with framing the debate in terms of who gets the 'final say', is not only that it delivers the wrong answers, but that it asks the wrong question.

In this book, I have tried to eschew these polarisations. Rather than being forced to choose between 'the legal constitution' and 'the political constitution', I have attempted to do justice to the (often complementary) legal and political methods of controlling Parliament, in order to ensure that Convention rights are protected in primary legislation. The British Constitution includes (and has always included) both legal and political constraints on Parliament's law-making power, though for various historical reasons, the orthodox picture of the Constitution has tended to emphasise only the political dimensions, and underplay the legal. This book has endorsed the important constitutional duties discharged by the courts in enforcing Convention rights, but it has also supported whole-heartedly, the immensely important work of the JCHR. These are comple-mentary mechanisms for enhancing the protection of Convention rights in primary legislation. They are not antagonistic. I advocated a contextual approach to the judicial choice between sections 3 and 4, such that one cannot say, in the abstract, which option is more favourable. Assessing this issue is not a matter of choosing between 'judicial supremacy' or 'parliamentary supremacy' – it is a nuanced, contextual task of determin-ing the limits of judicial law-making in the context of a particular case, combined with a (sometimes difficult) determination about the consti-tutionally appropriate degree of restraint which may be required. In what remains, I wish to draw out some of the implications of this approach for two fundamental principles of the British Constitution: the separation of powers and parliamentary sovereignty.

## The division of labour under the HRA: collaboration not separation

In this book, I have avoided relying on the term 'the *separation* of powers', because this nomenclature lends credence to a view which underestimates the legitimate interaction between the three branches of government and the interdependence between them. In these concluding remarks, I will highlight a few points about the interaction between Parliament and the courts, in their joint task of enforcing and implementing Conven-tion rights. As I have presented it, the protection and enforcement of Convention rights in primary legislation under the HRA is a collabora-tive enterprise between all three branches of government. Leaving aside complications about the executive dominance of Parliament in the UK parliamentary system, we can say that Parliament possesses the primary law-making power to give effect to Convention rights in legislative form. However, if that legislation is challenged in HRA litigation, the courts have the power to determine the meaning of that legislation at the point of application and to correct for rights violations, as far as possible, through interpretation. In carrying out this task of rendering legislation compatible with Convention rights on a case-by-case basis within the acknowledged limits of the adjudicative function, there is no doubt that judges must give effect to legislation enacted by Parliament and respect its terms, ensuring that their interpretive decisions 'go with the grain' of Parliament's legislative schemes. However, 'giving effect to' primary legislation is not their only task. They also perform the important constitutional function of ensuring that legislation is compatible with Convention rights, even when the legislative terms unambiguously and clearly flout them. As such, the courts are not just servants of Parliament's will – they are also partners in a constitutional collaboration, who are charged with the (often creative) task of furthering, determining, applying and sometimes modifying that will in order to achieve a Convention-compatible result. In terms of its constitutional position as the primary law-maker, Parliament is undoubtedly the senior partner. It has the power to make law on any subject, at any time, and virtually for any reason. In contrast, the courts have a much more limited law-making ability, and are constrained by the terms of the legislation enacted by Parliament and their constitutional role as the secondary decision-maker. But this does not detract from the fact that, within those admitted limits, they wield significant constitutional power – power which respects Parliament's enactments to a degree, but one which renders them more just at the point of application.

Parliament and the courts perform different roles – even though those roles sometimes overlap and sometimes cause tensions between the branches of government.[1] Throughout the various chapters of this book, I have sought to articulate what those different roles are, primarily by highlighting the constitutional dimension of the court's role in ensuring that legislation is compatible with Convention rights and by reiterating the limited nature of their law-making ability. The peculiarly constitutional features of the courts' powers of review and the limits on their role *vis-à-vis* Parliament, were key to understanding the proper division of labour between the three branches of government on the one hand, and the important supervisory role which courts play in enforcing and upholding Convention rights, on the other. This book defended the legitimacy of constitutional review, whilst denying that it should be a substitute for democratic government.

In presenting the relationship between Parliament and the courts as one of partnership rather than that of 'master and servant', I concentrated on the courts' powers of interpretation under the HRA. At various points

---

[1] By emphasising the interaction and collaboration between Parliament and the courts, I do not wish to suggest that it is always a cosy relationship. Constitutional review sometimes has the effect of preventing the elected bodies from pursuing policies they would like, or at least pursuing them in ways they might wish. Governments are not always happy to be constrained by the law. This is only one of the many potential sources of tension between the branches of government.

in the book, I described statutory interpretation as 'an inter-institutional meeting' between Parliament and the courts and highlighted its important (though often overlooked) constitutional dimension. When interpreting statutes, the courts take a stance on their constitutional role *vis-à-vis* Parliament and in so doing, must carry out an important 'institutional evaluation' in which the doctrine of deference features so prominently. This is one of the many features of adjudication under the HRA which highlights the continuity with pre-HRA statutory interpretation and underscores the truth of Lord Hoffmann's observation that the UK courts 'apply principles of constitutionality little different from those which exist in countries where the power of the legislature is expressly limited by a constitutional document'.[2]

## Interaction, interpretation and the metaphor of 'dialogue'

The forms of interaction, collaboration and partnership between Parliament and the courts, made explicit by adjudication under the HRA, have led some commentators to suggest that the HRA embodies a distinctive form of constitutionalism, namely, the 'dialogue model'.[3] 'Dialogue' and 'dialogue theory' are very much in vogue in those jurisdictions which have inherited the Westminster system of parliamentary democracy, but nonetheless adopt either a formally entrenched Bill of Rights or a 'statutory Bill of Rights' similar to the HRA. The idea of 'dialogue' has spawned a daunting and voluminous literature with various academic commentators advocating different variants of 'dialogue theory'.[4] Whilst I cannot do justice to this sophisticated array of positions in these concluding remarks, I nonetheless wish to explain briefly why I resist relying on the metaphor of 'dialogue' to describe the collaboration, interaction and partnership between Parliament and the courts endorsed in this book.

The main value of the metaphor of dialogue is that it counters an erroneous view about the relationship between Parliament and the courts which, following the traditional nomenclature, insists on a strict 'separation' between the branches of government. According to this view, the courts should carry out their tasks in an institutional vacuum – they

---

[2] R. v. *Secretary of State for the Home Department, ex parte Simms* [2000] 2 A.C. 115 at 131, *per* Lord Hoffmann.

[3] See e.g. Klug (2001); Hickman (2005).

[4] For an overview and analysis of the debates surrounding the idea of 'dialogue', as well as references to the vast literature on the subject, see Roach (2001).

should decide on the law and pay no attention to what is happening in the 'political' sphere. The courts have no business interfering or indeed interacting with Parliament, and to the extent that they do, they violate the 'separation' of powers. The advantage of the dialogue metaphor is that it highlights and embraces the interaction between the three branches of government, as well as the overlap and interdependence between them. It highlights the fact that the judiciary is not the exclusive protector of human rights.

Despite this advantage when compared with the misleading idea of a strict separation between Parliament and the courts, the dialogue metaphor can itself mislead. Those who claim that the HRA enacts a 'dialogue model of constitutionalism' tend to suggest that section 4 is the primary or most obvious instantiation of the interaction between Parliament and the courts, because it lends itself most obviously to the 'conversational' metaphor. It is said that in order to have true dialogue (as opposed to monologue), both partners have to be able to contribute on equal terms. This then generates the conclusion that interpretation under section 3 should be eschewed, because by interpreting compatibly with Convention rights, the courts have 'the last word' and the grand colloquy between Parliament and the courts is shut down. Much more desirable would be a 'routine' reliance on the declaration of incompatibility, because this can be more easily mapped onto the dialogue metaphor.

I addressed some of the problems with this type of argument in chapter 5.[5] However, I did not make explicit some broader reservations about the metaphor of dialogue, on which it rests. Whilst the metaphor provides some initial insight about the interaction between Parliament and the courts, when it is taken more literally to suggest that Parliament and the courts must interact in the fashion of a real dialogue or conversation, its power to illuminate the division of labour between Parliament and the courts begins to disintegrate. It creates a number of misleading impressions. First, it contributes to the already common tendency in public law scholarship to underestimate the interactive nature of statutory interpretation and the immense constitutional significance of that interpretation.[6] That judicial determinations of statutory meaning are, for practical purposes, effectively final, may well be true, but this does not detract from the fact that statutory interpretation is an important inter-institutional meeting point between Parliament and the courts of immense constitutional significance. It also highlights an aspect of the

---

[5] Chapter 5, 128–33.    [6] See further Kavanagh (2007).

interdependence between Parliament and the courts which is underplayed by advocates of the 'dialogue model of constitutionalism'.

Second, the dialogue metaphor overstates both the significance and nature of the declaration of incompatibility under section 4. It leads us to believe that when the courts issue a declaration of incompatibility, it is just like a conversation between two people, where one suggests a particular course of action and the other considers that option, but then suggests another. It urges us to characterise the declaration of incompatibility as merely a 'provisional determination'[7] about what Convention rights require. A closer analysis of the nature of the declaration of incompatibility reveals that it is nothing like this sort of unfreighted 'conversation'. The legal and political implications of the declaration of incompatibility are such that Parliament is under a strong (legal and political) obligation to change the law in light of the declaration. The misleading nature of the 'dialogue' metaphor is compounded by the fact that its advocates sometimes recommend that the declaration of incompatibility *should* be conducted as if it were merely a conversation between two people. They say that there should be a frequent 'back and forth' between Parliament and the courts, with declarations of incompatibility becoming a routine feature of the relationship between the two institutions, thus invigorating the political discourse.[8] Apart from ignoring the crucially important remedial concerns in carrying out the judicial task of upholding Convention rights under the HRA, this recommendation tends to underestimate the importance and value of inter-institutional comity between the three branches of government and obscures the important legal and political implications of any judgment of the higher courts that a legal wrong has been committed. The 'theory' of dialogue becomes radically divorced from constitutional practice. By issuing a declaration of incompatibility, the courts are not simply 'throwing the ball back into Parliament's court'[9] – they are pronouncing on what the law requires.

In these brief comments, all I have done is sketched my general reservations about the metaphor of dialogue and I have not sought to capture anyone's views in particular on the subject. A comprehensive consideration of the advantages and disadvantages of this metaphor for constitutional theory, will have to await another occasion. Throughout the book, I have sought to disambiguate ways of thinking about constitutional review and

[7] Campbell (2001), 99; Nicol (2002), 439.
[8] Nicol (2006) 744ff advocates an 'uninhibited use of declarations of incompatibility' on this basis.
[9] Nicol (2006), 747.

analyse the cogency and appeal of some common metaphors and concepts employed to explain it. My main aim in these brief concluding comments has been to give some indication why I do not necessarily subscribe to a 'dialogue theory', despite the fact that I understand the relationship between Parliament and the courts as one of constitutional partnership.

## The HRA and parliamentary sovereignty

This leads us back to constitutional fundamentals and the doctrine of parliamentary sovereignty. In chapter 11, I argued that although the HRA preserves the formalities of the principle of parliamentary sovereignty, there were many features of the HRA which placed substantial (and substantive) limits on the law-making power of Parliament. As I presented it, those who wished to preserve the orthodox doctrine, were compelled to rely on a combination of what I called *the argument from remote possibility* and *the argument from lack of legal limits*. The former involved placing reliance on theoretical possibilities about assertions of 'sovereignty' which its proponents accepted would not occur except in situations which were far fetched and remote from reality. I questioned whether a theory which placed such crucial reliance on remote possibility is not, itself, open to question. The latter argument tended to emphasise the political nature of the constraints on Parliament's ability to make law, at the expense of overlooking or marginalising the important legal constraints which exist. Both of those arguments were found wanting, when pressed in service of the claim that the HRA preserves parliamentary sovereignty. There was a tendency to underplay both the legal and political constraints on Parliament's ability to make law which violates Convention rights. Moreover, the effort to preserve parliamentary sovereignty contrived, yet again, to paint a picture of the constitutional relationship between Parliament and the courts, which severely underestimated the courts' powers of constitutional review and the extent to which they constrain (indeed legitimately constrain) Parliament's law-making ability. Of course, those who are concerned with the substance of Parliament's law-making powers (not merely their formal justification in accordance with orthodox doctrine), were alert to the fact that the significant powers of interpretation employed by the courts under section 3, create some unease. They note that the approach taken to section 3, especially the stance taken in *R. v. A,* is not one that it is entirely easy to feel comfortable with in terms of the doctrine of parliamentary sovereignty. But in acknowledging the constitutional potency of interpretive powers and the extent to which they place substantive limitations on Parliament's law-making powers, one has already stepped outside the absolutist tendencies of the orthodox doctrine. That doctrine stresses above all else that Parliament can make or remake *any* law and that no other body can *invalidate* primary legislation. The HRA was carefully crafted so as to ensure that, formally speaking, the courts are not empowered to 'invalidate' any law. This emphasis on formalities to the exclusion of the important substantive limitations on Parliament's power to violate Convention rights, led Lord Woolf to question whether the HRA merely enables 'those who enjoy fairytales to continue to do so'.[10]

When discussing parliamentary sovereignty, one is aware that one is treading on sacred constitutional ground. No doubt, many will believe that I have not trod softly enough. They may point out that I have underestimated the resources contained in Dicey's account of the British Constitution. Alternatively, they may suggest that I have underestimated the constitutional importance of formalities for constitutional theory. Finally, they may observe that I have not explored some sophisticated methods of refining the orthodox doctrine of parliamentary sovereignty, which remove some of its shortcomings, especially its absolutism.

It is unsurprising that a close textual exegesis of Dicey's writings would reveal his awareness of the constitutional function of the courts in upholding the rule of law, and his support for judicial interpretations of statutes which depart from Parliament's intention in various ways.[11] However, the issue of the compatibility of the HRA with parliamentary sovereignty, does not hinge on such textual exegesis. The mesmerising mantra that Parliament can make and unmake any law it wishes, unconstrained by any other institution, has taken on a life of its own and has become the prism through which generations of public lawyers have been led to understand what British public law is all about. This mantra has become the orthodoxy against which measures like the HRA are judged, even if it can be shown that its author did not subscribe to it in all its absolutist requirements.

The second strategy of emphasising the importance of the ceremonial forms of parliamentary sovereignty, despite the fact that they have little grounding in constitutional reality, does not rescue the doctrine either. It seems to me that this strategy purchases the theory of parliamentary

---

[10]  Woolf (2008), 87; Joseph (2004), 321ff.
[11]  See e.g. Dicey (1914) 488–90, where he notes that judges may 'indirectly limit or possibly extend, the operation of a statute' in ways that amount to 'judicial legislation'.

sovereignty at too high a price – it accepts as fit for purpose, a theoretical product which only has a tenuous grounding in constitutional practice. If one believes (as I do) that the purpose of constitutional theory is to illuminate the salient features of the constitutional practice and to uncover the values and ideals to which those practices aspire, then the orthodox principle of parliamentary sovereignty is found severely wanting.[12] Not only does the doctrine of parliamentary sovereignty not match constitutional practice (because we all know that Parliament cannot make or unmake any law it wishes), it also posits a dubious normative claim, namely, the idea that Parliament should not be limited by law or the rule of law in exercising its law-making powers. Moreover, it urges us to view EU law, the HRA and the traditional doctrines of statutory interpretation upholding constitutional principle, as aberrations, as something we should regret. The potentially pervasive reach of all three of these sources of limitation on parliamentary sovereignty, undercuts the plausibility of the suggestion that they are aberrations. It misrepresents the nature of the UK Constitution, if we present them as exceptions. It is just one of the ways in which the hegemony of the orthodox principles threatens to impoverish our understanding of the UK Constitution.

The last strategy is to accept that the orthodox presentation of the doctrine suffers from obvious shortcomings, and meet those objections by refining the doctrine, so that it is not so divorced from constitutional practice, and takes seriously the aim of seeking to illuminate that practice, capturing the true nature of the principles to which the practice aspires. Whilst these endeavours are worthwhile (and are indeed unexplored in chapter 11), I suspect that the degree of refinement required to save the doctrine is so great as to warrant a rejection of it altogether. After all, the salient feature of the orthodox doctrine of parliamentary sovereignty is its absolutism. It asserts the *unqualified* law-making power of Parliament and an aversion to *any* legal limits on that power. We are told that it is precisely this immunity to legal limits which distinguishes a system based on parliamentary sovereignty, from a system based on constitutional supremacy because the signature feature of the latter is an open acceptance of legal/constitutional limits on the law-making power of Parliament. Once we begin to refine the doctrine of parliamentary sovereignty by admitting the legitimacy of legal limits on Parliament's

---

[12] For the methodological presuppositions of this approach to legal theoretical inquiry, see e.g. Raz (1979), 181; Raz (1994), 44.

power, then this begs the question of what value remains in articulating these issues in terms of sovereignty at all.

My instinct is that nothing is lost, and a great deal gained, by eliminating the idea of sovereignty, and beginning instead with an attempt to characterise accurately the constitutional division of labour between Parliament and the courts, which simultaneously captures the necessary and desirable interaction and interdependence between them, but also highlights the significant differences which nonetheless obtain. This enables us to adopt a starting point for enquiry, which is not captive to the view that it is constitutionally illegitimate to limit Parliament's law-making powers. It releases us from the idea of a territorial division between constitutional actors, each one fighting for its own dominion, in order to rule the others. In this book, all I have done is sow the seeds of such an account obliquely through an analysis of the operation of the HRA with respect to primary legislation. In so doing, I sought to articulate and justify the important supervisory function which the courts exercise over Parliament. Central to this account was the distinction between the primary and secondary decision-maker. This distinction gave rise to the doctrine of judicial deference, which highlighted the constraints under which judges labour when seeking to uphold Convention rights. There was no attempt to supplant parliamentary sovereignty with judicial sovereignty. These (and other) polar opposites were rejected as false dichotomies, and as a misleading starting point from which to explore the true nature of the relationship between Parliament and the courts. In my view, a fixation on parliamentary sovereignty (or indeed on the idea of competing sovereignties with each institution carving out 'a province, in which it is the sovereign'[13]), threatens to deflect us from examining the real questions about the relationship between Parliament and the courts and exploring the justifications for them. The constitutional role of supervision for legality, even under an entrenched Bill of Rights, does not make the courts a rival for legislative power. It makes it a wielder of constitutional power which, whilst requiring some justification in a democracy, should not be 'stigmatised'[14] as inherently illegitimate, simply because it places limits on the power of Parliament.[15]

Trevor Allan argues that 'section 3 reproduces a fundamental feature of the common law constitution; that the common law also recognises

---

[13]  Kyritsis (2007), 19.     [14]  *A and Others* [2005] 2 W.L.R. 87 at [42], *per* Lord Bingham.
[15]  For similar questioning about the inhibiting effects of the doctrine of parliamentary sovereignty on constitutional thinking, see Elias (2003).

basic constitutional rights and requires their protection against unjustified encroachments'.[16] If the HRA has truly changed the Constitution, it is largely because 'it was planted in fertile soil'.[17] Much of the argument contained in this book points to a similar conclusion. However, this book has also sought to explore the subtle ways in which the HRA is beginning to change the constitutional and legal culture and fertilise that soil in various ways. This is manifest in the unequivocal adoption by the House of Lords of the standard of proportionality. It is also evident in the immensely important *obiter dicta* contained in *Jackson*.[18] It is true that, as *obiter* comments, they do not, in themselves, change the law or the constitutional principles on which that law is based. But as a strong judicial assertion of their constitutional role and legitimacy, they are important signposts to a subtle change in constitutional culture. They mark a significant break with the traditional judicial tendency to underplay the substantive nature of the courts' constitutional jurisdiction when exercising that jurisdiction. They are a signal that the judiciary no longer wishes to play a part in maintaining fairytales. So, although the methods of enforcing Convention rights are continuous with those which the courts have used in the past, the most profound influence of the HRA may well be in the impetus it gives the judiciary to be more explicit and more assertive about the nature of their constitutional role.

The HRA is, albeit slowly, subtly and incrementally, contributing to a change in how we understand constitutional law and how we characterise the appropriate relationship between Parliament and the courts and has begun to unleash the constitutional imagination in order to reassess the theoretical foundations of UK constitutional law. These subtle changes fall short of giving us a 'new legal order'. The analysis contained in this book rests on the belief that whilst the HRA is a valuable measure, one which enhances the protection of Convention rights, it gives rise to a type of constitutional review which is continuous with prior constitutional practice. This is a more modest understanding of both the nature and potential of an instrument like the HRA, than that which is embraced by many commentators. Whilst the HRA does not (and could not) fill Britain's 'morality gap',[19] nor has the democratic sky fallen since 1998. We may not have a civic religion, but nor do we have 'colonels in horsehair'.[20]

---

[16] Allan (2006a), 46.    [17] *Ibid.*, 31
[18] *R. (Jackson)* v. *Attorney General* [2006] 1 A.C. 262.    [19] Klug (1997).
[20] Sedley (2002).

## Statutory Bills of Rights and strong-form
## constitutional review

It seems as if the HRA may also be unleashing the constitutional imagination beyond the borders of the UK. There is now a body of international scholarship which celebrates the HRA as an instance of 'the new Commonwealth model of constitutionalism'.[21] We are told that the manner in which Convention rights are enforced under the HRA:

> amounts to a deliberate rejection of the American model of constitutionalism with its perceived excesses of judicial power. In its place, an attempt has been made to create institutional balance, joint responsibility, and deliberative dialogue between courts and legislatures in the protection and enforcement of fundamental rights that [countries like the UK] believe the legitimate core claims of parliamentary sovereignty require.[22]

The distinctive feature of the HRA is claimed to be that it 'emphasises the supremacy of legislative judgment'.[23] Of particular importance to this view is the declaration of incompatibility. Section 4 is described as 'the most unique and widely commented upon aspect of the HRA'[24] and the factor which makes the HRA a 'unique constitutional instrument'.[25] Thus, Francesca Klug observes that '*in contrast to* other models of rights protection, the courts cannot strike down primary legislation under the HRA. Instead, dialogue is established between the courts, Parliament and Government'.[26] These distinctive features of the HRA have even led Jeremy Waldron to soften his once unwavering faith in unlimited democratic majoritarianism and his fervent opposition to constitutional review. Whilst still maintaining his general opposition to 'strong form judicial review'[27] on the American model, Waldron now argues that there is some justification for what he characterises as the 'weak form judicial review' which operates under the HRA.[28]

A full analysis of Waldron's distinction between 'strong-form' and 'weak-form' review must await another occasion. However, a few comments on the general thrust of this type of argument are nonetheless warranted here, because they go directly to the issue of the nature, purpose

---

[21] Gardbaum (2001), 707.     [22] *Ibid.*, 710.     [23] Hiebert (2006), 7.
[24] Klug and Wildbore (2007), 232.     [25] Nicol (2005), 455.
[26] Klug (2001), 370, emphasis added.
[27] In the USA, 'judicial review' is not confined to administrative law, and is the term used to describe the courts' powers to review primary legislation for compatibility with constitutional rights. I will use the term 'constitutional review' here.
[28] Waldron (2006). For discussion of Waldron's views, see Dyzenhaus (2008), 138–54.

and value of the HRA. On Waldron's analysis, 'strong-form' constitutional review is where the courts have the:

> authority to decline to apply a statute in a particular case (even though the statute on its own terms plainly applies in that case) or to modify the effect of a statute to make its application conform with individual rights (in ways that the statute itself does not envisage).[29]

He contrasts this with 'weak-form' constitutional review, where courts:

> may scrutinise legislation for its conformity to individual rights but they may not decline to apply it (or moderate its application) simply because rights would otherwise be violated.[30]

On these definitions, statutory interpretation under the HRA is clearly an instance of 'strong-form judicial review', since the HRA case law makes it crystal clear that section 3 empowers the courts to modify the effect of statutory provisions in ways the statute may not envisage.[31] As Lord Bingham stated in a recent case: 'Section 3 provides an important tool to be used where it is necessary and possible to modify domestic legislation to avoid incompatibility with the Convention rights protected by the Act.'[32] Anyone reading R. v. A or some of the other House of Lords decisions which rectify statutory terms in order to render them Convention-compatible, would find it hard to accept that the type of adjudication employed there could be described as 'weak'.

Waldron's characterisation of the HRA as an instance of 'weak-form' constitutional review does not rest on interpretive power alone. Naturally, it also rests on the limited nature of the declaration of incompatibility under section 4, which falls short of the power to 'strike down' primary legislation. The analysis contained in this book suggests that, as a judicial tool to secure the protection of Convention rights in primary legislation, the declaration of incompatibility is far from weak either. Apart from its lack of direct remedial consequences for the individual litigant, it is very similar, both in form and effect, to a judicial 'strike-down' power. One of the main consequences of its apparently weak form (i.e. its remedial vacuity for the individual litigant), is that it forces the courts to engage in highly creative interpretation, when they might have otherwise preferred

[29] Waldron (2006), 1354.    [30] Ibid., 1355.
[31] Note that on these definitions, pre-HRA statutory interpretation which relies on the constitutional presumptions of statutory interpretation, is also an instance of 'strong-form judicial review', because the presumptions also enable the courts to modify statutory terms and depart from parliamentary intent.
[32] R. (Al-Skeini) v. Secretary of State for Defence [2007] UKHL 26 at [15].

simply to declare it to be null and void and leave it to the legislature to carry out the required law reform in the appropriate manner. So, when one examines both the similarities between the declaration of incompatibility and the judicial 'strike-down' power, and considers the practice that they have, in every single case of their use, been accepted and 'followed' by the government and legislature, the alleged distinction between strong- and weak-form constitutional review begins to look less clear cut and less convincing, than may at first have seemed.[33]

The analysis in this book has one further consequence for the claim about the distinctiveness of the HRA (and other statutory Bills of Rights), and the favourable contrast often drawn between it and the US Constitution. Those who celebrate the declaration of incompatibility and similar mechanisms which seem to give the legislature the 'last word' on matters of human rights, say that the great value of statutory Bills of Rights is that they emphasise the supremacy of legislative judgment. If my analysis is correct, they do not in fact emphasise the supremacy of legislative judgment, because they do not in fact give Parliament the 'last word' on matters concerning Convention rights. The real distinctiveness of statutory Bills of Rights like the HRA lies in the fact that they *seem* to give Parliament the last word, whilst nonetheless giving the courts powers of constitutional review, not hugely dissimilar from those possessed by the US Supreme Court. The other truly distinctive feature of the HRA (in contrast to an explicitly entrenched Bill of Rights combined with an explicit judicial 'strike-down' power) is the premium it places on statutory interpretation as a means of achieving consistency with human rights. The denial of a formal or express power to strike down legislative provisions, brings into sharp relief the constitutional significance of statutory interpretation as a judicial technique for making legislation rights compatible. This important point is sometimes obscured when the focus is drawn to the declaration of incompatibility, which, as interpreted by the House of Lords, is used as a matter of last resort when interpretation cannot do the job of law reform required by the aim of achieving Convention-compatibility.

---

[33] In fact, I think that an argument can be made (though it cannot be substantiated here) that once the courts are given the power to review for compliance with fundamental rights, there is no such thing as 'weak-form' constitutional review. Of course, constitutional review can have minimal political effect if the judges are not sufficiently independent to carry out their constitutional role properly, or if they capitulate too often to the various political pressures to defer substantially to the Executive or legislature. But these are contingent political factors, which say nothing about the *form* of constitutional review which generally exists under a statutory Bill of Rights.

Of course, there is good reason why the declaration of incompatibility attracts attention. Like the notwithstanding clause in Canada,[34] it is a novel constitutional solution to the age-old tension between constitutionalism and democracy. However, the fact that neither the declaration of incompatibility in the UK, nor the notwithstanding clause in Canada, have been used to assert the alleged supremacy of legislative judgment with respect to fundamental rights to any significant degree, may indicate that neither the Canadian Charter of Rights and Freedoms nor the UK HRA, embody a distinctive form of constitutionalism which can be contrasted so easily, and so favourably, with the US Constitution.

There is one further feature of constitutional adjudication under the HRA, which strengthens the doubts about the tenability of a straightforward contrast between it and adjudication under an entrenched Bill of Rights on the American model. It is sometimes claimed that a great virtue of the HRA is that, in contrast to the US Bill of Rights, many of the Convention rights contain express limitation clauses, which allow the rights to be limited, if it is 'necessary in a democratic society.' When assessing whether proportionality applied to qualified and so-called unqualified rights, I concluded that the method of judicial reasoning appropriate to both of these categories of rights, was not different in kind, though it was superficially different in form and presentation. The use of limitation clauses severs the definition of the right from its limitation creating a formal two-stage approach to assessing the justification for limiting the right, whereas under the so-called 'unqualified rights', the question of the degree of, or justification for, violating the right took place within the definition of the right itself and the judicial attempt to determine its proper scope.[35] Thus, though different in form and presentation, the evaluation of both explicitly qualified and unqualified rights, was not substantially different in kind. I imagine that the same is true of adjudication under Bills of Rights which do not contain express limitation clauses. The rights under the American Constitution are not absolute and the American Supreme Court engages in a similar (and similarly difficult) enterprise of isolating the values underlying the constitutional right, evaluating the

---

[34] The marked avoidance of the 'notwithstanding clause' in Canada, has led some commentators to wonder if it is too late to 'rehabilitate' it, see Hiebert (2004), 169ff. Its underuse has led Jeremy Waldron to characterise Canada as having a system of 'strong-form judicial review', see Waldron (2006), 1356–7.

[35] For an examination of the effect of limitation clauses on constitutional adjudication in the context of Canadian constitutional law, see Miller (2008), 93ff.

(countervailing) justification for the legislative provision under constitutional challenge and assessing the degree or severity of that violation in the context of the individual case. In other words, the inclusion of express limitation clauses with respect to some Convention rights, may not necessarily show that the HRA is distinctive along this dimension either.

## Conclusion

None of this is meant to deny the immense importance and value of the HRA for UK constitutional law or the judicial ability to protect rights. Nor is it meant to underestimate the immense political achievement of securing its successful enactment. When one considers some of the dismissive comments made by various members of the Labour Government, about how irritating it is to have to comply with court judgments upholding Convention rights and how it inhibits them from waging the 'war on terror' unconstrained by legal limits, one can indeed marvel that it was ever enacted. However, in seeking to understand the nature and importance of the HRA and the true division of labour it negotiates between Parliament and the courts, one has to separate myth from reality. There is no point celebrating the HRA for something it does not achieve. It has plenty of real achievements, albeit ones that do not grab headlines. Those real achievements have been the subject-matter of this book.

Through a detailed examination of the case law, I have attempted to show how the HRA has strengthened constitutional review in subtle ways, enhancing both the ability and willingness of the courts to intervene to uphold fundamental constitutional principles grounded, ultimately, in the rule of law. It has also given Parliament and the Government added incentives to take Convention rights seriously, in their law-making and Executive functions. The JCHR has been of immense importance in strengthening parliamentary review of legislative proposals for compliance with Convention rights and helped to 'mainstream' human rights thinking in legislative and Executive decision-making. The Act has given the courts a renewed sense of legitimacy in carrying out their traditional function of interpreting legislation compatibly with fundamental constitutional principle, injecting that principle into statutes wherever possible. Right from the beginning, the courts showed that they were willing to rise to the constitutional challenge, by rendering legislation compatible with Convention rights, even in highly sensitive areas. Historically, English lawyers have been sceptical about rights-based legal reasoning. Now, the courts are placed under a duty to consider legislation in an explicitly rights-based manner. The contrast between *Ghaidan* and *Fitzpatrick* in chapter 4 provided a vivid illustration of just how significant this new 'rights-based' approach is, in generating different legal outcomes post-HRA and more favourable outcomes for litigants.

The HRA has given the courts the impetus they needed to shake off the deferential baggage of *Wednesbury* unreasonableness once and for all, and explicitly adopt a more probing mode of scrutiny, based on the principle of proportionality. Rather than starting from the premise that review of democratically elected bodies is somehow constitutionally suspect, the courts now start from the premise that they have a democratic mandate to engage in strong constitutional review. A legal culture of demanding justification for inroads on fundamental rights now prevails. The courts are more prepared to intervene.[36] The HRA has prompted the courts to reject the doctrine of non-justiciability in cases involving national security. Judicial abstention has given way to judicial supervision combined with an appropriate degree of judicial deference. The shift from non-justiciability to deference may not be the sort of seismic legal change feared by democratic sceptics and hoped by rights enthusiasts, but it is nonetheless a significant development, whose effects are being felt in subtle ways throughout the legal system, perhaps most especially by those who have fallen foul of draconian anti-terrorist legislation which violates Convention rights. Finally, the HRA provides a catalyst for judges, politicians and scholars, to rethink the theoretical foundations of the UK Constitution. This book has responded to that catalyst by attempting to evaluate the nature, scope and justification of constitutional review, in a way which is closely attentive to its practical application in the case law, whilst remaining sensitive to the deeper constitutional, political and theoretical questions which attend it.

---

[36] Lord Sedley has argued that even pre-HRA, the gradual retreat from *Wednesbury* was part of 'a move in the direction of a rights culture compatible with constitutional adjudication in a democracy', see Sedley (1995), 395.

# BIBLIOGRAPHY

Abraham, A. (2008a) 'The Ombudsman and "Paths to Justice": a Just Alternative or just an Alternative?' (2008) *Public Law* 1.

(2008b) 'The Ombudsman and Individual Rights' (2008) 61 *Parliamentary Affairs* 370.

(2008c) 'The Ombudsman as Part of the UK Constitution: a Contested Role?' (2008) 61 *Parliamentary Affairs* 206.

Alexander, L. (ed.) (2003) 'Is Judicial Review Democratic? a Comment on Harel' (2003) 22 *Law and Philosophy* 277.

Alexy, R. (2002) *A Theory of Constitutional Rights*. Oxford University Press.

Allan, J. (2006) 'Portia, Bassanio or Dick the Butcher? Constraining Judges in the Twenty-first Century' (2006) 17 *Kings College Law Journal* 1.

Allan, T. R. S. (1997) 'Parliamentary Sovereignty: Law, Politics, and Revolution' (1997) 113 *Law Quarterly Review* 443.

(2002) 'The Constitutional Foundations of Judicial Review: Conceptual Conundrum or Interpretative Inquiry?' (2002) 61 *Cambridge Law Journal* 87.

(2003) 'Constitutional Dialogue and the Justification of Judicial Review' (2003) 23 *Oxford Journal of Legal Studies* 563.

(2004a) 'Legislative Supremacy and Legislative Intention: Interpretation, Meaning and Authority' (2004) 63 *Cambridge Law Journal* 685.

(2004b) 'Common Law Reason and the Limits of Judicial Deference' in Dyzenhaus, D. (ed.) *The Unity of Public Law*. Oxford, Hart Publishing, 289.

(2006a) 'Parliament's Will and the Justice of the Common Law: the Human Rights Act in Constitutional Perspective' (2006) 59 *Current Legal Problems* 27.

(2006b) 'Human Rights and Judicial Review: a Critique of "Due Deference"' (2006) 65 *Cambridge Law Journal* 671.

Alston, P. (1999a) *Promoting Human Rights through Bills of Rights*. Oxford University Press.

(1999b) 'A Framework for the Comparative Analysis of Bills of Rights' in Alston, P. (ed.), 1.

Amos, M. (2006) *Human Rights Law*. Oxford, Hart Publishing.

(2007a) 'The Principle of Comity and the Relationship between British Courts and the European Court of Human Rights'. Society of Legal Scholars Annual Conference: Civil Liberties Section (unpublished paper).

(2007b) 'The Impact of the Human Rights Act on the United Kingdom's Performance before the European Court of Human Rights' (2007) *Public Law*
655.

Arai-Takahashi, Y. (2002) *The Margin of Appreciation Doctrine and the Principle of Proportionality in the Jurisprudence of the ECHR*. Antwerp,
Intersentia.

Arden, Lady J. (2004) 'The Interpretation of UK Domestic Legislation in the Light
of European Convention on Human Rights Jurisprudence' (2004) 25 *Statute
Law Review* 165.

Ashworth, A. (1991) 'Interpreting Criminal Statutes: a Crisis of Legality?' (1991)
107 *Law Quarterly Review* 419.

Atrill, S. (2003) 'Keeping the Executive in the Picture: a Reply to Professor Leigh'
(2003) *Public Law* 41.

Austin, R. (2007) 'The New Constitutionalism, Terrorism and Torture' (2007) 60
*Current Legal Problems* 79.

Bagshaw, R. (2006) 'Monetary Remedies in Public Law – Misdiagnosis and Mis-
prescription' (2006) 26 *Legal Studies* 4.

Bamforth, N. (1998) 'Parliamentary Sovereignty and the Human Rights Act 1998'
(1998) *Public Law* 572.

(2003a) 'A Constitutional Basis for Anti-discrimination Protection?' (2003) 119
*Law Quarterly Review* 215.

(2003b) 'Courts in a Multi-layered Constitution' in Bamforth, N. and Leyland,
P. (eds.) *Public Law in a Multi-Layered Constitution*. Oxford, Hart Publishing,
277.

(2004) 'Understanding the Impact and Status of the Human Rights Act 1998
within English Law'. Global Law Working Paper 10/04. NYU School of Law,
New York, www.1.law.nyu.edu/nyulawglobal/.

(2007) 'Same-sex Partnerships: Some Comparative Constitutional Lessons'
(2007) *European Human Rights Law Review* 47.

Bankowski, Z. and MacCormick, N. (1991) 'Statutory Interpretation in the United
Kingdom' in MacCormick, N. and Summers, R. (eds.) *Interpreting Statutes:
a Comparative Study*. Aldershot, Dartmouth Press, 359.

Barak, A. (2002) 'A Judge on Judging: the Role of a Supreme Court in a Democracy'
(2002) 116 *Harvard Law Review* 16.

Barber, N. (2000) 'Sovereignty Re-examined: the Courts, Parliament, and Statutes'
(2000) 20 *Oxford Journal of Legal Studies* 131.

Baum, L. (2002) 'The Implementation of the United States Supreme Court Decisions' in Rogowski, R. and Gawron, T. (eds.) *Constitutional Courts in Comparison: the US Supreme Court and the German Federal Constitutional Court*.
Oxford, Berghahn Books, 219.

Beatson, J., Matthews, M. and Elliott, M. (2005) *Administrative Law*. Oxford
University Press.

Beitz, C. R. (1983) 'Procedural Equality in Democratic Theory: a Preliminary Examination' in Pennock, R. and Chapman, J. (eds.) *Nomos Xxv: Liberal Democracy.* New York University Press, 69.

Bell, J. (1983) *Policy Arguments in Judicial Decisions,* Oxford, Clarendon Press.

Bennion, F. (2000) 'What Interpretation is 'Possible' under s.3(1) of the Human Rights Act' (2000) *Public Law* 77.

(2002) *Statutory Interpretation: a Code.* London, Butterworths.

Bentham, J. (1843) *The Works of Jeremy Bentham. Published under the Superintendence of His Executor John Bowring.* Edinburgh, W. Tait.

Besson, S. (2005) 'The Paradox of Democratic Representation. On Whether and How Disagreement Should Be Represented' in Wintgens, L. J. (ed.) *The Theory and Practice of Legislation: Essays in Legisprudence.* Aldershot, Ashgate, 125.

BeVier, L. R. (1984) 'Judicial Restraint: an Argument from Institutional Design' (1984) *17 Harvard Journal of Law & Public Policy* 7.

Bickel, A. (1961) 'The Supreme Court 1960 Term. Foreword: the Passive Virtues' (1961) *75 Harvard Law Review* 40.

(1962) *The Least Dangerous Branch.* New Haven, Yale University Press.

Bingham, Lord T. (1996/7) 'The Courts and the Constitution' (1996/7) 7 *Kings College Law Journal* 12.

(1998) 'Incorporation of the ECHR: the Opportunity and the Challenge' (1998) 2 *Jersey Law Review* 257.

(2006) 'The Judges: Active or Passive?' (2006) 139 *Proceedings of the British Academy* 55.

Birch, D. (2000) 'A Better Deal for Vulnerable Witnesses?' (2000) *Criminal Law Review* 223.

(2002) 'Rethinking Sexual History Evidence: Proposals for Fairer Trials' (2002) *Criminal Law Review* 531.

Black-Branch, J. (2002) 'Parliamentary Supremacy or Political Expediency?: the Constitutional Position of the Human Rights Act under British Law' (2002) 23 *Statute Law Review* 59.

Blake, N. (2002) 'Importing Proportionality: Clarification or Confusion' (2002) 1 *European Human Rights Law Review* 19.

Boateng, P. and Straw, J. (1997) 'Bringing Rights Home: Labour's Plans to Incorporate the European Convention on Human Rights into United Kingdom Law' (1997) 1 *European Human Rights Law Review* 71.

Bogdanor, V. (2004) 'Our New Constitution' (2004) 120 *Law Quarterly Review* 242.

Bonner, D. (2007) *Executive Measures, Terrorism and National Security: Have the Rules of the Game Changed?* Aldershot, Ashgate.

Bonner, D., Fenwick, H. and Harris-Short, S. (2003) 'Judicial Approaches to the Human Rights Act 1998' (2003) 52 *International and Comparative Law Quarterly* 549.

Bradley, A. (2003) 'Judicial Independence under Attack' (2003) *Public Law* 397.

Bradley, A. and Ewing, K. (2003) *Constitutional and Administrative Law*. Harlow, Pearson Education.

Brennan, W. (1989) 'Why Have a Bill of Rights?' (1989) 9 *Oxford Journal of Legal Studies* 425.

Brown, L. (1994) 'Public Interest Immunity' (1994) *Public Law* 579.

Browne-Wilkinson, Lord N. (1992) 'The Infiltration of a Bill of Rights' (1992) *Public Law* 397.

Buss, S. (1999) 'Appearing Respectful: the Moral Significance of Manners' (1999) 109 *Ethics* 795.

Butler, A. (2000) 'Strengthening the Bill of Rights' (2000) 31 *Victoria University of Wellington Law Review* 129.

Calhoun, C. (2000) 'The Virtue of Civility' (2000) 29 *Philosophy and Public Affairs* 251.

Campbell, T. (2001) 'Incorporation through Interpretation' in Campbell, T., Ewing, K. and Tomkins, A. (eds.) *Sceptical Essays on Human Rights*. Oxford University Press, 79.

Chamberlain, M. (2003) 'Democracy and Deference in Resource Allocation Cases: a Riposte to Lord Hoffmann' (2003) 2003 *Judicial Review* 12.

Clapham, A. (1999) 'The European Convention on Human Rights in the British Courts: Problems Associated with the Incorporation of International Human Rights' in Alston, P. (ed.), 95.

Clayton, R. (2001) 'Regaining a Sense of Proportion: the Human Rights Act and the Proportionality Principle' (2001) *European Human Rights Law Review* 504.

(2002a) 'The Limits of what's "Possible": Statutory Construction under the Human Rights Act' (2002) *European Human Rights Law Review* 559.

(2004) 'Judicial Deference and "Democratic Dialogue": the Legitimacy of Judicial Intervention under the Human Rights Act 1998' (2004) *Public Law* 33.

(2007) 'The Human Rights Act Six Years on: Where are we now?' (2007) *European Human Rights Law Review* 11.

Clayton, R. and Tomlinson, H. (2000) *The Law of Human Rights*. Oxford University Press.

Cohen, J. (1998) 'Democracy and Liberty' in Elster, J. (ed.) *Deliberative Democracy*. Cambridge University Press, 185.

Cooke, Lord R. (1999) 'The British Embracement of Human Rights' (1999) *European Human Rights Law Review* 243.

(2004) 'The Road Ahead for the Common Law' (2004) 53 *International and Comparative Law Quarterly* 273.

Craig, P. (1991) 'Sovereignty of the United Kingdom Parliament after *Factortame*' (1991) 11 *Yearbook of European Law* 221.

(1999a) 'Unreasonableness and Proportionality in UK Law' in Ellis, E. (ed.) *The Principle of Proportionality in the Laws of Europe*. Oxford, Hart Publishing, 85.

(1999b) *Administrative Law*. London, Sweet & Maxwell.

(2001) 'The Courts, the Human Rights Act and Judicial Review' (2001) 117 *Law Quarterly Review* 589.

(2003) *Administrative Law*. London, Sweet & Maxwell.

Cross, R. (1995) *Statutory Interpretation*. London, Butterworths.

Cross, R. and Harris, J. W. (1991) *Precedent in English Law*. Oxford University Press.

Dahl, R. A. (1989) *Democracy and its Critics*. New Haven, Yale University Press.

Daley, J. (2000) 'Defining Judicial Restraint' in Campbell, T. and Goldsworthy, J. (eds.) *Judicial Power, Democracy and Legal Positivism*. Aldershot, Ashgate/ Dartmouth, 279.

Darrow, M. and Alston, P. (1999) 'Bills of Rights in Comparative Perspective' in Alston, P. (ed.), 465.

De Búrca, G. (1993) 'The Principle of Proportionality and its Application in EC Law' (1993) 13 *Yearbook of European Law* 105.

(1997) 'Proportionality and *Wednesbury* Unreasonableness: the Influence of European Legal Concepts on UK Law' (1997) 3 *European Public Law* 561.

Dicey, A. V. (1914) *Lectures on the Relation between Law and Public Opinion in England during the Nineteenth Century*, 2nd edition. London, Macmillan.

(1959) *Introduction to the Study of the Law of the Constitution*, 10th edition. London, Macmillan.

Dworkin, R. (1977) *Taking Rights Seriously*. London, Duckworth.

(1985) *A Matter of Principle*, Cambridge, Mass., Harvard University Press.

(1986) *Law's Empire*, Cambridge, Mass., Harvard University Press.

(1987) 'What is Equality? Part 4: Political Equality' (1987) 22 *University of San Francisco Law Review* 1.

(1995) 'Constitutionalism and Democracy' (1995) 3 *European Journal of Philosophy* 2.

(1996) *Freedom's Law: the Moral Reading of the American Constitution*. Cambridge, Mass., Harvard University Press.

(1997) 'The Arduous Virtue of Fidelity: Originalism, Scalia, Tribe and Nerve' (1997) 65 *Fordham Law Review* 1249.

Dyer, C. (1998) 'Transsexual Mother Goes Public'. *The Guardian*, 13 October 1998.

(2002) 'Sex Change Victory after 30 Years'. *The Guardian*, 10 December 2002.

Dyzenhaus, D. (1997) 'The Politics of Deference: Judicial Review and Democracy' in Taggart, M. (ed.) *The Province of Administrative Law*. Oxford, Hart Publishing, 279.

(2004) 'Intimations of Legality Amid the Clash of Arms' (2004) 2 *International Journal of Constitutional Law* 244.

(2007) 'Deference, Security and Human Rights' in Goold, B. and Lazarus, L. (eds.) *Security and Human Rights*. Oxford, Hart Publishing, 125.

(2008) 'The Incoherence of Constitutional Positivism' in Huscroft, G. (ed.) *Expounding the Constitution: Essays in Constitutional Theory*. Cambridge University Press, 138.

Edwards, R. (2000) 'Reading Down Legislation under the Human Rights Act' (2000) 20 *Legal Studies* 353.

 (2002) 'Judicial Deference under the Human Rights Act' (2002) 65 *Modern Law Review* 859.

Eisgruber, C. (2001) *Constitutional Self-Government.* Cambridge, Mass., Harvard University Press.

Elias, Rt Hon Dame, S. (2003) 'Sovereignty in the Twenty-first Century: another Spin on the Merry-Go-Round' (2003) 14 *Public Law Review* 148.

Elkin, S. (1993) 'Constitutionalism Old and New' in Elkin, S. and Soltan, K. (eds.) *A New Constitutionalism: Designing Political Institutions for a Good Society.* University of Chicago Press, 20.

Elliott, M. (2001a) 'Scrutiny of Executive Decisions under the Human Rights Act 1998: Exactly how "Anxious"?' (2001) 6 *Judicial Review* 166.

 (2001b) 'The Human Rights Act 1998 and the Standard of Substantive Review' (2001) 60 *Cambridge Law Journal* 301.

 (2002) 'Parliamentary Sovereignty and the New Constitutional Order: Legislative Freedom, Political Reality and Convention' (2002) 22 *Legal Studies* 340.

 (2003) 'Embracing Constitutional Legislation: Towards Fundamental Law?' (2003) 54 *Northern Ireland Legal Quarterly* 25.

 (2004) 'Parliamentary Sovereignty under Pressure' (2004) 2 *International Journal of Constitutional Law* 545.

 (2006) 'The Sovereignty of Parliament, the Hunting Ban and the Parliament Acts' (2006) 65 *Cambridge Law Journal* 1.

 (2007a) 'Bicameralism, Sovereignty and the Unwritten Constitution' (2007) 5 *International Journal of Constitutional Law* 370.

 (2007b) 'The "War on Terror" and the United Kingdom's Constitution' (2007) *European Journal of Legal Studies* 1.

Ely, J. H. (1980) *Democracy and Distrust: a Theory of Judicial Review.* Cambridge, Mass., Harvard University Press.

Endicott, T. (1996) 'Linguistic Indeterminacy' (1996) 16 *Oxford Journal of Legal Studies* 667.

 (1999) 'The Impossibility of the Rule of Law' (1999) 19 *Oxford Journal of Legal Studies* 1.

 (2002) ' "International Meaning": Comity in Fundamental Rights Adjudication' (2002) 13 *International Journal of Refugee Law* 280.

 (2003a) 'Constitutional Logic' (2003) 53 *University of Toronto Law Journal* 201.

 (2003b) 'The Reason of the Law' (2003) 48 *American Journal of Jurisprudence* 83.

Ewing, K. (1996) 'Human Rights, Social Democracy and Constitutional Reform' in Gearty, C. and Tomkins, A. (eds.) *Understanding Human Rights.* London, Mansell.

(1999) 'The Human Rights Act and Parliamentary Democracy' (1999) 62 *Modern Law Review* 79.

(2001) 'The Unbalanced Constitution' in Campbell, T., Ewing, K. and Tomkins, A. (eds.) *Sceptical Essays on Human Rights.* Oxford University Press, 103.

(2004) 'The Futility of the Human Rights Act' (2004) *Public Law* 829.

(2006) *The Funding of Political Parties – the Trade Union Case for Reform,* London, Amicus.

Ewing, K. and Gearty, C. (1990) *Freedom under Thatcher: Civil Liberties in Modern Britain.* Oxford, Clarendon Press.

(1997) 'Rocky Foundations for Labour's New Rights' (1997) *European Human Rights Law Review* 146.

Eylon, Y. and Harel, A. (2006) 'The Right to Judicial Review' (2006) 92 *Virginia Law Review* 991.

Fabre, C. (2000a) 'A Philosophical Argument for a Bill of Rights' (2000) 30 *British Journal of Political Science* 77.

(2000b) *Social Rights under the Constitution: Government and the Decent Life.* Oxford University Press.

Feldman, D. (1992) 'Public Interest Litigation and Constitutional Theory' (1992) 55 *Modern Law Review* 44.

(1998) 'Remedies for Violations of Convention Rights under the Human Rights Act' (1998) 6 *European Human Rights Law Review* 691.

(1999a) 'The Human Rights Act 1998 and Constitutional Principles' (1999) 19 *Legal Studies* 165.

(1999b) 'Proportionality and the Human Rights Act 1998' in Ellis, E. (ed.) *The Principle of Proportionality in the Laws of Europe.* Oxford, Hart Publishing, 117.

(2002) 'Parliamentary Scrutiny of Legislation and Human Rights' (2002) *Public Law* 323.

(2004) 'The Impact of Human Rights on the UK Legislative Process' (2004) 25 *Statute Law Review* 91.

(2006) 'Human Rights, Terrorism and Risk: the Role of Politicians and Judges' (2006) *Public Law* 364.

(2007) 'Institutional Roles and Meanings of "Compatibility" under the Human Rights Act 1998' in Fenwick, H., Phillipson, G. and Masterman, R. (eds.) *Judicial Reasoning under the UK Human Rights Act.* Cambridge University Press, 87.

Fenwick, H. (2000) *Civil Rights: New Labour, Freedom and the Human Rights Act.* Essex, Pearson Education Ltd.

(2007) *Civil Liberties and Human Rights.* Oxford, Routledge-Cavendish.

Fenwick, H. and Phillipson, G. (2006) *Media Freedom under the Human Rights Act.* Oxford University Press.

Finnis, J. (1985) 'The Fairy Tale's Moral' (1999) 115 *Law Quarterly Review* 170.

Fordham, M. (2004) 'Common Law Illegality of Ousting Judicial Review' (2004) *Judicial Review* 86.

Fordham, M. and De La Mare, T. (2001) 'Identifying the Principles of Proportionality' in Jowell, J., Cooper, J. and Owers, A. (eds.) *Understanding Human Rights Principles*. Oxford, Hart Publishing, 27.

Fredman, S. (2000) 'Judging Democracy: The Role of the Judiciary under the HRA 1998' (2000) 53 *Current Legal Problems* 99.

    (2001) 'Scepticism under Scrutiny: Labour Law and Human Rights' in Campbell, T., Ewing, K. and Tomkins, A. (eds.) *Sceptical Essays on Human Rights*. Oxford University Press, 197.

Freeman, S. (1990) 'Constitutional Democracy and the Legitimacy of Judicial Review' (1990) 9 *Law and Philosophy* 327.

Gardbaum, S. (2001) 'The New Commonwealth Model of Constitutionalism' (2001) 49 *American Journal of Comparative Law* 707.

Gardner, J. (2001) 'Legal Positivism: $5^{1}/_{2}$ Myths' (2001) 46 *American Journal of Jurisprudence* 199.

Gauthier, D. (1993) 'Constituting Democracy' in Copp, D., Hampton, J. and Roemer, J. (eds.) *The Idea of Democracy*. Cambridge University Press, 314.

Gavison, R. (1999) 'The Role of Courts in Rifted Democracies' (1999) 33 *Israel Law Review* 216.

Gearty, C. (2001) 'Tort Law and the Human Rights Act' in Campbell, T., Ewing, K. and Tomkins, A. (eds.) *Sceptical Essays on Human Rights*. Oxford University Press, 243.

    (2002) 'Reconciling Parliamentary Democracy and Human Rights' (2002) 118 *Law Quarterly Review* 248.

    (2003a) 'Civil Liberties and Human Rights' in Bamforth, N. and Leyland, P. (eds.) *Public Law in a Multi-Layered Constitution*. Oxford, Hart Publishing, 371.

    (2003b) 'Revisiting Section 3(1) of the Human Rights Act' (2003) 119 *Law Quarterly Review* 551.

    (2004) *Principles of Human Rights Adjudication*. Oxford University Press.

    (2005a) '11 September 2001, Counter-Terrorism and the Human Rights Act' (2005) 32 *Journal of Law and Society* 18.

    (2005b) 'Human Rights in an Age of Counter-Terrorism: Injurious, Irrelevant or Indispensable?' (2005) 58 *Current Legal Problems* 25.

Geiringer, C. (2005) 'Its Interpretation, Jim, but Not as We Know It: *Ghaidan* v. *Godin-Mendoza*, the House of Lords and Rights-Consistent Interpretation' in Morris, P. and Greatrex, H. (eds.) Human Rights Research (Victoria Human Rights Programme, 2005).

    (2008) 'The Principle of Legality and the Bill of Rights Act: a Critical Examination of *R. v. Hansen*' (2007) 6 *New Zealand Journal of Public and International Law* 59.

Gewirth, A. (1982) *Human Rights: Essays on Justification and Applications.* University of Chicago Press.

(1996) *The Community of Rights.* University of Chicago Press.

Goldsworthy, J. (1999) *The Sovereignty of Parliament: History and Philosophy.* Oxford University Press.

(2004) 'Parliamentary Sovereignty and the Statutory Interpretation' in Bigwood, R. (ed.) *The Statute: Making and Meaning.* Wellington, Lexis-Nexis, 187.

Greenawalt, K. (1983) 'Policy, Rights, and Judicial Decision' in Cohen, M. (ed.) *Ronald Dworkin and Contemporary Jurisprudence.* Totowa, N.J., Rowman & Allanheld.

Greenberg, D. (2006) 'The Nature of Legislative Intention and its Implications for Legislative Drafting' (2006) 27 *Statute Law Review* 15.

Hannett, S. (2003) 'Third Party Intervention: in the Public Interest?' (2003) *Public Law* 128.

Hare, I. (2000) 'Privacy and the Gay Right to Fight' (2000) 59 *Cambridge Law Journal* 6.

Harel, A. (2003) 'Rights-Based Judicial Review: a Democratic Justification' (2003) 22 *Law and Philosophy* 247.

Harlow, C. and Rawlings, R. (1992) *Pressure through Law.* London; New York, Routledge.

Harris, D. J., O'Boyle, M. and Warbrick, C. (1995) *Law of the European Convention on Human Rights,* London, Butterworths.

Hart, H. L. A. (1961) *The Concept of Law.* Oxford University Press.

(1982) *Essays on Bentham: Jurisprudence and Political Theory.* Oxford, Clarendon Press.

(1994) *The Concept of Law.* Oxford, Clarendon Press.

Hayek, F. (1960) *The Constitution of Liberty.* London, Routledge & Kegan Paul.

(1973) *Law, Legislation and Liberty: a New Statement of the Liberal Principles of Justice and Political Economy.* London, Routledge & Kegan Paul, vol. 1 'Rules and Order'.

Henderson, A. (2000) 'Readings and Remedies: Section 3(1) of the HRA and Rectifying Constructions' (2000) 5 *Judicial Review* 258.

Hickman, T. (2005) 'Constitutional Dialogue, Constitutional Theories and the Human Rights Act 1998' (2005) *Public Law* 306.

(2008) 'The Courts and Politics after the Human Rights Act: a Comment' (2008) *Public Law* 84.

Hiebert, J. (2004) 'Is it too Late to Rehabilitate Canada's Notwithstanding Clause?' in Huscroft, G. and Brodie, I. (eds.) *Constitutionalism in the Charter Era.* Markham, Ontario, Lexis-Nexis, 169.

(2006) 'Parliamentary Bills of Rights: an Alternative Model?' (2006) 69 *Modern Law Review* 7.

Hoffmann, Lord L. (1999a) 'The Influence of the European Principle of Proportionality upon UK Law' in Ellis, E. (ed.) *The Principle of Proportionality in the Laws of Europe.* Oxford, Hart Publishing, 107.

(1999b) 'Human Rights and the House of Lords' (1999) 62 *Modern Law Review* 159.

(2002) 'The Combar Lecture 2001: Separation of Powers' (2002) *Judicial Review* 137.

Hogg, P. (2003) *Constitutional Law of Canada.* Scarborough, Ontario, Thomson-Carswell, student edition.

Holmes, S. (1988) 'Precommitment and the Paradox of Democracy' in Elster, J. and Slagstad, R. (eds.) *Constitutionalism and Democracy.* Cambridge University Press, 195.

(1995) *Passions and Constraint: On the Theory of Liberal Democracy.* University of Chicago Press.

Holmes, S. and Sunstein, C. (1995) 'The Politics of Constitutional Revision in Eastern Europe' in Levinson, S. (ed.) *Responding to Imperfection: the Theory and Practice of Constitutional Amendment.* Princeton University Press, 275.

Hope, Lord D. (1999) 'The Human Rights Act 1998: the Task of the Judges' (1999) 20 *Statute Law Review* 185.

(2000) 'Human Rights – Where are we now?' (2000) 5 *European Human Rights Law Review* 439.

Horder, J. (2006) 'Moral Arguments in Interpreting Statutes' in Endicott, T., Getzler, J. and Peel, E. (eds.) *Properties of Law: Essays in Honour of Jim Harris.* Oxford University Press, 69.

Hunt, M. (1997) *Using Human Rights Law in English Courts.* Oxford, Hart Publishing.

(2003) 'Sovereignty's Blight: Why Contemporary Public Law Needs a Doctrine of "Due Deference"' in Bamforth, N. and Leyland, P. (eds.) *Public Law in a Multi-Layered Constitution.* Oxford, Hart Publishing, 337.

Hyland, J. (1995) *Democratic Theory: the Philosophical Foundations.* Manchester University Press.

Ingram, A. (1994) *A Political Theory of Rights.* Oxford, Clarendon Press.

Irvine, Lord D. (1996) 'Judges and Decision-Makers: the Theory and Practice of *Wednesbury* Review' (1996) *Public Law* 59.

(1999) 'Activism and Restraint: Human Rights and the Interpretative Process' (1999) *European Human Rights Law Review* 350.

(2003a) *Human Rights, Constitutional Law and the Development of the English Legal System.* Oxford, Hart Publishing.

(2003b) 'The Impact of the Human Rights Act: Parliament, the Courts and the Executive' (2003) *Public Law* 308.

Jaconelli, J. (1979) 'Constitutional Review and Section 2(4) of the European Communities Act 1972' (1979) 28 *International and Comparative Law Quarterly* 65.

Jones, P. (1994) *Rights*. Basingstoke, The Macmillan Press.

Jones, T. (1995) 'The Devaluation of Human Rights under the European Convention' (1995) *Public Law* 430.

Joseph, P. (2004) 'Parliament, the Courts, and the Collaborative Enterprise' (2004) 15 *King's College Law Journal* 321.

Jowell, J. (1999) 'Of *Vires* and Vacuums: the Constitutional Context of Judicial Review' (1999) *Public Law* 448.

(2000) 'Beyond the Rule of Law: Towards Constitutional Judicial Review' (2000) *Public Law* 669.

(2003a) 'Judicial Deference and Human Rights: a Question of Competence' in Craig, P. and Rawlings, R. (eds.) *Law and Administration in Europe: Essays in Honour of Carol Harlow*. Oxford University Press, 67.

(2003b) 'Judicial Deference: Servility, Civility, or Institutional Capacity?' (2003) *Public Law* 592.

(2006) 'Parliamentary Sovereignty under the New Constitutional Hypothesis' (2006) *Public Law* 562.

Jowell, J. and Cooper, J. (eds.) (2003) 'Introduction' in Jowell, J. and Cooper, J. (eds.) *Delivering Rights: How the Human Rights Act is Working*. Oxford, Hart Publishing, 1.

Jowell, J. and Lester, Lord A. (1987) 'Beyond *Wednesbury*: Substantive Principles of Administrative Law' (1987) *Public Law* 368.

(1988) 'Proportionality: Neither Novel nor Dangerous' in Jowell, J. and Oliver, D. (eds.) *New Directions in Judicial Review*. London, Stevens, 51.

Kateb, G. (1983) 'Remarks on Robert B. Mckay, "Judicial Review in a Liberal Democracy"' *Nomos XXV: Liberal Democracy*. New York University Press, 145.

Kavanagh, A. (2003a) 'The Idea of a Living Constitution' (2003) 16 *Canadian Journal of Law and Jurisprudence* 55.

(2003b) 'Participation and Judicial Review: a Reply to Jeremy Waldron' (2003) 22 *Law and Philosophy* 451.

(2004a) 'Comparative Perspectives on Constitutional Law: Implications for the Human Rights Act 1998' (2004) *European Public Law* 161.

(2004b) 'The Elusive Divide between Interpretation and Legislation under the Human Rights Act 1998' (2004) 24 *Oxford Journal of Legal Studies* 259.

(2004c) 'Statutory Interpretation and Human Rights after Anderson: a More Contextual Approach' (2004) *Public Law* 537.

(2004d) 'The Role of a Bill of Rights in Reconstructing Northern Ireland' (2004) 26 *Human Rights Quarterly* 956.

(2005a) '*Pepper* v. *Hart* and Matters of Constitutional Principle' (2005) 121 *Law Quarterly Review* 98.

(2005b) 'Unlocking the Human Rights Act: the "Radical" Approach to Section 3(1) Revisited' (2005) *European Human Rights Law Review* 260.

(2006) 'The Role of Parliamentary Intention in Adjudication under the Human Rights Act 1998' (2006) 26 *Oxford Journal of Legal Studies* 179.

(2007) 'Choosing between Section 3 and 4 of the Human Rights Act 1998: Judicial Reasoning after *Ghaidan* v. *Mendoza*' in Fenwick, H., Phillipson, G. and Masterman, R. (eds.) *Judicial Reasoning under the UK Human Rights Act.* Cambridge University Press, 114.

(2008) 'Deference or Defiance? the Limits of the Judicial Role in Constitutional Adjudication' in Huscroft, G. (ed.) *Expounding the Constitution: Essays in Constitutional Theory.* Cambridge University Press, 184.

Keene, D. (2007) 'Principles of Deference under the Human Rights Act' in Fenwick, H., Phillipson, G. and Masterman, R. (eds.) *Judicial Reasoning under the UK Human Rights Act.* Cambridge University Press, 206.

Keir, D. and Lawson, F. H. (1979) *Cases in Constitutional Law.* Oxford, Clarendon Press.

Kerrigan, K. and Plowden, P. (2007) 'Worth the Paper Its Written On? Declarations of Incompatibility and Exhaustion of Domestic Remedies in Convention Law'. Society of Legal Scholars Annual Conference. Durham.

Kibble, N. (2000) 'The Sexual History Provisions: Charting a Course between Inflexible Legislative Rules and Wholly Untrammelled Judicial Discretion?' (2000) *Criminal Law Review* 274.

(2001) 'The Relevance and Admissibility of Prior Sexual History with the Defendant in Sexual Offence Cases' (2001) 32 *Cambrian Law Review* 27.

(2004) 'Judicial Perspectives on Section 41 of the Youth Justice and Criminal Evidence Act 1999'. Research Report for the Criminal Bar Association.

King, J. (2007) 'The Justiciability of Resource Allocation' (2007) 70 *Modern Law Review* 197.

(2008) 'The Pervasiveness of Polycentricity' (2008) *Public Law* 101.

Kirk, J. (1997) 'Constitutional Guarantees, Characterisation and the Concept of Proportionality' (1997) 21 *Melbourne University Law Review* 1.

(2001) 'Rights, Review and Reasons for Restraint' (2001) 23 *Sydney Law Review* 19.

Klug, F. (1997) 'Can Human Rights Fill Britain's Morality Gap?' (1997) 68 *Political Quarterly* 143.

(1999) 'The Human Rights Act 1998, *Pepper* v. *Hart* and All That' (1999) *Public Law* 246.

(2000) *Values for a Godless Age: the Story of the UK's New Bill of Rights.* London, Penguin.

(2001) 'The Human Rights Act – a "Third Way" or "Third Wave" Bill of Rights' (2001) *European Human Rights Law Review* 361.

(2003) 'Judicial Deference under the Human Rights Act 1998' (2003) *European Human Rights Law Review* 125.

(2005) 'The Long Road to Human Rights Compliance' (2005) 57 *Northern Ireland Legal Quarterly* 186.

(2007) 'A Bill of Rights: Do we need one or do we already have one?' (2007) *Public Law* 701.

Klug, F. and Starmer, K. (2001) 'Incorporation through the "Front Door": the First Year of the Human Rights Act' (2001) 2001 *Public Law* 654.

(2005) 'Standing Back from the Human Rights Act: How Effective is it Five Years on?' (2005) *Public Law* 716.

Klug, F. and Wildbore, H. (2007) 'Breaking New Ground: the Joint Committee on Human Rights and the Role of Parliament in Human Rights Compliance' (2007) *European Human Rights Law Review* 231.

Kyritsis, D. (2006) 'Representation and Waldron's Objection to Judicial Review' (2006) 26 *Oxford Journal of Legal Studies* 733.

(2007) 'Principles, Policies and the Power of Courts' (2007) XX *Canadian Journal of Law and Jurisprudence* 1.

Landfried, C. (1992) *Constitutional Review and Legislation: an International Comparison*. Baden-Baden, Nomos.

Laws, J. (1995) 'Law and Democracy' (1995) *Public Law* 72.

(1998a) 'The Limitations of Human Rights' (1998) *Public Law* 254.

(1998b) '*Wednesbury*' in Forsyth, C. and Hare, I. (eds.) *The Golden Metwand and the Crooked Cord: Essays in Honour of Sir William Wade Q.C.* Oxford, Clarendon Press, 185.

Laws, L. J. (1999) 'An Overview' in Beatson, J., Forsyth, C. and Hare, I. (eds.) *The Human Rights Act and the Criminal Justice and Regulatory Process*. Oxford, Hart Publishing, xiii.

(2004) 'The Impact of the Human Rights Act 1998 on the Interpretation of Enactments in the UK' in Bigwood, R. (ed.) *The Statute: Making and Meaning*. Wellington, Lexis-Nexis, 245.

Le Sueur, A. (1995) 'Justifying Judicial Caution: Jurisdiction, Justiciability and Policy' in Hadfield, B. (ed.) *Judicial Review. A Thematic Approach*. Dublin, Gill & Macmillan, 228.

(1996) 'The Judicial Review Debate; from Partnership to Friction' (1996) 31 *Government and Opposition* 8.

(2005) 'The Rise and Ruin of Unreasonableness' (2005) *Judicial Review* 32.

Leigh, I. (2002) 'Taking Rights Proportionately: Judicial Review, the Human Rights Act and Strasbourg' (2002) *Public Law* 265.

(2007a) 'Concluding Remarks' in Fenwick, H., Phillipson, G. and Masterman, R. (eds.) *Judicial Reasoning under the UK Human Rights Act*. Cambridge University Press, 424.

(2007b) 'The Standard of Judicial Review after the Human Rights Act' in Fenwick, H., Masterman, R. and Phillipson, G. (eds.) *Judicial Reasoning under the UK Human Rights Act*. Cambridge University Press, 174.

Leigh, I. and Lustgarten, L. (1999) 'Making Right Real: the Courts, Remedies and the Human Rights Act' (1999) 58 *Cambridge Law Journal* 509.

Lester, Lord A. (1998) 'The Art of the Possible – Interpreting Statutes under the Human Rights Act' (1998) *European Human Rights Law Review* 663.

(2001) 'Developing Constitutional Principles of Public Law' (2001) *Public Law* 684.

(2002a) 'The Magnetism of the Human Rights Act 1998' (2002) 33 *Victoria University of Wellington Law Review* 53.

(2002b) 'Parliamentary Scrutiny of Legislation under the Human Rights Act 1998' (2002) 4 *European Human Rights Law Review* 432.

(2005) 'The Utility of the Human Rights Act: a Reply to Keith Ewing' (2005) *Public Law* 249.

Lester, Lord A. and Pannick, D. (2000) *Human Rights Law and Practice*. London, Lexis-Nexis Butterworths.

(2004) *Human Rights Law and Practice*, London, Lexis-Nexis Butterworths.

Letsas, G. (2006) 'Two Concepts of the Margin of Appreciation' (2006) 26 *Oxford Journal of Legal Studies* 705.

Limbach, J. (2001) 'The Concept of the Supremacy of the Constitution' (2001) 64 *Modern Law Review* 1.

Lively, J. (1975) *Democracy*. Oxford, Basil Blackwell.

Loveland, I. (2006) *Constitutional Law, Administrative Law and Human Rights: a Critical Introduction*. Oxford University Press.

MacCormick, N. (1978) *Legal Reasoning and Legal Theory*. Oxford, Clarendon Press.

(1993) 'Argumentation and Interpretation in Law' (1993) 5 *Ratio Juris* 12.

Macklem, T. (2006) 'Entrenching Bills of Rights' (2006) 26 *Oxford Journal of Legal Studies* 107.

Mahoney, P. (1990) 'Judicial Activism and Judicial Self-Restraint in the European Court of Human Rights: Two Sides of the Same Coin' (1990) 11 *Human Rights Law Journal* 57.

Malik, M. (2001) 'Minority Protection and Human Rights' in Campbell, T., Ewing, K. and Tomkins, A. (eds.) *Sceptical Essays on Human Rights*. Oxford University Press, 277.

Malleson, K. (1999) *The New Judiciary: the Effects of Expansion and Activism*. Aldershot, Ashgate.

Mammen, L. (2001) 'A Short Note on the German Federal Constitutional Court and its Power to Review Legislation' (2001) *European Human Rights Law Review* 433.

Manin, B. (1997) *The Principles of Representative Government*. Cambridge University Press.

Manning, J. (1997) 'Textualism as a Non-Delegation Doctrine' (1997) 97 *Columbia Law Review* 673.

Marks, S. (1995) 'Civil Liberties at the Margin: the UK Derogation and the European Court of Human Rights' (1995) 15 *Oxford Journal of Legal Studies* 69.

Marmor, A. (2005) *Interpretation and Legal Theory*. Oxford, Hart Publishing.

Marshall, G. (1998) 'Interpreting Interpretation in the Human Rights Bill' (1998) *Public Law* 167.

    (2002) 'Metric Martyrs and Martyrdom by Henry VIII Clause' (2002) 118 *Law Quarterly Review* 493.

    (2003) 'The Lynchpin of Parliamentary Intention: Lost, Stolen or Strained?' (2003) *Public Law* 236.

Masterman, R. (2007) 'Aspiration or Foundation? the Status of the Strasbourg Jurisprudence and the "Convention Rights" in Domestic Law' in Fenwick, H., Phillipson, G. and Masterman, R. (eds.) *Judicial Reasoning under the UK Human Rights Act*. Cambridge University Press 57.

McColgan, A. (1996) 'Common Law and the Relevance of Sexual History Evidence' (1996) 16 *Oxford Journal of Legal Studies* 275.

McLachlin, B., Chief Justice (1999–2000) 'Charter Myths' (1999–2000) 33 *University of British Columbia Law Review* 23.

    (2001) 'The Supreme Court and the Public Interest' (2001) 64 *Saskatchewan Law Review* 309.

Miller, B. (2008) 'Justification and Rights Limitations' in Huscroft, G. (ed.) *Expounding the Constitution: Essays in Constitutional Theory*. Cambridge University Press, 93.

Munro, C. (1999) *Studies in Constitutional Law*. London, Butterworths.

Nelson, W. (1980) *On Justifying Democracy*. London, Routledge & Kegan Paul.

Nicol, D. (2002) 'Are Convention Rights a No-Go Zone for Parliament?' (2002) *Public Law* 438.

    (2004a) 'Gender Reassignment and the Transformation of the Human Rights Act' (2004) 120 *Law Quarterly Review* 194.

    (2004b) 'Statutory Interpretation and Human Rights after *Anderson*' (2004) *Public Law* 273.

    (2005) 'The Human Rights Act and the Politicians' (2005) *Legal Studies* 451.

    (2006) 'Law and Politics after the Human Rights Act' (2006) *Public Law* 722.

Oliver, D. (2003) *Constitutional Reform in the UK*. Oxford University Press.

Oliver, D. and Drewry, G. (1996) *Public Service Reforms: Issues of Accountability and Public Law*. London, Pinter.

Palmer, E. (2000) 'Resource Allocation, Welfare Rights – Mapping the Boundaries of Judicial Control in Public Administrative Law' (2000) 20 *Oxford Journal of Legal Studies* 63.

(2007) *Judicial Review, Socio-Economic Rights and the Human Rights Act* Oxford, Hart Publishing.

Pannick, D. (1998) 'Principles of Interpretation of Convention Rights under the Human Rights Act and the Discretionary Area of Judgment' (1998) *Public Law* 545.

Pearce, D. and Geddes, R. (2001) *Statutory Interpretation in Australia.* Sydney, Butterworths.

Perry, S. (1989) 'Second-Order Reasons, Uncertainty and Legal Norms' (1989) 62 *Southern California Law Review* 913.

Pettit, P. (1989) 'The Freedom of the City: a Republican Ideal' in Hamlin, A. and Pettit, P. (eds.) *The Good Polity: Normative Analysis of the State.* Oxford, Basil Blackwell, 141.

(1997) *Republicanism: a Theory of Government and Freedom.* Oxford, Clarendon Press.

(1998) 'The Consequentialist can Recognise Rights' (1998) 38 *Philosophical Quarterly* 42.

(1999) 'Republican Freedom and Contestatory Democratisation' in Shapiro, I. and Hacker-Cordon, C. (eds.) *Democracy's Values.* Cambridge University Press, 163.

(2001a) 'Deliberative Democracy and the Case of Depoliticising Government' (2001) 24 *University of New South Wales Law Journal* 724.

(2001b) 'Is Criminal Justice Politically Feasible?' (2001) 5 *Buffalo Criminal Law Review* 427.

(2004) 'Depoliticising Democracy' (2004) 17 *Ratio Juris* 52.

Phillips, A. (1995) *The Politics of Presence.* Oxford, Clarendon Press.

Phillips, Lord N. (2002) 'The Interpretation of Contracts and Statutes' (2002) 68 *Arbitration* 17.

Phillipson, G. (2003) '(Mis)-Reading Section 3 of the Human Rights Act' (2003) 119 *Law Quarterly Review* 183.

(2006) 'Deference, Discretion, and Democracy in the Human Rights Act Era' (2006) *Current Legal Problems* 40.

Pieterse, M. (2004) 'Coming to Terms with Judicial Enforcement of Socioeconomic Rights' (2004) 20 *South African Journal of Human Rights* 383.

Pillay, A. (2007) 'Courts, Variable Standards of Review and Resource Allocation: Developing a Model for the Enforcement of Social and Economic Rights' (2007) *European Human Rights Law Review* 616.

Poole, T. (2008) 'Courts and Conditions of Uncertainty In " Times of Crisis"' (2008) *Public Law* 234.

Rawlings, R. (2005) 'Review, Revenge and Retreat' (2005) 68 *Modern Law Review* 378.

Rawls, J. (1971) *A Theory of Justice.* Cambridge, Mass., Harvard University Press.

Raz, J. (1978) 'Professor Dworkin's Theory of Rights' (1978) 26 *Political Studies*
123.

    (1979) *The Authority of Law: Essays on Law and Morality.* Oxford, Clarendon
Press.

    (1994) *Ethics in the Public Domain: Essays in the Morality of Law and Politics.*
Oxford, Clarendon Press.

    (1995) 'Rights and Politics' (1995) 71 *Indiana Law Journal* 27.

    (1996a) 'Why Interpret?' (1996) 9 *Ratio Juris* 349.

    (1996b) 'Intention in Interpretation' in George, R. (ed.) *The Autonomy of Law.*
Oxford University Press, 249.

    (1998a) 'On the Authority and Interpretation of Constitutions: Some Prelim-
inaries' in Alexander, L. (ed.) *Constitutionalism. Philosophical Foundations.*
Cambridge University Press, 152.

    (1998b) 'Disagreement in Politics' (1998) 43 *American Journal of Jurisprudence*
25.

    (1999) *Engaging Reason: On the Theory of Value and Action.* Oxford University
Press.

Rinken, A. (2002) 'The Federal Constitutional Court and the German Political
System' in Rogowski, R. and Gawron, T. (eds.) *Constitutional Courts in Com-
parison: the US Supreme Court and the German Federal Constitutional Court.*
Oxford, Berghahn Books.

Rishworth, P. (2004) 'The Inevitability of Judicial Review under "Interpretive"
Bills of Rights: Canada's Legacy to New Zealand the Commonwealth Con-
stitutionalism' in Huscroft, G. and Brodie, I. (eds.) *Constitutionalism in the
Charter Era.* Markham, Ontario, Lexis-Nexis, 233.

Rivers, J. (2002) 'Translator's Introduction: a Theory of Constitutional Rights and
the British Constitution' in Alexy, R. (ed.).

    (2006) 'Proportionality and the Variable Intensity of Review' (2006) 65 *Cam-
bridge Law Journal* 174.

Roach, K. (2001) *The Supreme Court on Trial: Judicial Activism or Democratic
Dialogue.* Toronto, Irwin Law.

Rodger, L. (2002) 'The Form and Language of Judicial Opinions' (2002) 118 *Law
Quarterly Review* 226.

Rogowski, R. and Gawron, T. (eds.) (2002) 'Introduction: Constitutional Litigation
as Dispute Processing: Comparing the US Supreme Court and the German
Federal Constitutional Court' in Rogowski, R. and Gawron, T. (eds.) *Constitutional Courts in Comparison: the US Supreme Court and the German Federal
Constitutional Court.* Oxford, Berghahn Books, 1.

Rose, D. and Weir, C. (2003) 'Interpretation and Incompatibility: Striking the
Balance' in Jowell, J. and Cooper, J. (eds.) *Delivering Rights: How the Human
Rights Act is Working.* Oxford, Hart Publishing, 37.

Sales, P. and Hooper, B. (2003) 'Proportionality and the Form of Law' (2003) 119 *Law Quarterly Review* 426.

Sandalow, T. (1981) 'The Distrust of Politics' (1981) 56 *New York University Law Review*.

Scalia, A. (1989) 'Judicial Deference to Administrative Interpretations of the Law' (1989) *Duke Law Journal* 511.

Schaeffer, A. (2005) 'Linking *Marleasing* and s.3(1) of the Human Rights Act 1998' (2005) *Judicial Review* 72.

Schauer, F. (1995) '*Ashwander* Revisited' (1995) *The Supreme Court Review* 71.

Schokkenbroek, J. (1998) 'The Basis, Nature and Application of the Margin of Appreciation Doctrine in the Case Law of the European Court of Human Rights' (1998) 19 *Human Rights Law Journal* 30.

Sedley, Lord S. (1994) 'The Sound of Silence: Constitutional Law without a Constitution' (1994) 110 *Law Quarterly Review* 270.

(1995) 'Human Rights: a Twenty-first Century Agenda' (1995) *Public Law* 386.

(2002) 'Colonels in Horsehair' (2002) *London Review of Books* 17.

(2004) 'The Last Ten Years' Development of English Public Law' (2004) 12 *Australian Journal of Administrative Law* 9.

(2005) 'The Rocks or the Open Sea: Where is the Human Rights Act Heading?' (2005) 32 *Journal of Law and Society* 3.

(2008) 'No Ordinary Law' (2008) 5 June *London Review of Books* 20.

Smith, A. T. H. (1999) 'The Human Rights Act: the Constitutional Context' in Beatson, J. (ed.) *The Human Rights Act and the Criminal Justice and Regulatory Process*. Oxford, Hart Publishing, 3.

Soper, P. (2002) *The Ethics of Deference: Learning from Law's Morals*. Cambridge University Press.

Sossin, L. (1999) *Boundaries of Judicial Review: the Law of Justiciability in Canada*. Toronto, Carswell.

Starmer, K. (2003) 'Two Years of the Human Rights Act' (2003) 1 *European Human Rights Law Review* 14.

(2007) 'Setting the Record Straight: Human Rights in an Era of International Terrorism' (2007) *European Human Rights Law Review* 123.

Steyn, Lord J. (1997) 'The Weakest and Least Dangerous Branch of Government' (1997) *Public Law* 84.

(1998) 'Incorporation and Devolution – a Few Reflections on the Changing Scene' (1998) *European Human Rights Law Review* 153.

(2000) 'The New Legal Landscape' (2000) *European Human Rights Law Review* 549.

(2001) '*Pepper* v. *Hart*; a Re-examination' (2001) 21 *Oxford Journal of Legal Studies* 59.

(2002a) 'Democracy through Law' (2002) *European Human Rights Law Review*
    723.

(2002b) 'The Case for a Supreme Court' (2002) 118 *Law Quarterly Review* 382.

(2004a) 'Dynamic Interpretation amidst an Orgy of Statutes' (2004) *European
    Human Rights Law Review* 245.

(2004b) 'Lord Steyn's Comments from the Lester and Pannick Book Launch'
    (2004) 9 *Judicial Review* 107.

(2005a) 'Deference: a Tangled Story' (2005) *Public Law* 346.

(2005b) '2000–2005: Laying the Foundations of Human Rights Law in the United
    Kingdom' (2005) *European Human Rights Law Review* 349.

(2006) 'Democracy, the Rule of Law and the Role of Judges' (2006) *European
    Human Rights Law Review* 243.

Stone-Sweet, A. (2000) *Governing with Judges. Constitutional Politics in Europe.*
    Oxford University Press.

Sullivan, D. (1998) 'The Allocation of Scarce Resources and the Right to Life under
    the European Convention on Human Rights' (1998) *Public Law* 389.

Summers, R. (1991) 'Statutory Interpretation in the United States' in MacCormick,
    N. and Summers, R. (eds.) *Interpreting Statutes: a Comparative Study.* Alder-
    shot, Dartmouth Press, 407.

Sunstein, C. (1988) 'Constitutions and Democracy: an Epilogue' in Elster, J. and
    Slagstad, R. (eds.) *Constitutionalism and Democracy.* Cambridge University
    Press, 327.

(1993) *The Partial Constitution.* Cambridge, Mass., Harvard University Press.

Supperstone, M. and Coppel, J. (1999) 'Judicial Review after the Human Rights
    Act' (1999) *European Human Rights Law Review* 301.

Sypnowich, C. (2007) 'Ruling or Overruled? the People, Rights and Democracy'
    (2007) 27 *Oxford Journal of Legal Studies* 757.

Taylor, J. (2004) 'Human Rights Protection in Australia: Interpretation Provisions
    and Parliamentary Supremacy' (2004) 32 *Federal Law Review* 58.

Temkin, J. (1993) 'Sexual History Evidence – the Ravishment of Section 2' (1993)
    *Criminal Law Review* 3.

Tierney, S. (2005) 'Determining the State of Exception: What Role for Parliament
    and the Courts?' (2005) *Modern Law Review* 668.

Tomkins, A. (2001) 'Introduction: On Being Sceptical About Human Rights' in
    Campbell, T., Ewing, K. and Tomkins, A. (eds.) *Sceptical Essays on Human
    Rights.* Oxford University Press, 1.

(2002a) 'In Defence of the Political Constitution' (2002) 22 *Oxford Journal of
    Legal Studies* 157.

(2002b) 'Defining and Delimiting National Security' (2002) 118 *Law Quarterly
    Review* 200.

(2002c) 'Legislating against Terror: the Anti-Terrorism, Crime and Security Act
    2001' (2002) *Public Law* 205.

(2003) *Public Law.* Oxford University Press.

(2005a) 'Readings of A v. Secretary of State for the Home Department' (2005) *Public Law* 259.

(2005b) *Our Republican Constitution.* Oxford, Hart Publishing.

(2008) 'The Rule of Law in Blair's Britain' (2008) *University of Queensland Law Journal* 1.

Tremblay, L. (1984) 'Section 7 of the Charter: Substantive Due Process' (1984) 18 *University of British Columbia Law Review* 201.

Tribe, L. (1978) *American Constitutional Law.* Mineola, N.Y., The Foundation Press.

(2001) 'Trial by Fury: Why Congress Must Curb Bush's Military Courts' (2001) *The New Republic* 18.

Turpin, C. and Tomkins, A. (2007) *British Government and the Constitution.* Cambridge University Press.

Tushnet, M. (2003) 'New Forms of Judicial Review and the Persistence of Rights- and Democracy-based Worries' (2003) 38 *Wake Forest Law Review* 813.

Van Zyl Smit, J. (2005) *Rights-Compatible Interpretation of Statutes.* M.Phil. Thesis, University of Oxford.

(2007) 'The New Purposive Interpretation of Statutes: HRA Section 3 after *Ghaidan* v. *Godin-Mendoza*' (2007) 70 *Modern Law Review* 294.

Vogenauer, S. (2005) 'A Retreat from *Pepper* v. *Hart?* a Reply to Lord Steyn' (2005) 25 *Oxford Journal of Legal Studies* 629.

Wade, S. W. (1955) 'The Basis of Legal Sovereignty' (1955) *Cambridge Law Journal* 172.

(1996) 'Sovereignty – Revolution or Evolution?' (1996) 112 *Law Quarterly Review* 568.

(1998) 'Human Rights and the Judiciary' (1998) *European Human Rights Law Review* 520.

Wadham, J. (1997) 'Bringing Rights Half-way Home' (1997) *European Human Rights Law Review* 141.

(2001) 'The Human Rights Act: One Year on' (2001) 6 *European Human Rights Law Review* 620.

Waldron, J. (1990) *The Law.* London, Routledge.

(1993a) 'Rights and Majorities: Rousseau Revisited'. *Liberal Rights: Collected Papers 1981–1991.* Cambridge University Press, 392.

(1993b) 'A Right-based Critique of Constitutional Rights' (1993) 13 *Oxford Journal of Legal Studies* 18.

(1999) *Law and Disagreement.* Oxford, Clarendon Press.

(2003) 'Security and Liberty: the Image of Balance' (2003) 11 *Journal of Political Philosophy* 191.

(2006) 'The Core of the Case against Judicial Review' (2006) 115 *Yale Law Journal* 1346.

(2008) 'Do Judges Reason Morally?' in Huscroft, G. (ed.) *Expounding the Constitution: Essays in Constitutional Theory.* Cambridge University Press, 36.

Walker, N. (1999) 'Setting English Judges to Rights' (1999) 19 *Oxford Journal of Legal Studies* 133.

(2001) 'Human Rights in a Postnational Order: Reconciling Political and Constitutional Pluralism' in Campbell, T., Ewing, K. and Tomkins, A. (eds.) *Sceptical Essays on Human Rights.* Oxford University Press, 119.

Waluchow, W. J. (2007) *A Common Law Theory of Judicial Review: the Living Tree.* New York, Cambridge University Press.

Warbrick, C. (2007) 'The European Convention on Human Rights and the Human Rights Act: the View from the Outside' in Fenwick, H., Philipson, G. and Masterman, R. (eds.) *Judicial Reasoning under the UK Human Rights Act.* Cambridge University Press, 25.

Weale, A. (1989) 'The Limits of Democracy' in Hamlin, A. and Pettit, P. (eds.) *The Good Polity: Normative Analysis of the State.* Oxford, Basil Blackwell, 35.

(1999) *Democracy.* London, The Macmillan Press.

Wicks, E. (2000) 'The United Kingdom Government's Perceptions of the European Convention on Human Rights at the Time of Entry' (2000) *Public Law* 438.

(2005) 'Taking Account of Strasbourg? the British Judiciary's Approach to Interpreting Convention Rights' (2005) 11 *European Public Law* 405.

Wikeley, N., Ogus, A. I. and Barendt, E. M. (2002) *The Law of Social Security.* London, Butterworths.

Willis, J. (1938) 'Statute Interpretation in a Nutshell' (1938) 16 *Canadian Bar Review* 1.

Wintemute, R. (2000) 'Lesbian and Gay Inequality 2000: the Potential of the Human Rights Act 1998 and the Need for an Equality Act 2002' (2000) *European Human Rights Law Review* 603.

(2003) 'Same-Sex Partners, "Living as Husband and Wife", and Section 3 of the Human Rights Act 1998' (2003) *Public Law* 621.

(2006a) 'The Human Rights Act's First Five Years: Too Strong, Too Weak, or Just Right?' (2006) 17 *Kings College Law Journal* 209.

(2006b) 'Same-Sex Couples in *Secretary of State for Work and Pensions* v. *M*: Identical to *Karner* and *Godin-Mendoza*, yet no Discrimination?' (2006) *European Human Rights Law Review* 722.

Wiseman, D. (2001) 'The Charter and Poverty: Beyond Injusticiability' (2001) 51 *University of Toronto Law Journal* 425.

Woodhouse, D. (2007) 'The Constitutional Reform Act 2005 – Defending Judicial Independence the English Way' (2007) 5 *International Journal of Constitutional Law* 153.

Woolf, Lord H. (1995) '*Droit Public* – English Style' (1995) *Public Law* 57.

(2001) '*Droit Public* – English Style' (1995) *Public Law* 57.

(2003) 'Are the Courts Excessively Deferential to the Medical Profession?' (2001) 9 *Medical Law Review* 1.

(2004) 'The Rule of Law and a Change in the Constitution' (2004) 63 *Cambridge Law Journal* 317.

(2008) *The Pursuit of Justice.* Oxford University Press.

Young, A. (2002) 'Judicial Sovereignty and the Human Rights Act 1998' (2002) 61 *Cambridge Law Journal* 53.

(2005) '*Ghaidan* v. *Godin-Mendoza:* Avoiding the Deference Trap' (2005) *Public Law* 23.

(2006) 'Hunting Sovereignty: *Jackson* v. *AG*' (2006) *Public Law* 187.

(2008) *Parliamentary Sovereignty and the Human Rights Act.* Oxford, Hart Publishing.

Zedner, L. (2007) 'Preventive Justice or Pre-Punishment? the Case of Control Orders' (2007) 60 *Current Legal Problems* 174.

# INDEX